MW01534607

Networking Administration for NetWare™
Versions 4.11 and 5

Richard A. McMahon, CNA, CNI
Conroe, Texas

VISIT US ON THE INTERNET
www.swep.com
www.thomsonlearning.com

South-Western
EDUCATIONAL PUBLISHING
Thomson Learning™

Australia • Canada • Denmark • Japan • Mexico • New Zealand • Phillipines
Puerto Rico • Singapore • South Africa • Spain • United Kingdom • United States

Acquisitions Editor:	John Wills
Managing Editor:	Carol Volz
Editor:	Shannon O'Connor
Consulting/Technical Editor:	Alan Rowland, CNI, CNE
Art/Design Coordinator:	Mike Broussard
Marketing Manager:	Larry Qualls
Electronic Prepress, Production and Design:	A. W. Kingston Publishing Services

ISBN: 0-538-69089-5

1 2 3 4 5 6   CK   04 03 02 01 00 99

Printed in the United States of America

For permission to use material from this text or product, contact us by
- web: www.thomsonrights.com
- Phone: 1-800-730-2214
- Fax: 1-800-730-2215

Prepare for Certification

Networking Administration for NetWare™ Versions 4.11 and 5 from South-Western is directly correlated to Novell's CNA exam objectives and insures quality preparation for professional industry certification. It begins with an introduction to networking terms and technology, then proceeds through network installation and access. From there, move into learning about network structure and use. Followed by information on careers in the networking industry.

- *Networking Administration for NetWare™ Versions 4.11 and 5* (McMahon)
  Student book, soft cover   0-538-69089-5
  Study Guide   0-538-69090-9
  Electronic Instructor CD-ROM   0-538-96651-3
  Testing CD   0-538-69244-8

Other Technical Certification Courseware from South-Western

- *A+ Certification* (MindWorks)
  Student book, soft cover   0-538-68669-3

- *Microsoft Visual Basic 6.0 Introduction to Programming* (Sprague, Phillips)
  Student book, hardcover   0-538-68818-1

- *Microsoft Windows NT 4.0: Getting Started* (Meinster) Exam # 70-067 & 70-068
  Student Text, (perfect bound, soft cover)   0-538-71938-9

- *Networking Essentials* (Meinster, Craver, Wang) Exam # 70-058
  Student Text, (perfect bound, soft cover)   0-538-68477-1

- *Introduction to TCP/IP Internetworking* (Bush) Exam # 70-059
  Student Text, (perfect bound, soft cover)   0-538-68870-X

- *Microsoft Windows 98 Implementation and Support* (Helmick) Exam # 70-098
  Student Text, (perfect bound, soft cover)   0-538-68905-6

- *Microsoft Internet Information Server 4.0* (Helmick) Exam # 70-087
  Student Text, (perfect bound, soft cover)   0-538-69101-4

The Electronic Instructor CD-ROM contains tests, Lesson Plans, solutions, and much more.

South-Western
EDUCATIONAL PUBLISHING
Thomson Learning™

Join Us On the Internet
www.swep.com

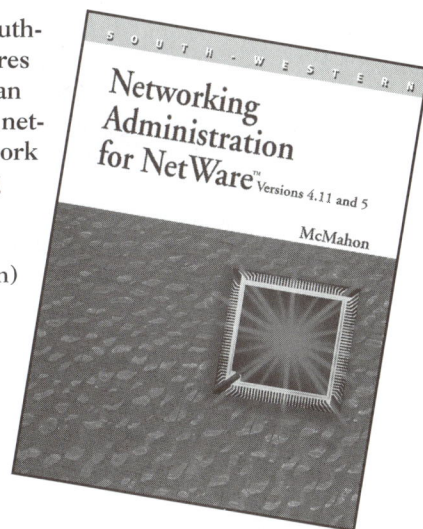

CONTENTS

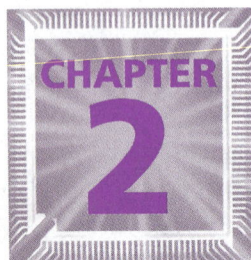

iv

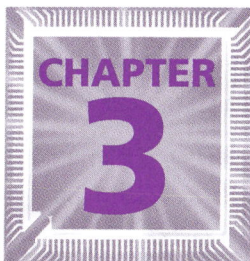

CHAPTER 3

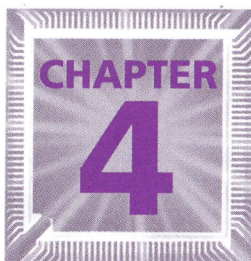

CHAPTER 4

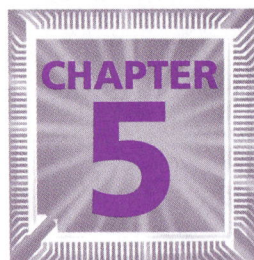

CHAPTER 7

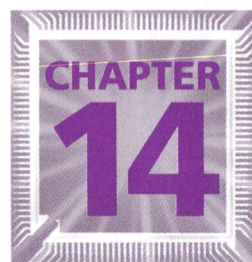

CHAPTER 15

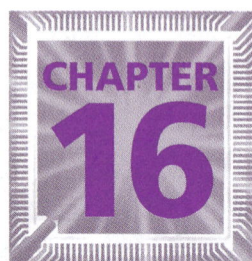

CHAPTER 16

PREFACE

Purpose of the Textbook

This textbook is the result of my experience teaching the Certified Novell Administrator (CNA) course as a Certified Novell Instructor in both high school and college environments under the Novell Education Academic Partner program. This textbook is also the result of my involvement with Microsoft as an Approved Academic Training Partner. At the time, the only materials available for CNA candidates were self-paced home study programs from local bookstores or intensive five-day courses at Novell Authorized Education Centers. I was unable to find materials to help me prepare middle-grade students and high school students to pass the CNA test. This text-workbook is the main portion of the instructional package designed for an Introductory Novell Networking Administration course. The complete package also includes a study guide, an Instructor's manual, an Electronic Instructor CD-ROM with text-book/workbook answers, tests and answer keys, test banks, transparencies, and recommended teaching schedules, and a Testing Tools test generator package.

Course Design

This course is designed to lead a moderately computer-literate person into the complex world of networking through a hands-on, developmentally structured laboratory setting. Ideally, that individual will have already completed the typical computer literacy course and acquired familiarity with computers in general, including operating systems like Windows 95/98 and applications such as Microsoft Office. To allow for variations in previous experience, this course includes sections for the advanced user as well as the beginner.

Businesslike Setting

Networking and Network Administration are sought-after business skills. This course uses a simulated business environment to teach Novell networking. Class members will role-play as employees, applying what they learn in the classroom to a business situation. That situation changes during the course as the members of the class rotate through various positions in a simulated company which includes corporate-level, management-level and worker-level networked computer needs.

Classroom Needs

Your classroom will not need computer equipment set up before starting this course. Members of your class will first examine the need for a computer network and then build it as the need evolves.

Ultimately, the ideal classroom will provide a personal computer workstation for each learner, at least one personal computer to be used as a server, several different types of printers, and the appropriate networking tools necessary to assemble and test networked computers. This ideal classroom would also include a telephone connection with modem capabilities and a modem on the server, along with dial-up Internet access through a local Internet Service Provider (ISP).

The *minimum* networking computer requirements for a classroom setup (listed by version) include:

Minimum Hardware/Software Requirements

		NetWare 4.11	NetWare 5
1	1 PC server w/CD	486-66 (16 Meg RAM)	Pentium 75 (48 Meg RAM)
2	1 Win95 Workstation w/CD	486-66 (16 Meg RAM)	Pentium 75 (16 Meg RAM)
3	Network interface cards for each computer		
4	Category 5 wiring for connecting the computers together		
5	Novell NetWare software with sufficient user licenses		
6	At least one printer		
7	*At least* 500 Meg hard disk drives on each computer		

Additionally, because these computers will be built and rebuilt as needed, the equipment for this course should not be used in any other regularly scheduled classes.

To obtain optimum results and minimize delays, the minimum hardware requirements listed above should be increased if possible. If possible, upgrade each workstation with at least a Pentium 75Mhz processor with 32 megabytes of RAM and provide at least 64 megabytes of RAM for the computer used as a file server.

Information for the Learner

Textbook Orientation

Effective use of this textbook will help you prepare to take the Certified Novell Administrator examination. Should you desire to obtain Novell's CNA designation, the objectives you need to master are covered in the business simulations of this text. The textbook requires you to become an active participant in a simulated working environment where the need for computers to communicate with each other and other devices ultimately leads to the need for a network. The step-by-step developmental approach is used in this course because it better explains how the conceptual relates to the actual. Rather than learning by memorizing, you gain experience by doing (or not doing) things that affect you and your coworkers.

Become an Active Participant

At the beginning of the semester, you will be assigned a position within a company called "TPUP" (based upon an actual manufacturing company). You will be responsible for the computer duties associated with that position. Much of the initial work is completed manually but will later be used in your computer network. Within one semester the actual company went from near computer illiteracy to using a fully-functional network connecting all managers (such as yourself) with each other and with the company headquarters several miles away. That real company went from almost total dependency on handwritten work to the nearly unlimited potential of network immersion. The same thing should happen with your computing abilities and networking prowess as you work through the simulations included in this text.

Need for a Network

When you begin the class, you will be required to fill out a job application and submit a handwritten resume to apply for your preferred position with TPUP. Everyone in the class will be doing the same thing and no one will know who is "hired" for what position. It really does not matter because the jobs will rotate in order to provide experience in lateral job shifting and additional job "experience." This type of activity will help demonstrate the need for computers and, later, the need for effective network administration. As you accumulate more and more data about yourself and your involvement with TPUP's operations, the need for a network should become apparent. Your network will develop out of that need through various growth patterns. At first, you will become familiar with networking activities as they are needed to do your job function. You determine what goes on in the network and how it is released for viewing and use by your coworkers. From these simple beginnings, the need for better organization and more structure will make you seek change in your network. The result will be a more complex, useful network design that can expand as the company's needs evolve. Everyone involved eventually becomes an administrator of TPUP's network. The final network structure will be influenced by how each person relates to others and by your perception of the company's need for security and data access.

About the Author

Rich McMahon began his Novell networking training at Conroe High School in Conroe, Texas, where he taught drafting, AutoCAD 13, computer graphics, and construction graphics as he assisted with the networking administration duties on the department's NetWare 3.12 network. He later moved to the school's business department and began teaching Microcomputer Applications, Visual Basic Programming, and World Wide Web Page Development. He also began managing that department's computer laboratories along with the Novell 4.0 network installed for those laboratories. In addition, he began teaching drafting courses at the local Montgomery College.

Rich went on to complete every Novell NetWare 4.11 course offered at the local NAEC facilities for his CNE and Master CNE track. He completed the Certified Technical Trainer certification and received his Certified Novell Instructor rating. Additionally, Rich recently was invited by Microsoft to become involved in the new Microsoft Train-The-Trainer program. Under this worldwide pilot program, Rich became one of the first nine AATP mentors trained to help spread the Microsoft networking program to more colleges and high schools.

Having seen the potential for training at the high school level (or earlier), and having learned firsthand what it is like to teach such a course without proper materials, Rich determined to prepare a textbook to fill this need. It is through this textbook series that Rich hopes your job will be made easier so that more individuals will have the opportunity to enter the field of networking.

Acknowledgments

Most of all to Sheronna, Lauren, and Ricky—my loving family—for their patience and understanding of all the time this textbook and all the training and certifications leading up to it have taken.

To South-Western Educational Publishing and Novell, Inc. for having the foresight to initiate this program at the high school and middle school levels and for inviting me to be one of the first Novell Education Academic Partners in the nation.

To Matthew and Madeleine Feinberg, of AVATAR Computer Solutions, for their support while I was pursuing both Novell and Microsoft certification.

To Pat Hosford for allowing the use of his company's structure and his support throughout this text's creation.

Finally, to all of those individuals in my elementary, middle school, high school, and college classes for helping me recognize the need for this series of textbooks.

Thank you, one and all!

Rich McMahon

UNIT 1

Network Introduction

CHAPTER 1

INTRODUCTION TO TPUP

Because the needs of a particular company will determine the structure of the network you develop, you will be introduced to the organizational structure of the company and to its individual workers. In the introductory process you will:

- become familiar with the company's background.

- be introduced to individuals within the company and decide which position you will assume in this portion of the simulation.

- read the company's advertisement for positions available.

- decide which positions best match your interests.

- create, fill out, and submit a job application and handwritten resume for your desired position.

- go through a selection process and obtain "employment."

- create a manual filing system for all of the documents you will use throughout the semester, and another for any documents produced while filling the role for which you have been "hired."

- understand the term "unique identifier."

- devise "naming standards" for data acquisition.

- format your workstation's hard disk (optional—only with Instructor approval).

TPUP Background Information

TPUP is a fictitious company based on a real manufacturing company in Willis, Texas. Texas Pup, Inc. is a manufacturing firm whose main products are oil and gas well tubulars (pup joints) and forged drill rods for the horizontal drilling industry. The owner's efforts to update his workers' computer technology capabilities provide an excellent case study for teaching purposes. Mr. Pat Hosford, owner and president of Texas Pup, Inc., wanted to increase his company's involvement in computer technology. He began in the accounting section of the company, and soon expanded company-wide after purchasing a work-in-progress tracking system.

The TPUP Organization

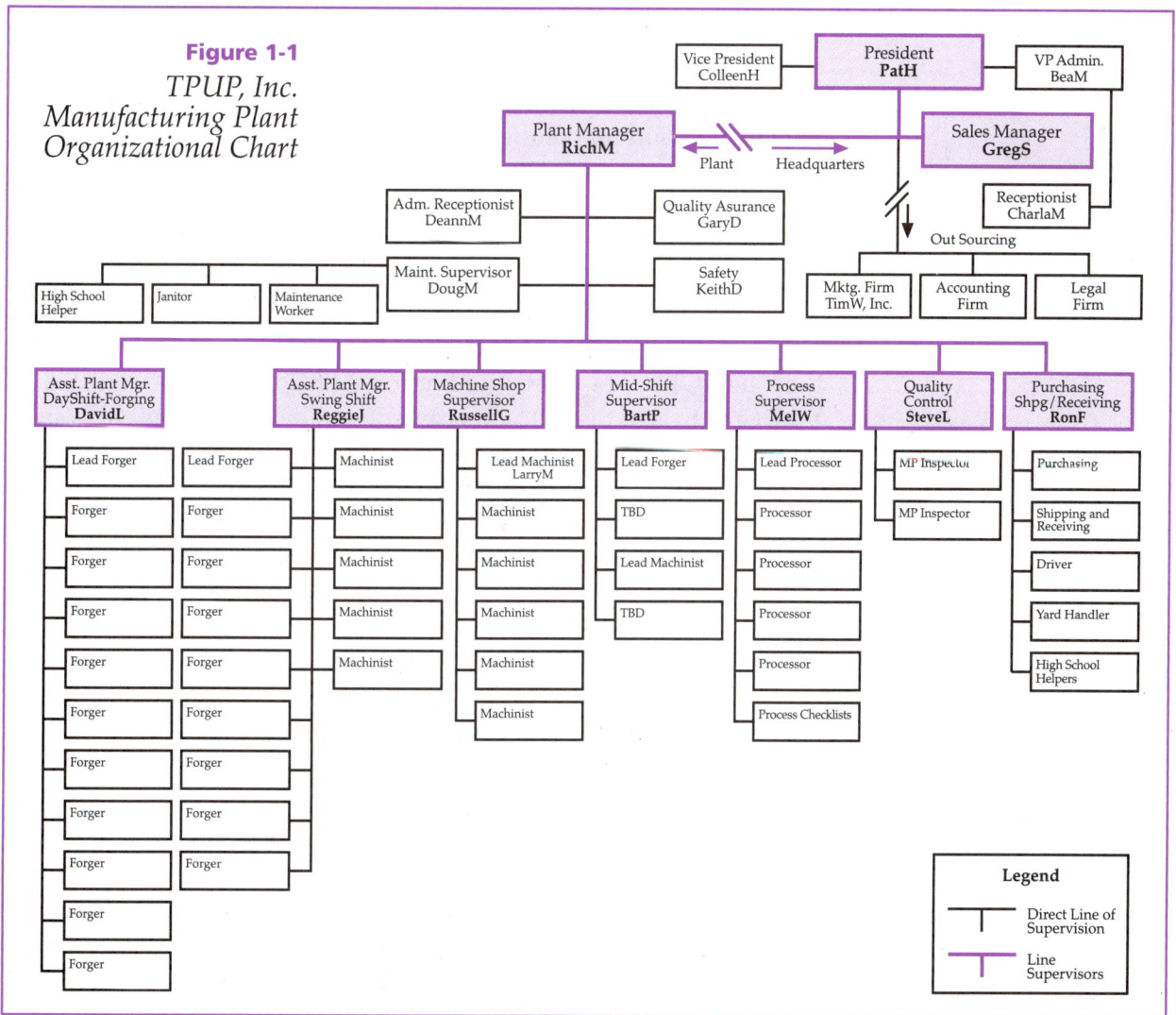

Figure 1-1

TPUP, Inc. Manufacturing Plant Organizational Chart

TPUP's Current Situation

Job Announcement Posting

As you start this semester, TPUP has just posted an announcement in the local papers listing several management positions within the company. You will be role-playing as one of the candidates trying to get hired as a manager. After learning what job you are "hired" for, refer to TPUP's organization chart (see Figure 1-1), which shows each person's position within the company.

An Introduction to TPUP Management

TPUP is divided between two main facilities—the corporate headquarters, located in a growing suburb of a major city, and the manufacturing plant, situated in a smaller town nearby. The headquarters facility is the home of the executive management of the corporation, a group which includes the president and vice-president, the corporate administration department, and the sales department. Some additional corporate functions, including legal, accounting, telephone sales, and marketing are "outsourced" (supplied by another firm whose principal business involves one of these departments).

The president, Pat H., spent many years working in and later running his own oil exploration companies. Just over ten years ago Pat and his wife, Colleen, took over executive management of TPUP when the previous partnership dissolved. Many things have changed since that time, but the employee who has been with TPUP the longest, Bea M., is the Vice President of Corporate Administration. Greg S. is in the sales department and has just joined the company. Greg has worked in the oil industry for many years and came to TPUP from a continuing purchaser of TPUP's products. The last employee at the corporate office is Charla M., the receptionist, a recent addition who performs much of the company's data entry.

All other corporate activities are conducted at the manufacturing plant. These include plant management (up to three shifts), quality assurance, safety, maintenance, forging, machining, processing, inventory control, plant administration, and operation of the quality control lab. Rich M., the plant manager, has the least amount of experience in the oil or drill rod industries, but came to the plant with much previous management training and experience and a high level of involvement in computer technology. Rich's night shift manager was Reggie J., who was recently promoted from the forging and processing departments. Mid shift was headed by Bart P., who is the most recent member of the management team and came from the machining side of the plant's operations. Reggie and Bart just came back to day shift as assistant shift supervisors in their respective departments. Bart has been quickly learning data base management in order to help the plant convert to the new data tracking software system.

Gary D. heads the Quality Assurance department, which includes the Quality Control section run by Steve L. Both Gary and Steve have been with the company from its formation in 1980. Doug M., the maintenance supervisor, has a master's degree in marine biology and has worked directly with Pat's operations in oil field exploration and in TPUP's plant operations. David L. is the forging manager as well as the assistant plant manager, and has significant experience with forging operations at all levels. Russell G. is the machine shop manager and also performs all of TPUP's drafting work.

Mel W. worked his way up through numerous positions to Process Supervisor in the plant. Inventory control, purchasing and shipping/receiving are handled by Ron F., who recently transferred to the plant from sales at the corporate office. Plant administration functions are handled by DeannM., who also acts as the purchasing representative, controlling all input and output documents. In addition there are approximately forty other hourly employees working at the plant.

Your Employment Objective

Read the TPUP employment announcement below and choose a job for which you will complete an application and resume.

Help Wanted

Small manufacturing firm in need of entire management team to replace a recently transferred group of highly trained, dedicated supervisors. Positions available immediately include: 1) Machine Shop Supervisor to supervise 14 machinists and oversee operation of four CNC lathes, 2) Forging Supervisor to oversee twenty employees and manage operation of an AJAX 4-1/2 inch forging machine, 3) Swing shift and Mid-shift Supervisors, 4) Process Manager to control in-process activities including painting, phosphating, hydrostatic testing, and control all in-process checklist procedures, 5) Inventory Control Supervisor, 6) Quality Control Laboratory Manager to check and calibrate all measurement tools and testing equipment, 7) Sales Manager, 8) Plant Manager, 9) Administration Manager and two assistants, 10) Quality Assurance Manager, 11) Safety Manager, 12) Maintenance Supervisor, 13) Executive Vice President, 14) Substitute President. Additionally, a new marketing consulting firm, accounting firm, and legal firm are needed for outsource responsibilities. A manager capable of starting and operating an education department and another to initiate and maintain a Research and Development Department are also needed.

Interested Individuals should apply in person at: TPUP.
A hand-written resume and application must be submitted.

ACTIVITY 1-1   Apply for a job at TPUP

Appendix A contains information and a sample form required for completing your job application. Appendix B contains the information you need in your resume and an example of a format that has been used at TPUP in the past. Read Appendices A and B thoroughly and plan how you will complete both the application form and your resume. Using the information in Appendices A and B, create the job application and resume. Remember that although you are applying for the job that interests you the most, someone else may be selected. You should ensure that your qualifications make you eligible for at least two alternate positions. ■

ACTIVITY 1-2   Obtain "Employment" at TPUP

Submit your application and resume to your Instructor. The company president will be selected by the Instructor, and all other positions in TPUP will be assigned by your new president according to your Instructor's criteria discussed in class. ■

Your Manual Filing System

> **Effectively organizing your filing system at this early stage will simplify the process of converting the information to an automated system later.**

You have already begun collecting data that will later become part of TPUP's company records. Begin now to file the material so that you or anyone in the office will be able to retrieve the records easily. Effectively organizing your filing system at this early stage will simplify the process of converting the information to an automated system later.

As you consider the filing project you are working on, ask yourself the question: what is data? Simply defined, *data* is a piece or pieces of information. While a single piece of information can be unimportant, when combined with other pieces of information it can help describe something or someone that is important to a business. It is the collection and proper manipulation of many seemingly unimportant segments of information, and the effective tracking of them, that makes information management so important.

Using information about yourself, let's gather some data. Enter the pieces of information about you requested below:

1. Your first name: _____
2. Your middle initial: _____
3. Your last name: _____
4. Your street address: _____
5. Your city: _____
6. Your state (XX): _____
7. Your ZIP code (99999-9999): _____
8. Your home phone (999-999-9999): _____
9. Your Social Security number (999-99-9999): _____
10. Your date of birth (MMDDYY): _____
11. The school subject in which you earned your highest grade: _____
12. Your current employer ("school" if unemployed): _____

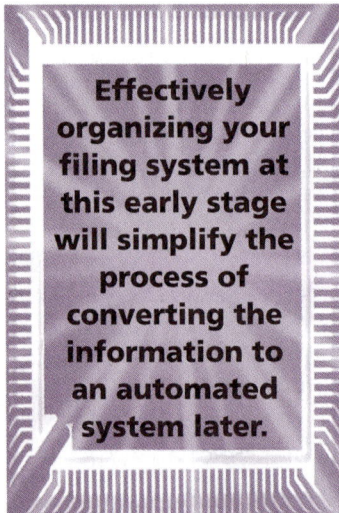

Note that the *format*, or the manner in which you enter some of the data above, is very important. The number 123456789, for instance, could be either a ZIP code or a Social Security number. If it is formatted as 123-45-6789, you know that it is a Social Security number. What if you were told to make a payment to the bank on 010203? When would you make the payment? Would it change if the format for that date were year-month-date? Of course it would. Format, then, is important!

Using Your Own Data

As you have seen, pieces of data are relatively unimportant individually. Put them all together, though, and items 1 through 12 identify a person. If your Instructor wants to keep a book with information about all the members of the class, you can now provide that to him. If all the class members print out their information on a sheet of paper and give them to your Instructor, you will be giving him a *record* of your information. When the Instructor puts them together in a folder, they become a *file*. The individual pieces of data (item numbers 1 through 12) are called *fields*. Once in a while, there may be a *multiple entry field* in which more than one entry is permissible when filling in the field. The phone number in item 8 could be an example of a multiple entry field if there are multiple phones in your household.

A field, then, is a single piece of information. When grouped together with other single interrelated pieces of information, fields join to become a record. When records are combined with other similar records, they are classified as a file. This is the development of a *hierarchy of data* (see Figure 1-2). A hierarchy is a ranking of entities from least to most important. In a hierarchy of data, the data of the entity you are describing becomes more detailed as you go further up the hierarchy. A single field, such as a "name" field, does not provide much information about the person. However, when you add the other fields which form the record, you gain more information about that person. On the other hand, you still don't have enough information if you want to know about all the individuals in a class. You could accomplish this only by combining all the individual records to form a file.

Continuing on in the hierarchy, all of the Instructors in a school combine their class rolls to obtain information about all of those enrolled at a given school. Then, all of the schools in a district combine their information to have data on everyone enrolled in their district, and the districts combine their data for statewide information. And finally, if you wanted information about all of the students in the United States, each state would offer its information to form a collection of data listing all of the students enrolled in all of the schools throughout the country. Thus, files can consist of large amounts of data. Organization is the key.

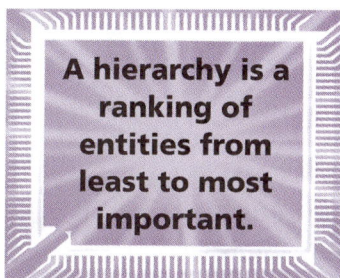

> A hierarchy is a ranking of entities from least to most important.

Figure 1-2
Hierarchy of Data

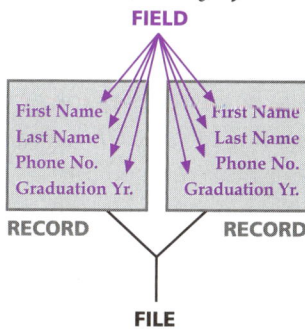

Unique Data Records

Storing and retrieving data accurately depends heavily on the existence of one record with exactly the same information and storage path. That is, there can only be one of you in your math class today. Although it may seem a simple concept when stated about individuals in a school, the "unique records" concept creates a lot of problems in a typical company's data structuring.

> **Storing and retrieving data accurately depends heavily on there being one record with exactly the same information and storage path.**

Looking back to classes in previous years, you may remember a class that had two people with the same name. Especially during the first few days of school, the Instructor experienced "uniqueness of data" difficulties when one student's name was called and two people responded. Usually there was some obvious difference between the two, and everyone grew accustomed to the problem and compensated for it in some way. Maybe one of them went by a nickname, or by their middle name, or had a "1" or "2" placed after his name. Maybe one was taller or older. The point is that in some way those students were differentiated and a way was devised to address them properly.

Data within a file is not very different. Using our hierarchy of data example of the school system in the United States, you would need increasingly refined data if you wanted to get score results for a person named John. Which individual named John? Starting from the least and going to the most refined data, you would have to know that John was from the U.S., that he was born in California, moved to Modesto, went to school at Valley High School, was in the eleventh grade, had fourth period in room 119, and sat in the third seat in the fourth row during that period. Then you could find out that John's last name is Smith. There could have been another John anywhere along this hierarchical path who was not the one we were looking for. There even could have been another one in the same room, and we would have found ours only if we went to his particular seat.

There is a better way to get there. If the data record has a unique identifier in it, we can arrive there directly. In TPUP's case, our data record has your Social Security number in it. A Social Security number is considered a *unique identifier,* because we can search all the data for that identifier and immediately identify our John.

Naming Standards

Now that you have your data and understand the difficulty of unique identifiers, it is time to develop the *naming standards* that you will use throughout the course. We already have some of the information needed—your own personal data—but what has to be determined now is how that relates to the company. If you look at Figure 1-1 on page 3, you will see a company organization chart for TPUP. The job you were selected for in Activity 1-2 should be listed in TPUP's organization chart, and you will find the current employee's user name in the associated organization chart entry.

Depending on the number of people in your class and the position that you were hired for, your user name will come right from the chart, or, if you are an assistant, you will use your first name and the first letter of your last name to form your user name. This is how it was done at TPUP, and it is done similarly at other companies. Normally your user name is the first letter of your first name combined with your last name; "rmcmahon" would be my user name using that naming standard. Either way is fine provided you use the same standard and there is a solution for cases of identical user names. For example, if a Rich Martin were hired, his user name would also be RichM.

With the *user name*, whether or not a letter is capitalized does not affect the computer's acceptance of it. It reads the name as all lower case letters and will accept it even though it looks different to us. This means that a user name is *case insensitive*. It only has to have the same letters. Watch out for spaces and other special characters, though. They still have to be there.

Passwords, on the other hand, are sometimes a different matter. They can be *case sensitive*. If "TeacheR" were my password, typing "TEACHER" would not work; typing "teacher" would not work either. The fact that we call it a pass "word" is confusing, too. It does not have to be a word. It can even be made up entirely of special characters, like ΦϑΠΩ. You have to remember it though, and type it in exactly when they are case sensitive. Note that Novell NetWare passwords are *not* case sensitive.

> ... a user name *is* case insensitive.
>
> Passwords ... *can be* case sensitive.
>
> Novell NetWare passwords *are not* case sensitive.

ACTIVITY 1-3   Select Your Own Password

In this activity you will select your own password and give it to your Instructor to keep in case you forget it. Your password should be easy enough for you to remember, but difficult enough for someone else to determine what it is. If someone else has your password, they have access to your information and may damage it or pass it along to someone else. That someone else may be just the person or business you did *not* want to see it.

When you select your password, you should protect it. Do not write it down anywhere other than on the sheet for your Instructor. You should not let anyone else know what your password is—no matter what! Your class should come up with some penalty for breaking this rule. Then tracking passwords can be informative and fun. You will change your password four times during the semester, and you will not be allowed to reuse any of them. If your password is lost or discovered, you will need to come up with another one.

A good password should be more than seven characters long, be made up of letters, numbers, and special characters, and be easily remembered by its user. Once your password is in the Novell network, not even the network administrator—the person who controls the network—can look at it. He can change it, but he cannot see what

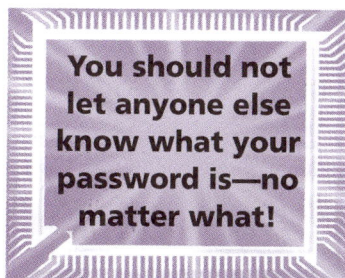

> You should not let anyone else know what your password is—no matter what!

it was. Moreover, you know when it has been changed because your old one will no longer work, and he will have to give you another one.

Passwords are serious business. Start protecting yours now even though you are not yet on a networked computer. ■

Build Your Own Disk Operating System

> To build your own disk operating system, you must begin by understanding the structure of what you want on your hard disk drive.

To build your own disk operating system, you must begin by understanding the structure of what you want on your *hard disk drive*. Your hard drive has circular discs inside on which you electronically store your data. These discs circulate at extremely high rates of speed. As they rotate, a read/write head is raised and lowered to store or retrieve data from the surface. You can imagine some of the problems of trying to do this if you put a small dot on the surface of a *Compact Disk (CD)* and rotate it at about 3000 revolutions per minute (RPM). As the disc rotates, have a classmate touch the dot every 100th revolution without touching anything else on the CD and without slowing the CD down. That person would have to be *very* fast!

It is easy for the computer to do this, however, because it is extremely fast, and it has an unfair advantage because it can "see" the dot. The problem the computer faces, however, should become more apparent when you imagine that the dot is invisible and that your classmate still has to touch it each 100th revolution without impeding the CD's speed. Sound impossible? Not for the computer!

First, you must know the speed of the disc. That is very important, because all the adjustments you make as you go nearer to or further from the center of the disk are based on mathematical calculations and corrections determined by speed and distance. As you go closer to the center of a turning disc, you complete a revolution around that disk faster.

Next you need to be able to determine your starting point. If you know where you start and how fast you are traveling, you can always compute where you are. If you are a computer, this is an easy matter. You simply bounce a laser beam down and "read" where you are. Then you adjust for time and speed to calculate where the information you want will be at a time you can be there to get it. Then, when it gets there, you "read" the information at that estimated time. It's simple—if you are a computer.

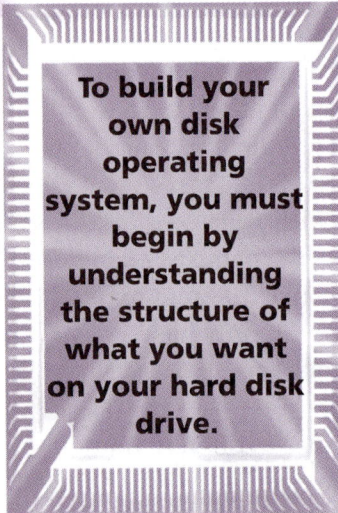

ACTIVITY 1-4　　Be the Disk Drive

Try it yourself. Be the hard drive's disk. Get a classmate to be the computer-controlled disk drive head. Have that classmate close his eyes and hold one hand in front of himself at approximately waist level with his palm down, ready to "pat" the disk as it goes by. You, as the disk, set the speed, but you have to simulate the drive head's ability to locate itself on you by making audible sounds (like counting a one, two, three beat). Tell your classmate that at each count of one, your hand will be at his left side, at two it will be directly below his hand, and at three it will be at his right side. Keep the beat steady and start with your hand at the "number one position" as you say "one." Move it to the "two position" as you say "two." Then go on to the "three position" as you say "three." From there go back to the "two position" and then to the "one position." Keep the beat steady and continue. Tell your classmate to touch the "disc" slightly (so as not to impede it) each time it is in front of him.

You should notice that as soon as the embarrassment of doing this activity wears off and your classmate gets in sync with the beat you are giving him, he finds the disk each time. If you increase your speed, the success rate will remain constant up to a point. (You can go too fast for even you to keep up with yourself!) Alter your pattern again and have your classmate touch the disk every other or every third pass. On the last alteration, have him touch your hand on the left side, then skip a beat and touch it on the right side. When he does that, your classmate is performing much as your computer does as it locates items on the disk!

In this activity, you have simulated the retrieval of data from the designated storage area on a rotating disk. Each time your classmate touched the "disk" as it went by, he was in effect reading or writing data to the correct location.

In this exercise you also "*formatted* your disk drive" when you told your classmate when to lower his hand to touch yours. He needed to know when you started. From then on, he knew where your hand was and only had to anticipate where it would be next, and touch it when he thought it would be where he could reach it. He knew your "format," and was ultimately successful at "retrieving" your data. He could have been more effective if you had had a more precise method of telling him where to look for information. For instance, you could have used letters in addition to numbers to specify when you were closer to or further away from your classmate. He could have placed his hand nearer to the actual data's location if, for example, "2" still meant in front of him but "2A" meant closer to his waist, while "2B" indicated the middle of his reach in front, and "2C" that your hand was far out in front of him.

Your number system would roughly equate to the hard disk's *sectors*, the pie-wedge "slices" of a disk used as areas where data is stored. When you specified A, B, or C to your classmate (indicating closer or further from him), you gave information similar to that which the disk drive uses when it stores data on *tracks*, the concentric circles where data is stored around a disk. The combination of the two, tracks and sectors, even during your imitation of a disk drive, would make accurate "data retrieval" more likely to occur. With the precision of a computer, the two combine to ensure that the disk drive finds the data it is looking for every time. ■

Your Workstation

Right now, you are probably working at a typical stand-alone work-station computer. If you are, this portion of the chapter will fit your circumstances somewhat better than if you are using an atypical computer setup, such as a laptop computer, dumb terminal, or a Macintosh system. Regardless of which computer system you use, or even if you are not at a workstation at all, you should be able to understand the following discussion. If you have trouble following the discussion, or think you need to refresh your memory on the basics of computing or computer accessories, refer to Appendix C and to this chapter's references in the back of the textbook.

The typical stand-alone workstation at high schools and colleges is made up of four main parts—a *mouse*, a *keyboard*, a *monitor*, and the *Central Processing Unit (CPU)*. You can read about the first three in Appendix C, along with a brief physical description of the CPU. You must read and understand that section of the text so that you recognize the physical components. However, this section of our discussion goes beyond the physical description of the principal parts. We look into how they coordinate within your CPU.

It is time to actually set up and use your computer. It is best if you gain the knowledge of and respect for the computing environment you are entering by building your own set-up. The exercises in this part of the text, however, may be ones your Instructor does not want you to perform. Some schools do not have the luxury of allowing their class participants to disassemble the software structure of the classroom workstations. Therefore, do not proceed with this section until your Instructor tells you to do so. Doing so without the Instructor's consent may result in irreparable damage to someone else's files, or require someone to restore the items you removed. This section will completely remove *all* traces of everything you have on your computer.

> **WARNING**
>
> Do not proceed with this section until your Instructor tells you to do so. Doing so without the Instructor's consent may result in irreparable damage to someone else's files.
>
> **WARNING**

Removing the Operating Instructions

This section is fundamental to your understanding of the way your computer works and the interconnectivity of the network you are studying. Your computer may be operational right now, but soon you will destroy everything in it and replace only the pieces your network activities will use. Although it may sound ominous at this point, you will not damage your computer. You will simply remove the operating instructions your computer is currently using and install the ones you will need for this course.

In this section you will use the other three main physical parts of your computer, but you will primarily work with your hard drive. In order to do that you will use your CD drive and your *floppy disk drive*, additional physical components within your CPU. This discussion requires that you already have the DOS diskettes (6.22 preferably) and the *Original Equipment Manufacturer (OEM)* Windows 95 CD. The Windows 3.1x diskettes with the Windows 95 upgrade (on diskettes or CD) produce basically the same operating system configuration, and Windows 98 CD is a newer version but is also a similar operating system. If you have anything other than the 6.2x diskettes and the Windows 95 CD, make the appropriate adjustments to the process by using the directions that you receive as you install the software.

Rebuild Workstation's Hard Drive – Optional (Instructor Approval *Required*)

This discussion about formatting is important because your computer's hard disk needs to be formatted. Your processor retrieves the data you store on the hard drive based on its format. In this exercise, you will erase everything on the disk in the CPU of your workstation and re-format it as specified below. The steps to do that are as follows:

- Restart your Windows 95 Pentium 75 (or higher) computer (others will be similar but not exactly the same) in DOS.

- Use the DOS **FDISK** command to remove all the partitions presently on your hard drive.

- Reestablish the new partition required for this course.

- Format your hard drive. (You need disk overlay software for older model computers.)

- Install DOS.

- Install Windows 95 (or Windows 98, or Windows NT). (You need CD driver software if Windows is on a CD.)

> **CAUTION**
>
> If your computer is an older model and cannot handle hard drives larger than 512 MB, do not execute this procedure without verifying your reformatting capability using a large disk allocation system. In Figure 1-3, the warning window illustrates some of the difficulties that you will encounter if this is done improperly. If you are unsure about your ability to properly format your workstations, skip the **FDISK** steps.
>
> **CAUTION**

Figure 1-3

```
Your computer has a disk larger than 512 MB. This version of Windows
includes improved support for large disks, resulting in more efficient
use of disk space on large drives, and allowing disks over 2 GB to be
formatted as a single drive.

IMPORTANT: If you enable large disk support and create any new drives on this
disk, you will not be able to access the new drive(s) using other operating
systems, including some versions of Windows 95 and Windows NT, as well as
earlier versions of Windows and MS-DOS. In addition, disk utilites that
were not designed explicitly for the FAT32 file system will not be able
to work with this disk. If you need to access this disk with other operating
systems or older disk utilities, do not enable large drive support.

Do you wish to enable large disk support (Y/N)...........? [N]
```

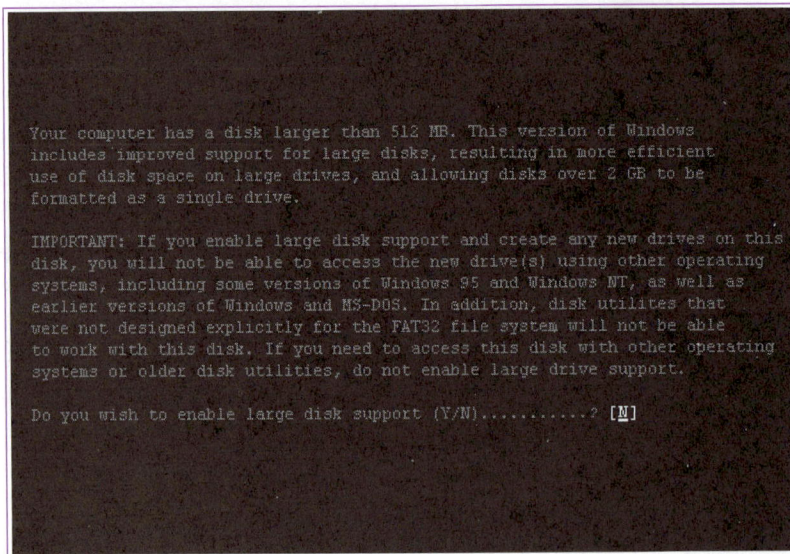

> **Restart the computer by turning it off and then back to on. This ensures that the computer goes through a "cold start" and that all settings are re-initialized.**

Procedure:

1. Insert the DOS diskette number 1 into the 3-1/2" floppy disk drive. Restart the computer by turning it off and then back to on. This ensures that the computer goes through a "cold start" and that all settings are re-initialized.

2. The computer will start up on the floppy disk and warn you that you are about to replace the operating system. Cancel out of this by hitting **F3**. Cancel out of the next item with another **F3**, and you should end up at a DOS "A:" prompt.

3. Type **fdisk** and press **<ENTER>**. This DOS command is the first step to partitioning your fixed disk.

4. The **FDISK Options** window in Figure 1-4 appears.

Figure 1-4

```
                        Microsoft Windows 95
                        Fixed Disk Setup Program
              (C)Copyright Microsoft Corp. 1983 - 1995

                             FDISK Options

        Current fixed disk drive: 1

        Choose one of the following:

        1. Create DOS partition or Logical DOS Drive
        2. Set active partition
        3. Delete partition or Logical DOS Drive
        4. Display partition information


        Enter choice: [1]




        Press Esc to exit FDISK
```

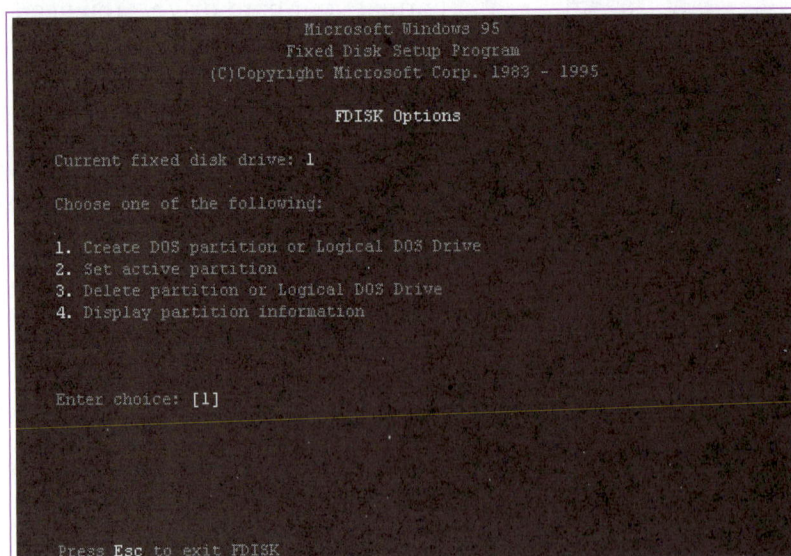

5. Choose option **4** to display partition information (see Figure 1-5) and to ascertain what you have when you start. This procedure

accounts for one partition's removal, but you should delete all partitions. Note the partitions installed on your computer so that you can delete each one. Hit **<ESC>** to return to the previous window (see Figure 1-4) when finished.

Figure 1-5

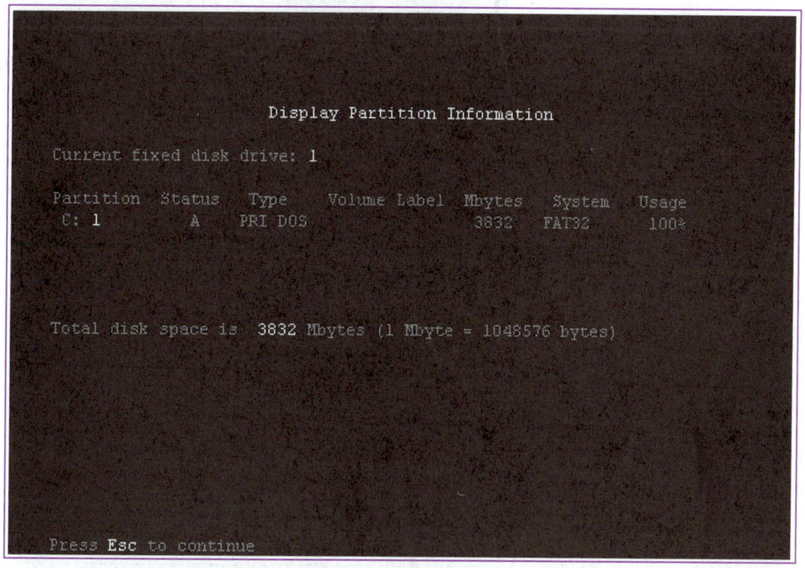

```
                    Display Partition Information

Current fixed disk drive: 1

Partition   Status   Type    Volume Label   Mbytes   System   Usage
C: 1          A     PRI DOS                   3832    FAT32    100%




Total disk space is  3832 Mbytes (1 Mbyte = 1048576 bytes)







Press Esc to continue
```

Figure 1-6

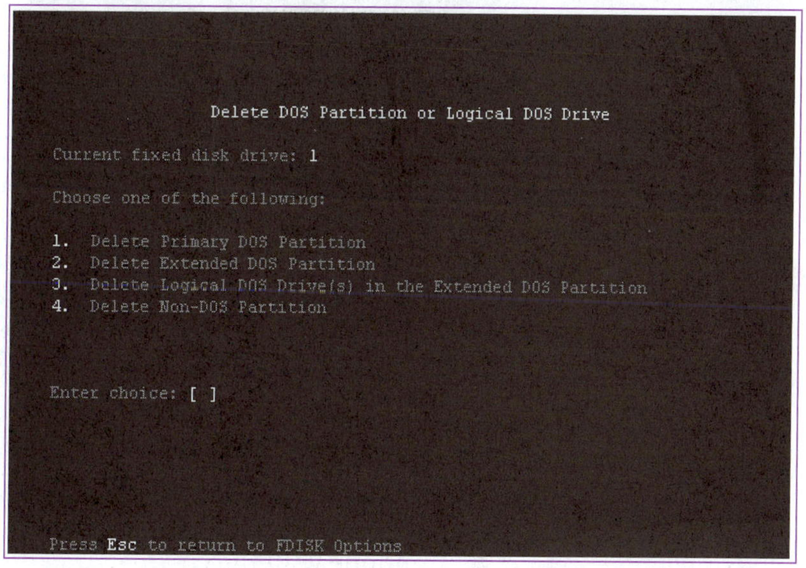

```
              Delete DOS Partition or Logical DOS Drive

Current fixed disk drive: 1

Choose one of the following:

1.   Delete Primary DOS Partition
2.   Delete Extended DOS Partition
3.   Delete Logical DOS Drive(s) in the Extended DOS Partition
4.   Delete Non-DOS Partition


Enter choice: [ ]




Press Esc to return to FDISK Options
```

6. Choose Option **1** to delete the Primary DOS Partition (see Figure 1-6). You will have to confirm this command and enter the partition's name before the computer allows you to delete the partition.

Figure 1-7

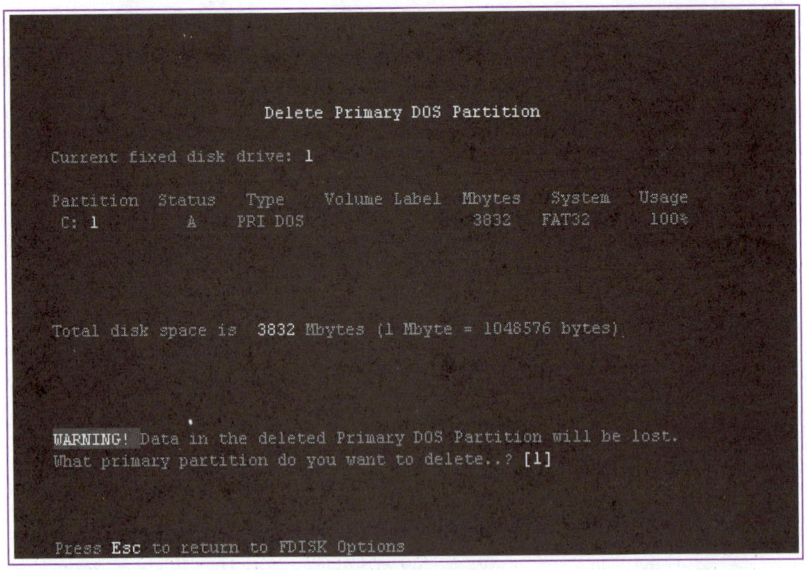

```
                        Delete Primary DOS Partition

Current fixed disk drive: 1

Partition  Status   Type     Volume Label   Mbytes   System   Usage
C: 1         A      PRI DOS                   3832    FAT32    100%




Total disk space is  3832 Mbytes (1 Mbyte = 1048576 bytes)




WARNING! Data in the deleted Primary DOS Partition will be lost.
What primary partition do you want to delete..? [1]


Press Esc to return to FDISK Options
```

7. You will receive a warning (see Figure 1-7) that the data in the primary DOS partition will be lost. Specify the number of the primary DOS partition and press <ENTER>.

Figure 1-8

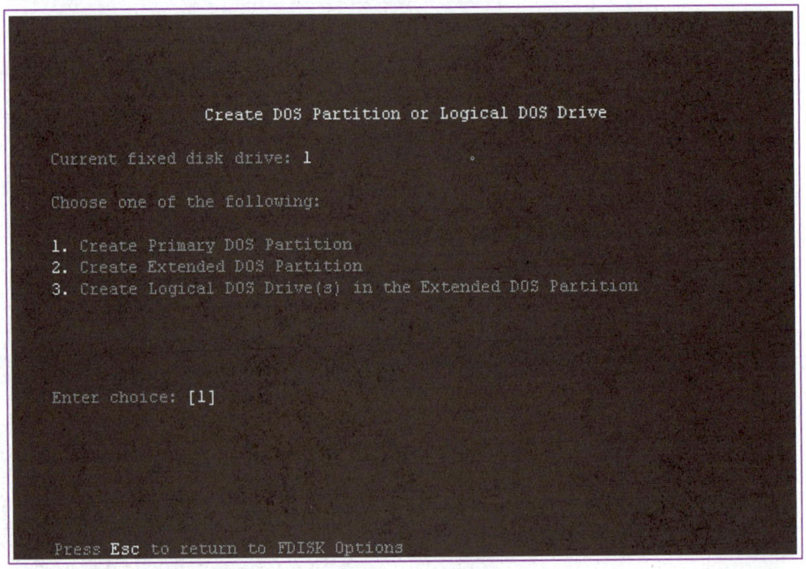

```
                  Create DOS Partition or Logical DOS Drive

Current fixed disk drive: 1

Choose one of the following:

1. Create Primary DOS Partition
2. Create Extended DOS Partition
3. Create Logical DOS Drive(s) in the Extended DOS Partition




Enter choice: [1]




Press Esc to return to FDISK Options
```

> **Shut down your computer and restart it with the DOS diskette number 1 in your floppy disk drive. This will initiate the DOS installation to your computer.**

8. Continue with the *Create DOS Partition or Logical DOS Drive* window by choosing number 1. You will name and specify the size of the partition. Let the computer take all of the hard disk space available to use in the DOS partition.

9. Press <ESC> to return through the *FDISK* windows to the initial *FDISK Options* window and then again to exit **FDISK**.

10. Shut down your computer and restart it with the DOS diskette number 1 in your floppy disk drive. This will initiate the DOS installation to your computer. (See Appendix D)

11. If your Windows program is on diskettes, begin your Windows installation. If you have Windows on CD, you must install your CD driver software first and restart your computer before installing Windows.

Chapter Summary

> In this chapter, you met TPUP. It is a fictional company based on a real manufacturing firm.

In this chapter, you met TPUP. It is a fictional company based on a real manufacturing firm. You will develop your network while acting as a member of their management staff. After reading their classified advertisement, you created a job application and resume and applied for a position at TPUP. While the position you were "hired" for is unimportant with respect to learning about networking, the way that position fits into the company and the data used in that position will bear directly on your developing network skills.

The pieces of information accumulated during this class discussion will remain important throughout the entire course. Effective organization of this information as you begin using this text will assist you during your employment with TPUP. When combined, the data, or pieces of information, help describe entities important to your system. Data is collected initially in fields. When the fields are combined, records are formed. In the hierarchy of data model, records are then combined to form files.

Some fields have required formats which render data recognizable as a particular type of data. Occasionally a data field will have multiple entries, as when a person has two phone numbers. No records can be comprised of files with exactly the same information; there must be a unique identifier that distinguishes records from each other.

A naming standard must be utilized to assure that only properly authorized people have access to information.

The way disk drives work and how they are formatted was illustrated through an exercise in which the learners were active participants.

Finally, the information on the class workstations was deleted and replaced with the information necessary for the remainder of this course.

Networking Terms Used in Chapter 1

data	user name	mouse
format	case insensitive	keyboard
record	password	monitor
file	case sensitive	Central Processing Unit (CPU)
field	hard disk drive	floppy disk drive
multiple entry field	Compact Disk (CD)	Original Equipment
hierarchy of data	format	Manufacturer (OEM)
unique identifier	sectors	**FDISK**
naming standard	tracks	

CHAPTER 1
TPUP

1. Explain why simulated employment at TPUP is used for your networking activities during this course.

2. What caused TPUP's company-wide technology expansion?

3. Define the term *data*.

4. Relative to data collection, define the term *format* as used in the text.

5. Explain why format is important for some data.

6. Fill in the three blanks on the following diagram with the term that describes the item shown.

Hierachy of Data

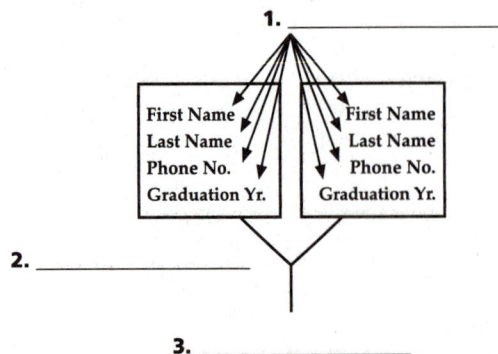

1. _____

First Name	First Name
Last Name	Last Name
Phone No.	Phone No.
Graduation Yr.	Graduation Yr.

2. _____

3. _____

■ Associated Chapter Problems

1. With respect to the collection and use of data in your TPUP simulation, how would the distance between the plant and corporate office affect your filing system? Explain.

2. If you were directed to implement a technologically-driven data collection system, which employees in TPUP would you expect to have more difficulty accepting that system? Explain.

3. Describe some of the difficulties encountered because of the "handwritten" requirements for your job application and resume.

4. Explain the term "hierarchy of data" relative to the way you would sort your classmates' records created from the data you collected in your manual filing system.

5. A "unique identifier" is needed to distinguish each record. Why are they needed? How do they work?

6. In the absence of the hierarchy of data model and a unique identifier, how would you locate the information of a specific individual in your class?

7. Explain the importance of a unified naming standard and discuss the value of settling on that standard at an early stage in a network's development.

CHAPTER 2
WHAT IS A NETWORK?

Now that you have begun to amass data relative to this course and your involvement in TPUP, the next step is to store and share that data. These functions are some of the main reasons for forming networks. In this chapter you will:

- understand the need for a network.

- describe the typical components of a network.

- understand the different types of networks.

- distinguish between the different types of cabling.

- create network connections.

- install and configure a network interface card.

Network Basics

In its broadest sense, a network consists of two or more entities sharing resources and information. For example, when you were born you joined a "human network" in which the adults who raised you shared their resources and information in your family network. As you grew older, your network expanded when you added friends, relatives, and classmates.

In the business world, especially when job hunting, you are encouraged to increase the number of people who know you by "networking." The business contacts network you establish can be used to share information about yourself with others in the network who might have a job position available.

A Networking Need

From the first day of this course, you and your classmates began sharing information and resources. You also began compiling data in chapter one that will be used in your computer network. The human networks mentioned above demonstrate that networking between people is also necessary and that networking is not an activity restricted to computers. However, you enrolled in this class to learn about connecting computers and having them communicate with each other. The network you have selected to learn operates with Novell NetWare software.

A *network* of computers consists of two or more computing devices that are connected in order to share resources and information with each other. The network expands and becomes more usable when additional computers join and add their resources. The power of networking becomes even more pronounced when a network is able to communicate and share resources with other computer networks. The communication and resource sharing activities of the joined network are shared with your network as you become part of its networking community.

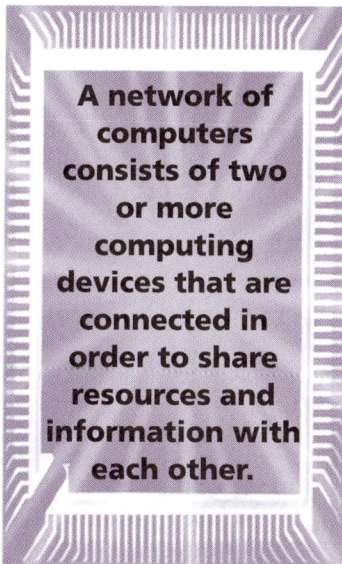

> A network of computers consists of two or more computing devices that are connected in order to share resources and information with each other.

Figure 2-1

A network consists of two or more computing devices connected together and able to communicate.

You will agree that this situation can quickly become unmanageable and confusing as you try to control which computer communicates with and shares resources with other computers. In your network of friends do you share everything? In your family network would you want your parents or guardians to know your every thought? Similar concerns must be taken into consideration while designing your network. Before you even connect your first computers and attempt to communicate between them, there must be a plan.

The Hierarchy of Data

The hierarchy of data model from Chapter 1 will be the basis of our plan. Simply put, the lower you are in the hierarchy, the more you should be able to share your information. As data accumulates and is stored higher in the chain, the access requirements should be stricter and the number of people able to obtain your information fewer. We can illustrate the point using the data you gathered in Chapter 1. Because it is your own information, you can share your phone number and Social Security number with as many people as you like. When you turn it in for this class, though, it should not be freely shared by the person gathering it without your approval. How much you can trust that person determines the security level of the information you are willing to share over your network. After considering this simple example, you will agree that data sharing has security issues and that network access to data must be evaluated carefully so that only those who need that data can access it. Security will be of prime concern later in this text.

> ... network access to data must be evaluated carefully so that only those who need that data can access it.

Let's examine the fundamental components of a computer network. You already have the first component—the data you collected in Chapter 1. You now wish to share that data in an electronic fashion that is more convenient than storing handwritten documents in your Instructor's folder. You want to enter that data in a computer and allow it to be viewed and used by at least one other computing location. You have developed a need for a computer network.

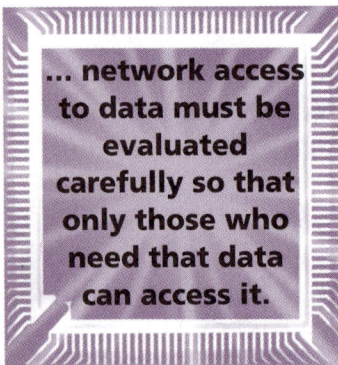

Fundamental Network Components

Figure 2-2
Server

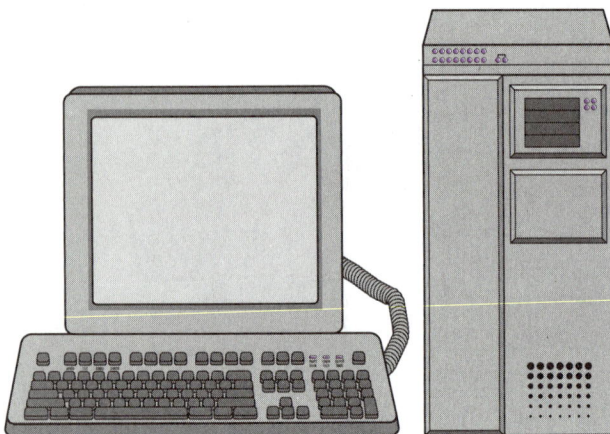

Let's evaluate the equipment you have and then look at what you still lack in your network. You have the data that you want to share and you have two computers, one that stores your data and another that needs to access the data. You already have the basic structure of all networks. The computer you wish to store your data in wishes to "serve it up" to the other computer. The first computer is commonly referred to as the *server*. The other computer is trying to gain access to your data in order to use your information. In our simple example that second computer is referred to as a *workstation*. It becomes a *client* when it requests services from the network server.

Figure 2-3
Server and Clients

Server

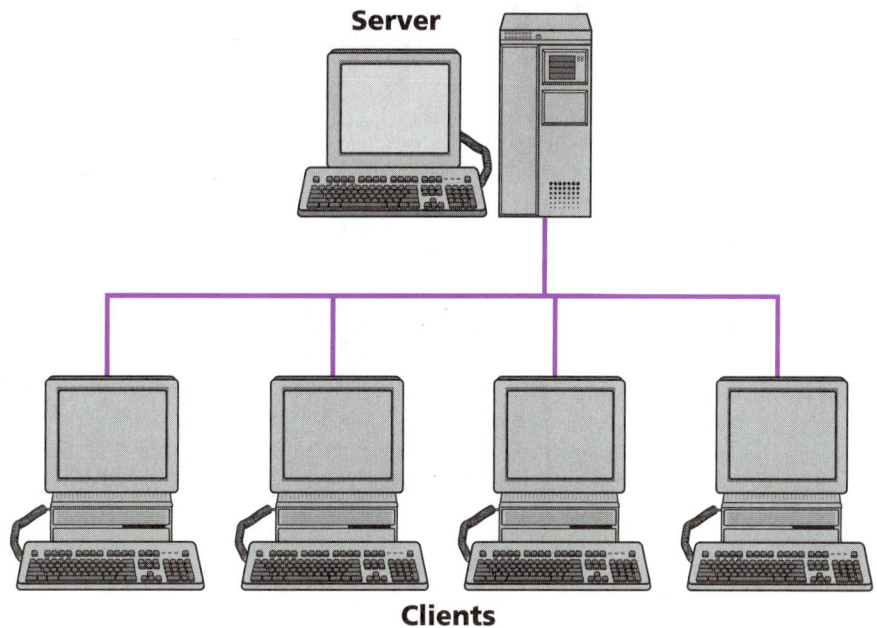

Clients

> A server is a computer that offers its services and resources to clients and workstations over a network.

> A client is any device on a computer network that requests services or resources from a server.

A server is a computer that offers its services and resources to clients and workstations over a network. Some of the services a server provides to other computers on the network are centralized management of resources, security, and expanded access to networked resources. See Figure 2-3.

A client is any device on a computer network that requests services or resources from a server. Clients can be printers, workstations, servers or any other device on a network. The most common clients are workstations. See Figure 2-4 for typical examples of clients.

Figure 2-4
Typical Clients

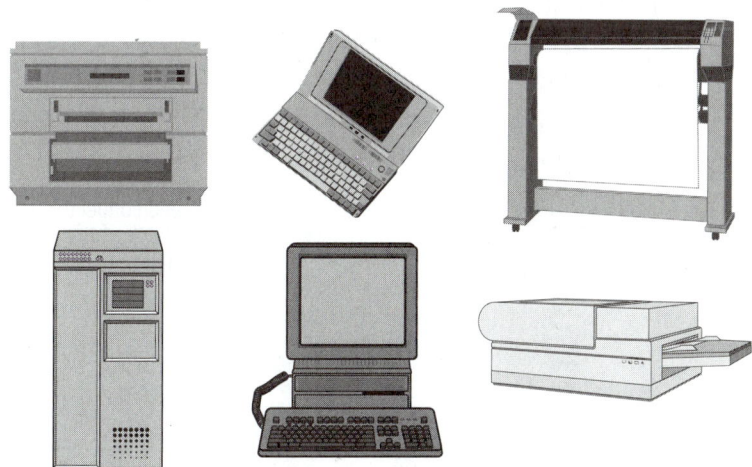

> A workstation is a computer that is able to operate independently of the network and manage its own files and processing.

A workstation is a computer that is able to operate independently of the network and manage its own files and processing. Most computers in a typical network are stand-alone workstations able to function without the network. Connecting to the network allows them to access networked resources. The security and centralized management of networked resources are two of the main reasons workstations join a network. See Figure 2-5 for examples of typical workstations.

Figure 2-5
Workstations

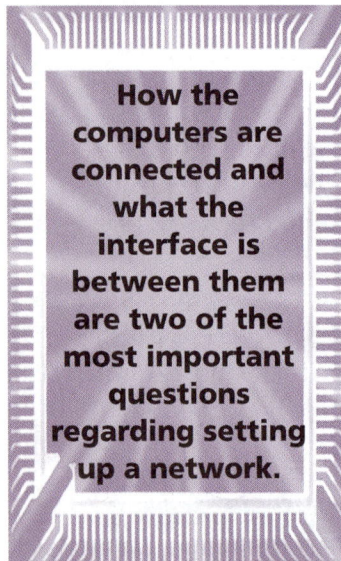

Essential Network Hardware

Once you combine a server and at least one client, such as a workstation or printer, you have the majority of the basic network's hardware. You have the "who needs to get information and services from whom" and the "what needs to communicate where," but something very important is still missing. The pathway and interconnection have not been discussed. How the computers are connected and what the interface is between them are two of the most important questions regarding setting up a network.

How networked computers are connected involves the *communication medium* or *cabling*. This normally takes the form of either *coaxial cable* (similar to wiring used for cable TV, Figure 2-6) or *twisted pair wiring* (similar to telephone wiring in your home, Figure 2-7). Recently, *fiber optic cabling* (insulated glass or hard plastic fibers over which light passes and transfers data, Figure 2-8) has gained widespread acceptance as a network communication medium.

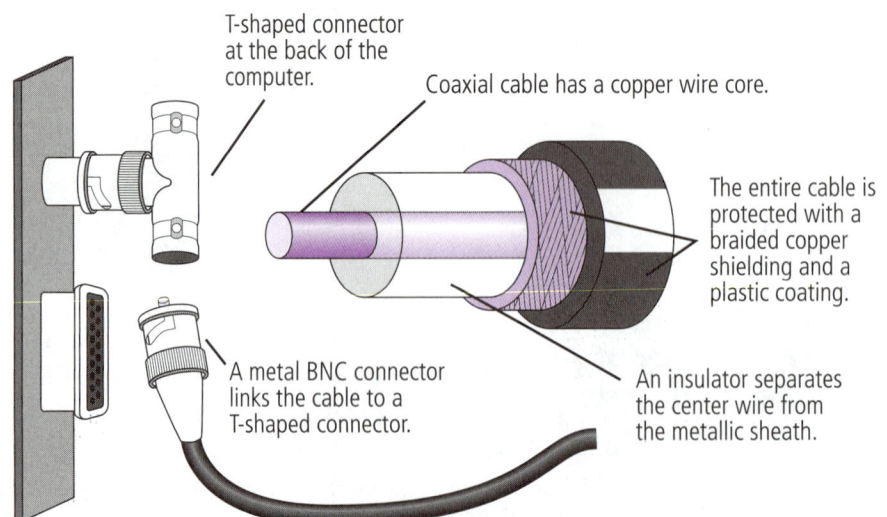

> How the computers are connected and what the interface is between them are two of the most important questions regarding setting up a network.

Figure 2-6
Coaxial Cable

T-shaped connector at the back of the computer.

Coaxial cable has a copper wire core.

The entire cable is protected with a braided copper shielding and a plastic coating.

A metal BNC connector links the cable to a T-shaped connector.

An insulator separates the center wire from the metallic sheath.

Figure 2-7
Twisted-Pair Cable

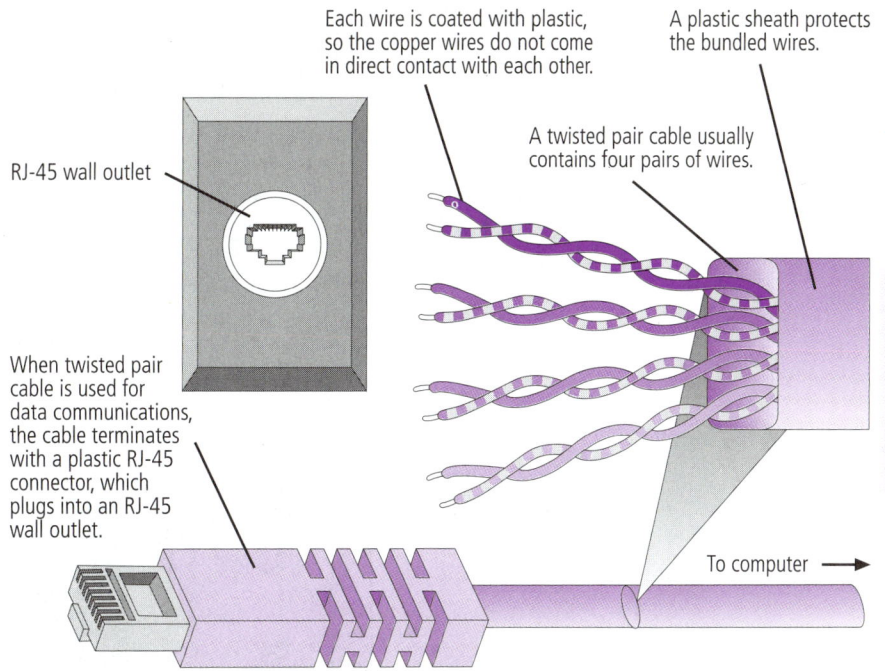

RJ-45 wall outlet

Each wire is coated with plastic, so the copper wires do not come in direct contact with each other.

A plastic sheath protects the bundled wires.

A twisted pair cable usually contains four pairs of wires.

When twisted pair cable is used for data communications, the cable terminates with a plastic RJ-45 connector, which plugs into an RJ-45 wall outlet.

To computer →

Figure 2-8
Fiber Optic Cable

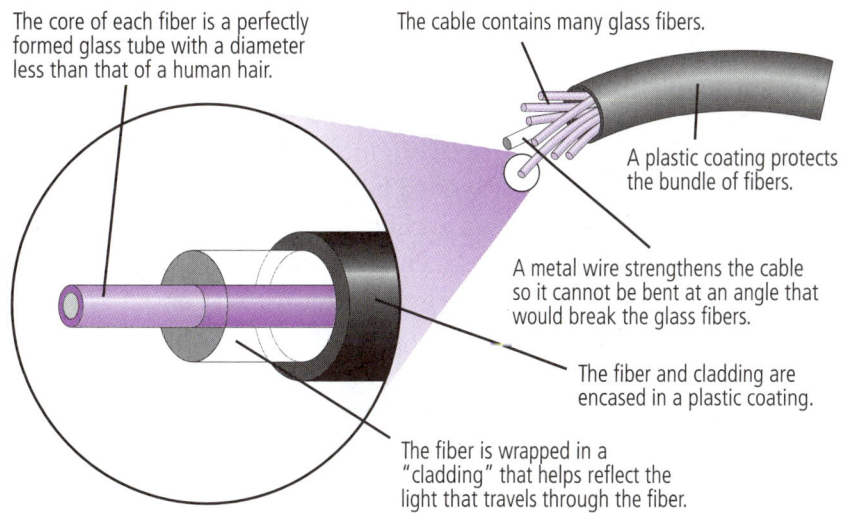

The core of each fiber is a perfectly formed glass tube with a diameter less than that of a human hair.

The cable contains many glass fibers.

A plastic coating protects the bundle of fibers.

A metal wire strengthens the cable so it cannot be bent at an angle that would break the glass fibers.

The fiber and cladding are encased in a plastic coating.

The fiber is wrapped in a "cladding" that helps reflect the light that travels through the fiber.

Figure 2-9
A typical network

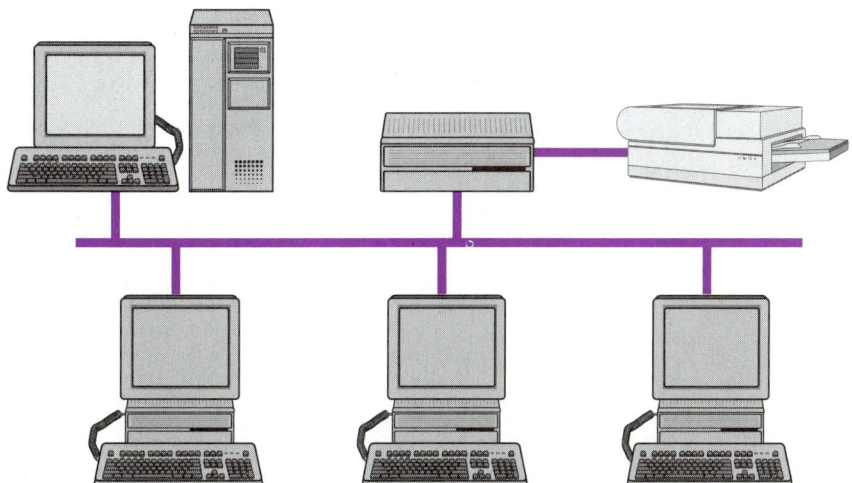

The principal hardware components which might comprise a typical network are shown connected together in Figure 2-9. A server (top left) is connected to a print server (top center) sharing its printer (top right). It is also connected to various network clients. The components are connected above but the network connection has not yet been explained. Your network requires a *Network Interface Card (NIC)*, or network board, for most components. This *network board* serves both as a physical connection and as a translator between every computing device on the network.

Figure 2-10

A network interface card

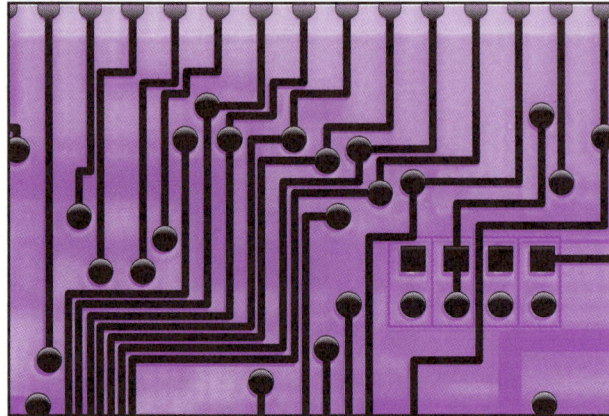

> **The network board serves both as a physical connection and as a translator between every computing device on the network.**

> **The hub simply acts as a central meeting point for the information as it is gathered for the server.**

Each server, then, connects to the network cabling through its network interface card. However, there are additional components needed because the computer cabling cannot physically connect to each client directly. You need a network *concentrator* or *hub* to connect the many client cables together and channel them to the server. See Figures 2-11 and 2-12. The hub simply acts as a central meeting point for the information as it is gathered for the server. If the server had enough ports, or connection points, for each client on the network, there would be no need for a hub or concentrator. Because it is more economical to use a hub to gather the information for the server, they are widely used in most computer networks.

There are additional connection devices in networks as well. Hubs are the simplest and merely act as a central connection location. *Intelligent hubs* perform the same type of service for the network but add the capability of network monitoring and selective configuration. *Bridges* divide the network into segments and pass information from one segment to another, often joining dissimilar network sections in the process. *Routers* are the most sophisticated of the concentrators and are able to send specific portions of messages directly to their intended destination.

Figure 2-11
Hub/Wiring Concentrator

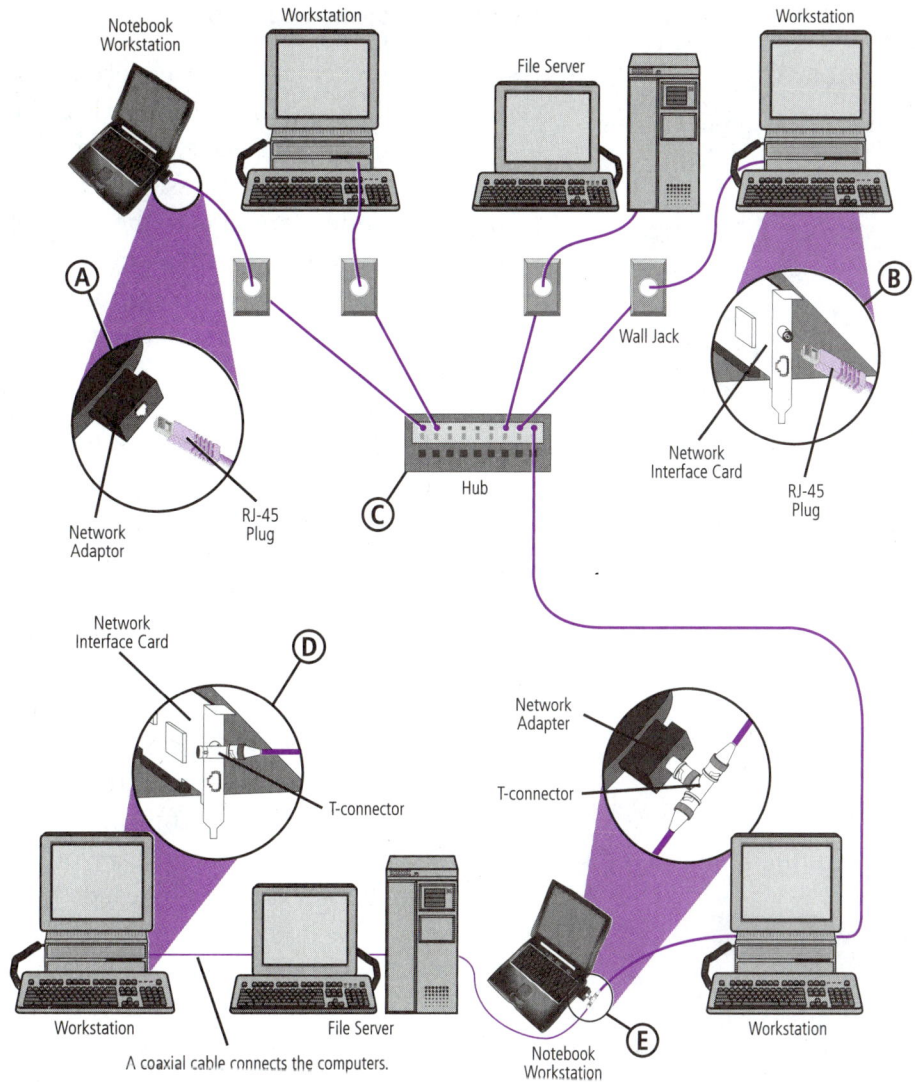

Labels: Notebook Workstation, Workstation, File Server, Workstation, Network Adaptor, RJ-45 Plug, Hub, Network Interface Card, RJ-45 Plug, Wall Jack, Network Interface Card, T-connector, Network Adapter, T-connector, Workstation, File Server, Notebook Workstation, Workstation

A coaxial cable connects the computers.

(A) A network adapter plugs into the parallel port of a notebook computer. An RJ-45 connector and twisted pair cable connect the laptop's network adapter to the wall plug.

(B) A network interface card plugs into the main board inside the desktop and tower computers. An RJ-45 connector at one end of the twisted pair cable plugs into the network interface card. An RJ-45 connector at the other end of the cable plugs into a wall jack that looks similar to a telephone jack.

(C) A wiring hub, or concentrator, provides a central connecting point for the cables on the network. Here, the hub connects a series of computers that use twisted pair cable and another series of computers that use coaxial cable. The cables branch out from the hub through the wall jack to the computers at the top of the page. The computers at the bottom of the page are connected to each other in a series.

(D) A T-connector is attached to the network interface card. The T-connector is then attached to the coaxial cable's BNC connector. A "terminating resistor" is added to the T-connector on the last computer on the cable.

(E) A network adapter plugs into the parallel port of a notebook computer. A T-connector connects the network adapter to the coaxial cable.

Figure 2-12
Network Concentrator

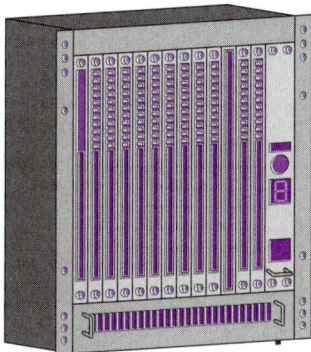

> When two computers "speak" on a network, they are exchanging digital information. Computers use 1's and 0's to form their "language."

> When one computer wants to communicate with another computer within its own network, or even in another network, a source address is created which specifies where the transmitted information originates, and a destination address is created which specifies where the information goes.

Network Communication

As you learn when you take a speech class, members of a network cannot effectively communicate unless there is at least one sender, at least one receiver, a message, and a method (or medium) of transmission. In addition, the message sent by the sender must be in a form that is understandable to the receiver; they must "speak" the same language. Just as in speaking, if there is a translator between the sender and receiver, the communication between networked components may not be as effective.

When two computers "speak" on a network, they are exchanging digital information. Computers use 1's and 0's to form their "language." The 1 represents an electrical connection that is "on" and a 0 represents one that is "off." The word *bit* (from the words binary digit) is used to represent a single "on" or "off" (1 or 0). This can also be represented by either light pulses or electrical current. The computer interprets a light pulse or electrical current as a binary 1. The absence of the light or the current is read as a binary 0.

For this method to work there must be another step or the individual bits would be dispersed in a random, unrecognizable manner. A computer combines groups of eight bits into a *byte*. Each byte is used to represent a character, digit or symbol that is understood by humans. When a computer communicates with another computer, it assembles groups of bytes to form words and other meaningful data. The combination of bits and bytes, then, forms the basis of computer languages.

Bits are also combined to form computer messages sent over the network. Each computer on a network has a unique address or *physical address*. That physical address is a number assigned to the network interface card by its manufacturer or set by the installer by means of jumpers or switches placed in the "on" or "off" position. It is commonly referred to as the *hardware address*.

Along with the hardware address, a unique *node address* is created for every computer on a network. This works well for all communication between computers on the same local area network, but another step is necessary for communication to occur beyond the boundaries of a computer's own network. Since each node address is designated to the specific network to which it is attached, another number is assigned arbitrarily by the network when it communicates with another network. The combination of all those addresses then becomes the computer's *network address* and uniquely identifies it to all others on the network.

When one computer wants to communicate with another computer within its own network, or even in another network, a *source address* is created which specifies where the transmitted information originates, and a *destination address* is created which specifies where the information goes. The uniqueness of the networking address system ensures that effective communication takes place.

Figure 2-13
Network addresses

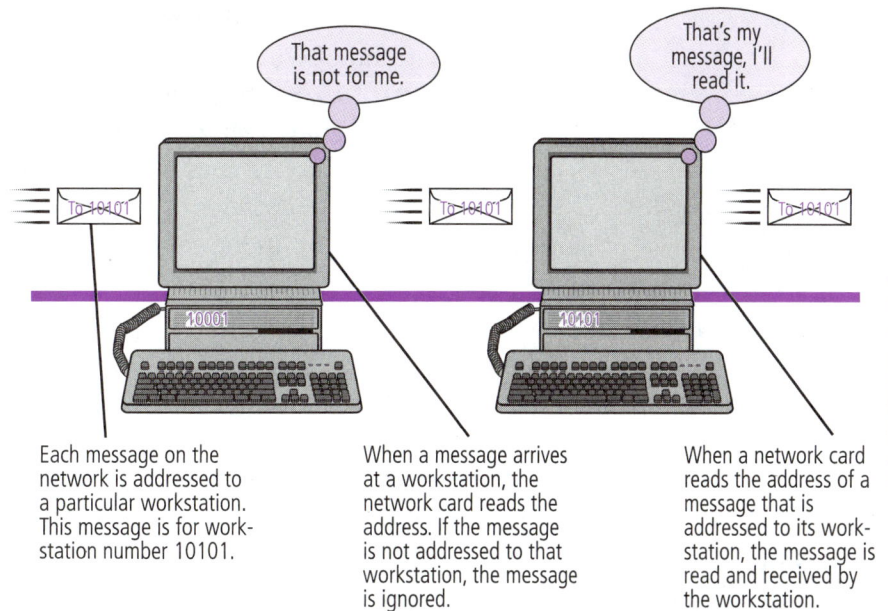

The source and destination addresses are added to the data being transmitted to make sure that the message is routed properly. It is examined by the receiver and if it is not completely understood, the receiver asks the sender to retransmit the message. When it is completely understood, the receiving computer acknowledges receipt and the sending computer stops repeating the transmission. See Figure 2-13.

Figure 2-14
How computers are connected together determines the topology

Types of Networks

The physical layout or arrangement of computers within a network is referred to as its *topology*. See Figure 2-14. While the physical connections for the network determine its topology, the information's logical flow through that network may not actually follow the physical configuration. The three most common types of physical topologies are the bus, ring, and star topologies.

In a *bus topology* all computers are attached to what amounts to a single strand of wire directly connecting each computer in the chain. See Figure 2-15. Such connection is called *daisy chaining* computers together. The main connection in a bus topology is also called the "bus" or "backbone," and every end on the bus must be either connected to a computer or *terminated* with a special end piece signifying an end in the cable.

Figure 2-15
Bus topology

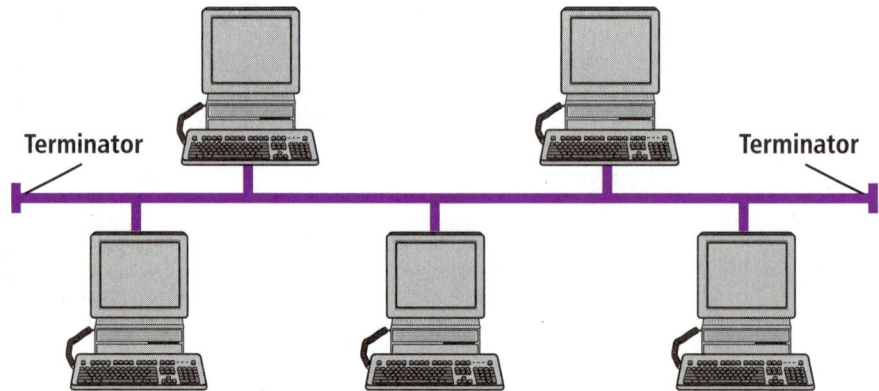

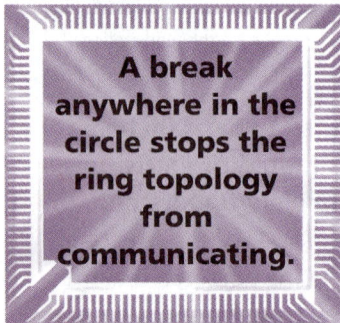

A break anywhere in the circle stops the ring topology from communicating.

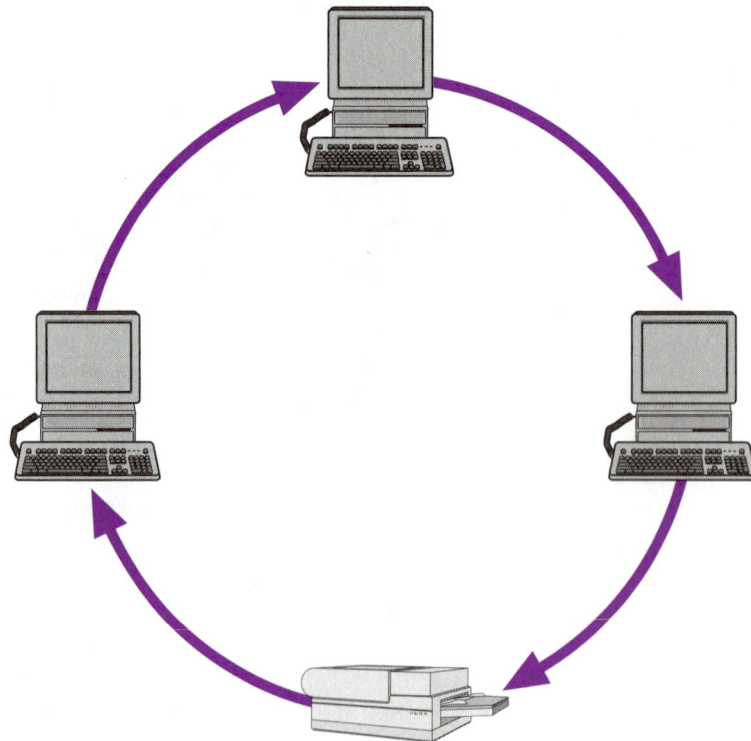

In a *ring topology*, the computers are attached to each other in a large circle, as shown in Figure 2-16. The signal flows around the circle to the next working station. If one is not operating properly, it is simply bypassed as long as the circle remains unbroken. A break anywhere in the circle stops the ring topology from communicating.

Figure 2-16
Ring topology

Star topology is the most commonly used topology in the classroom ...

Star topology is the most commonly used topology in the class-room, mainly because it is the easiest to maintain. See Figure 2-17. Hubs play an important role in the star topology because all data passes through the hub to each of the spoke-like connections of the star. This creates a slight increase in cabling cost but makes the system relatively easy to troubleshoot. The points of the star are made up of independent network segments running directly from the computer to the hub. If the hub stops working, the workstations cannot communicate. If only one machine cannot communicate, it is likely that a problem exists with that machine's connection to the hub.

Figure 2-17
Star topology

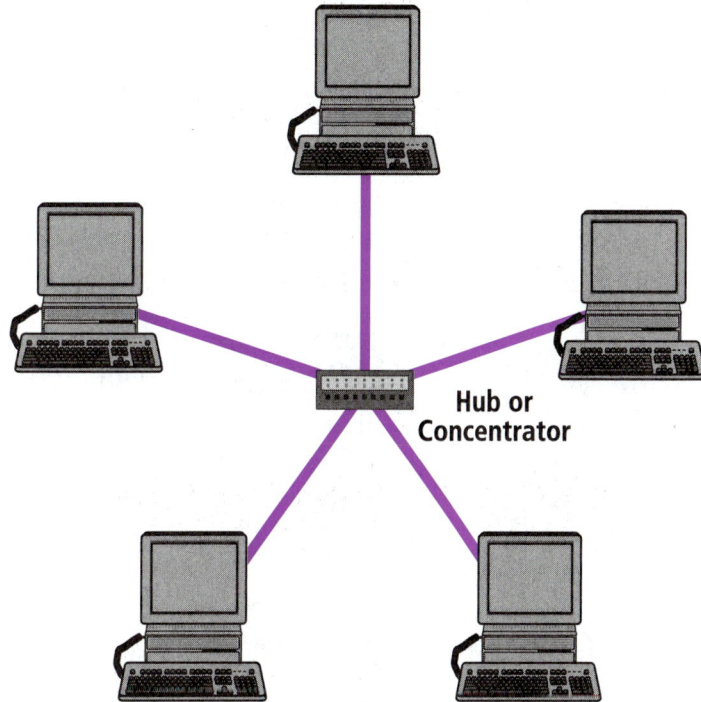

Hub or Concentrator

Network Geography

Networks are frequently classified according to the geographical boundaries spanned by the network itself ...

Networks are frequently classified according to the geographical boundaries spanned by the network itself, as shown in Figure 2-18. If the network is contained within a relatively small area such as a classroom, school, or campus, it is commonly referred to as a *Local Area Network*, or *LAN*.

If the network spans the distance of a typical metropolitan city, it can be referred to as a *Metropolitan Area Network*, or *MAN*.

When the network spans a larger area than a single large city it is classified as a *Wide Area Network*, or *WAN*.

Figure 2-18
LAN, MAN, and WAN networks

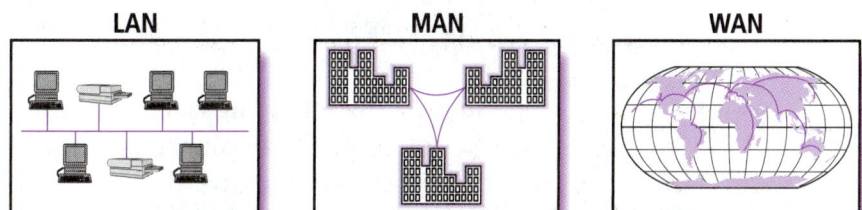

Activity 2-1	Let's Get Connected

Now that you have an idea about what networks are and how they are cabled together, let's connect some computers and begin networking over your own cables. In this activity you will create your own network cables to connect your computer either to another computer or to a concentrator (hub).

You will need the following items:

1. Network Interface Card (NIC) (one per computer or networked device)
2. *RJ-45 Connectors* (one for each planned cable end, plus lots of spares for practice)
3. *Category 5 (Cat 5) Unshielded Twisted Pair (UTP) Wire* (sufficient wire should be available for short pieces of "practice" cable in addition to the wiring you will make to link your computer to the server connection)
4. RJ-45 Wire Crimping Tool
5. Wire Cutters
6. *10Base-T* Wire Continuity Tester
7. Hub (with sufficient capacity to connect each computer in the class to the server)

Making a Straight Through Cable—Practice

Step 1 Cut off a 3-inch section of *Cat 5 wire*.

Step 2 Being careful not to nick the insulation off the internal twisted pairs of wire inside the Cat 5 wire piece, cut back 3/8-inch of the outer covering from your piece of wire. This should expose the internal four pairs of twisted wiring inside the external cover.

Step 3 Pull off the entire external cover from the twisted pairs within. Do not untwist pairs.

Step 4 Note whether the internal wires have solid or striped colors on the plastic coating.

Step 5 Untwist the first inch of each pair of wires. The colors (or striping) will play an important role when connecting the wires to the connectors.

Step 6 Notice that the pairs of wires are twisted together but that the spacing of the twists on one pair is different from the spacing of the twists on another pair. These twists help filter out interference from one pair to another.

Step 7 The following is for practicing cable placement for insertion to the RJ-45 connector. Turn connector around so that the flat side is toward you and the plastic tang is away from you. Pin 1 is to your left.

Step 8 Arrange the single wires in the following *straight through cable* order from left to right, and pinch all eight close together side by side and between your index finger and thumb.

Straight Through Cable		
Pin	**If Striped Colored Wiring:**	**If Solid Color Wiring:**
1	White/Orange	Green
2	Orange	Yellow
3	White/Green	Blue
4	Blue	Red
5	White/Blue	Black
6	Green	Orange
7	White/Brown	Brown
8	Brown	Gray

Step 9 Slide all eight wires completely into the end of an RJ-45 connector. It will be seated properly in the RJ-45 when you can look through it and see the wire ends completely pushed up against the inside end.

Step 10 If done properly, this connection is ready to crimp and be used as a network termination. Do not *crimp* this connection.

Step 11 Get Instructor confirmation before removing your wire pieces from your RJ-45 connector.

Step 12 Before you remove your wire pieces, note where the outer cover of the wiring (stripped off in step 4 above) would have fit inside the RJ-45 connector. When you crimp down with the crimping tool, that external cover should be crimped in the outermost section of the connector. That cover will give the cable support and help keep the smaller wires from being pulled out if the cable is tugged.

Step 13 Remove the wire pieces from your RJ-45 connector

Making a Straight Through Cable—Actual

Step 1 Obtain your first real networking cable from your Instructor. Depending on where the Instructor wants to use your cable, it could be anywhere from 6' to 100' long.

Step 2 Being careful not to nick the insulation off the internal twisted pairs of wire inside the Cat 5 wire piece, carefully cut back 3/8" from the outer covering from your piece of wire. This should expose the internal four pairs of twisted wiring inside the external cover.

Step 3   Untwist the exposed 3/8" section of each pair of wires.

Step 4   Arrange the single wires for insertion to the RJ-45 connector in the following "Straight Through Cable" order from left to right, and pinch all eight close together side by side and between your index finger and thumb.

Straight Through Cable		
Pin	**If Striped Colored Wiring:**	**If Solid Color Wiring:**
1	White/Orange	Green
2	Orange	Yellow
3	White/Green	Blue
4	Blue	Red
5	White/Blue	Black
6	Green	Orange
7	White/Brown	Brown
8	Brown	Gray

Step 5   Slide all eight wires completely into the end of your RJ-45 connector. It is properly seated in the RJ-45 when you can look through it and see the wire ends completely pushed up against the inside end, and the external covering is also inside the RJ-45.

Step 6   When inserted properly, use the crimping tool to crimp your RJ-45. It can now be used as a network termination.

Step 7   Get Instructor confirmation before continuing with the other end of your RJ-45 connector. Stop here if you have completed both ends of your cable.

Step 8   If your Instructor tells you to continue making a Straight Through Cable, repeat the steps above beginning with Step 2. When you get back to this point after crimping the second end on, test your cable using the cable tester. If it passes the continuity check, you have a working cable.

If your Instructor tells you to finish your cable as a *crossover cable*, perform the following steps.

Making a Crossover Cable—Actual

Step 1   Being careful not to nick the insulation off the internal twisted pairs of wire inside the Cat 5 wire piece, carefully cut back 3/8" from the outer covering from your piece of wire. This should expose the internal four pairs of twisted wiring inside the external cover.

Step 2   Untwist the exposed 3/8" section of each pair of wires.

Step 3 Arrange the single wires for insertion to the RJ-45 connector in the following "Straight Through Cable" order from left to right, and pinch all eight close together side by side and between your index finger and thumb.

Crossover Cable (one end only)		
Pin	If Striped Colored Wiring:	If Solid Color Wiring:
1	White/Green	Blue
2	Green	Orange
3	White/Orange	Green
4	Blue	Red
5	White/Blue	Black
6	Orange	Yellow
7	White/Brown	Brown
8	Brown	Gray

Step 4 Slide all eight wires completely into the end of your RJ-45 connector. You have seated it correctly in the RJ-45 when you can look through it and see the wire ends completely pushed up against the inside end, and the external covering is inside the RJ-45.

NOTE

Maximum cable segment distance for this type of system is 100 meters.

NOTE

Step 5 When inserted properly, use the crimping tool to crimp your RJ-45. After testing it with the cable tester your cable can be used as a network crossover cable.

Congratulate yourself! You have just completed a wiring task that would have cost the school approximately $2.50 per foot if they had had a network-wiring specialist make the cable. As you can see, becoming a network-wiring specialist would prepare you for a lucrative career should you choose that path. Completing your first network cable and understanding (or completing) crossover cables has given you a great start on a network wiring career path. For those of you still interested in network administration, cabling is just one important part of the position's requirements. ■

Something To Connect To

There should be plenty of network cables for everyone in your class now that you have all become familiar with cable termination. However, you need network interface cards in your computers so that you can speak to one another over the network. If your Instructor did not strip them out of the computers before you re-installed Windows, your system may already recognize your network card. If that is the case, and there are two communicating computers, you can skip this section and wait while the other individuals install NIC cards into classroom computers.

Otherwise, it is time to install a NIC card so you can continue with your networking project. In case you forgot, the network interface card is a small circuit board that plugs into the expansion ports of the motherboard in your computer's CPU. That circuit board then allows your computer to "speak" over the network and be "heard" by computers at the other end of the network connections.

Activity 2-2	NIC Card Installation

During this activity, you will be working on the inside of your computer.

WARNING

The computer operates with voltages that can be lethal. Before you remove the computer cover, observe the following steps to protect yourself and those around you, and to prevent damage to the system's components.

a. Turn off the computer and unplug the unit from its power source.

b. Disconnect all cables connected to the CPU.

c. Remove any jewelry from your hands and wrists or anything that may dangle into your working environment.

d. Use only insulated or nonconductive tools.

WARNING

Step 1 Remove the computer's cover and choose an empty expansion slot appropriate for the type of NIC card you are installing.

Step 2 Remove the expansion slot's backplate, if it has one installed.

Step 3 Insert the NIC card into the expansion slot and secure it with the screw removed from the expansion slot's backplate removal. *Note:* make sure that the card is securely seated in the expansion slot. It may take firm downward pressure to ensure proper installation. When correctly seated, the gold fingers on the NIC card will not be visible.

Step 4 Replace the computer's cover.

Step 5 Reconnect all cables to the computer and connect a crossover networking cable from your computer to another computer in your classroom.

Step 6 Turn the computer on.

Step 7 Windows 95, 98, or NT Workstation installed on a Pentium computer will detect the new network interface card's presence and will initiate driver installation.

Step 8 If your NIC card is not recognized by your computer upon startup, your Instructor will have to initiate troubleshooting procedures. Other steps may be necessary such as driver installation and/or communication with the manufacturer of either your computer or the card or both.

Step 9 If the network interface card is installed properly and Windows correctly recognizes the card, your Windows desktop will include a *Network Neighborhood icon* as shown in Figure 2-19.

Figure 2-19

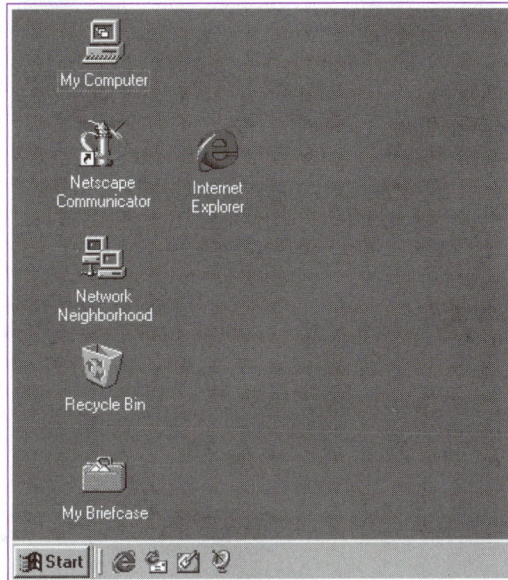

Step 10 Right click the *Network Neighborhood* icon and choose **Properties** from the drop-down menu.

Step 11 On the *Network* window, select Client for Microsoft Networks and left click on File and Print Sharing….

Figure 2-20

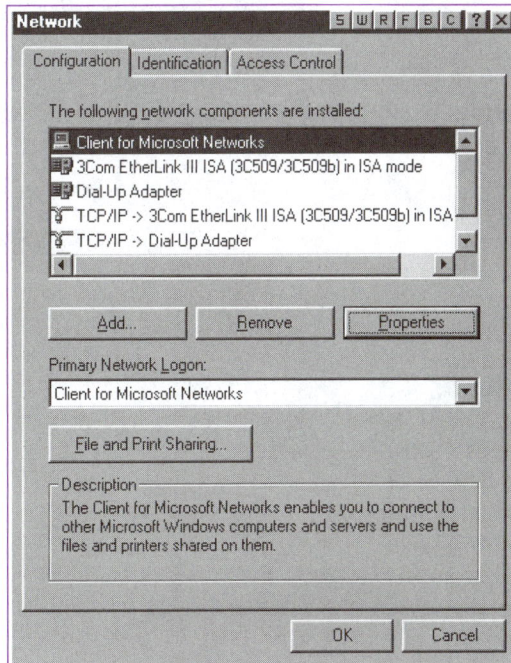

Step 12   Activate both boxes to give access to files and to printers.

Figure 2-21

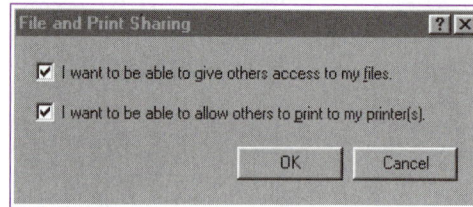

Step 13   • Right click on *Network Neighborhood*; select **Properties** again.
  • Click on **Add**.
  • Select **Protocol**.
  • Select **Microsoft**.
  • Highlight NetBEUI.
  • Click **OK** to install the NetBEUI protocol on your computer. Your computer will need to be restarted after installation.

Figure 2-22

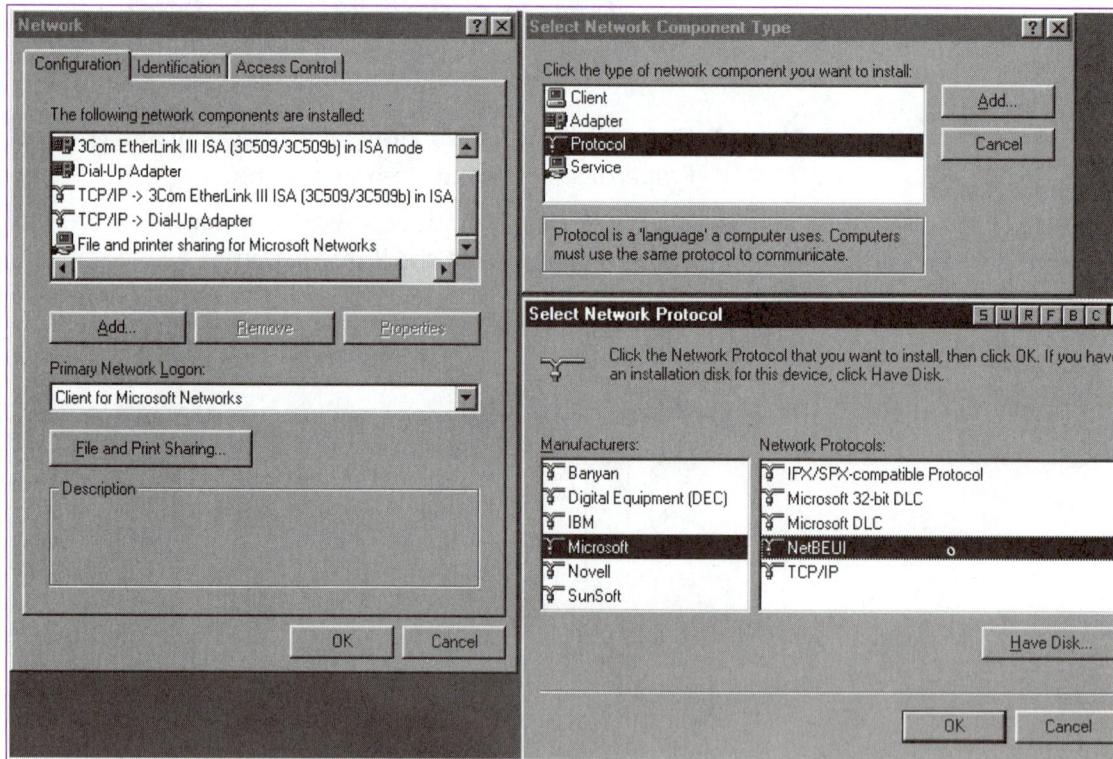

Step 14 After restarting and double clicking on *Network Neighborhood*, you should see the other computer you are "networked" to, provided that the computer has already shared at least one file.

Figure 2-23

Step 15 If "Nothing" has been shared on either computer, left click on the *C:* Drive, choose the **File** menu, click on **Sharing**, and click on the **Shared As** radio button to activate sharing.

Figure 2-24

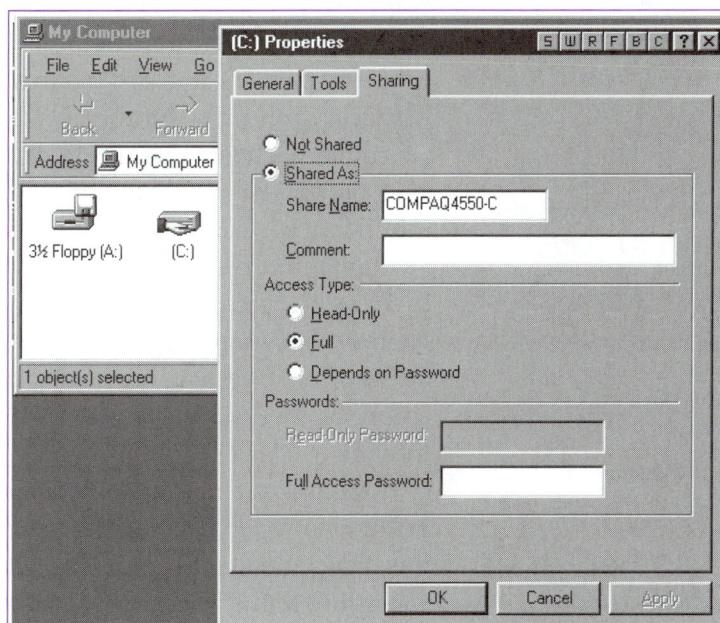

Congratulate yourself. You have created your own network!

Chapter Summary

Even before reading this chapter, you began developing a need for a network. That need was explained and clarified through a discussion of computer networks. Computer networks consist of two or more computers that are connected and able to communicate. They share resources and information. Powerful networks result as additional computers add to the communication possibilities. As more and more data becomes available over a network, a control system must be established. The hierarchy of data model used in this context allows those lower in the hierarchy to share their information with many people. Higher up in this chain, access is more strictly controlled, and fewer people can obtain the data as a result.

Once you have data that you want to share and two computers to share it, you have the basic components of a computer network. The computer able to "serve up" information is commonly referred to as the server. The other computer becomes the client, because it is requesting services or resources from the server and is commonly a stand-alone workstation.

The networked computers are interconnected with cabling. It is comprised of either twisted pair wiring, co-axial cabling, or fiber optic cabling. The cabling connects the computers through network interface cards or network boards which act as both translators and physical connectors for the network. A hub serves as a concentrator when many clients attempt to connect to a server. Intelligent hubs, bridges, and routers also act as connections in a network and furnish additional services for passing information around the network.

Digital information "spoken" on a network is made up of bits and bytes which are interpreted at the other end as a computer's words. Network messages are sent over the network and picked up at the appropriate physical, hardware, or node address. This requires the source address of the sender and the destination address of the intended receiver.

Topology refers to the physical layout or arrangement of computers in a network. The three most common types of topologies are the bus, ring, and star topologies. Networks are also frequently classified according to the geographical boundaries spanned by the network. The three most common are the Local Area Network, Metropolitan Area Network, and Wide Area Network.

This chapter also had classroom participants make network cables from Cat 5 cable. RJ-45 connectors and crimping tools were used to connect properly sequenced wiring into either a straight through cable or a crossover cable. The installation and configuration of a network interface card, along with setting up a network protocol, allowed a basic network connection to demonstrate networking capability.

Networking Terms Used in Chapter 2

network
server
workstation
client
communication medium
cabling
coaxial cable
twisted pair wiring
fiber optic cabling
Network Interface Card (NIC)
network board
concentrator
hub
intelligent hub
bridge

router
bit
byte
physical address
hardware address
node address
network address
source address
destination address
topology
bus topology
daisy chaining
terminated
ring topology
star topology
Local Area Network (LAN)

Metropolitan Area Network
   (MAN)
Wide Area Network (WAN)
RJ-45 connector
Category 5—Unshielded
   Twisted Pair (UTP)—wire
10Base-T
Cat 5 wire
straight through cable
crimp
crossover cable
Network Neighborhood icon
Client for Microsoft Networks
File and Print Sharing…
NetBEUI

CHAPTER 2
Network

■ **Chapter Review Questions**

1. Explain how the concept of networking can assist with a job search.

2. Define the phrase *network of computers.*

3. Eventually, a hierarchy of data must be established. Explain.

4. Describe the fundamental network components.

5. Explain the concept of a *network client.*

6. Why do workstations join a network?

7. Describe the three primary communication mediums.

8. What connects the pieces of a network to the network itself?

9. What is a *hub*?

10. What is the difference between a bridge and a router?

11. How do computers speak to each other on a network?

12. Explain the networking address scheme.

13. What are the different types of networks?

14. Define the term "topology."

15. What is "daisy chaining?"

16. What can stop the ring topology from communicating?

17. What is the most widely used topology in the typical classroom?

18. How does a network's geographical span play a role in its classification?

19. What should you remember before opening the cover of any computer?

20. Explain the difference between a straight through cable and a crossover cable.

21. What is the maximum cable segment distance for a 10Base-T network?

22. How can you tell if your computer recognizes the network interface card when Windows starts?

23. Why are the wires in a twisted pair cable twisted?

24. What Microsoft protocol is used in a simple computer-to-computer network?

25. What must you do on one computer before another computer can access its resources?

■ Associated Chapter Problems

1. Write a procedure for wiring the typical classroom. Include all aspects of cable creation.

2. Record all the steps necessary for the installation of a network interface card in the computer you use in this classroom.

3. Why is it important to ensure that all the computers on a network have the same or compatible software installed?

4. Design a hybrid network using the three topologies discussed in this chapter.

Now it is time to create your own network. The components from the first two chapters need to be assembled into a functional network which will serve your needs for the remainder of the course. In this chapter you will:

- assemble the necessary hardware, software, and cabling required for a simple network.

- choose the type of network and its topology.

- rebuild the computer that you will use as your NetWare server (change the partitions, install DOS, load the mouse and CD drivers, and install your network interface card drivers).

- perform an installation of NetWare 5 (or the alternate 4.11 if applicable).

- become familiar with the selections made during installation which involve devices and drivers necessary for proper server operation.

- down the server from its console, reboot your computer to the *C:* prompt, and begin server operation using server console commands.

Preparing for the Installation

Normally, the server is the strongest, fastest, and most powerful computer a company can afford.

Now that you have information to store, multiple users, and more than one computer with which to share information, you need a network. Once you have the applicable version of Novell NetWare networking software, you are ready to begin the TPUP server installation.

First you need a computer to act as that server. For the TPUP installation, you can simply obtain a computer similar to those at your workstations. Normally the server is the strongest, fastest, and most powerful computer a company can afford. It is the central point of all the company's users. Everyone on the network must use it for authentication, storage, retrieval, printing, and running network applications. The server should be fast and capable of handling high loads. When it comes to server selection, the more powerful, the better.

In our case, the server will probably be more powerful than the workstations, but not as strong as that needed in a typical company. For a NetWare 5 server used in a classroom setting, Novell recommends *NetWare minimum hardware requirements*, which include a computer with a Pentium (or compatible) processor, 48 megabytes of RAM, and at least 500 megabytes of available hard disk space. For a NetWare 4.11 server, Novell recommends a computer with a 486/66 processor, 24 megabytes of RAM, and at least 500 megabytes of available hard disk space. In both cases, Novell requires a CD-ROM drive, a network interface card, and the most recent version of the network operating system software (NetWare 4.11 or NetWare 5) that you plan to install. In addition, for the Windows workstations supported by the network server Novell recommends the most recent version of its client software.

Note: Fast computers with a lot of RAM are not always available in classroom situations. Classroom server setups with NetWare 4.11 can run satisfactorily on a 486/33 processor with only 16 megabytes of RAM. NetWare 5 does "require" 48 megabytes of RAM for the server software. The installation of 50 megabytes will give you 47 megabytes of usable RAM. The result is that a warning message may appear, but the program will load and operate without problems. The installation of only 32 megabytes on a 486/66 processor will result in the same warning message appearing. Again, the software will load and operate without problems. There may be cursory warnings during installation, and the system may run slowly. Provided you understand DOS and the **NetWare Client's** operation reasonably well, you can even load the server software from another computer's CD-ROM drive and avoid the need for a CD-ROM drive on your server.

Remember, if you intend to take the Certified Novell Administrator (CNA) exam, it is important to know the official as well as the "real" minimums.

Remember, if you intend to take the *Certified Novell Administrator (CNA)* exam, it is important to know the official as well as the "real" minimums. Novell's official minimums are based on extensive product testing. You must know their stated minimums when you take their test even though you may have experienced successful installations in settings with less than their stated minimums.

CHAPTER 3
Install

You will probably also have to rebuild the computer that you select as your server. You should make sure that the primary DOS *partition* is the only partition on your hard drive when you start the server installation. As in Chapter 2, use **FDISK** (the DOS command for partitioning fixed disks) to delete all the existing partitions, including the primary DOS partition, and recreate only a primary DOS partition. When asked for the size of the partition, change the megabytes from 100 percent to 50 megabytes. That partition size will work if you install NetWare 4.11 or NetWare 5 software on your server.

When using a computer that was previously running Windows NT:

> **HINT**
>
> Should you decide that you want to reuse a Windows NT server or workstation as a NetWare server, it may be difficult to remove NT prior to reformatting the drive. You should check your NT drive with **FDISK** as you did above to verify whether your system is on a FAT (File Allocation Table) partition or an NTFS (or NT File Structure) partition.
>
> **HINT**

■ If your system is on a FAT partition, you must remove the Windows *NT Boot Loader* (the initial segment of the NT operating system that loads into a computer and boots the system in Windows NT) and Files. To do this you must:

a. Boot the drive with a Win95 or DOS system diskette that has the file *SYS.COM* (with the operating system commands) on it.

b. Transfer the system file from the diskette to the hard drive partition by typing **SYS C:** (directing the computer to transfer the operating system to the C: drive) from the A: prompt.

c. Remove the diskette and restart the computer.

d. Delete the following files from the C: drive (some must be *unmarked* as hidden, *system*, and *Read-Only files*):

C:\PAGEFILE.SYS

C:\BOOT.INI

All files whose names begin with "NT" (i.e. NT*.*)

C:\BOOTSECT.DOS

The *\WINNT_ROOT* folder

The *\WINDOWS NT* folder in the *\PROGRAM FILES* folder

■ If your system is on an NTFS *partition*, you need to remove Windows NT from the partition. To do this you must:

a. Boot the drive with the WinNT set-up diskettes.

b. Continue the NT installation until asked to verify the partitions used for your NT system. Select the NTFS partition and press **D** to delete it.

c. Press **F3** to exit setup.

d. Reboot the computer with the DOS installation diskette.

e. Exit the setup, repartition the drive, and load DOS as in Chapter 2.

With the advent of Windows, users have become accustomed to working with graphical interfaces by pointing at icons and clicking on buttons, thus operating with something ostensibly more concrete than text.

As you did in Chapter 1 for the workstations, reinstall DOS onto your rebuilt server's hard disk drive. Refer to Appendix D for the installation steps. While you could use the NDOS that Novell includes with its installation software package, you obtain the results indicated here by installing the MS-DOS operating system. Since both NetWare software packages install from CD-ROMs, you will need to run your CD-ROM player installation software and install your player in DOS. At the same time, you should also load your mouse drivers if you plan to install NetWare 5.

Mouse drivers will be needed with a NetWare 5 file server because unlike a NetWare 4.11 server, the newer software includes a *Graphical User Interface*, or *GUI*. A user interface is simply what communicates with another computer. In past versions of Novell's operating system, this was usually a screen in which you typed text. Now Novell's NetWare 5 has a more graphically-oriented interface. With the advent of Windows, users have become accustomed to working with graphical interfaces by pointing at icons and clicking on buttons, thus operating with something ostensibly more concrete than text. Server console operation has become more user-friendly.

Hint: Installing the mouse software and including the drivers in your DOS setup statements ensures that the mouse works when NetWare 5's Graphical User Interface launches. That, coupled with remembering whether your mouse is a *PS/2* version or connected via one of your *communications ports* (usually COM 1 or COM 2), will prevent your having to re-install NetWare 5. Otherwise, you will be in a "mouseless mode" during and after server installation. While it is possible to navigate with the keyboard, you will probably have to install a serial mouse later.

Your installation will go more smoothly if you connect both your hard drive and your CD-ROM player directly to your motherboard as *IDE drives*, rather than using disk controller cards. There will be fewer configuration errors when the installation needs to know which driver to use.

Speaking of drivers, you should have your network interface card's installation disks available when you start the server installation. Both 4.11 and 5 need your network card settings. You should confirm that your NIC manufacturer has an updated NetWare 5 driver. Most manufacturers have new drivers available on the Internet. As part of your classroom's preparation, your Instructor has probably already checked the Web for your driver's availability.

The final items you will need for your network installation are a hub (unless you still have sufficient room on your other hub network), and the network wiring, so that you can connect the server to your other workstations. If you still have one of the crossover cables you made in the chapter two, you may be able to use it to connect your server.

Now you need to make a preparation checklist to ensure that you have everything needed for a server installation. Before starting, you should have with you or have completed the following:

1. NetWare Operating System software

2. A computer to act as a file server

3. Run the DOS diskettes to load DOS

4. Installed the CD-ROM drive and installed the software drivers

5. Connected the mouse and installed the software drivers (for GUI on NetWare 5)

6. Installed the Network Interface Card (NIC) and installed the software drivers

7. Connected the Server to the hub (depending on topology, may need crossover cable)

8. Networking cables

Activity 3-1   NetWare 5 Server Installation (Primary)

NetWare 5 has one installation method with several options for the different types of installations.

After this careful preparation for the installation, your server should now be ready for Novell's NetWare 5 networking software. NetWare 5 has one installation method with several options for the different types of installations. TPUP's server needs are relatively small, so one of the simplest installations will suffice. Later in the course, you may elect to rebuild your server using the much more customized installation possibilities.

For a NetWare 5 server installation, you may choose from several options. Because of your classroom needs, many of the decisions regarding these options have already been made. It has already been decided, for example, that the server meets the equipment needs, that the DOS partition contains at least 35 MB, that a CD-ROM rather than a network installation will be performed, that both IP and IPX protocols will be used on the network, and that a new NDS Tree will be created.

To perform an installation of Novell's NetWare 5 server software:

1. Reboot the computer.

2. From the C: prompt, change to the applicable drive designation for your CD-ROM drive (i.e. `D:`).

3. Type `Install` `<ENTER>`.

4. Accept the license agreement by pressing the `F10` key.

5. On the *Welcome to the NetWare server installation* screen accept the **Continue** option as shown in Figure 3-1, accept **New server** as the type of installation, and *C:\NWSERVER* as the startup directory (the default responses) by pressing **<ENTER>**.

Figure 3-1

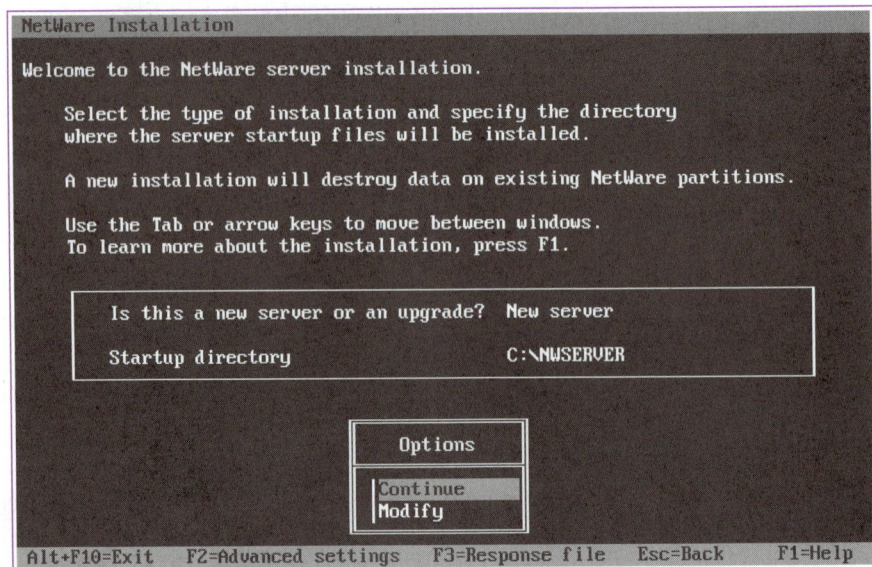

While not the best option for a production setting, servers with less RAM should work satisfactorily in a school setting if the stated minimum requirements cannot be met.

6. In Figure 3-2, you can see the result of installing insufficient RAM on your server. However, the installation with 32 MB of RAM did finish when **<ENTER>** was pressed, and the system operated properly. While not the best option for a production setting, servers with less RAM should work satisfactorily in a school setting if the stated minimum requirements cannot be met.

Figure 3-2

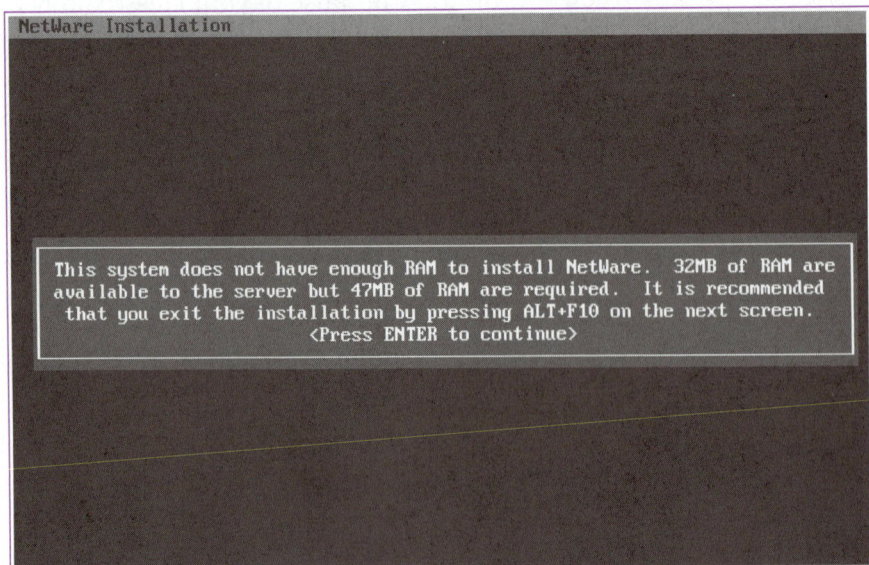

7. ***Select the regional settings for the server*** by pressing <ENTER> to select the default values as indicated in Figure 3-3.

Figure 3-3

```
NetWare Installation

Select the regional settings for the server.


                    Country:    001  (USA)

                    Code page:  437  (United States English)

                    Keyboard:   United States




                              Options

                              Continue
                              Modify




Alt+F10=Exit                    Esc=Back                    F1=Help
```

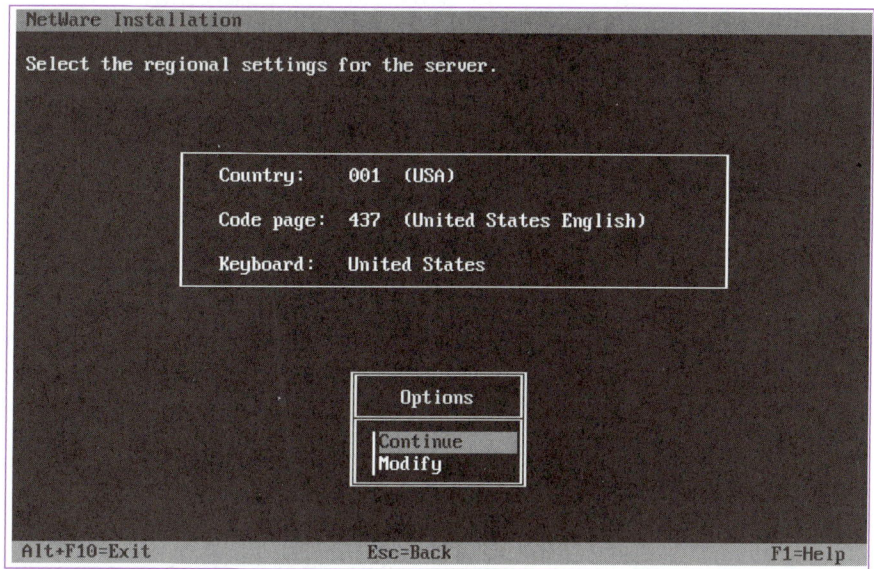

8. ***Select the mouse type and video mode for the server*** by pressing <ENTER> to select the default values as indicated Figure 3-4.

Figure 3-4

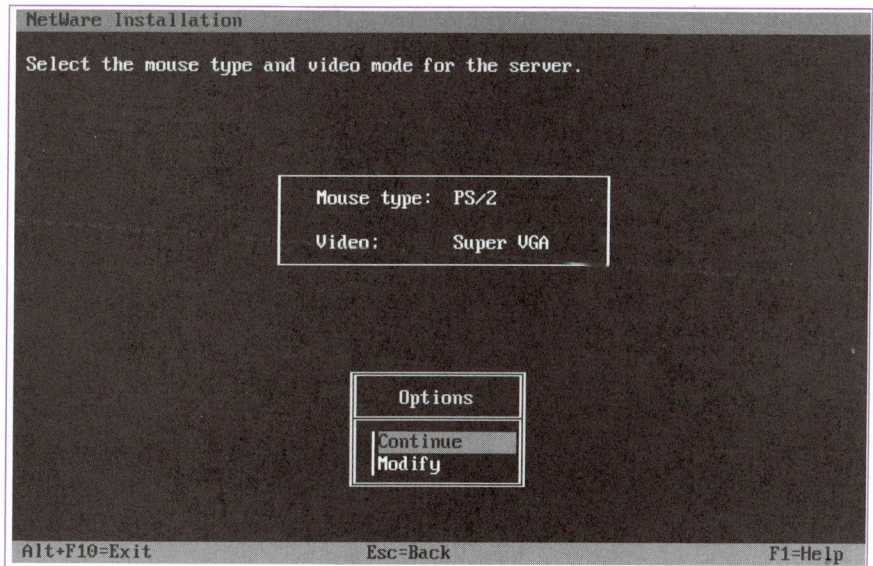

IMPORTANT NOTE

NetWare 5 assumes that the mouse type is PS/2. You must select **Modify** in the **Options** window to change this type if your mouse is not PS/2. Otherwise, you will be in the **Mouseless** category when using Novell's new Graphical User Interface at the server console.

IMPORTANT NOTE

```
NetWare Installation

Select the mouse type and video mode for the server.




                    Mouse type:  PS/2

                    Video:       Super VGA




                              Options

                              Continue
                              Modify




Alt+F10=Exit                    Esc=Back                    F1=Help
```

CHAPTER 3
Install

9. If you do not have a PS/2 mouse, use the down arrow to change to **Modify** in the *Options* window and press **<ENTER>**. Use the down arrow to select the **COM1** or **COM2** serial mouse as indicated in Figure 3-5 if that is the type and location for your mouse.

Figure 3-5

```
NetWare Installation

Select the mouse type and video mode for the server.




                              Mo┌──────────────────────┐
                              Vi│     Mouse Types      │
                                │                      │
                                │ PS/2                 │
                                │ Serial COM1          │
                                │ Serial COM2          │
                                │ No Mouse             │
                                └──────────────────────┘


                                ┌──────────────────────┐
                                │       Options        │
                                │                      │
                                │ Continue             │
                                │ Modify               │
                                └──────────────────────┘


Alt+F10=Exit                 Enter=Select/View                 F1=Help
```

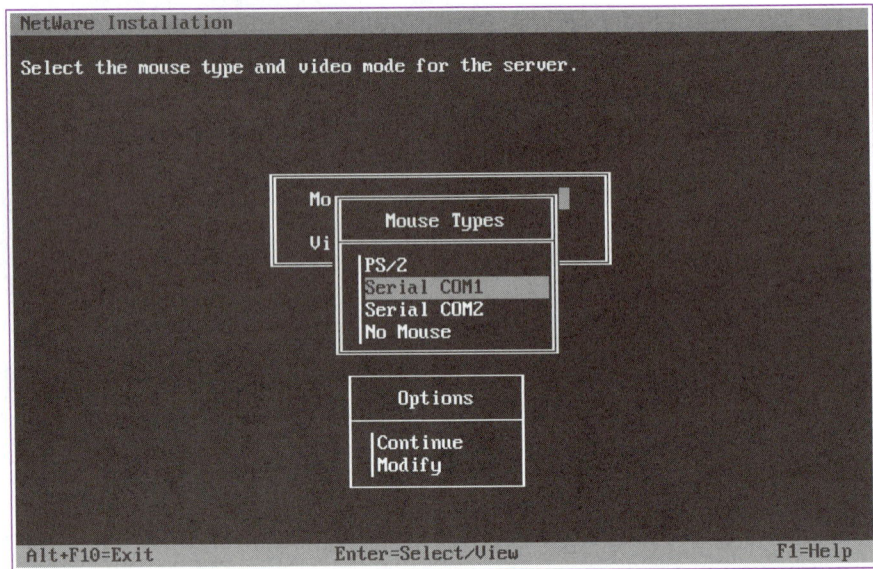

10. If you have changed the mouse type, you should see the window shown in Figure 3-6. Select **Continue** and press **<ENTER>** to accept the modifications you have made.

Figure 3-6

```
NetWare Installation

Select the mouse type and video mode for the server.




                    ┌──────────────────────────────────┐
                    │  Mouse type:   Serial COM1       │
                    │                                  │
                    │  Video:        Super VGA         │
                    └──────────────────────────────────┘




                              ┌──────────────────────┐
                              │       Options        │
                              │                      │
                              │ Continue             │
                              │ Modify               │
                              └──────────────────────┘


Alt+F10=Exit                    Esc=Back                       F1=Help
```

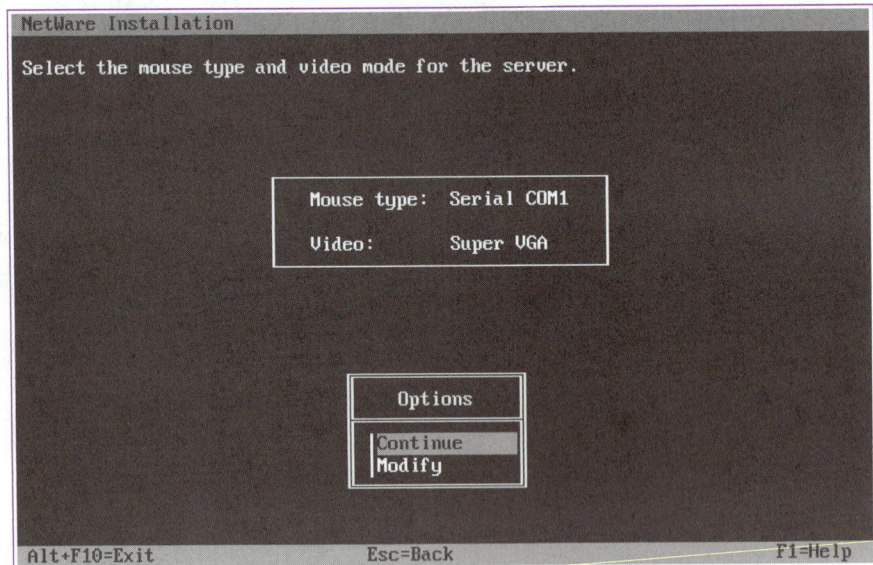

11. The *Copying Files . . . Please Wait* screen appears. (If there is an error on loading, a blank *NetWare Installation* screen remains on your screen without the "Copying Files" annotation. In this case, your installation will abort and will have to be restarted.)

12. After a short wait, the *Matching drivers to hardware devices. . . Please Wait* message appears and then returns to the *Copying Files. . . Please Wait* screen.

13. In the ***The following*** *device drivers* ***were detected for this server. Add, change or delete device drivers as needed.*** window press **<ENTER>** to select the devices found and accept the **Continue** highlighted in the **Options** window as indicated in Figure 3-7.

Figure 3-7

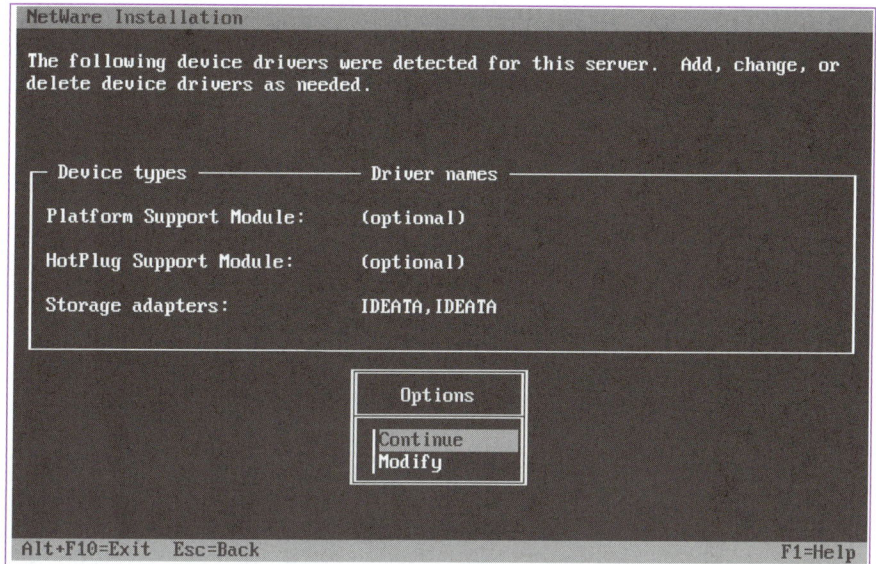

IMPORTANT NOTE

If the proper driver is not listed, pressing the **INS** key will allow the installation of an unlisted driver. Your Instructor should have already verified that your NIC card drivers operate properly with NetWare 5 and should have the drivers available for your use during this installation.

IMPORTANT NOTE

14. A second ***The following device drivers were detected for this server. Add, change or delete device drivers as needed.*** window appears. This time it shows the storage devices and the network boards found during the installation. In the event that no network boards are found (as in Figure 3-8), select **Modify** and press **<ENTER>** to select a network board. See note on bottom left.

Figure 3-8

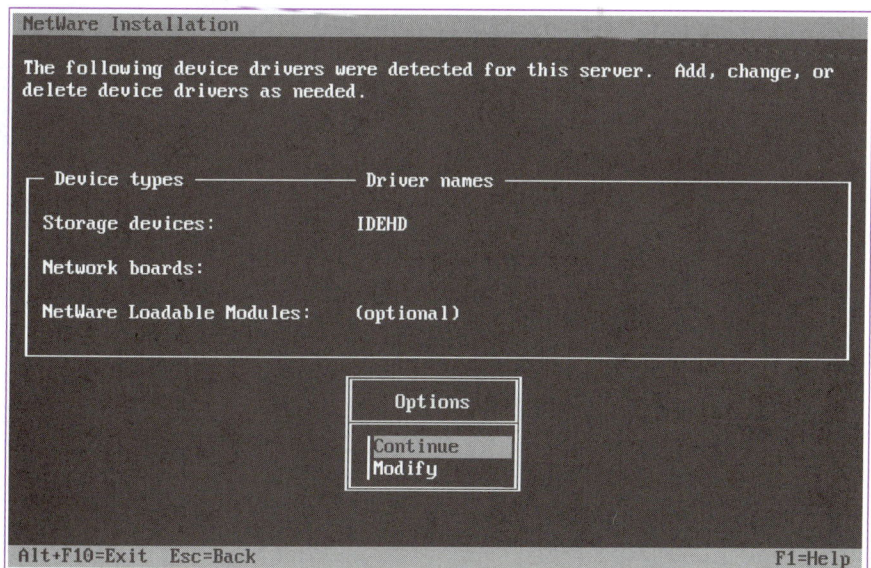

NOTE

If your network board was found and appears in the screen at right, go to item 21 on page 58 to continue.

NOTE

15. If you press **\<ENTER\>** and accept the default **Continue** as highlighted above without entering a network board, the reminder
***You must select a storage device driver and a network board driver
to continue.*** appears as indicated in Figure 3-9. Press **\<ENTER\>** to
return to the screen in item 14.

Figure 3-9

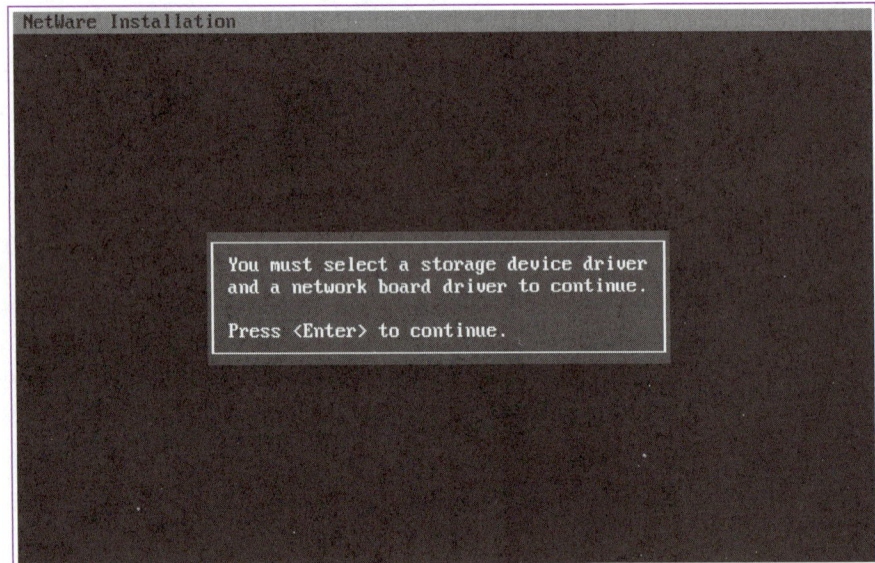

16. After selecting **Modify** and pressing **\<ENTER\>** in item 14, the
following screen appears with the **Network boards** area highlighted as indicated.

Figure 3-10

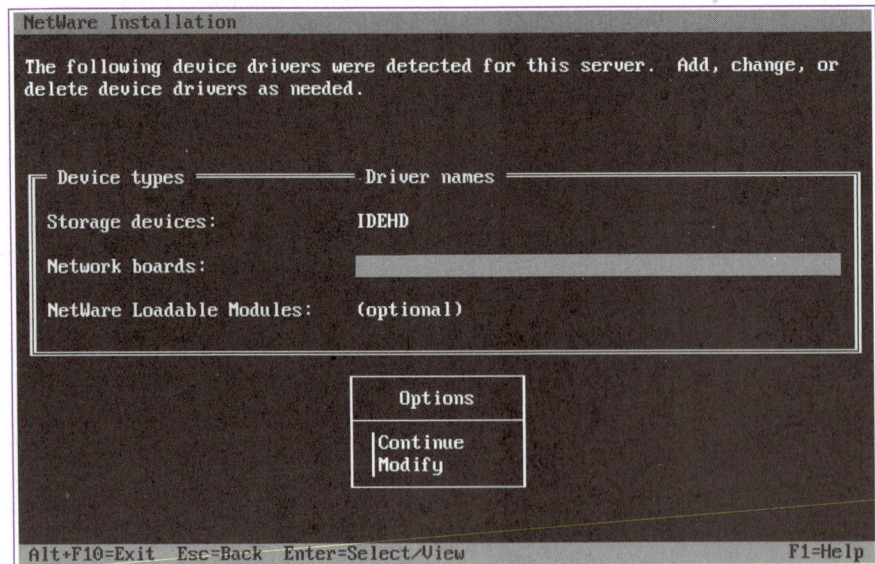

17. Press **\<ENTER\>** and the ***Select a driver for each network board in this server.*** appears as indicated in Figure 3-11. *Note*: the **3Com EtherLink III Family Driver v4.0** was selected for the sample server's network driver. You must select the proper driver for your own network interface card. Press **\<ENTER\>** when you have selected the correct driver.

Figure 3-11

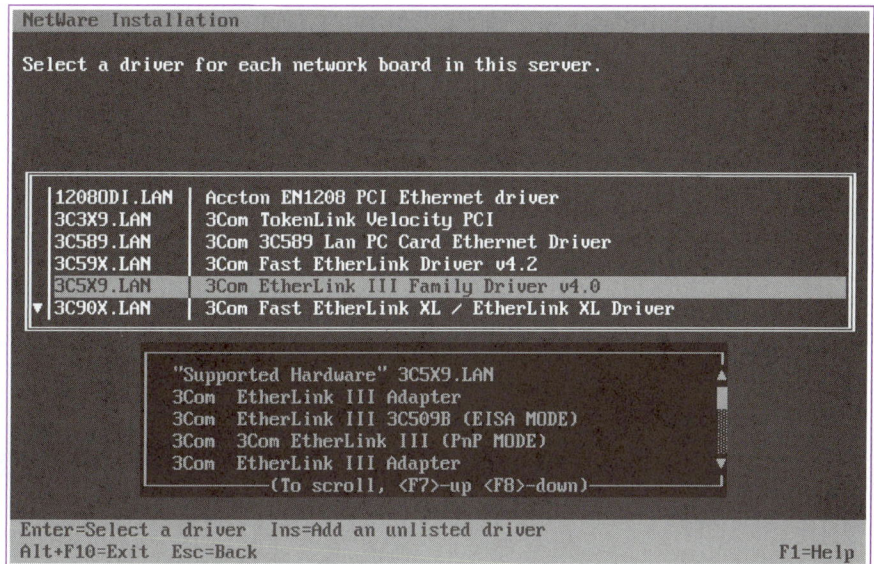

18. After selecting the proper driver, you may also have to ***Verify/ Enter the driver properties so that they match the hardware in this server.*** as indicated in Figure 3-12. Highlight **Modify driver properties** and press **\<ENTER\>**.

Figure 3-12

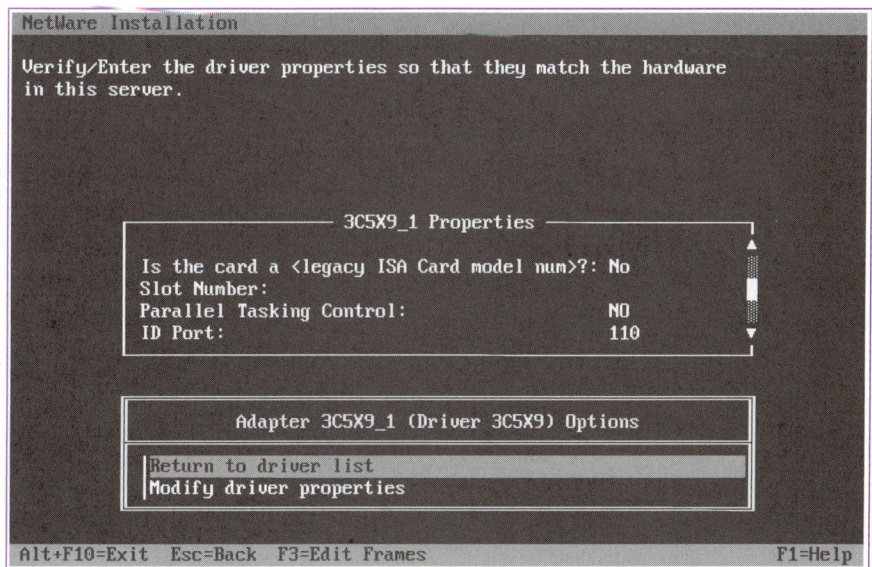

19. For the ***3C5X9_1 Properties*** window shown in Figure 3-13, the question **Is the card a legacy ISA Card model number?** is shown with the response changed to **Yes**. This indicates whether the card's parameters are recognizable by the server's hardware. Press **<ESC>** to go back to the screen in item 18, select **Return to driver list** and press **<ENTER>**.

Figure 3-13

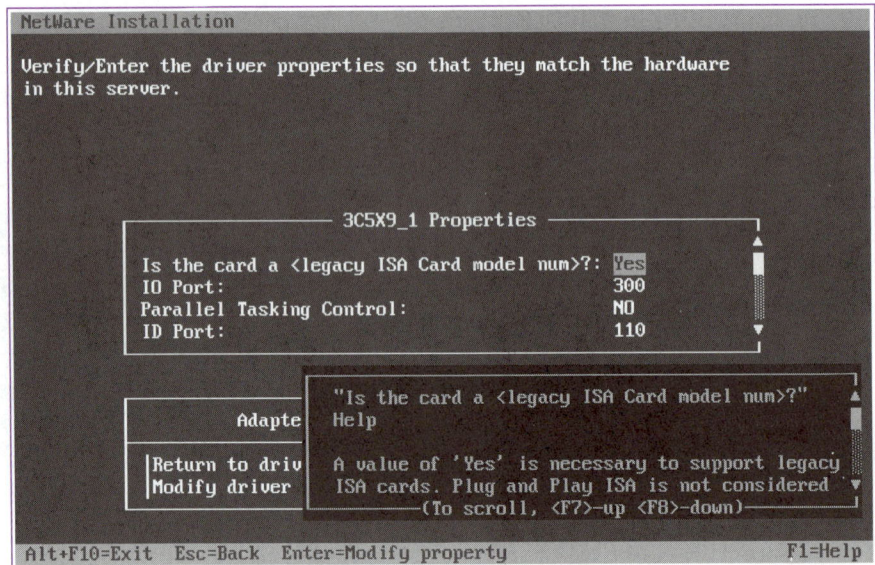

20. In the ***Add, edit or delete network board drivers*** window, highlight the **Return to driver summary** selection in the ***Additional Driver Options*** window as indicated in Figure 3-14 and press **<ENTER>**.

Figure 3-14

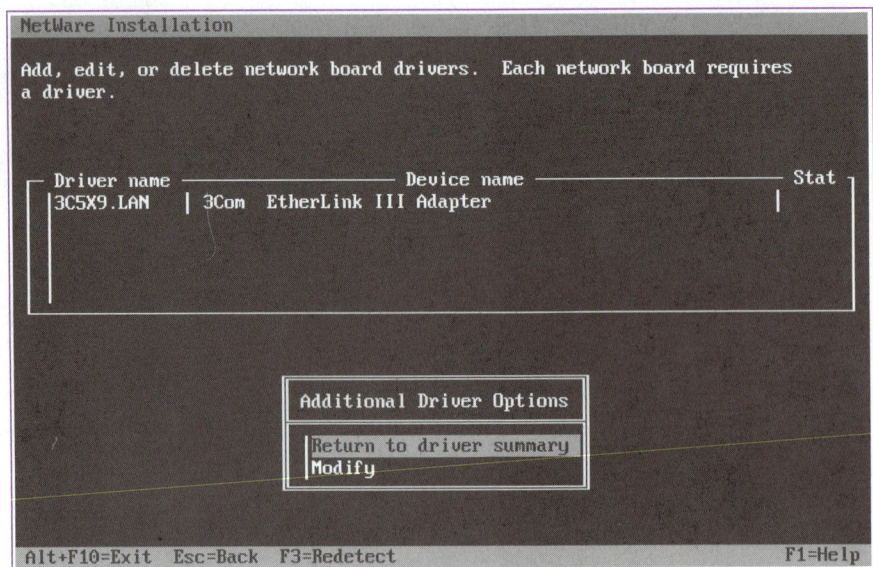

21. This returns you to the window in item 14 but has the **Network board driver name** indicated as shown in Figure 3-15. Use your down arrow to highlight the **Continue** option in the *Options* window and press <ENTER>.

Figure 3-15

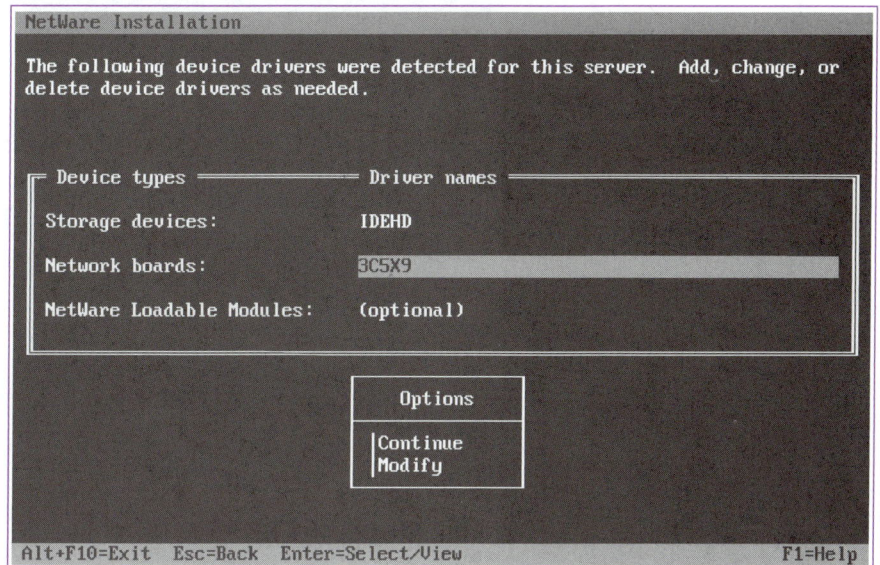

22. The *Scanning for hardware devices* window appears, followed immediately by the *Loading driver...* window as shown in Figure 3-16.

Figure 3-16

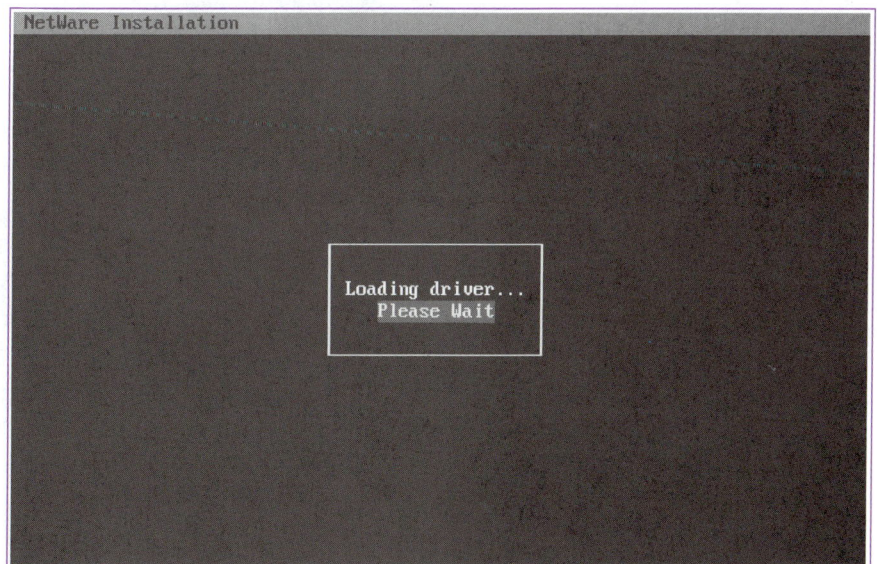

23. Next, the ***Looking for Disk Devices... Please wait*** appears as indicated in Figure 3-17.

Figure 3-17

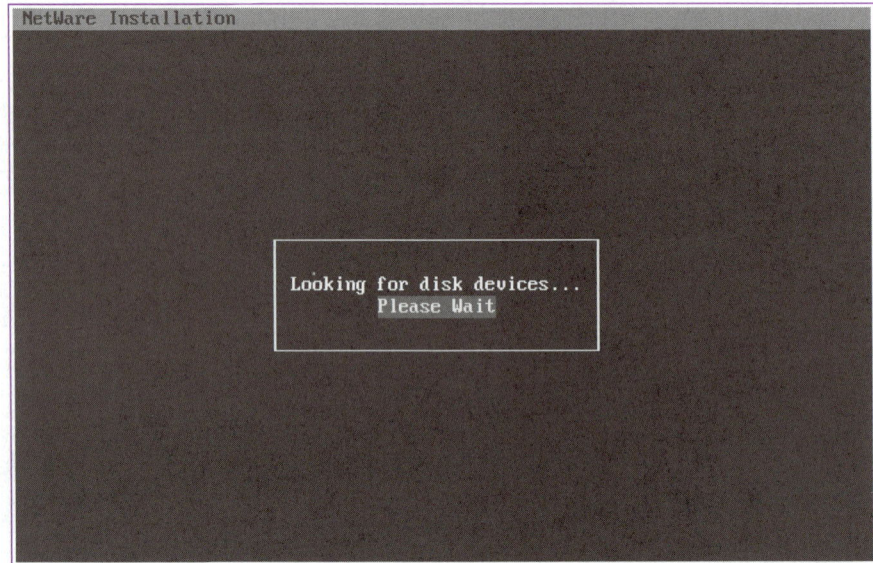

24. ***Create a NetWare partition and volume SYS.*** as indicated in Figure 3-18. Accept the default values and press **<ENTER>** to select **Continue**.

Figure 3-18

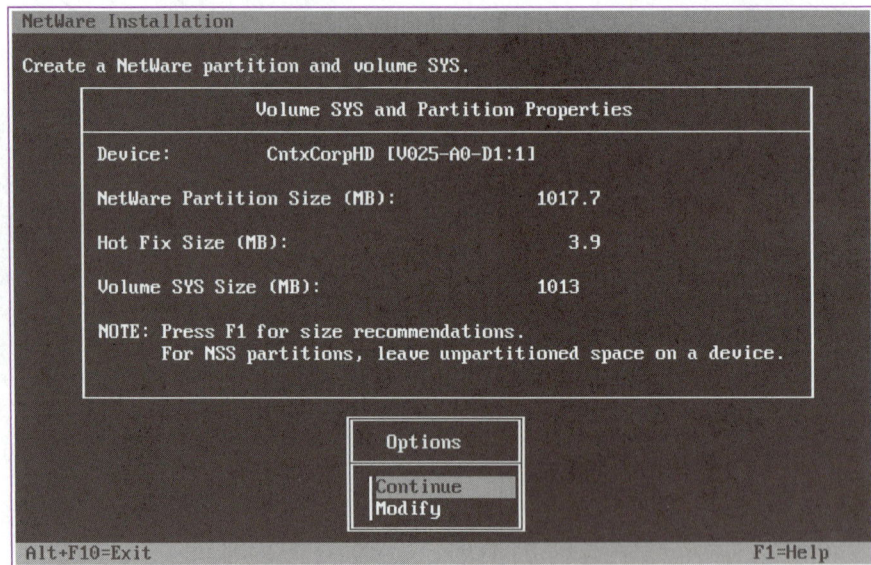

25. A *File Copy Status window* appears and tracks the installation of the files to the *SYS:* volume as shown in Figure 3-19.

Figure 3-19

```
NetWare Installation

                        File Copy Status

  ▮▮▮▮▮▮▮▮▮▮▮▮▮▮▮▮▮▮▮▮▮▮▮▮▮▮▮▮▮▮▮▮▮▮▮▮▮▮▮▮▮▮▮▮▮▮▮▮▮▮
                             3%

  File group: NetWare JVM
  Source path: NETWARE5:\SYS\JAVA_INS
  Destination path: SYS:

   ->Installing "System files".
   ->Installing "NetWare JVM".
   ->Copying file "TAR.NLM".
   ->Copying file "NJCL.TAR".
```

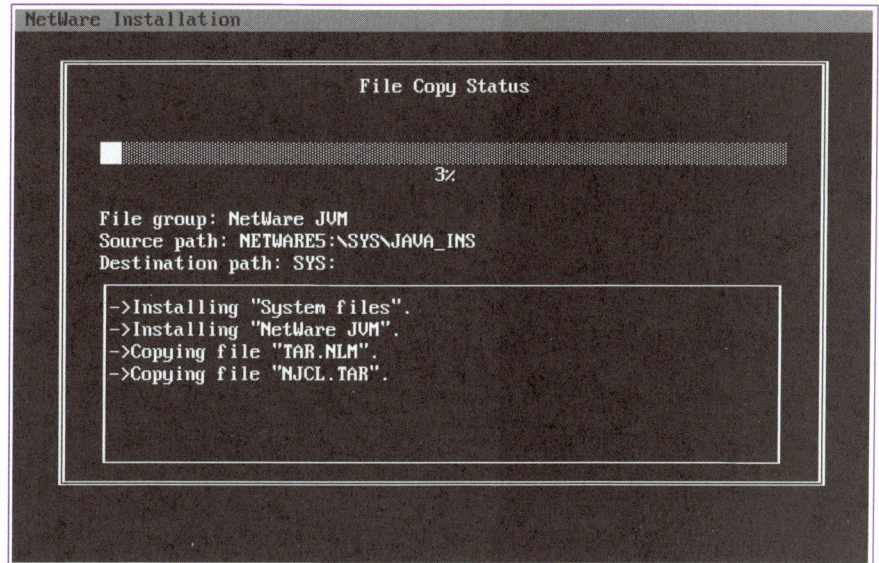

26. Numerous instances of the following *File Copy Status* screen occur showing the names of the NetWare files that are loading or have loaded another *NetWare Loadable Module (NLM)*. Wait while these screens process.

Figure 3-20

```
NetWare Installation

                        File Copy Status

  ▮▮▮▮▮▮▮▮▮▮▮▮▮▮▮▮▮▮▮▮▮▮▮▮▮▮▮▮▮▮▮▮▮▮▮▮▮▮▮▮▮▮▮▮▮▮▮▮▮▮
                             98%

  File group: Installation Modules
  Source path: NETWARE5:\SYS\JAVA_INS
  Destination path: SYS:
   ->    Other Products di | Please Wait | iles are being extracted
   ->Removing file "SYS:\P
   ->Copying file "CONSOLE
   ->    Console One directories and files are being extracted
   ->Removing file "SYS:\CONSOLE1.TAR".
   ->Copying file "MACH1.TAR".
   ->    Mach directories and files are being extracted
```

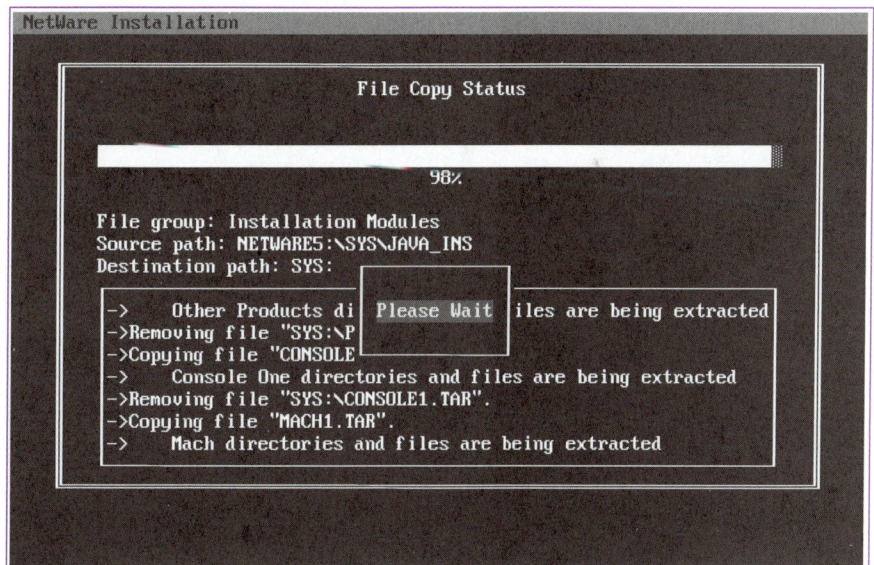

27. If a mouse was not installed (or the incorrect type was selected), a *Mouseless Mode cursor movement instructions* window appears and remains on the screen until **OK** is selected.

28. The screen then shifts from the normal installation black background to the Graphical User Interface with a picture background. This initiates a more user friendly means of continuing the installation, as illustrated in the *Initializing the NetWare 5 Installation* screen shown in Figure 3-21.

Figure 3-21

29. The *Server Properties* window appears as shown in Figure 3-22. Moving your cursor to the *Server Name* window you name the NetWare 5 server in this screen, and at this point the NetWare installation generates a server ID number. Type in the server name **Plant** and use your mouse pointer to click on the **Next >** button.

Figure 3-22

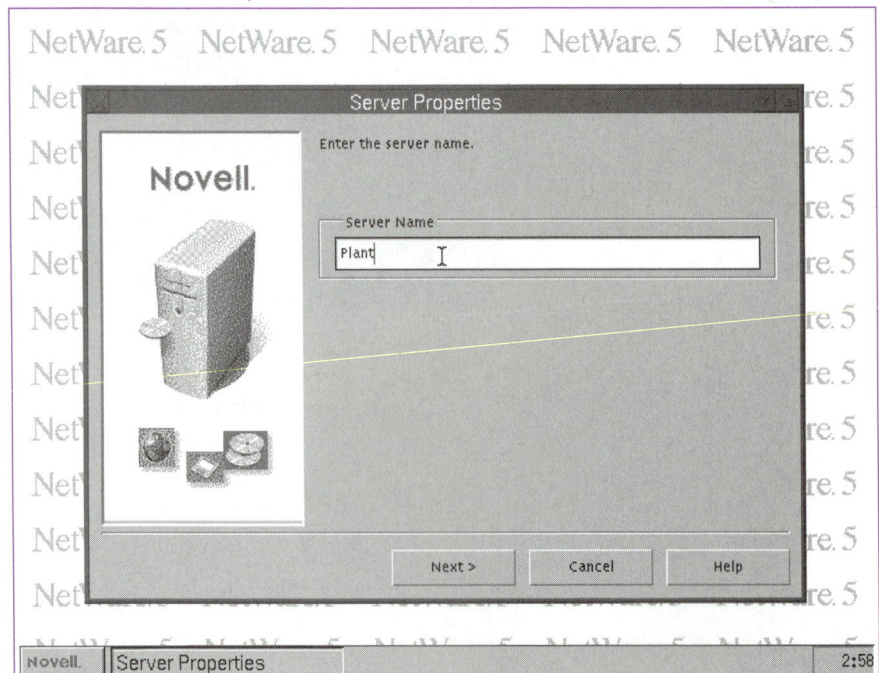

30. The **Configure File System** window appears as indicated in Figure 3-23. In this window you are able to modify, delete, or create volumes. Use your mouse pointer to click on the **Next >** button when you have finished modifying your volumes.

Figure 3-23

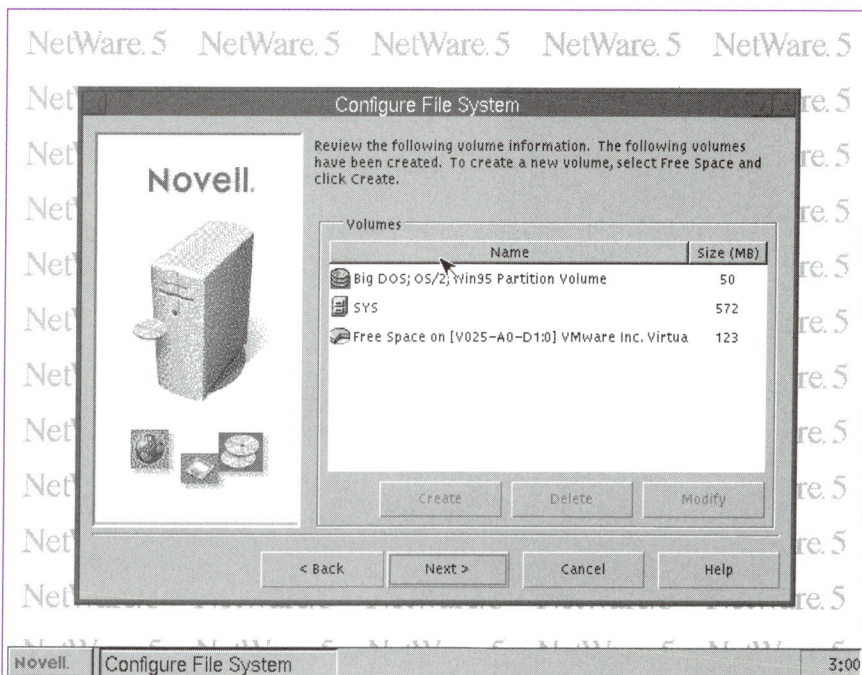

31. In the first **Protocols** window, you are shown the network interface cards detected during the earlier phase of the installation. Select the board with which you wish to associate (or bind) this protocol by clicking on the network board's name to highlight it. Do not click on the **Next >** button until you have highlighted the board and selected the desired bindings.

Figure 3-24

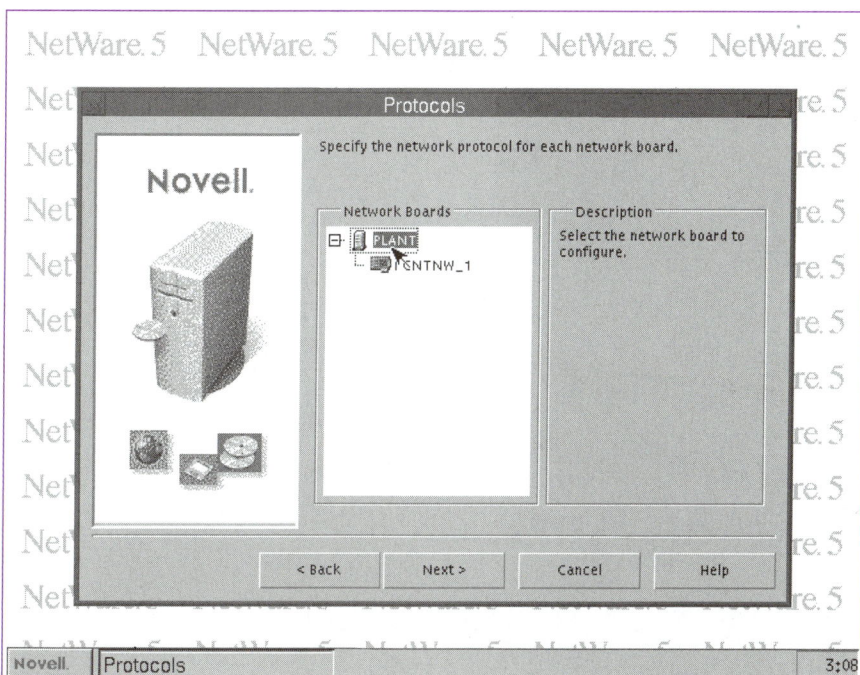

32. In the second *Protocols* window, which appears when you click on your network board, you are able to bind the applicable protocols to each of your network boards. TPUP will be using both IP and IPX. To activate the IP protocol, click the **IP** box in the right panel. Then insert the IP address specified by your Instructor (in the example below `192.168.1.100`) in the IP Address box and change the Subnet Mask box setting to the setting specified by your Instructor (`255.255.255.0` in the example shown). Finally, click on the **IPX** box to activate it too. Unless you have a router that you must use, do not enter any information in the Router (Gateway) box. Click on the **Next >** button when complete.

Figure 3-25

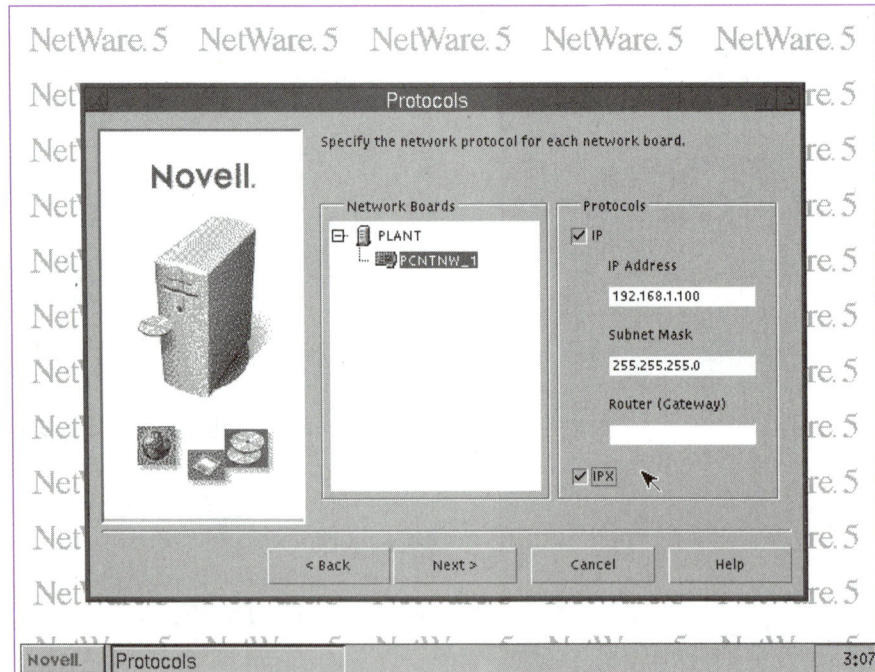

33. Enter the time zone information in the **Time Zone** window and if appropriate for your location, check the box that will **Allow the system to adjust for Daylight Saving Time**. Click on the **Next >** button when complete.

Figure 3-26

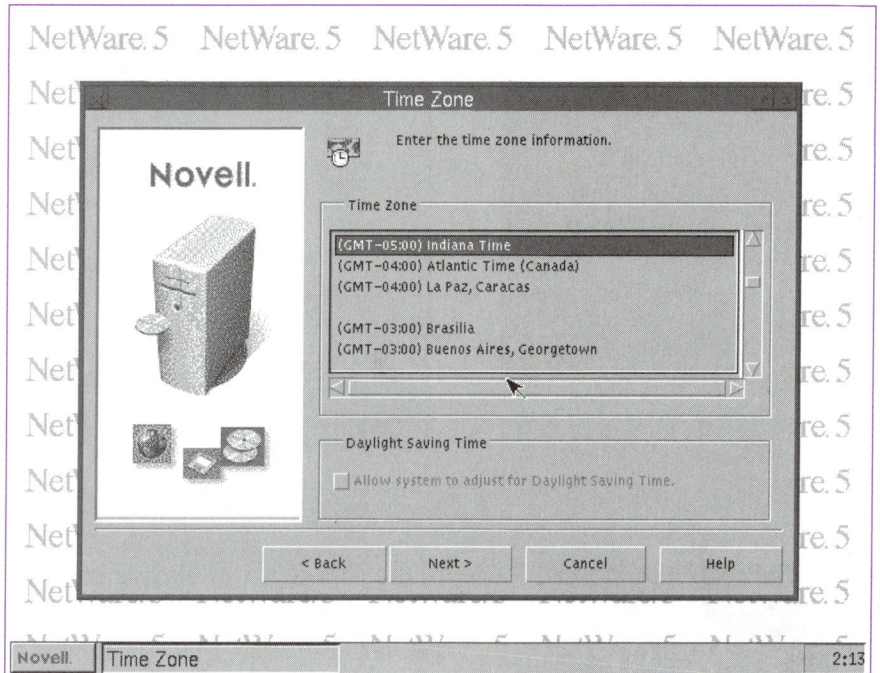

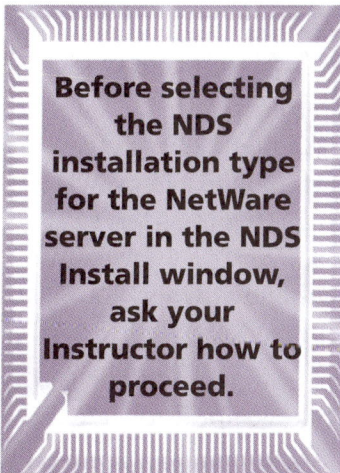

Before selecting the NDS installation type for the NetWare server in the NDS Install window, ask your Instructor how to proceed.

34. Before selecting **the NDS installation type for the NetWare server** in the **NDS Install** window, ask your Instructor how to proceed. Your Instructor will explain why clicking the **Create a new NDS tree** *radio button* is the usual selection at this point. If you will be installing more than one server, however, your Instructor will tell you which server will be selected for the primary NDS tree, and all the other servers will be installed into that tree. Click on the **Next >** button when complete.

Figure 3-27

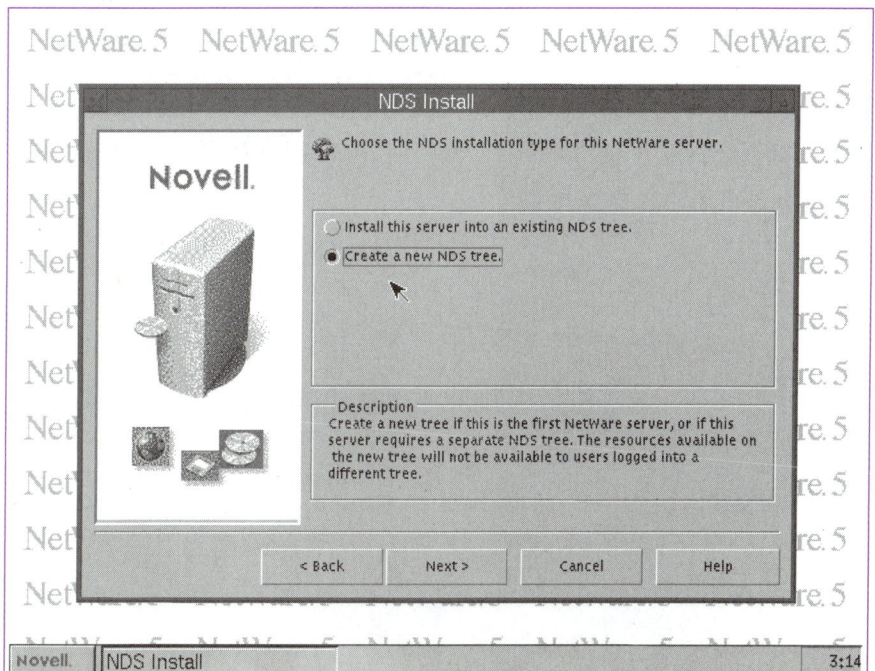

Figure 3-28

> ... creating a new NDS tree requires a unique tree name and an administrator password.

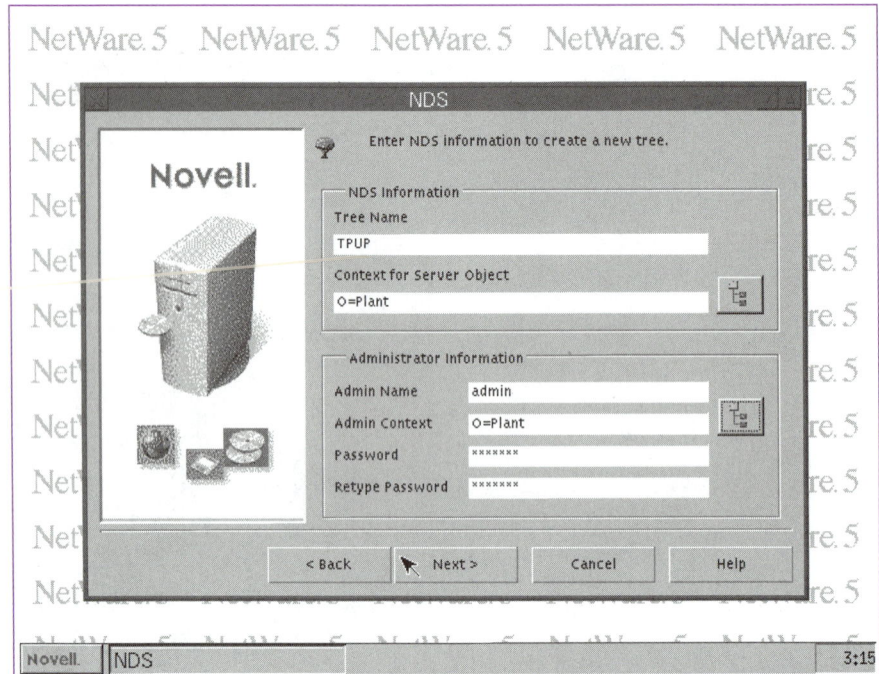

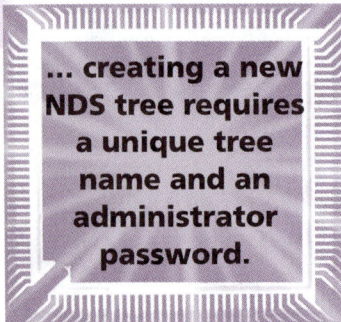

35. In the **NDS** window shown in Figure 3-28, enter NDS information. Remember that creating a new NDS tree requires a *unique tree name* and an *administrator password*. Enter **TPUP** as your Tree Name and **Plant** as your server object's context. Leave the Admin name as is and enter your Admin password as **Novell5** (unless your Instructor tells you otherwise). Retype your Admin password on the second password line. Note that when you type passwords, they are hidden. Click on the **Next >** button when complete.

36. An **NDS Install** window opens while NDS looks for duplicate tree names.

37. You may be given an **NDS Install** warning. Once this window is passed you will not be able to change the names of the NDS objects you have made thus far. If you are not sure about those selections, you may use the Back button to review your settings. Click on the **OK** button when ready.

38. The window shown in Figure 3-29 appears and informs you that your system is Installing *Novell Directory Services (NDS)*.

Figure 3-29

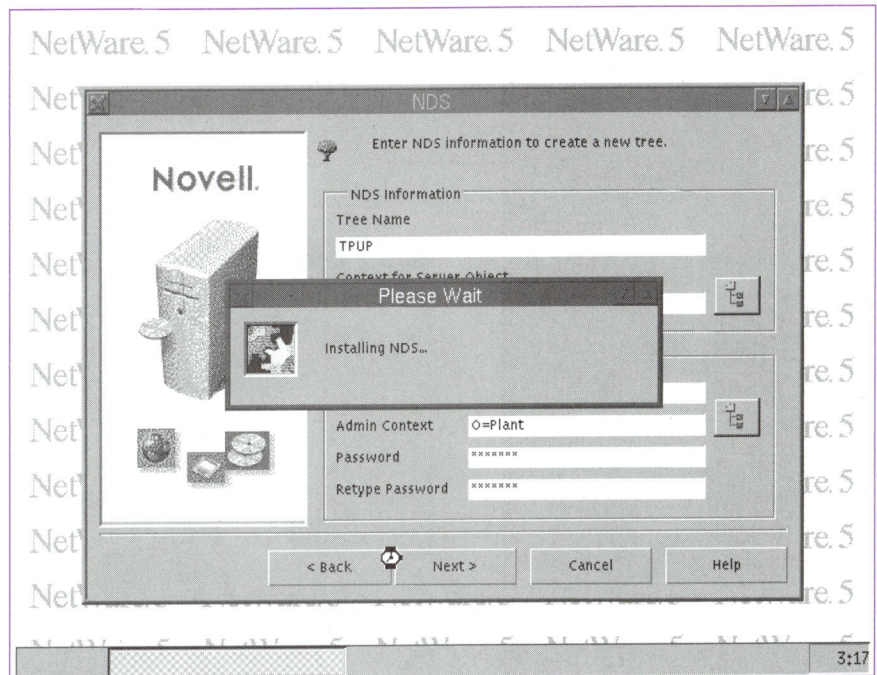

39. The **NDS Summary** window appears. Write down all the information for future reference. This is the information NDS will use for subsequent logins by your Admin user. Click on the **Next >** button when complete.

Figure 3-30

Write down all the information for future reference. This is the information NDS will use for subsequent logins by your Admin user.

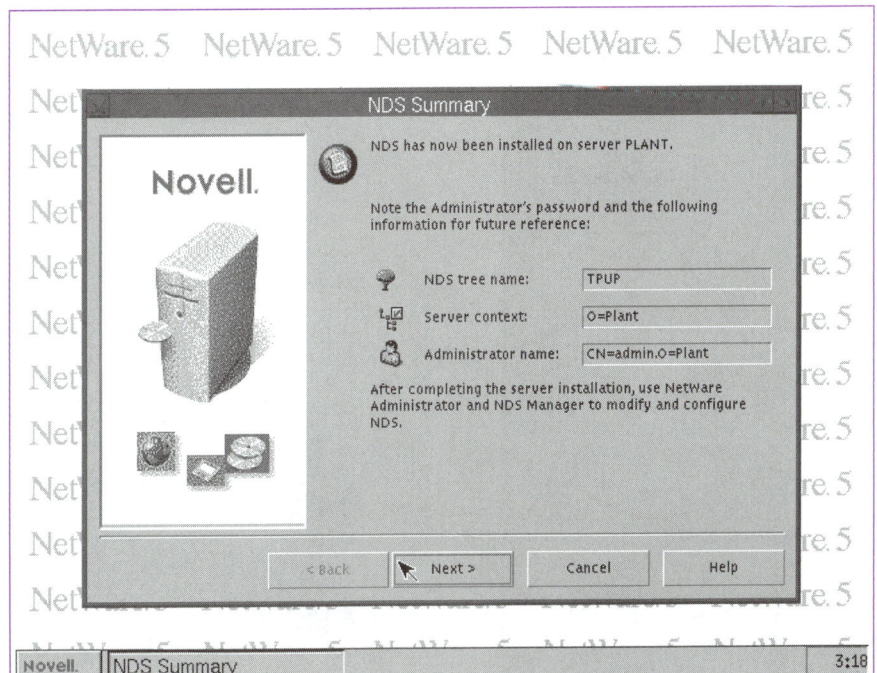

CHAPTER 3
Install

40. On the *License* screen, the installation asks for the location of your license information. Insert the floppy disk with your license information on it and use the Browse button to locate it on the *A:* drive. If you check the **Install without licenses** box, the server will continue loading. You will need to install your *server license* at a later time. Click on the **Next >** button when ready to continue.

Figure 3-31

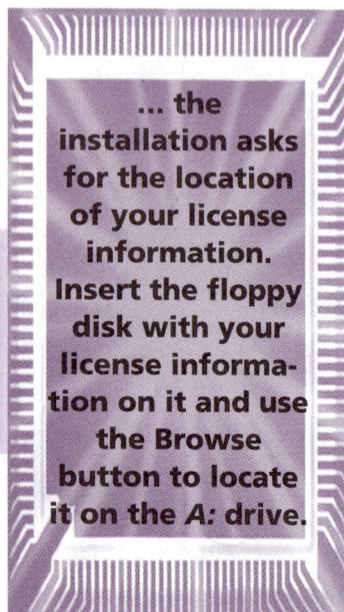
... the installation asks for the location of your license information. Insert the floppy disk with your license information on it and use the Browse button to locate it on the *A:* drive.

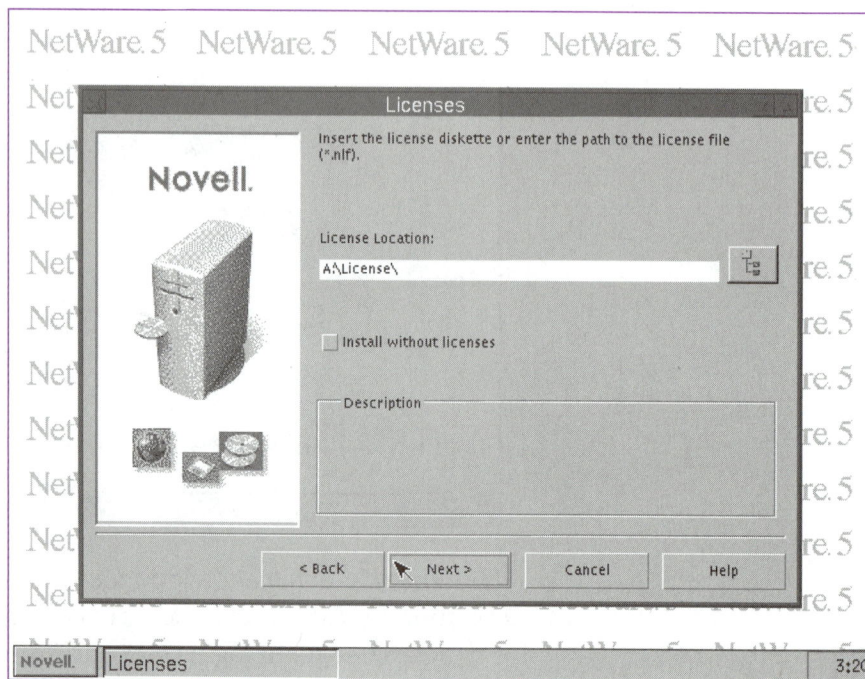

41. If more than one license is found, a *Multiple License Files* warning window appears informing you that a browser will automatically appear. This allows you to select which license to install. Click on the **OK** button when complete.

Figure 3-32

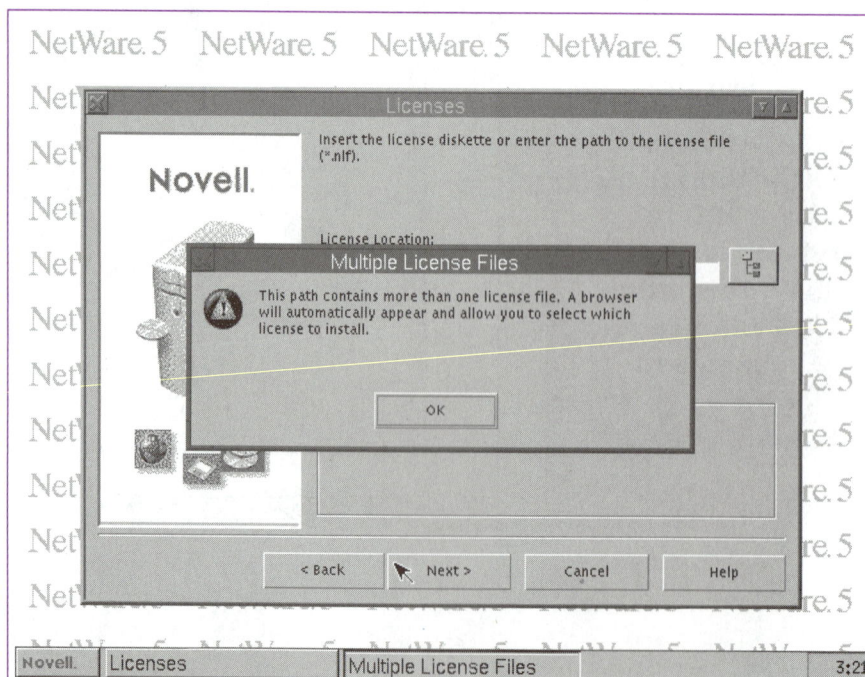

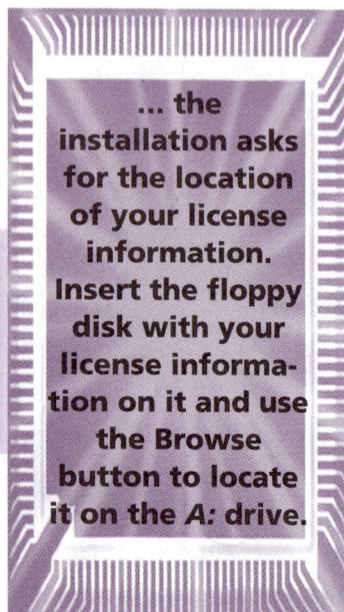

42. A ***Select a license*** window appears. Choose one of the license numbers available and click on the **OK** button when ready to proceed.

Figure 3-33

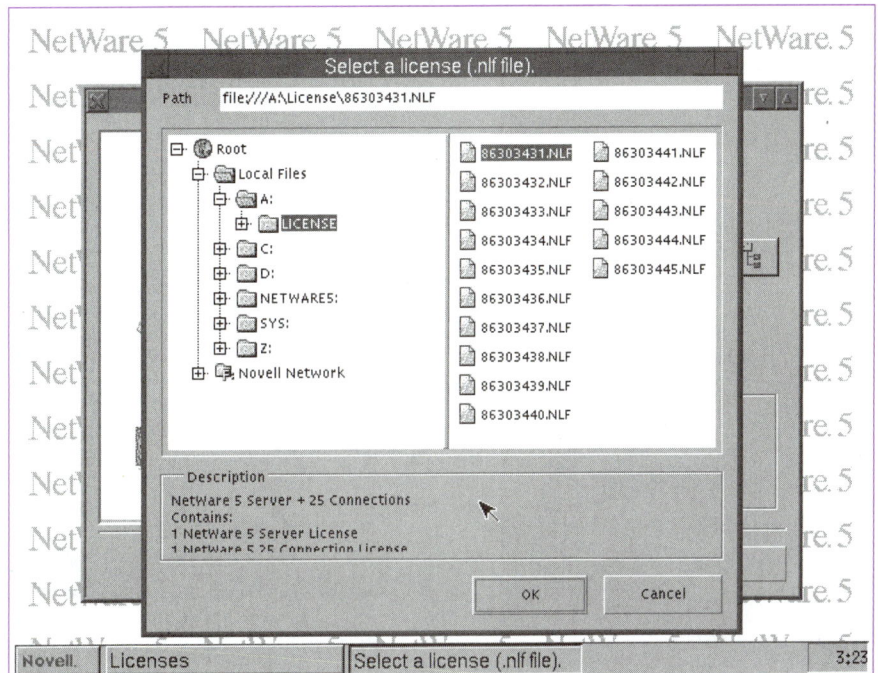

43. This brings you back to the window in item 40 with the addition of the license you have selected. Click on the **Next >** button when you are ready to proceed.

Figure 3-34

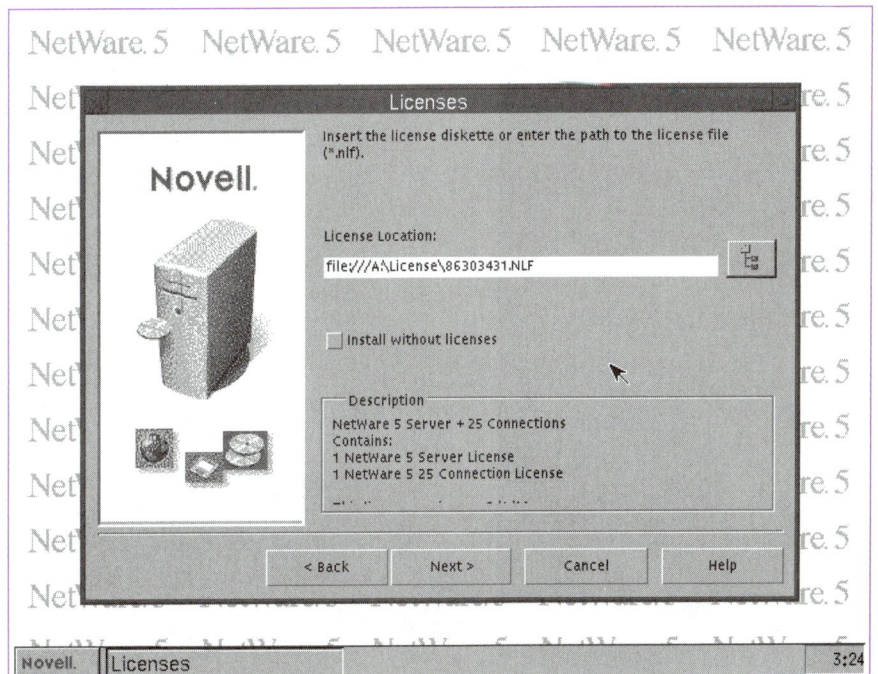

44. An *Other Products and Services* window appears. Uncheck all the checked boxes except Novell Distributed Print Services and Storage Management Services, then click on the **Next >** button.

Figure 3-35

Use the scroll bar to the right to make sure you uncheck all the boxes.

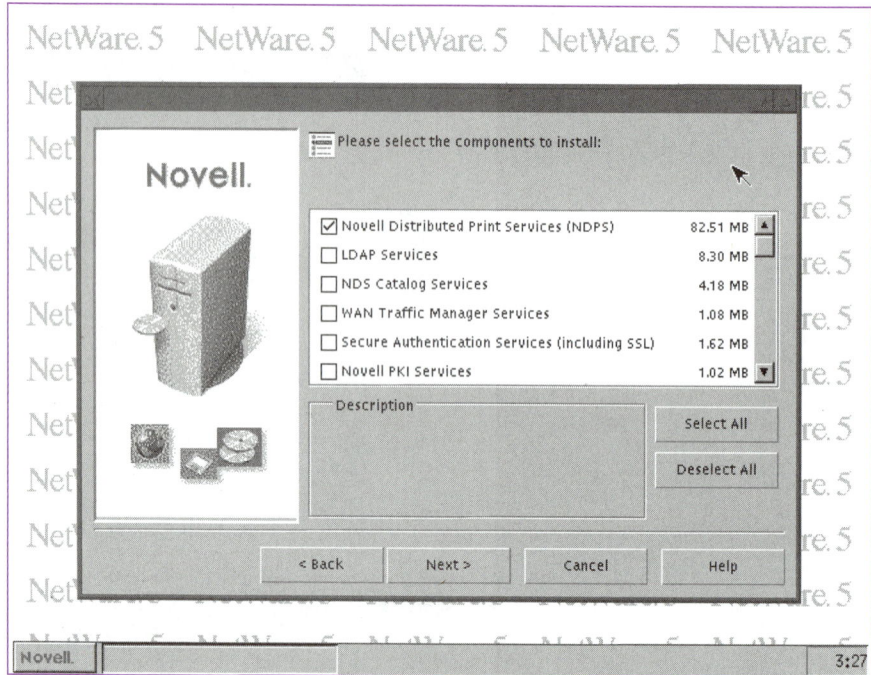

45. A *Summary* window appears showing what services will be installed. Click on the **Finish** button when ready to proceed.

Figure 3-36

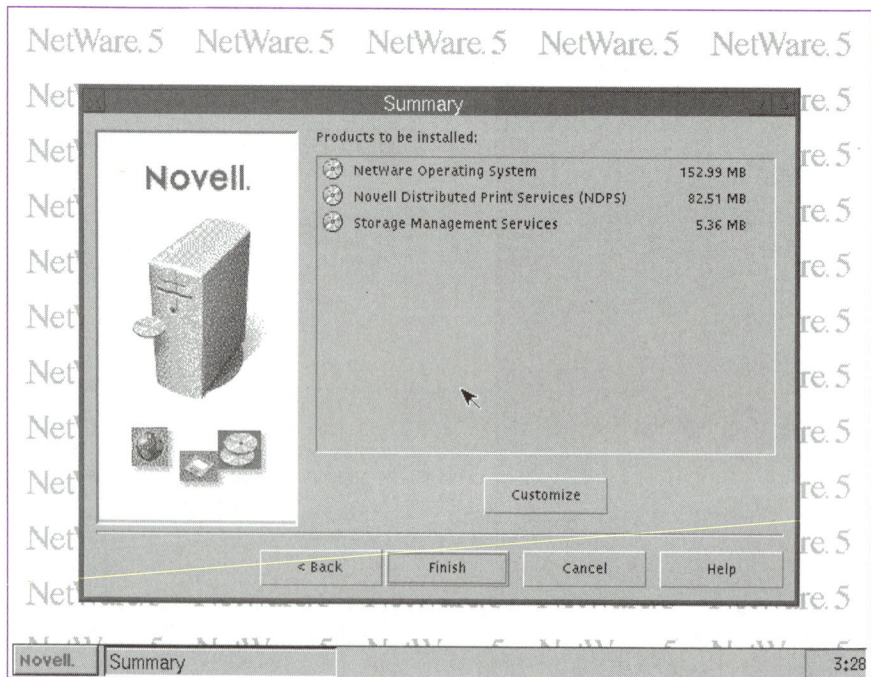

46. A ***Please Wait. . . Analyzing objects*** window appears, followed by a ***Preparing for file copy*** window. Wait for these steps to complete.

47. These screens are followed by a ***progress indicator*** and an additional Novell product information screen as shown in Figure 3-37.

Figure 3-37

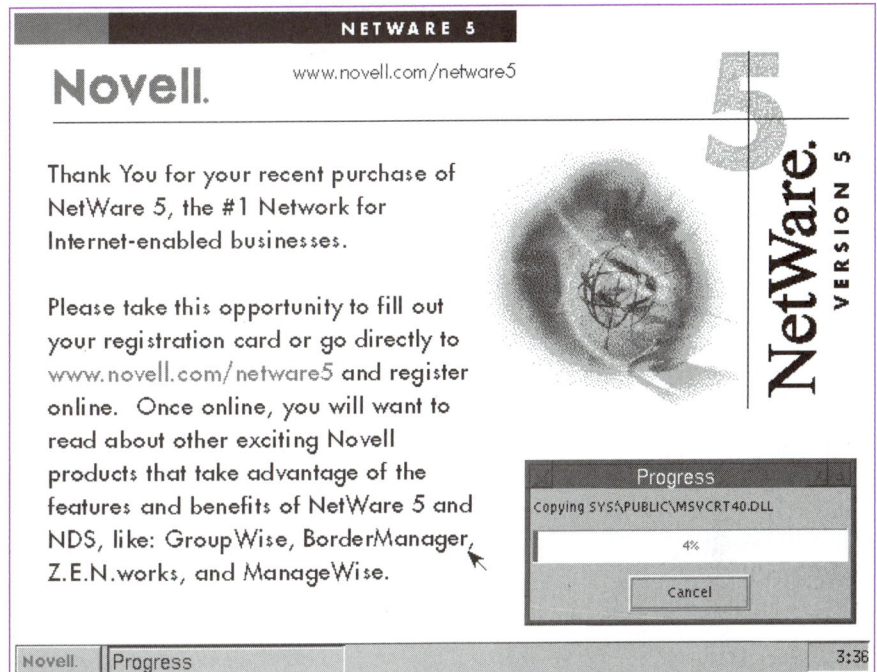

48. If there were any errors during installation, an ***Installation complete*** notice would appear which showed the number of errors and offered a *ReadMe* file for viewing. You would be able to either **View** the *ReadMe* file, **Close** the information window, or **Reboot** your server. Click on the **Reboot** button when ready to proceed.

49. If the reboot ends at the server console GUI, click on the **Novell** button in the lower left and **Exit** the GUI. At the console prompt, type **down** to down the server. Then press **<CONTROL>-<ALT>-<DELETE>** to restart your server.

50. When your server starts, it will end at the *C:* prompt. Type in **CD NWSERVER** and press **<ENTER>**. Then type **Server** and press **<ENTER>** to activate the server.

51. If you do not want to type in the indicated commands each time you restart the server, you can add them to your *AUTOEXEC.BAT* file on your *C:* drive.

Additional Information

The **NDPS Install** window shown in Figure 3-38 will appear if you left the **NDPS** product checked in the **Other Products and Services** window.

Figure 3-38

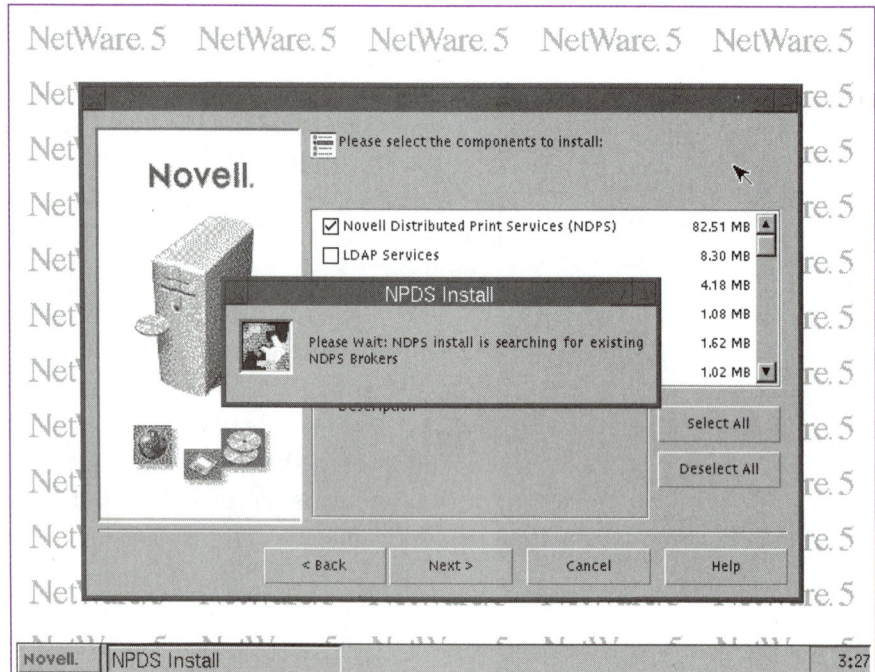

The ***Storage Management Services Setup*** window shown in Figure 3-39 will appear if you left the **SMS** product checked in the ***Other Products and Services*** window.

Figure 3-39

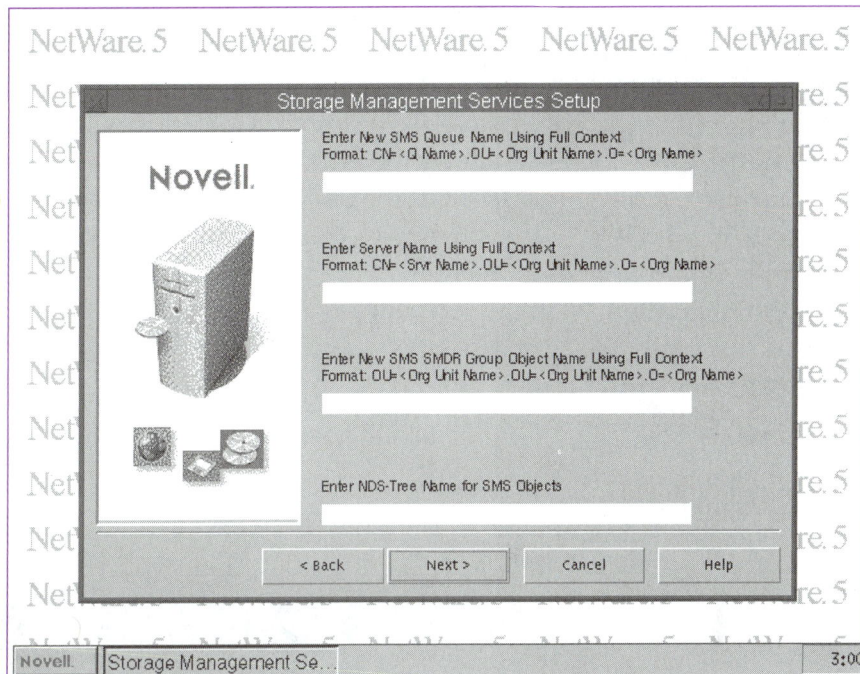

Congratulations. You have completed your server's installation and now have an operational Novell NetWare 5 Server at your disposal. The ease and usefulness of your new server depend on the speed of your processor and on how much remaining space it has on its hard drive. Regardless of how useful your first server may be, the steps you just completed are the same ones you will use to create another server in the future.

The server you have now will be important for you during the remainder of this course, but its speed and capacity are not. The server's speed and capacity do become important when you apply your ability to create a Novell NetWare 5 server to your employer's environment in an actual production setting. The knowledge you gain from installing these Novell NetWare 5 servers helps you to understand how they are created. Usually the servers do not need rebuilding, and a newcomer may wait a long time before installing another.

Activity 3-1   NetWare 4.11 Server Simple Installation (Alternate)

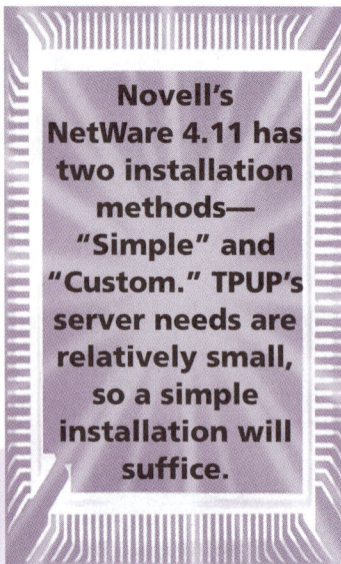

Novell's NetWare 4.11 has two installation methods—"Simple" and "Custom." TPUP's server needs are relatively small, so a simple installation will suffice.

After carefully preparing for a simple installation, your server should now be ready for Novell's NetWare 4.11 network operating system software. Novell's NetWare 4.11 has two installation methods—"Simple" and "Custom." TPUP's server needs are relatively small, so a simple installation will suffice. The custom installation allows the installer more control over settings and modifications, such as the use of additional NetWare volumes. Later in the semester you may elect to rebuild your server using the "custom install" at that time.

To perform a simple install:

1. Reboot the computer

2. From the *C:* prompt, insert the NetWare 4.11 CD and change to the applicable drive designation for your CD-ROM drive (i.e. `D:`)

3. Type `Install <ENTER>`.

Figure 3-40

```
NetWare Install                                              NetWare Install

                    ┌─────────────────────────────────────────┐
                    │              NetWare Install              │
                    ├─────────────────────────────────────────┤
                    │ Diese Zeile für deutsche Installation auswählen │
                    │ Select this line to install in English    │
                    │ Seleccione esta línea para instalarlo en español │
                    │ Sélectionner cette ligne pour installer en français │
                    │ Selezionare questa riga per installare in italiano │
                    │ Selecione esta linha para instalar em Português │
                    └─────────────────────────────────────────┘

```

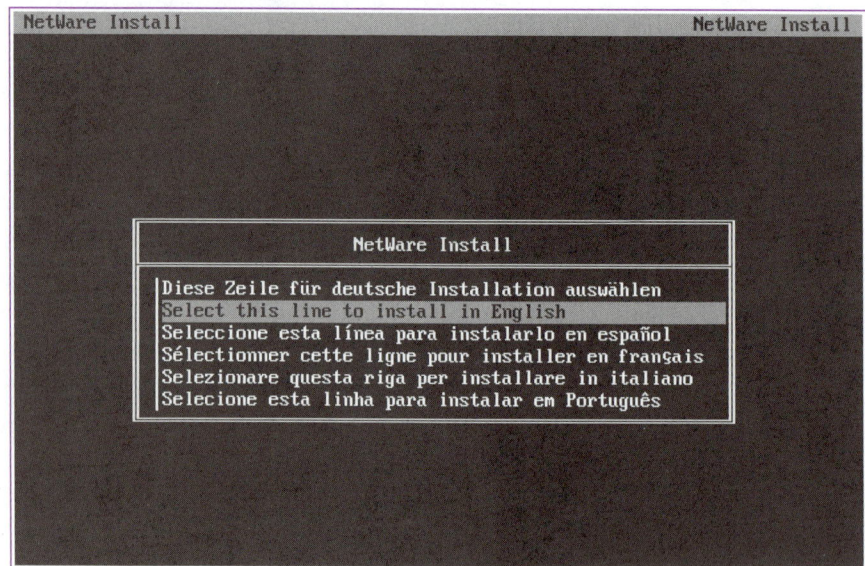

4. Highlight **Select this line to install in English** as shown in Figure 3-40 and press `<ENTER>`.

5. Read *Novell Terms and Conditions* shown in Figure 3-41. Press `<PAGE DOWN>` to scroll through the terms, then press `<ENTER>` when finished to accept the terms and conditions.

Figure 3-41

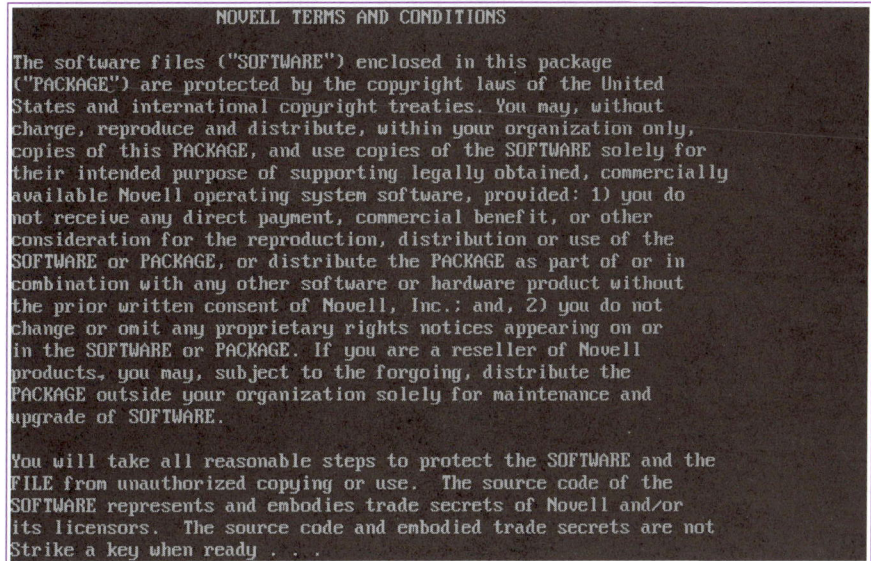

6. Select **NetWare Server Installation** from the choices shown in Figure 3-42 and press `<ENTER>`.

Figure 3-42

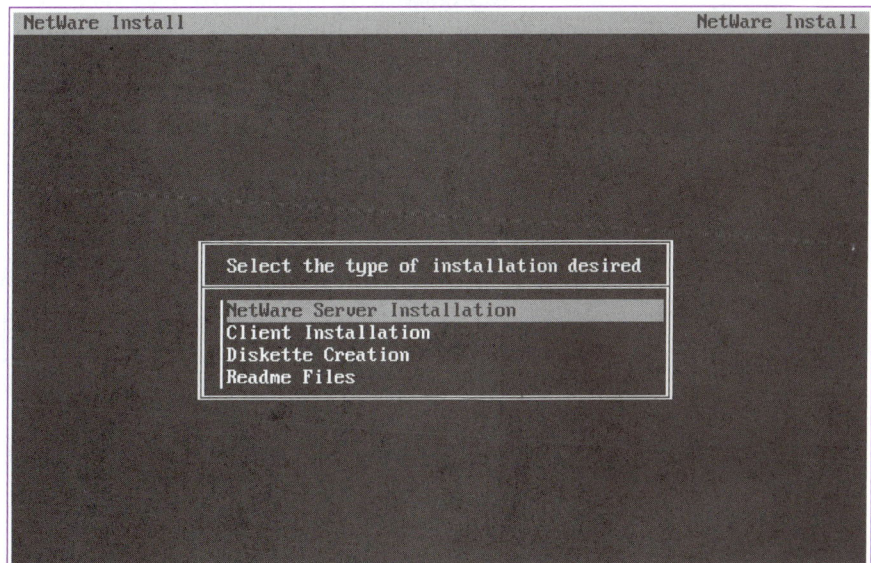

7. Choose **NetWare 4.11** as the product you want to install from the choices shown in Figure 3-43 and press **<ENTER>**.

Figure 3-43

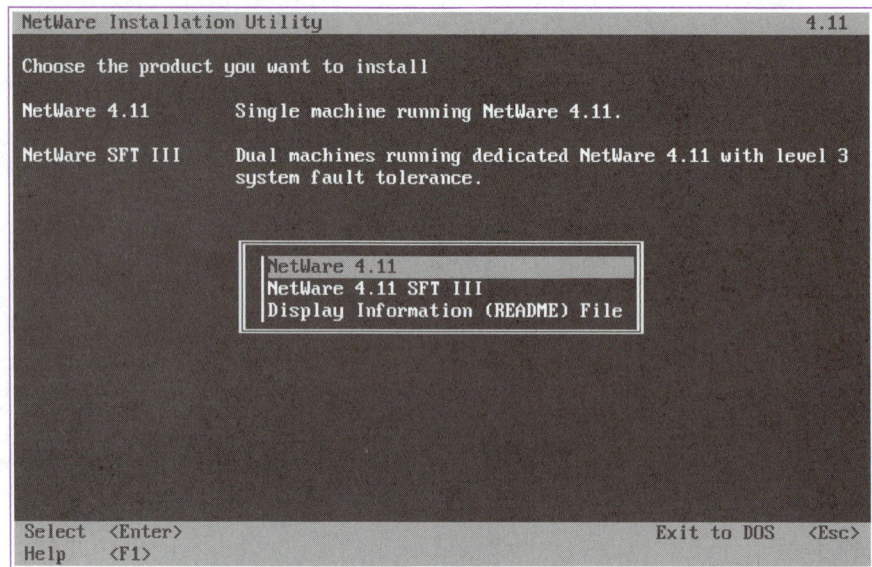

8. Select **Simple Installation of NetWare 4.11** from the choices shown in Figure 3-44 and press **<ENTER>**.

Figure 3-44

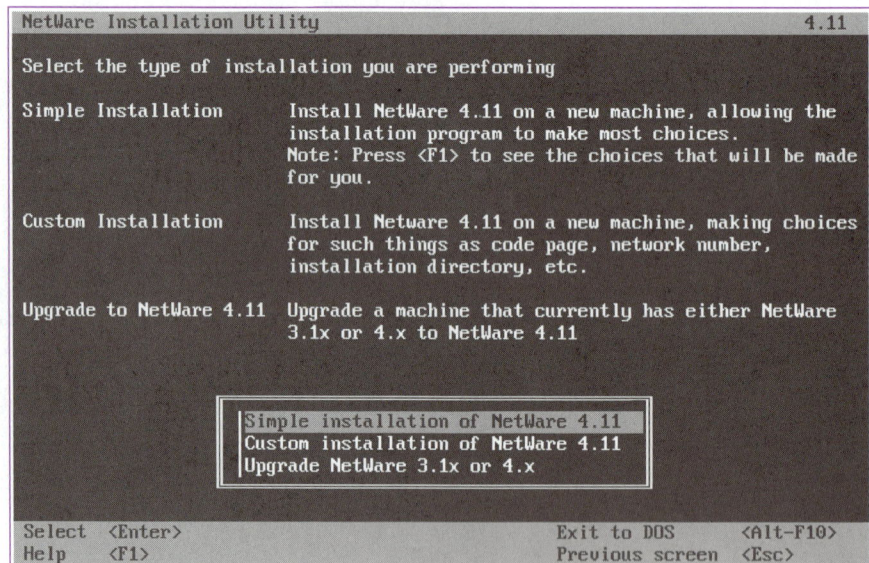

9. Specify the server name **TPUP-HQ** as shown in Figure 3-45 and press **<ENTER>**.

Figure 3-45

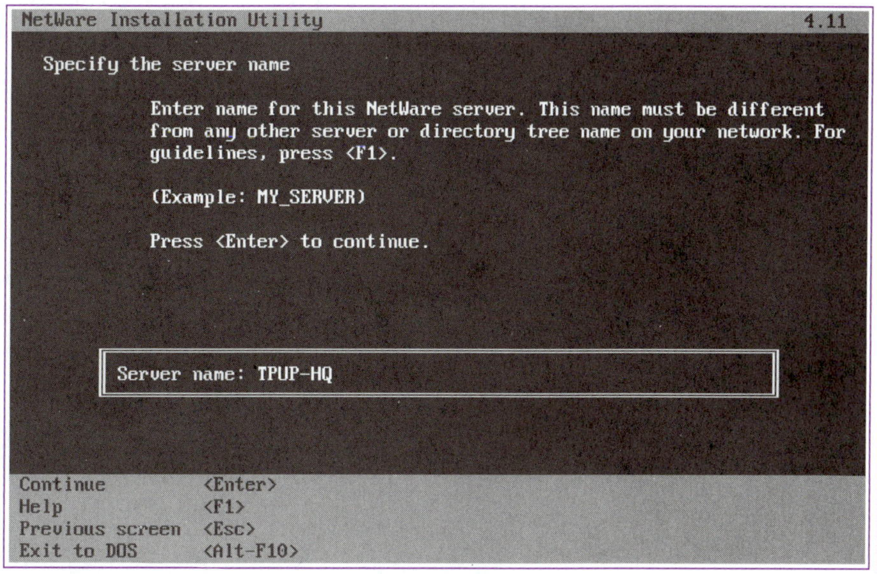

```
NetWare Installation Utility                                          4.11

  Specify the server name

           Enter name for this NetWare server. This name must be different
           from any other server or directory tree name on your network. For
           guidelines, press <F1>.

           (Example: MY_SERVER)

           Press <Enter> to continue.




           ┌──────────────────────────────────────────────────────────┐
           │ Server name: TPUP-HQ                                       │
           └──────────────────────────────────────────────────────────┘



 Continue          <Enter>
 Help              <F1>
 Previous screen   <Esc>
 Exit to DOS       <Alt-F10>
```

10. Copy the server boot files to the DOS partition. This is done automatically and tracked with a progress indicator as shown in Figure 3-46:

Figure 3-46

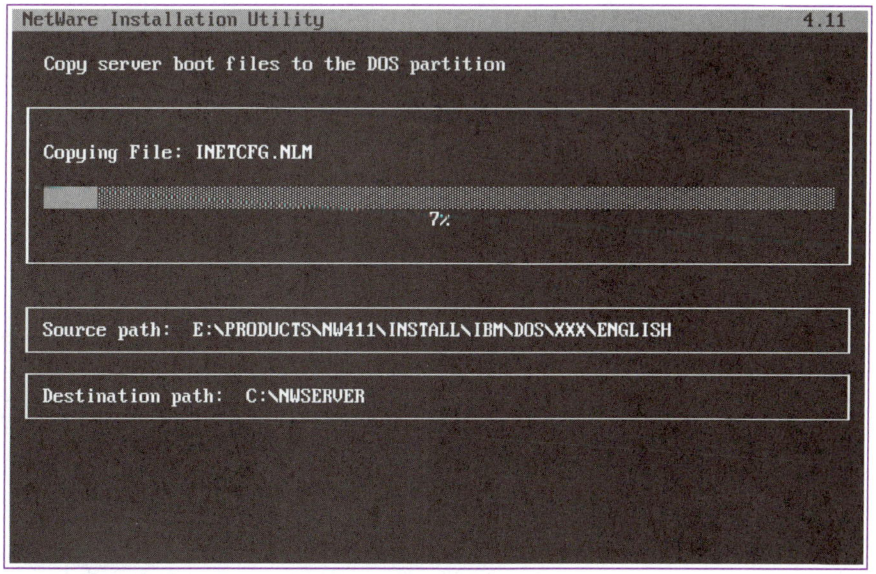

```
NetWare Installation Utility                                          4.11

  Copy server boot files to the DOS partition

 ┌─────────────────────────────────────────────────────────────────────┐
 │ Copying File: INETCFG.NLM                                             │
 │                                                                       │
 │ ▓▓▓░░░░░░░░░░░░░░░░░░░░░░░░░░░░░░░░░░░░░░░░░░░░░░░░░░░░░░░░░░░░░░░░░░░ │
 │                              7%                                       │
 └─────────────────────────────────────────────────────────────────────┘

 ┌─────────────────────────────────────────────────────────────────────┐
 │ Source path:   E:\PRODUCTS\NW411\INSTALL\IBM\DOS\XXX\ENGLISH          │
 └─────────────────────────────────────────────────────────────────────┘

 ┌─────────────────────────────────────────────────────────────────────┐
 │ Destination path:   C:\NWSERVER                                       │
 └─────────────────────────────────────────────────────────────────────┘
```

> **NOTE**
>
> The Source path shown in Figure 3-46 indicates where the files are located on the installation CD-ROM and that the default destination path is C:\NWSERVER.
>
> **NOTE**

When the server boot files are finished being copied to the DOS partition, the system automatically executes *SERVER.EXE* and restarts the server. It scans for and loads disk and LAN drivers and their settings.

11. Choose the **Server Drivers – Network Driver** as shown in
    Figure 3-47. *Note:* the *3C5X9.LAN* for the 3Com Etherlink III
    Family Driver v 4.0 is currently selected and represents the
    LAN driver in the server being built in this demonstration.

Figure 3-47

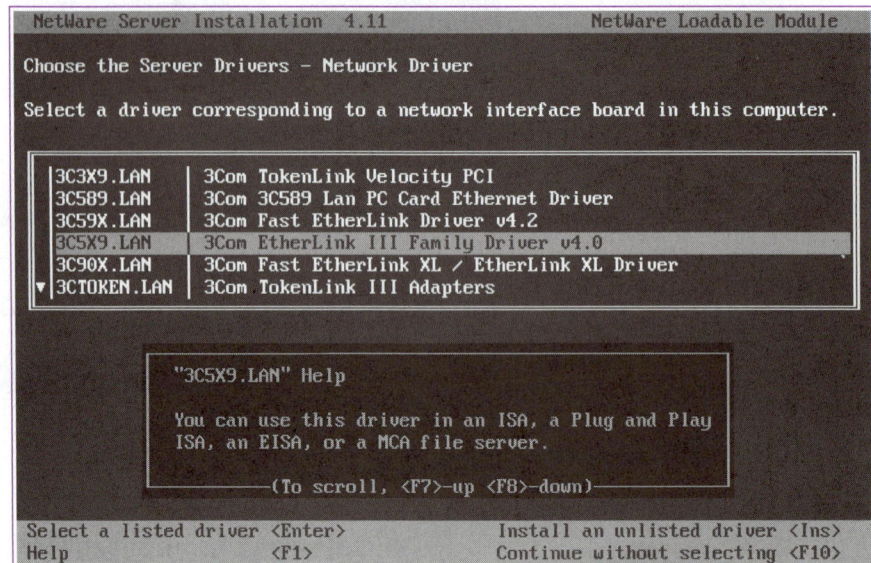

12. Choose the **Server Drivers – Network Driver Parameters** as indicated
    in Figure 3-48. Use the **<UP ARROW>** to scroll to the top window
    and highlight the **No** on **Is the card a Legacy ISA Card Model
    number?** (which means "Is this card automatically detectable?")
    Change it to **Yes**. The parameters will then appear. Scroll back
    down to the **Save parameters and continue** and press **<ENTER>**.

Figure 3-48

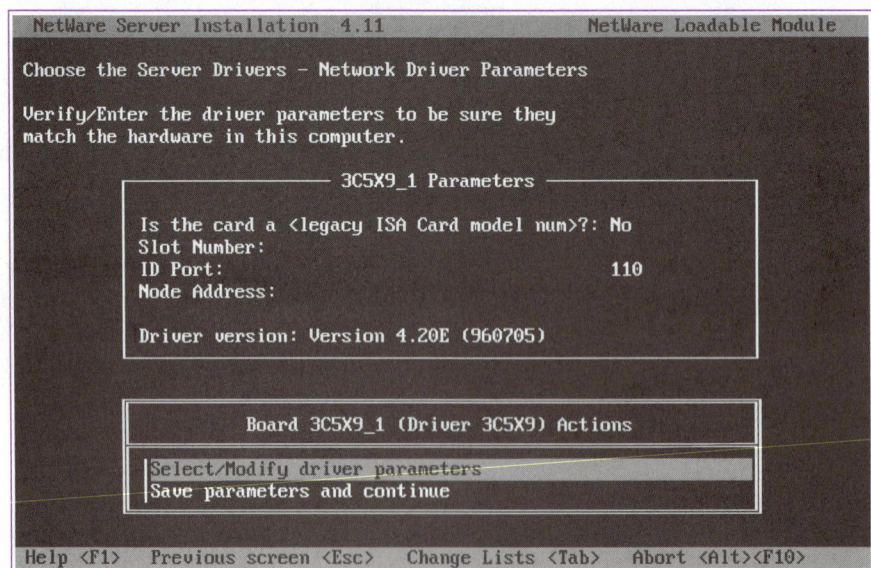

13. Select **No** when you do not want to select any additional network drivers as indicated in Figure 3-49 and press **<ENTER>**.

Figure 3-49

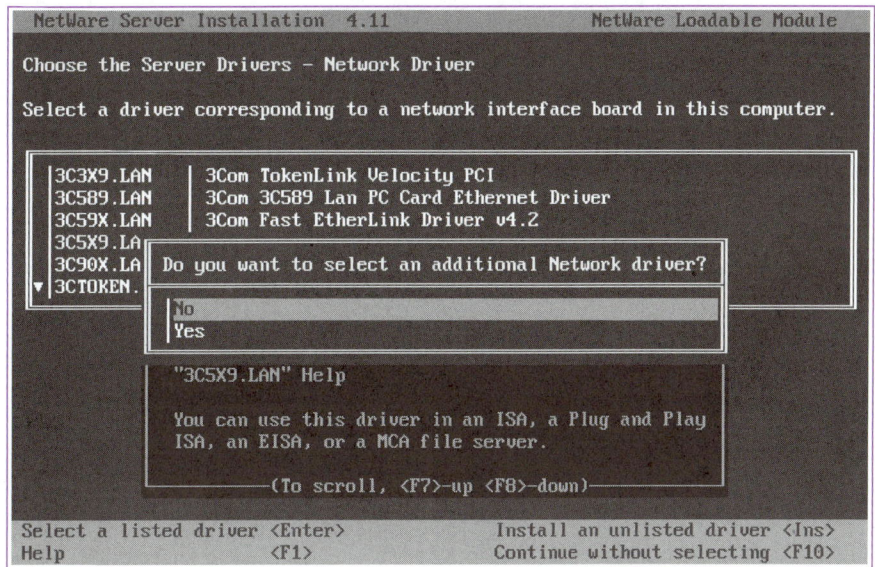

14. Review the ***Server Drivers – Summary*** as shown in Figure 3-50
and, if correct, press **<ENTER>**.

Figure 3-50

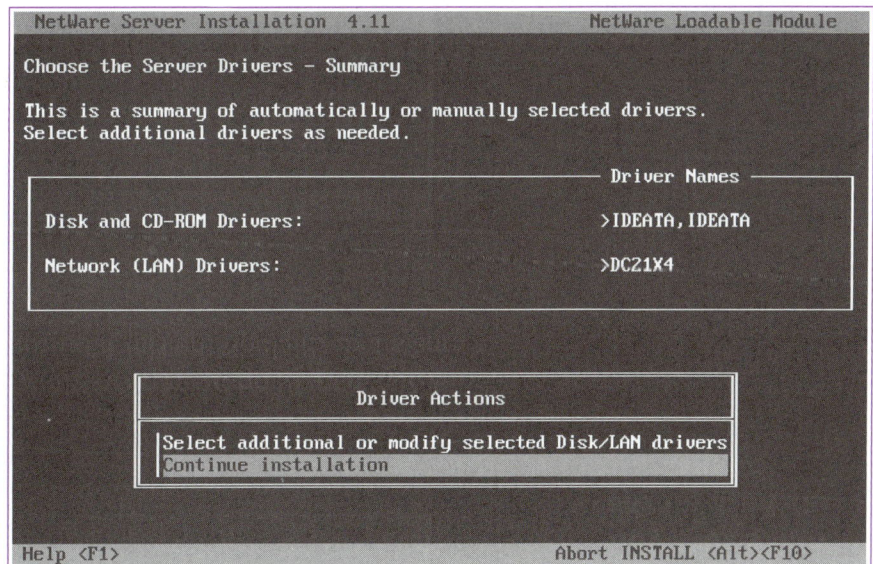

> **NOTE**
>
> An IPX number is assigned automatically after this point.
>
> **NOTE**

15. Read the *Warning* shown in Figure 3-51. Select **Continue accessing the CD-ROM via DOS** and press **<ENTER>**.

Figure 3-51

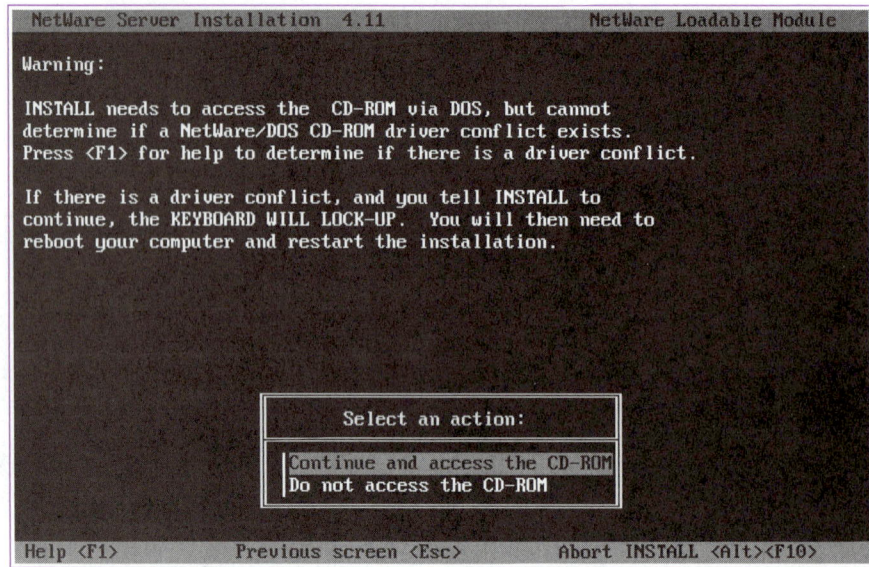

NOTE

The *SYS:* volume is mounted, and a preliminary copy is started at this time.

NOTE

16. If the previous installation was not completely removed, the message shown in Figure 3-52 could appear. Press **<ENTER>** to continue.

Figure 3-52

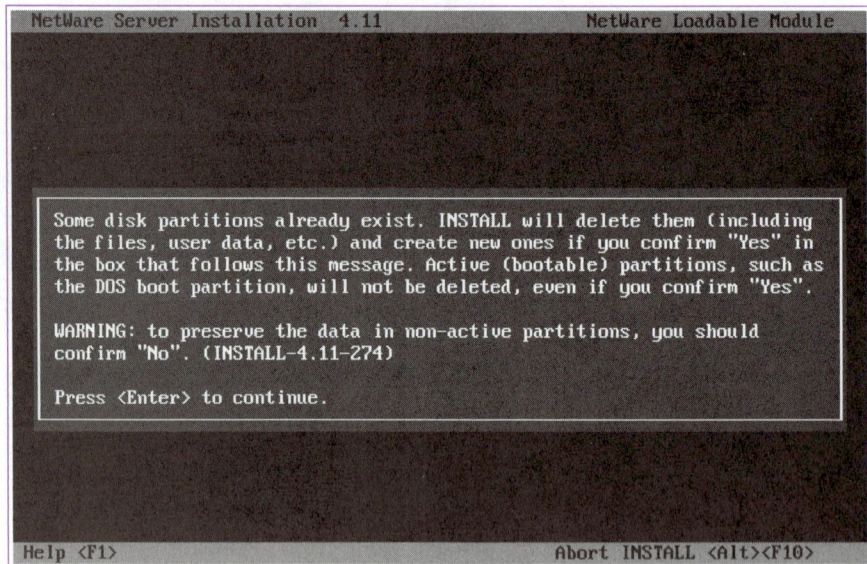

CHAPTER 3
Install

17. Delete existing non-bootable disk partitions if they were not already removed by selecting **Yes** from the choices shown in Figure 3-53.

Figure 3-53

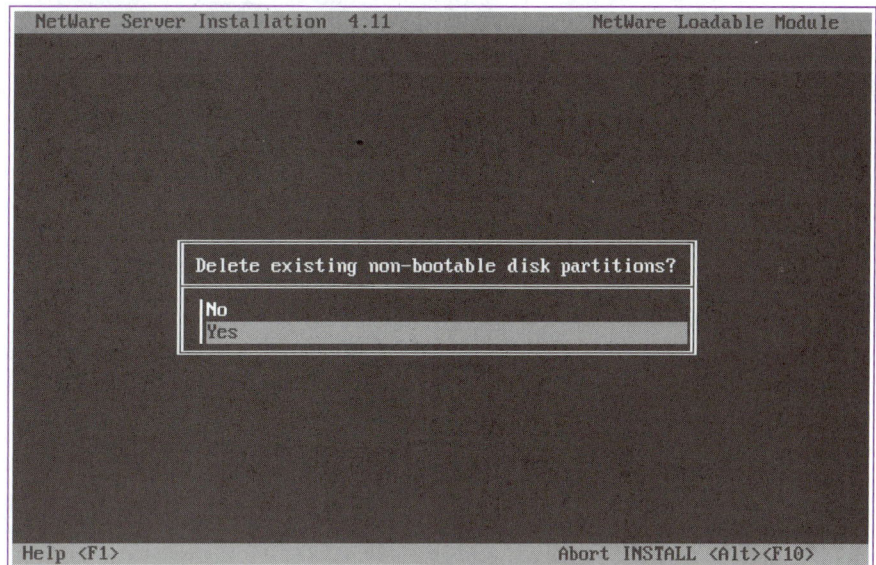

18. *File Copy Status (Preliminary Copy)* shown in Figure 3-54 tracks the installation's progress.

Figure 3-54

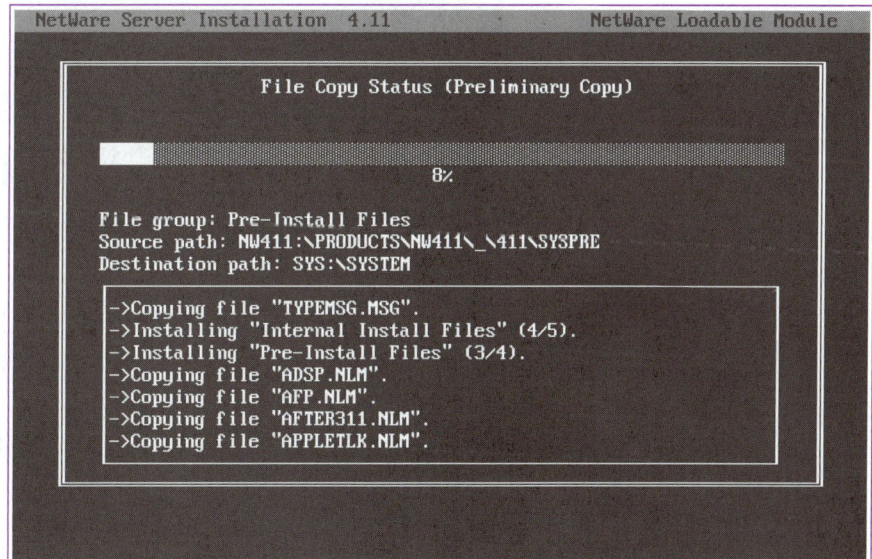

19. **Install NetWare Directory Services (NDS)** by selecting **Yes, this is the first NetWare 4 server** in the window shown in Figure 3-55.

Figure 3-55

```
NetWare Server Installation  4.11              NetWare Loadable Module

Install NetWare Directory Services (NDS)

No other NetWare 4 servers are accessible on any networks visible to this
server. Either this is the first NetWare 4 server, or there is a network
problem that prevents this server from seeing other NetWare 4 servers.




                 Is this the first NetWare 4 server?

                 Yes, this is the first NetWare 4 server
                 No, connect to existing NetWare 4 network




Previous screen <Esc>                          Restore NDS     <F3>
Help <F1>                                       Abort INSTALL <Alt><F10>
```

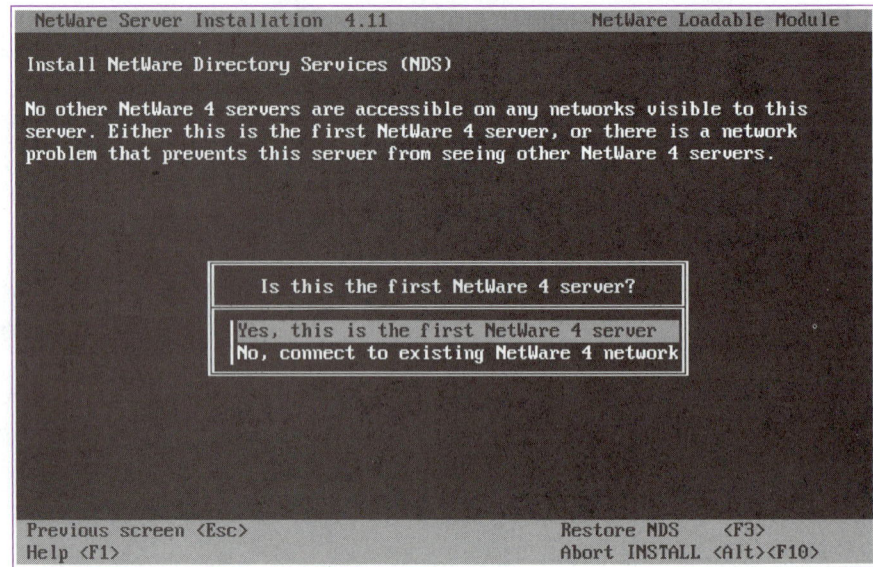

20. Highlight your time zone as indicated in Figure 3-56 and press **<ENTER>**.

Figure 3-56

```
NetWare Server Installation  4.11              NetWare Loadable Module

Choose Time Zone

Choose the time zone where this server will be installed.



        ▲ Spain: Peninsula and Baleares
          Taiwan, Taiwan Time
          United Kingdom, Greenwich Mean Time
          United States of America, Alaskan Time
          United States of America, Atlantic Time
          United States of America, Central Time
          United States of America, Eastern Time
          United States of America, Hawaiian-Aleutian Time
          United States of America, Mountain Time
          United States of America, Pacific Time



Select a time zone listed                  <Enter>  Previous screen   <Esc>
Enter parameters for a time zone not listed <Ins>
Help                                       <F1>    Abort INSTALL <Alt><F10>
```

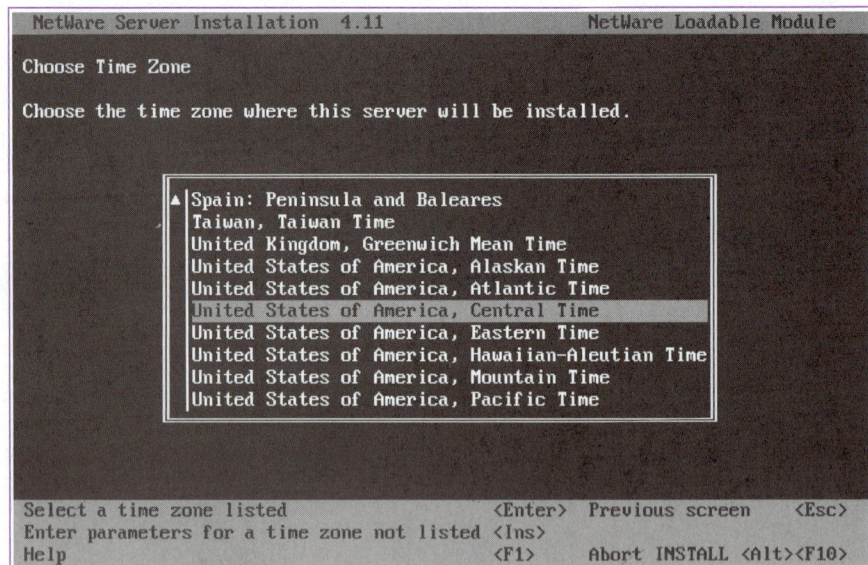

21. Type in the name of your **Organizational Unit** provided by the Instructor and press **<ENTER>**.

22. Type in the **Network Administrator's Password** provided by the Instructor and press **<ENTER>**.

23. Retype in the **Network Administrator's Password** and press **<ENTER>**.

24. ***For Your Information***—Record the information from the screen shown in Figure 3-57. This is the information NDS will use for subsequent logins by your Admin User. Press **<ENTER>** when complete.

Figure 3-57

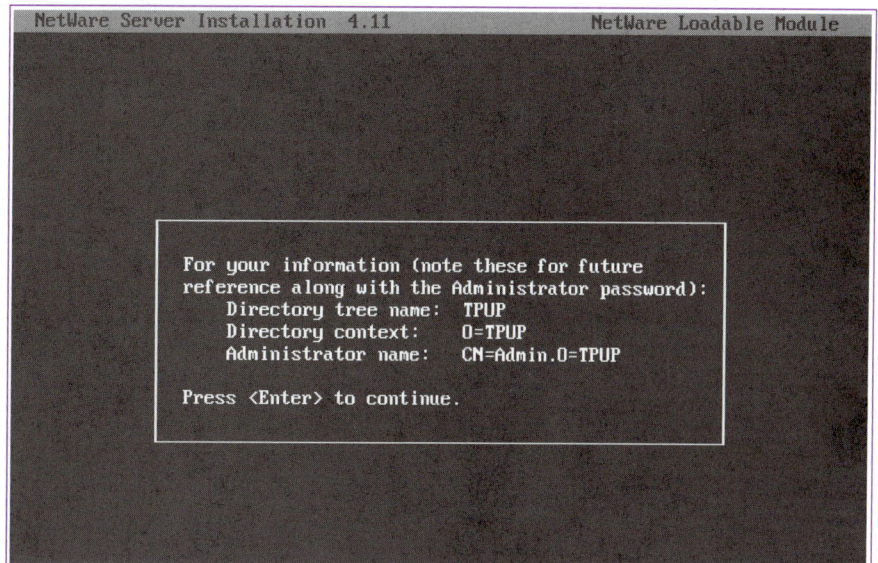

```
NetWare Server Installation  4.11                         NetWare Loadable Module




                    For your information (note these for future
                    reference along with the Administrator password):
                         Directory tree name:   TPUP
                         Directory context:     O=TPUP
                         Administrator name:    CN=Admin.O=TPUP

                    Press <Enter> to continue.
```

25. ***NetWare License***—You will now be asked to license your software. (This defaults to 0 users if you do not insert a licensing diskette at this time, but still allows up to two users to connect.) Insert your license diskette into the floppy drive (*A:*) when the screen shown in Figure 3-58 appears and press **<ENTER>**. The computer will read the file *SERVER.MLS* from the diskette.

Figure 3-58

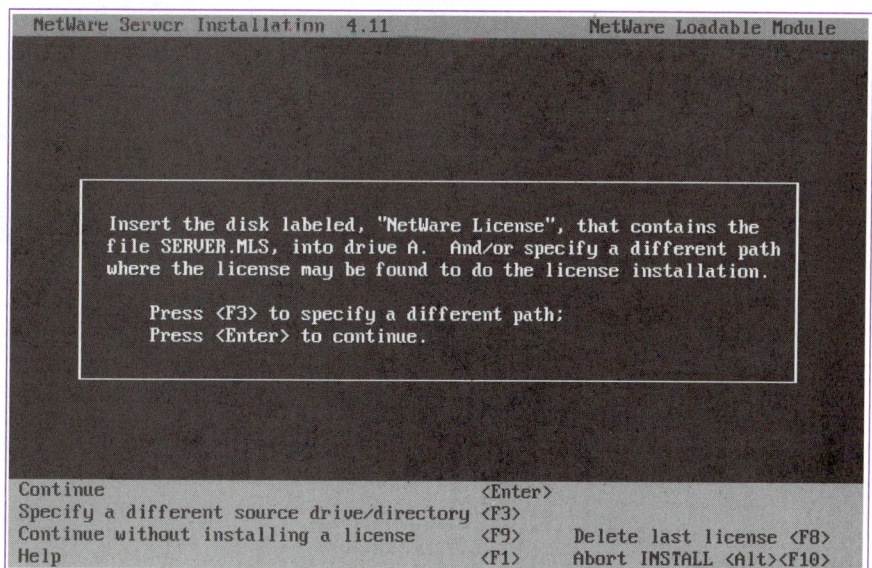

```
NetWare Server Installation  4.11                         NetWare Loadable Module



             Insert the disk labeled, "NetWare License", that contains the
             file SERVER.MLS, into drive A.  And/or specify a different path
             where the license may be found to do the license installation.

                  Press <F3> to specify a different path;
                  Press <Enter> to continue.




Continue                                         <Enter>
Specify a different source drive/directory <F3>
Continue without installing a license            <F9>        Delete last license <F8>
Help                                             <F1>        Abort INSTALL <Alt><F10>
```

CHAPTER 3
Install

26. The ***File Copy Status (Main Copy)*** screen appears as indicated in Figure 3-59. This is the point during the installation that NetWare copies the *SYSTEM, PUBLIC,* and other necessary files on the *SYS:* volume.

Figure 3-59

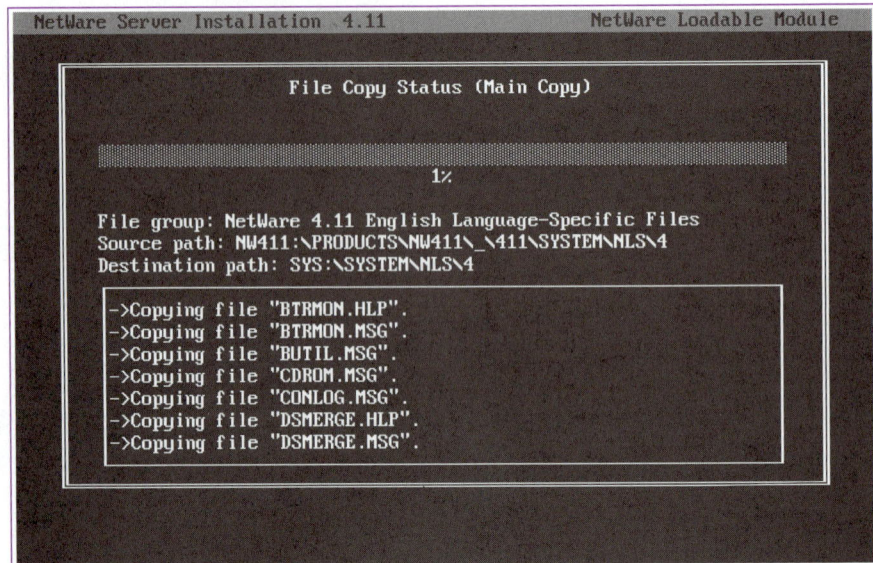

27. Upon completion of the Main Copy you will be offered ***Other Installation Options***. See Figure 3-60. Select **Continue Installation** and press **<ENTER>** when complete.

Figure 3-60

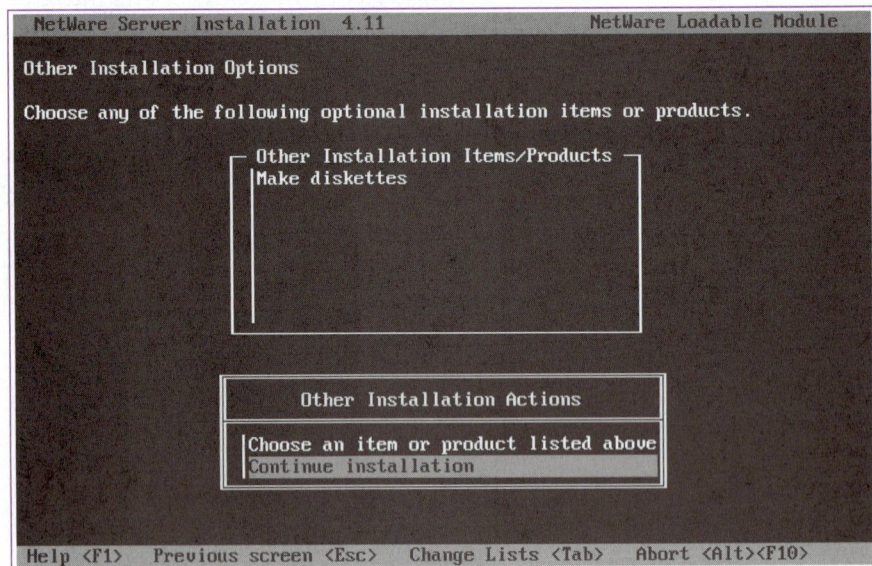

28. Press **<ENTER>** when *The Server Installation of NetWare 4.11 is complete* screen appears. This exits from the installation program and brings you to the *System Console* screen.

Figure 3-61

```
NetWare Server Installation  4.11                NetWare Loadable Module



     ┌──────────────────────────────────────────────────────────────┐
     │                                                                │
     │  The server installation of NetWare 4.11 is complete. It is recommended │
     │  that you reboot the server after exiting the installation.     │
     │                                                                │
     │  Continue by installing NetWare client software, and setting up access │
     │  to the online documentation.                                  │
     │                                                                │
     │  Refer to the "Installation" manual for information on installing │
     │  client software.  Refer to "Installing and Using Novell Online │
     │  Documentation for NetWare 4.11" for information on installing online │
     │  documentation.  Refer to the online documentation manuals,     │
     │  "Supervising the Network" and "Utilities Reference", for information │
     │  on administering your network, creating user accounts, etc.     │
     │                                                                │
     │  Press <Enter> to exit to the system console screen.           │
     │                                                                │
     └──────────────────────────────────────────────────────────────┘


Continue and exit INSTALL <Enter>           Previous screen      <Esc>
Help                     <F1>               Abort INSTALL <Alt><F10>
```

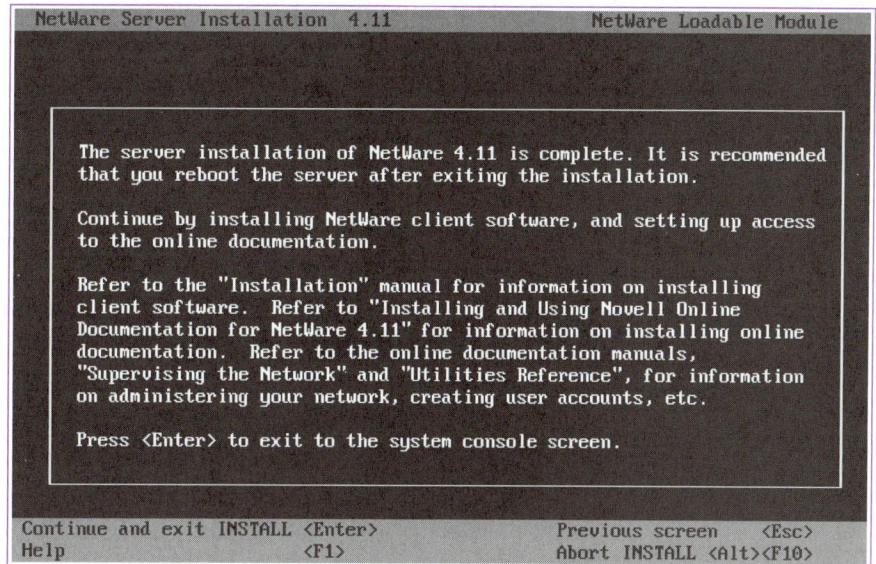

29. You should "Down" the server by typing in the word **Down** and pressing **<ENTER>**. At the next screen type in the word **Exit** and press **<ENTER>** again. These actions bring you to the *C:* prompt. You should be in the *NWSERVER* directory.

30. At this point you should restart your computer. It will boot up to the *C:* prompt again. You will need to type in **cd nwserver** and press **<ENTER>** to change to the *NWSERVER* directory. Then type in **server** and press **<ENTER>** again to start the server.

    If you do not want to be required to change to the *NWSERVER* directory and manually start the server by typing in **server**, you can simply add those two commands to your *AUTOEXEC.BAT* file and let them automatically execute when your computer restarts.

Congratulations. You have now successfully completed your Novell NetWare 4.11 server's installation and have a Novell NetWare 4.11 server at your disposal. The ease of use and usefulness of your new server depend on the speed of its processor and on how much remaining space it has on its hard drive. Regardless of how useful your first server may be, the steps you just completed are the same ones you will use to create another NetWare 4.11 server in the future.

The NetWare 4.11 server you have now will be important for you during the remainder of this course, but its speed and capacity are not. The server's speed and capacity do become important when you apply your ability to create a Novell 4.11 server to your employer's environment in an actual production setting. The knowledge you gain from installing these classroom servers helps you understand how they are created. Usually the servers do not need rebuilding, and a newcomer may wait a long time before installing another. ■

Chapter Summary

At the beginning of this chapter you prepared for the installation of your Novell NetWare server. You set aside a computer that would act as that server. In a real work environment, it would usually be the most powerful computer, but in your school setup it can be like your other workstations. A server is the central point for all authentication, storage, retrieval, printing, and network applications. The minimum hardware requirements for a server to run Novell's networking software were discussed. You used the information studied in chapter two about rebuilding computers and built your server by repartitioning it, formatting it, and installing DOS and all the necessary drivers for your mouse, CD-ROM player, and your Network Interface Card.

The remainder of this chapter concerned the actual installation of your NetWare server's software. Whether you installed the recently-released Novell NetWare 5 or the NetWare 4.11 software, the steps you completed were accompanied by figures of the screens you saw on your computer. Hopefully, this reassured you that all was going smoothly. If you run into problems later and a reinstallation is necessary, you should refer to this chapter for the hints and graphical assistance it provides.

Networking Terms Used in Chapter 3

NetWare minimum hardware requirements
NetWare Client
Certified Novell Administrator (CNA)
partition
FDISK
NT Boot Loader
unmarked files
system files
Read-Only files

NTFS partition
Graphical User Interface (GUI)
PS/2
communications ports
IDE drives
`Install`
C:\NWSERVER
device drivers
3COM EtherLink 3 Legacy Card

SYS: volume
NetWare Loadable Module (NLM)
radio button
unique tree name
administrator password
server license
Novell Directory Services (NDS)

■ Chapter Review Questions

1. What are the items that lead to a need for a computer network?

2. Explain why the computer used for a server is usually the strongest, fastest, and most capable computer in an organization.

3. List the hardware, software, and cabling requirements needed for a ten-workstation computer network.

4. Why is it necessary to rebuild the computer used as the server in this chapter's networking project?

5. What are the minimum hardware requirements for a Novell NetWare 5 server?

6. Explain why Novell's minimum requirements are higher than what is actually necessary for a server to operate.

7. What is NetWare Client software?

8. Explain the steps used to **FDISK** your computer's hard drive when preparing your server.

9. Explain the use of the term *Graphical User Interface*.

10. Why are passwords "hidden" when they are typed in?

■ **Associated Chapter Problems**

1. Re-create your server repeatedly until you do so without mistakes. (From the **FDISK** command through server reboot).

2. Explain the installation process in your own words. This should be done conceptually by explaining what was accomplished rather than how it was done.

3. Defend or refute the following statement: "A Graphical User Interface lets a user accomplish more."

4. The NetWare Graphical User Interface at the Server Console is a new concept for Novell. How could Novell make its interface more useable? Write ten additions that you would make to the GUI if you were one of the Novell programmers on the NetWare 5 project. Sketch out any icons you would use and explain how they would operate.

OBJECTIVES

At this point, you understand why you need a network and you have actually created your own NetWare file server. Now you need to gain and control access to the resources of your network. By the end of this chapter, you will be able to:

■ install the NetWare Client at the workstation.

■ log on to your new NetWare network as an Admin user.

■ explain the need for network security.

■ decide on your basic network structure.

■ create additional User objects.

■ implement your Network Design.

■ use basic security measures on your network.

Installing Novell Client Software

The previous chapters introduced you to the organizational structure of the TPUP environment, demonstrated the need for a network, and taught you how to create your own workstations and build your own NetWare server. Now you only need to start using your network. To do this you must have resources that you need to use and someone who will grant you access to those resources over your network connection.

Before you can arrive at that point, however, you return to the problem you had when you and your classmates assembled in your classroom and wanted to share information. You needed an orderly way to transfer that information from one learner to another. Now that your computers are connected, you must make sure that they are able to "speak" to one another.

We have already discussed the topology of your computers. Your network is probably an Ethernet 10baseT network, most likely connected in a type of star topology. Thus, they are capable of communication. Your workstation has files on it which you would like to share with others in your class through your server and over your network. All of the elements for networking seem to be there. How then does it actually happen? What is the missing piece?

In Chapter 2, you learned that a network requires a server offering its services or resources and a client requesting those services or resources. These are the elements missing right now. How does your workstation become a client of your server?

The answer lies in *Novell NetWare's client software*. While there are many editions of this software, this textbook will discuss the newest Novell client software. For this reason, the client software that accompanied Novell NetWare 5 networking software (client version 3.0 at the time of this writing) will be the client of choice for the remainder of this course. Most client programs perform similar functions. They allow a workstation to make a request by *logging in* to the server and obtain authorization to use the services and resources of the network.

Already, a user account is established on your server. It is the *Admin user* created during installation. As you recall, you specified "Novell5" as the *password*. Without that user account already on your server, you would not be able to gain access to any resources. The security on a Novell NetWare server is designed to prevent unauthorized users from gaining access without the Admin user's authorization.

Now that your computers are connected, you must make sure that they are able to "speak" to one another.

The security on a Novell NetWare server is designed to prevent unauthorized users from gaining access without the Admin user's authorization.

**CHAPTER 4
Access**

Activity 4-1	Installing Novell Client on Your Workstation

In order to access that user account on the server, you must install the Novell Client on your workstation. Your server should be running. Ensure that no applications are running on your workstation. The CD set currently distributed with the NetWare 5 operating system includes both the Windows 95 and Windows NT client software and operates with both NetWare 5 and 4.11 networks. The client installation runs a program called *WINSETUP.EXE* on your workstation and copies the NetWare login files to your workstation so that you are able to login using Novell Client.

> **NOTE**
> When in Novell's graphical mode, selections are done similar to those in HTML and only a single click with the hand icon activates your choice.
> **NOTE**

1. Close all open windows and insert the *Novell NetWare 5 Client CD*. The CD should self-start (*autorun*) and the *Z.E.N.works* screen should appear. (Z.E.N. stands for Zero Effort Networking.) The window shown in Figure 4-1 should appear. Place your cursor (the hand) over the word **English** and click once.

Figure 4-1

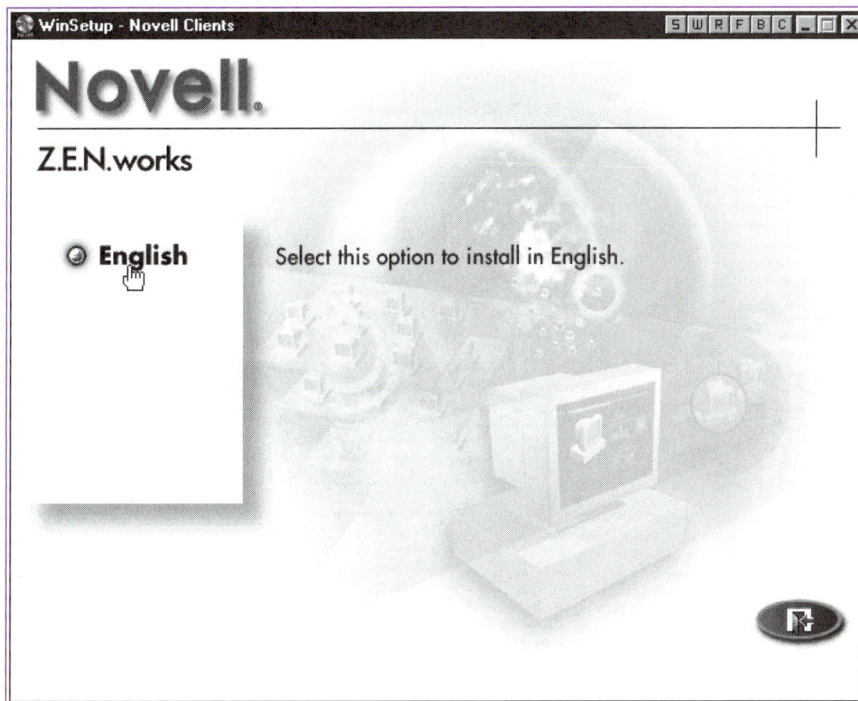

2. The window shown in Figure 4-2 appears. Slide your cursor over the **Windows 95** and click once to begin installation of the Windows 95 workstation client software.

Figure 4-2

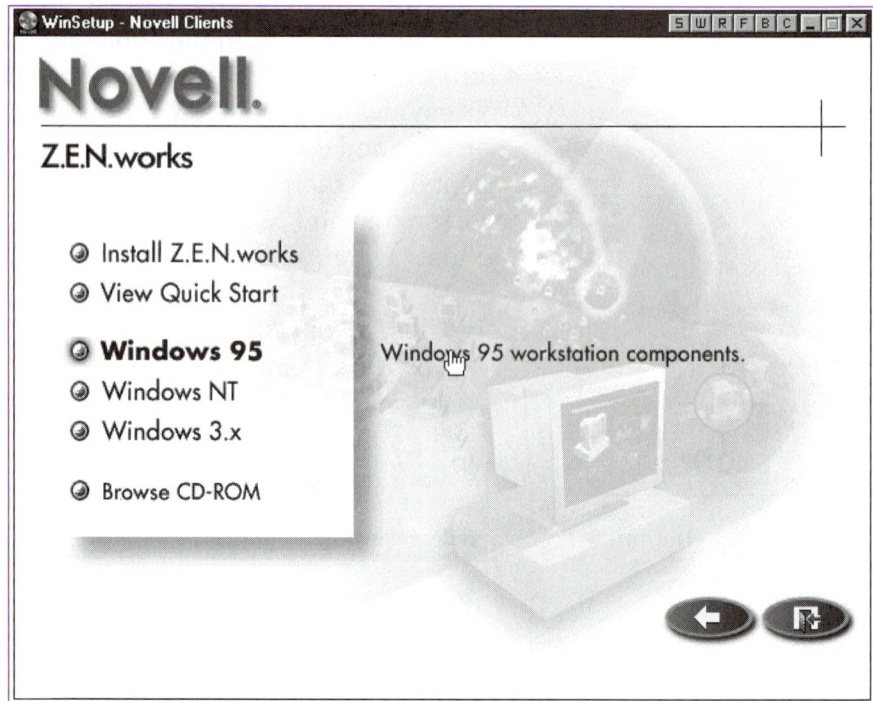

3. The window shown in Figure 4-3 appears. Move the cursor over **Install Novell Client** and click once to install the Novell Client software for Windows 95.

Figure 4-3

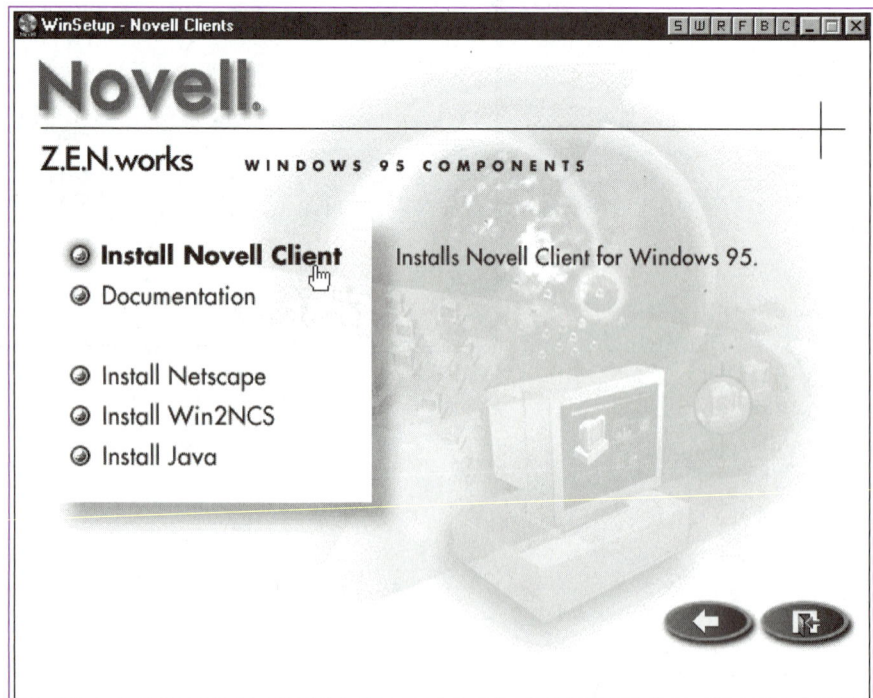

4. The ***Novell Terms and Conditions License Agreement*** window shown in Figure 4-4 appears. Move your cursor to the **Yes** button after reading and agreeing to the terms, and click once to continue.

Figure 4-4

Novell Client for Windows 95 License Agreement

Please read the following license agreement.

NOVELL TERMS AND CONDITIONS

The software files ("SOFTWARE") enclosed in this self extracting file ("FILE") are protected by the copyright laws of the United States and international copyright treaties. You may, without charge, reproduce and distribute, within your organization only, copies of this FILE, and use copies of the SOFTWARE solely for their intended purpose of supporting legally obtained, commercially available Novell operating system software, provided: 1) you do not receive any direct payment, commercial benefit, or other consideration for the reproduction, distribution or use of the SOFTWARE or FILE, or distribute the FILE as part of or in combination with any other software or hardware product without the prior written consent of Novell, Inc.; and, 2) you do not change or omit any proprietary rights notices appearing on or in the SOFTWARE or FILE. If you are a reseller of Novell products, you may, subject to the forgoing, distribute the FILE outside your organization solely for maintenance and upgrade of SOFTWARE.

You will take all reasonable steps to protect the SOFTWARE and the FILE from

Do you accept all of the terms of the preceding Novell License Agreement? If you choose No, Setup will close. To install the Novell Client for Windows 95, you must accept this

Yes   No

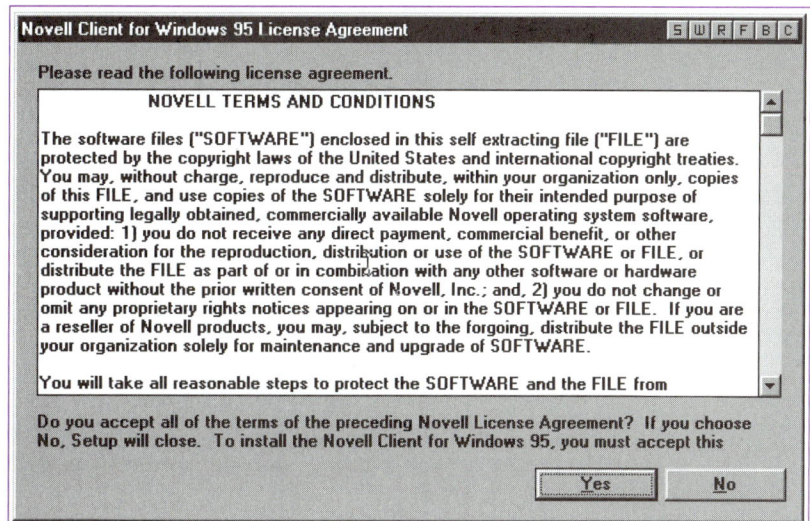

5. The ***Select an installation option*** window shown in Figure 4-5 appears. Leave the radio button clicked on **Typical** and press the **Install >** button when ready to proceed.

Figure 4-5

For late breaking information not available in the printed documentation, view the README file.

Welcome to the Novell Client for Windows 95 Install

Novell.
CLIENT INSTALLATION

Select an installation option:

⊙ Typical   The Novell Client for Windows 95 will be automatically installed and configured with default settings. Recommended for most computers.

○ Custom   The Novell Client for Windows 95 and selected components will be installed and configured. For system administrators or advanced users only.

For late breaking information not available in the printed documentation, view the README file.   View README

< Back   Install >   Cancel   Help

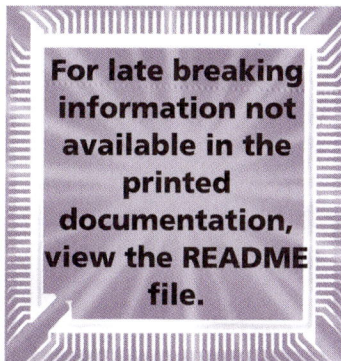

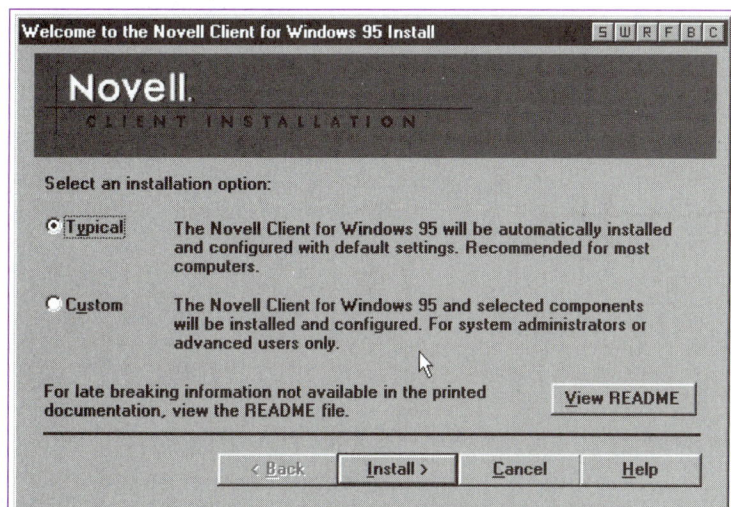

6. A ***Status*** window appears, informing you that your existing client is being removed.

CHAPTER 4
Access

7. The **Copying Files** window shown in Figure 4-6 appears and shows you the copying progress.

Figure 4-6

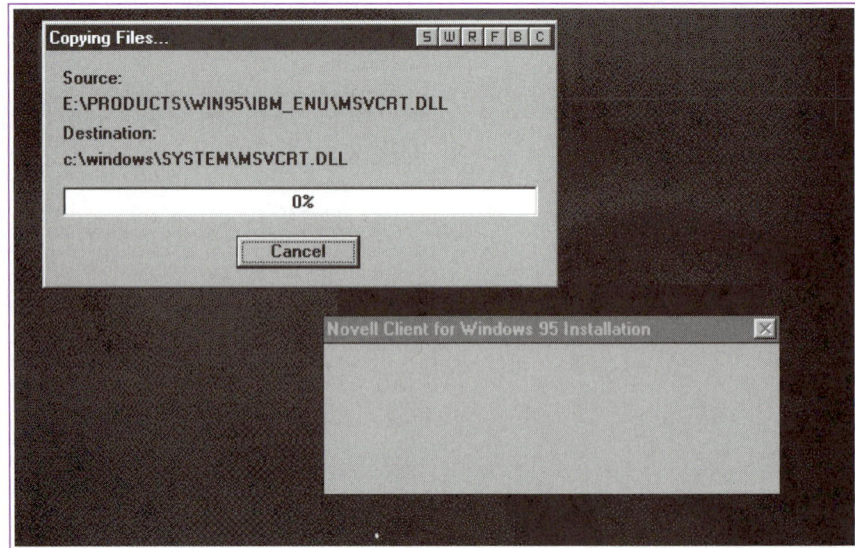

8. The informational window shown in Figure 4-7 appears, giving you a choice of actions available now that your client installation has completed. Click the *Reboot* button.

Figure 4-7

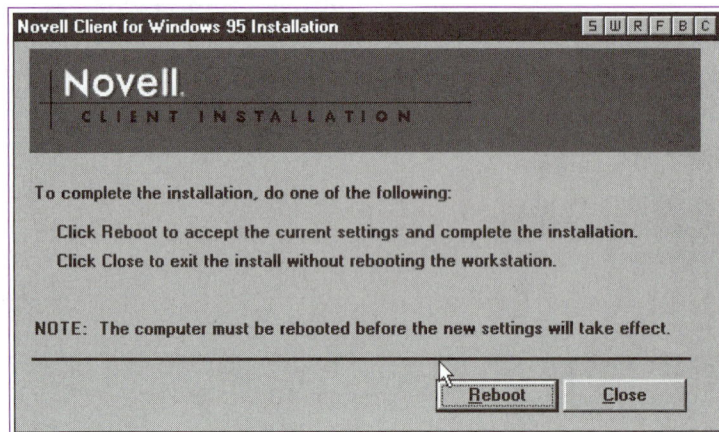

9. The **Novell Login** window shown in Figure 4-8 appears after your computer is finished rebooting. This confirms that your Novell Client installed correctly.

Figure 4-8

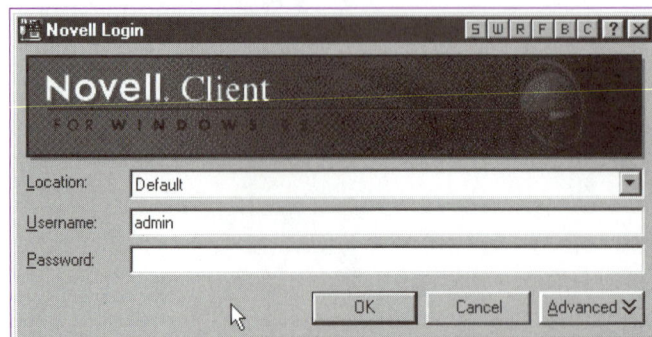

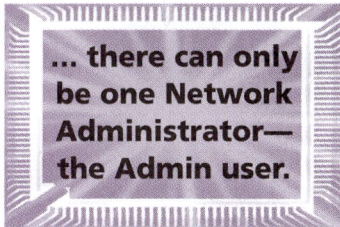

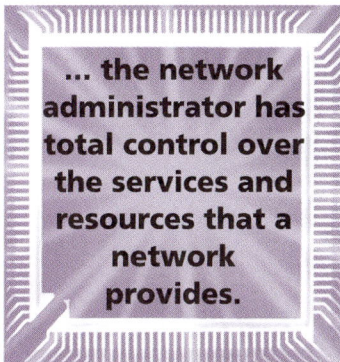

Only One Admin User

There are several learners in your class, but there can only be one *Network Administrator*—the Admin user. The network administrator is the person responsible for overall network security. That person normally creates the network and is responsible for its safekeeping. Some of the network administrator's duties include creating additional users, creating the organizational structure of the network itself, securing individuals' files, and making applications to multiple users. Additionally, the network administrator issues and changes other users' passwords. Because a password is required for entry to the network, the network administrator has total control over the services and resources that a network provides.

For the above reasons, you must select only one class member to be your network administrator. This role can be rotated to others at a later time (possibly when the server is rebuilt later in the course), but the control should be absolute. No one should be able to undo what the administrator does to the network structure and security. It is the administrator's job to maintain the network and it is the Admin's responsibility to correct problems. When you choose your administrator, be aware that whoever is chosen will be working much harder than anyone else on the network. Choose that person wisely.

> ... there can only be one Network Administrator— the Admin user.

> ... the network administrator has total control over the services and resources that a network provides.

Activity 4-2	Logging In as the Admin User

The new administrator should first do a *login* to the network as Admin and change the Admin's password, because everyone in class currently knows the password. Now that your administrator has the required components for logging into a network, he or she should log in properly and begin preparing the network for additional users. Complete the chapter exercises before changing your Admin password, and then make sure that only one person and your Instructor know it.

Login procedures assure that only authorized network users gain access to your network services and resources. When you log into the network, your identity is verified using what the network administrator has recorded about you, and your right to access resources or services is controlled. Login procedures protect your network. Everyone on the network *must* log in. With the advent of NetWare 4.0 (and later versions), most users will have only one login name and password with which to access any of his or her authorized resources.

1. From the login screen in the previous exercise, click on the **Advanced** button in the lower right of the screen. The window shown in Figure 4-9 should appear if your network is operating properly. Type in your Admin user's password (**Novell5**) and click the **OK** button when ready to proceed.

CHAPTER 4
Access

Figure 4-9

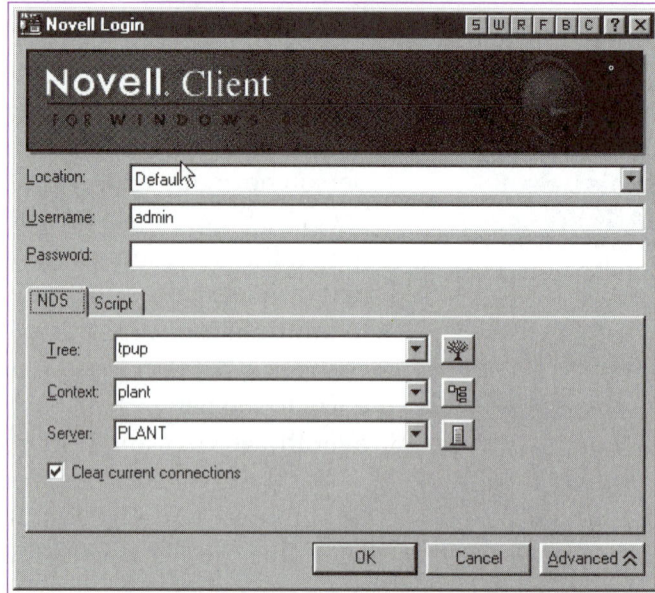

2. The window shown in Figure 4-10 should flash on your screen and close automatically as the login procedure continues. This is another verification that your login procedures are working properly. You will notice that your *local drives* (the drives physically attached to your computer) are indicated as *mapping to a local disk*. Additionally, drive *N:* shows *Plant_SYS:\SYSTEM*. This is the Novell method for specifying files and directories on *NetWare Volumes*. (This will be discussed in later chapters.)

Figure 4-10

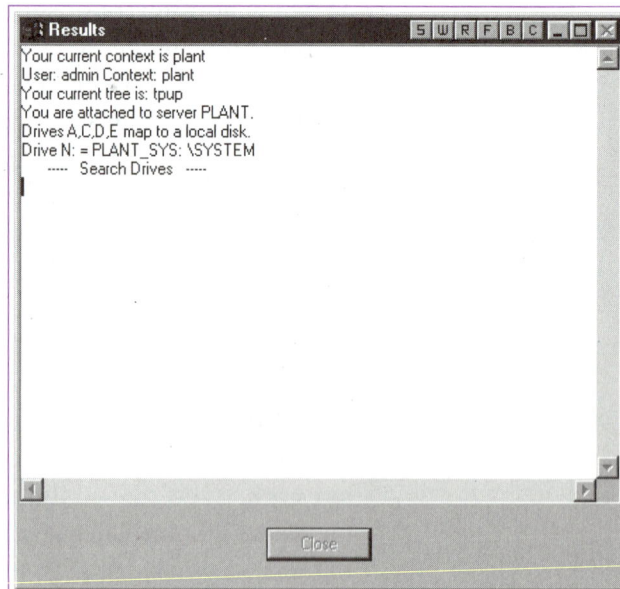

Network security is quickly lost when a user fails to log out from his active connection. An *unauthorized user* could sit down at an unattended but still logged in computer and gain access to private files. That user could damage the network or cause irreparable harm to the files that you thought were safe on your network. Get into the habit of logging out of your network as soon as you are finished using the services.

> Network security is quickly lost when a user fails to log out from his active connection. An unauthorized user could sit down at an unattended but still logged in computer and gain access to private files.

Your class could create a password and login program that is similar to the one in operation at the real TPUP manufacturing facility. The plant supervisors agreed that network security is very important. File security and network access had presented a problem to the supervisors because they were not accustomed to such security measures. Networking was new to all of them, and they wanted to devise a way to help them remember their passwords and remind them to log out when they were finished with the network. They agreed to impose a small monetary "fine" on any violator of either security measure. Each time anyone walked away from an unattended network computer with an active connection and another supervisor noticed it, the violator was "fined" for carelessness. Because they considered forgetting a password an even greater breach of security, a supervisor who forgot his or her password was fined even more each time. The money was then donated to the Employee of the Month account and thus contributed to another worthy program. Your class can invent a penalty for security violations. Monetary penalties work best, but the point will be made regardless of your method. ■

Components of Logging In

What are the components of a login procedure? You have been developing them since the first chapter of this text. You created a system for assigning user names. Whatever system you decided to use, you should adhere to that naming convention now. Use your *user name* for your first login component to gain access to your network. You may remember that TPUP used the employee's first name combined with the first letter of his last name. Using this convention, my user name would be RichM. It does not matter whether you use upper or lower case letters in user names or passwords so RichM is the same as richm or RICHM.

Remember, too, that two people can have the same user name provided their accounts do not exist in the same *network container*. If you developed your own naming standard, it will work provided the login procedure does not have to distinguish between two people in the same department at the same time with the same name. User names, like passwords, can be composed of a specified maximum number of letters, numbers, or special characters. The limit is 64 characters for a user name and 128 characters for a password.

The second component of logging in is the password, and there are several *password rules* governing their creation and use. Only the user should know it. Initially, the fact that the password is given by the administrator violates this rule, but you can easily remedy this situation by requiring each user to change his password the next time he logs in. Although the administrator has the power to change a user's password, when that user's old password no longer works it is immediately clear that the administrator has changed it. Passwords should be difficult for others to figure out, but easy for the user to remember. They should be a combination of letters and numbers.

They should not be a user's initials, last name, first name, date of birth, spouse's date of birth, child's name, pet's name, or anything else that is readily attributable to the user. "*Hackers*" are people who try combinations of items such as these to "break in" to a network. With a user name and password, a hacker is authorized to do anything with the network resources that the valid user could do.

Another component to logging in is the user's *context*. A user's context is the location where the computer can locate his user object. Using the organization chart from the first chapter of this text, you can compare the context concept with the job function of each of the workers at the plant. Therefore, because MelW, BartP, SteveL, and DaveL are all supervisors, their context could be "Manufacturing Managers." If there is another Bart whose last name begins with the letter P (even if the user is not our BartP), there would be a conflict. At some time, the computer will have to decide which BartP to allow to log on, but the computer will not know what to do given that choice. The unique identifier concept is violated in this case.

On the other hand, if one of the BartPs at the plant were a supervisor and the other the janitor, there would not be a problem. The computer would locate one BartP by checking all the managers and the other by checking all the janitors. No single container lists them both as members, so the computer is not forced to decide between two individuals with the same user names. Using notation similar to Novell's identifier, the first BartP would be located by checking the following location: TPUP, Manufacturing-Plant, Supervisors : \BartP, while the second would be found at TPUP, Manufacturing-Plant, Janitors : \BartP. Because they are clearly different, the computer finds the right person. Knowing where to look, who to look for, and what the password is, the computer can easily verify whether an individual is authorized to access the network.

> Knowing where to look, who to look for, and what the password is, the computer can easily verify whether an individual is authorized to access the network.

Activity 4–3   Installing Z.E.N.works on the NetWare 5 Server

If your server is a NetWare 4.11 server, you already have the interface required for network operation. You have client software loaded on your workstation, and your server has the software necessary to be the central point or the network.

However, as you may have noticed when installing the client on your workstation, Novell NetWare 5 also allows installation of the Z.E.N. Starter Pack to the NetWare 5 server.

> ... Novell NetWare 5 also allows installation of the Z.E.N. Starter Pack to the NetWare 5 server.

1. Close all open windows and insert the *Novell Client CD*. The CD should self-start and the autorun feature of Z.E.N.works should start. The first window in Activity 4-1 should appear. Place your cursor over the word **English** and click once. The window shown in Figure 4-11 should appear when you place your cursor over the **Install Z.E.N.works** selection. With the cursor still in that location, click once when ready to proceed with the installation.

Figure 4-11

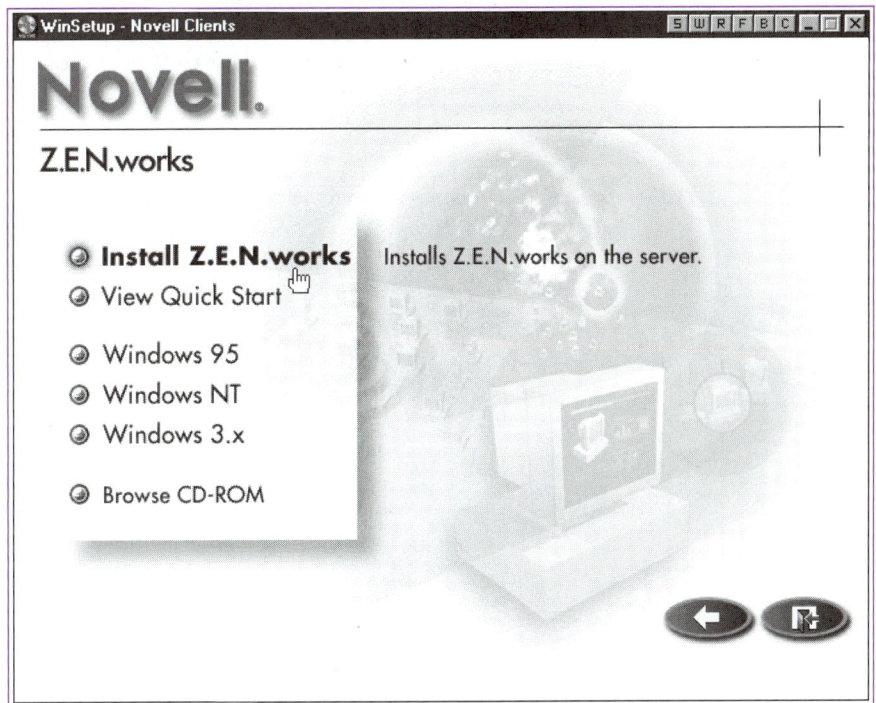

2. The **Setup** window shown in Figure 4-12 appears showing the progress of the Starter Pack Wizard installation to the server.

Figure 4-12

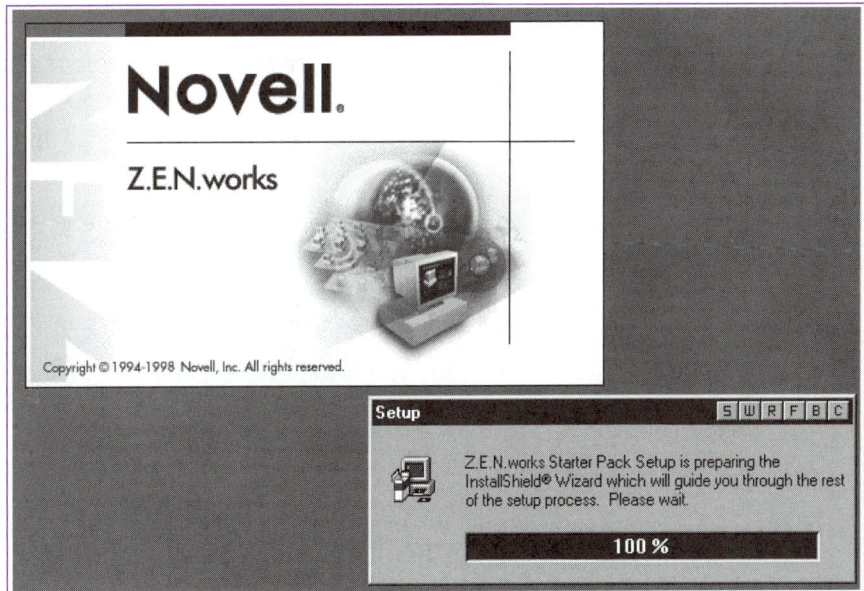

3. The ***Welcome to Z.E.N.works*** window shown in Figure 4-13 appears requesting that you close all programs using files in *Sys:Public* (on the server). Click on the **Next >** button when ready to proceed.

Figure 4-13

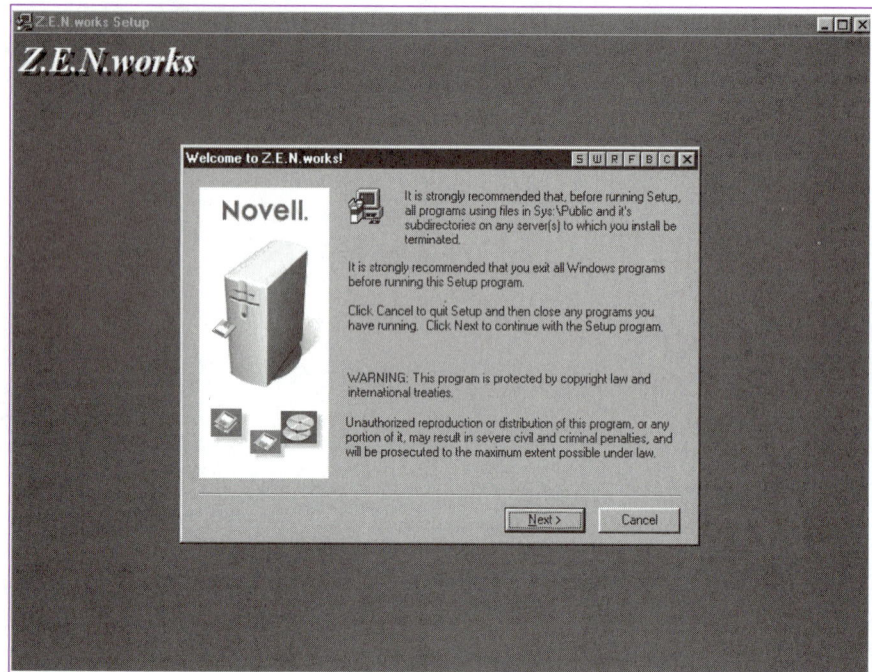

4. The ***Software License Agreement*** window shown in Figure 4-14 appears. Move your cursor over the **Yes** button after reading the agreement and agreeing to it. Click once to continue.

Figure 4-14

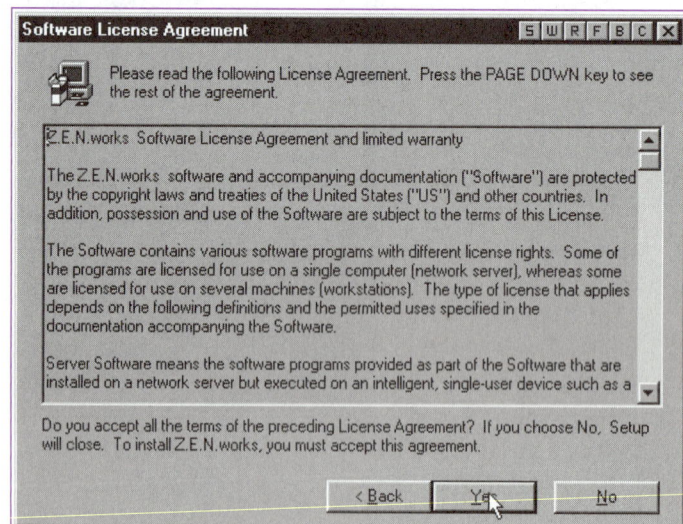

5. The *Z.E.N.works Setup Type* window shown in Figure 4-15 appears. Leave the radio button set on **Typical** and click the **Next >** button when ready to proceed.

Figure 4-15

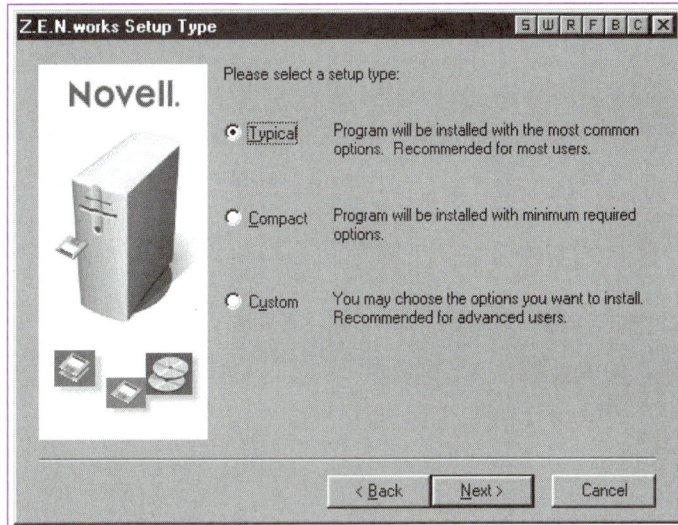

6. The *Z.E.N.works List of Tree/Servers* window shown in Figure 4-16 appears. Note that although the NetWare 4.11 server TPUP-HQ was available on the network, it could not be selected for Z.E.N.works installation. Make sure the check mark remains in the server that you want to install onto and click the **Next >** button when ready to proceed.

Figure 4-16

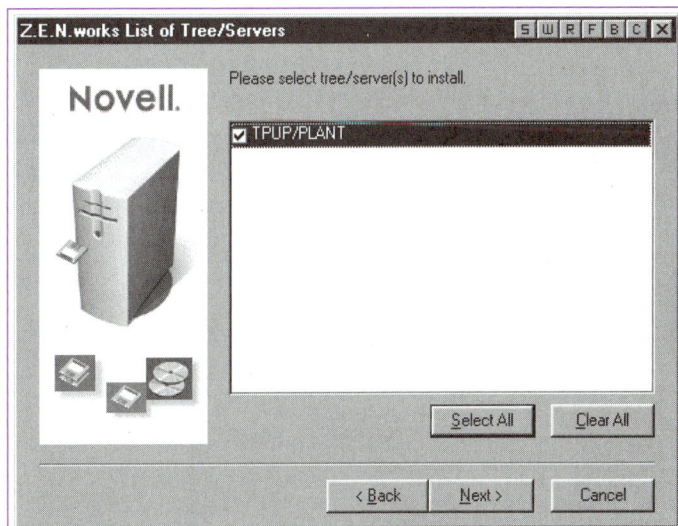

CHAPTER 4
Access

7. The ***Z.E.N.works Language Selection*** window shown in
   Figure 4-17 appears. Make sure that **ENGLISH** is checked
   and click the **Next >** button when ready to proceed.

Figure 4-17

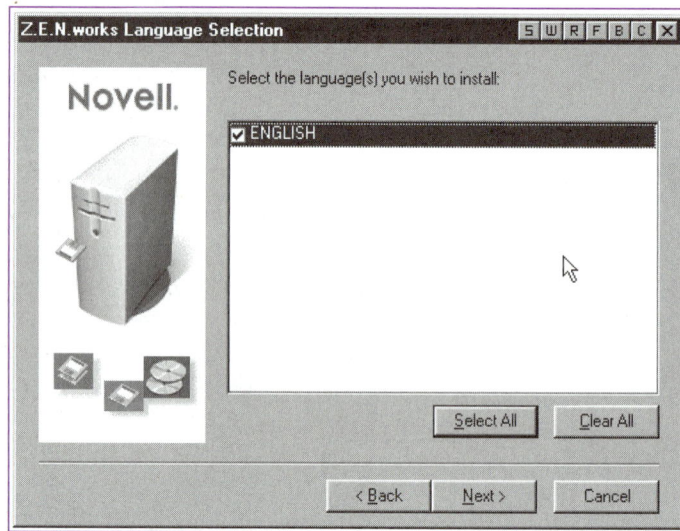

8. The ***Start Copying Files*** window shown in Figure 4-18
   appears. Click the **Next >** button when ready to proceed.

Figure 4-18

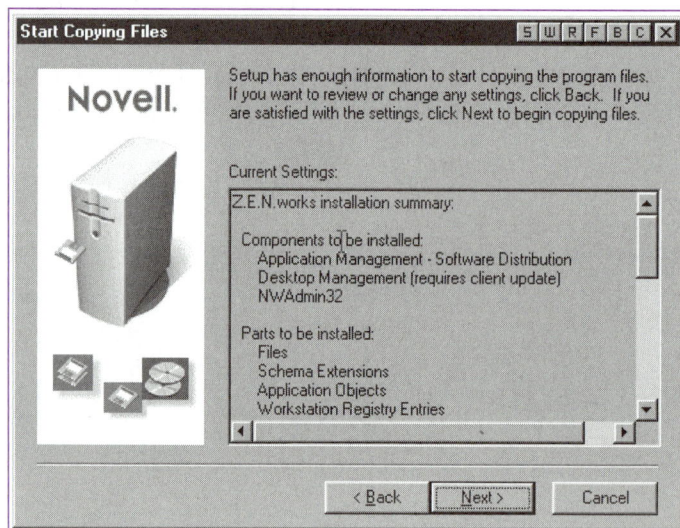

9. The **Z.E.N.works Setup** window shown in Figure 4-19 appears showing the installation progress.

Figure 4-19

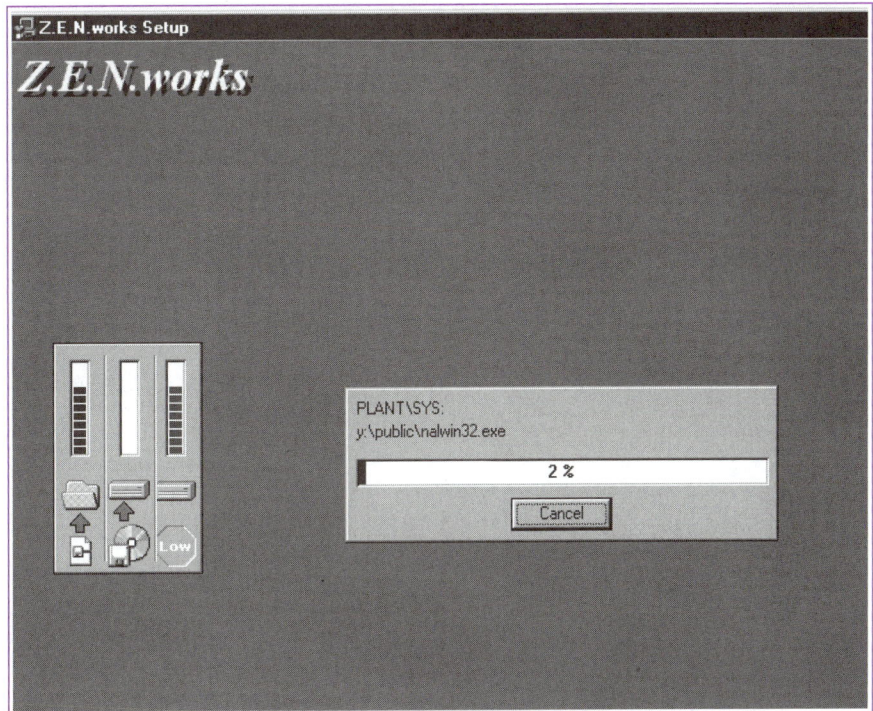

10. The **For Server PLANT, installing schema extension, new NDS objects** window shown in Figure 4-20 appears.

Figure 4-20

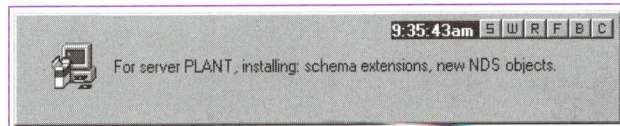

11. The **Novell Z.E.N.works rights granting** window shown in Figure 4-21 appears informing you that workstations must be granted appropriate rights and asking for a context to grant the rights to the users.

Figure 4-21

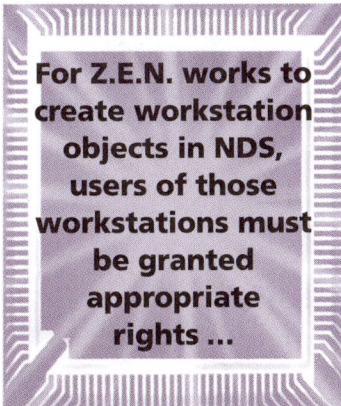

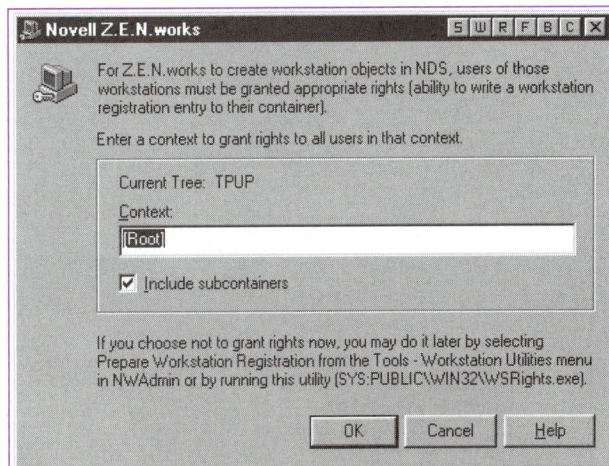

12. The **Z.E.N.works Workstation Auto-Registration rights were successfully set up** window appears. See Figure 4-22.

Figure 4-22

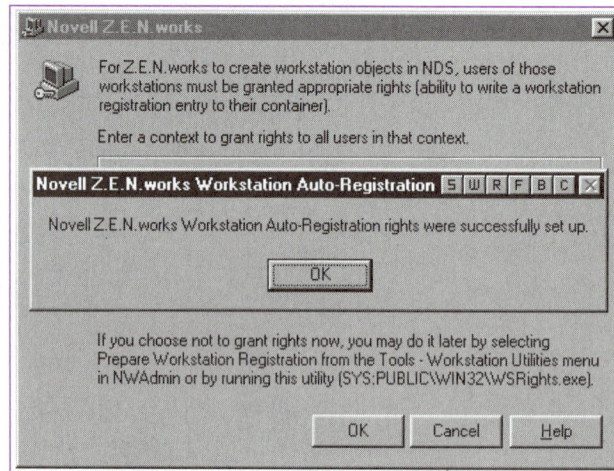

13. The **Z.E.N.works Setup** window appears informing you that Setup has finished installing Z.E.N.works on the server and giving you the option of *Launch Read-Me* file or the *Launch Setup Log* file. Click the **Finish** button when ready to proceed.

Figure 4-23

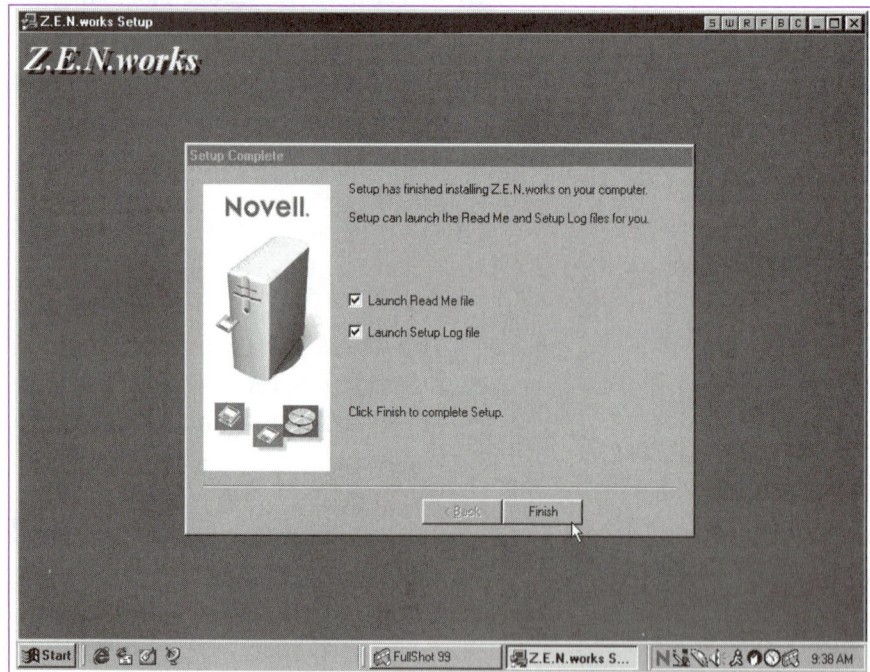

CHAPTER 4
Access

14. The ***readme - Notepad*** window appears if you leave the appropriate check in the window previously shown in step 13.

Figure 4-24

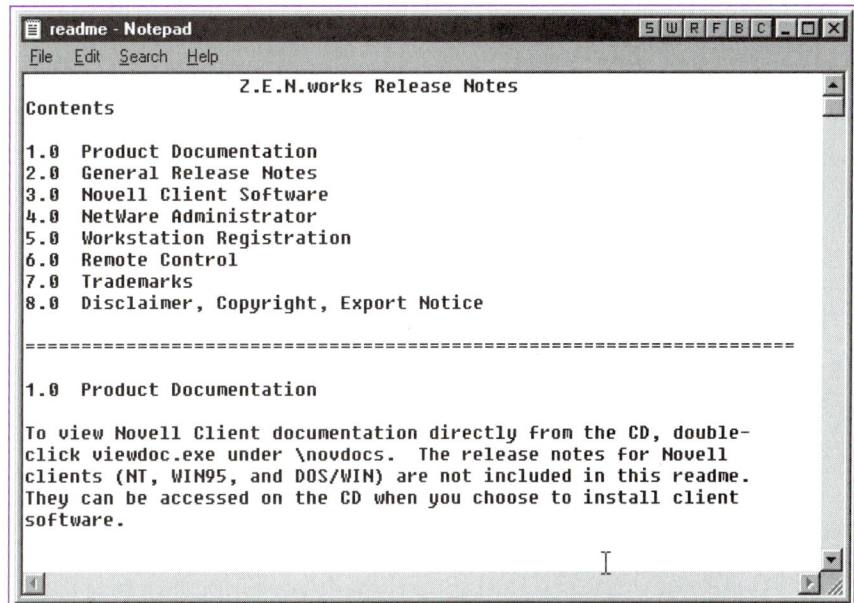

15. The ***setuplog - Notepad*** window appears if you leave the appropriate check in the window previously shown in step 13.

Figure 4-25

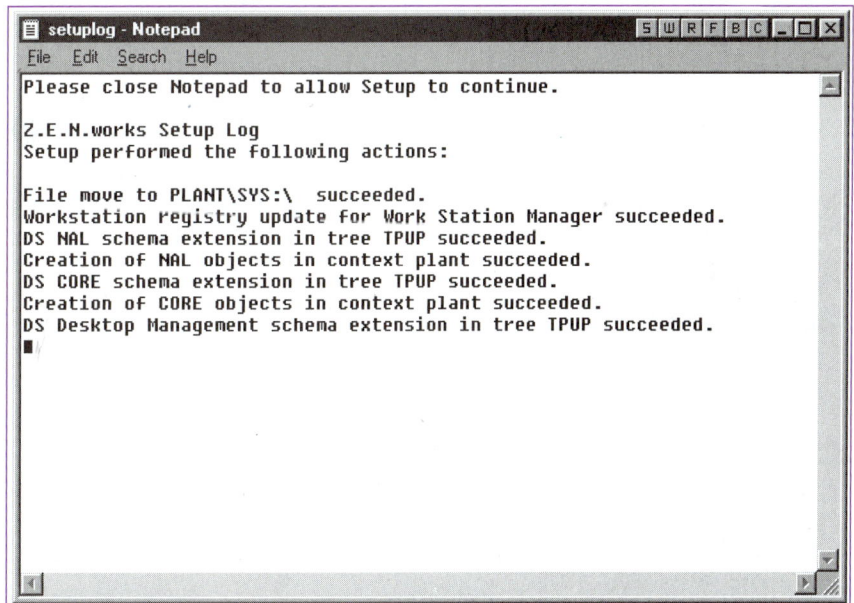

Administering the Network

When *administering the network*, you will use the Admin User object to login to the network and a utility called NetWare Administrator, or NWADMIN32, to manage it. As you saw in the installation portion of this class, your Admin object was created as a default user during the installation process. It is the only user object to which the operating system gives *administration rights* when the NetWare Directory is created. Your Admin user object gains the responsibility for network creation as the network administrator, and the installation process ensures that you have the authority by giving you *supervisory rights* to everything on the server.

More than one person can have administrative responsibility for your network and can, therefore, also have supervisory rights to the server. The Admin user must create them, however, during the network implementation process. Your Admin user object should not be deleted or modified (except possibly to change the password) unless you are absolutely sure that other user objects have administrative rights over all portions of the network.

When you log in as the Admin object you will be able to use **NWADMIN32** to administer the network. To run *NetWare Administrator* (**NWADMIN32**), click on the Windows **Start** button and go to **Run**. Type in the command **NWADMIN32** and press **<ENTER>**. The window shown in Figure 4-26 should appear. It is through this window that the Admin User object manages the NDS database.

Figure 4-26

> Your Admin User object should not be deleted or modified ... unless you are absolutely sure that other user objects have administrative rights over all portions of the network.

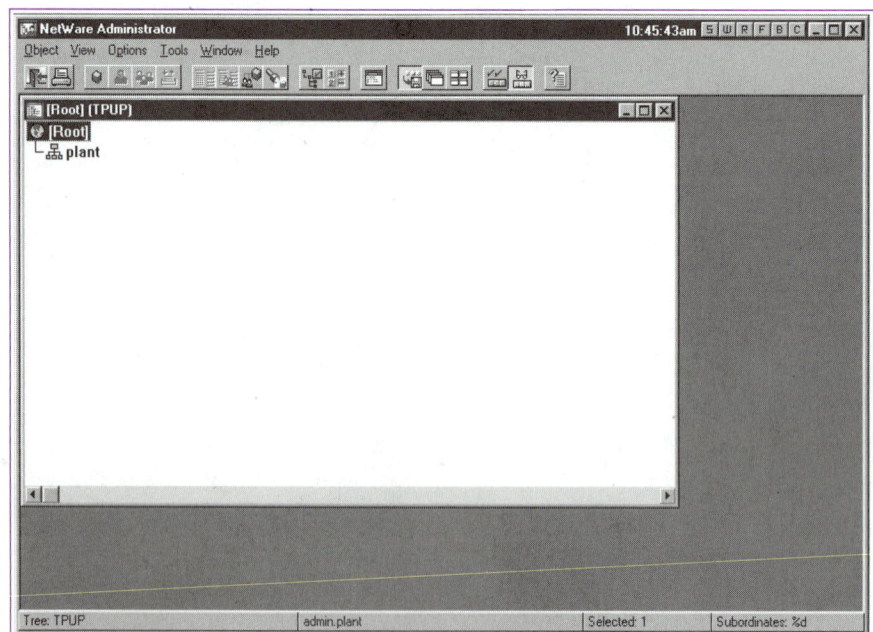

Double clicking on some objects in the view above will show results similar to those in *Windows Explorer*. Double clicking on the Plant object, however, will show you that there are vast differences in what will be there. When you double click on the Plant object, the window shown in Figure 4-27 appears. It is in this window that your Admin user creates user objects and organizational objects for the rest of the class.

Figure 4-27

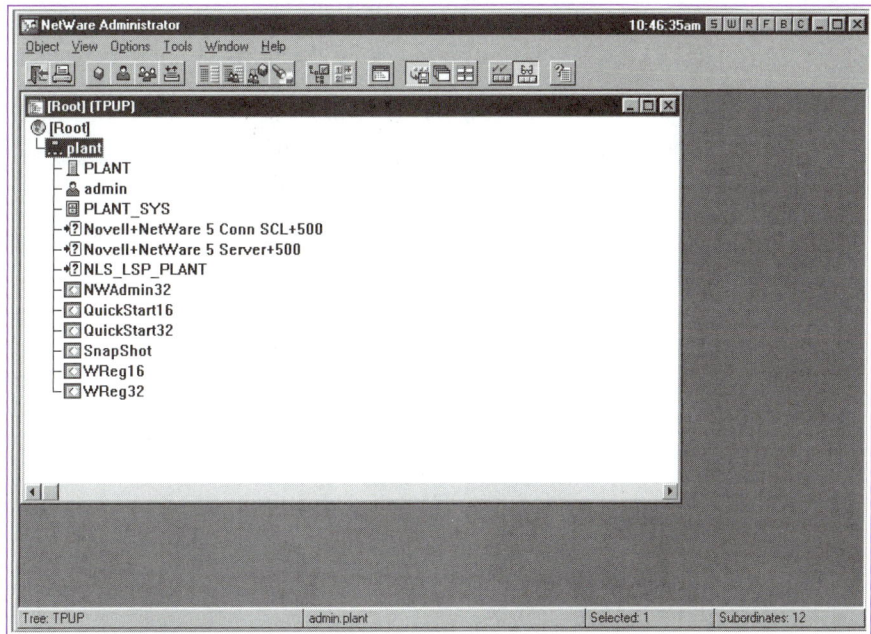

All objects in NDS have similar property buttons.

It is through the window shown in Figure 4-27, that the Admin user arrives at specific properties for each of the objects in NetWare. Double clicking the Plant object reveals an *object properties* window which contains information concerning the object itself. See Figure 4-28. Each of the property buttons on the right side contains information about the object. All objects in NDS have similar property buttons.

Figure 4-28

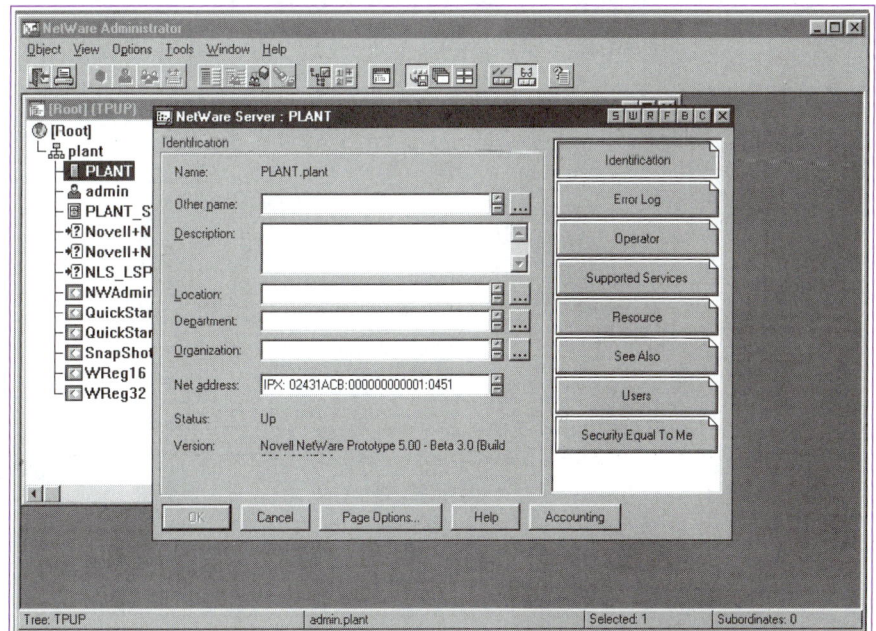

Right clicking the Admin user object reveals the window shown in Figure 4-29. Moving over to **Details** and clicking that item opens the same window series that you opened for the Plant in Figure 4-28.

Figure 4-29

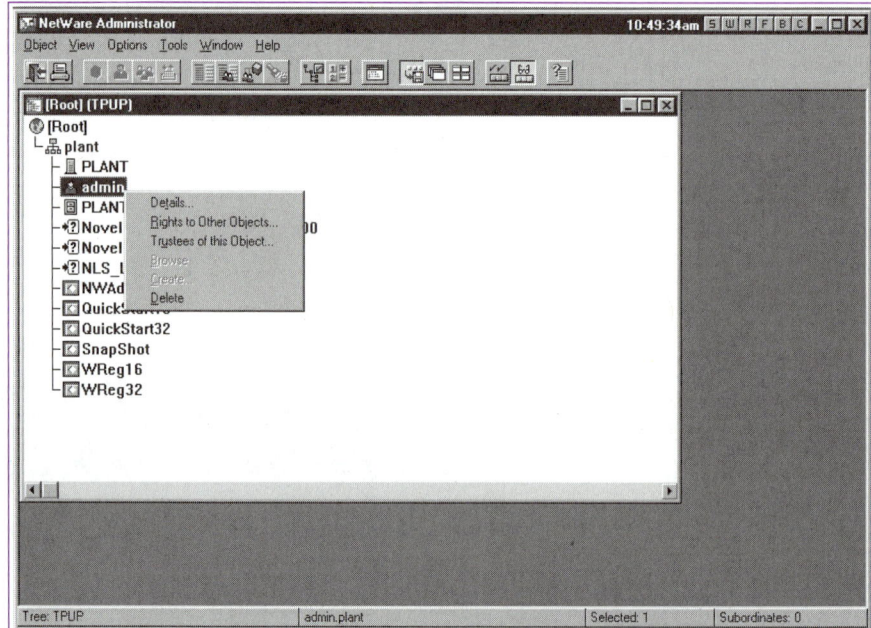

Figure 4-30 shows the opened Admin user window filled in with the information necessary for TPUP's administrator.

Figure 4-30

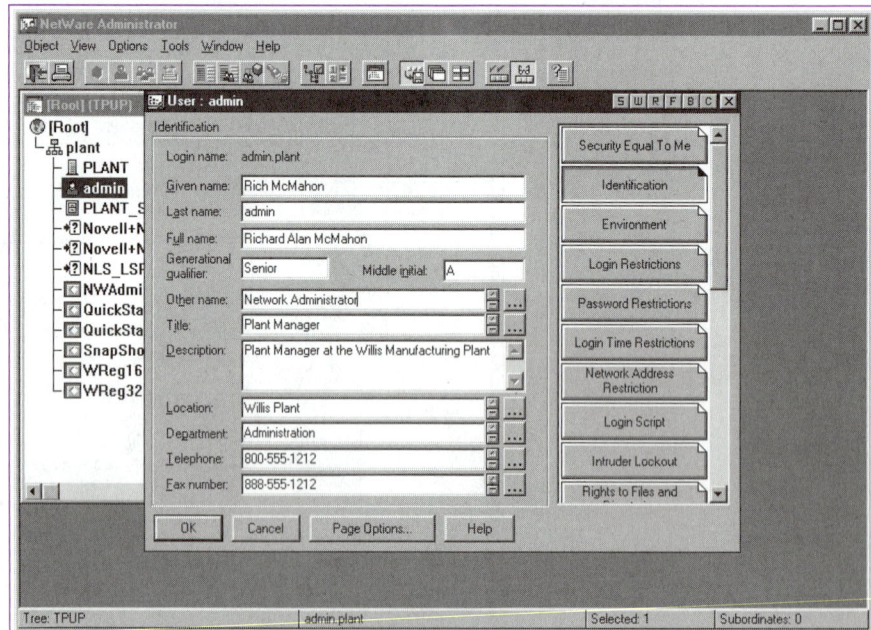

Navigate your NetWare 5 Network

> **If you do accidentally damage the network, the worst that can happen at this point is that you may have to rebuild the network again and again until no damage occurs.**

Now that you are finally in, have some fun "navigating" around your network. Get to know it well, and your job for the rest of this course will be much easier. Run NetWare Administrator and investigate the NDS tree structure. If you only explore and view things to see how your TPUP network is put together, you will not do any damage. If you have malicious intentions, you will be caught, because networking leaves a record of when actions occur. If you do accidentally damage the network, the worst that can happen at this point is that you may have to rebuild the network again and again until no damage occurs. The purpose of this chapter is to assure that no real damage occurs—yet! Later, when your server design takes on more shape, with many more objects and services available, you will have even more reason to protect your server. Explore it now while we are still in the practice mode.

Part of the experimentation at this point should include adding another user. Change the logging in constraints placed on that user, then try logging in as that user during the times you have constrained him or her as well as when you have not. See what the difference is. Remember, do not make any changes to your Admin user object until after you have completed the chapter review exercises and have selected a single person as your Network Administrator.

Chapter Summary

> **Since it is the Admin user who provides all network users with passwords and assigns the rights to files and network resources, he or she should be a very trustworthy individual.**

While previous chapters illustrated the *need* for a network and showed you how to build your own workstations and server, this chapter was designed to help you *create* a network. Although you had the hardware for an operational network, you lacked Novell's client software, the necessary link between what you had and what you needed. You loaded the client software on your workstation (and your server as well if you are on a Novell NetWare 5 system) using the Z.E.N.works package on your installation CD-ROM. The Admin object's ability to add additional users and resources to share demonstrated its importance in the server as a default user. You should remember that a network should have only one person who can log in as the Admin user in order to provide the security control necessary for networked assets. Since it is the Admin user who provides all network users with passwords and assigns the rights to files and network resources, he or she should be a very trustworthy individual.

To log into the network as your Admin user, you must have a workstation with a network interface card connected to the network, client software installed, a server with a network interface card connected to the same network, a valid user name and network context, and a valid password. Login is a security measure designed to make sure only authorized users gain access to the network. Your user name standard was planned in the first chapter, and you should adhere to the naming standard you devised at that time.

The context in which you find your user will also be important for logging into the network. Your context refers to the location of your user object in the NDS tree. Passwords help prevent someone from gaining unauthorized access to a network. Most of the other elements necessary to access a network can be easily figured out by someone who wants to get in. Passwords should be easy for you to remember but difficult for someone else to figure out. Once you have a password, you should protect it. Protecting your network by properly logging out is also important.

Installing the server software did not build your company information into the computer. The Admin user has to do that or has to provide the framework for others to enter that information. The network Administrator has the authority to do this deriving from the supervisory rights assigned him or her. Supervisory rights can also be entrusted to other individuals to alleviate the burden of administering a large network, but the overall responsibility for the network should remain with a sole Network Administrator.

When your Admin user logs in to manage your network he or she should be using NetWare Administrator (**NWADMIN32**) to gain access to all the objects in the NDS Tree. NetWare Administrator provides a Windows tool to navigate the NDS tree structure. Each object is located in a container within the NDS database. Each object has specific properties stored in the NDS database. These properties are entered through the Details section of the object and can be filled out using the many buttons of the properties window.

Networking Terms Used in Chapter 4

Novell NetWare client software	login	context
logging in	local drives	administering the network
admin user	mapping to a local disk	**NWADMIN32**
password	NetWare volumes	administration rights
autorun	unauthorized user	supervisory rights
Z.E.N.works	user name	NetWare Administrator
reboot	network container	Windows Explorer
network administrator	password rules	object properties
	hackers	

■ Chapter Review Questions

1. What piece of the networking environment allows a workstation to speak to a server once all the hardware pieces and connectivity are in place?

2. Explain the term *Admin user*.

3. Which executable file (.EXE) does Novell's Z.E.N.works use to prepare your workstation for connection to your server?

4. Defend or refute the following statement: "There should be only one Administrator on a network."

5. Does the recent move toward using the Internet alter the position you took in the statement in question 4?

6. List the job responsibilities of a Network Administrator.

7. How does something as simple as a password protect your network?

8. Why should you change your Admin user's password from the *Novell5* password that you used when installing your server software?

9. What is as important as protecting your password when logging into a network?

10. What are the components of a login procedure?

11. Explain how two people can have the same password and user name and still log into the network without difficulty.

12. Explain the term *context*.

13. Which user object is the only default user installed during server installation?

14. Can an Admin user object be deleted?

15. Explain where the information about users is stored inside the server.

■ **Associated Chapter Problems**

1. List the job responsibilities of your classroom Network Administrator in relation to safeguarding your network.

2. Use NetWare Administrator to navigate your server's objects prior to creating TPUP's other objects.

3. Should files stored on a server have the same pieces of information kept on them as user objects? Why or why not?

4. Describe how you would change your Admin user's password.

5. Which property page in the Admin user's information details has information regarding which hours that user can use the network? How are those hours set?

6. What is the default number of times a user's login can be attempted before the system "locks" him or her out? Did you cover this in the reading?

UNIT 2

Network Structure

CHAPTER 5

NOVELL DIRECTORY SERVICES

Now that you have navigated the network that you developed and built in the first unit of this textbook, it is time to begin adding to the structure of the network. When you logged into your network, there were not many places to explore. Now it is time for TPUP to take form and for your class to gain network access as users. By the end of this chapter, you will be able to:

- explain the term *Novell Directory Services (NDS)*.

- explain how NDS organizes the structure of a network with objects.

- explain how NDS gives users access to the resources of your Novell network.

- compare NDS objects with those of typical databases and DOS.

- create a container object within the NDS Directory tree of TPUP.

- create users individually and with User Template objects.

- identify objects as either [Root], container, or leaf objects.

- refer to NDS objects using the correct naming techniques.

- create the TPUP user objects and assume the identity of a TPUP employee.

Novell Directory Services (NDS)

NDS manages the resources of the network by grouping similar objects together hierarchically and assigning attributes to each object.

Excluding network communication, NDS is the most fundamental service a Novell NetWare network provides.

A Directory can have only one [Root].

When you worked with the basic organizational structure of TPUP in the first chapter, you were to begin thinking about adapting the company's hierarchy to your network. With that hierarchy as our model, we will now begin creating users for our network.

Novell NetWare stores and organizes information about users and groups in a database called *Novell Directory Services*, or *NDS*. The NDS Directory is an integral component of NetWare 4.11 and NetWare 5, and the key to managing the network. NDS manages the resources of the network by grouping similar objects together hierarchically and assigning attributes to each object. The objects that NDS tracks include users, groups, servers, and volumes. NDS organizes each of the network resources and makes them available to a user by assigning or removing access rights, depending on the user's need to access those resources. It is, therefore, a database that provides information about the location, characteristics and authorized users for every resource on your entire NetWare network.

Using its information about all the objects on the network, NDS processes network client requests for services to and from those objects. Processing client requests involves locating the resource on the network, *validating* the client's rights to that resource, and providing the connection between the client and the resource. Excluding network communication, NDS is the most fundamental service a Novell NetWare network provides. One of the most important features provided by NetWare is its ability to create a single, unified network with a single point for accessing and managing objects. Every resource on the network has a unique name. You do not need to know where the resource is located on the network. NDS can locate a resource if you provide a unique identifier.

Like the TPUP organization chart, NDS's structure resembles an *inverted tree*. The root of the upside-down tree is at the top of the organization chart and usually represents its geographical boundaries. As you descend in the typical organization chart, divisions, organizations, and departments fan out in a tree-like fashion. The lowest level employee is located at the bottom of the tree.

In NDS the *[Root]* object is the highest object in the tree. (The brackets ([ ]) are required when referring to the [Root] object.) As you descend through the company in NDS, the tree-like structure of the *Directory* resembles that of a company organization chart. NDS structure is also similar to that of the DOS file system, and many of the DOS commands with which you are familiar have equivalents in NDS. If there were different country locations within the company, they could be the next NDS dividing points under the [Root]. A Directory can have only one [Root].

Figure 5-1

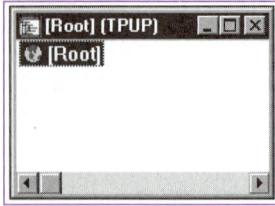

Figures 5-1 and 5-2 show the TPUP tree using the Windows-based **NWADMIN** utility. In addition, **NETADMIN**, a 4.11 text utility, performs some of the same NDS management tasks.

Figure 5-2

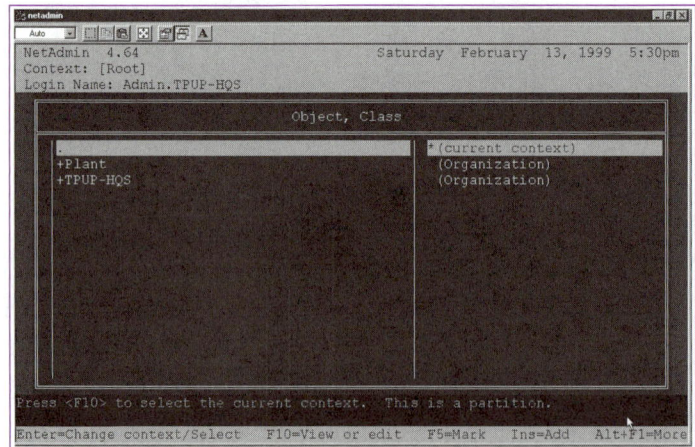

Figure 5-3

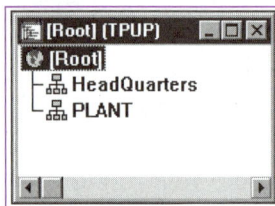

The [Root] can hold only Country container objects or Organization container objects. (Alias objects can also be used, but we will not use them in the TPUP company design). The TPUP [Root] is shown in Figure 5-3, with the Plant organization *container* as an offshoot of the [Root]. A comparable view of the NetWare 4.11 con-figuration with two organization containers is shown in Figure 5-4.

Figure 5-4

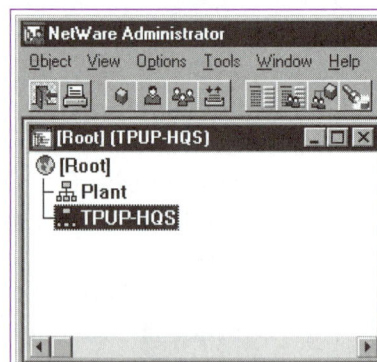

NDS is a *fundamental networking service* on a Novell NetWare network. Whenever you refer to NDS as the "Directory," use a capital "D." This helps differentiate it from a lower level *directory* in the file system, which you will study later. You became familiar with the terms files, folders, and directories when referring to your floppy disk storage and hard disk storage, so using capitalization when referring to Novell's Directory in NDS highlights the difference between them.

All Netware 4.0 and higher servers on the same network share their information about the network resources, because that information is in the Directory to which they all contribute. The servers share the lists they maintain about such resources. These lists include the server's users, the groups to which those users belong, the printers connected to the servers or directly to the network, information about the servers themselves, and information about all other resources that they share. Network security responsibilities can easily be distributed proportionately if desired, or they can be kept centralized by assigning them to a single administrator. It depends on how much security and control the company desires. In any case, network administrators need to create a user only once. The resources which that user accesses on the network are controlled using that one user object's attributes.

Although it is already apparent that a network can have more than one NDS tree (and therefore multiple Directories), such a situation produces separate and distinct databases and negates the benefits of a unified database for all networked resources. Two TPUP networks are used in this textbook only to illustrate the differences between the two software packages at the same level between servers. Otherwise, the two servers would be merged into one more powerful Directory.

What Makes Up Novell Directory Services (NDS)

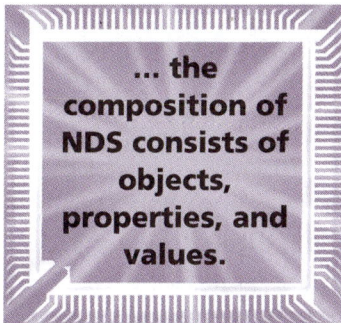

> ... the composition of NDS consists of objects, properties, and values.

Novell Directory Services (NDS) is extremely efficient because it can keep track of the many *objects* it manages by subdividing the information that describes them into smaller pieces of data. The information NDS maintains on each resource or service it provides on the network is divided into the *properties* of the object, which NDS uses to depict the service or resource, and the *values* NDS uses when it describes each of those properties. Therefore, the composition of NDS consists of objects, properties, and values.

Objects

The objects themselves become units of information about the resources or services NDS makes available on the network. The objects resemble database *records*. In the database that describes those enrolled in your school, you are an object. The information stored about you makes it possible to access you for administrative purposes. Similarly, a principal can find a student because she knows his identity and where he is located at any point during the school day. The system may malfunction at the beginning of the school year, when administrators tried to find one of two people with the same name.

Properties

> Properties are very similar to database fields.

NDS stores information about an object in the form of categories, called properties. Properties are very similar to database fields. In the example above, when the principal tries to find a student, she decides which properties will fully describe the student. If those properties include the student's last name, his scheduled location during the period in question, and his class ranking, there would probably be multiple students fitting the principal's description.

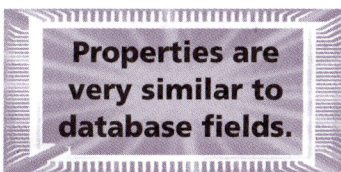

The more properties the principal adds when trying to narrow the choice of students, the more likely she will succeed in finding him. Successful searches would be ensured if the principal were to use a unique property that no other student could have, like a Social Security number.

The previous example illustrates that some properties are more important than others. When logging onto a network, for example, the username, context, and password properties are all vital pieces of information. The user's job title is not. Similarly, when looking for a student, his class ranking was not as important as his Social Security number.

Taken together as a set, the different properties associated with an object determine the *class* of that object. For instance, properties of a user object and the values in those properties are different from the properties and values associated with a printer. They both may have a name and a unique network node number, but it is doubtful that the printer will have a telephone number or mother's last name for security reasons. NDS determines which properties each object should possess.

Values

Like the data in a database, the pieces of information within the property fields that describe an object are the property values of the object. For example, "Jones, Room 105, junior" are the values the principal had in mind when specifying the "properties" she wanted searched. However, because names like Jones are common, there could be two Joneses in Room 105 who are both in their junior year at the school. The principal would have increased her chances of finding the student if she had added more properties and their applicable values to her description.

Some property values are *required*. If the principal wants to find her students, she should require students to furnish their Social Security numbers before allowing them to enter school. In NDS, a user's last name property value is mandatory when creating a new user. Other properties may have multiple values. For example, when a student filled out school paperwork, he or she may have written a cellular phone number, pager number, home number, parent's work number, guardian's number, nearest relative's number, or some other telephone number in that property's field.

Types of Objects

There are only three NDS object types, or classes of objects. Each NDS object is either a [Root] object, container object, or leaf object.

[Root] object

The *[Root] object* is a *placeholder* and does not contain the information found in most other objects. Right clicking on the [Root] object as in the screen in Figure 5-5 shows that the "*Details*" selection is not available.

Figure 5-5

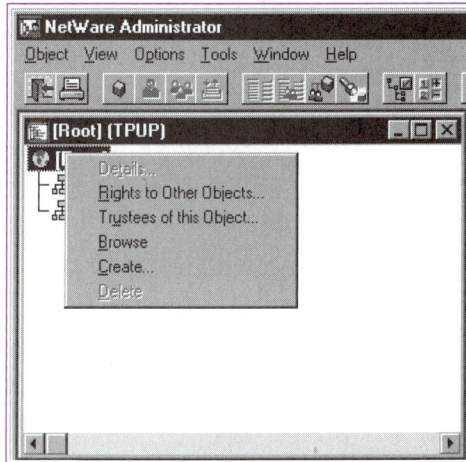

Figure 5-6

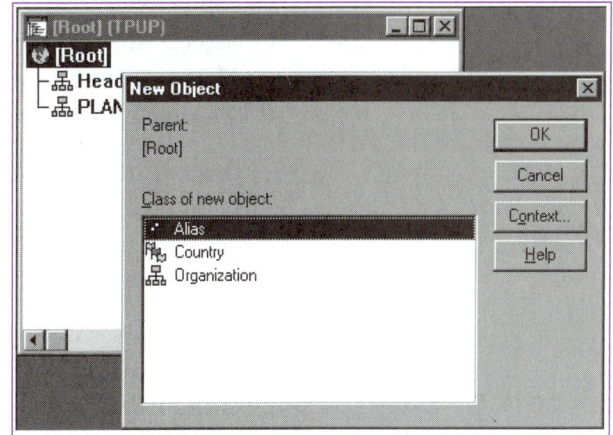

The [Root] can be created only during the original network software installation. The [Root] cannot be moved, renamed, or deleted, and as you can see in Figure 5-6, the [Root] has no properties. Additionally, as shown in Figure 5-5, the [Root] object can have *trustees* and can have *rights* to other objects. Often, the [Root] and the tree name are the same. This leads to naming confusion because the tree name can be changed after original installation, while the [Root] name cannot. The NDS [Root] object is similar to the root directory in DOS.

Although the [Root] object contains no actual information, as shown in Figure 5-6, Country container objects, Organization container objects, and *alias* objects (under special circumstances) can be created immediately under a [Root] object.

Container Objects

NDS treats every resource or service on your network as an object. You organize the Directory by placing objects within other objects or "containers." These *container objects* are special locations in which other objects are placed for administrative purposes. The containers help group other container objects or the final resource objects for access or rights assignment. Container objects are similar to directories in DOS. A container object is referred to as a *parent object* if it contains other objects.

Three major classes of container objects will concern us: *Country*, *Organization*, and *Organizational Unit*. (There are actually five classes, but we will not be working with either *locality* or *licensed product container objects*.) Each of these classes helps organize the objects in your NDS tree into logical groupings. One of the benefits of grouping objects into containers is that it allows creation of group login procedures.

Country (C) Container Objects

Novell created country container objects because of *X.500 directory specification certification* requirements. Novell does not recommend use of country container objects and its documentation states

> **The NDS [Root] object is similar to the root directory in DOS.**

> **Container objects are similar to directories in DOS.**

that "… using the Country object might add an unnecessary level of complexity." They are, therefore, optional. If country container objects are used, however, they will help organize your network's NDS tree by country. They can hold only a valid two-character country abbreviation and can exist only below the [Root] object.

Organization (O) Container Objects

Each Directory tree must have at least one organization (O) container object. Unless a country container (or locality container) is used, the organization container object must be directly below the [Root] object. Although it can hold additional container objects (organizational units), the organization container is the first level that can contain leaf objects (besides an alias object representing an organization). Organization container objects usually designate companies, divisions of companies, and organizations with subsequent departments, or the departments themselves, depending on the desired NDS structure. Organization container objects cannot contain additional organization container objects. A use in DOS similar to organization container objects would be a major applica-tion's primary folder in either the root directory or the *Windows Program Files* folder such as the *MS Office 97* folder. It is a major division of items, which helps organize and categorize all other items below it.

> **Each Directory tree must have at least one organization (O) container object.**

Organizational Unit (OU) Container Objects

Use of the organizational unit (OU) container object is also optional but it is the most commonly used container object. OUs help organize the lower levels of an organization. They can be used as lower level containers themselves or can contain NDS objects directly. They are frequently used to designate business units within a company, departments within a larger entity, or separate projects within a department. When used, an OU must be placed directly below an Organization container object or another Organizational Unit container object. In DOS, an embedded folder within a major application's primary folder on the root directory or in the program files folder is similar to an OU type container. The *clipart* folder inside the *MS Office 97* folder in the *Program Files* folder on the root directory is an example.

> **Use of the organizational unit (OU) container object is also optional but it is the most commonly used container object.**

Leaf Objects

The Directory-tree metaphor extends to the resources themselves, which are referred to as *leaf objects*. As in a tree, leaves in NDS are the final division and cannot "contain" any other objects. They represent the resources and services available on your network. You can find leaf objects in container objects. Leaf objects are similar to the actual files in DOS.

In Figure 5-7, the [Root] is the placeholder, HeadQuarters and Plant are containers, and the Plant server, Admin user, and *Plant_Sys* volume are all leaf objects.

> **Leaf objects are similar to the actual files in DOS.**

Figure 5-7

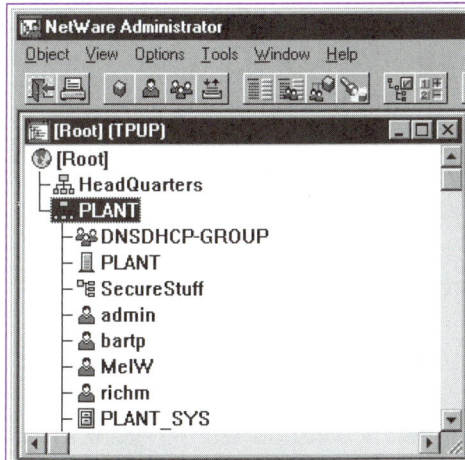

Figure 5-8

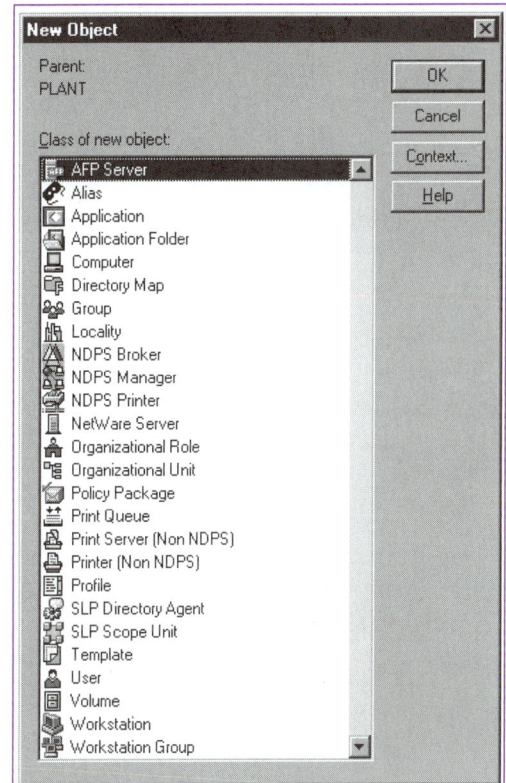

Some of the different objects that you can add to the NDS tree in NetWare 5 are shown Figure 5-8.

Calling NDS Objects by Name

It is important to remember that an *NDS search* does not include its entire database when it locates a service or resource. If you want access to networked resources or services, you must provide NDS with the correct object name for that resource or service. When NDS receives a request for a resource or service, the applicable server checks its own copy of the Directory. It then locates the object, controls your user's status validity, and verifies that you have the permission (rights) to do what you are asking to do with that object. NDS inspects the property values of the object and your user before connecting or denying a connection to the object.

If all networks had all their objects in a single container and a single list within that container, finding a particular object would be a relatively simple task. Networks are no longer designed in that way. For efficiency and ease of administration, network directories consist of multiple containers representing a multitude of combinations of functions, geography, and other uses. It is no longer efficient for a server to search its entire database when seeking a particular object.

You can access any object in the Directory simply by knowing its name and location in the tree. Each object in the Directory has only one name and, therefore, one path to it from any other given resource. If you know the entire name (or one of the shortcuts that represents it) you will access that resource. Without it, you will not. Precision in naming is the key. Using precise naming ability permits you to log onto the network and make services start up properly. In order to devise an object's precise name, it is beneficial for users to understand *context* naming conventions.

> You can access any object in the Directory simply by knowing its name and location in the tree.

Object Names

Simplicity is usually the key when devising a name for an object.

Novell Directory Services names every object in the Directory tree. Each object therefore has its own *object name*, and it is through that name that NDS tracks all information associated with the object. Simplicity is usually the key when devising a name for an object. Some form of a person's name would be best as the name of his user object.

The organization chart in Chapter 1 lists the naming convention names for each of the applicable employees at TPUP. Ron F. became ronf on the organization chart, and his user object should now bear the same name. In addition, because the NDS name for the object is also called the *common name* or (CN), Ron F.'s common name would also be ronf. In NDS, the leaf name shown next to the leaf icon for Ron F.'s user object would be his common name—ronf in this case. The designation CN=RONF is also an appropriate common name.

However, as you learned when the principal looked for the student named Jones, the common name is not enough to uniquely identify an object. NDS allows two objects to have the same common name provided the two are not located in the same container. Therefore, you must know the location of an object as well as its common name to uniquely identify an object to NDS.

Context

An object's exact location in the NDS tree is specified by its context.

An object's exact location in the NDS tree is specified by its *context*. Because you can designate an object's location by fully describing the container in which the object resides, context can also be considered the name of the parent container of the object. Context is simply a list of all the container objects leading from an object to the [Root] object. In DOS, it is similar to the directory path statement. In our principal example, the context for the student Jones was OU=RM105.O=SCHOOLNAME, because it fully describes the container in which Jones was sitting. As we saw, however, this naming technique did not preclude finding multiple Joneses in the same room. NDS allows multiple examples of the same name, but never in the same location. In our example, the initial of the students' first name would have differentiated the JJONES from the PJONES that the principal was seeking.

You can locate or use objects in the current context simply by typing their common name without contextual reference.

NDS also tracks where a user object is currently working. This is referred to as the user object's *current context* and is commonly called the *name context*. You can locate or use objects in the current context simply by typing their common name without contextual reference. It can also be specified by using the CN= before the common name designation. For example, you could type PJONES's current context, or PJONES. (Remember that user names are not case sensitive). The current context is the first place NDS looks for a resource when its full name and location as unique identification are not specified. Similarly, if Jones were to call the principal over the

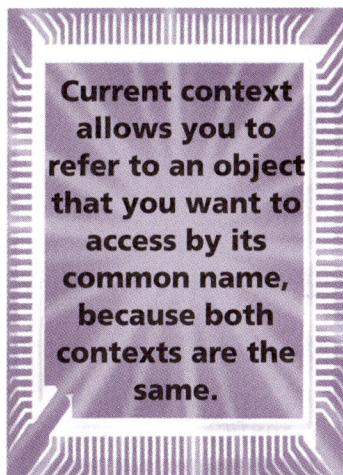

intercom but the principal could not verify Jones's location, the principal would have to assume that Jones was where his schedule showed him to be at that time.

If Jones were to ask the principal the location of a specific object in his classroom, the principal would have to describe the location of the object based on her knowledge of the room. If, however, Jones's class has been moved to another room, and Jones does not tell the principal, the principal will not adjust her contextual description for Jones's search. Jones has been "taken out of context," and his user object would not be located.

Current context identifies the default container to the Novell Client. It affects the amount of detail you are required to provide when seeking resources. Current context allows you to refer to an object that you want to access by its common name, because both contexts are the same.

> **Current context allows you to refer to an object that you want to access by its common name, because both contexts are the same.**

Distinguished Name

When you refer to an object by its common name and its context, you provide exact identification. This is referred to as an object's *distinguished name* (*fully distinguished name* in previous software versions). The name .PJONES.RM105.YOURSCHOOL completely identifies the user and ensures that NDS will not find two of the same users in the same location at the same time. Two objects cannot have the same distinguished name.

Note the use of a leading period in the above example. A distinguished name always begins with a leading period. The format also requires the use of periods between each object's name. Trailing periods, used in relative distinguished names, are not allowed in distinguished names. Although such a format technique is similar to the backslash used in DOS, the flow from smaller to larger object is the opposite of that used when locating DOS files.

Relative Distinguished Name

NDS can also use your current location in the Directory tree to help locate the resource you seek. Your *relative distinguished name* is determined by your current context rather than by the [Root] object, as is the case in distinguished names. By default, then, common names are relative distinguished names. Relative distinguished names do not start with a period, and any name that starts without a period is considered a relative distinguished name.

> **Relative distinguished names list the path of all the objects leading from the object you seek to your current context.**

Relative distinguished names list the path of all the objects leading from the object you seek to your current context. If the object is not in your current context, you can adjust your relative distinguished name by using a trailing period to indicate that you wish to move up one level in the Directory tree. For each trailing period that you add to your relative distinguished name, one object is removed from the left side of your current context. This feature is similar to the **CD..** feature DOS uses when navigating its directory structure.

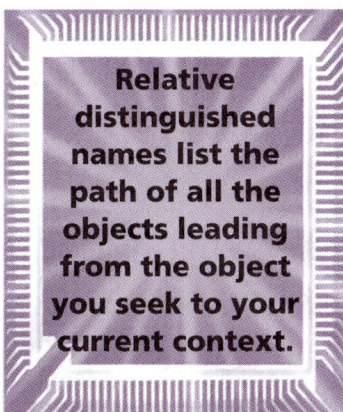

> **When you use a typeless name, NDS calculates the missing attributes and adds them to the name.**

Typeless Names

All of the names used in the examples above are *typeless names*. Although they include the names of all the objects in the proper sequence, they do not include the objects' attribute types. When you use a typeless name, NDS calculates the missing attributes and adds them to the name. In rare instances, the utility used for this calculation makes a mistake and the objects fail to communicate.

Typeful Name

To make *typeful names*, you add the attribute type abbreviation and differentiate between the different container types and leaf objects in either distinguished or relative distinguished names.

Returning to our example above, the student's typeful name would be the following, more descriptive name: .CN=PJONES .OU=RM105 .O=YOURSCHOOL, and NDS would not have to append any information.

Typeful names are *optional*, but they assist NDS in locating objects.

Before Novell Directory Services

> **When NetWare 4.0 was introduced, all NetWare servers on the same network combined to form a large pool of services to share the information about the resources available from any location with all users.**

Before Novell began incorporating NDS in its NetWare network operating system software, a user could use only the resources of the server which he was logged on to. If he wanted to use the resources on another server, he had to log on to that server and seek authorization. A user often had multiple passwords encompassing numerous security levels and spanning several servers.

Resources on NetWare networks before NDS were in flat files or lists of resources for one server at a time. They resembled a phone book, and their networks were "*server-centered;*" concerned primarily with how the server provided the services. This arrangement functioned well with relatively small networks. However, as the network controls more objects, networking efficiency diminishes rapidly. Consider how long it takes to find someone in a large phone book when you are not sure how to spell his or her name. When you do not know their city, it becomes very difficult. When you are not sure of their name, do not know their city, and cannot find the phone book it is similar to trying to remember what server a user belongs to, where the resource he wants is located, and what his password is for the first server, the resource, and any servers he has to pass through to get to the resource.

When NetWare 4.0 was introduced, all NetWare servers on the same network combined to form a large pool of services to share the information about the resources available from any location with all users. This pool of services is the NDS tree and its system of containers and leaf objects. Networks became *network-centered*, focusing on a *unified access* to resources. A *single password* would allow a user to access the entire network, and the same security level would follow that user on the entire network.

Benefits of Novell Directory Services

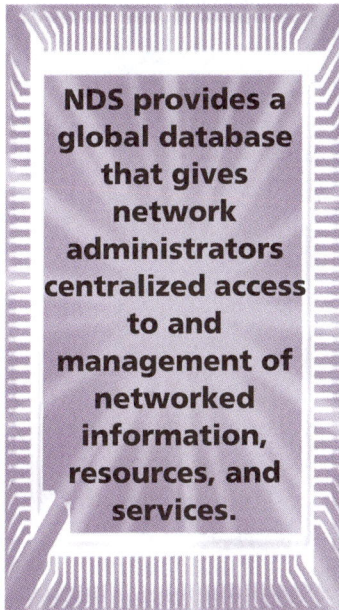

NDS provides a global database that gives network administrators centralized access to and management of networked information, resources, and services.

NDS provides a global database that gives network administrators *centralized access* to and management of networked information, resources, and services. It standardizes the method of managing, viewing and accessing these items. It also provides logically organized network resources that are independent of physical network configuration and *dynamic mapping* between an object and its actual physical resource.

NDS makes it easier to administer the network. Users and NDS objects are managed using NetWare Administrator (or **NWADMIN**), a user-friendly GUI program located on the server. Administration can be accomplished by a central administrator or divided among various levels where additional administration is required.

The Directory's ability to provide administrators with more manageable groupings of objects makes network design and organization more logical and provides greater security.

In addition, because the Directory (or at least pieces of it) is stored on numerous servers around the network, fault tolerance is increased and the inevitable loss of an occasional server becomes much less critical. The Directory information needed to become operational again is available on more than one server, and can be used to restore the Directory on malfunctioning servers.

Browsing Novell Directory Services

There are three utilities available for browsing the Directory tree. Primarily you will use **NWADMIN** when you navigate and administer your Directory, but **CX** and **NETADMIN** are also available. Each of the three different Directory browsing utilities are shown in Figures 5-9, 5-10, and 5-11.

Figure 5-9

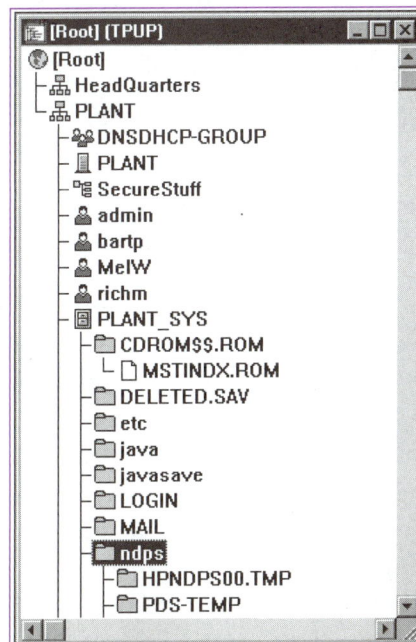

Figure 5-10

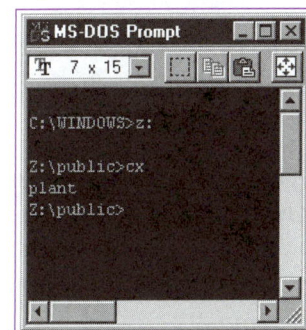

**CHAPTER 5
NDS**

Figure 5-11

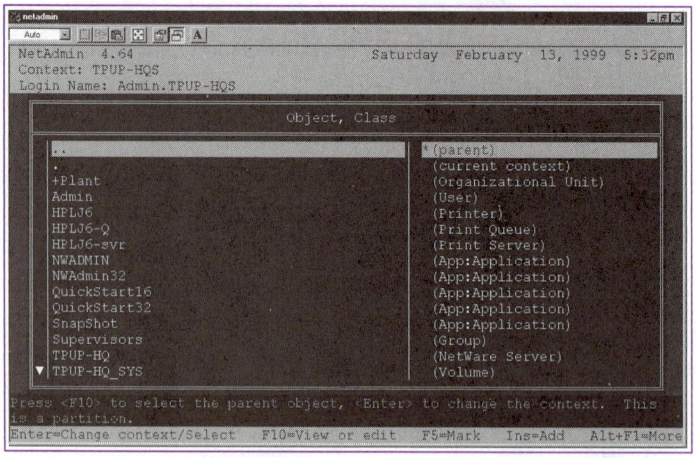

Some differences between the three utilities are readily perceived from the screen depictions. **NWADMIN** is the browsing method of choice in a Windows environment and will be used in the remainder of this course. You should be cognizant of the others, however, especially if you intend to take Novell's CNA certification exam.

CX is the utility used to browse the Directory from a command line. The syntax for using **CX** is shown in Figures 5-12 and 5-13.

Figure 5-12

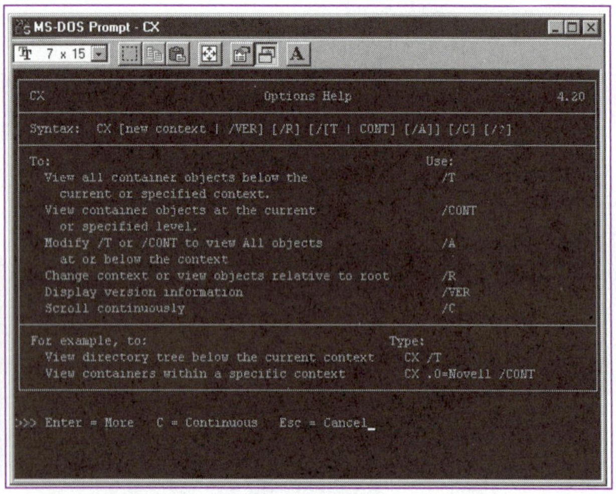

Figure 5-13

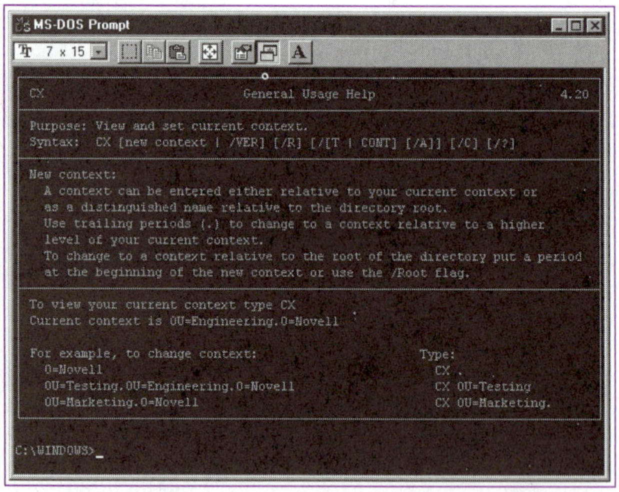

Activity 5–1   Creating NWADMIN Shortcuts

1. Log onto your server as Administrator (admin). You should become accustomed to using the advanced section of the *Novell Client Login* window as shown in Figure 5-14. You will note that the Tree is TPUP, the server is PLANT, and the Admin user's context is plant. That equates to your user object (admin) logging into PLANT server, which is located on the TPUP tree. The object is located within the Plant container object. Note also that although the password is entered correctly as "Novell5," the letters are not visible. Remember that this is a security measure to keep your password secret. *Note*: 4.11 classes will be on the

TPUP-HQ server, on the TPUP-HQS tree, and in the TPUP-HQS context with "Novell411" as the password. The Client software used in both instances is the newest version available, so the remainder of these steps are the same.

Figure 5-14   **Figure 5-15**

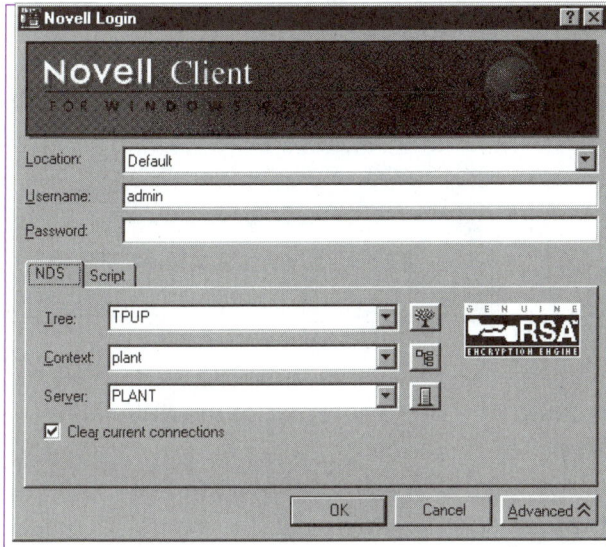   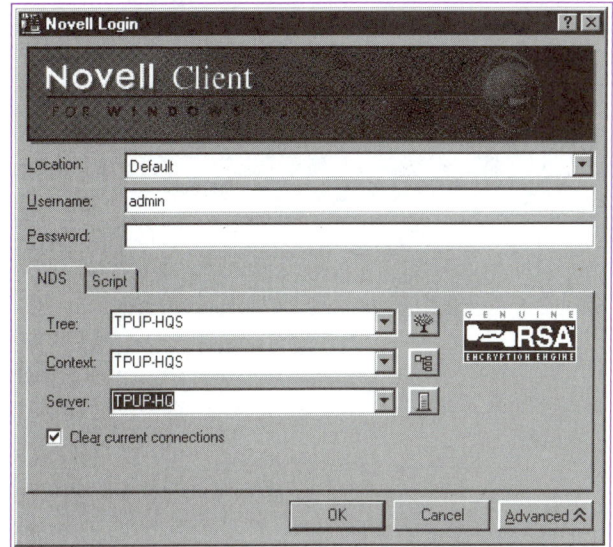

Figure 5-16   2. Click on the Windows **Start** button, then scroll up to and click on the **Run** command as shown in Figure 5-16.

   3. Type **NWADMIN32** in the **Open:** box and click on the **Browse...** button.

                                                   4. Navigate through **Network Neighborhood** as shown in Figure 5-17 to the *NWAdmin32.exe* file (located in the *win32* folder, inside the *Public* folder, on the *SYS* volume, in the *Plant* icon, on your *Network Neighborhood*). Click the **Open** button.

Figure 5-17

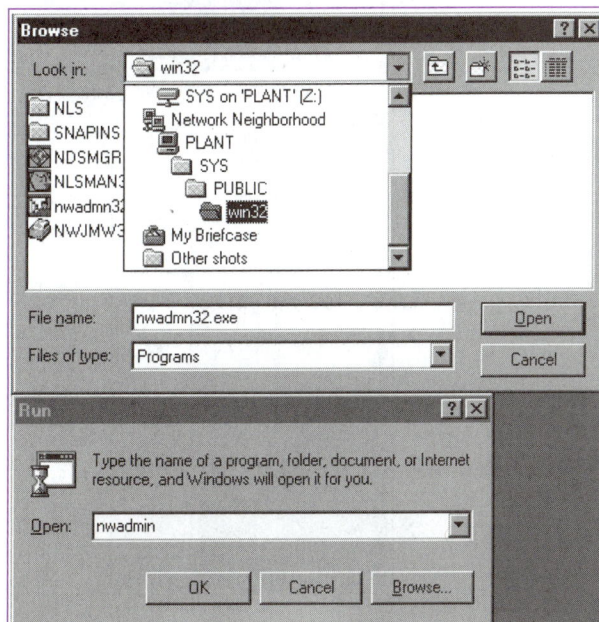

5. When you click on **Open** as shown in Figure 5-17, the **NWAdmin32** command that you typed in earlier changes to match what is shown in Figure 5-18. When you click the **OK** button as shown in Figure 5-18, you will execute the **NWAdmin** command and enter that command in the *Run* window's *pull down window* for future use (as shown in Figure 5-19).

Figure 5-18

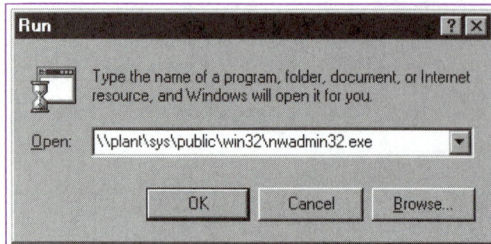

Figure 5-19

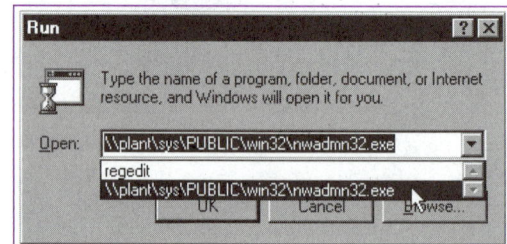

6. There is another way to navigate to that same file on your server. We will use that method to locate a *shortcut* of the **NWAdmin** icon on your desktop. This will make it easier for you to enter **NWAdmin** for the remainder of this course. Start with all windows on your computer closed. Double click on your *My Computer* icon. Double click on the *Z: drive* icon (*SYS:* on Plant), then on the *Public folder*, and then on the *Win32 folder*. Within that *Win32* folder, you should see the *NWAdmin* icon as shown in Figure 5-20. If you were to double click on that icon now, you would execute **NWAdmin** and be able to administer your network from your workstation. You will be using **NWAdmin** extensively throughout this course, so it best to locate a shortcut to this icon on your desktop.

Figure 5-20

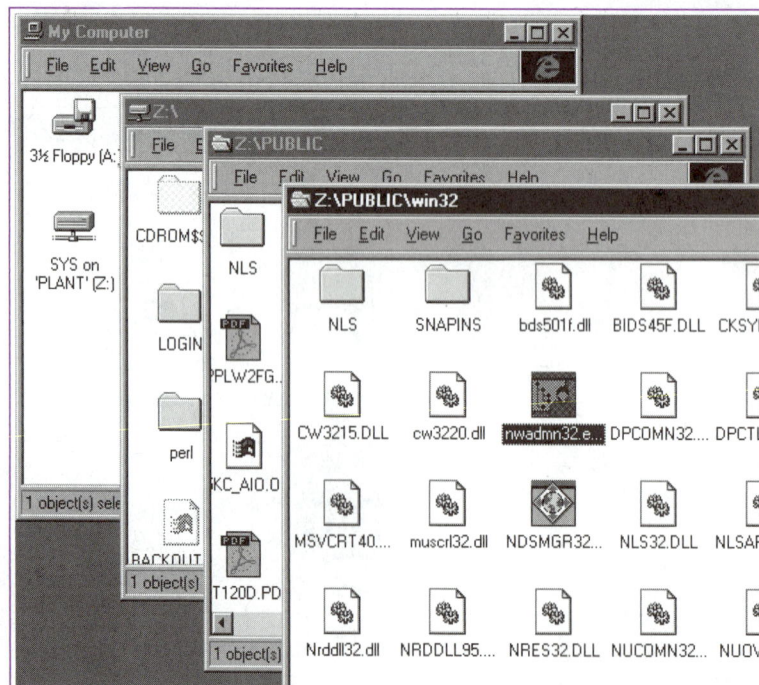

7. To put a shortcut icon for *NWAdmin* on your desktop, right click on the icon and drag down to Send To..., and then over to **Desktop as Shortcut**. Click on that item to create an icon for **NWAdmin** on your desktop. Provided you are logged into the server, this icon will immediately connect you to **NWAdmin** when you want to administer the network. It will be on your desktop.

Figure 5-21

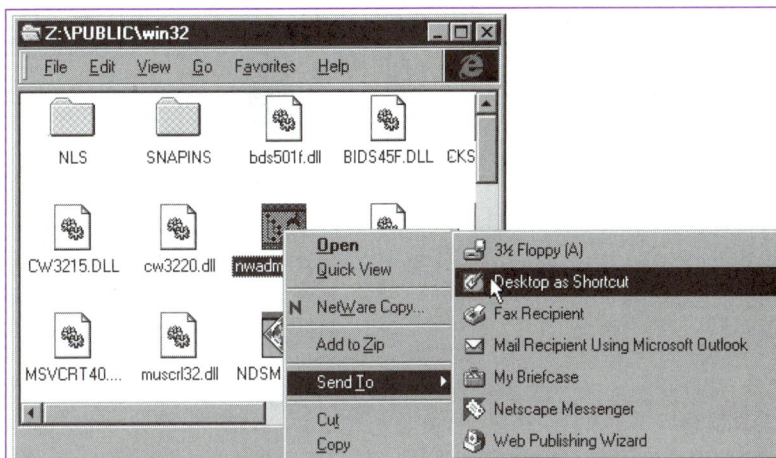

Activity 5–2　　　Creating an Organization Container Object

Figure 5-22

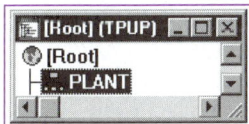

1. Now that you have two methods from which to choose, select one to start **NWAdmin**. Whichever way you enter it, you should arrive at the window shown in Figure 5-22. With Windows there are many ways to accomplish a task, including shortcut positioning. You may have another location from which you want to start **NWAdmin** each time you need it. Locate it wherever you are most comfortable using it. The two shortcuts you created in Activity 5-1 were only two of the most common. *Note:* unlike the NetWare 5 classes, the NetWare 4.11 classes should start with a Headquarters and add a Plant. Later in the year the two can be merged, so it will not matter at that point. For now, however, the NetWare 4.11 classes will substitute Headquarters for their server whenever we discuss the Plant server.

Figure 5-23

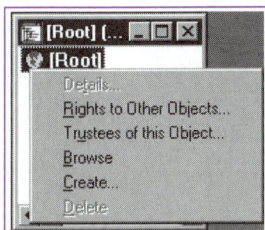

2. Once in **NWAdmin**, you can begin adding necessary objects. The first will be an additional container object for "Headquarters." Again, there are many ways to accomplish the same task, and we will discuss the two most common here. In Figure 5-23, either: 1) right click on the [Root] object, then click on Create, or 2) select [Root], click on the **Object** menu, and then click on **Create**. Either way will take you to the next step shown in Figure 5-24.

Figure 5-24

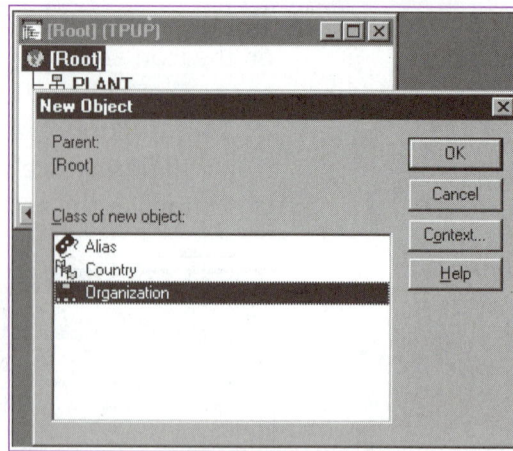

3. If you put a check mark in the *Define additional properties* box as shown in Figure 5-25, the window in Figure 5-26 appears, allowing you to complete information about the object you are creating.

Figure 5-25   **Figure 5-26**

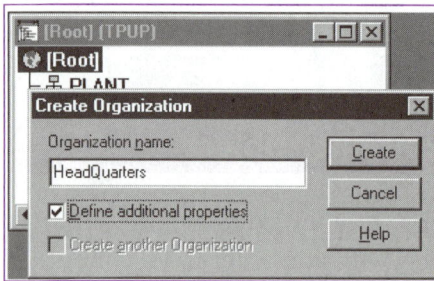

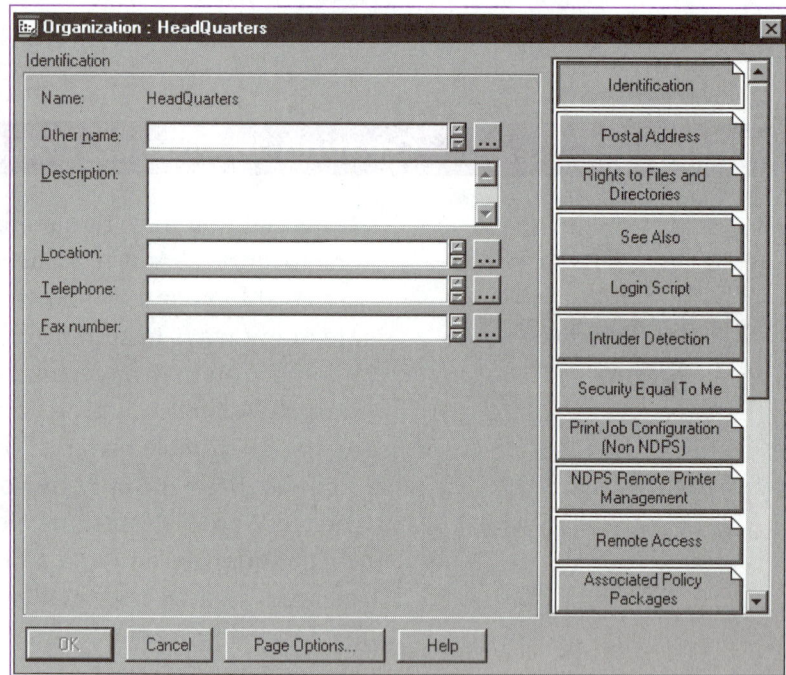

4. Figure 5-27 shows the same type of information for the NetWare 4.11 classes using the TPUP-HQ server on the TPUP-HQS tree.

Figure 5-27

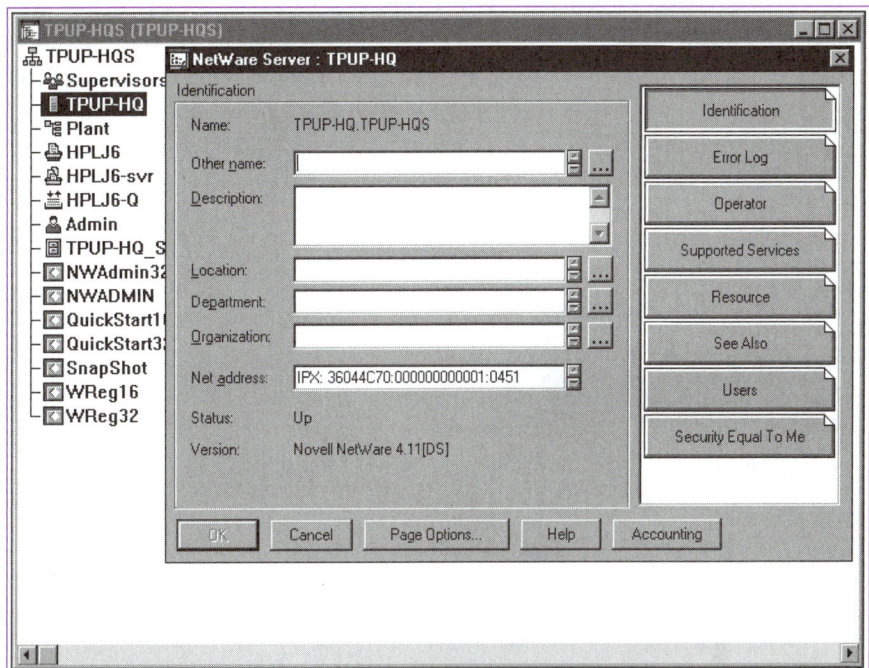

5. When completed, you should have your TPUP [Root] and two organization containers below it, as shown in Figure 5-28. In Figure 5-29, you can compare the screen that you obtain using the NetWare 4.11 server information.

Figure 5-28   **Figure 5-29**

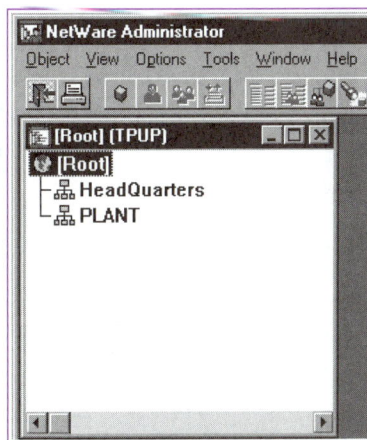   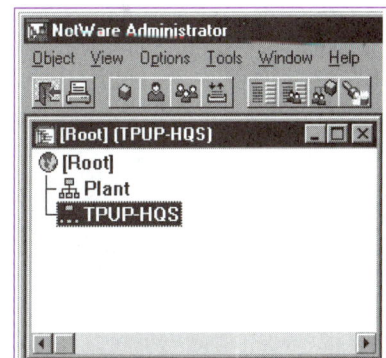

At this point it is sufficient that we have created the new organization container object. It will not matter whether you are using Plant as your NetWare 5 server or Headquarters as your NetWare 4.11 server. However, the subtle differences should be pointed out. It is important to have your server set up in the proper container and to be aware of the difference in order to adjust accordingly. Later in this course, you could *migrate* the actual 4.11 Headquarters server over to NetWare 5 and see how the old server changes as a result of that migration. ■

Administering Your TPUP Network

The TPUP organization chart in Figure 5-30 shows two organization objects representing the two separate geographical locations for the segments of the company. NetWare 4.11 and NetWare 5 classes should have the same graphic (as shown by comparing Figures 5-30 and 5-31 with Figures 5-32 and 5-33), although the structure within the respective containers will be somewhat different.

Figure 5-30

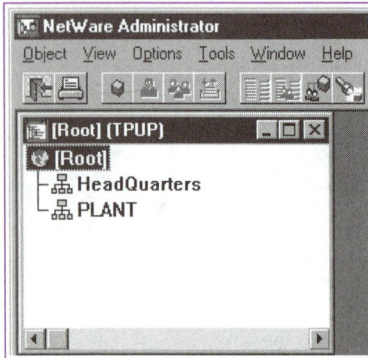

Figure 5-32

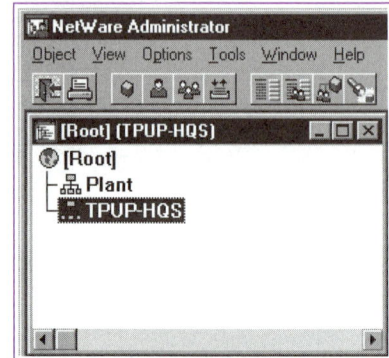

Figure 5-31

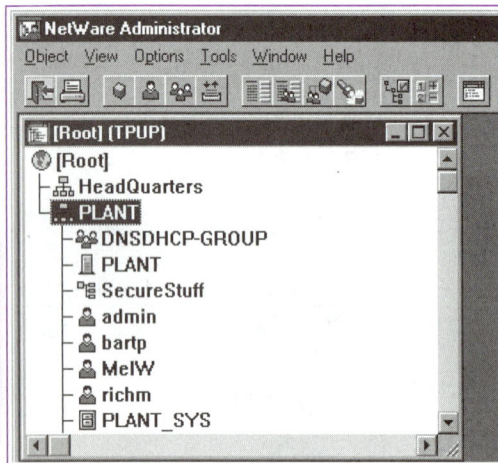

Figure 5-33

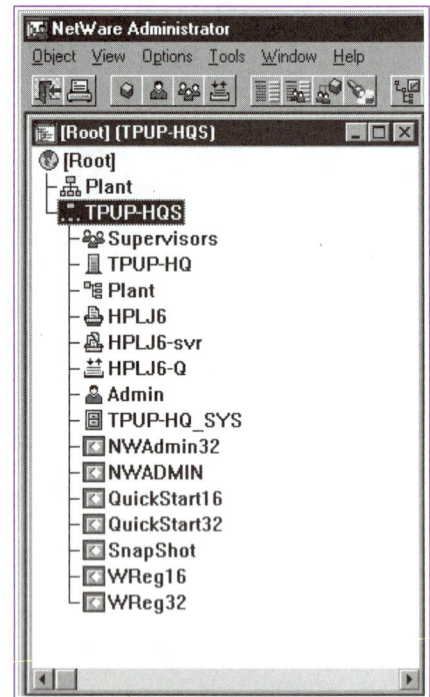

As mentioned previously, for the sake of simplicity the majority of the remaining text will be about NetWare 5 at the plant. Currently there is a NetWare 4.11 server for the Headquarters as shown in the previous set of graphics. We will use that server only when there are *significant* differences between the two operating systems.

You can see in Figure 5-31 that the graphical nature of the Directory does not look as neat as the graphics we used when we formed the organization chart in the first chapter. The organization chart now looks more horizontal and gives a more accurate depiction of the company's span. As shown in Figure 5-33, however, the vertical nature of the Directory becomes more apparent as you view additional objects.

When more than a few objects are viewed it becomes even more evident, as shown in Figure 5-34. (4.11's **NETADMIN** is also shown in Figure 5-35 for comparison. If you plan to test for your 4.11 CNA, you will need to be familiar with **NETADMIN**, but this class will not use it further.)

Figure 5-34

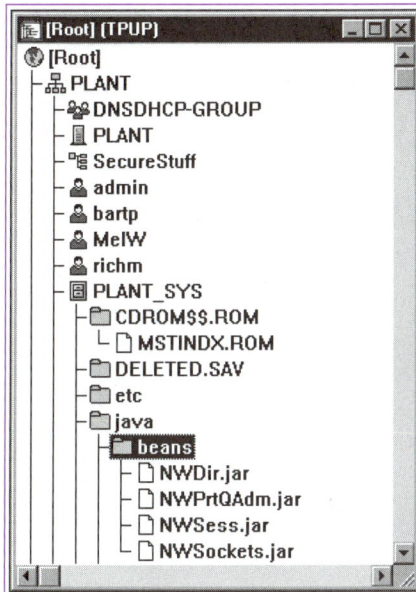

Figure 5-35

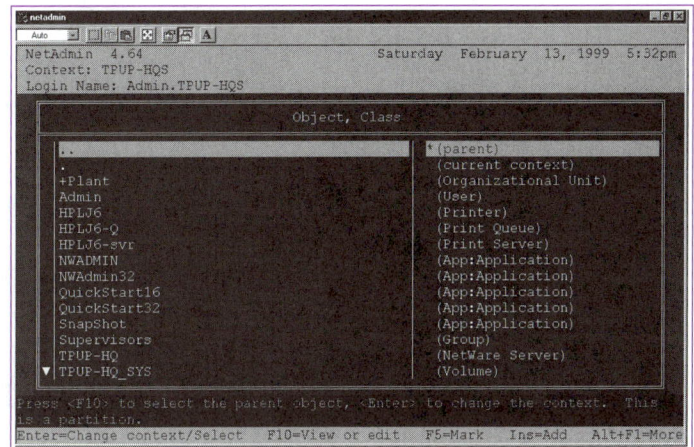

This course teaches you network administration. As a network administrator, you will be responsible for maintaining the Directory. It is one of the fundamental job functions of your position. At times, it is the most important function you provide to the networking community where you work. You control the database that gives your users information about every facet of their computerized neighborhood. If they cannot access something that they should be able to access, they will call you and demand that you make *your* system work. When they can access the resources they want, they will tell you that they are able to command *their* network.

**CHAPTER 5
NDS**

Activity 5–3   Adding Users and Groups to Your TPUP Network

1. Log into the Plant server.
2. Double click the *My Computer* icon and open your *Public* folder on the NetWare server.

3. Add a new *Users* folder in your *Public* folder on your NetWare server as shown in Figure 5-36.

Figure 5-36

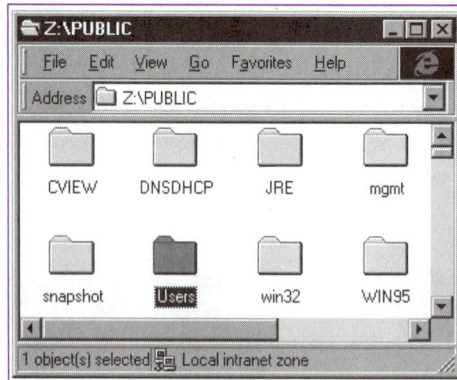

4. If it is not already running on your desktop, start **NWAdmin**.
5. Navigate to the window shown in Figure 5-37.

Figure 5-37

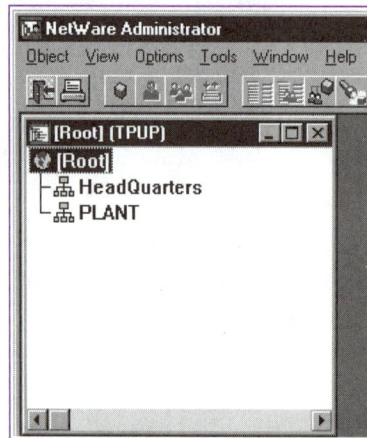

6. Select the **PLANT** icon and use the pull down **Object** menu to select **Create**. In the *New Object* window, scroll to **Group** and click the **OK** button as indicated in Figure 5-38.

Figure 5-38

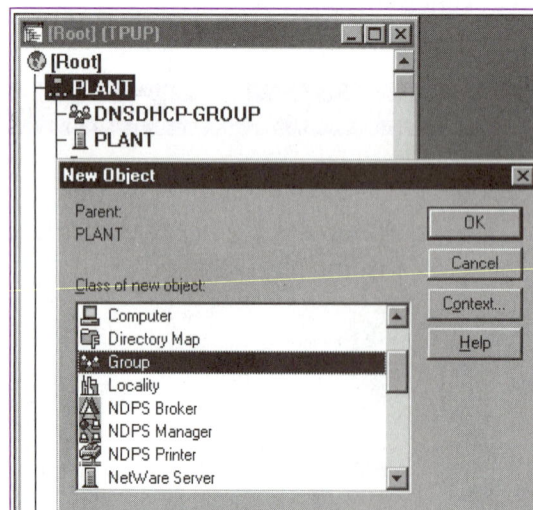

7. Create a Supervisors Group as indicated in Figure 5-39. Put a check mark in **Define additional properties** and click the **Create** button.

Figure 5-39

8. Complete the Supervisors Group properties in the window shown in Figure 5-40.

Figure 5-40

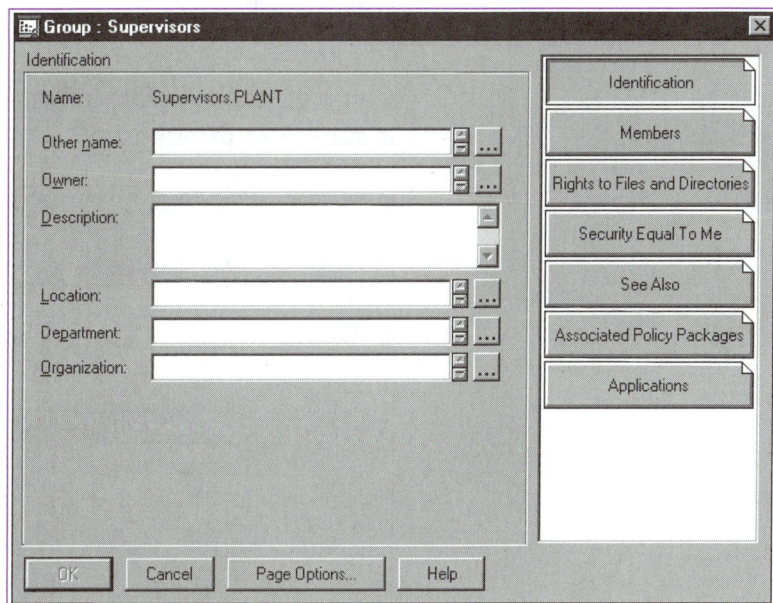

9. When you close the completed Supervisors Group Object, you should see the tree shown in Figure 5-41.

Figure 5-41

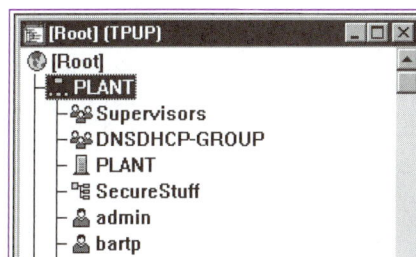

CHAPTER 5
NDS

10. Create a SupervisorsTMPL template to help you create additional users.

Figure 5-42

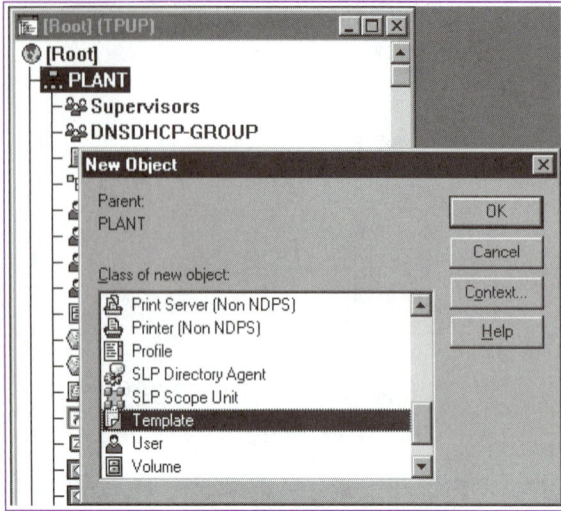

Figure 5-43

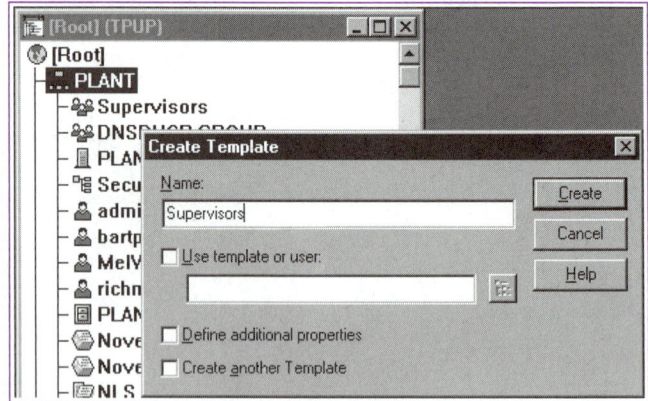

11. Complete the template information in the pages as shown in Figures 5-44 through 5-50.

Figure 5-44

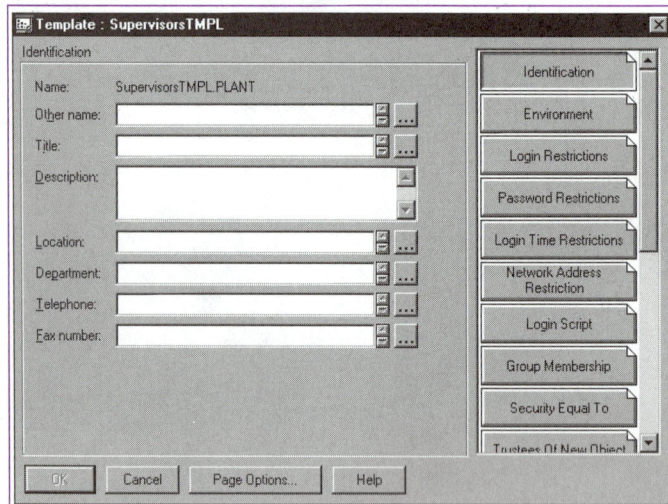

Figure 5-45

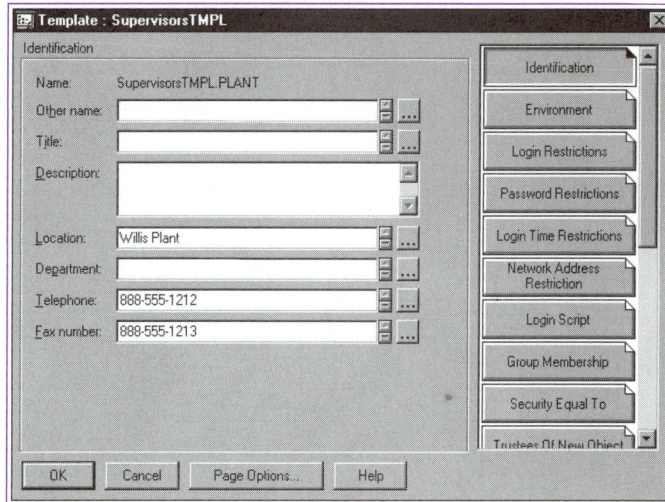

Figure 5-46

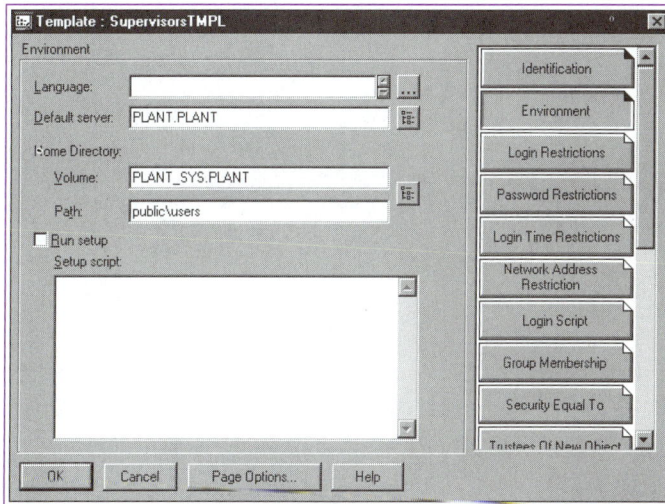

Figure 5-47

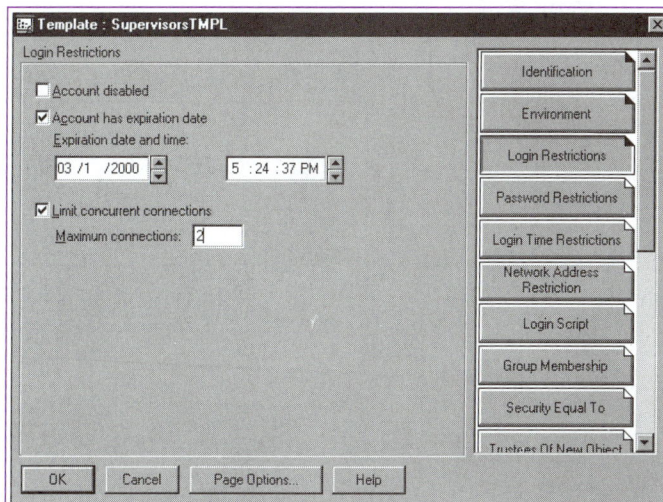

Figure 5-48

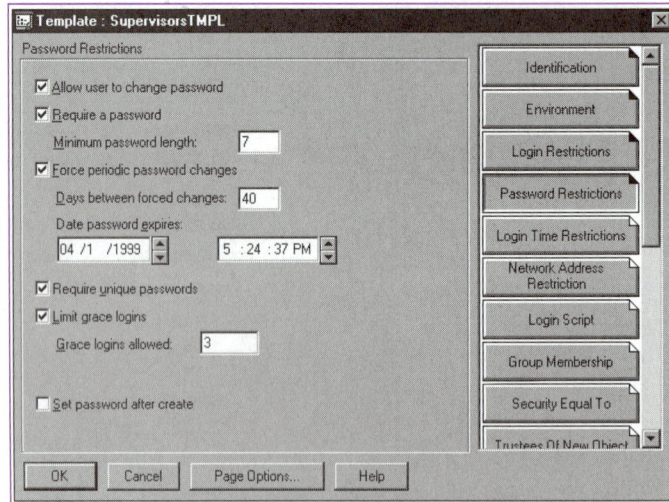

Figure 5-49

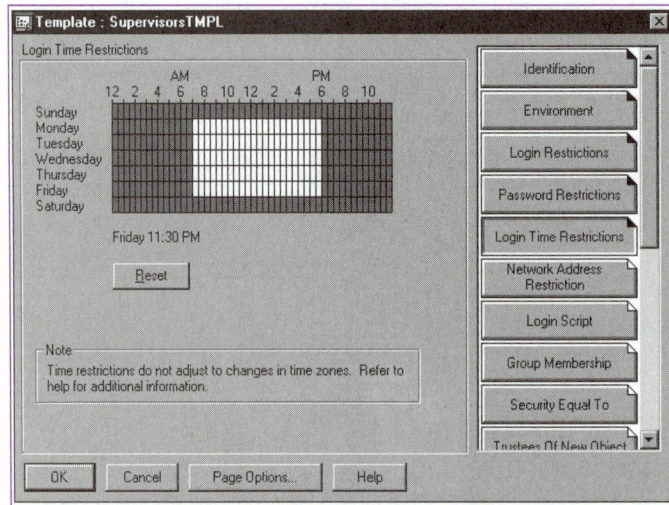

Figure 5-50

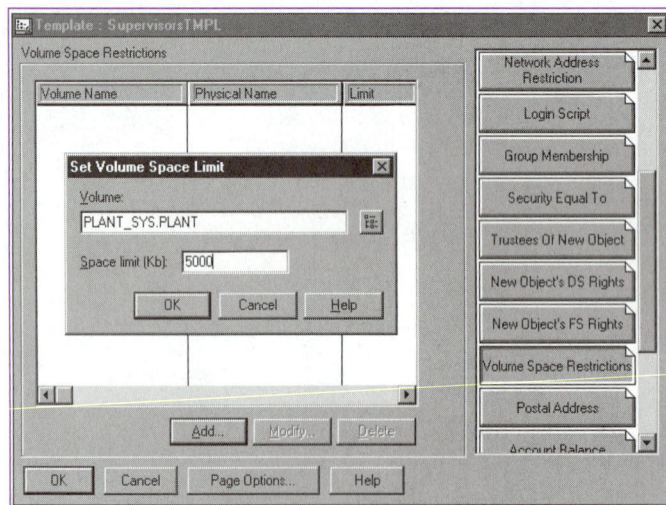

12. Create multiple users in the Plant Organization container with the template object you just created. Fill the Plant container with the workers in the organization chart from Chapter 1. See Figures 5-51 through 5-54 for reference.

Figure 5-51

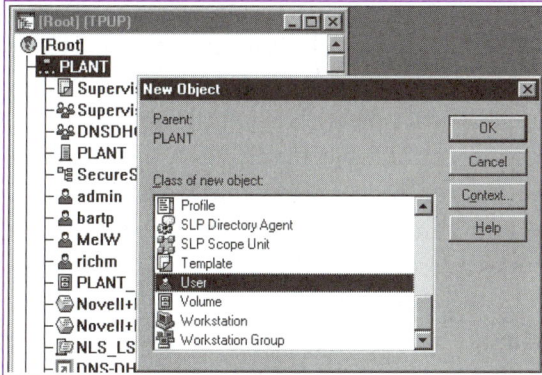

Figure 5-52

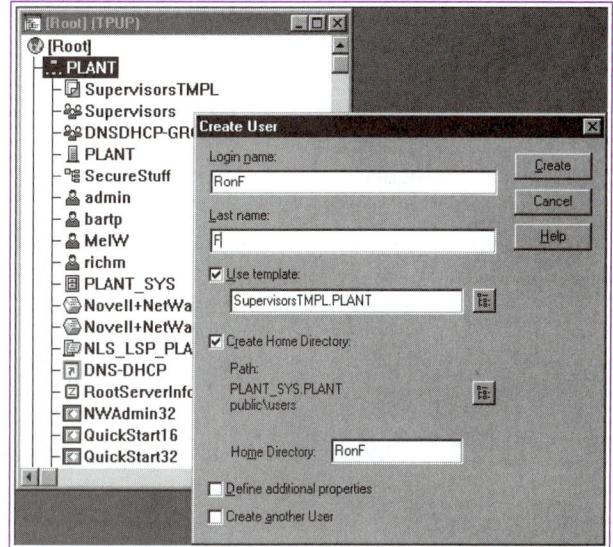

Figure 5-53

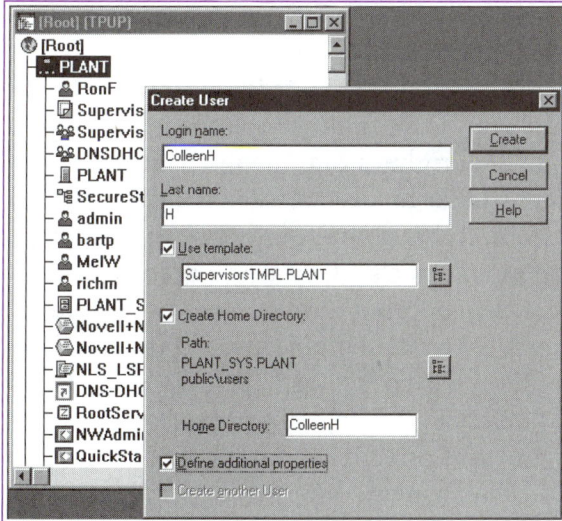

Figure 5-54

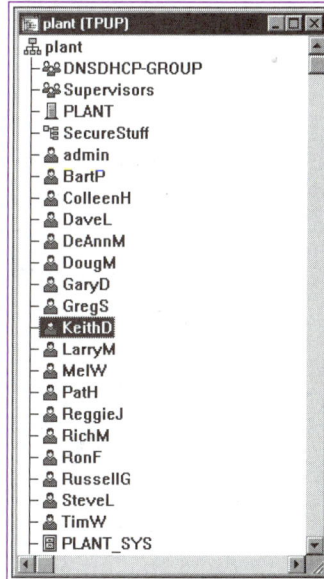

Chapter Summary

In this chapter you were introduced to Novell Directory Services (NDS). When referring to the NDS Directory, the initial "D" in Directory should be capitalized. NDS allows NetWare to manage the network by grouping similar objects hierarchically and assigning attributes to each object. NDS organizes the data and makes it available to all network users as it processes requests for services, locates the resource, validates the client's rights, and provides the connection between the user and the resource. Apart from network communication, NDS is the most fundamental service a Novell network provides.

In an NDS tree the [Root] is the highest object. As you descend through the company's organizational structure, its tree-like nature is reflected in the network design. The NDS hierarchy is similar to DOS's filing system, but it imposes restrictions on object placement. A Directory can have only one [Root] object. The [Root] object can hold only country objects, organization objects, or alias objects.

> **NDS manages objects by subdividing the information that describes them into properties and values.**

NDS manages objects by subdividing the information that describes them into properties and values. Objects are units of information about resources or services available on the network. NDS stores information about objects in categories, called properties. The different properties associated with an object determine the class of that object. NDS determines which properties each object will possess. Values are the data within the property fields that describe an object. Some property values must be filled in before the object can be created. Other properties have multiple values, such as multiple user telephone numbers.

> **NDS objects are either [Root] objects, container objects, or leaf objects.**

NDS objects are either [Root] objects, container objects, or leaf objects. The [Root] object is a placeholder and does not contain information about other objects. The [Root] object can be created only during initial network installation. The [Root] cannot be moved, renamed, or deleted. The [Root] object is not a container object.

The Directory is organized by grouping individual resource or service objects within containers. The container objects help group other container objects and allow rights assignments to multiple objects. container objects are similar to directories in a database. A parent object is a container object that contains other objects. There are three main types of container objects—Country, Organization, and Organizational Unit container objects. Novell does not recommend using the optional country container object, but if it is used, it must be placed directly under the [Root] object. Each directory must have at least one organization container object, and, unless a country container object is used, it must be directly below the [Root]. The organization container object can contain other container objects (except another organization container object), and is the first level that can contain leaf objects. The optional organizational unit container object is the most commonly used container object. Organizational Unit container objects help organize the lower levels of an organization and can also be used as lower level containers.

Leaf objects are found within containers in an NDS tree and cannot contain other objects. They represent the actual resources and services of the network. Leaf objects are similar to files in a database.

> **NDS does not search its entire database when locating a resource.**

NDS does not search its entire database when locating a resource. You must provide NDS with the correct object name. NDS then locates the object, controls your status on the network, and verifies that you are permitted to use the object before connecting you to it.

Networking Terms Used in Chapter 5

Novell Directory Services (NDS)
validating
inverted tree
[Root]
Directory
NWADMIN
NETADMIN
container
fundamental networking
   service
directory
object
properties
values
record
class
required value property
multiple value property
[Root] object
placeholder
details selection
trustee

rights
alias
container objects
parent object
Country container object
Organization container object
Organization Unit container
   object
locality container object
licensed product container
   objects
X.500 directory specification
   certification
leaf objects
NDS search
context
object name
common name
current context
name context
distinguished name
fully distinguished name

relative distinguished name
unified database
typeless name
typeful name
server-centered
network-centered
unified access
single password
centralized access
dynamic mapping
CX
Run command
pull down window
shortcut
Z: drive
SYS:
Public folder
Win32 folder
Send to…
Create
Define additional properties
migrate

■ Chapter Review Questions

1. What is NDS?

2. What does NDS use to process requests for services by network clients?

3. What three actions are required when NDS processes client requests?

4. What is the most fundamental service a Novell NetWare network provides?

5. Why is the ability of a NetWare network to provide a single unified network important?

6. Where is the [Root] located in a NetWare tree?

7. How many [Root] objects are allowed in a NetWare tree?

8. Why is the word Directory capitalized when referring to NetWare Networking components?

9. What types of objects can the [Root] contain?

10. How many NetWare servers on the same network contain object information?

11. How many NDS trees can exist on a NetWare network?

12. Define the term *Object*.

13. Define the term *Properties*.

14. Define the term *Values*.

15. Which NDS object is a placeholder that does not contain any information?

16. Is the [Root] object a container?

17. Define the term *parent container*.

18. Which container object is the most frequently used type?

19. Which object is the final division of the NDS tree?

20. When searching for an object, how much of the tree does NDS search?

21. Define the term *common name*.

22. What is the most effective way to go directly to an object in NDS?

23. Define the term *context*.

24. Compare a distinguished name to a relative distinguished name.

25. Compare a typeless name to a typeful name.

26. What are the three utilities used to browse NDS?

■ Associated Chapter Problems

1. Create the remainder of TPUP's NDS structure based on the organization chart in chapter one.

2. What are the important features of NetWare's NDS?

3. Explain how a client's network service request is processed.

4. Compare NDS components to a typical database's components.

5. Compare NDS structure to that of DOS.

6. Create an NDS structure with your school district as the [Root] object, your class as the leaf objects, and all the appropriate levels in between.

7. Explain why NDS is considered "efficient."

8. Create a chart showing the different types of objects on a NetWare network and the allowable structure considering all constraints.

9. Explain why it is important that NDS does *not* search the entire database.

10. Explain the different object naming options.

11. Explain how it is possible for two NDS objects to have the same common name.

12. Explain how leading and trailing periods are used.

13. Explain why NDS was a welcome innovation for the networking community.

14. Create a list showing the benefits of NDS and provide an example
    of each.

15. Explain how to use the three utilities for browsing NDS.

16. Explain two different ways to enter **NWAdmin**.

OBJECTIVES

You now have nearly all of the components of a network and you can sign in to your TPUP server. But when you logged in and wandered around the Directory tree, getting familiar with TPUP, you found nothing to use. It is now time for you to put something there that your users can share. By the end of this chapter, you will be able to:

- describe the components of the NetWare's Network File System (NFS).

- explain the use of the term Volume.

- explain the use of Directories and Subdirectories.

- use the correct syntax for NFS operation.

- explain why Files are important to NFS.

- describe the file management utilities used with NFS.

- compare **NWAdmin** and **FILER** when used with NFS.

- create a Drive Mapping.

Novell NetWare's Network File System (NFS)

NetWare's *Network File System (NFS)* stores data and applications for users to share throughout the network. Novell does not usually refer to its network file system as NFS, but for the sake of simplicity, this text will. Using NFS helps organize the data into another hierarchical system that is similar to the *filing cabinet system* used in the typical office, and quite similar to *DOS's organizational structure*.

During installation, the NetWare operating system creates some of the file system that is later used by administrators and users when developing or using their network resources. Some of the files on the network are offered for sharing by other users. They share resources because they are clients on the network, and the resources they wish to share are resources on the network, residing in disk drives attached to the NetWare servers. The file system stores the data and shares it with network users. It also stores networked applications and shares them with network users.

NFS is on all NetWare servers. Its components include *servers, volumes, directories, subdirectories,* and *files*. NFS provides *centralized access* to these components and allows users to share applications and data. The structure formed by these components is another example of NetWare's orientation toward *hierarchical filing systems*.

Figure 6-1

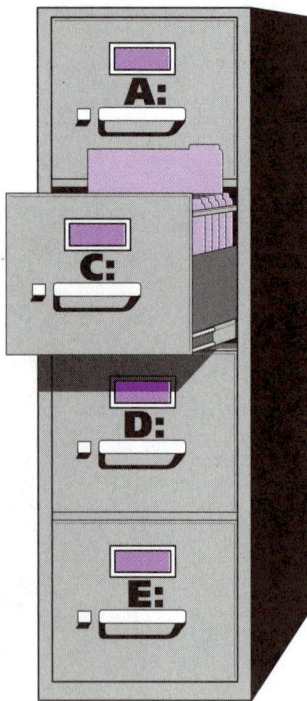

Server

Use Figure 6-1 to think of the entire NetWare Server as a typical filing cabinet in an office. It is the top level of the NFS structure, where all the other components are organized. As illustrated in Figure 6-2, the volumes are separate drawers inside the server. The directories are folders in the drawers. The subdirectories are folders within other folders. The files are individual documents stored in the folders (either volumes, directories, or subdirectories). *Server naming convention* allows them names that contain from two to 47 characters. However, they cannot use any of the following reserved characters in the name: = < > ? " * + , : ; \ / | [ ] .

Figure 6-2

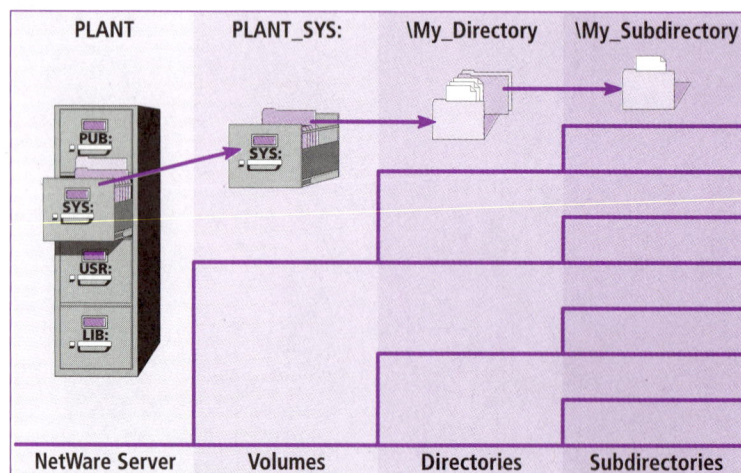

Volume

A volume is a physical device used for storage and either installed in or attached to the server. It is commonly a hard disk drive, but can also be a CD-ROM drive, a tape drive, or any other large storage device. Volumes are similar to DOS disk drives. Like DOS disks, NetWare volumes can be either separate hard drives or major subdivisions within a hard drive, created to separate the information from everything else on the drive. This is similar to partitioning DOS disks with **FDISK**.

When you set up your DOS partition on your TPUP NetWare server, the remaining space was available for subdividing into NetWare volumes. During installation, we chose to use only one volume for this part of the course. Your NetWare server initially boots up in the DOS partition that you created. It contains the main server executable file—*Server.exe*—that starts your NetWare operating system.

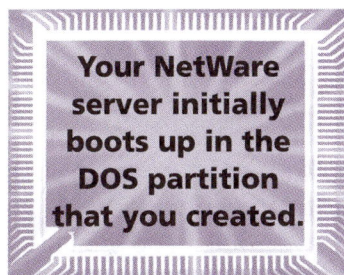

Your NetWare server initially boots up in the DOS partition that you created.

The *server.exe* file loads some additional system files and then switches to the NetWare partition for all other operating system functions. The first NetWare volume created on a server is always the *SYS: volume*. Each NetWare server must have at least one NetWare volume, the *SYS:* volume, where the operating system files are stored for server operation. Deleting or changing the name of this volume will cause the server to operate improperly and possibly to fail to start. Additionally, administrators should monitor the available disk space on the *SYS:* volume because if it becomes full, the server could crash.

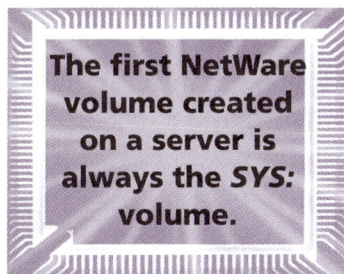

The first NetWare volume created on a server is always the *SYS:* volume.

Volumes are located on NetWare servers, and some servers contain more than one volume. Unlike DOS drives configured using **FDISK**, however, NetWare volumes can also span more than one physical hard drive and continue to be considered single volumes. NDS represents volumes on NetWare networks as *Volume objects* and automatically gives them an object name. Volume object names are a combination of the name of the server and the name of the volume, connected by an underscore.

Thus, the volume object name for the volume you created on your PLANT server should, therefore, have been *PLANT_SYS:*, with a filing cabinet icon representing it in the tree (see Figure 6-3). Because all servers have a *SYS:* volume, and, as we discussed in the previous chapter, all objects must have unique names in NetWare, this naming scheme provides the objects with unique names.

Figure 6-3

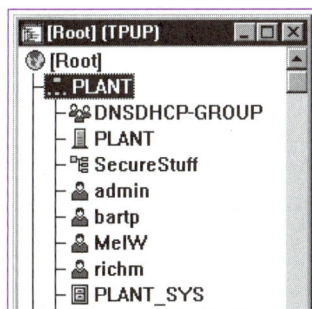

If you create additional volumes, your NetWare server automatically names them *Vol1:*, *Vol2:*, etc., unless you specify individual names during installation. You can change these default names later if you wish. For clarification, you may name your additional volumes for the geographical location (*plant 1:*, *Florida:*, *West Coast:*, etc.), department (*finance:*, *drafting:*, etc.), or any other descriptor that will help clarify your structure. Usually, the *SYS:* volume is available only for system-required files, while the additional volumes are available for everything else. Because this first installation

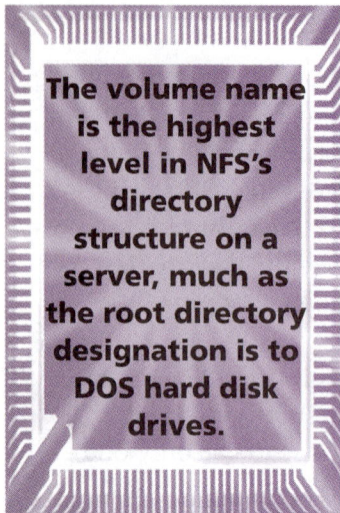

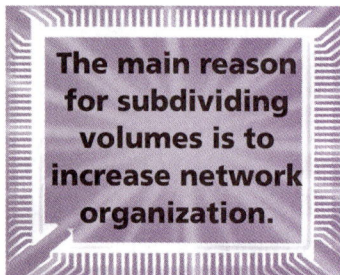

did not permit a second volume on your server, this separation is not yet important.

The volume name is the highest level in NFS's directory structure on a server, much as the root directory designation is to DOS hard disk drives. Also similar to DOS, NetWare's file system directory structure is "tree-like," with directories and subdirectories branching out from the root directory, with stored files as the lowest level in the structure.

Directory

A directory is an area on a NetWare volume where files or additional directories (called subdirectories) are stored. The main reason for subdividing volumes is to increase network organization. The more you can subdivide and group like objects together, the more organized a network tends to be. Think of the filing cabinet mentioned earlier. When you wish to store and later retrieve a file, good general organization and adequately subdivided file folders make it easier for you to find the file you want. Creating a folder in Windows 95 is similar to creating a directory in NFS.

When you perform your duties as the network administrator in this class, you will find that administering networks often involves creating and working with directories. Most of the directories with which you will work are those you create on your own. However, there are several directories that are created by the installation program when you first install NetWare.

The following are some of the required directories that NetWare automatically installed on your server (provided it contains a NetWare 4.0 or higher operating system). You will be working with these directories frequently as you administer your TPUP network on either the NetWare 5 or the NetWare 4.11 operating system.

SYSTEM—The majority of the tasks you will perform on your server will use the configuration files, NLMs, and utilities contained in this directory. They are accessible only to those individuals designated as administratively responsible for the network. These files affect how your NetWare server functions and should be protected from access by unauthorized users.

PUBLIC—The files and programs that you want available to all users after they have logged in can be placed in this directory. Many of these are necessary for users when gaining access to or using any network services. By default, all users on a network are granted Read access to the *PUBLIC* directory.

LOGIN—These files can be accessed by users prior to their logging in to the network. Merely connecting to the network gives all individuals access to these files and programs. Users can see what servers are available for them to log onto and they can attempt to log onto any of those servers. Whether or not they are successful in their

---

The volume name is the highest level in NFS's directory structure on a server, much as the root directory designation is to DOS hard disk drives.

The main reason for subdividing volumes is to increase network organization.

attempt determines whether they gain access to the network itself. Network administrators should be very careful when placing programs in the *LOGIN* directory because anyone, authorized or not, has access to those programs at all times.

MAIL—Configuration files for users are stored in this directory. The *MAIL* directory also facilitates backward compatibility with Novell servers prior to NetWare 4.0 (using "Bindery" emulation), thus allowing users from those servers access to services on the newer networks.

In addition, you will usually see several more directories on a typical Novell Network. It will be your job, as the network administrator, to create and maintain these directories.

APPLICATION—Applications that the network administrator determines should be available to multiple users over the network are placed in an *APPLICATION* (or *APPS*) directory. Create a separate directory below *APPS* for each application. A separate location for applications is created so that your most frequently used items are segregated from other files. In case of failure or data corruption, your more important files (such as your *SYSTEM* files) are not affected. All authorized users will have access granted to run these applications.

USERS—All users will usually have files that they wish to store on the server in order to access their information from any workstation on the network. These files and associated documents are customarily stored in a *HOME directory* located below the folder labeled *USERS*. Think of it as their "home base," or location where they keep their personal "possessions." When you created new users on your TPUP server, you were asked to designate their *HOME* directory, and you specified the *USER* directory. Therefore, all users on your TPUP network now have their *HOME* location in your *USERS* directory. Typically, the name of their directory is also their user's name. Usually only the users will be granted access to their *HOME* directory.

SHARED—Frequently, your users will also have files, like a client database, that they wish to share over the network. Such items are usually stored in a *SHARED* directory created by the administrator. Users who are permitted to share all of the information in the directory should be granted access to the entire *SHARED* directory.

Subdirectory

Some of the directories identified above are directories within other directories—or subdirectories. For example, the *USERS* directory you created on your TPUP server is actually a subdirectory within the *PUBLIC* directory on your *PLANT_SYS:* volume, and your own user's directory is actually a subdirectory of that *USERS* subdirectory. Therefore, a subdirectory is merely a directory within another directory. It is a further subdivision of the information contained in the category

> Network administrators should be very careful when placing programs in the login directory because anyone, authorized or not, has access to those programs at all times.

> All users will usually have files that they wish to store on the server in order to access their information from any workstation on the network. These files and associated documents are customarily stored in a HOME directory located below the folder labeled USERS. Think of it as their "home base," ... where they keep their personal "possessions."

... your user's storage area should be a separate folder within that *USERS* directory to avoid mixing your information with that of another user.

of the higher-level directory. In the *USERS* directory category, for example, you are one of the users on the network. Therefore, your user's storage area should be a separate folder within that *USERS* directory to avoid mixing your information with that of another user. You have your own subdirectory within the *USERS* directory. The terms directory and subdirectory are typically used interchangeably.

Syntax

The normal *syntax* for referring to NetWare Volume directories requires a colon between the volume name and the directory. An example using your TPUP server information is *PLANT_SYS:PUBLIC*.

The normal syntax for referring to NetWare Volume subdirectories specifies the entire volume-directory-subdirectory by using a colon between the volume name and the directory and a backslash between the directory and subdirectory names. An example using your TPUP server is *PLANT_SYS:PUBLIC\USERS\MelW*.

Because you can also refer to other servers on a network with multiple servers, you may need to specify the full path as well, all the way from the server through the file. To do this, you begin with the name of the server (*PLANT*), followed by a slash (*/*), followed by the name of the volume (*SYS*), followed by a colon (*:*), followed by the directory syntax referred to above. Therefore, the proper syntax used when specifying Dave L.'s home directory on your TPUP PLANT server would be as follows:

PLANT/SYS:PUBLIC\Users\Davel

The above location is shown in Figure 6-4, which also contains the correct syntax showing the Server through File format.

Figure 6-4

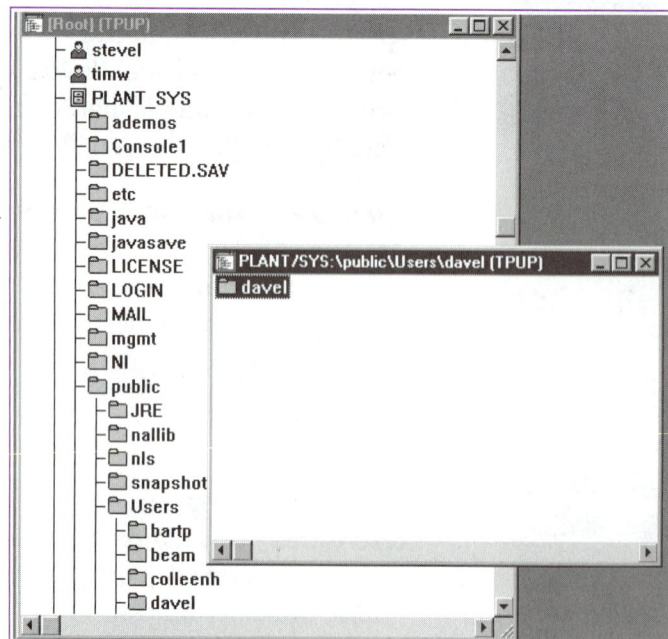

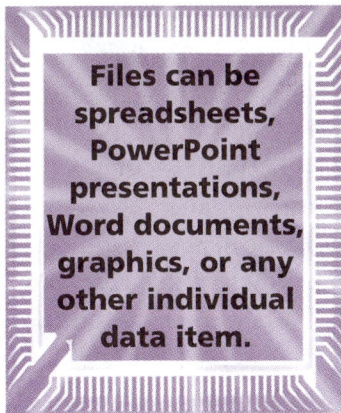

Files can be spreadsheets, PowerPoint presentations, Word documents, graphics, or any other individual data item.

Files

The data actually stored in NFS comprises what is referred to as a file. Although files are at the end of the NFS description and may seem insignificant at this point in your studies, remember that we developed a network to allow you to share such information with your classmates. You wanted to share the files that you and your classmates already had and those you have created so far this year.

Files can be spreadsheets, PowerPoint presentations, Word documents, graphics, or any other individual data item. They can also be application programs, or any other blocks of data you wish to share with someone on the network.

Managing NetWare's Network File System (NFS)

Much of what you already know about managing files in the Windows environment is also applicable to managing NetWare files. You should already know how to create new folders in Windows, how to move or copy them from one location to another (on the same hard drive or between networked storage devices), and how to navigate between drives, directories, folders and files. Once you know all that about Windows, you can do similar things on NetWare Volumes.

This will become evident when you log onto your TPUP tree and look in your *Network Neighborhood*. The NetWare icons for TPUP appear as indicated in Figure 6-5, and you can navigate through them as you can through any Windows folders.

Some differences, however, will also become apparent. For example, when you right click on the *PLANT* icon as shown in Figure 6-6, several NetWare actions such as **WhoAmI**, **Logout**, **Authenticate**, and **Login to Server** are available.

Figure 6-5

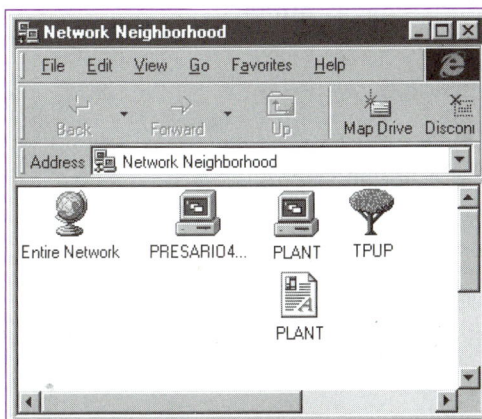

Figure 6-6

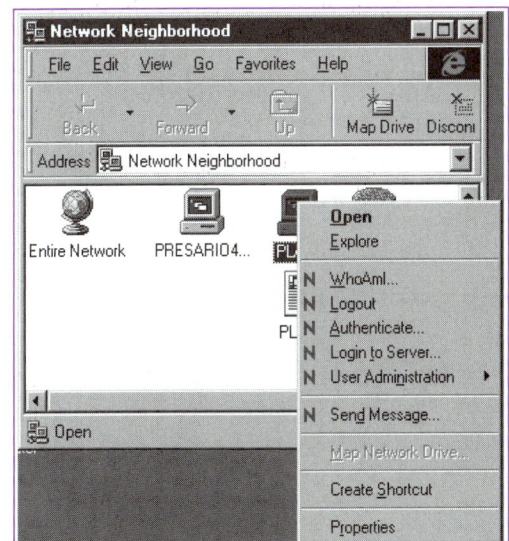

Along with the typical Windows methods you have for navigating and exploring access to your new NetWare directories, the *PUBLIC* directory contains additional utilities for you to use. These include the following: **NetWare Administrator**, **FILER**, **FLAG**, **NDIR**, **NCOPY**, **RENDIR**. As the network administrator, you will use these utility programs to create and manage your directory and subdirectory structure, your files, and your volume space.

You noticed when you worked with Novell Directory Services in the last chapter that you could work with NDS at the DOS prompt and with a limited utility—**NETADMIN**—in a non-GUI environment. Similarly, you will find that Novell's GUI utility for working with Network File System is the most powerful. You will primarily be using either of the first two—**NetWare Administrator** and **FILER**—but the following two charts will give you an idea of how you can use each of the above utilities.

Chart 1	
Task to Perform (directory management)	**Utility to Use**
View directory information	**NetWare Administrator** **FILER** **NDIR**
Change directory information	**NetWare Administrator** **FILER**
Create directory	**NetWare Administrator** **FILER**
Rename directory	**NetWare Administrator** **FILER** **RENDIR**
Delete directory contents	**NetWare Administrator** **FILER**
Remove directory and contents	**NetWare Administrator** **FILER**
Remove multiple directories	**NetWare Administrator** **FILER**
Copy directory structure	**NetWare Administrator** **FILER** **NCOPY**
Move directory structure	**NetWare Administrator** **FILER**

Chart 2	
Task to Perform (file management)	**Utility to Use**
View file information	NetWare Administrator FILER NDIR
Change file information	NetWare Administrator FILER
Copy files	NetWare Administrator FILER NCOPY
Copy files with attributes	NetWare Administrator FILER NCOPY
Salvage deleted files	NetWare Administrator FILER
Purge deleted files	NetWare Administrator FILER
Change file to purge automatically	NetWare Administrator FILER FLAG

NDIR

As shown in Figure 6-7, **NDIR** is a command line utility and not a GUI type utility. It is similar to, but much more powerful than, the DOS **DIR** command. **NDIR** stands for Network Directory and lists files in directories on network hard disk drives. In addition to the file name, size, date, and time, **NDIR** displays the owner, *effective rights*, *last update*, *last access*, and the *attributes of the file*.

Figure 6-7

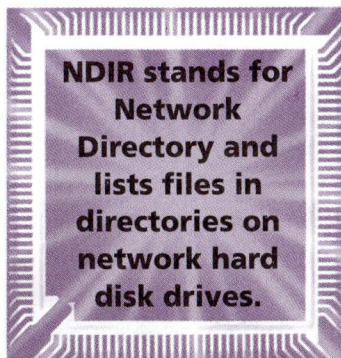

NDIR stands for Network Directory and lists files in directories on network hard disk drives.

NetWare Administrator (NWAdmin)

As you noted in the charts, you can use **NetWare Administrator** when performing all of the tasks indicated. You used the same **NWAdmin** when working with NDS in the previous chapter. However, its uses with NFS are vastly different, as illustrated in Figures 6-8 through 6-11, which show the four different attribute windows for a user's home directory.

Activity 6-1 · Managing with NWADMIN

1. Log onto your TPUP PLANT server.
2. Activate **NWAdmin** and browse the tree to each of the following sixteen windows. Become familiar with the options available to you in each applicable page.

Figure 6-8

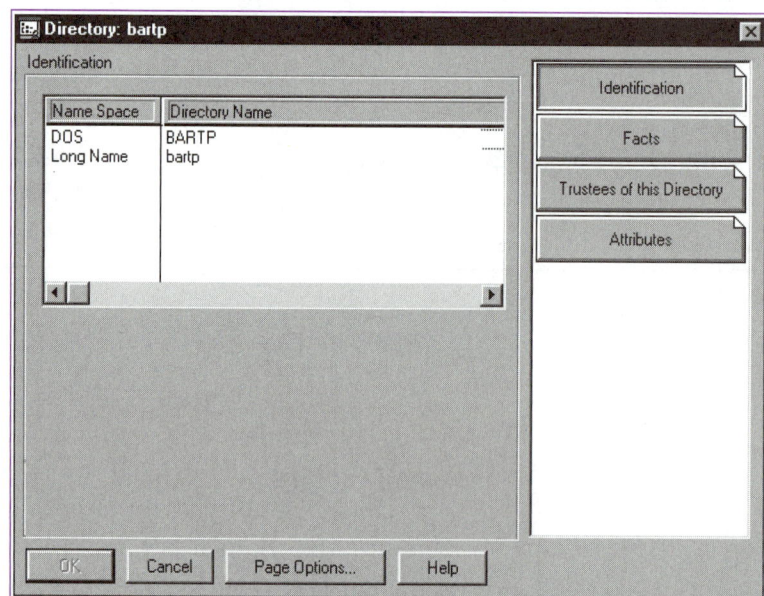

Figure 6-9

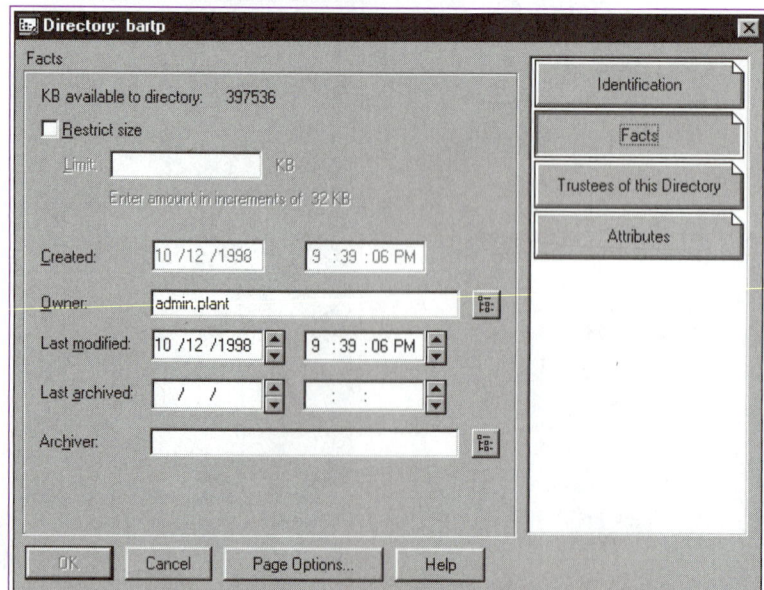

Figure 6-10

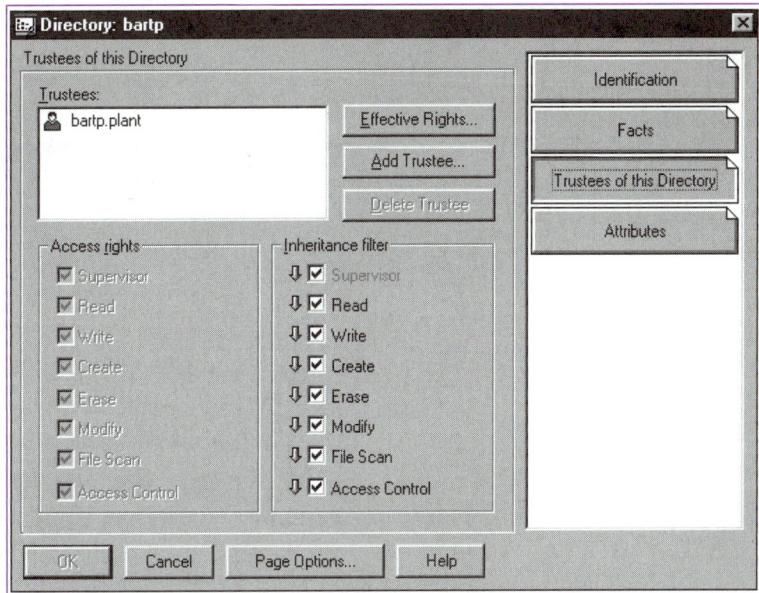

Figure 6-11

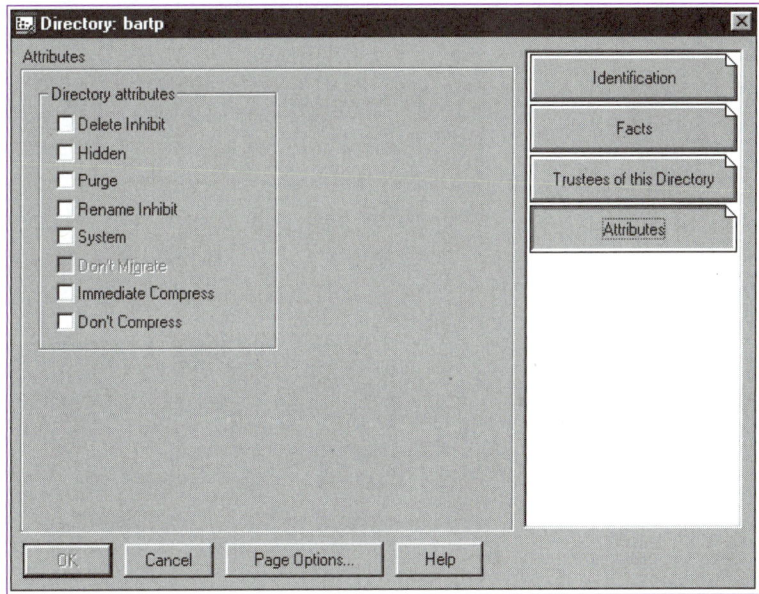

When you created the TPUP Plant server, the installation software installed two objects—the Server Object and the Volume Object. These objects can be seen in Figure 6-12.

Figure 6-12

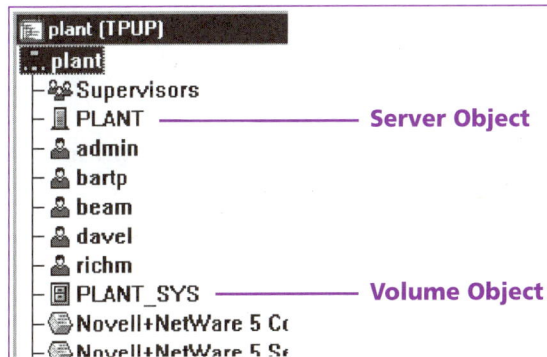

If you right click on the Server Object as shown in Figure 6-13, you will see the server properties information that we viewed in the previous chapter on NDS.

Figure 6-13

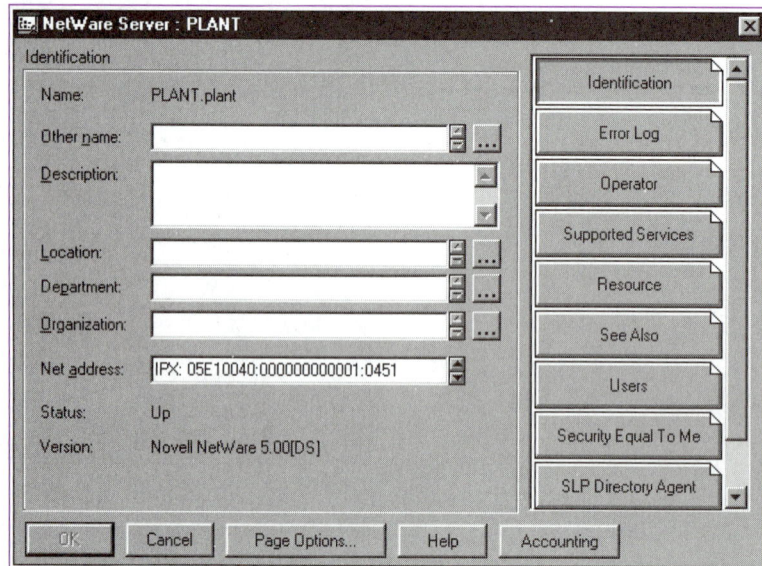

However, when you right click on the Volume Object as shown in Figure 6-14, you will notice that you gain access to information about the file system. This property page allows you to provide optional information that can help when searching for the Volume object. It also shows the NetWare server, *NetWare version number*, and *physical volume* for the Volume object.

Figure 6-14

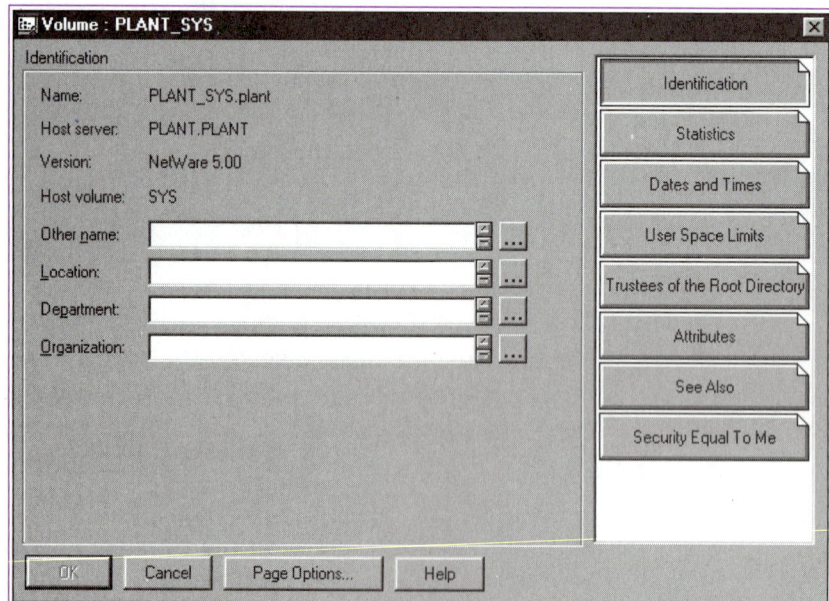

The *Statistics* property page, shown in Figure 6-15, depicts statistical information about the volume. This includes such information as its block size and used disk space. It also lists the Name spaces and other features installed on the volume. In addition, it shows the deleted and compressed file status.

Figure 6-15

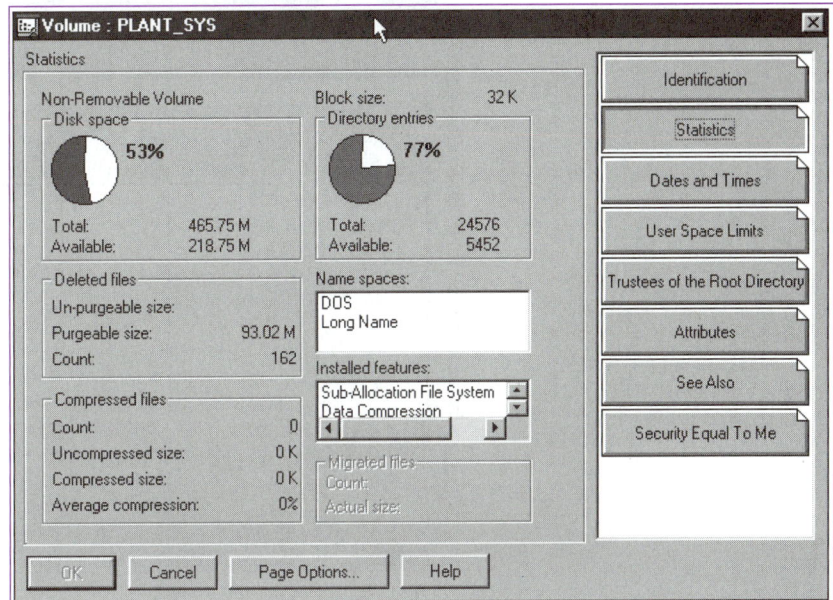

The *Dates and Times* property page shown in Figure 6-16 gives the date and time the volume was created and when it was last archived (backed up). It displays and allows you to change the owner of the volume. It also shows who last performed a back up.

Figure 6-16

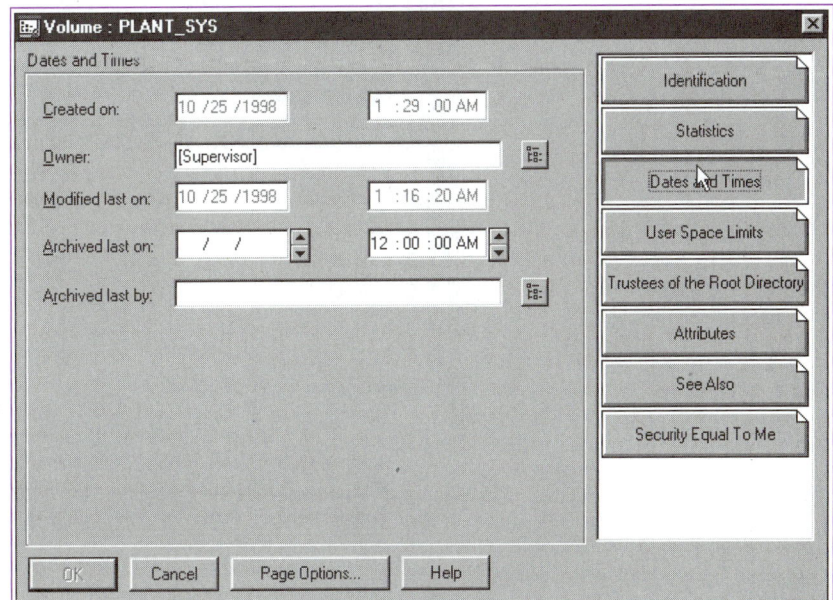

The *User Space Limits* property page shown in Figure 6-17 allows you to set a limit on the amount of disk space a user can use on the volume. This is optional, but it can be helpful if storage resources are limited.

Figure 6-17

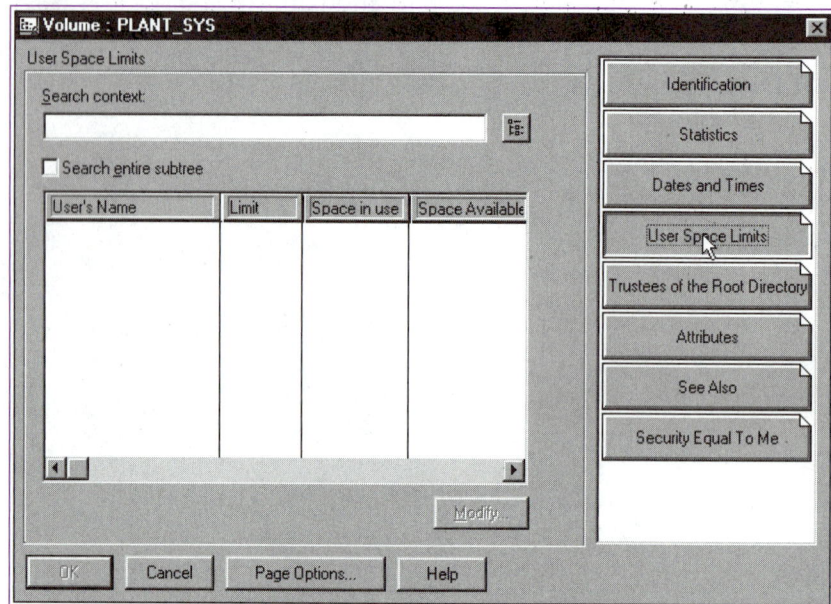

Note in Figure 6-18 that *user space restrictions* are listed when you specify the context of the User objects you want listed. (This is done by choosing the **Browse** button next to *Search context*).

Figure 6-18

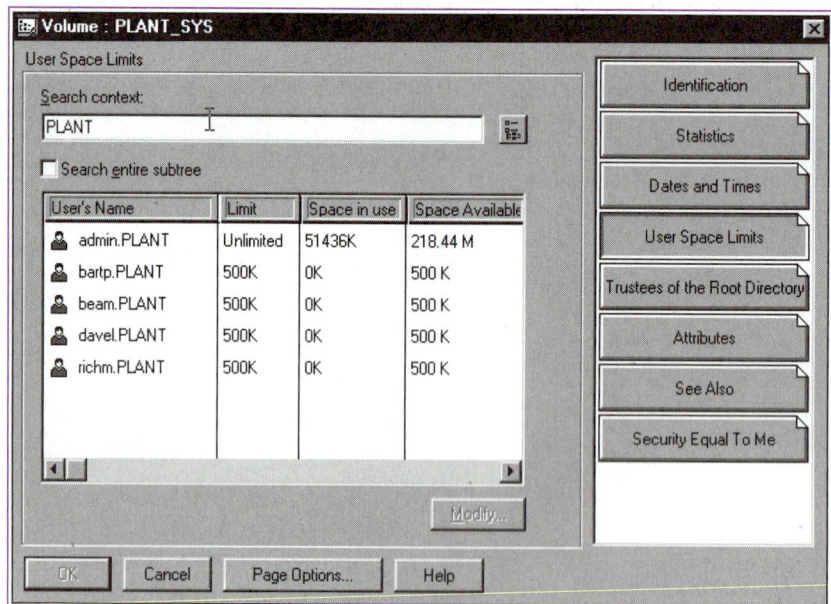

The *Trustees of the Root Directory* property page, as shown in Figure 6-19, permits you to assign trustees of the root directory and their explicit rights to the applicable file or directory.

Figure 6-19

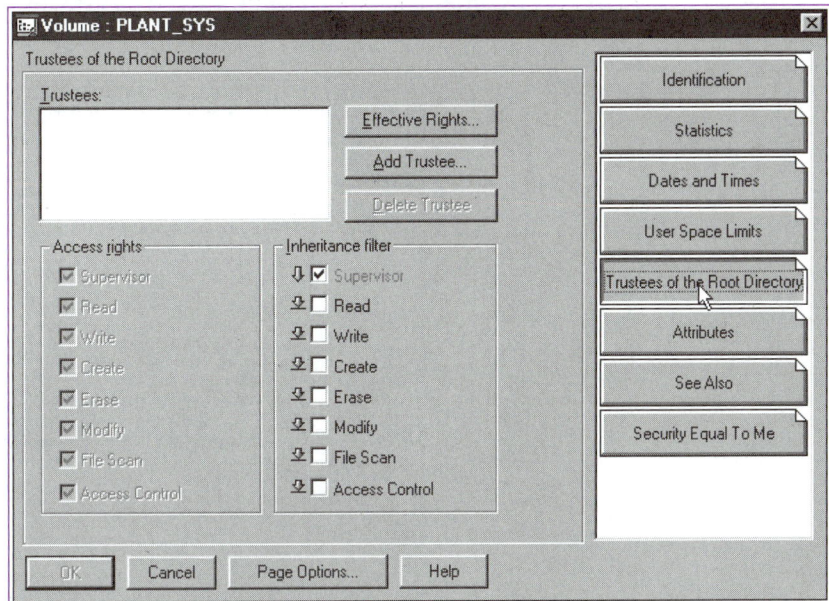

The *Attributes* property page allows you to edit the attributes for the applicable directory. If you chose a volume, as in Figure 6-20, the attributes are for the root directory of the volume.

Figure 6-20

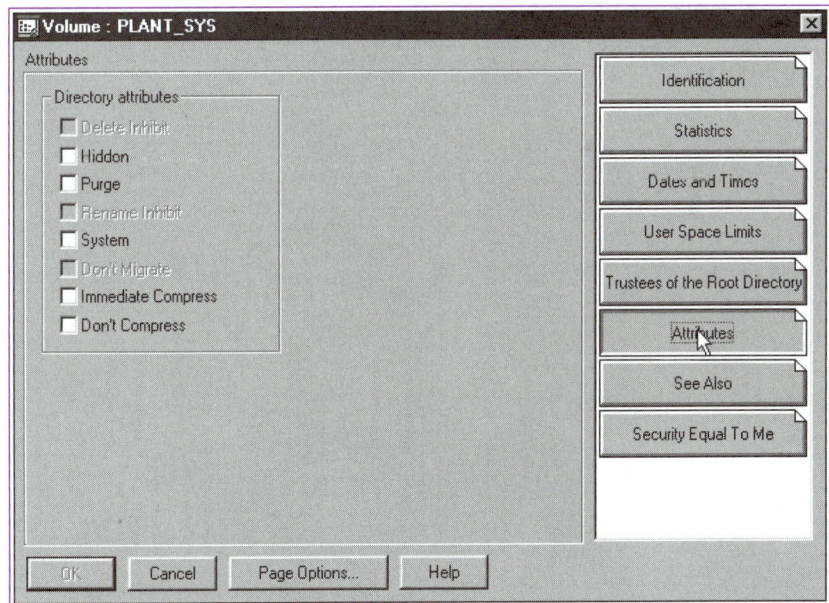

NetWare Administrator also lets you view information about files, as indicated in Figure 6-21. This shows the file's name and extension in both DOS and Long Name format. The same four pages of information shown in Figures 6-21 through 6-24 are available for directories as well.

Figure 6-21

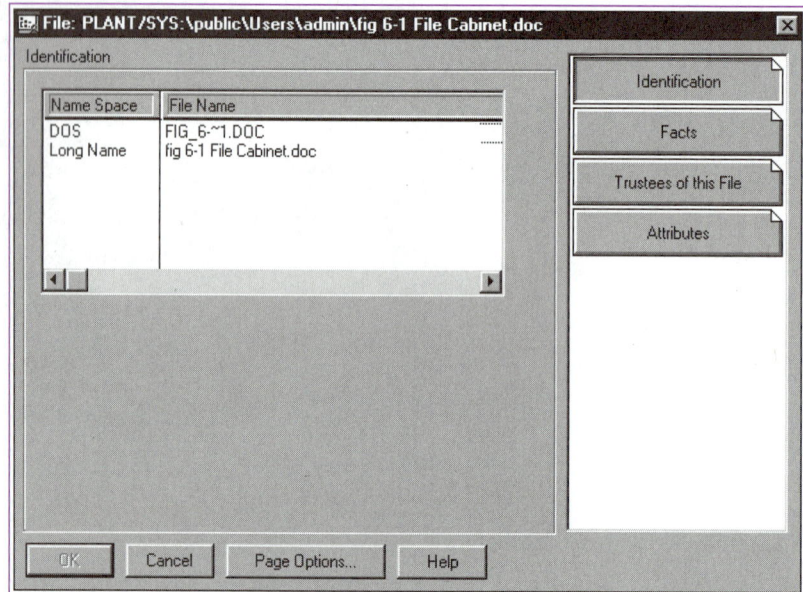

The same information available earlier on Volumes is shown being made available for files in Figure 6-22.

Figure 6-22

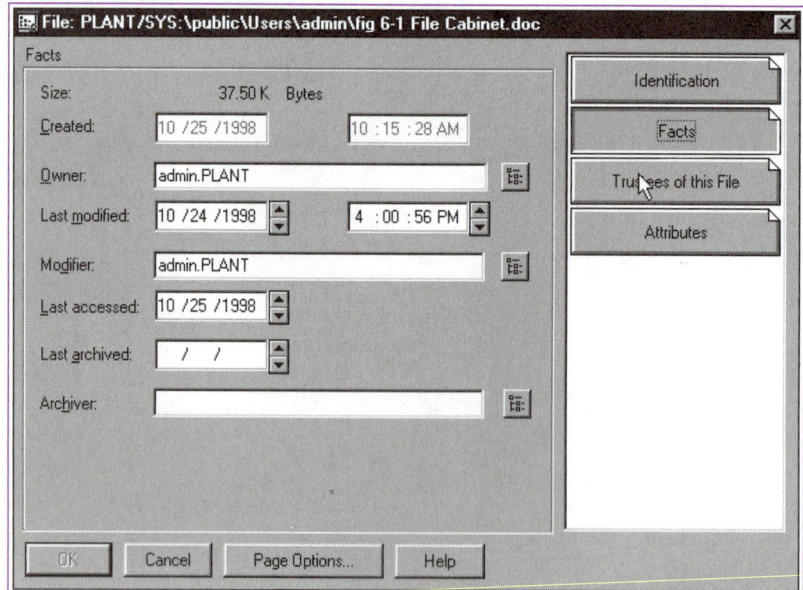

You can also check your effective rights to files in NWAdmin. After entry into the *Trustees of the File* page is the **Effective Rights** option that displays after clicking on the **Effective Rights** button, as shown in Figure 6-23.

Figure 6-23

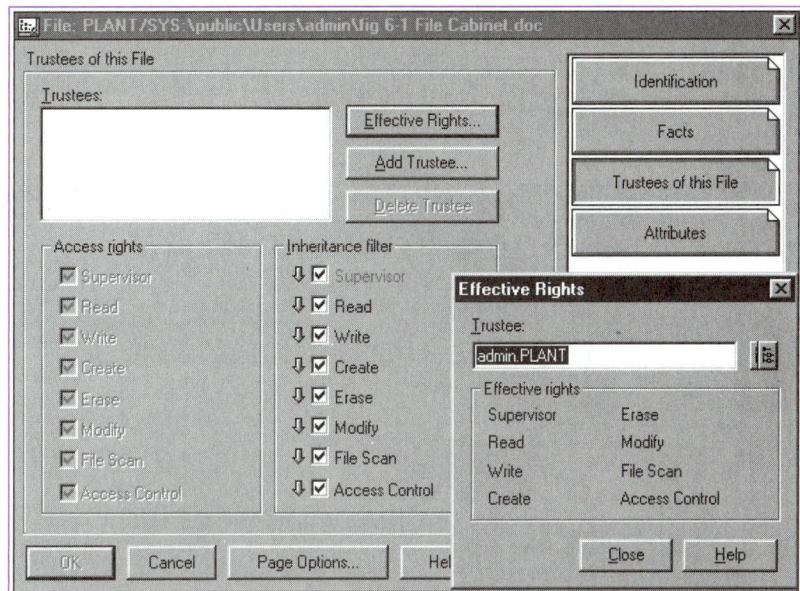

Additionally, the file's attributes can be reviewed and altered, as in Figure 6-24.

Figure 6-24

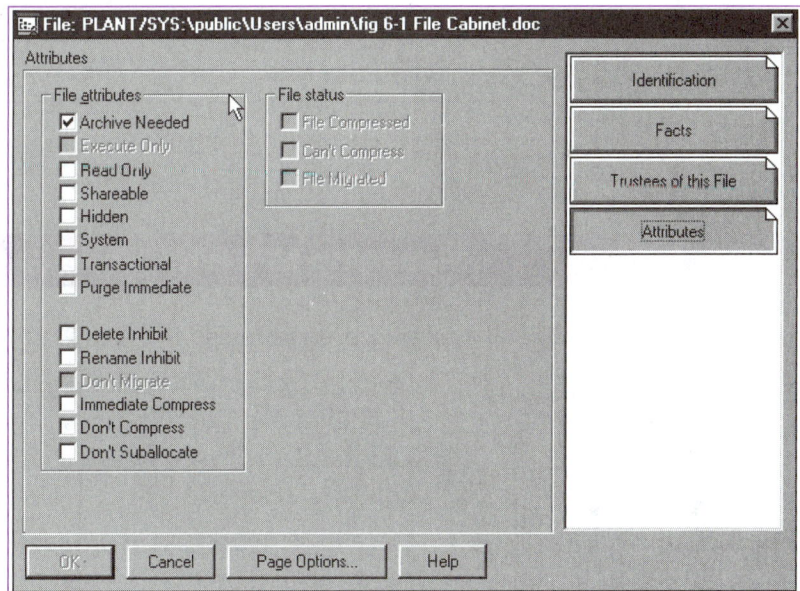

Novell Client

Much of the same information shown above through **NWAdmin** is also available for viewing in *Network Neighborhood,* as shown in Figure 6-25. Starting in the top left of the screen and going clockwise, you begin by opening *Network Neighborhood,* go to the *SYS:* volume on *PLANT,* then to *PUBLIC,* then to *PUBLIC\USERS,* and finally (in the top center window) to an individual file.

Figure 6-25

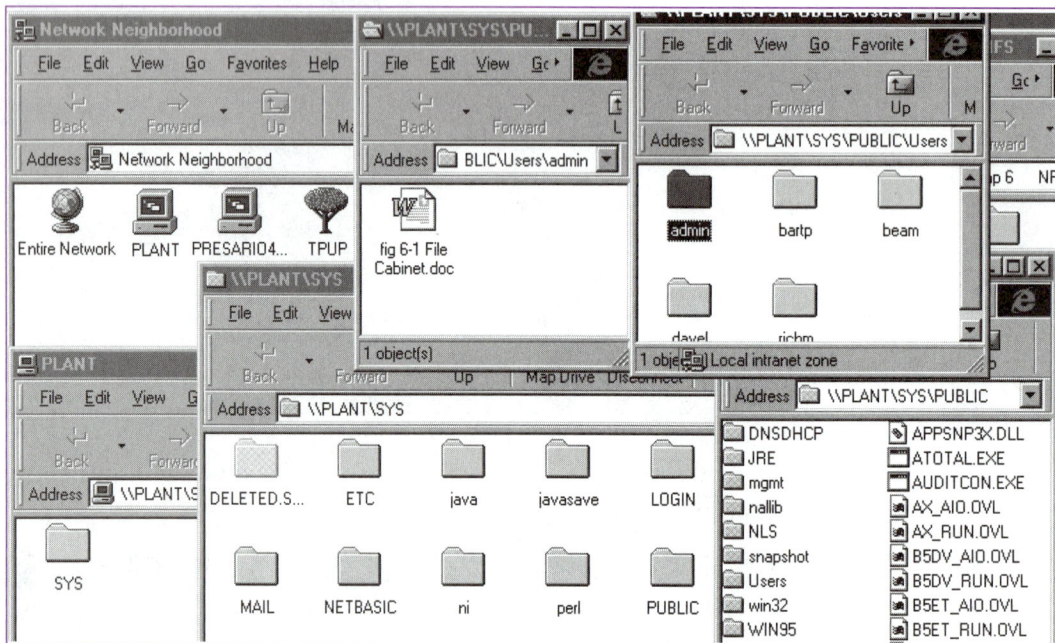

Activity 6-2   **Managing NFS with Novell's Client**

> **Once in Network Neighborhood, you can obtain information by right clicking on the desired icon and viewing the properties.**

1. Log onto your TPUP PLANT server.

2. Double click on **Network Neighborhood** and navigate to each of the following four windows shown in Figures 6-26 through 6-29. Familiarize yourself with the options available to you in each applicable page.

Once in **Network Neighborhood**, you can obtain information by right clicking on the desired icon and viewing the properties. The volume information and statistics and the NetWare information and NetWare rights can be managed through the four windows shown in Figures 6-26 through 6-29.

Figure 6-26

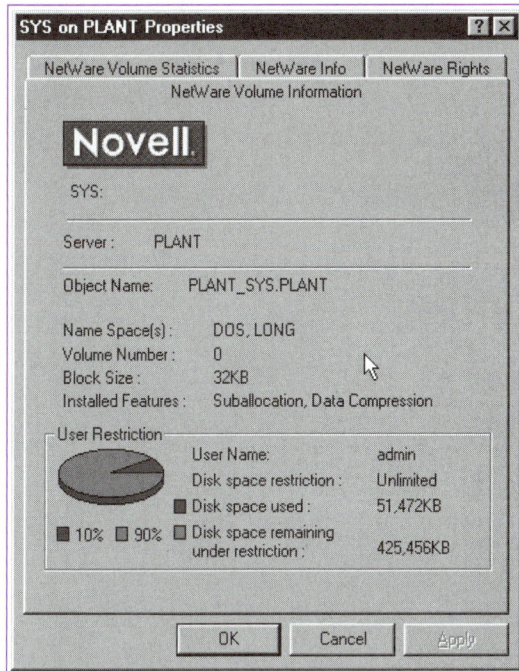

Figure 6-27

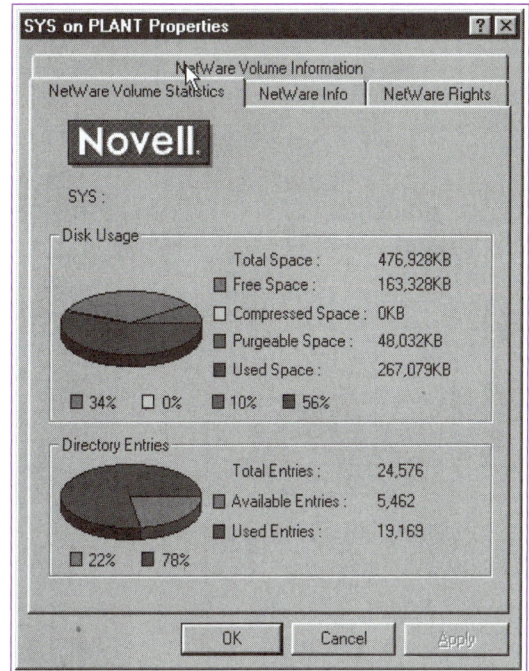

Figure 6-28

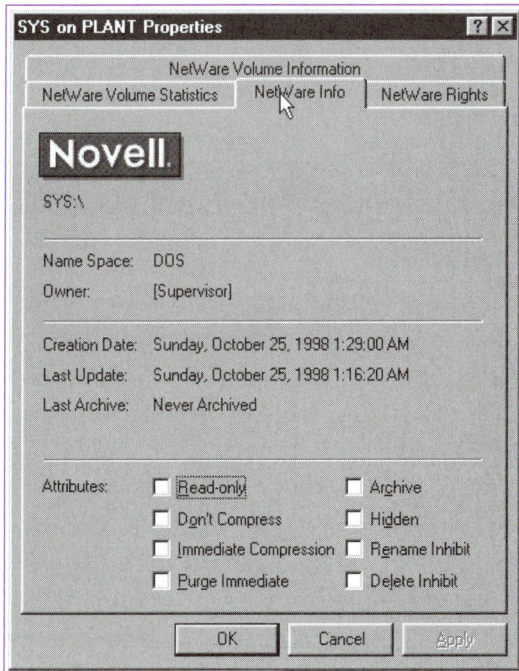

Figure 6-29

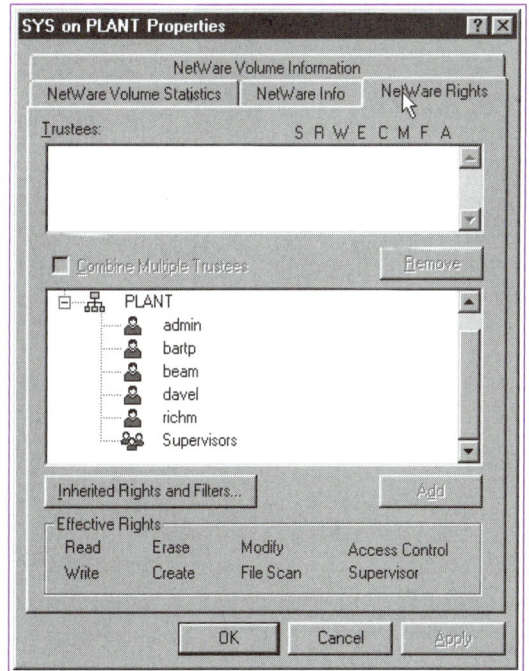

Filer

FILER is a text-based utility, as you can see in Figure 6-30, but it performs the same file system functions as **NetWare Administrator**. It is not used for NDS tree operations. You can confirm this by comparing the two utility programs in the charts on pages 154 and 155.

Figure 6-30

> FILER is a text-based utility, as you can see in Figure 6-30, but it performs the same file system functions as NetWare Administrator.

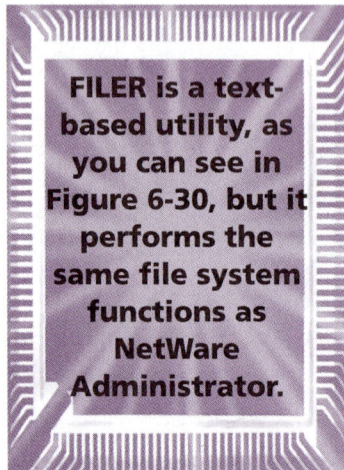

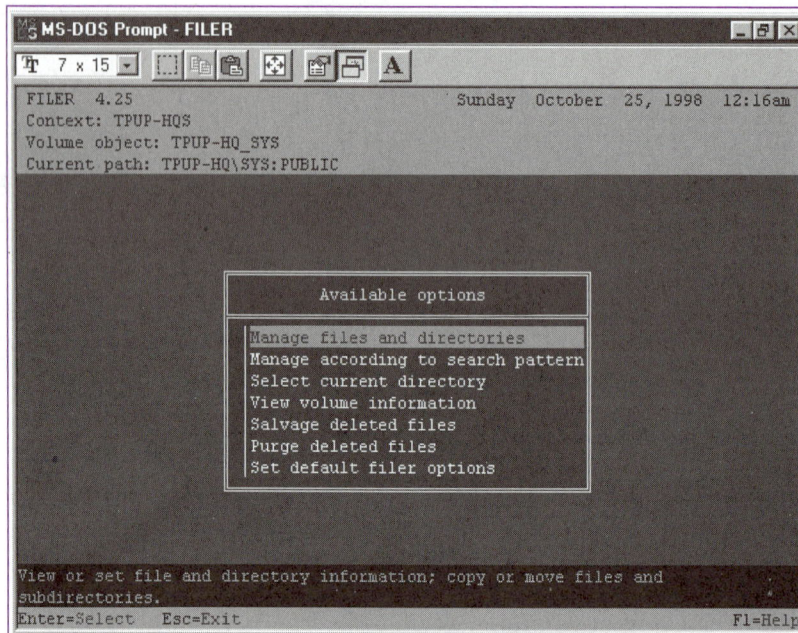

Gaining Access to NetWare's Network File System (NFS)

NetWare aware applications are those able to access the file system by using the server/volume or volume object name, as discussed earlier in this chapter. However, many applications are unable to address NetWare applications directly through the networking name. In those cases, *drive mapping* is available, and you can create *drive pointers* to indicate to the program where the drives are located.

Using the *Hard Drive* name in the *My Computer* designation on your Windows desktop depicted in Figure 6-31, for example, shows how this concept works. If you want to load a program to the *Apps* folder on your hard drive in your **My Computer** window, you will be unable to accomplish the task using those designators. Windows does not understand those names. They are there for your benefit only.

However, Windows does understand the drive designation *C:*, and it knows that the *C:* drive is on your *My Computer* system. It can, therefore, load the program to the *Apps* folder on the *C:* drive without difficulty. Thus, the drive pointer is the designator *C:*. By convention, the *A:* drive is now the 3-1/2" floppy drive, the *B:* (if you still

Figure 6-31

... the shortcut icon you place on your desktop does not contain the program or folder itself, but serves as a convenient location for you to go to when you do want access to the folder.

have one) is another floppy drive, and the *D:* drive is usually the CD-ROM drive as shown in Figure 6-31. If you had another hard drive or another partition added to a single hard drive, the *D:* drive would probably be that additional drive or partition. The *D:* pointer, then, would be telling the system to use that additional storage space whenever there is a reference to the designator *D:*. The CD-ROM drive in this case would probably be the *E:* drive.

NetWare drive pointers and drive mappings behave as described above. They will be discussed in more detail later in this text, but a basic understanding of them is necessary at this point for successful file system design. If you have become proficient at using shortcuts on your Windows desktop for easy access to folders you frequently access, you have already been working with a pointer-like system of your own. The folder for which you created the shortcut could be embedded within 10 or 12 other folders. Without the shortcut, you would have to open each of them every time you accessed your desired folder.

You know that the shortcut icon you place on your desktop does not contain the program or folder itself, but serves as a convenient location for you to go to when you do want access to the folder. You simply activate the icon and enter the folder. You clicked on the shortcut and it pointed the computer in the direction of the folder. Once you create the shortcut on your desktop, you can even rename it and the original folder will still open.

Much the same occurs with drive mappings and drive pointers. If you want ready access or an application needs access at a specific level on a disk drive (at the root, for instance), you can create a drive mapping that places the NetWare item at that location. If you have the folder embedded somewhere on your server, and an application won't accept it unless it was created in the root directory, you can map a new drive pointer and cause it to think it is loaded at the root directory.

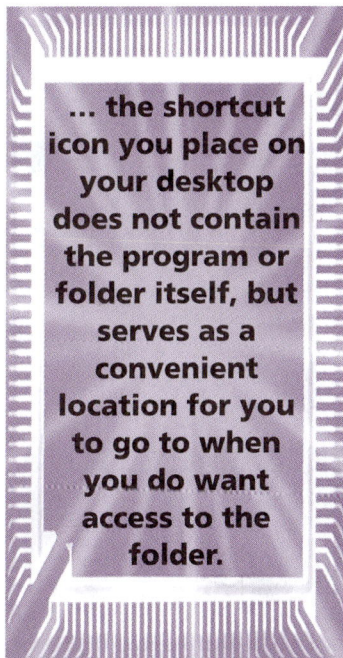

Activity 6-3   Mapping a Drive

1. Log into the network as administrator.

2. Double click on your *Z:* drive in your **My Computer** window. This should open the *SYS:* volume as indicated in the upper right portion of Figure 6-32.

3. Double click on your *PUBLIC* folder. This will open the *PUBLIC* folder as indicated in the left front portion of Figure 6-32.

4. Highlight and right click on the *Users* folder to bring up the **Novell Map Drive** window as shown in Figure 6-32.

5. We do not wish to have this folder each time we reconnect, so do not click in the **Reconnect at Login** box. Do check in the **Map Root** box so that the *Users* folder is the only one shown, and change the **Device** to *U:* (for Users) by pulling down the drop down arrow to the right of the **Device** designator.

Figure 6-32

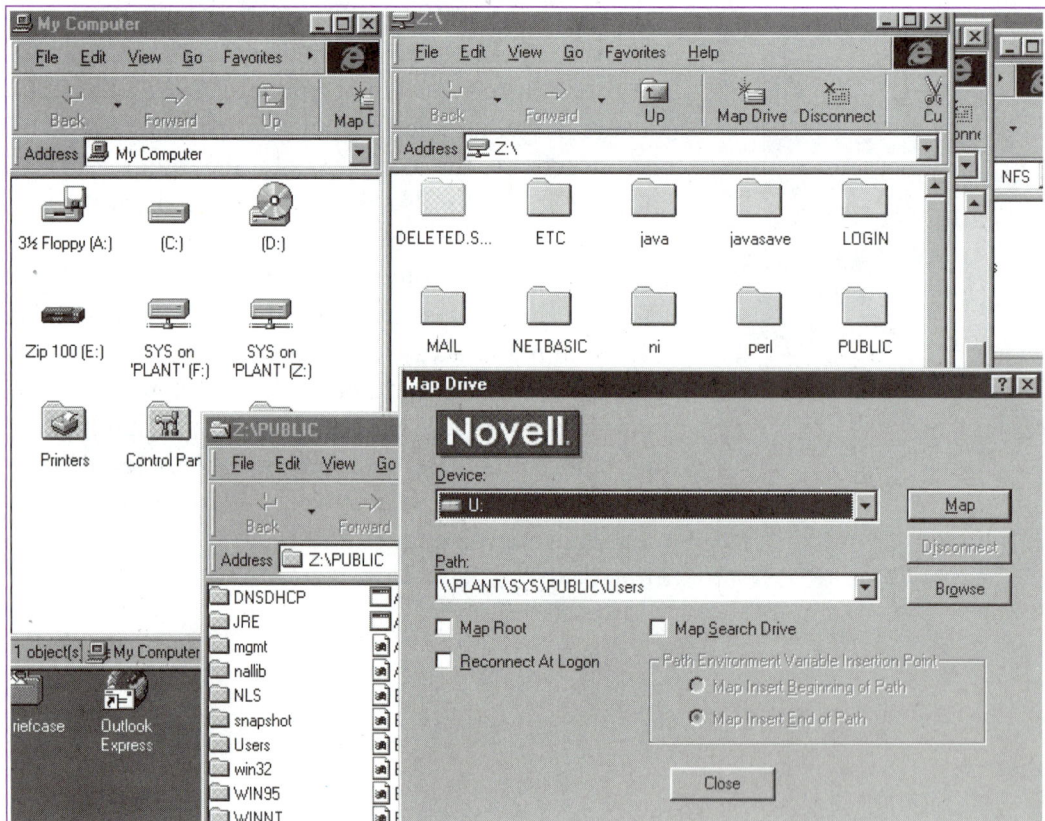

Figure 6-33

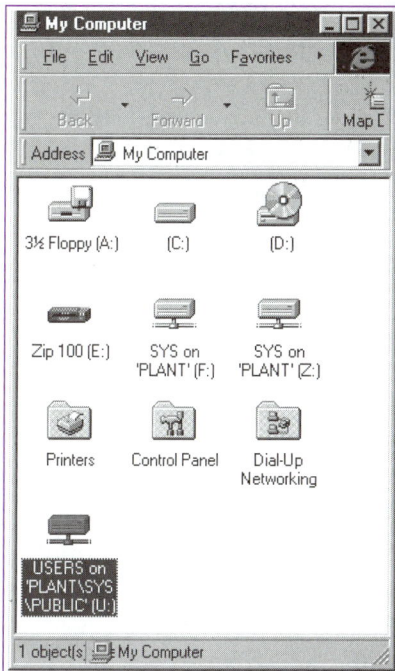

Figure 6-34

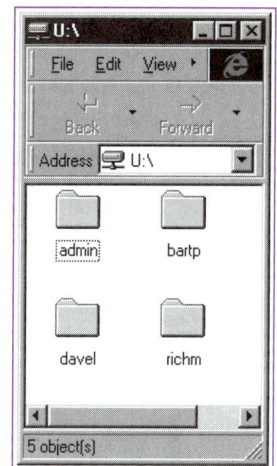

6. A **Mapping Drive** indicator will appear briefly.

7. The result of the successful drive mapping operation will be shown in the **My Computer** window. (See Figure 6-33)

8. Open your new *U:* drive by double clicking on the *U:* drive pointer shown in Figure 6-33.

9. The *Users* folder on your *SYS:* volume should open up to resemble Figure 6-34.

10. Because you did not check the **Reconnect at Login** box, this window will not be available after restarting your computer or after logging back into your server.

Chapter Summary

Novell's Network File System (NFS) is used to store data and applications for users to share throughout the network. It is another hierarchical system of container components, and is similar to a typical office's system for filing documents in filing cabinets. Some of the network file system is created during installation of the operating system, while the remainder is built as the network is designed and implemented. Files and applications on the network are shared by users.

NFS components include Servers, Volumes, Directories, Subdirectories, and Files. The server is the top level of the NFS structure. Like a filing cabinet, it organizes all the other components. Volumes are separate storage devices within the server that are similar to the cabinet drawers. Directories and subdirectories are the hanging folders, and files are the pieces of data or documents that the filing system tracks.

Volumes can be compared to DOS disk drives. The entire file system is tree-like, with directories and subdirectories branching out from the root directory. *Server.exe* is the main executable file when starting the server. It loads the system files from the DOS partition and switches to the NetWare partition's *SYS:* volume for the remaining NetWare files. NDS represents volumes on NetWare networks as Volume objects and gives them an object name. That name is a combination of the name of the server and the name of the volume, connected by an underscore. Additional volumes are automatically named *Vol1:, Vol2:,* etc., unless other names are given. The volume name is the highest level in NFS's directory structure on a server and is similar to the root directory designation in a DOS hard disk drive.

CHAPTER 6
NFS

A directory is an area on a NetWare volume where files or additional subdirectories are stored. Their main purpose is to facilitate organization. Creating a folder in Windows resembles creating a directory in NFS.

During installation, several directories, such as *SYSTEM*, *PUBLIC*, *LOGIN*, and *MAIL*, are created by the operating system, and the remaining organization is done by the administrator. *SYSTEM* contains the configuration files, NLMs and utilities necessary for server operation. *PUBLIC* files and programs are available to all users after they have logged in, while login files are available to anyone connected to the network regardless of their log in status. Subdirectories are directories within other directories.

The syntax for referring to NetWare volume directories requires using a colon between the volume name and the directory. For subdirectories, add a backslash between the directory and subdirectory names. Because you can refer to other servers on a network with multiple servers, the full path from the server to the file can be specified. Begin with the name of the server, followed by a slash, followed by the name of the volume, followed by a colon, followed by directory, a backslash, and finally the subdirectory.

> The actual data stored in NFS comprise the files. They are the reason the Network File System exists.

The actual data stored in NFS comprise the files. They are the reason the Network File System exists. They can be the spreadsheets, briefings, documents, or applications that network users wish to share with other network users. Managing network files with NFS is similar to managing files in Windows 95. Creating folders and managing documents by moving, copying, or navigating between them in Windows is comparable to file management in NFS. Novell's Client 32 software includes additional utilities such as **NetWare Administrator**, **FILER**, **FLAG**, **NDIR**, **NCOPY**, and **RENDIR** for managing NFS. **NetWare Administrator** and **FILER** are the two most powerful of these utilities.

Networking Terms Used in Chapter 6

Network File System (NFS)	*PUBLIC*	**NCOPY**
filing cabinet system	*LOGIN*	**RENDIR**
DOS's organizational structure	*MAIL*	effective rights
server	*SYSTEM*	last update
volume	*HOME* directory	last access
directory (small d)	*USERS*	attributes of the file
subdirectory	*SHARED*	NetWare version number
file	syntax	physical volume
centralized access	**WhoAmI**	user space restrictions
hierarchical filing system	**Logout**	Search context
server naming convention	**Authenticate**	Trustees of the Root Directory
Server.exe	**Login to Server**	drive mapping
SYS: volume	**FILER**	drive pointers
volume objects	**FLAG**	
PLANT_SYS:	**NDIR**	

CHAPTER 6
NFS

■ Chapter Review Questions

1. What is the purpose of NetWare's network file system?

2. Explain how NFS is similar to a filing cabinet.

3. What does the network file system do for its network users?

4. Define the five main NFS components found on all NetWare servers.

5. Explain the naming convention for directories and subdirectories.

6. A _____ is a physical device used for storage and either installed in or attached to the server.

7. The NetWare server initially boots up in the operating system using the *SERVER.NLM* file. True or False?

8. Servers can have only one volume—the *SYS:* volume. True or False?

9. Explain volume object naming and your resulting TPUP volume names.

10. What is the highest level in NFS's directory structure?

11. What action in Windows is similar to creating a directory in NFS?

12. Name four of the required directories automatically installed on NetWare servers.

13. Why is it likely that you will limit the size of your users' home directory?

14. Explain the naming syntax convention for referring to NetWare Volume directories in a multiple server network.

15. What is the difference between drive mapping and drive pointers?

■ Associated Chapter Problems

1. Draw a diagram that illustrates the relationship between a filing cabinet system and NetWare's network filing system.

2. Explain the term *centralized access* and its importance to users of NFS.

3. Develop a plan for the directories you intend to install in your TPUP filing system.

4. Explain how each of the filing system management utilities is used.

5. Defend the following position: "Novell's NetWare Administrator is the most useful of the network management utilities."

6. Locate and list the Name Spaces installed on your *SYS:* volume.

7. Calculate the Space in Use and Space available after locating the space limit imposed on each of your users in your *SYS:* volume.

8. Explain the concept behind drive mapping.

9. Explain drive pointer conventions concerning local disk allocation.

10. How can you ensure that a drive mapping that you want to occur each time you operate your computer is ready when you are?

CHAPTER
7
PRINTING

You have probably noticed that it is a great inconvenience when you cannot print what you want to print, wherever you want to print it. Network printing makes printing more convenient. In this chapter, you will learn to:

■ describe the Network Printing Environment.

■ configure a Network Printing Environment.

■ explain the components of Network Printing with Novell Distributed Print Services (NDPS).

■ explain the NDPS printer types.

■ contrast Public Access printers to Controlled Access printers.

■ configure NDPS.

■ setup a workstation to operate with NDPS.

■ manage print jobs using NDPS.

■ explain the management roles for printer access control.

Network Printing

Before connecting to a network, you could print only if you had a printer connected directly to a printer port on your computer. No one else could print to your printer without saving his or her work on a disk and bringing it to your computer for printing. Likewise, if someone else had a printer you wanted to use, you, too, had to do the *floppy swappy* and shuffle your disk over to that person for printing. If the file you wanted to print was too large for a floppy, you were usually unable to print it from the additional printers possibly available to you.

Once you created your Windows 95 workstations and connected them using the Cat 5 wiring and network interface cards, some of you probably began printing using the sharing feature available with Windows. If you had a printer connected to your computer, you could declare it shareable and allow your fellow workers to use it for their print jobs. Because you were printing over a network, you were *Network Printing*. But NetWare's printing capabilities involve much more than simply sharing printers.

Network printing saves money. All computer users do not need their own attached printer. They can share printer resources to save money and provide backup capability in the event a printer fails. In addition, when there are multiple types of printers available, users can print to the printer that best fits their need. One print job may need the color available from one printer, and the next may require a paper size available only on another printer.

In the preceding chapters, we discussed Novell's networking capabilities first with NetWare 5 and then with 4.11. In this chapter, it will be more beneficial to discuss printing with NetWare 4.11 first, and then with NetWare 5.

We will follow this sequence for two main reasons. First, the newer software with NetWare 5 provides many advantages over previous printing methods. Knowing something about the earlier version will provide a greater appreciation for the new product's capabilities. Secondly, it will help you recognize how much easier the newer software is to use.

> **Network printing saves money. All computer users do not need their own attached printer. They can share printer resources to save money and provide backup capability in the event a printer fails.**

Novell NetWare 4.11 Printing

NetWare 4.11 printing services are not installed by default. You must install them and execute an elaborate setup procedure to make the various printing components work together. Similar to the stand-alone computers mentioned above, networked computers can also print if they are directly connected to their own printers. Like Windows, they can also share printers if desired. However, Novell networked computers can also send output to printing devices connected directly to the network.

Printers are usually connected directly to a computer. The port used for this connection is ordinarily on the back of the computer, and is typically the first line printer port, or *LPT1*. Once you connect that computer to a network, it becomes a network object and can be shared. Often, the capability for sharing printers is sufficient justification for installing networking software. Depending on the number of LPT ports a computer has, multiple printers can be attached to computers and each can be shared on the network.

The network printing operation begins with the user's need to print something and ends with the printed material being output. There are several steps and components involved in accomplishing this operation.

Print Job

> **The print job is the most important of the individual printing components.**

The print job is the most important of the individual printing components. A *print job* is the information a user sends from his computer for printing. If a printer is not connected to his or her computer, a print job would be stored as a file on a floppy disk and carried to another computer for printing. Print jobs can be documents you created in your word processor, graphics, or database applications, as well as anything you want in hard copy format from the digital version inside your computer. In order for the job to be printed correctly, the job's format must be correct. If you are sending a job out to a company that does printing, their definition of camera-ready copy includes the format and settings they need to accomplish the job. Print jobs on the network are no different. They are normally set up according to the specifications of the printer to which the job is being sent.

NDS Print Operation Components

> **In NDS, three main components comprise a successful print operation. They are the Printer, the Print Queue, and the Print Server.**

In NDS, three main components comprise a successful print operation. They are the *printer*, the *print queue*, and the *print server*. Each is an NDS object and has information stored about its features in the NDS database.

Printer

The printer is the device to which the print job is sent. It accomplishes the printing. It can be a laser or ink jet printer, plotter, engraver, or any other similar device capable of performing the necessary print job. All printers on the network should have a printer object. Its name and attributes are viewed in NWAdmin by checking the details pages for that object.

Workstations with directly connected printers are those computers with printers connected to an LPT port on the computer itself. When a computer prints to a direct printer, it bypasses the network altogether. This helps reduce network traffic and is the fastest way to print.

> A local printer is one that is directly connected to the network's print server.

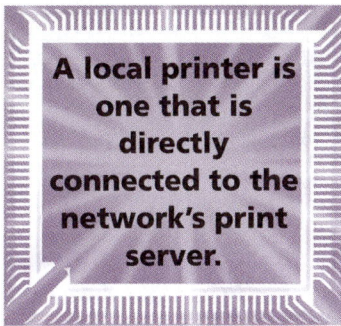

There are three ways printers can be connected to the network—through a *local connection*, a *remote connection*, or a *direct connection*. A local printer is one that is directly connected to the network's print server. While this term may seem confusing, "local" refers to the computer that runs the print server software (**PSERVER**).

On the other hand, when a computer with a printer that is shared over the network is printed to by someone on a second computer, that second printer is printing to a remote printer. Remote printers are available only when the workstation to which they are attached is turned on and attached to the network. A software program must also be running on the workstation itself to "announce" that there is a network available printer in operation from the workstation.

Some other printers are *network ready*, with a network card already installed, and can be attached directly to the network cabling. When so connected, these printers are called direct connection printers and can be used by authorized network workstations. Because they have their own network interface card, they take one of the licensed connections allowed by the network software license.

Print Queue

When you go somewhere and have to stand in a line, you participate in a *queue*. We prefer that the operation of that line be fair, and that the first one there be served before all others, but that does not always happen. Sometimes someone with higher priority goes ahead of the first one in the line. Print queues operate in the same way. It is an area where print jobs go when waiting for a printer to become available.

The existence of an area for print jobs to go when waiting for printers implies that multiple computers are able to send jobs to printers. In addition, multiple jobs can be sent from those computers for printing. *Print job prioritization* is then necessary. If you own the printer it is obvious that you should be able to print your jobs first. Your alternative would be not sharing your printer at all. Then it would always be available to you and your jobs would always be given top priority.

Print Server

Just as guards can stop people from cutting ahead of you in lines, there is an *order keeper* for maintaining smooth print queue operation. The print server keeps the printer and print queue working without interruption. It monitors the print server and the print queue, and sends a print job waiting in a print queue to the printer when the printer is finished and it is that job's turn.

In NetWare 4.11, a print server is a computer running **PSERVER** software that can monitor up to 256 printers. Up to five of these printers can be connected directly to the server itself. These five are called local printers. The remaining printers are called remote printers, and they can be connected to other servers, to network computers, or directly to the network.

In the network operating system software, *PSERVER.NLM* is the *NetWare Loadable Module (NLM)* that enables a NetWare file server to operate as a print server as well. It is executed at the server and loads such print server information as passwords, user lists, and applicable printers serviced by the printer into memory.

Activity 7-1   Printer Setup (4.11 Accomplish, All others Read)

1. Start NWAdmin and log into TPUP-HQS as your Admin user.

2. Highlight the *TPUP-HQS* Organization Container.

3. From the menu bar, select **Object**, **Create**, and **Printer**. You should arrive at the window shown in Figure 7-1.

Figure 7-1

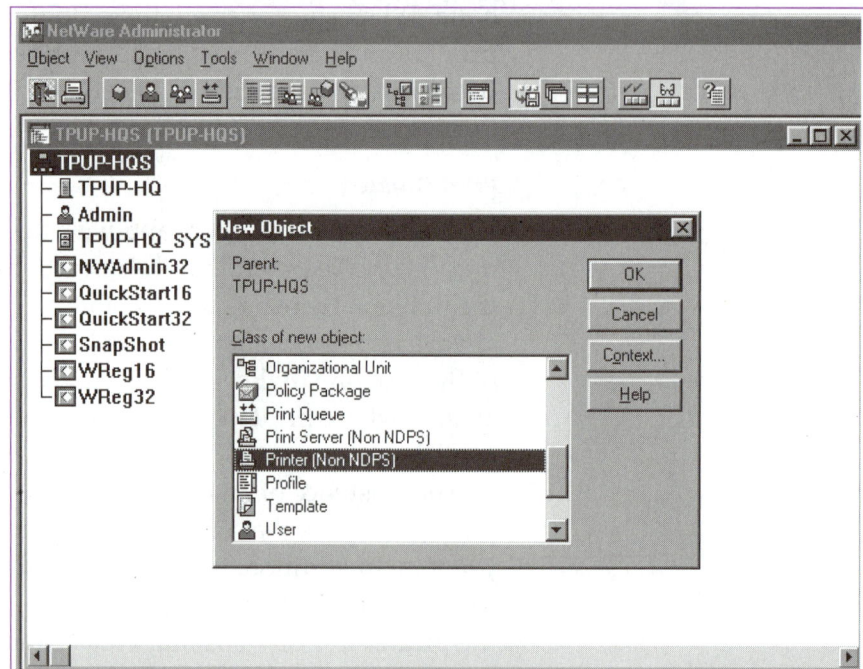

4. Type in the name of your printer (**HPLJ6** will be used in this example), and click the **Create** button, as shown in Figure 7-2.

Figure 7-2

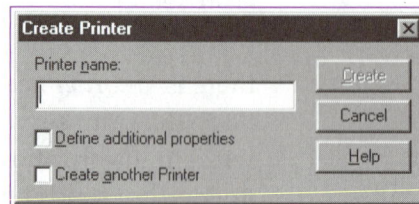

5. This will result in the *NWAdmin* screen.

6. Click the **Add Print Queue** button on the Toolbar to continue setting up network printing. Notice that a *Queues* directory is added to the *TPUP_SYS* Volume, and a subdirectory with a randomly generated name is also created. See Figure 7-3.

Figure 7-3

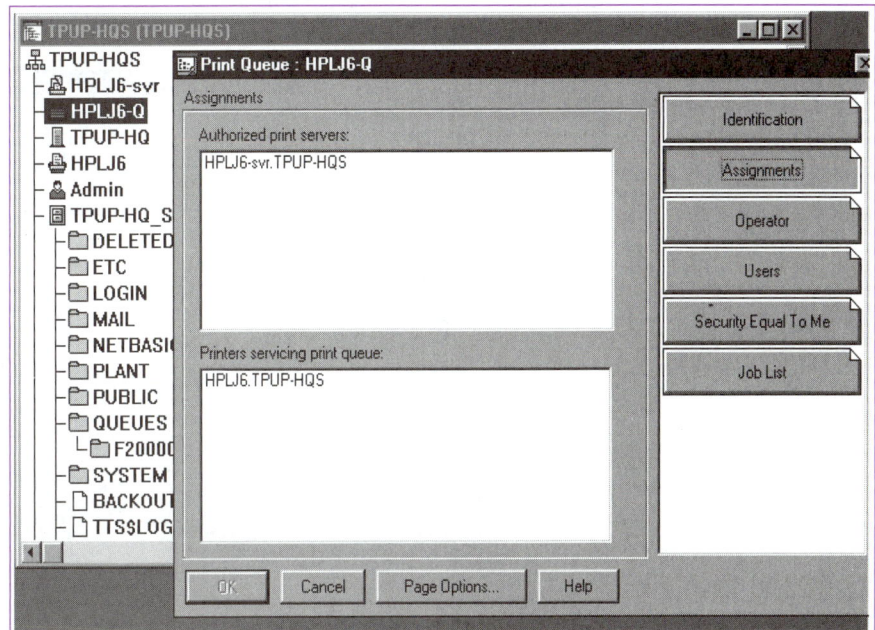

7. In **NWAdmin**, continue by adding a print server (*HPLJ6-svr* in the example). Add the printer assignment to the printer as shown in Figure 7-4. Then add the server to the printer queue as indicated.

Figure 7-4

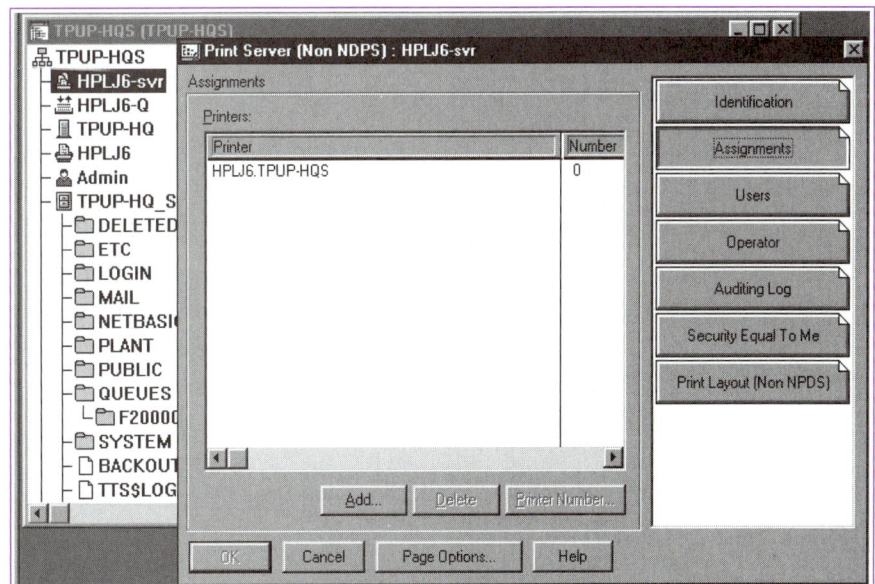

8. Verify that all three objects are linked together by returning to the details window for the printer and ensuring that the printer, print queue, and print server are all shown linked together. See Figure 7-5.

Figure 7-5

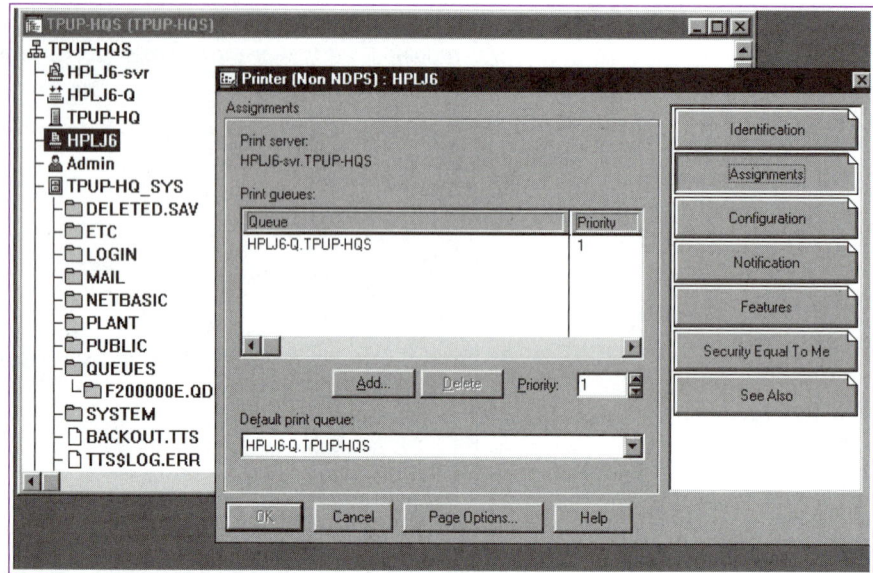

9. At the server console, type **LOAD PSERVER**.

10. The print server software (*PSERVER.NLM*) will load and request the name of the server. When you press **<ENTER>** with your current context of *TPUP-HQS*, the server finds your print server (*HPLJ6-svr* in our case).

11. It offers you your printer in a **Contents of current context** window. Highlight the print server you wish to load and press **<ENTER>**.

12. An **Attaching to the network** window appears while it loads the server. An **Available Options** window appears giving you Printer Status or Print Server Information.

13. Now it is necessary to allow the workstations access to printing. At the workstation, click on **My Computer** and scroll through your **Z:** drive to the *Public* directory's folder, and then to the *NPTWIN95.EXE* file as shown in Figure 7-6.

Figure 7-6

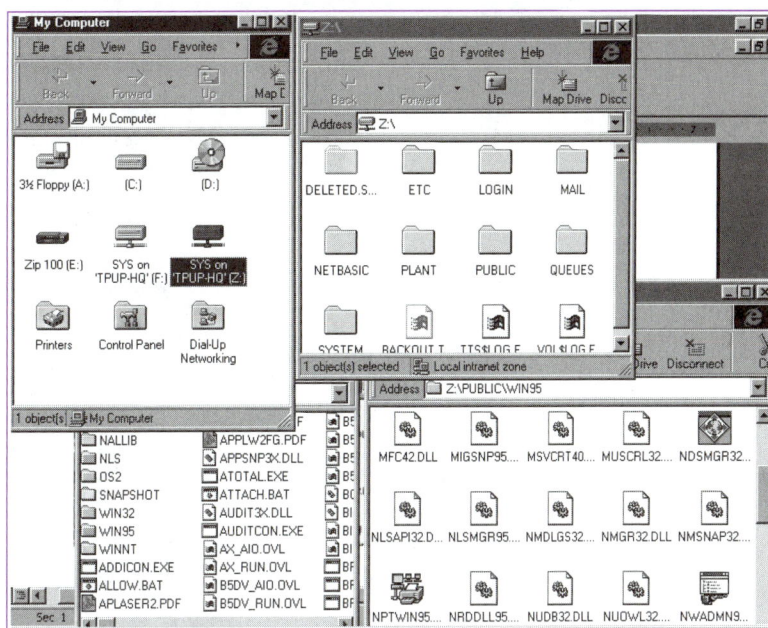

14. Right click and hold on the *NPTWIN95.EXE* file, then drag it to your desktop to place a shortcut there for future use. While in this folder, you could also put shortcuts to the other two items you will be using—*NDSMGR32.EXE* and *NWADMN95.EXE*.

15. Once you have the shortcuts on your desktop, close the *Z:* drive windows and the **My Computer** window, and double click on the **NPTWIN95.EXE** shortcut that you just placed on your desktop.

16. The NetWare **Nprinter Manager** window will appear, offering you the **Add Network Printer** option as shown in Figure 7-7. Select the **NDS Printer** window by clicking in the radio button next to the selection and then clicking in the **Browse** box to the right of the selection box.

Figure 7-7

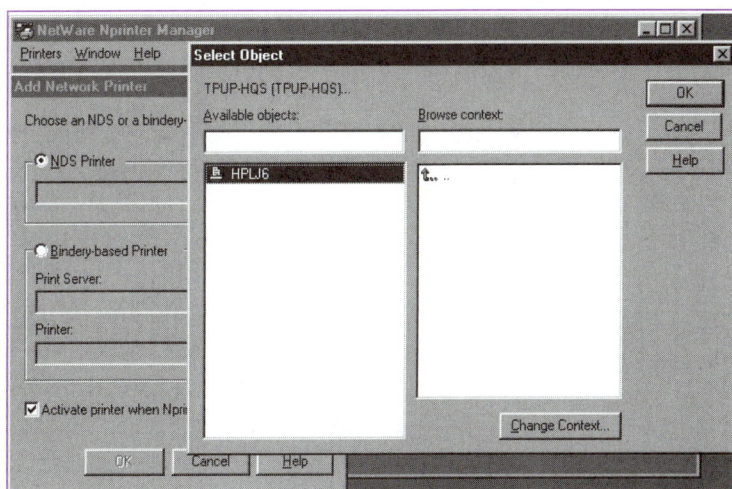

17. When you click **OK**, the *Select Object* appears. Double clicking that printer object puts the information for that printer in your NetWare *Nprinter Manager* window as indicated in Figure 7-8. This verifies proper printer operation. Viewing the printer status at the server in **PSERVER** will also give additional information about the printer's status.

Figure 7-8

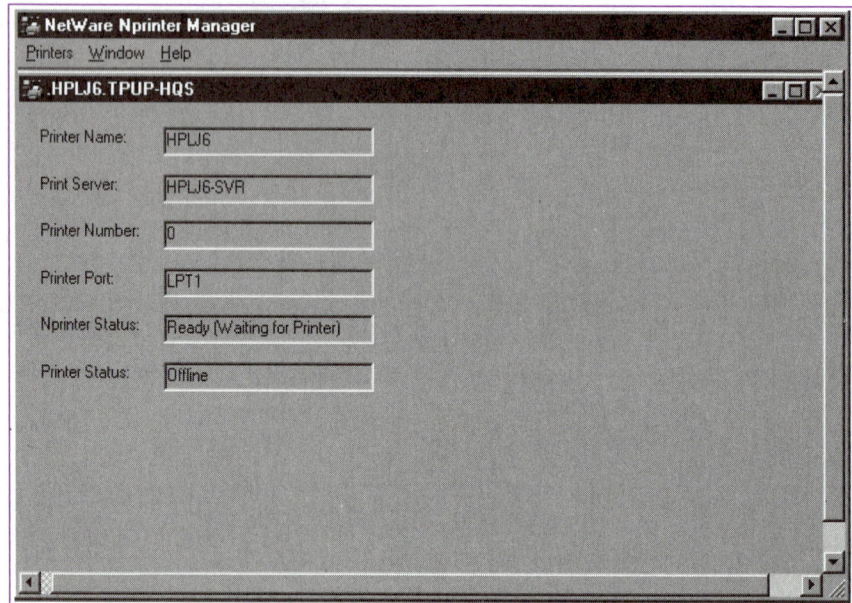

18. Closing the Figure 7-8 window will not take the printer out of operation. *Terminate and Stay Resident (TSR)* portions will keep the printer available until you shut down the workstation. You can also automate the activation of the **NPTRWIN95** by entering its use in your *AUTOEXEC.BAT* file or the Windows Startup group.

OPTIONAL

19. If you wish, you can add that same network printer to your other networked computers. Do this by going to your *My Computer* window and then to your *Printers* folder. Highlight the printer you are adding to your network (*LaserJet 6*, in this case), right click, and select properties as shown in the third window below. Next to the *Print to the following port* window, press the **Add Port** button. The fourth window below appears. When you click the **Browse** button next to the *Specify the network path to the printer* window, the *Browse for Printer* window below appears. Browse to the printer you are using as shown in Figure 7-9, and double click.

Figure 7-9

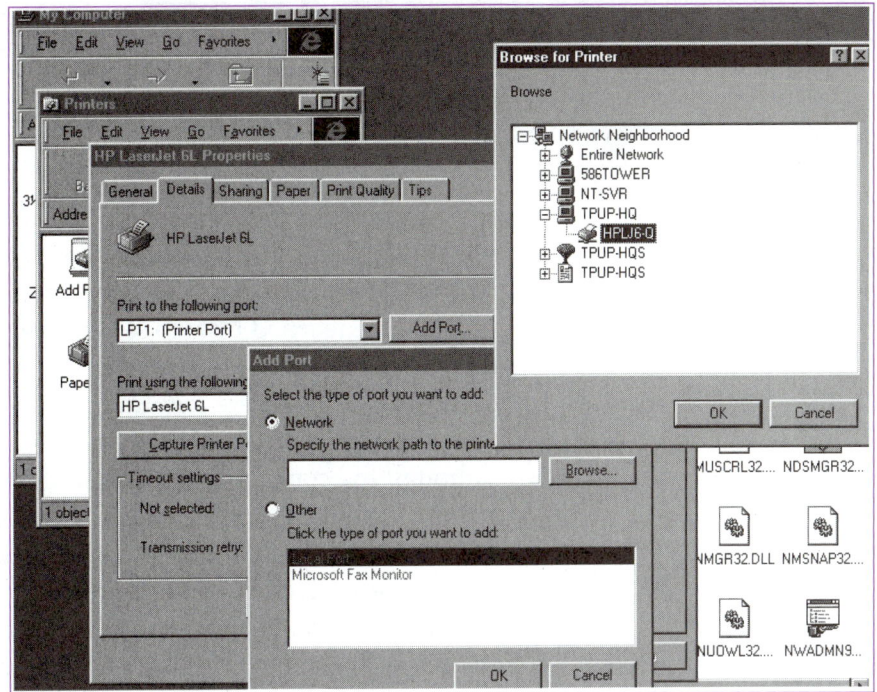

20. The printer's path is added to the ***Add port*** window. Pressing **<ENTER>** will complete the network printer setup, and your computer will now print over the network to that printer. See Figure 7-10.

Figure 7-10

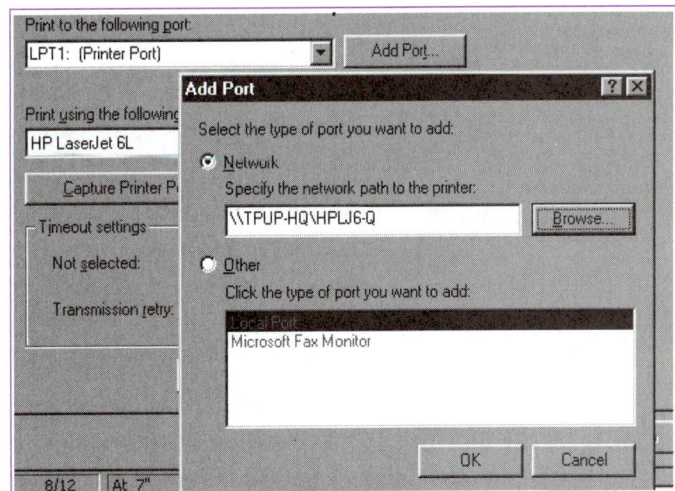

Novell Distributed Print Services (NDPS)

Now that you have followed the procedures for setting up printing in NetWare 4.11, you should have a feeling for how network printing works. As mentioned earlier, the print job is the reason for the printing operation. Without something to print, there would be no need for printers. Being able to direct the print job to the appropriate printer is the reason for network printing.

You have learned how to set up printing in a 4.11 network. There are many elements involved in initiating the process. All of the elements must be there and functioning before the process works—something to print, a waiting line for print jobs, and an output device. Although the concept is easy, often the implementation is not. Most printing problems arise from difficulties with the print queue.

Novell's NetWare 5 does away with the print queue completely. It is no longer necessary to create the main pieces in what became a "printing puzzle." Linking a printer, print queue, print server, and printers is no longer the difficult process you witnessed in the first half of this chapter. *Novell Distributed Print Services (NDPS)* replaces many of the setup steps from NetWare 4 operating systems.

NDPS has a *printer agent* instead of the NetWare 4 printer, print queue, and print server. The printer agent serves to combine all of these elements in to one object. NDPS focuses on the printer, and manages its configuration and use through NDS. NDPS handles the drivers used at the workstations, with the result that print drivers are no longer stored directly at a user's location. Instead, they are downloaded to the workstation by NDPS before printing.

Because NDPS reduces the setup time and maintenance actions required to maintain the printing environment, NetWare 5's printing operations render the newer operating system more "administrator friendly" and more efficient to use. Setting up printers and print queue logic was often the administrator's most unpleasant chore, and troubleshooting was dreaded by even the best administrator. The simplicity of the new printing operation both improves network performance and reduces printing problems.

> **Novell's NetWare 5 does away with the print queue completely.**

> **NDPS has a printer agent instead of the NetWare 4 printer, print queue, and print server.**

NDPS Components

There are four basic components in the NDPS printing operation. They are the Printer Agent, the NDPS manager, the Gateway, and the NDPS Broker. Newer printers have NDPS printer capabilities embedded in their hardware. Thus, they operate immediately in an NDPS printer environment.

Printer Agent

The printer agent represents Novell's efforts to focus printing on the printer. As mentioned above, the printer agent combines three separate items from the Novell NetWare 4.0 printing process. These are the printer, the print queue, and the print server. As in the print queue process, every printer must have an NDS object that represents it before it can be printed to over the Novell network. In NetWare 5, this object is the printer agent. Each printer can have only one network printer agent, and each printer agent can represent only one printer.

Printer agents can be software items running on a server that represent printers attached directly to the network, to servers, or to workstations. They also can be embedded in the printer attached directly to the network.

Printer agents manage the processing of the print job. They also manage many of the printer's own internal functions, and they respond to network clients' requests for information about their print job status or about the capabilities of the printer. Events can be set up so that the relevant individuals are notified when jobs finish, when problems are encountered, or when a job's status changes. The new printer agent allows printing to a wider range of printers. Printer agents also ensure scalability of the printing environment when changing from LAN to WAN or even Enterprise situations.

NDPS Manager

The *NDPS manager* creates and makes available for play the printers (printer agents) that it manages. Like the printer agent, the NDPS manager is also an NDS object that the administrator creates. Then it is through the manager that the printer agent is created. Therefore, an NDPS manager must be created in NDS *before* the server-based printer agent is created.

Each NDPS manager can control an unlimited number of printer agents. A server can have only one NDPS manager loaded. NDPS manager is a utility that runs on a NetWare server when printer agents are created in NWAdmin. It can also be loaded manually through the server's console command line when controlling printers attached directly to that server. If NDPS manager is not running when you create the first printer agent, NetWare will ask you if you want it loaded.

Gateways

For printers whose agent is not hardware-embedded and thus not "NDPS aware" right out of the box, Novell has created *Gateways*. Gateways are configured to provide printer specifics on the network. They translate requests sent to the printers into printer-recognizable machine code. Gateways allow non-NDPS-aware printers to receive print jobs over the network, and facilitate their management and use.

Novell NetWare 5 includes three gateways that provide access to printers that are not NDPS-aware. They are the Hewlett Packard, Xerox, and Novell gateways. The first two are company-specific and provide more detailed information on those company's printers for use on NDPS networks. Novell's gateway is for printers with neither NDPS nor a specific company gateway.

NOTE

For backward compatibility with earlier versions of Novell's operating system, you can still use the NDS print queue and printer objects. They are set up using the techniques mentioned in the 4.11 portion of this chapter.

NOTE

Gateways allow non-NDPS-aware printers to receive print jobs over the network, and facilitate their management and use.

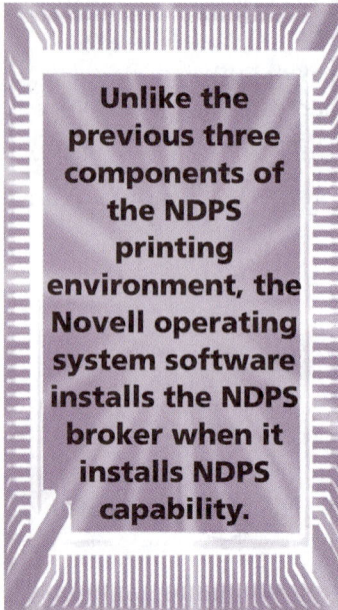

NDPS Broker

Unlike the previous three components of the NDPS printing environment, the Novell operating system software installs the NDPS broker when it installs NDPS capability.

Unlike the previous three components of the NDPS printing environment, the Novell operating system software installs the *NDPS broker* when it installs NDPS capability. In addition, each time the server starts, the NDPS broker logs in and authenticates itself for each of three services it provides: *Service Registry Services (SRS)*, *Event Notification Services (ENS)*, and *Resource Management Services (RMS)*. The services supported by the broker start when NDPS is loaded. When installing NDPS on an additional server, the software verifies that another broker is needed before one is created. If the new server will be no more than three hops (connections through three network devices), it will not add another broker.

Service Registry Services (SRS) allow printers to announce their own presence on the network so that they can be identified and used by potential network clients.

Event Notification Services (ENS) allow printers to communicate with users about their print jobs. NetWare pop-up windows, log files, and e-mail notifications are available through ENS.

Resource Management Services (RMS) provide central distribution of printing resources. Some of these resources include print drivers, definition files, fonts, and banner use.

NDPS Printer Types

There are two types of printer configurations available under NDPS. They are both available to the hardware-installed NDPS-aware machines as well as to the software-activated non-NDPS-aware machines. The two types of configurations are Public Access and Controlled Access printers.

Public Access Printers

... the Public Access printer is available to anyone on the network, without restrictions.

As the name implies, the *Public Access printer* is available to anyone on the network, without restrictions. This type does not have an NDS object or any security levels available. However, these printers provide "plug and print" capability, and are immediately available to anyone. They are managed through NetWare Administrator using the Tools menu.

Controlled Access Printers

As the name implies, *Controlled Access printers* allow the network administrator a higher degree of control than that available with Public Access printers. Unlike the Public Access printers, Controlled Access printers have an NDS object associated with them, and the full range of network security selections and printer configurations is available for their use.

When you create a Controlled Access printer in an NDS container, all users in that container automatically have access to the printer. All other network users must be granted access to use Controlled Access printers.

A Public Access printer can be converted to a Controlled Access printer by creating an NDS object for the printer. You then use NetWare Administrator to change the printer's associated values.

Activity 7-2	Network Printer Setup (NetWare 5)

1. Start NWAdmin and log into TPUP as Admin.

2. Highlight the *PLANT* Organization Container as shown in Figure 7-11.

Figure 7-11

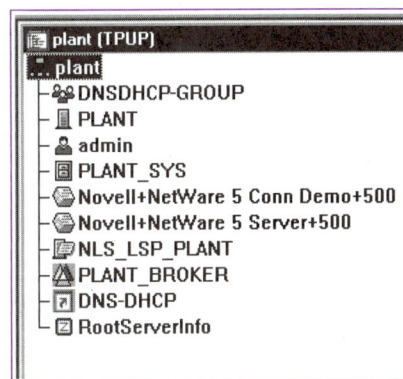

3. Click the menu bar, select **Object**, **Create**, and **NDPS Manager** to display the window shown in Figure 7-12. Click on the **OK** button.

Figure 7-12

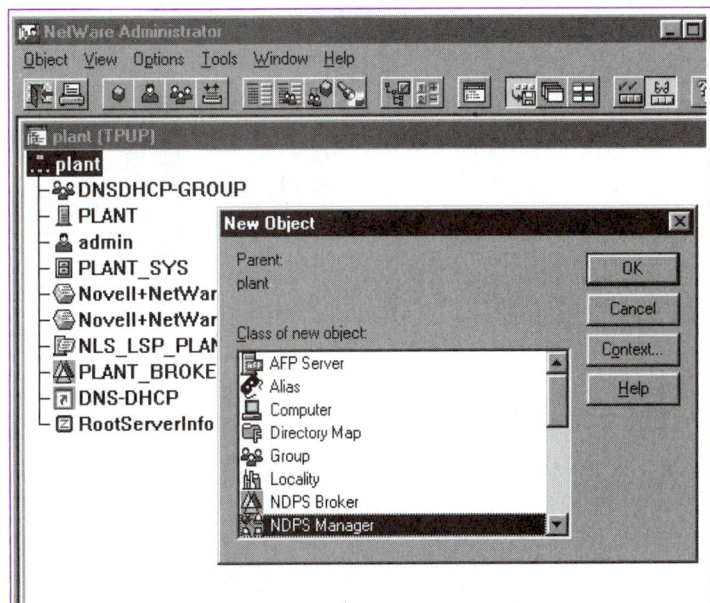

4. Enter the NDPS Manager name, press the **Browse** button on the *Resident Server* window, and double click on the **Plant** server icon. This loads the server information into the *Resident server* window. (See Figure 7-13.)

Figure 7-13

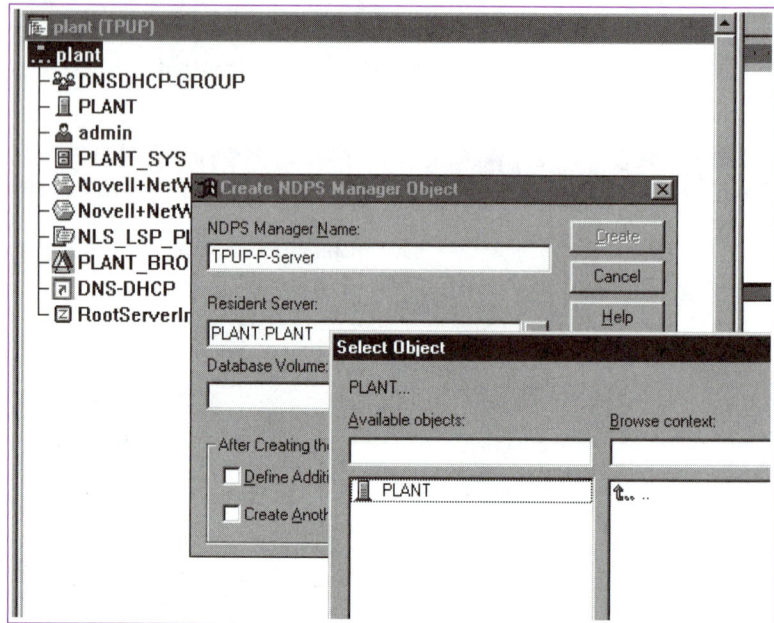

5. Click the **Browse** button on the side of the *Database Volume* window. This loads the volume information into the *Database Volume* window. (See Figure 7-14.)

Figure 7-14

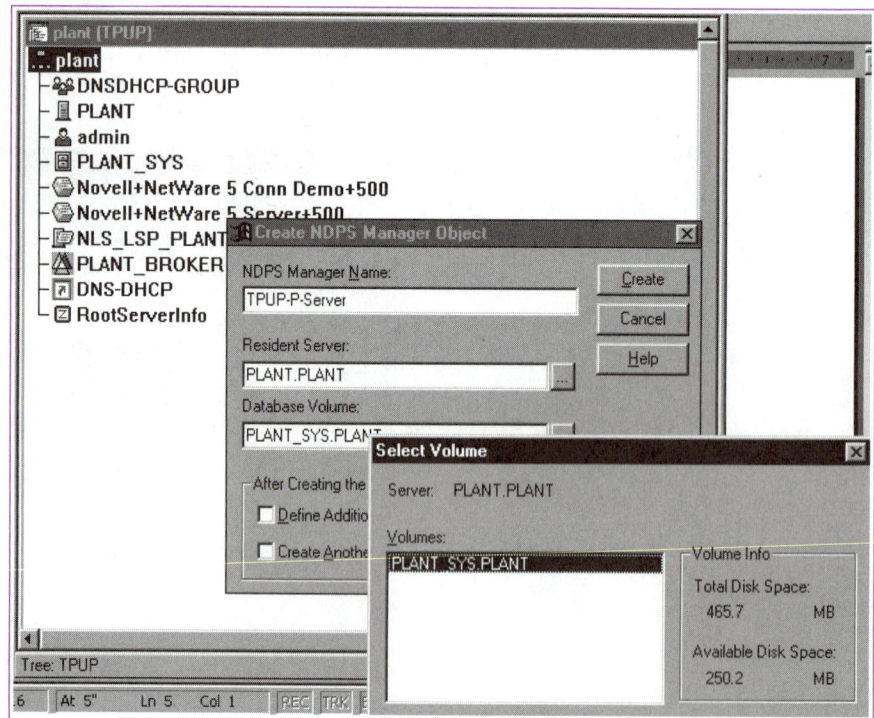

6. Click the **Create** button and create the *TPUP-P-Server* as shown in Figure 7-15.

Figure 7-15

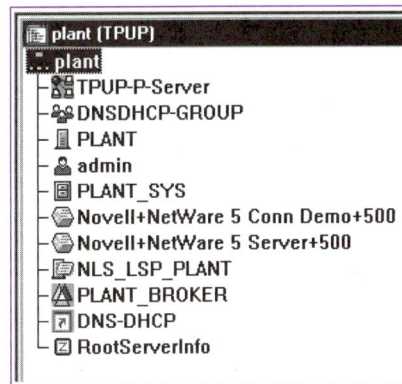

7. To create a controlled printer as the first printer managed by this manager, select **Object**, **Create NDPS Printer**, and **Create Printer agent**. Use the browse buttons to locate the gateway and NDPS manager name. (See Figure 7-16.)

Figure 7-16

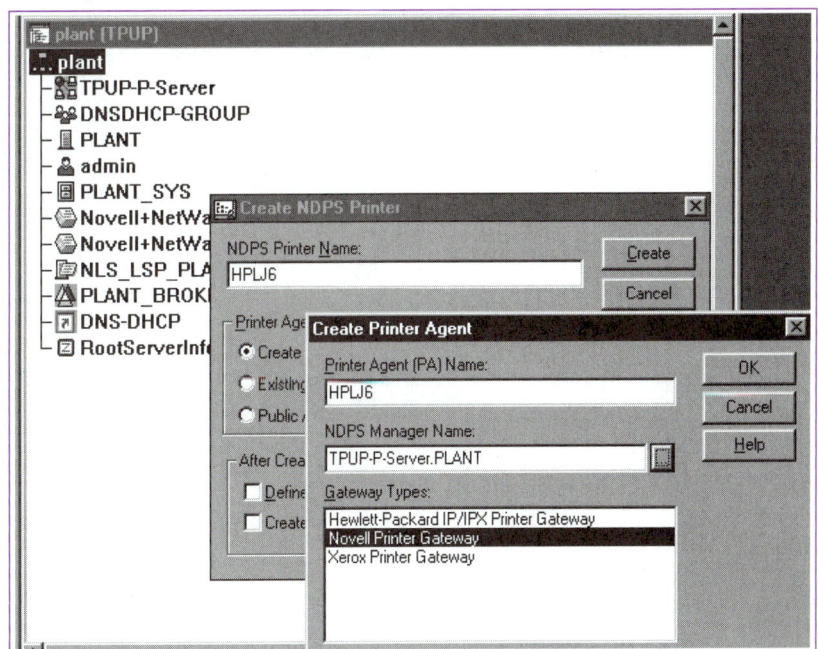

8. The window in Figure 7-17 appears, informing you that NDPS manager is not loaded and offering to load it for you. Click the **OK** button.

Figure 7-17

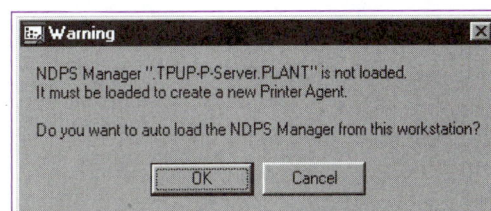

9. The informational window shown in Figure 7-18 appears.

Figure 7-18

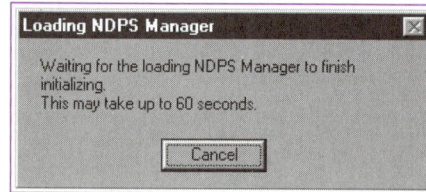

10. When loading is complete, the window shown in Figure 7-19 will appear. Click the **OK** button.

Figure 7-19

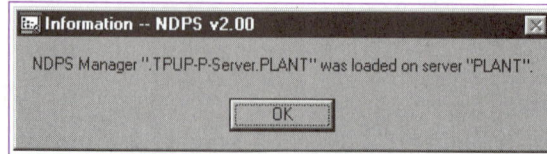

11. Check to see that the **HPLJ6** icon was loaded in the container you chose. By double clicking on the printer object, the printer information pages appear as shown in Figure 7-20.

Figure 7-20

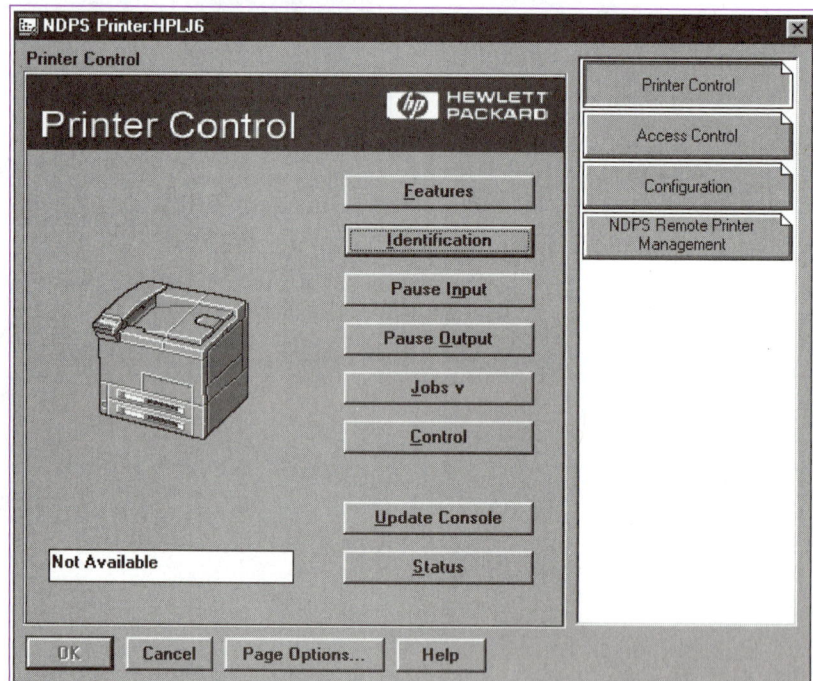

12. To verify the information contained in your new manager, double click its manager object in **NetWare Administrator**. The window in Figure 7-21 appears.

Figure 7-21

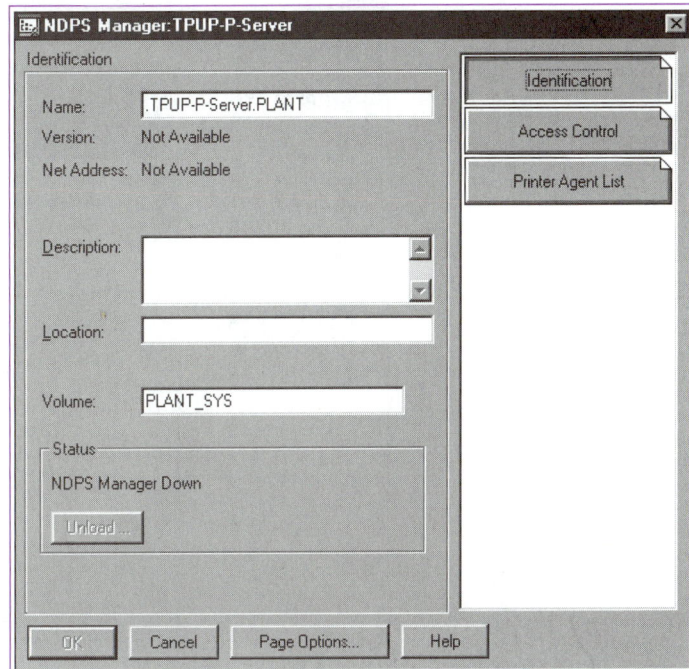

13. Click on **Access Control** to see the window in Figure 7-22. This step is for information only.

Figure 7-22

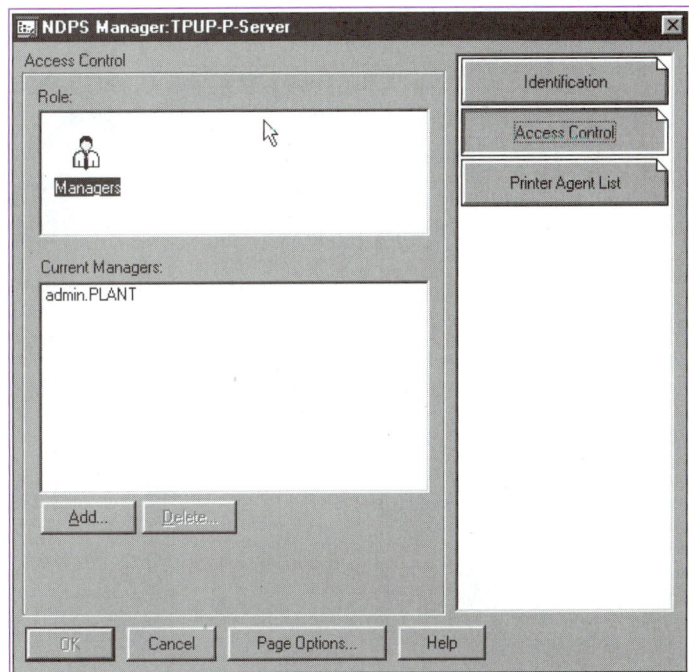

14. Click on the **Printer Agent List**. Figure 7-23 shows a printer error on the HPLJ6 printer. This step is for information only at this point.

Figure 7-23

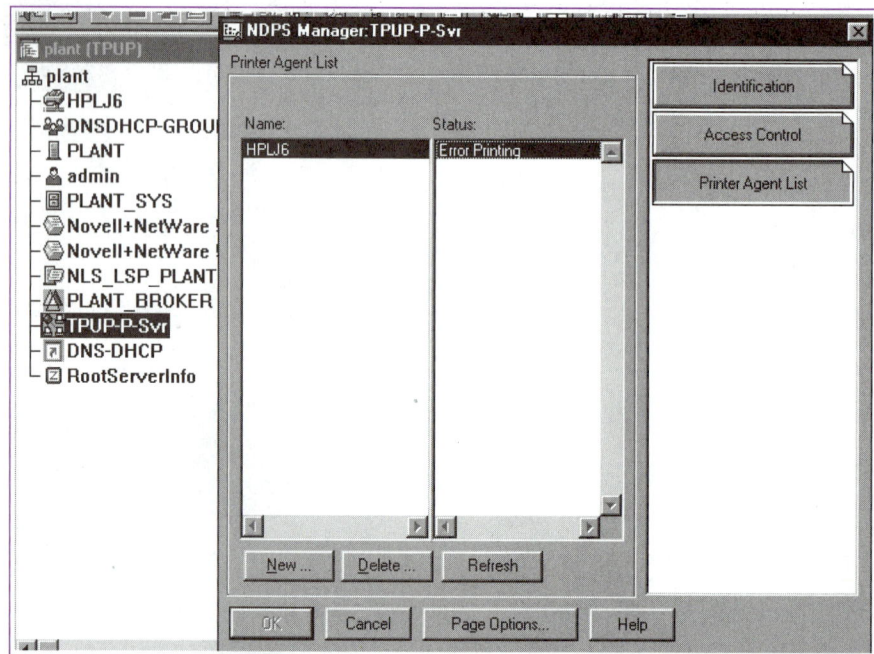

15. To create a Public Access printer as the next printer managed by this manager, double click on the NDPS manager name. Type the name of the Printer Agent as shown in Figure 7-24 (**Brother 720**, or the appropriate printer for your lab).

Figure 7-24

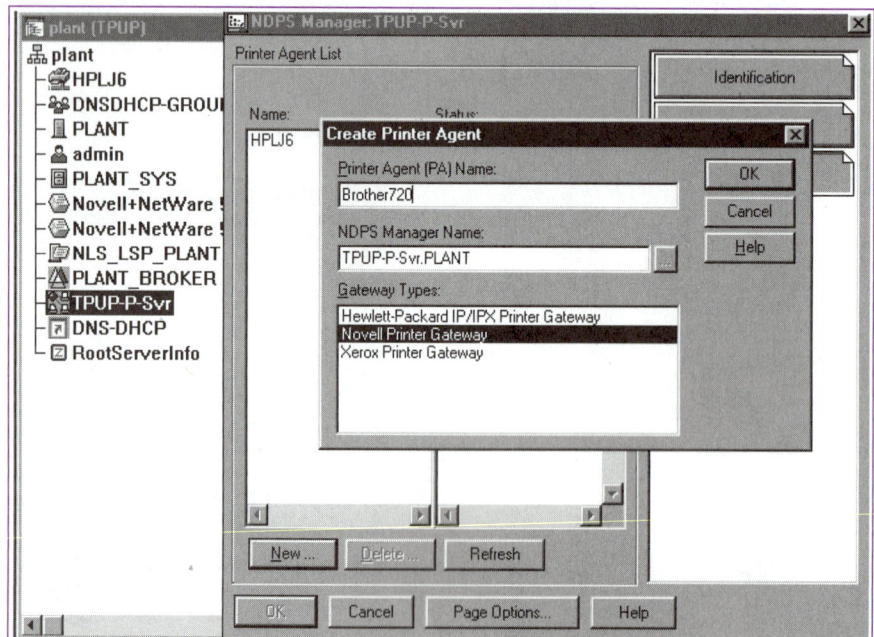

16. Clicking the **OK** button will cause the window in Figure 7-25 to appear, where the printer type is selected. Scroll down to your printer type, and it will be added to the listing of printer agents.

Figure 7-25

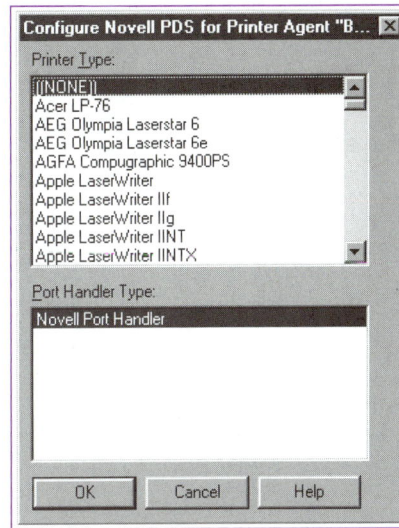

17. Choose the appropriate printer port in the window shown in Figure 7-26. Leave the **Remote** radio button selected and click on the **Next >** button to continue.

Figure 7-26

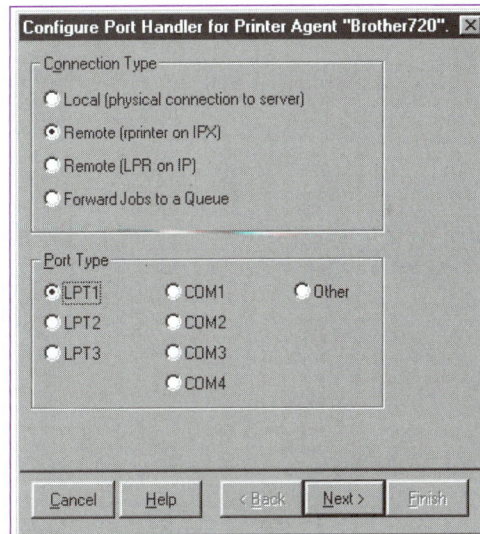

18. Select (or leave alone) the *SAP* name and ***Network Address Restriction*** as shown in Figure 7-27. Click on the **Next >** button.

Figure 7-27

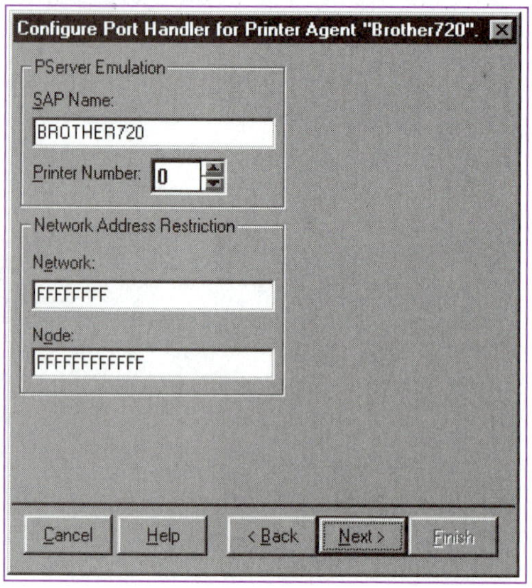

19. Select the correct *IRQ* number. If you do not know it, select **None** (polled mode). Click on the **Finish** button. (See Figure 7-28.)

Figure 7-28

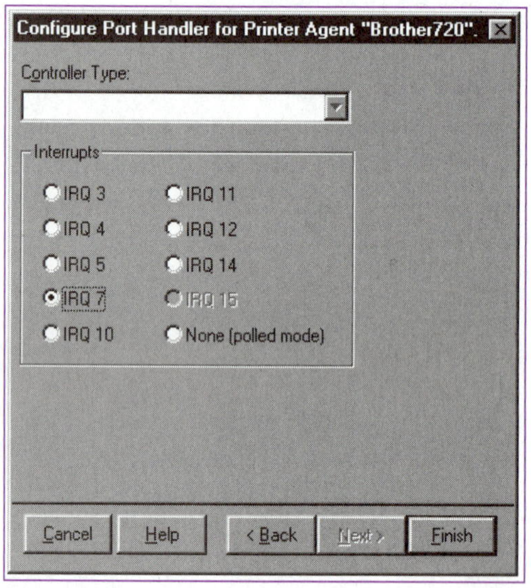

20. Verify the information in the manager windows.

Workstation Configuration

NDPS includes a *database* of printer configuration information that includes printer drivers for Windows 3.1, Windows 95, and Windows NT operating systems. Additional drivers may be added to this database as they become available. This configuration information can be downloaded to the workstations and automatically updated as new drivers are obtained.

Workstations must have the Novell Client (version 2.2 or higher) in order to use NDPS.

Workstations must have the Novell Client (version 2.2 or higher) in order to use NDPS. The workstation can be configured to use NDPS printers. This is accomplished either by setting NDS to automatically download and configure printing automatically, or by using Novell Printer Manager to manually set up the workstation for printing. NDPS printer objects can be set to be automatically updated so that users do not have to install or configure printers at their workstation.

The automatically updated option is selected by viewing the details of the container object at the printer manager location. Click on the NDPS Remote Printer Management options page. Choose the settings to update or limit the printer selection on the workstations as desired. Click the **OK** button when complete. (See Figure 7-29.)

Figure 7-29

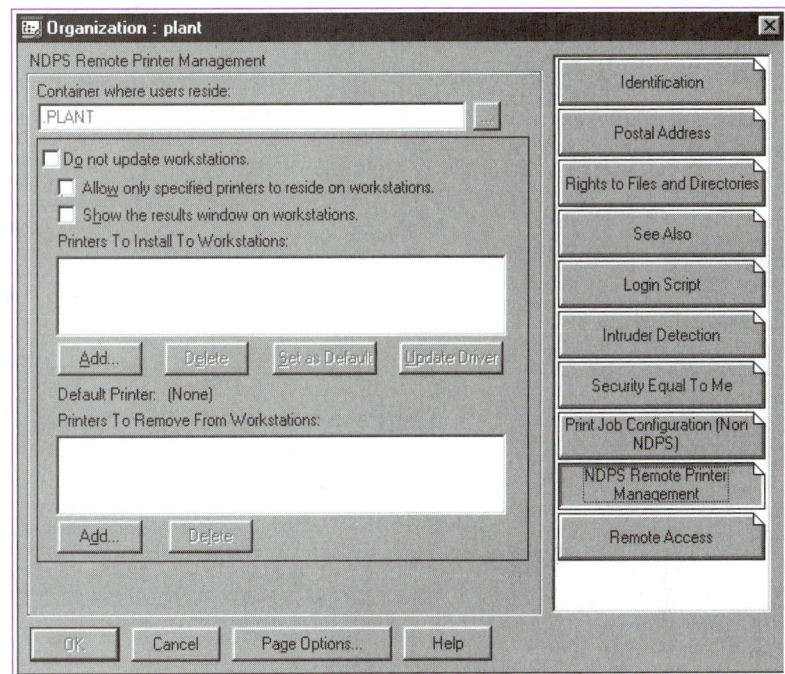

NDPS printer objects can be set to be automatically updated so that users do not have to install or configure printers at their workstation.

Managing NDPS Printing

... the duties and responsibilities of managers and operators, as well as their capabilities, are greater than those of users.

NDPS allows every element of the printing process to be managed. This includes managing access first to the printer, and then to the print jobs.

When managing printer access, there are three roles available under the *Access Control* window of the printer object. (See Figure 7-30.) You will note that the *Managers* and *Operators* role has only *admin.plant* as a user, while the *Users* role also has all of the residents of the *PLANT* container as current users. This is important, because the duties and responsibilities of managers and operators, as well as their capabilities, are greater than those of users.

Managers usually have the most control over printer objects. They are usually the ones who create and manage the printer. This includes configuration, troubleshooting problems, creating profiles, and creating, modifying, and deleting printer configurations.

Operators perform the second most important role with respect to access levels. They maintain the printer on a day-to-day basis. They reorder jobs, abort printing, restart the printer, and pause or reinitialize the printer.

Finally, the user sends, reconfigures, or removes his own print jobs. Users can move print jobs only to a lower priority status, never to a higher one.

Figure 7-30

> **Managers usually have the most control over printer objects.**
>
> **Operators perform the second most important role with respect to access levels.**

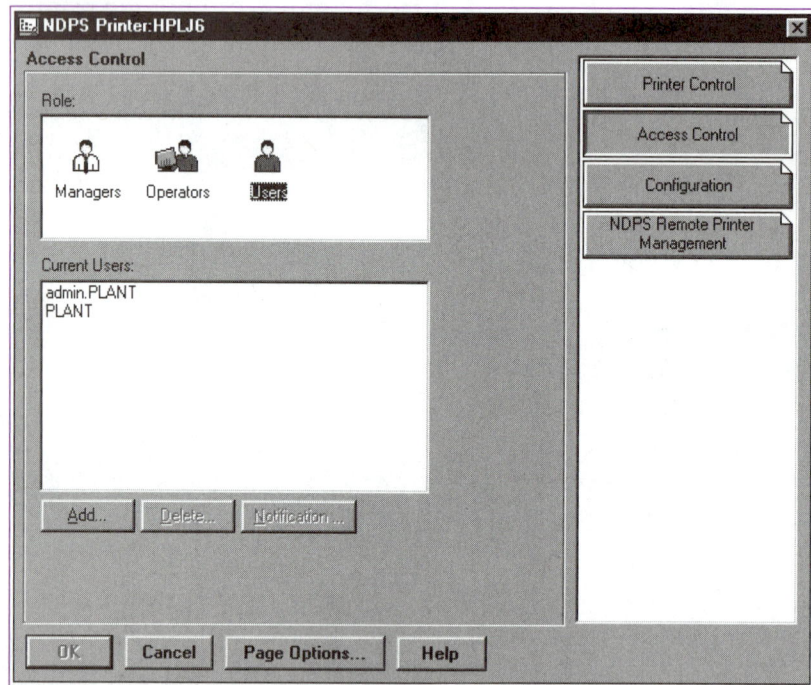

Chapter Summary

In this chapter, we examined network printing. Without network printing, you would have to do the "floppy swappy," shuffling floppy disks from one computer to another in order to print. Network printing allows multiple users to access a company's resources and tailor their printer output by selecting the appropriate printers. Because of the logical development for adding and maintaining printers in the NetWare 4.11 printing environment, we began by creating a 4.11 print setup. NetWare 4.11 printing is not installed by default, but through a series of steps and procedures. Networked computers can print directly to their own printers if one is attached directly, but they can also use printers attached to other computers. The printer port typically used for connecting printers is LPT1. The ability to share printers over a network alone often justifies installing networking software. The print job is what needs to be printed.

Without a print job, printing would be unnecessary. Print jobs consist of anything you want to transform into a hard copy format from the digital information inside your computer. Print jobs must be formatted correctly for the printer doing the job.

In NDS there are three main components used in a successful print operation: the printer, the print queue, and the print server. The printer is the device to which the print job is sent. It can be a laser or ink jet printer, plotter, engraver, or other similar device that creates output. Printers can be connected to the network in three ways: through a local connection, remote connection, or direct connection. Local printers are connected directly to the print server computer's printer port. Remote printers are connected to the printer port of a workstation or file server. Direct-connected printers are network ready and plug right in to the network wiring. The print queue is a print job's waiting area. Print job prioritization is necessary if someone must print before someone else. The print server is the order keeper. *PSERVER.NLM* is the NLM that enables servers to operate as a print server.

> **In NDS there are three main components used in a successful print operation: the printer, the print queue, and the print server.**

In NDPS, the difficult process of adding multiple pieces to the printing puzzle is replaced by a process that focuses on the printer. Linking the printer, print server, and print queue is no longer necessary. They are replaced by a printer agent object. NDPS handles the drivers used at the workstation and removes the need for updating workstations individually.

There are four basic components in the NDPS printing system: the printer agent, the NDPS manager, the Gateway, and the NDPS broker. Some printers have their NDPS capabilities embedded in their hardware. The printer agent combines the printer, print server, and print queue into one NDS object. Printer agents can be software items running on a server that represent printers attached directly to the network, to servers, or to workstations, or they can be embedded in the printer attached directly to the network cabling. Printer agents manage the processing of the print job. The NDPS Manager creates and makes available the printers that it manages. NDPS is also an NDS object created by the administrator. Printer agents are created through the NDPS manager, so the manager must be created before the first agent is created. Managers can control an unlimited number of printer agents, but a server can have only one NDPS manager loaded. The NDPS manager is a utility that runs on the server. Gateways are for printers without the NDPS-aware hardware installed. It is a software equivalent which translates requests sent to printers into printer recognizable machine code. NDPS Brokers are installed with NDPS and are loaded each time NDPS is loaded as the server is started.

> **There are four basic components in the NDPS printing system: the printer agent, the NDPS manager, the Gateway, and the NDPS broker.**

There are two types of printer configurations available under NDPS: Public Access printers and Controlled Access printers.

> **There are two types of printer configurations available under NDPS: Public Access printers and Controlled Access printers.**

Networking Terms Used in Chapter 7

floppy swappy
network printing
LPT1
print job
printer
print queue
print server
local printers connection
remote printers connection
direct connection
network ready
queue
print job prioritization
order keeper
PSERVER.NLM

NetWare Loadable Module
   (NLM)
NPTWIN95.EXE
NDSMGR32.EXE
NWADMN95.EXE
Terminate and Stay Resident
   (TSR)
Novell Distributed Print
   Services (NDPS)
printer agent
NDPS manager
gateways
NDPS broker
Service Registry Services (SRS)

Event Notification Services
   (ENS)
Resource Management Ser-
   vices (RMS)
Public Access printers
Controlled Access printers
SAP
IRQ
polled mode
database
NDPS remote printer management
managers
operators
users

■ Chapter Review Questions

1. Explain how you would print to a printer not connected to your computer if you did not have a network.

2. What is the *floppy swappy*?

3. What are the benefits of network printing?

4. When is network printing installed?

5. Which port is the most commonly used port for printers?

6. Describe a print job.

7. What are the three main components of a successful print operation?

8. Describe the three ways printers can be connected to a network.

9. Define *Network Ready*.

10. Explain print queue operations.

11. How many printers can a print server monitor?

12. What NLM enables servers to operate as print servers?

13. Where are most of the print problems found in NetWare 4.11?

14. Which three facets of NetWare 4.11 does the NetWare 5 printer agent replace?

15. What are the four basic components of the NDPS printing operation?

16. Does the manager or the agent come first in NDPS?

17. Describe NDPS Gateways.

18. When is the NDPS broker installed?

19. How many hops are required before an additional broker is added to NDPS?

20. What are the two printer types available under NDPS?

■ Associated Chapter Problems

1. Explain the need for network printing.

2. Compare the printing environment of NetWare 4.11 to that of NetWare 5.

3. Describe the typical printing environment.

4. Describe the similarities between network printing and taking a print job to a printing company.

5. Explain the need for print job prioritization.

6. Fully explain the four main components of the NDPS printing environment.

7. Explain the phrase *NDPS aware*.

8. Explain the three services available in NDPS.

9. Compare Public Access printers to Controlled Access printers.

10. Explain how NDPS allows print management.

CHAPTER 8
APPLICATION LAUNCHING

Let us assume that you have not been running any applications from your network. You probably have been using them on your computers and storing the data on the file server, but now we will discuss how an administrator installs applications and makes them available through the network. In this chapter, you will learn to:

- understand network licensing requirements.

- create an Application Object.

- create the login script necessary for Application Launcher operation.

- set container Application options.

- describe the basic components of the NetWare Application Launcher.

- launch an application from NetWare Application Launcher.

- launch an application from the NetWare Application Explorer.

- describe the Application Snap-in.

- describe snAppShot.

- explain the benefits of the NetWare Application Launcher.

Software Licensing

Before we start talking about launching applications over a network, you need to take a moment to discuss *software licensing* and *software piracy*. In the early 1980's, Bill Gates, chairman of Microsoft Corporation, took a stand against the common practice of copying other people's work and distributing it freely. He took out an advertisement and chastised people who did not pay for the software they were using. He essentially said that everyone was doing it and that they were all thieves. Needless to say, Bill's advertisement agitated many people who did not consider themselves thieves. The term "software pirates" has become widely used when describing people who use software without proper permission.

The controversy over whether using someone else's software constitutes theft still rages today among software users. However, the courts have protected software and given its authors the same protection afforded authors of books, music, and similarly crafted works. In October 1998 the government got involved. "We are declaring war on software piracy," Vice President Al Gore said in a statement in The New York Times, "The message is clear: Don't copy that floppy. At home or abroad, intellectual property must be protected." Later that year, Bill Gates took out full page ads in some of the largest newspapers across the country and again chastised people who use software without a license. This time most people were not agitated by the ad. It is, after all, illegal to use someone else's software without their permission. Most times this permission is in the form of a license, which you purchase. Sometimes the permission to use a piece of software is given freely (*Freeware*) or shared for a time with payment expected after the shared period (*Shareware*).

As the person responsible for controlling the network, you should make sure that all software installed on your servers is legal and that everyone in your company follows proper licensing procedures. Some software runs only on individual workstations and cannot run from a network file server. This type of software should not pose a network licensing problem. However, installing multiple copies of it on workstations is also illegal and you should make sure that does not happen either. Other software can run over networks as either *single installations* or *network licenses* (called *site licenses*). There are almost as many different license agreements as there are different pieces of software, so you should be very familiar with your licensing agreement *before* installing any software and releasing it for use by anyone on your network. You are the responsible agent and could be held financially liable!

> **As the person responsible for controlling the network, you should make sure that all software installed on your servers is legal and that everyone in your company follows proper licensing procedures.**

NetWare's Application Launcher (NAL)

Once you consider and account for the legalities of software use, you should begin sharing applications over the network wherever you can. When the number of users on a network is relatively small, installing individual applications on each workstation does not seem like such a difficult task. However, as the number of users, workstations, and locations increase, that task increases rapidly. Installing Microsoft Word for two or three network users does not seem too difficult, but when there are 500, 1000, or 10,000 users it becomes very difficult indeed. Assuming the present rate of software revisions, updates, and major new releases, network administrators could spend the majority of their time running from workstation to workstation keeping Office 97 current (there are 38 versions of Office 97) or trying to keep them communicating with workstations operating Office 95 or Office 2000. Instead, installing whatever version of Word you want on the server and giving multiple users access to that one location makes a lot of sense.

The benefits of using *network applications* include easier network maintenance for the administrator, uniform application setups for network users, and a more efficient distribution of available resources. However, some software produces extreme traffic on the network even though it is capable of being networked. For this reason, you should always test the software you plan on offering over your network both in the stand-alone configuration as well as the networked launcher configuration discussed below. When you determine the best configuration for your network, that is the one you should release to your users.

NetWare 4.11 first used the *NetWare Application Manager (NAM)* for running applications over the network. The applications had to be properly configured by the network administrator *before* their use. This included creating an NDS network object for the application and storing all the necessary information about that application in its information pages. Once the administrator created the application and the information was properly stored in the NDS object, the user could launch that application with the *NetWare Application Launcher (NAL)* from his/her workstation's desktop. The user's workstation NAL contained icons for all the applications that they could run. There were three operating systems *application objects* available: Windows 95, Windows 3.1, and DOS.

NetWare 5 takes the 4.11 NetWare Application Manager and NetWare Application Launcher operations and makes them a part of the new *Z.E.N.works*. You still have the option of installing applications individually on stand alone workstations but you also have an expanded application launcher system. NetWare 5 makes using the application launcher much easier for the administrator and the network user, too. Unlike the 4.11 NAL's use of different icons for different operating systems, NetWare 5's Application Launcher uses the same icon for all operating systems. It does, however, let you specify and optimize for the operating systems which will run the application.

NetWare 5's Application Launcher gives the network administrator the ability to centrally control application use and maintain all applications available to network users. Additionally, this centralized control is available to the administrator logging in from any workstation with access to the necessary network application files. Since all these files should be available to the administrator from any location, it means that administration of applications can be accomplished from anywhere on the network.

In Exercise 8-1, the network administrator will be creating an application object in the TPUP-HQS container for anyone on a NetWare 4.11 network or in the TPUP container for those on a NetWare 5 network. (TPUP-HQS is used in the example but both work the same way with the newest Novell Client installed.)

Activity 8-1 — Creating an Application Object for NWAdmin

1. Log in to your network as the Admin.

2. Start **NWAdmin** using the icon on your desktop that you created earlier in this course.

3. Use the pull down **OBJECT** menu and click on **Create**. The *New Object* window shown in Figure 8-1 appears. Highlight the **Application** icon as indicated and click the **OK** button.

Figure 8-1

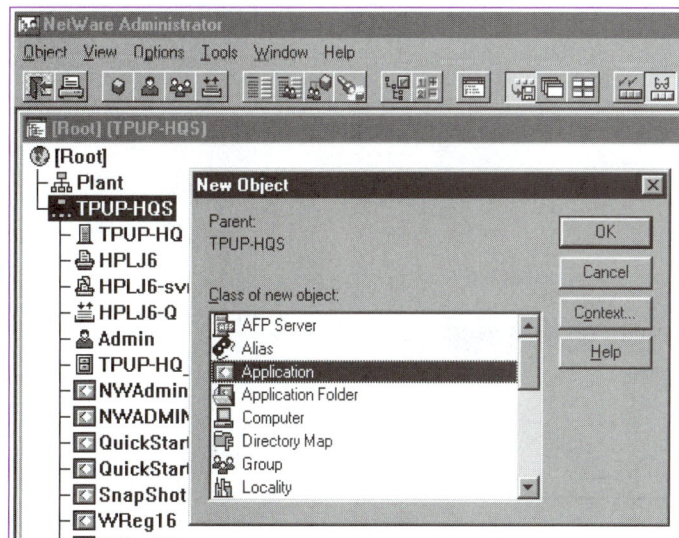

4. The *Create Application Object* window appears as shown in Figure 8-2. Leave the radio control button clicked on the **Create a single Application object (no .aot/.axt file)** and click the **Next >** button.

Figure 8-2

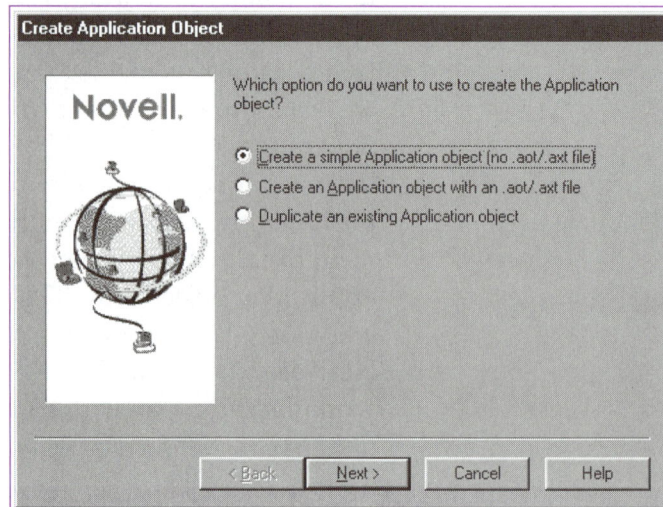

5. The window shown in Figure 8-3 appears. Type in the object name as indicated and use the **Browse** button to the right of the *Path to executable:* window and locate the file. (You could simply type it in but browsing lets you see that it actually does exist before exiting from the create object procedure.) Click the **Finish** button.

Figure 8-3

Figure 8-4

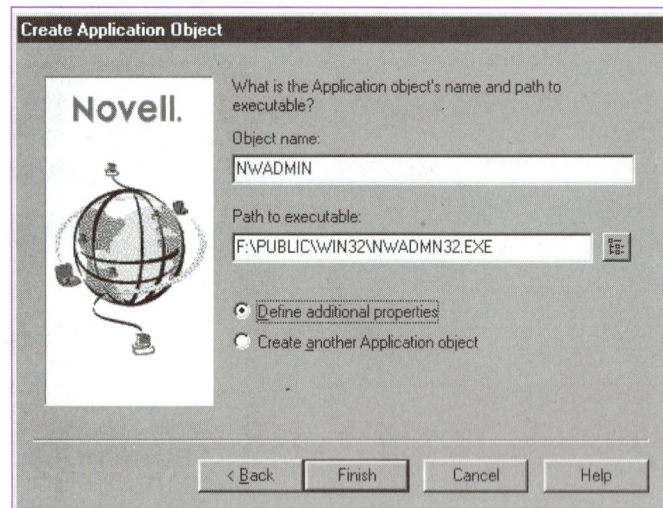

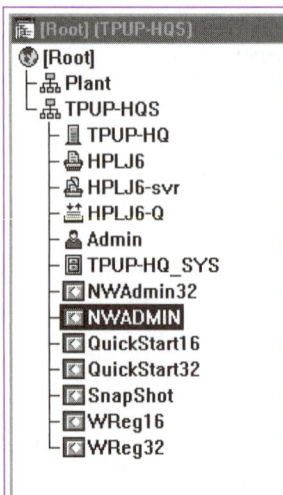

6. When you close the TPUP-HQS container object and reopen it, your **NWAdmin** object will appear. (See Figure 8-4.)

7. Right click on that **NWAdmin** object and click on **Details**. The *Application* window appears as shown in Figure 8-5.

Figure 8-5

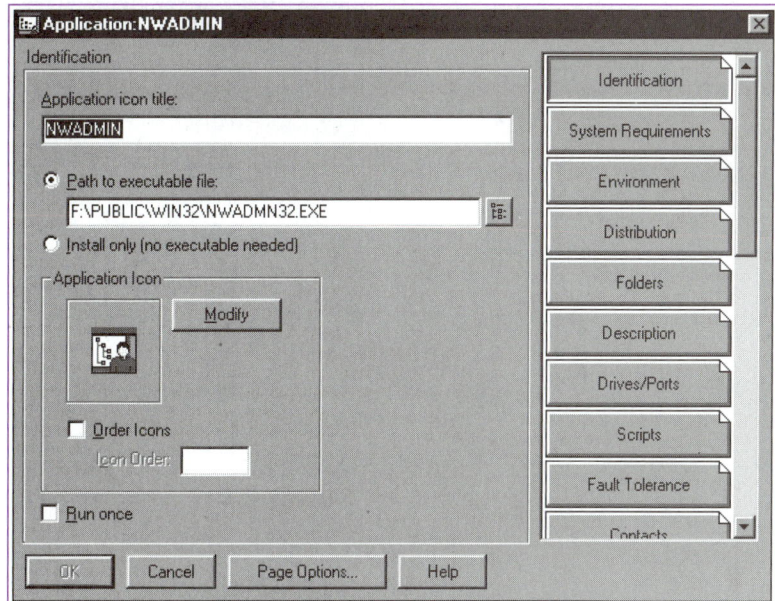

8. Scroll down and click on the **Associations** button. The window shown in Figure 8-6 will appear.

Figure 8-6

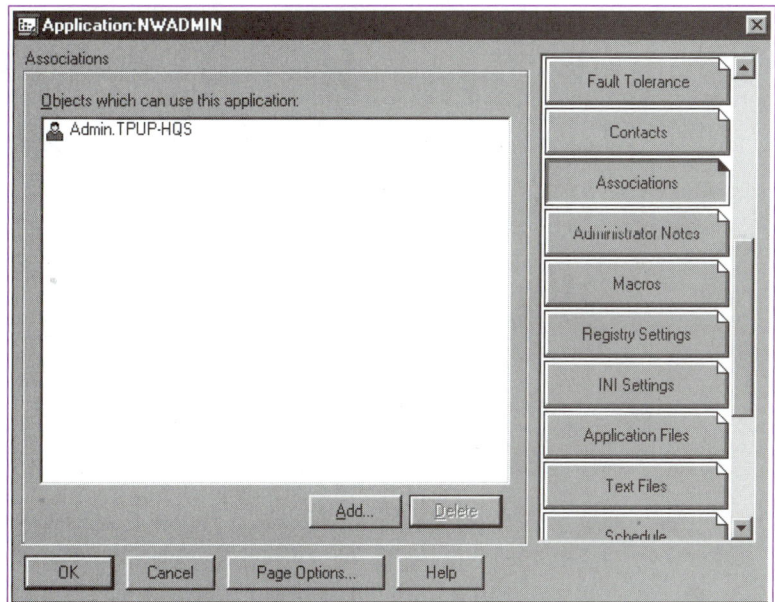

9. Click on the **Add** button. Scroll on the **Browse context** side to locate the **TPUP-HQS** container. Click the **OK** button. (See Figure 8-7.)

Figure 8-7

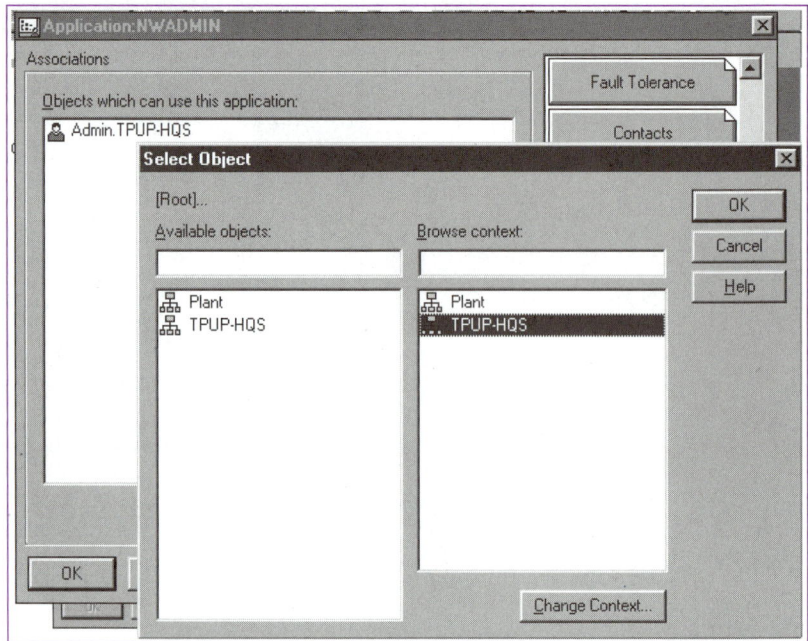

10. The window shown in Figure 8-8 appears with the **TPUP-HQS** container added. Click the **OK** button.

Figure 8-8

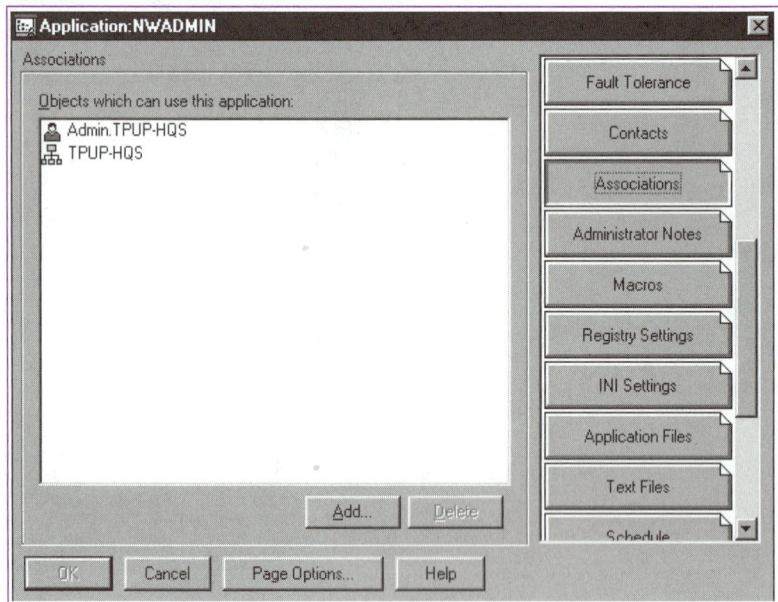

11. Right click on the **TPUP-HQS** container and click on **Details**. The window shown in Figure 8-9 appears.

Figure 8-9

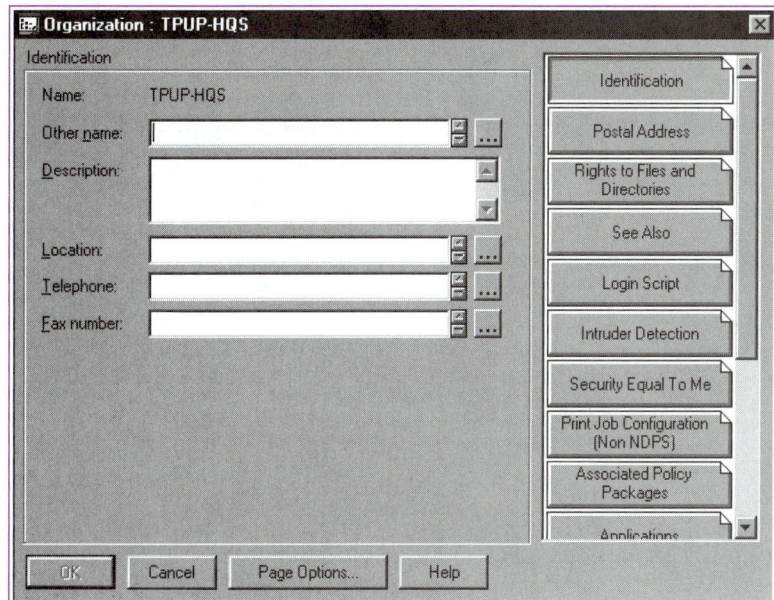

12. Click on the Login Script button and type the text shown in Figure 8-10. (Login scripts will be discussed later in the text.)

Figure 8-10

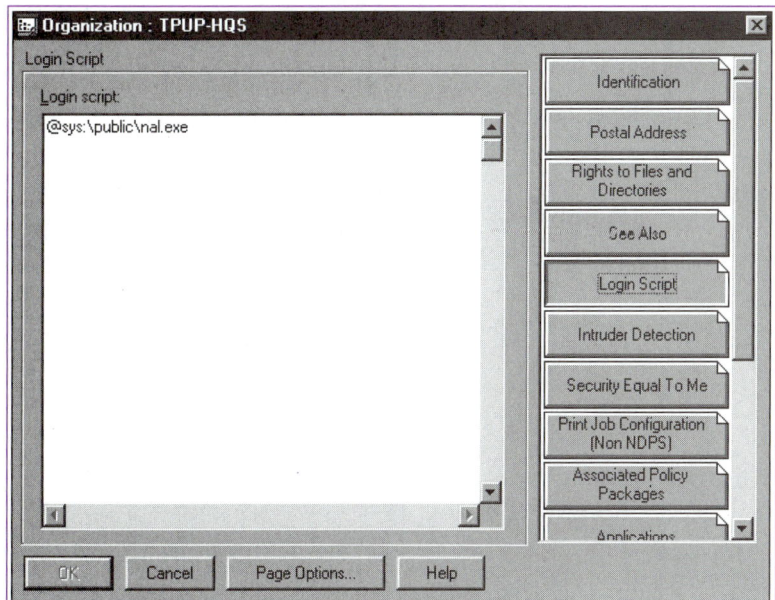

13. Scroll down and click on the **Applications** button and the window shown in Figure 8-11 will appear. Click on the three items indicated in Figure 8-11 to place an icon for the **NWAdmin** application in your application launcher, in your **Start** menu, and on your desktop.

Figure 8-11

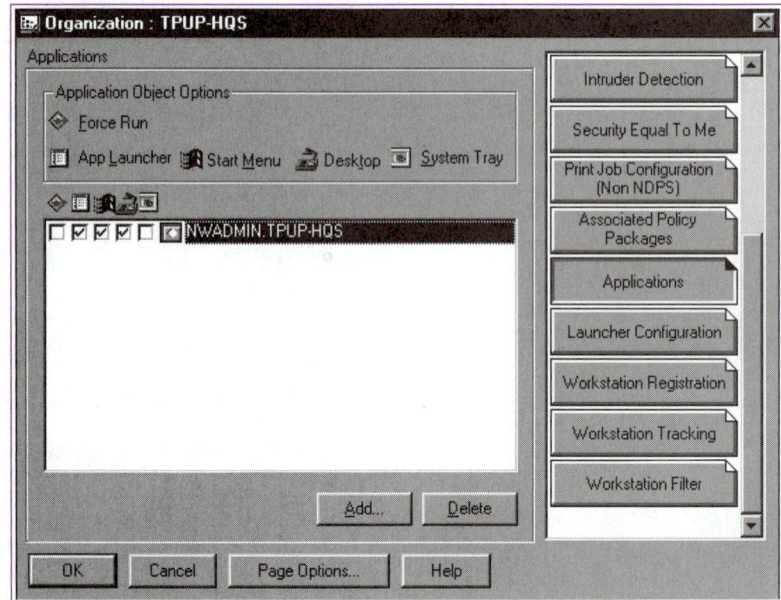

14. Click the **OK** button. Log out and log back in as a user in the TPUP-HQS container.

15. The Application Launcher window shown in Figure 8-12 will open on your desktop.

Figure 8-12

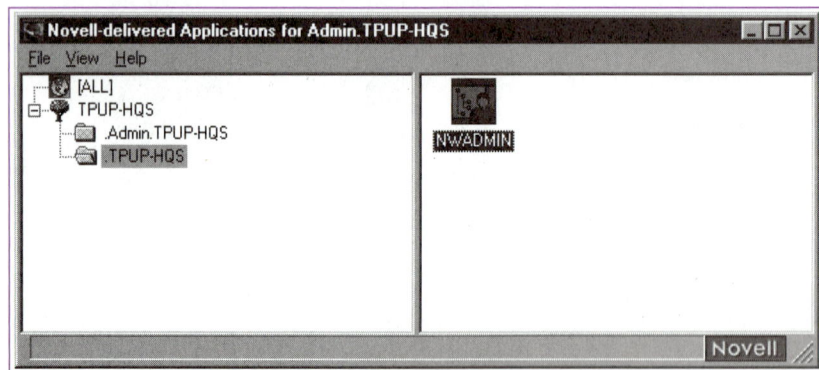

16. The **Start** button and the desktop will have **NWAdmin** icons in addition to the Application Launcher, as shown in Figure 8-13. Note the *red* shortcut arrow in the lower left corner of the desktop icon as opposed to the usual *black* arrow on the shortcut that you placed on your desktop earlier in this text.

Figure 8-13

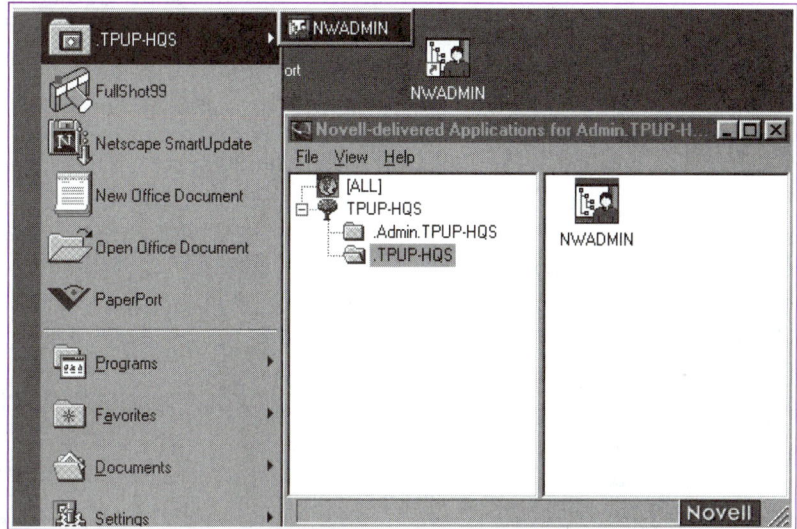

17. Exit **NWAdmin**. Test each of your three new **NWAdmin** icons to ensure that they operate properly.

NAL Basic Components—Administrator

Application Snap-In

The same process discussed above can be used by the administrator for associating application icons with software installed on the server. The primary component of this launcher is the *Application Launcher Snap-in*, a segment of NetWare written to activate and manage the launcher. The snap-in also adds administrator features to the **Tools** pull down menu of NetWare Administrator, as shown in Figure 8-14.

Figure 8-14

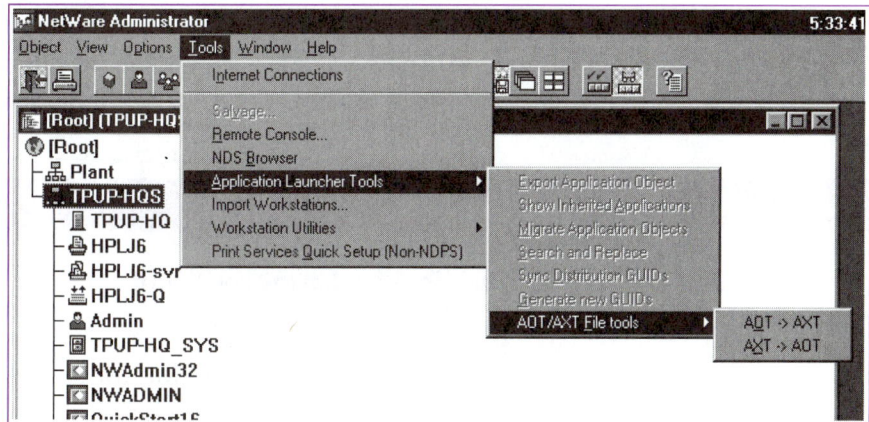

Using the snap-in with NetWare Administrator gives you the ability to create and configure the objects necessary for the launcher's operation. It also allows you to view and manage the application objects you created. You can manage the applications through the property pages of the object and the containers in which the objects reside. The launcher snap-in also lets you sort out the applications you wish to launch and decide which users are allowed access.

snAppShot

> Another of the main components of the application launcher is the ability to keep track of all the supporting bits and pieces of software that get installed when a major software application gets added to a computer.

Another of the main components of the application launcher is the ability to keep track of all the supporting bits and pieces of software that get installed when a major software application gets added to a computer. When you run it the *snAppShot* portion of the launcher records (or takes a "snapshot" of) the current workstation configuration before the software installation. It then keeps track of the changes as you perform the installation and then takes another snapshot of your workstation after the installation. Comparing the two snapshots and the actions during the installation allows the launcher to create a template for you to use when creating additional application objects. That application's required configuration can thus be copied to additional workstations without actually performing a complete software installation.

What should be evident in Exercise 8-1 is that applications were already loaded on the server prior to the association step of the application launcher setup. Our example used a relatively small application, which was installed on the server during server/client setup. You may have to install your software application on the server using snAppShot before making it available to your network users.

Note for 4.11 users

You should create the *long name space* on your 4.11 server that is needed when you start storing Windows 95 files whose file names are longer than the DOS conventional 8.3 naming standard. (A DOS name has eight characters followed by a "." and then by a three-character extension, as in *AUTOEXEC.BAT*.)

At the 4.11 server console prompt type:
`load long` and press `<ENTER>`. Then type:
`add name space long to volume sys` and press `<ENTER>`.

NAL Basic Components—User

Application Launcher Window

Once again, the same basic steps are used by the administrator above to set up a user's workstation for use with application launcher. The user then logs into the network and has a window appear for him to choose an application to launch if he wishes. The *application*

launcher window may even be configured so that it replaces the normal Windows desktop startup window. This method ensures the users only have access to the files designated through the launcher window. An example appears in Figure 8-15.

Figure 8-15

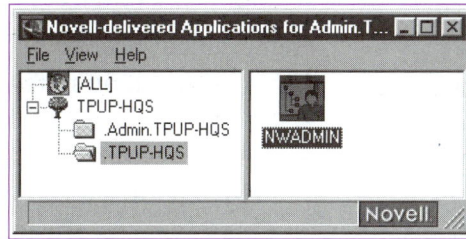

Application Explorer Window

By placing the text (shown in Figure 8-16) in the user's container login script, the user will have the option of launching applications from either the application launcher window or the Application Explorer, as shown in Figure 8-17.

Figure 8-16

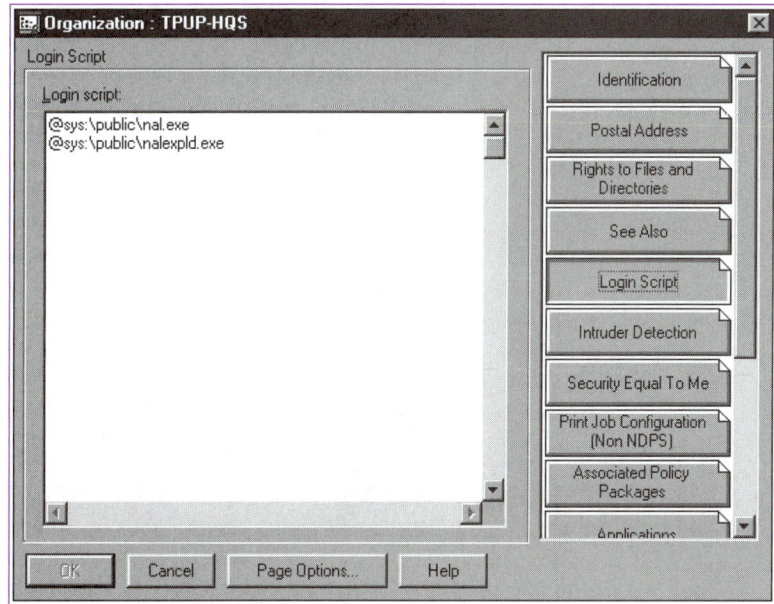

Figure 8-17

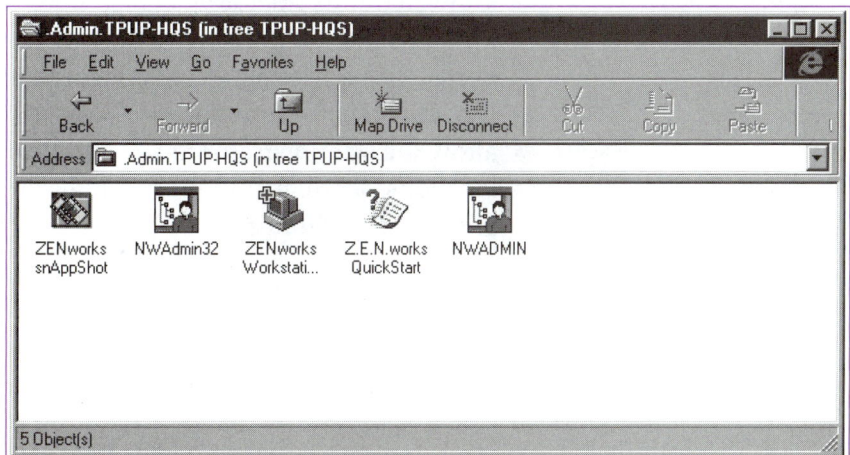

User Benefits

A network that is fault tolerant is designed with redundant components available in the event that a main component fails. Users are able to continue working without noticing the failure.

Not only does the administrator benefit from using NetWare's Application Launcher capability, the user benefits as well. The benefit users will be aware of is the fact that they are able to launch the same application software from any workstation attached to the network and it operates the same each time. The user does not have to tell the server where he is or where the drives that he needs to use with the application are. The launcher has been configured to locate the applications, then deliver the icons to the desktop.

Other benefits also come with using the application launcher. With backup servers available, the user will not even be aware of which server he is logging onto to run the application. If one server goes down, another will take its place and provide access to the desired application This is called *fault tolerance*. Fault tolerance is very important to networking. A network that is fault tolerant is designed with redundant components available in the event that a main component fails. Users are able to continue working without noticing the failure.

Additionally, the network can select an alternative installation of the application in the event too many users are trying to use the same application. This balances the load and allows the network to run more efficiently in times of peak demand for services. The launcher senses the increased demand and sends additional users elsewhere for their copy.

All of these benefits to the user depend on the proper installation of both the application launcher and the applications themselves. This includes multiple installations of the software and may include multiple servers as well. A properly designed network helps the administrator and the user perform their respective tasks.

Other Application Launcher Features

The application launcher is able to specify a title for an application's icon, the path for starting it, and everything the program needs to know about its operating environment. You entered the Identification information in Exercise 8-1 and the pages for entering the other items (**System Requirements**, **Environment**, **Distribution**, and **Registry Settings**) are shown in Figures 8-18 through 8-21. These pages allow the administrator to set environments, filter activities or locations, set distribution schedules and recipients, and decide *load balancing* and fault tolerance.

Figure 8-18

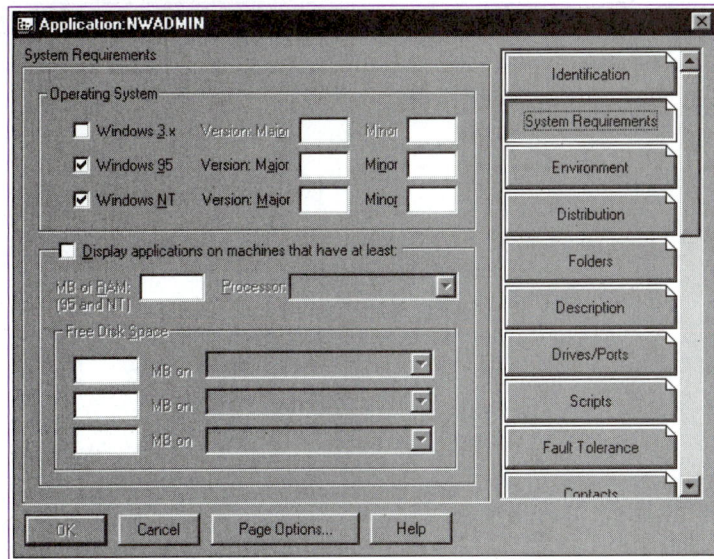

Figure 8-19

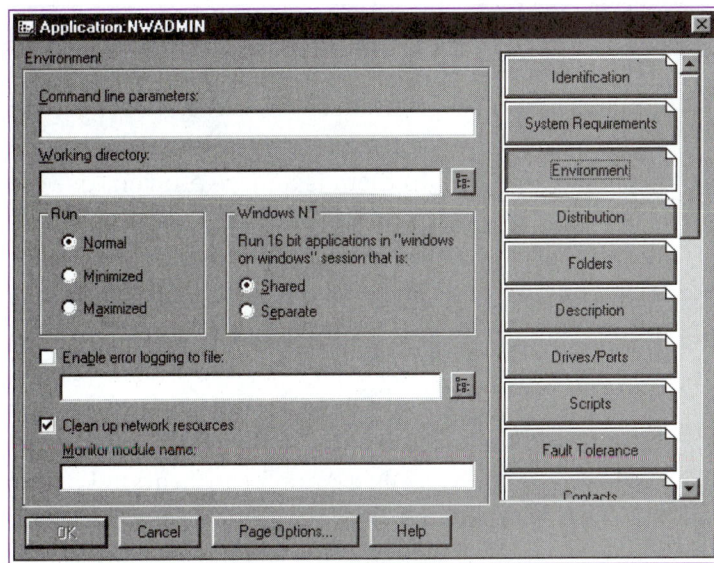

Figure 8-20

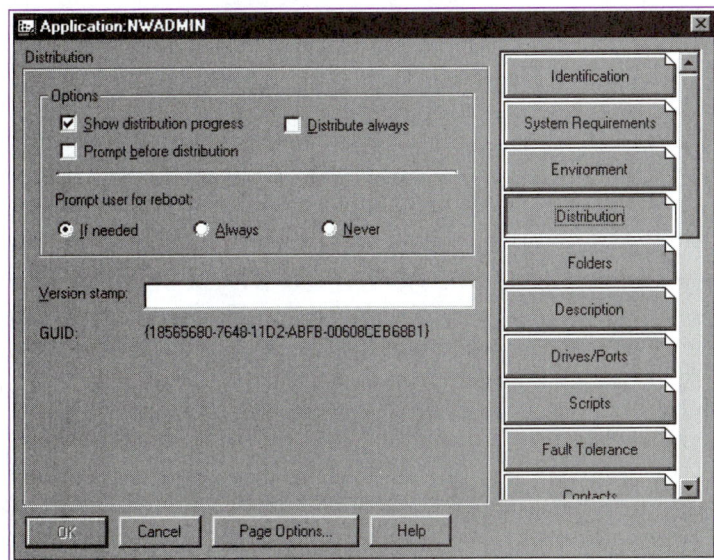

Figure 8-21

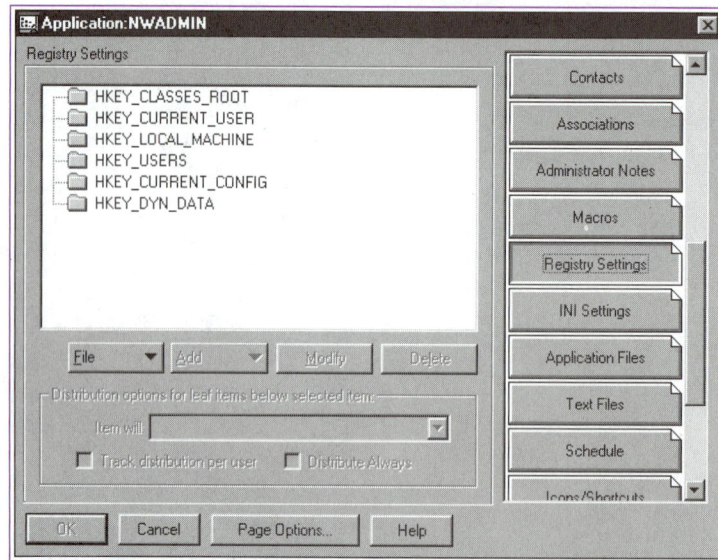

Chapter Summary

Provided you have the proper licensing agreements, installing software applications on a network and giving multiple users access to them is a more efficient use of a company's resources. Software piracy is allowing users to install copies of software for which they do not have a license. Providing network applications for users makes the job of a network administrator easier and ensures more uniform application installation techniques. Although some software drastically impacts network efficiency when running more than one copy over the network, most software will allow network installation and distribution.

NetWare 5 Application Launcher is part of the new Z.E.N.works addition to Novell's operating system. The same icon is used for all operating system installations of the application but the options pages allow the administrator to set specifications and optimize the software for each environment.

In Exercise 8-1 you created an application object for the frequently used NWAdmin application on your server. Although the exercise showed this on the 4.11 server, the same actions happen when setting up applications on NetWare 5 stations.

The basic administrator component of the application launcher is the Snap-In, which allows the launcher to be produced and managed. It also adds administrator tools to the **Tools** pull down window in NWAdmin. The next administrator component of the launcher is snAppShot. This component allows launcher to record the configuration settings before, during, and after software installation on a workstation. These settings are then compared and the necessary changes for the software to operate are set into the launcher's configuration settings on the application. When another workstation is set up for running the application, the software itself no longer needs to be installed in order to obtain the necessary settings.

The basic user components of the NetWare 5 Application Launcher are the Application Launcher Window and the Application Explorer Window.

The basic user components of the NetWare 5 Application Launcher are the Application Launcher window and the Application Explorer window. Either is available to the network user when attempting to launch an application to which he has both access and rights to operate.

The user benefits from application launcher use because the same application software setup is available from any workstation on the network. The user does not have to tell the server where he is or what he wants set up when running the application. The launcher has already taken care of all those settings. The user also benefits from the network's ability to provide access to the applications from backup servers without user knowledge. If a server is down when the user requests an application, an alternate server provides the service to the application. Additionally, if there are multiple users accessing a particular server's copy of the application, a load balancing shift to another server's copy will go unnoticed by the user.

Other launcher features that the administrator can set include identification path, system requirements, environment, distribution, and registry settings. These are all found on the options pages of the application or its container object's option pages. They allow setting the environment, filtering activities or locations, setting distribution schedules and recipients, and decisions about load balancing and fault tolerance.

Networking Terms Used in Chapter 8

software licensing	network applications	login script
software piracy	**NetWare Application Manager**	Application Launcher Snap-in
freeware	**(NAM)**	**snAppShot**
shareware	**NetWare Application Launcher**	long name space
single installations	**(NAL)**	application launcher window
network licenses	application object	fault tolerance
site licenses	**Z.E.N.works**	load balancing

■ Chapter Review Questions

1. What is *software piracy*?

2. Compare *shareware* to *freeware*.

3. Who is responsible for ensuring that all copies of software are legal copies in a company?

4. Describe the use of network licensing.

5. What is the primary benefit of using the NetWare Application Launcher?

6. What kind of test should you always run on software before distributing it over the network?

7. What is one difference between the NetWare 4.11 and the NetWare 5 Application Launcher?

8. Who has the ability to centrally control application use?

9. Describe the steps to creating an application object.

10. What is the path to the *NWADMIN32.EXE* file?

11. On the identification page of an application object, which two items must be filled in?

12. Which options page would you use to filter out any workstations that do not have a predetermined amount of available hard disk space remaining?

13. How many locations can you set up to receive icons for application objects?

14. What is the primary component to the application launcher?

15. From your desktop, how can you tell whether the **NWAdmin** you are clicking on is the one you made earlier in this text or the one put there by the application launcher?

■ **Associated Chapter Problems**

1. Take a position on the controversy surrounding software piracy and defend your position in three to five paragraphs.

2. Describe the steps for installing Office 97 to 100 networked workstations if the network is not operating at all.

3. Describe the components of the application launcher.

4. What are the benefits of snAppShot?

5. List and explain the benefits of using application launcher.

UNIT

3

Network Use

CHAPTER

9

FILE SYSTEM SECURITY

Everyone is currently able to view, change, or even delete the files on your server. Now it is time to learn how to secure them. This is accomplished using file system security features that give the network administrator control over user access to directories and files. Upon completing this chapter, you will be able to:

- describe the network file system security components.

- explain file system rights and how they are assigned.

- describe Inherited Rights and the use of Inheritance Rights Filters.

- explain the default rights assignments created automatically by the system.

- list the rights required for commonly performed tasks.

- describe the use of trustees and the Access Control List (ACL).

- assign users rights to files, directories, and subdirectories.

- calculate effective rights.

- list the utilities available to verify or change file attributes.

File System Security

File System Security gives the network administrator control over who has access to items stored on the network.

A user cannot access anything unless the administrator assigns him the right to do so.

Until now, everyone in your class has been able to explore the contents of the entire file system, uninhibited by security concerns. In Chapter 6, you learned that the file system consists of volumes, directories, subdirectories, and files. This chapter will teach you how to control who can use (or even see) these file system components.

File System Security gives the network administrator control over who has access to items stored on the network. The administrator does this by granting individuals or groups the levels of authority necessary for them to perform their assigned tasks. That *authority* is granted based on their *need for access*, and users are then granted the *right of access* to particular files. Effective administrators grant rights based on a strict *need-to-know* analysis. If a user needs access to certain information in order to perform a job function, he should have the right to access the information he needs. However, users should not obtain access rights to more information than they need. This concept of rights is not confined to file system security. The NDS database is also regulated through rights. Both security systems give the administrator the authority to assign rights, but there are significant differences between the two systems. We will discuss each system separately. NDS security is the subject of the next chapter.

File System Security revolves around a set of *File System Rights*. These rights regulate both who has access to information stored in network volumes and how access to them is obtained. A user with access to a file or folder on a network volume is referred to as a *trustee*. The act of giving that user particular rights is referred to as *granting rights* or *assigning rights*. Once an administrator grants rights to a trustee at some directory level within the file system, those rights flow down through the folders to the lower levels of the file system in a particular way. By default, rights flow downward. As a result of that downward flow, rights to the lower levels are *inherited*, and become a user's *inherited rights*. This prompts the use of *Inherited Rights Filters (IRF)* to block unwanted transference of access rights. The different rights assigned and inherited by a user down through the tree, minus the rights blocked by filters along the way, comprise the *effective rights* a user has to a particular file at a specific level. Each item in the file system maintains a list of all trustees with rights of access to its information. This list is a *trustee list*, commonly called an *Access Control List (ACL)*.

The administrator controls the type of access he gives a user through the *access rights* he grants. A user cannot access anything unless the administrator assigns him the right to do so. Once a right is granted, what the user can do with the file system component depends on which right was granted. Different rights allow different actions, depending on the type of access granted by the right.

NetWare File System Rights

> Although an individual's access rights to a directory and to the files within that directory are usually the same, they can be set differently if an administrator wishes to limit access to certain files.

There are eight different rights assigned to files and directories in the file system. The files and the directories are secured by the same eight rights, but they can be set independently. Although an individual's access rights to a directory and to the files within that directory are usually the same, they can be set differently if an administrator wishes to limit access to certain files. The eight file system rights are: *Supervisor*, *Read*, *Write*, *Create*, *Erase*, *Modify*, *File Scan*, and *Access Control*.

Each of the rights has a full right name, a single letter abbreviation, and a description of the capabilities of the user granted that right. They are as follows:

Supervisor (S): Granting this right assigns the user all rights to the file system component (directory, subdirectory, and/or file), and to *any* sub-components below it, because Supervisor is the *only right* that cannot be blocked by an Inherited Rights Filter. It also grants the user the right to grant rights to other users.

Read (R): Granting this right assigns the user the right to open and read files in the directory. It also allows the user to run programs that reside within the directory.

Write (W): Granting this right assigns the user the right to open and change or add data to the contents of the directory.

Create (C): Granting this right assigns the user the right to create new files and subdirectories.

Erase (E): Granting this right assigns the user the right to delete the directory and/or any files or subdirectories it contains.

> ... Supervisor is the *only right* that cannot be blocked by an Inherited Rights Filter.

Modify (M): Granting this right assigns the user the right to change the name of a file, directory, or subdirectory, or to change their attributes. It does not allow a user the right to modify the contents of a file, directory, or subdirectory.

File Scan (F): Granting this right assigns the user the right to see a directory listing of file, directory, and subdirectory names.

Access Control (A): Granting this right assigns the user the right to grant another user access to the file, directory, or subdirectory, or to remove such access. It also allows the user to change IRFs and trustee assignments. It does not allow the user to make any changes to the Supervisor right by alteration or by setting IRFs.

These rights are important, and you should remember them, particularly if you plan to take the Novell CNA exam. Devise a technique to remember them. The most common mnemonic device uses the single letter abbreviation of each file right to form a sentence. A sentence frequently heard in Novell classes is:

Some Rights Will Cause Extreme Mental Fatigue, Always!

This sentence is easy to remember. That is why it is so effective. You can see these rights listed as access rights in the Figure 9-1.

Figure 9-1

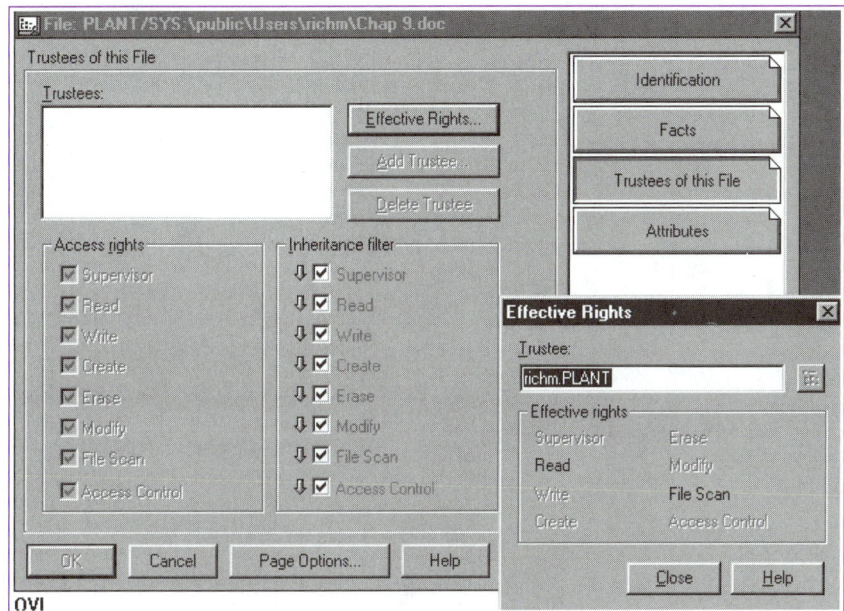

This graphic shows the effective rights that were assigned automatically in a user's home directory by the system for a file that the user did not create. These are referred to as *default rights*. Examples of these *default rights assignments* follow:

■   The user who created the server object, and any objects given NDS Supervisor right to the server object, receive all rights, including the Supervisor right to the server object.

■   Any users in the same container as the *SYS:* volume receive the Read (R) and File Scan (F) rights to *SYS:PUBLIC*. Other users must be assigned these rights by the administrator.

■   All users created in NDS User object creation with **NWAdmin** or **NETADMIN**, and assigned a home directory, are granted all rights to their own home directories, except the Supervisor (S) right. This is shown in Figure 9-2, using **NWAdmin** to view the directory.

Figure 9-2

NOTE

To prevent a user from assigning other users rights to their home directory, you should immediately remove the Access Control (A) right from any users' home directories that are automatically created for you.

NOTE

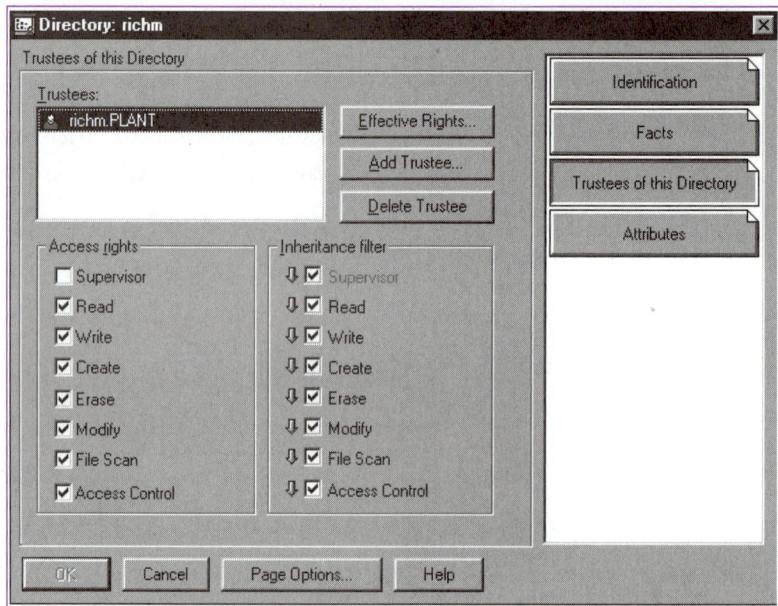

The same directory and rights information is shown in Figure 9-3. This time Network Neighborhood is used to view the user's home directory and the rights to the file placed within that directory.

Figure 9-3

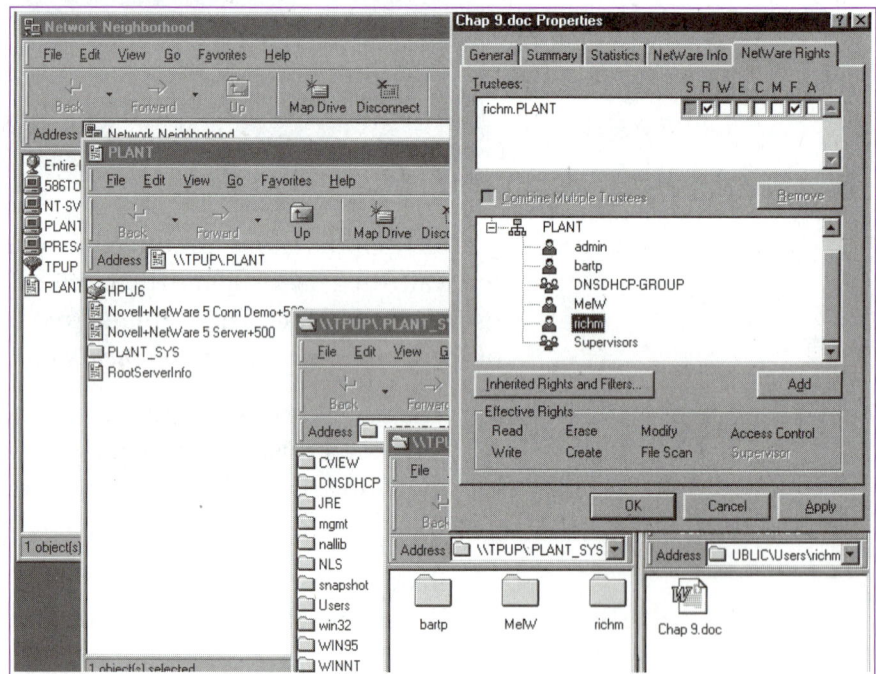

Other rights are required for a user to complete commonly performed file system tasks. Some of these include:

Rights Required for Common Networking Tasks	
Commonly Performed Task	**Rights Required**
Execute .EXE, .COM, or .BAT files	R, F
Delete a file	E
Salvage a deleted file	R, F at the file level C at the directory level
See a directory listing	F
See a file name	F
Open and read a file	R
Open and write to an existing file	W, C, E, M (M not always required)
Copy files from a directory	R, F
Copy files to a directory	W, C, F
Create a new directory	C
Rename or change a file or directory	M

As demonstrated previously, a user can check these rights using different tools. Another example of rights checked using the Network Neighborhood utility is shown in Figure 9-4.

Figure 9-4

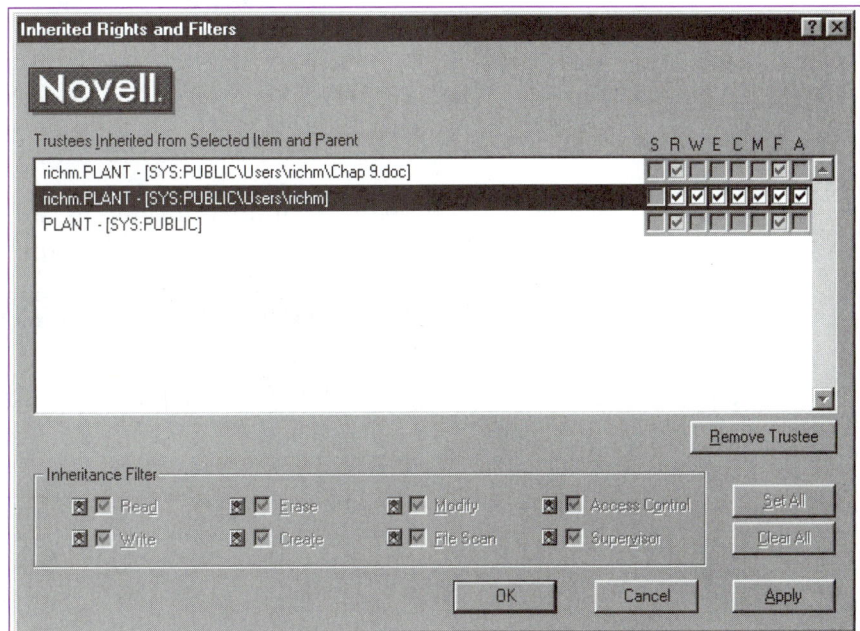

Attribute Security

There is an additional subset of file system security called *attribute security*. It uses the characteristics of files and directories. The attributes can be associated with either files or directories. Their function is to limit user manipulation of a file or directory. Attributes give the administrator an override capability that can prevent users from doing something that they would otherwise be authorized to do by virtue of their effective rights assignment. For example, if the following graphic's Read-only box were checked, the file could not be changed by any user, regardless of his assigned or effective rights. The window shown in Figure 9-5 can be found through **Network Neighborhood**, and the attributes shown can be changed there.

Figure 9-5

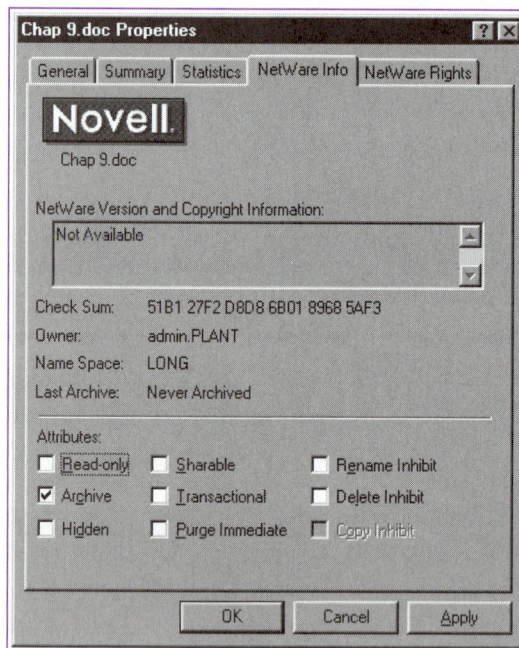

The same attribute information can be viewed and changed through **NWAdmin**, as shown in Figure 9-6.

Figure 9-6

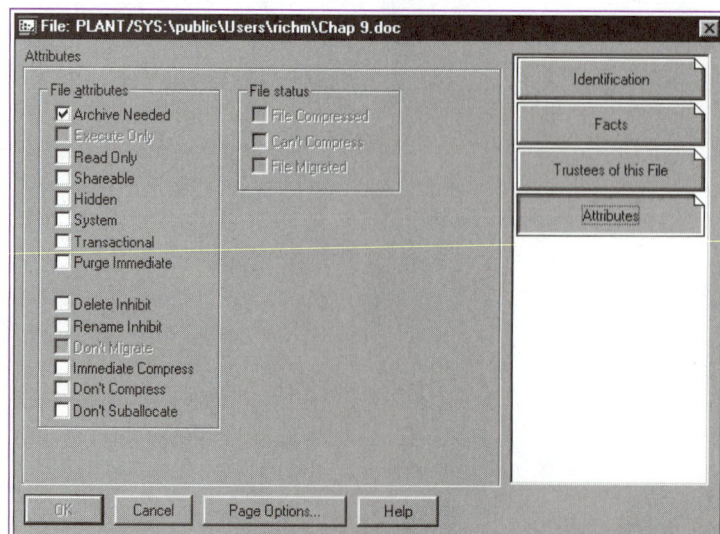

A brief list of some of the file and directory attributes follows:

Archive Needed (A)—assigned automatically to files when their contents are modified, making it possible to backup only files that have been changed since the last backup.

Can't Compress (Cc) or **Compressed (Co)**—both are set by the operating system automatically. They show either that no appreciable space savings can be achieved by compressing (Cc), or that the file has already been compressed using NetWare's file compression function.

Copy Inhibit (Ci) or **Delete Inhibit (Di)**—both are usually set by the administrator to protect files from being copied or deleted.

Don't Compress (Dc), **Don't Suballocate (Ds)**, or **Don't Migrate (Dm)**— all can be set by the user to prevent files from being compressed, suballocated, or migrated.

Execute Only (X)—used by the administrator to protect *.EXE* and *.COM* files from being copied illegally. Once set, this attribute cannot be changed by anyone. To remove it, you must delete the file and reinstall it.

Hidden (H)—commonly used in DOS to hide files and directories from utilities and application programs. Hidden files can also be set to prevent users from exploring directories.

Normal (N)—when no other attributes are specifically set, Normal is the default attribute. It is a combination of Read-Write and Non-Shareable.

Purge Immediate (P)—used when a file should be purged from the system as soon as it is deleted, so that it cannot be salvaged.

Read Only (Ro)—used on files only to protect them from being modified or deleted. Upon initiation, the Read only attribute also sets the Rename Inhibit (Ri) and Delete Inhibit (Di) to prevent the files from being renamed or deleted. Both the rename and delete inhibit can be reset later.

Shareable (Sh)—used after files are created to allow more than one user access to the file at the same time.

System (Sy)—used to designate files as part of the operating system; it also hides files from DOS applications.

As demonstrated earlier, the attributes can be set in either **NWAdmin** or *Network Neighborhood* as well as in **FILER**, a NetWare Menu Utility. **FILER** is text-based and allows you to manage files through text menus. You enter **FILER** through a DOS prompt, as shown in Figure 9-7.

Figure 9-7

Once in **FILER**, you move through the various screens by using the `<UPARROW>` and `<DOWNARROW>` keys and pressing the `<ENTER>` key. The options are shown in Figure 9-8.

Figure 9-8

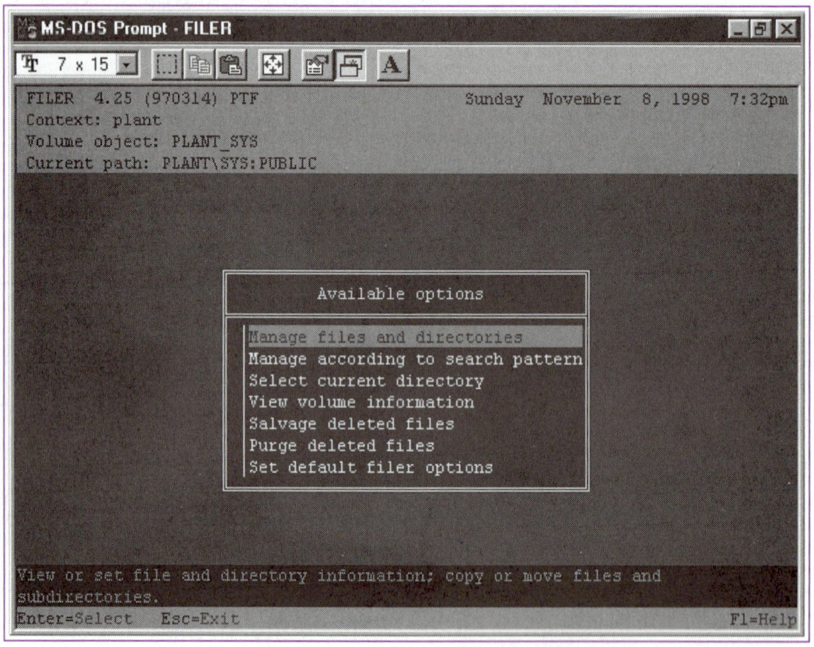

After pressing <ENTER> to select **Manage files and directories**, the graphic shows that the current path was changed to the location of the document whose name begins with *CHAP_9*. (See Figure 9-9.)

Figure 9-9

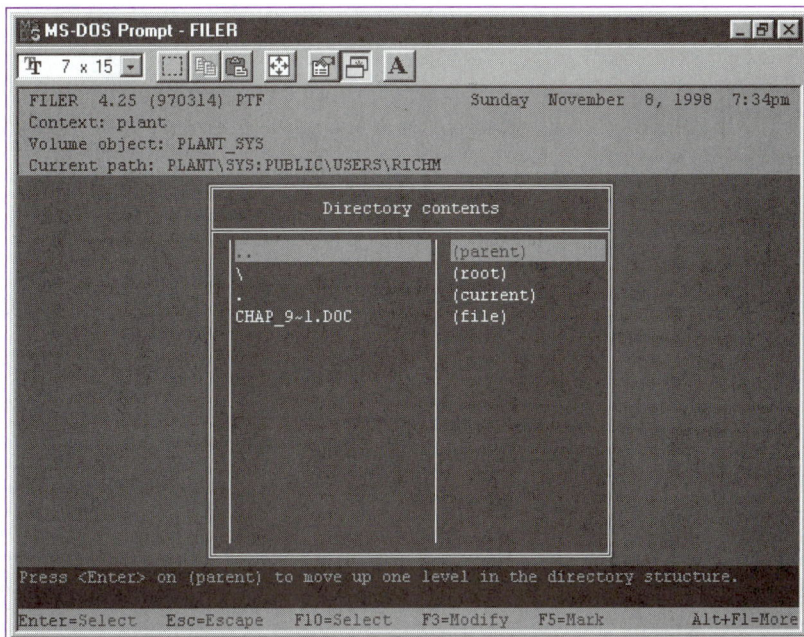

NOTE

Remember **FILER** is a DOS utility and follows the DOS file name rules. The file used in this example has more characters than DOS can display in its 8.3 file name size limitation. It has been shortened and the ~/ added to limit the name to 8 characters.

NOTE

Highlighting that file and pressing <ENTER> again will display the options shown in Figure 9-10.

Figure 9-10

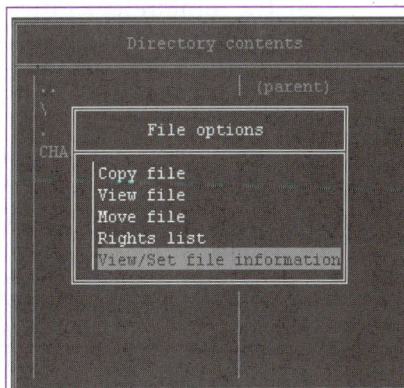

Finally, selecting the **View/Set file information** and pressing `<ENTER>` displays the window showing the status of the file information. (See Figure 9-11.)

Figure 9-11

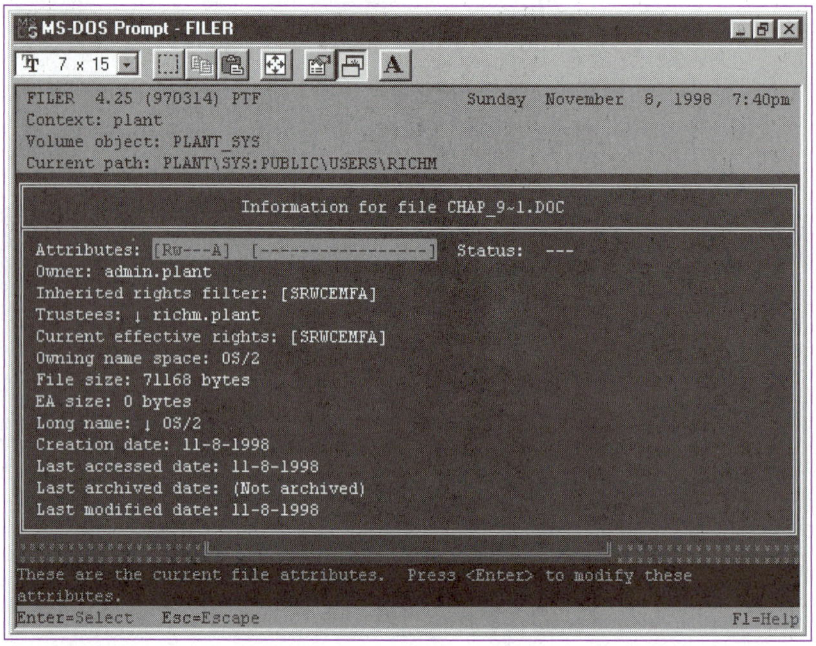

```
MS-DOS Prompt - FILER                                                _ | 8 | x |
 T   7 x 15 ▾    [ ]  🗐 🖺  🔳   🖻 🖨  A
FILER  4.25 (970314) PTF                        Sunday  November  8, 1998  7:40pm
Context: plant
Volume object: PLANT_SYS
Current path: PLANT\SYS:PUBLIC\USERS\RICHM
┌──────────────────────────────────────────────────────────────────────────┐
│                      Information for file CHAP_9~1.DOC                      │
├──────────────────────────────────────────────────────────────────────────┤
│  Attributes: [Rw---A] [----------------] Status:  ---                       │
│  Owner: admin.plant                                                        │
│  Inherited rights filter: [SRWCEMFA]                                       │
│  Trustees: ↓ richm.plant                                                   │
│  Current effective rights: [SRWCEMFA]                                      │
│  Owning name space: OS/2                                                   │
│  File size: 71168 bytes                                                    │
│  EA size: 0 bytes                                                          │
│  Long name: ↓ OS/2                                                         │
│  Creation date: 11-8-1998                                                  │
│  Last accessed date: 11-8-1998                                            │
│  Last archived date: (Not archived)                                       │
│  Last modified date: 11-8-1998                                            │
│                                                                            │
└──────────────────────────────────────────────────────────────────────────┘
These are the current file attributes.  Press <Enter> to modify these
attributes.
Enter=Select   Esc=Escape                                            F1=Help
```

While **FILER** is not fast to use, it is another method for making necessary changes to the file system. However, it will not be used in the remainder of this text.

RIGHTS (shown in Figure 9-12) and **FLAG** (shown in Figure 9-13) are other NetWare utilities that can be used to manage files and attributes. Both of these utilities are beyond the introductory level of this text, and neither will be used in the remainder of this course.

Figure 9-12

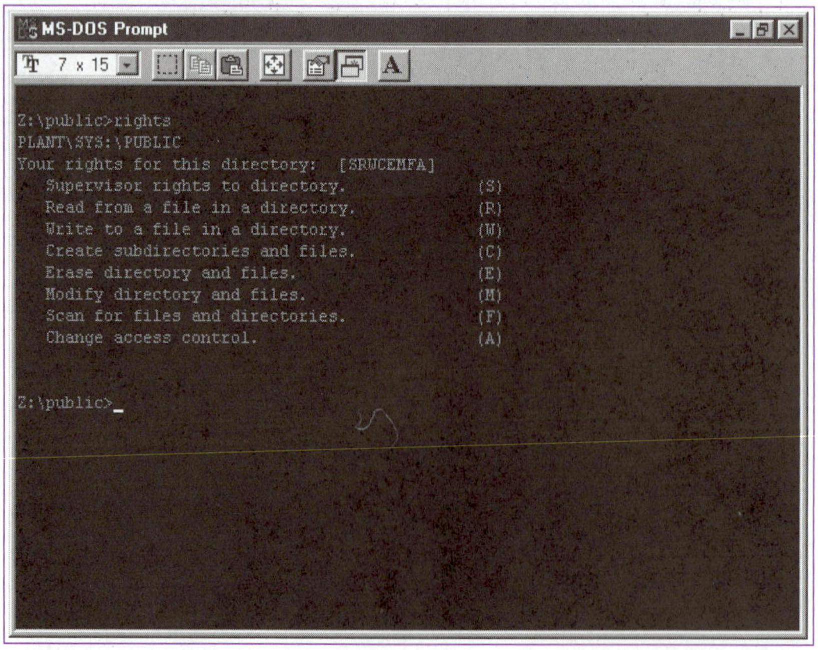

```
MS-DOS Prompt                                                        _ | 8 | x |
 T   7 x 15 ▾    [ ]  🗐 🖺  🔳   🖻 🖨  A
Z:\public>rights
PLANT\SYS:\PUBLIC
Your rights for this directory:  [SRWCEMFA]
    Supervisor rights to directory.                (S)
    Read from a file in a directory.               (R)
    Write to a file in a directory.                (W)
    Create subdirectories and files.               (C)
    Erase directory and files.                     (E)
    Modify directory and files.                    (M)
    Scan for files and directories.                (F)
    Change access control.                         (A)


Z:\public>_
```

CHAPTER 9
FSS

Figure 9-13

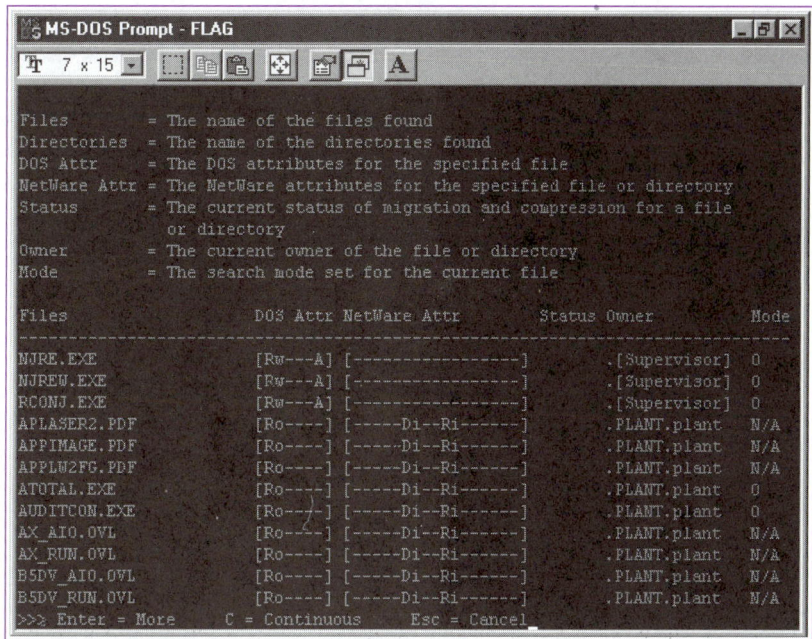

Access Control List (ACL)

Files and directories have embedded lists that show their trustees and their rights. Such a list is sometimes referred to as a trustee list or, more commonly, the Access Control List (ACL). The ACL shows all the current trustees of a directory. In the example shown in Figure 9-14, richm is the only trustee for the richm directory shown on the far left.

Figure 9-14

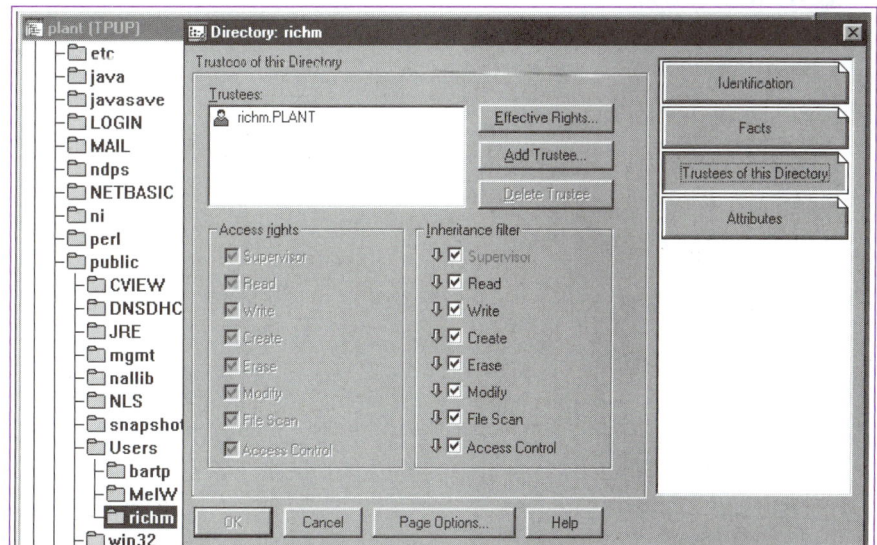

Remember that trustees are NDS objects that have been assigned rights. It is much easier to manage trustee relationships if the objects granted the rights are equally high in the Directory. Giving rights to a group object and placing users in that group is an efficient way to provide rights to several users at the same time. The group or container to which the rights are granted passes its rights on to all the users within them.

> **Giving rights to a group object, and placing users in that group, is an efficient way to provide rights to several users at the same time.**

Receiving File System Rights

As has already been stated, those rights granted directly to a user are *assigned rights*. Assigning rights directly is one way to issue rights to users. However, as mentioned above, assigning rights to containers or groups is a much more efficient way for an administrator to manage the rights assigned to individuals. There are seven ways a user can receive file system rights. User rights can be

1. granted directly to the *user object*.

   Grant rights directly to a user object only when that assignment is unique and non-recurring, as when a user is assigned rights to his home directory.

2. granted to a *group* of which the user is a member.

   Grant rights to a group when more than one user will need the same rights. The users can be in the same container or anywhere else in the NDS Directory.

3. granted to an *organizational role* that the user is occupying.

   Grant rights to an organizational role when the rights apply more to the position than to the individual holding the position. If the person were not in that role, the rights would not be necessary. For example, you could create an organization role for the Help Desk.

4. granted to a *container object* in which the user object is located.

   Grant rights to a container when they are required by all users in that container or anywhere below the container. All container objects can be used to pass rights in this way, and are referred to as *natural groups*.

5. granted to another user object to which the first user is a *security equivalent*.

   Grant rights through security equivalence when you want one user object to have the same rights that another object has. It should be used very sparingly, and only as a temporary measure.

6. granted to the *[Public] trustee*.

   Grant rights to the [Public] trustee only when you want to assign access to all users even before they log in to your network. Any object connected to the network will inherit the rights associated with the [Public] trustee.

7. granted to a *parent container* of a group or container to which the user is a member. (This is commonly referred to as inheritance.)

   Grant rights to a parent container when you want the rights to flow down to all of the container's sub-containers and to any objects within them. The container below automatically adds the rights from above through what is commonly referred to as inheritance.

> **All container objects can be used to pass rights ...**

> **Any object connected to the network will inherit the rights associated with the [Public] trustee.**

Blocking Inherited File System Rights

In file system security, the Supervisor right cannot be blocked by either the new trustee assignment or the IRF method.

The rights granted to a higher container object, which flow down to all the container objects and users within that container, can be blocked in two ways. First, you can block the inheritance of rights by creating a new trustee assignment that replaces those inherited rights either to the object itself or to the object's container. You can also place an Inherited Rights Filter (IRF) on the object or its container to block the downward flow of rights to the object. In file system security, the Supervisor right cannot be blocked by either the new trustee assignment or the IRF method.

Let us use the examples in Figure 9-15 to explain how inherited rights are blocked using filters. In the first example, your rich uncle wants to treat you to a fine dinner that is served by the waiter on the left. The food is in your parent container and is trying to reach you. The hockey goalie, however, is blocking delivery to you (and probably planning to eat your dinner). That waiter is not going to reach you! Because no one else has anything for you to eat, you will not eat any dinner. The rights from your uncle do not reach your present container, and you do not have any added in that container, so you do not receive any food.

In the second example, your uncle tries to give you that dinner again. Again, it is blocked. This time, however, your mom comes to your rescue with rights to a hamburger, and brings it to your room. Although you still do not get the dinner, you do get the burger.

Finally, while the goalie sleeps in the third example, your uncle's dinner does reach you, and your mom also brings you the burger. You receive all the rights from above, as well as those from your present container.

CHAPTER 9 FSS

Figure 9-15

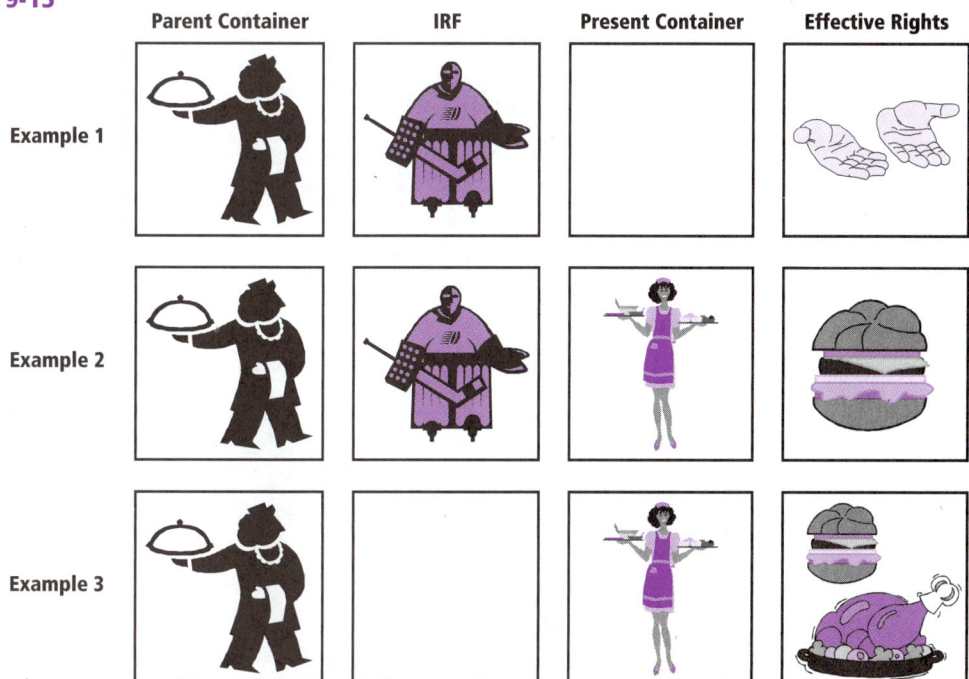

	Parent Container	IRF	Present Container	Effective Rights
Example 1				
Example 2				
Example 3				

> **Creating individual trustee assignments assures that your users obtain only the rights you want them to have.**

Creating a new trustee assignment lower in the directory is the most common way to block rights from flowing to an individual user. You simply go to the user object that you want blocked and assign him the rights you want him to have. For example, imagine that you had recently become a vegetarian in our third example above. Although everyone else in your room would eat your uncle's dinner and your mom's burgers, you would eat only the vegetables that came with them. Your new trustee assignment would prevent only you from eating anything else.

Creating individual trustee assignments assures that your users obtain only the rights you want them to have. It is effective when assigning rights to a small number of users in a large container. If the goal is to block the flow of rights to all individuals in the container, however, the IRF is the better method.

Remember that an IRF cannot block rights assignments made in the container where the IRF resides. They are used only when blocking the flow from a higher container object into a lower one. The goalie can only block what tries to get through him. He cannot block what happens further down the line.

Effective rights are all of those rights an object is assigned or inherits, minus any rights blocked by IRFs or by new trustee assignments. When calculating a user's effective rights, you need to be aware of all IRFs, all new trustee assignments, and all objects where the user was granted rights.

Activity 9–1   Determine Effective Rights

1. Log in as your own user.
2. Create a text file in **WordPad** and save it as *TEST.doc* in your user's home directory, as indicated in Figure 9-16.

Figure 9-16

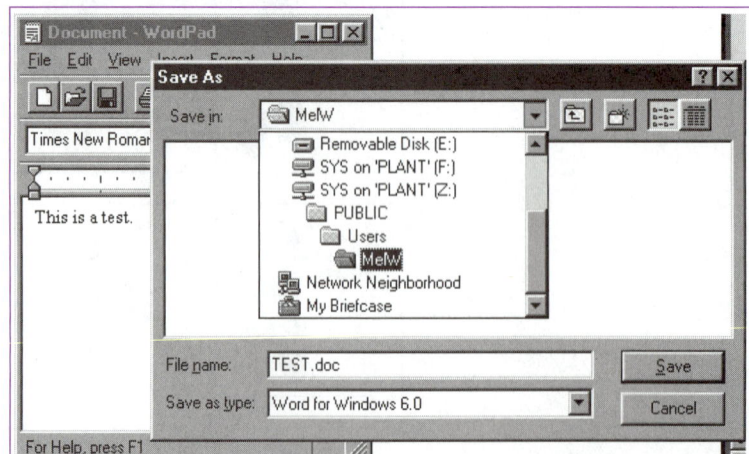

3. Log back in as the Administrator.
4. Start **NWAdmin**.

5. Navigate to the *TEST.doc* file that you just created in your user's home directory, and right-click on the document to check the details. (See Figure 9-17.)

Figure 9-17

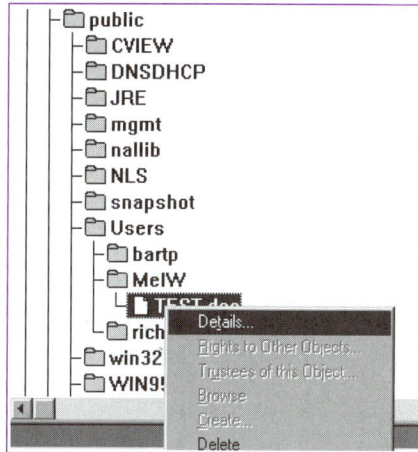

6. Click on **Trustees of this File**, and open the window showing the rights you have to that file based on your ADMIN status. This should resemble Figure 9-18.

Figure 9-18

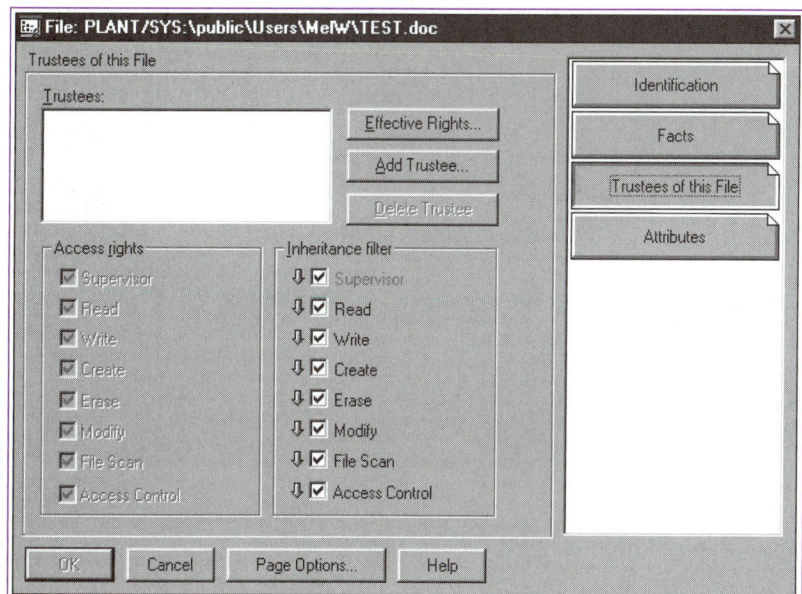

7. As shown in Figure 9-19, rights are verified by clicking on the **Effective Rights** button and displaying the rights for the Admin user.

Figure 9-19

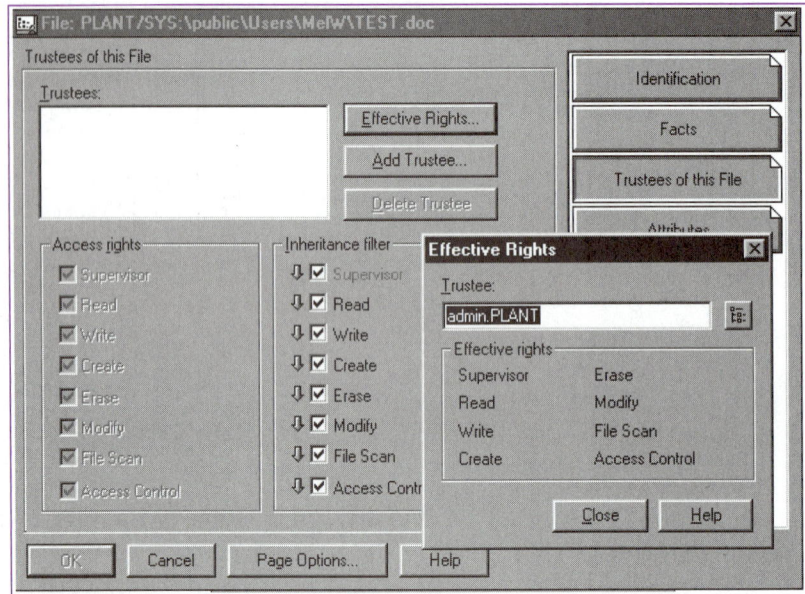

8. Click the **Browse** button on the right of the *Effective Rights* window. Browse to your user's object (*MelW* in this case) to display your rights to the file you just created. Notice that you have all rights except Supervisor, and that ADMIN has all rights.

Figure 9-20

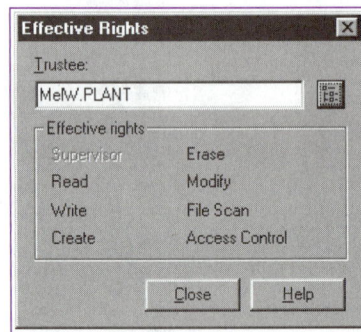

9. Now click the **Browse** button, and check the effective rights of a user other than yourself or ADMIN. In this case, BartP's rights to the file you just created are only the Read and File Scan rights. Remember that these rights are the default rights given to users.

Figure 9-21

10. Click **Close** on the *Effective Rights* window, click **Add Trustee** on the *Details* window, and select a user other than yourself or ADMIN (BartP in the example shown). Notice that you can now grant access rights, including the Supervisor access right, and that the Read and File Scan are automatically selected for you when you add a trustee. You should de-select them if they are not the ones you wish to grant. You can also place Filters, but you cannot add a Supervisor Inheritance Right Filter (because it is grayed out). (See Figure 9-22.)

Figure 9-22

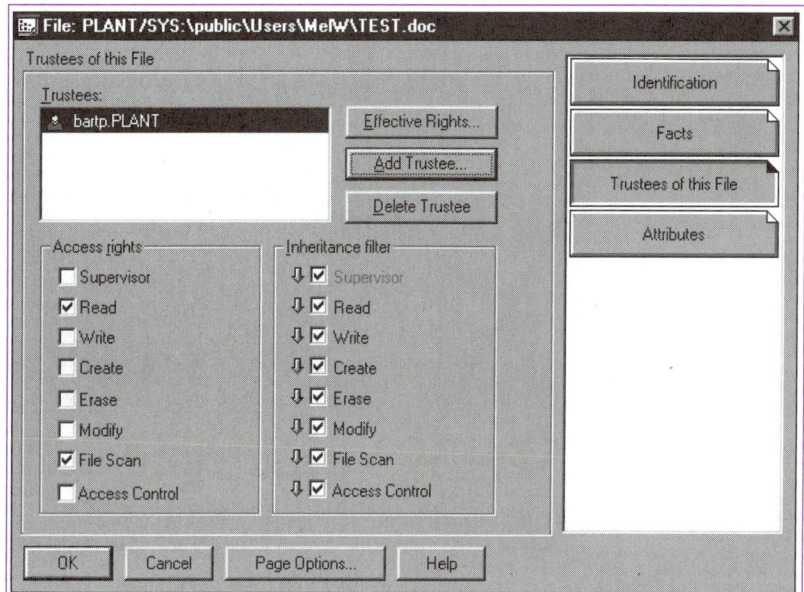

11. Note that removing the check marks from the Access rights side for that user, and clicking the **OK** button to apply the change, does not ensure that the Read and File scan rights have been removed. (See Figure 9-23.)

Figure 9-23

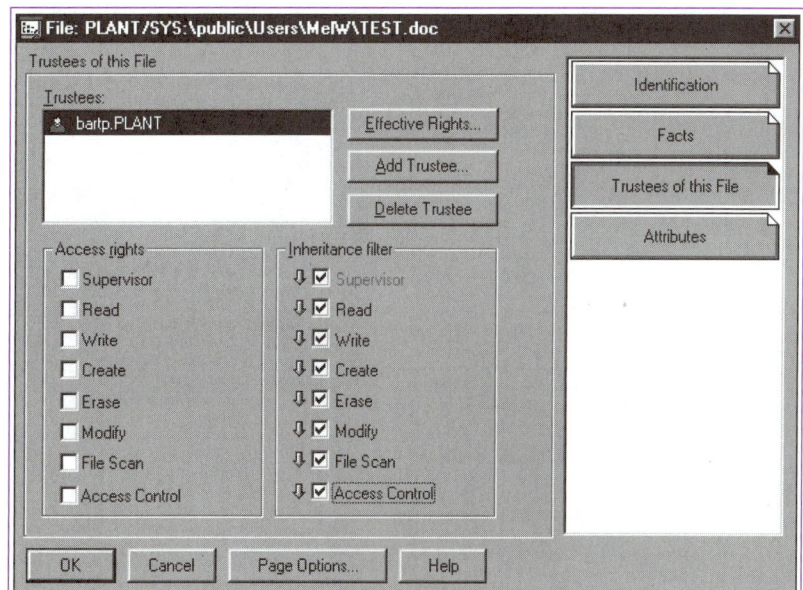

12. Verify this by clicking the **Effective Rights** button and checking that user's rights. Note that BartP in this example still has the Read and File scan rights. This is because the inheritance filters were set to allow the flow of rights from above to continue. Thus, the two rights were inherited from the user's container above.

Figure 9-24

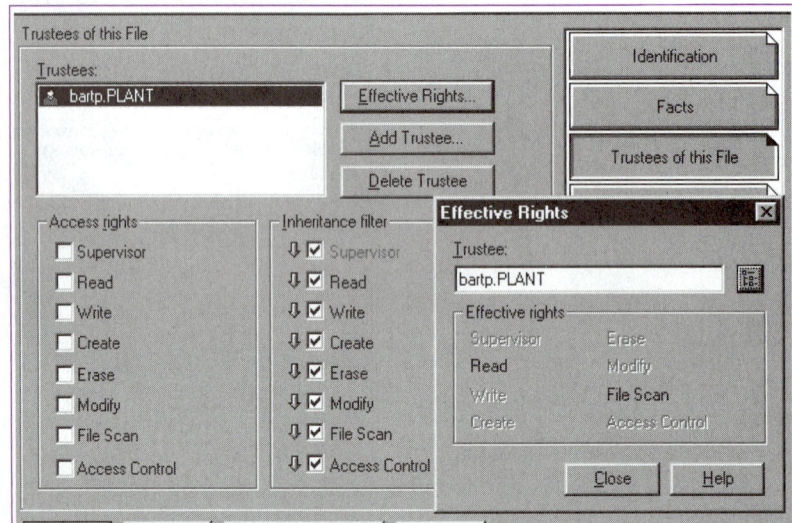

13. To ensure that the new trustee assignment grants only the rights you wish to grant, you should assign the rights you desire and use an IRF to filter out the rights you do not wish to flow to the user. This is shown in Figure 9-25, after assignment and filtering were set and the file re-checked. Note that the supervisor right still cannot be filtered.

Figure 9-25

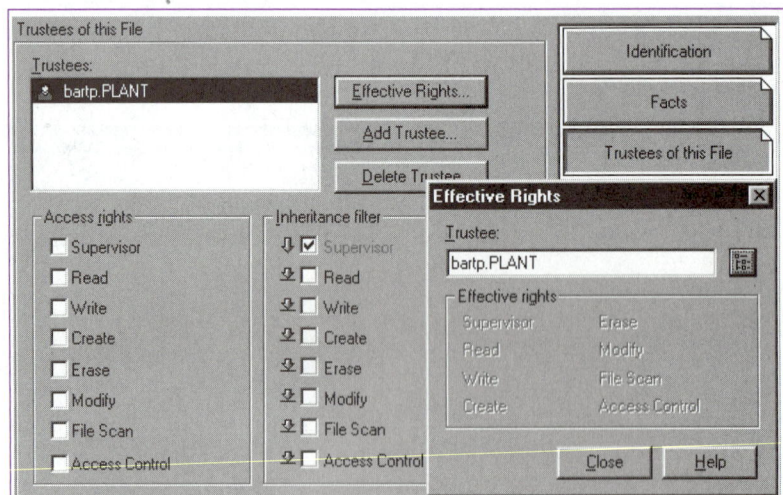

14. Note, too, that the file's access can be checked, as indicated below through the **Network Neighborhood** window. BartP is shown as a trustee whose rights have been removed. (See Figure 9-26.)

Figure 9-26

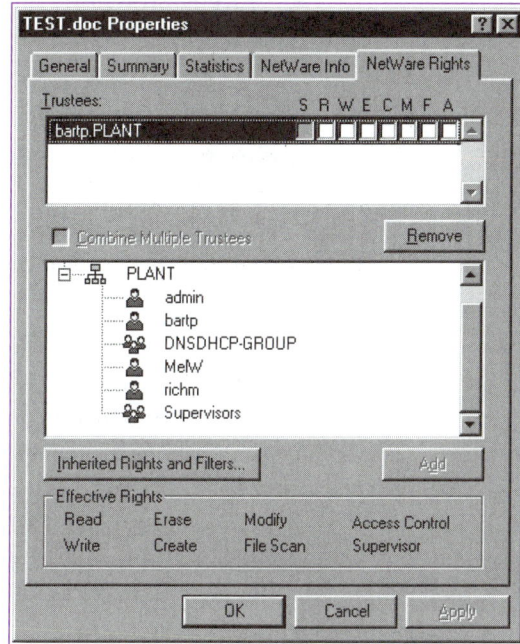

Planning Rights in File System Security

Avoid excessive rights granted high in the directory, because inheritance will allow them to flow downward.

Plan Top Down Rights Assignment

Plan rights in a directory structure so that the majority of users have fewer rights near the top of the directory structure. Grant additional rights as necessary as you move further down the directory structure. Avoid excessive rights granted high in the directory, because inheritance will allow them to flow downward. At each level in the directory structure, grant only those rights that users need to perform necessary functions. Use IRFs to block rights that should not flow down (remembering that the Supervisor right cannot be blocked).

Plan Largest to Smallest Group Assignments

By assigning rights to large groups, administrators do not have to make those rights assignments to all individual users. Where necessary, the user object can be assigned rights, but this should occur only when group and container assignments will not grant the desired rights to a user.

Chapter Summary

This chapter introduced File System Security. The administrator grants authority, in the form of rights of access, based on a user's need to use file and directory resources. File System Rights regulate who accesses an item and how that access is obtained. A user with access is a trustee. Giving rights is referred to as granting or assigning rights. Rights assigned to a user flow down and apply to the containers below through inheritance, unless they are blocked by an Inherited Rights Filter. The resulting list of rights a user has at a particular level in the tree is his effective rights. All trustees granted access to information are contained in that information's Access Control List (ACL).

There are eight different rights assigned to files and directories in the file system. The rights are the same for both files and directories, but can be set differently. The eight rights are: Supervisor, Read, Write, Create, Erase, Modify, File Scan, and Access Control. They are designated either by their full name or by their single letter identifier. The Supervisor (S) right assigns the user all rights to the file system component, and to any sub-components below it. Supervisor is the only right that cannot be blocked by an Inherited Rights Filter. The Read (R) right grants a user the right to open and read files in the directory, and to run programs that reside within the directory. The Write (W) right assigns the user the right to open and change or add data to the contents of the directory. The Create (C) right assigns the user the right to create new files and subdirectories. The Erase (E) right assigns the user the right to delete the directory and/or any files or subdirectories it contains. The Modify (M) right assigns the user the right to change the name of a file, directory, or subdirectory, or to change their attributes, but does not permit content modifications.

Remember the names of rights by using the phrase "Some Rights Will Cause Extreme Mental Fatigue Always!"

Rights assigned automatically by the system are referred to as default rights. The user who creates the server objects, and any objects given NDS Supervisor right to the server object, automatically receives all rights, including the Supervisor right to the server object. Any user in the same container as the *SYS:* volume automatically receives the R and F rights to *SYS:PUBLIC*. All users created in NDS User object creation with **NWAdmin** or **NETADMIN**, and assigned a home directory, are automatically granted all rights, except the S, to their own home directories. Rights can be checked using *Network Neighborhood* in addition to **NWAdmin** and **NETADMIN**.

Attribute security is an additional subset of file system security for files and directories. Its function is to keep the operating system informed as to what can be done to the associated file. It gives the administrator an override capability that prevents users from doing things that they would otherwise be authorized to do through other rights assignments. These override capabilities include Archive Needed (A), Can't Compress (Cc), Copy Inhibit (Ci), Don't Compress (Dc), Execute Only (X), Hidden (H), Normal (N), Purge Immediate (P), Read Only (Ro), Shareable (Sh), and System (Sy). These attributes can be set in **NWAdmin**, *Network Neighborhood*, and **FILER**. Other NetWare utilities that can be used when working with files and attributes include **RIGHTS** and **FLAG**.

There are seven ways to assign file system rights to a user. They can be assigned: 1) directly to the user object; 2) to a group of which the user is a member; 3) to an organizational role which the user is occupying; 4) to a container object in which the user object is located; 5) to another user object to which the first user is a security equivalent; 6) to the [Public] trustee; and 7) to a parent container of a group or container to which the user is a member (commonly referred to as *inheritance*).

Rights granted to higher containers that flow down to all container objects and users within them can be blocked, either by creating a new trustee assignment, or by using Inherited Rights Filters (IRF). An IRF can only block rights, not grant them. The Supervisor right in the file system cannot be blocked. Effective rights are all rights assigned and inherited by the user, minus any rights blocked by IRFs.

Rights assignments should allow users fewer access rights at higher positions in the directory, and grant only those rights necessary to perform job functions at other directory locations. Assigning rights to large groups reduces the administrator's workload by eliminating the need to assign a similar set of rights to every user.

Networking Terms Used in Chapter 9

File System Security	trustee list	attribute security
authority	Access Control List (ACL)	**FILER**
need for access	access rights	assigned rights
right of access	Supervisor (S)	user object
need-to-know	Read (R)	group
File System Rights	Write (W)	organizational role
trustee	Create (C)	container object
granting rights	Erase (E)	natural groups
assigning rights	Modify (M)	security equivalence
inherited	File Scan (F)	[Public] trustee
inherited rights	Access Control (A)	parent container
Inherited Rights Filter (IRF)	default rights	
effective rights	default rights assignments	

■ **Chapter Review Questions**

1. What is the central concept of File System Security?

2. Define *authority* as it relates to the rights a network administrator grants to individuals or groups in order for them to accomplish their assigned tasks.

3. Why should the level of rights given to individuals or groups be determined by how much they *need-to-know*?

4. What do *File System Rights* regulate?

5. Define *trustee*.

6. The act of giving a user particular rights is referred to as _____.

7. How do *rights* flow?

8. Explain *inherited rights*.

9. What is an *Inherited Rights Filter*?

10. Explain *effective rights*.

11. What is a *trustee list*?

12. Explain each of the *NetWare File System rights*.

13. What is the only right that cannot be blocked by an Inherited Rights Filter?

14. What is the right that grants the right to users to grant rights to any other user?

15. Which right allows the user to run programs in the applicable directory?

16. Does the *Modify* right allow the user to modify the contents of a file?

17. What are *default rights assignments*?

18. What are *attributes*?

19. What utilities can check or set *attributes*?

20. List the file and directory *attributes*.

21. Explain how FILER is used.

22. What are two other utilities used to work with files and attributes in the DOS prompt mode?

23. What is an *ACL*?

24. How are rights transferred?

25. What are two ways to block *inherited rights*?

■ Associated Chapter Problems

1. Explain the need for File System Security.

2. Define each of the eight File System Rights.

3. List all the rights given by default rights assignments.

4. Show all the ways rights assignments can be checked.

5. Check the attributes on three files in different locations on your *Z:* drive, and report your findings.

6. Explain the process for verifying effective rights using **NWAdmin**.

7. Describe all methods for receiving file system rights.

8. Explain the two ways inherited rights can be blocked.

9. What are your user object's rights to files that you place in your own home directory?

10. Why should group assignments be planned from largest to smallest?

CHAPTER
10
DIRECTORY SERVICES SECURITY

Much like File System Security, Novell Directory Services Security provides a method for Administrators to control object access. In this instance, that access involves NDS objects. Upon completing this chapter, you will be able to:

- describe the Novell Directory Services (NDS) Security components.

- explain the NFS and NDS Security similarities.

- list and explain Object rights.

- list and explain Property rights.

- compare the All Properties method of rights assignment to the Selected Properties method.

- explain Effective rights.

- state when multiple administrator security systems are likely to be utilized.

- explain when NDS rights *do* flow into NFS.

NDS Security

You already learned in Chapter 5 that after network communication, Novell Directory Services (NDS) is the most fundamental service a NetWare network provides. You also learned that NDS is your network's single point for accessing and managing network resources. Now you will learn how administrators control that single point through *NDS Security*.

Just as NDS is composed of Objects, Properties, and Values, NDS Security is made up of *Object rights* and *Property rights* (with the latter controlling the ability of a user to alter Values). Through NDS Security, an administrator controls who has access to the network's objects, who can see the information stored in those objects, and whether or not users with access can alter what they see. Therefore, NDS Security gives network objects rights to other network objects.

Like NetWare File System Security, NDS Security involves assigning network resource rights to trustees, computing their *Effective rights* (all granted and *Inherited rights*), and accounting for *Inherited Rights Filters (IRF)*. To gain access to an object or its properties, a user must be made a trustee of that object on its *Access Control List (ACL)*, and be granted the specific rights to that object.

Once a user has logged into an NDS tree, granting *trustee assignments* is the administrator's main tool for controlling the resources of his network. Through trustee assignments, the administrator can secure access to the network resources, and maintain control by granting users only those rights necessary to perform their job tasks. The trustee list is also an integral part of NDS Security, because it is stored as a property of the object in the access control list. You must be a trustee of an object and be on that object's ACL to be granted rights to the object.

NDS Security works in two directions. If a User object is granted rights to a targeted resource, the targeted resource will also have the User object in its list of trustees. Once a user is in the ACL of another object, it has access to the object, and depending on the rights he has, he may be able to alter the information stored in the object's properties.

Figure 10-1 shows the trustees of the NetWare 5 [Root] object in your TPUP Plant network.

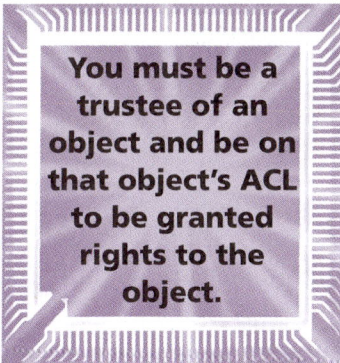

You must be a trustee of an object and be on that object's ACL to be granted rights to the object.

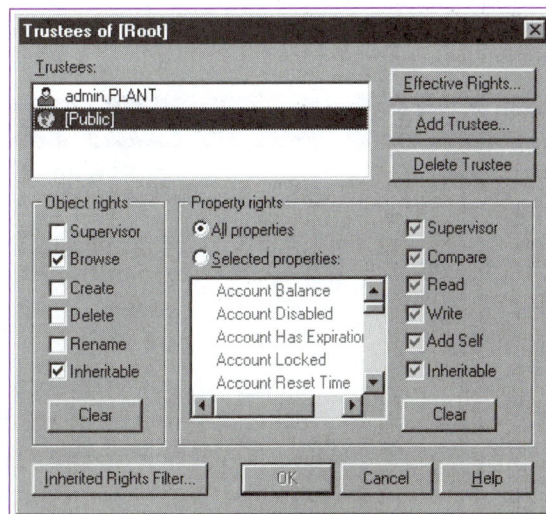

Figure 10-1

CHAPTER 10
DSS

Figure 10-2 shows the same trustee information for the NetWare 4.11 TPUP Headquarters network.

Figure 10-2

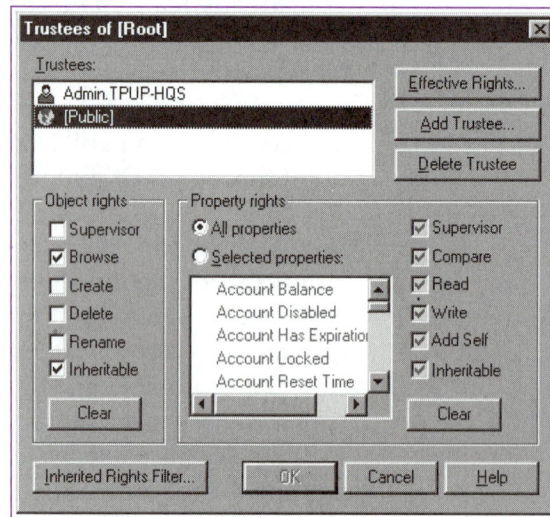

NOTE 4.11 USERS

These screen shots are based upon the most recent Novell Client (version3). Previous versions of the Novell Client did not use the **Inheritable** object right shown in Figure 10-2.

NOTE 4.11 USERS

Any object can be made a trustee of an object.

You can also grant rights to all users connected but not yet logged into the network by assigning [Public] as a trustee of an object.

Any object can be made a trustee of an object. You will recall that NDS has several objects that represent more than one other NDS object. A *Group object*, for example, represents several users. When objects that represent more than one network resource are made trustees of another object, all members of the represented group receive the rights from that trusteeship. As you learned in Chapter 5, Group objects, *containers* and *Parent containers*, and the *Organizational Role object* are multiple representation items. Multiple users can also gain *trusteeship* through security equivalence if the administrator uses this function.

Special circumstances may warrant assigning rights to all network users. In those circumstances, an administrator may grant object access to everyone authenticated to the network by making the [Root] object a trustee of the object. This is not recommended, but it may be useful in certain situations.

You can also grant rights to all users connected but not yet logged into the network by assigning [Public] as a trustee of an object. Recall that users not yet authenticated to the network inherit the rights assigned to the [Public] object.

Two Categories of NDS Security Rights

Unlike the NetWare File System Security, NDS security has two different types of rights: Object rights and Property rights. These rights are shown in the lower half of the two graphics used in the previous section on Trustee assignments and are discussed on the following pages.

Object rights determine the actions a trustee can perform on an object (with the exception of the new "Inheritable" right). These rights are shown on the left portion of Figure 10-3, which lists the Trustees of the **TPUP-HQS** container object.

Figure 10-3

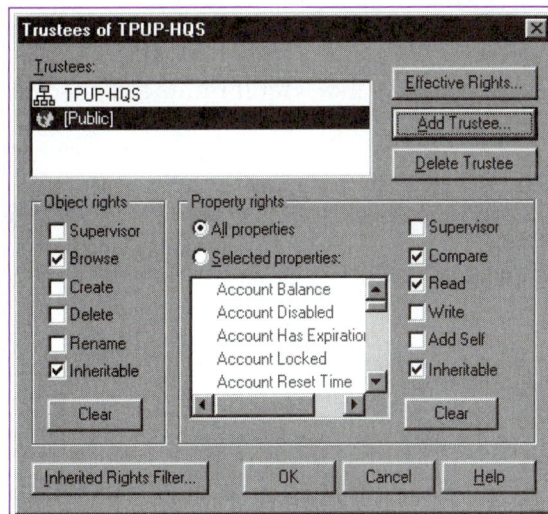

CHAPTER 10
DSS

> **NOTE**
>
> Versions of NetWare before version 5 did not include "Inheritable" as a right.
>
> **NOTE**

Object rights consist of *Supervisor*, *Browse*, *Create*, *Delete*, *Rename*, and *Inheritable* rights.

Object Rights Chart

Object Rights	Description
Supervisor (S)	This right grants the trustee all of the access rights to an object listed in this table, and access to all of the object's property rights. Unlike the NFS Supervisor right, the NDS Supervisor right can be blocked by an Inherited Rights Filter (IRF).
Browse (B)	This right grants the trustee the ability to see an object in the Directory.
Create (C)	This right is available only in Container objects, and grants the trustee the ability to create new objects within the applicable container object.
Delete (D)	This right grants the trustee the ability to delete an object from the Directory.
Rename (R)	This right grants the trustee the ability to change the name of the object in the Directory.
Inheritable (I)	This right is available only in Container objects, and grants the trustee the ability to inherit the assigned rights he has to objects and child objects inside the applicable container.

Admin is the only user created automatically by the operating system. It is automatically granted the Supervisor object right to the [Root] object. Confirm this by checking your TPUP Admin User object.

1. Open **NWAdmin**.
2. Scroll to the **[Root]** object.
3. Right click and then click on **Trustees of this Object**.

4. Notice in Figure 10-4 that the **Supervisor** and **Inheritable** object rights are already checked for the admin user. These are the default rights assigned to the Admin User object. Click the **OK** button.

Figures 10-4   **Figure 10-5**

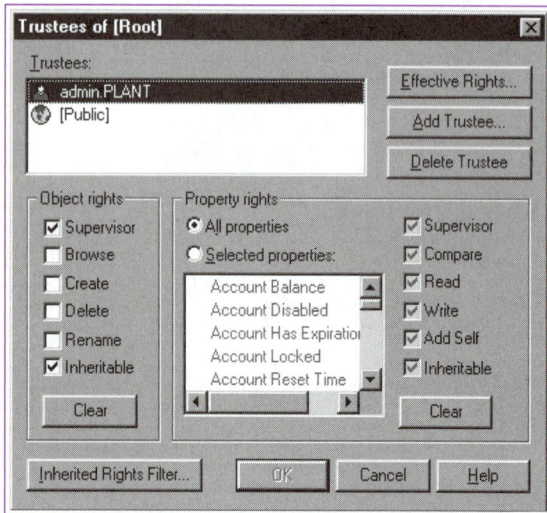
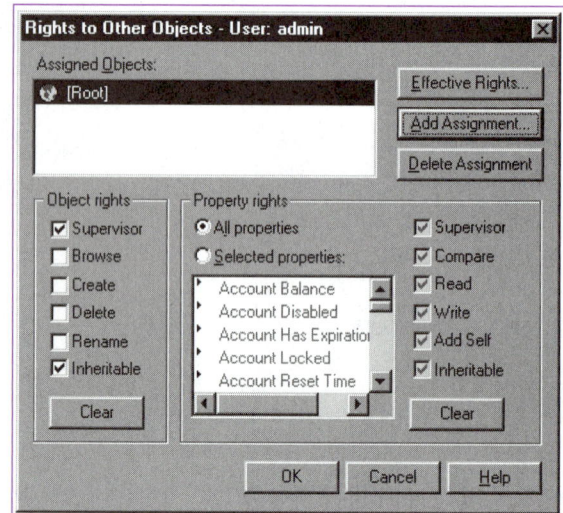

5. This can be verified by scrolling to the Admin user object.

6. Right click on the Admin user, and click on **Rights to Other Objects** as shown in Figure 10-5. The same two default rights are shown pre-selected.

Remember that the Supervisor object right grants all Object rights, whether they are checked or not. The Inheritable right is granted automatically when the Supervisor right is assigned, but it may be taken away to secure containers at lower levels within the Directory. If you attempt to clear the Supervisor right, however, you will find that the Supervisor right to the [Root] object may not be removed from the Admin User object.

It is through this automatic rights assignment that the Admin user obtains all of its rights. Supervisor to the [Root] gives the supervisor right to all objects attached to the Directory, including all NFS servers, and to the root of all volumes attached to the servers. If this one rights assignment were not done automatically, no object would be able to create additional objects. Verify that the Admin object has Supervisor rights to the Server object.

7. Click the **OK** button.

8. Scroll to the **Plant** Server object.

9. Right click on the Server object, and click on **Trustees of this Object**.

> Supervisor to the [Root] gives the supervisor right to all objects attached to the Directory, including all NFS Servers, and to the root of all volumes attached to the servers.

10. Click the **Browse** button next to the ***Object name*** window, and scroll to the **admin** user. The information in Figure 10-6 should appear. Notice that some Object rights are not available on the Server object. This is because the Server can only be created during installation. Click the **Close** button when you have finished viewing these rights.

Figure 10-6

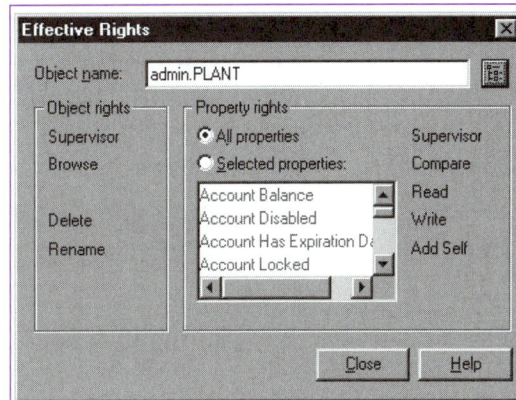

Property rights determine the actions a trustee can perform on an object's properties (with the exception of the new "Inheritable" right). Property rights also control a user's ability to use network resources. Property rights can also be granted to trustees using the *All properties* button, as shown below, or by using the *Selected properties* button. Property rights are listed in the center and right portion of Figure 10-7.

Figure 10-7

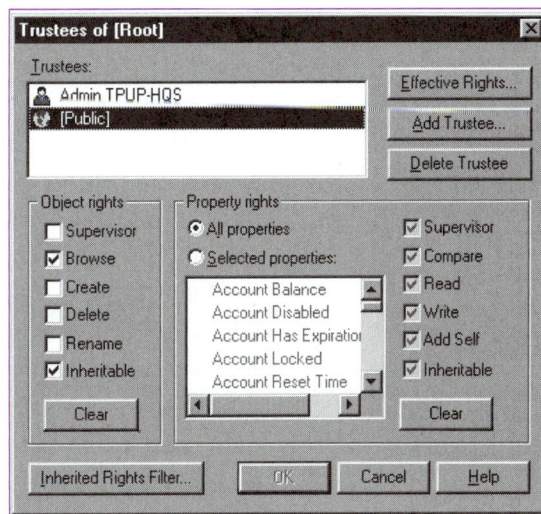

Property rights consist of *Supervisor*, *Compare*, *Read*, *Write*, *Add/Remove Self*, and *Inheritable* rights.

Property Rights Chart

Property Rights	Description
Supervisor (S)	This right grants the trustee all of the object's property rights. Unlike the NFS Supervisor right, this NDS Supervisor right can be blocked by an Inherited Rights Filter (IRF).
Compare (C)	This right grants the trustee the ability to compare a value to a value in the applicable property. The comparison responds either True or False, but does not allow the trustee to view the actual property value. This right is automatically granted when a trustee is assigned the Read right.
Read (R)	This right grants the trustee the ability to view the property value. This right also automatically grants the Compare (C) right.
Write (W)	This right grants the trustee the ability to add, delete, modify, or change an object's property value. This right also automatically grants the Add/Remove Self (A) right.
Add/Remove Self (A)	This right grants the trustee the ability to add or delete itself as a value of the object's property value. This right is automatically granted when the Write (W) right is assigned.
Inheritable (I)	This right allows the trustee to inherit the assigned property rights to objects within the container. It is available only on container objects, and is automatically granted when the All Properties option is selected. However, it must be manually selected when the Selected Properties is used.

NOTE

In previous versions of NetWare, rights applied with the **Selected properties** option were not inherited. In NetWare 5, the **Inheritable** button allows the rights to flow down to the next levels.

NOTE

Property rights can also be granted using the **All properties** button (the rights checked on the side are applied to all of the object's properties in the center). They can also be granted using the **Selected properties** button (the administrator can scroll through the object's properties to choose the ones he wants the rights applied to property). The **Inheritable** button is selected by default when the **All properties** selection is chosen, but it must be granted manually to each property when the **Selected properties** button is chosen. Rights granted with the **Selected properties** option overwrite the properties previously granted by the **All properties** option.

When you create a user, that User object is automatically granted rights to itself. Check this by performing the following steps.

1. Scroll to a user (**BartP** in the example), right click, and click **Trustees of this Object**. Note in Figure 10-8 that the Property right **Read** is on **All properties**.

Figure 10-8

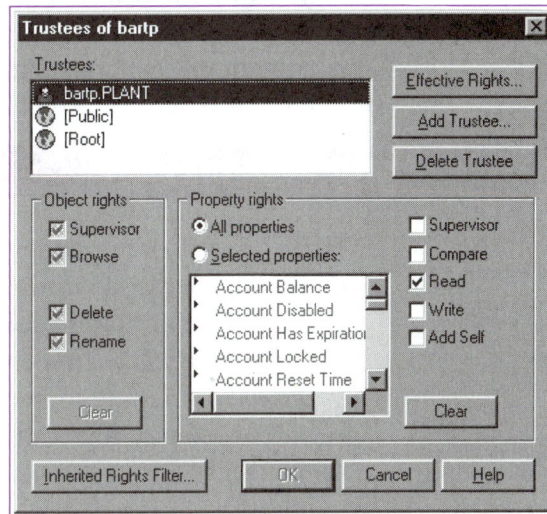

2. Check the individual properties affected by this assignment by clicking on the **Selected properties** radio button, then scroll through the property list.

When you grant property rights using the All Properties method, the rights you select are applied to all of the object's rights at the same time. The All Properties method does not allow additional adjustment of these rights to fine tune what the user is able to do. For this reason, assigning rights using the All Properties method is not recommended. Although it is easier to grant rights using this method, it frequently results in granting additional rights to objects that do not need them.

It is better to choose the rights you want the object to have and grant them individually using the Selected Properties method. It is an extremely flexible way to choose which rights you want to grant. Although it is more work for an administrator to use this method, it provides more accurate rights placement and a more secure network. Only the rights you want a user to have are given, and it requires you to make decisions about each right before it is given. This method helps ensure network security, although rights can still be incorrectly assigned or excessively granted.

In addition, rights granted through the Selected Properties method supersede those previously assigned through All Properties. For example, if you first assign a user the Read and Write rights (RW) to an object's Phone Number property using the All Properties method, and then go back and give him the Read right using the Selected Properties (but not the Write right), you will have granted him read and write to all properties, but he will only be able to read the phone number, not write a new one.

The All Properties method does not allow additional adjustment of these rights to fine tune what the user is able to do.

... rights granted through the Selected Properties method supersede those previously assigned through All Properties.

This ability to tailor security to the exact level you wish is an extremely powerful tool. The price of that tool is the inconvenience of individually planning and executing the security of every property of every object for every user. In a small network, this may be a manageable task for one individual. In a large network, however, it may be more than one person can handle.

Multiple Administrator Networks

How you assign the duties of maintaining network security depends on the size of the network itself. Your classroom network, for example, is small, so it is probably best to use a single, or *centralized network administration* role. If your network were large, however, you could designate separate administrators for the NFS and NDS security systems. You could even place multiple security administrators on each side of the network if the system warranted them. In either case, you would be creating a *distributed administration network* with multiple security administrators.

In the *multiple security administrator network*, there would probably be security monitors for individual container objects, and higher security control for more sensitive information areas like payroll and industrial or customer data files. This ability to divide the administration role is one of the principal advantages of NDS security. When setting up this type of security, however, you should remember to keep an emergency administrator object with full rights to the entire Directory tree. That user would be essential if a portion of the tree were inadvertently left without an administrator, and would be used when creating the distributed network administrators.

Using the Organizational Role object to administer NDS container objects is the most logical way to create multiple security administrators. To grant the administrators the rights you wish them to have, you can create the organizational role object, assign the object whatever rights it needs, and make your chosen individuals (or individual) occupants of the Organizational Role. They could then administer the container and all the objects within the container. When it is time to remove those rights from that individual, you need only remove their object from the Organizational Role object ACL. You could then reassign someone else to the position as necessary.

Once you have created an Organizational Role object with security rights over a container object, you are able to create *exclusive security administrators*. NDS does not allow you to filter the security right, unless you have already given it to a container object. Once you have given the security right to a container object, you can filter out all other Supervisor rights and create a container with a single, or exclusive, administrator. However, be careful. If that Organizational Role object is deleted after being made the exclusive

Using the Organizational Role object to administer NDS container objects is the most logical way to create multiple security administrators.

CHAPTER 10
DSS

administrator, you could lose control over that portion of the Directory tree. For this reason, it is wise to grant the Supervisor right, as well as the Organizational Role, to a designated individual for backup in case of emergencies.

| Activity 10-1 | Exclusive Security Administrator |

Let us try to assign exclusive security rights to an object—RichM in this case—by removing all other Supervisor rights to a container we create called "Secure Stuff." We will do this by creating the container "Secure Stuff," then creating the Organizational Roll "Security" and finally adding RichM to the Organizational Role, with Supervisor rights to the Secure Stuff container.

1. Create a container object called **Secure Stuff**, and an Organizational Role called **Security**, as indicated in Figure 10-9.

Figure 10-9

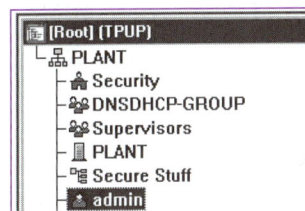

2. Check the trustees of **Secure Stuff** by right clicking on the container object, and then on **Trustees of this Object**. The object **Secure Stuff.PLANT** should be the only trustee shown in the *Trustees* window, as indicated in Figure 10-10.

Figure 10-10

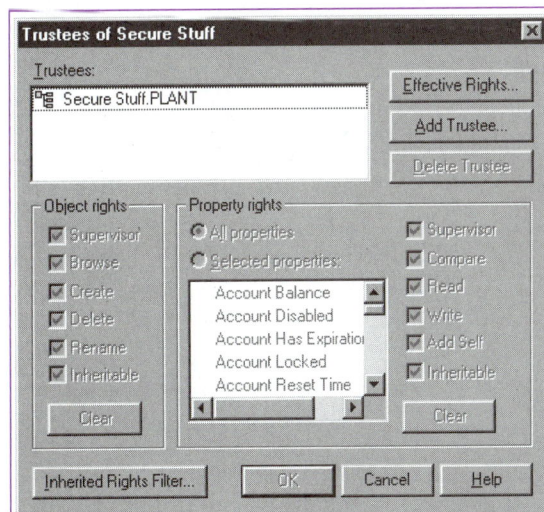

3. Click the **Effective Rights** button, and use the **Scroll** button to check the Admin object's rights to this object, as shown in Figure 10-11. Note that Admin has Supervisor Object and Supervisor Property rights. Click the **Close** button.

Figure 10-11

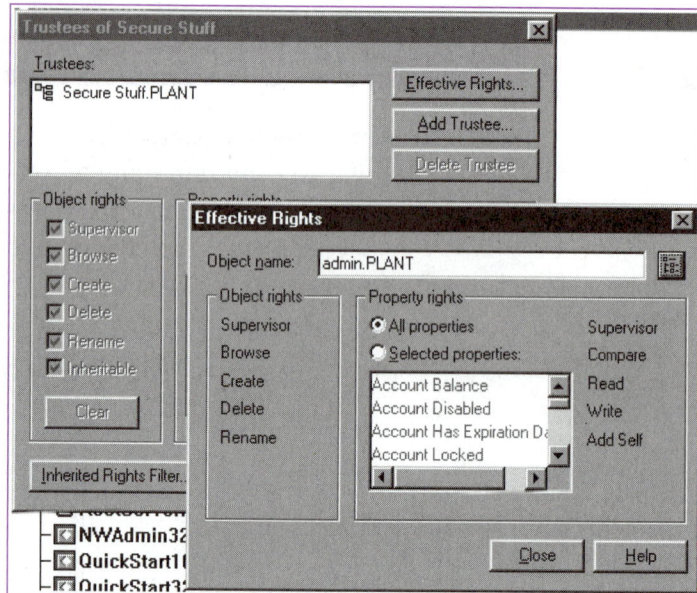

4. Click the **Effective Rights** button again. Then scroll to the **RichM** user object. Note in Figure 10-12 that **RichM** has only the default Browse right. Click on the **Close** button.

Figure 10-12

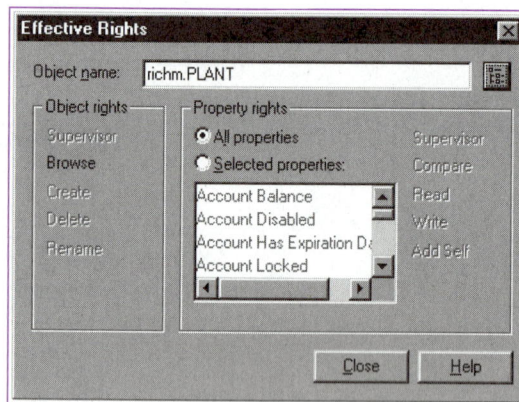

5. Click **Add Trustee**, and select the **Security** Organizational Role by double clicking on the object from the list. The following graphic should appear. (See Figure 10-13.)

Figure 10-13

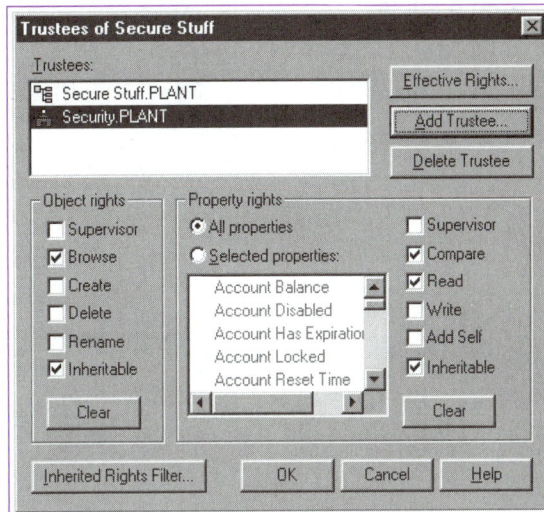

6. Click on the **Supervisor** object right, **Supervisor** property right, and then all other unchecked rights to assign the Security object all rights, as shown in Figure 10-14.

Figure 10-14

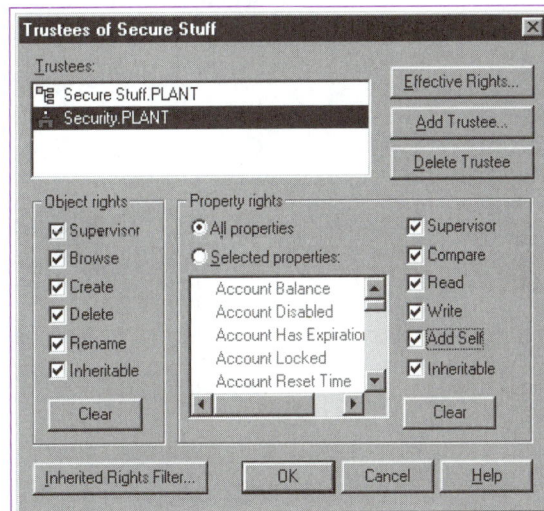

7. Click the **Inherited Rights Filter** button, and try to clear the **Supervisor** right to block it. The warning shown in Figure 10-15 should appear. Click **OK**, and **Cancel** the *IRF* window. Click **OK** on the *Trustees of this Object* window.

Figure 10-15

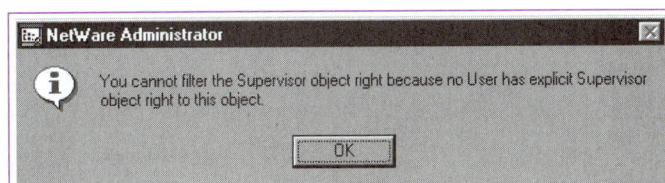

8. Double click the **Security** Organizational Role object and assign **RichM** as an Occupant, as indicated in Figure 10-16. Click **OK** on the *Occupant* and **OK** on the *Organizational Role: Security* window.

Figure 10-16

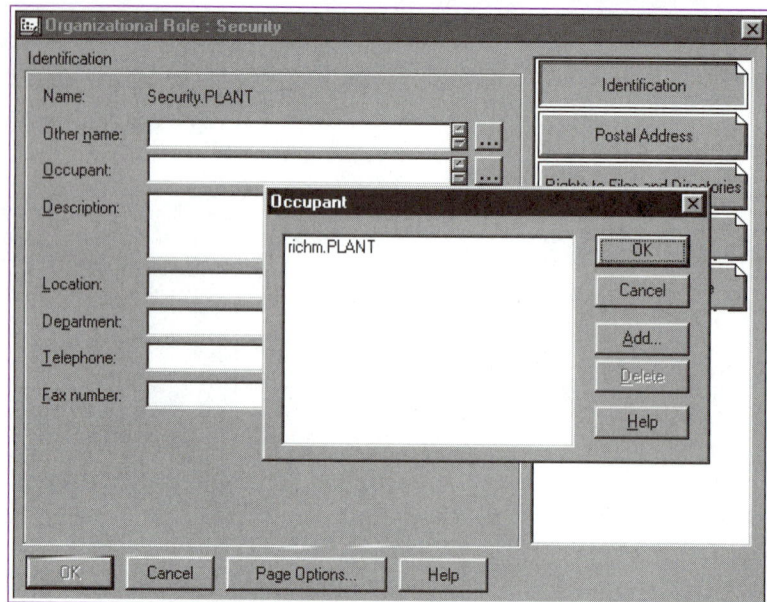

9. Right click on the **Secure Stuff** Container object, and click on the **Trustees of this Object** listing. Note that RichM is still not listed as a trustee of this object. Click on the **Effective Rights** button and scroll to **RichM** as shown in Figure 10-17. Note that RichM has been granted all rights, because he is an occupant of the **Security** Organizational Role object. Click the **Close** button.

Figure 10-17

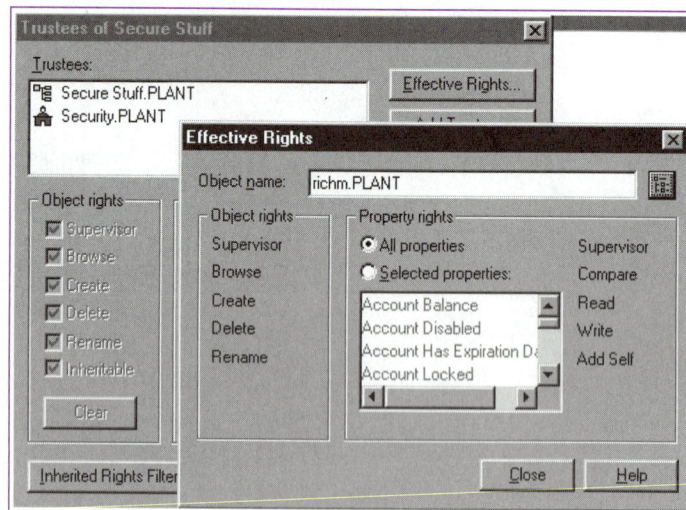

10. Click the **Inherited Rights Filter** and try to block the **Supervisor** right again by clicking on it. Note that you still cannot block this right because there is not yet an object with *explicit* Supervisor rights to the object.

11. Click **OK** and **Close**, and then **Add User**. Select **RichM** and grant him **Supervisor** object rights, but uncheck all other rights assignments as shown in Figure 10-18.

Figure 10-18

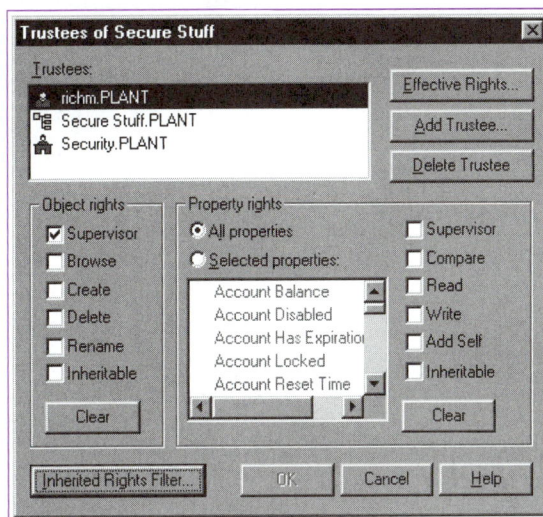

12. Check **RichM**'s effective rights, and note that he still has all rights because of the Organizational Role object rights assignments. Click **OK** to finish checking his effective rights.

13. Click the **Inherited Rights Filter** button again, and try to uncheck the supervisor right to block it. This time, as shown in Figure 10-19, you should be able to set the Inherited Rights filters to block the Supervisor object and Property rights.

Figure 10-19

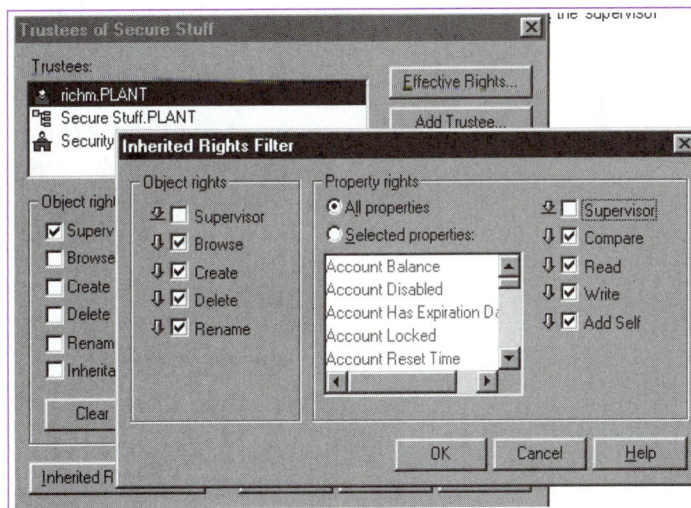

14. Now go back and check the effective rights of **Admin** on the **Secure Stuff** container. You will notice a difference immediately when the window in Figure 10-20 appears, informing you that your Admin user is not authorized to read the trustee list.

Figure 10-20

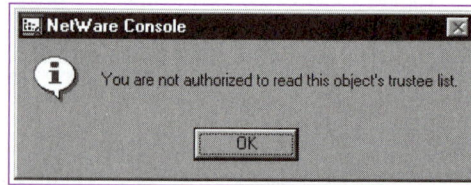

15. When you click **OK**, the *Effective Rights* window shown in Figure 10-21 indicates that your Admin user is now authorized only to browse the container's objects.

Figure 10-21

You have thus created an exclusive container administrator for the Secure Stuff container that you created in this exercise.

16. To verify the security of such an administrator, try to access and change any of the information regarding the Secure Stuff container. If you did this exercise properly, you should not be able to do so. You can even try to delete this object, but you should not be able to do this either.

17. To access the information in that container, you must either log in as RichM, because of his Supervisor status, or make yourself an occupant of the Organizational Role object, which includes the Supervisor status.

18. Add your **Admin** user as an occupant of **Security**. This will demonstrate that controlling access to a container is not enough. You must also lock down all other avenues which grant control to that container.

19. Once you are convinced that securing a network is often difficult because of the many ways access is granted to objects, undo the restrictive IRFs limiting the Admin user's rights, and remove **Admin** as an occupant of **Security**.

NDS Rights Flow Into NFS

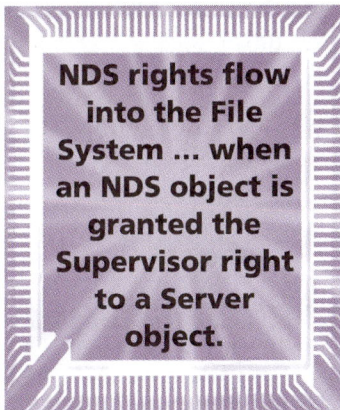

> NDS rights flow into the File System ... when an NDS object is granted the Supervisor right to a Server object.

NDS rights flow into the File System in only one instance. This occurs when an NDS object is granted the Supervisor right to a Server object. This assignment also immediately grants the Supervisor right to all volumes attached to that Server object, and gives the object Supervisor rights to all Volumes attached to that Server.

Passing this right to the NFS may be an intentional and desired result. However, this assignment may be granted unintentionally, and you should be careful that this does not occur. If a user is granted the Write (W) right to the Object Trustee ACL property of the Server object, that user is able to assign himself the file system Supervisor right at the root of all the server's volumes. This could result in the excessive granting of rights. Any way by which a user can be assigned rights to the Server or the Write right to the ACL should be carefully monitored, so that only the proper rights are granted.

Security Equivalence

Rights can also be granted to an object through *security equivalence*. An object can be made security equivalent to another object. This grants an object the same rights as the second object. Although rights normally flow down through the tree, and can be blocked by an IRF, security equivalence rights are independent of any other rights. An object whose rights have been blocked by an IRF and through an implicit rights assignment to a particular container may still have those rights if the object is security equivalent to another object with those rights.

All objects are also security equivalent to all the container objects that comprise its distinguished name. This is called *implied security equivalence*.

Determining Effective Rights

An object's effective rights to another object are comprised of all rights received from every available means of rights assignment, minus any rights blocked by an Inherited Rights Filter.

The sources of rights assignments for an object follow:

1. [Root]
2. [Public] trustee
3. All containers in the object's distinguished name
4. Groups of which the object is a member
5. Organizational Roles of which the object is an occupant
6. Rights explicitly assigned to the object
7. Security equivalences

Two methods can be used to display the effective rights an object has to another object. You can right click the first object, click on **Rights to Other Objects**, and browse to the object you want checked. In the example shown in Figure 10-22, checking **BartP** shows that he has only the Browse right on the container Secure Stuff.

Figure 10-22

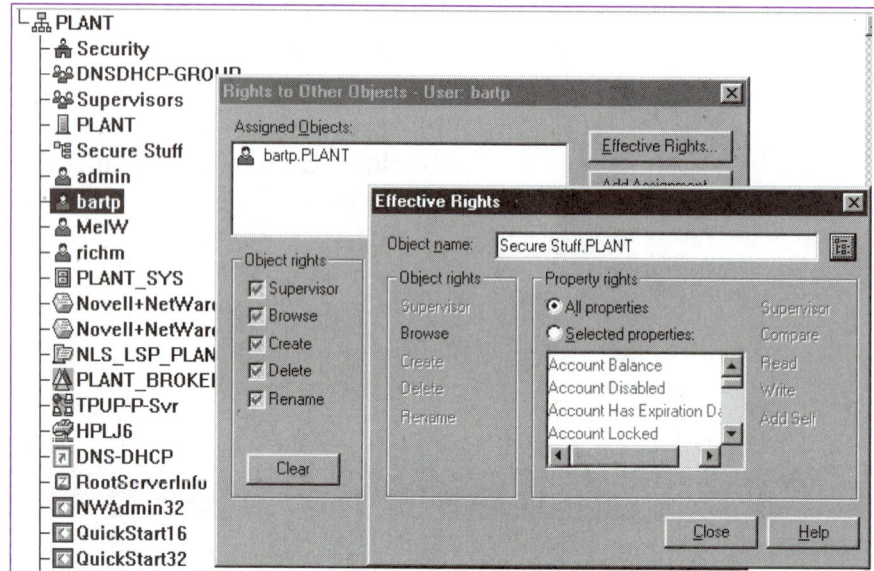

The other method requires you to go to the object you want checked and list the trustees of that object. Right clicking on **Secure Stuff** and selecting **Trustees of this Object** allows you to verify that BartP still has only the Browse right to the Secure Stuff container. This is shown in Figure 10-23.

Figure 10-23

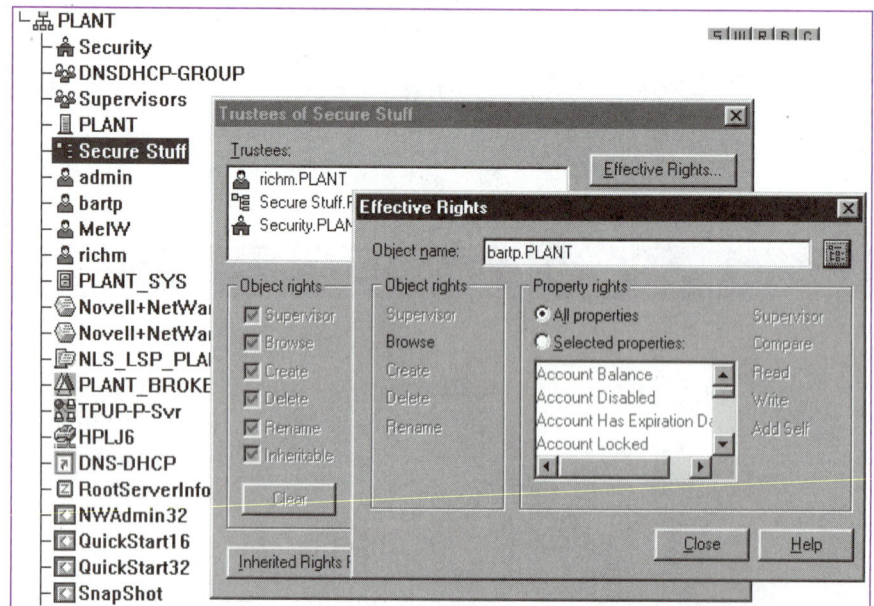

Identifying Sources of Effective Rights

Once you know an object's effective rights, it is sometimes difficult to determine where those rights originated. You may have to search the entire tree for evidence of the source of those rights.

When searching the tree, you may have to go to each of the seven sources of rights assignments for an object, listed above in this section. You would need to check both explicit rights assignments and inherited rights for each. To discover the origin of the rights for your object's assignments, you would primarily use the "Trustees of this Object" window of each object.

When the desired rights are not being transferred to a user, on the other hand, the same method is used to discover where the rights are being dropped. You would need to control each of the seven sources of rights assignments. This is also difficult, and you may have to search the entire tree before finding the source of the problem.

Troubleshooting NDS Security

As mentioned in the section above, two instances would require an administrator to troubleshoot NDS security—when a user has too many or not enough rights to perform a particular function. In either case, you should first determine the object's effective rights, and then determine the sources of those rights. Once you have completed those two steps, you can either add the missing rights or delete unnecessary rights. Although this may seem an easy task, it is one of the more difficult ones an administrator will encounter.

Chapter Summary

It is primarily through NDS Security that administrators control access and manage network resources. NDS Security is made up of Object rights and Property rights. Property rights determine the user's ability to alter an object's Values. Using NDS Security, an administrator controls who has access to the information stored in the network's objects, and determines whether those users with access can alter what they see.

NDS Security involves assigning rights to network resources to trustees and computing their effective rights. Effective rights are calculated by accumulating all instances of granted and inherited rights, and accounting for all inherited rights filters. An object can gain access to another object or its properties only by being made a trustee of that object on its access control list, and by being granted the specific rights to it.

NDS Security actually works in two directions. A User object may be granted rights to a targeted resource, but the targeted resource will also have the User object in its list of trustees. Either action produces the same result.

Any object can be assigned as trustee of another object. When objects that represent more than one object are made trustees of another object, all members of the represented group receive the rights from trusteeship. Multiple objects include Group objects, containers and Parent containers, and the Organizational Role object. Multiple users can also gain trusteeship through security equivalence. Granting rights to all network objects is possible through the [Root] object and the [Public] trustee.

There are two different types of rights in the NDS Security system: Object rights and Property rights.

Object rights determine the actions a trustee can perform on an object (with the exception of the new Inheritable right). Object rights consist of Supervisor, Browse, Create, Delete, Rename, and Inheritable rights. Admin is the only user automatically created by the operating system, and it is automatically granted the Supervisor object right to the [Root]. This allows Admin to manage the creation of the remainder of the objects in the NDS tree.

Property rights determine the actions a trustee can perform on an object's properties (with the exception of the new Inheritable right), and control a user's ability to use network resources. Property rights consist of Supervisor, Compare, Read, Write, Add Self, and Inheritable rights. Property rights can be granted using the **All properties** button, or by using the *Selected Properties* window. Rights granted with the **Selected properties** option overwrite the properties previously granted with the **All properties** option.

The size of your network determines whether a single administrator should be used. In larger networks, multiple administrators may be required. In multiple security administrator networks, there are usually security monitors for individual container objects, and higher security control for more sensitive information areas. This ability to divide the administration role is one of the most important advantages of NDS Security. The Organizational Role object is the most logical way to create multiple security administrators. Exclusive security administrators, rather than the Admin user, can be responsible for administrating a portion of the network. Be careful, however, to designate an emergency user to ensure that portions of the network are not left without an administrator.

NDS rights can flow into the File System when an object is granted the Supervisor right to a Server object. It immediately grants the object the Supervisor right to the root of all volumes attached to that server, and gives the object Supervisor rights to all volumes attached to that server.

Rights also flow to an object using Security Equivalence, which grants an object the same rights as another object. These rights are independent of any other rights, and are not blocked by an IRF or implicit rights assignment.

There are seven sources of rights assignments for an object. They are [Root], [Public] trustee, containers, groups, organizational roles, explicit rights assignment, and Security equivalence. An object's effective rights are all of these rights, less any IRFs.

There are two methods to check the effective rights an object has to another object. You can click on the **Rights to Other Objects** and browse to the object you want checked, or you can check the listing of the trustees of the object.

It is sometimes difficult to determine where rights originate. You may have to search the entire tree to find their source. You would primarily use the Trustees of this Object window for each object. You would also have to do the same search if not enough rights are being transferred to the user's object. You would have to find the source for each right, and discover where the intended right is being dropped.

Networking Terms Used In Chapter 10

NDS Security	Supervisor (Object right)	Add/Remove Self (Property right)
Object rights	Browse (Object right)	Inheritable (Property right)
Property rights	Create (Object right)	centralized network adminis-
Effective rights	Delete (Object right)	tration
Inherited rights	Rename (Object right)	distributed administration
Inherited Rights Filter (IRF)	Inheritable (Object right)	network
Access Control List (ACL)	All properties	multiple security administra-
trustee assignments	Selected properties	tor network
Group object	Supervisor (Property right)	exclusive security administra-
containers	Compare (Property right)	tor
Parent containers	Read (Property right)	security equivalence
Organizational Role object	Write (Property right)	implied security equivalence
trusteeship		

■ Chapter Review Questions

1. What is the primary way administrators control their single point for accessing and managing their network resources?

2. What two types of rights comprise NDS Security?

3. What does an administrator control through NDS Security?

4. What does NDS Security give network objects?

5. What is the only way by which users can gain access to an object or its properties?

6. When is a user affected by NDS Security?

7. What is the main tool an administrator has to control the resources on his network?

8. What kind of rights should administrators grant to users?

9. What must you be to be granted rights to an object?

10. How does the assignment of trustee rights in NDS work in two directions?

11. Which objects can be assigned trustee of another object?

12. What are the multiple representation items?

13. Who gains rights to an object when rights are assigned to the [Root] object?

14. Who gains rights to an object when rights are assigned to the [Public] trustee?

15. Define *Object rights*.

16. Define *Property rights*.

17. List the different Object rights.

18. List the different Property rights.

19. What are the two ways to grant Property rights to trustees?

20. What is the most logical way to create multiple security administrators?

21. What is the one instance when NDS rights flow into the NFS?

22. Define *security equivalence*.

23. What are the sources of effective rights?

24. How do you check the sources of effective rights?

25. How should you troubleshoot NDS security?

■ Associated Chapter Problems

1. Describe the similarities and differences between the NFS and NDS Security systems.

2. Explain how an administrator secures and maintains control over his system.

3. Show why it is best to assign security to multiple representation items first.

4. Describe instances in which you would want to use the [Public] trustee or the [Root] object.

5. Explain the two categories of NDS Security rights.

6. When is it preferable to use the All properties option instead of the Selected properties option? Why?

7. What does an administrator give up when he chooses to use multiple administrators or exclusive administrators on his network?

8. Explain the use of the Organizational Role object.

9. Explain *security equivalence*.

OBJECTIVES

Login scripts automate repetitious actions for users, making it easier for them to gain access to the network and its resources. Upon completion of this chapter, you will be able to:

- describe the types of login scripts.

- explain when the types of login scripts are executed.

- understand Planning for login scripts.

- understand components of typical login scripts.

- explain and use the **MAP** command.

- explain the **SEARCH DRIVE** commands.

- use the **MAP ROOT** and **MAP NEXT** commands.

- use Mapping within Windows.

- describe Directory Map objects.

Login Scripts

> **Login scripts are designed to help the user so that he or she will not need to remember the settings and long commands each time he or she accesses his or her computer.**

You may have noticed that a list of commands appears each time you log into the network. These commands are part of your login script. They are instructions that are executed immediately every time you log in. Like *DOS batch files*, they set the defaults that you will use while logged into the network. These defaults can predetermine the drives you will use, the way the network searches those drives, how the printers are configured, which printers you will use, any variable settings you need, and any additional commands that must be run before you log into the network (such as a *greeting message*). After these commands run, your user environment is automatically set up, and you no longer need to remember any of the commands.

Login scripts are designed to help the user so that he or she will not need to remember the settings and long commands each time he or she accesses his or her computer. Although the login process is still complicated, and still requires the same settings and commands, they are executed automatically by the scripts that the administrator creates. Apart from the window that pops up when the user logs on, the scripts go unnoticed. They are part of the magic that makes the network operate for him. You, as the administrator, are the magician who puts those scripts together.

There are three types of login scripts that an administrator may create or edit. They are the Container, Profile, and login User scripts. All three are optional, and have a *Login Script property* that can be created or edited in **NWAdmin**. In addition, there is a fourth login script that cannot be edited. This is the default script, and will be executed if a user does not have a user script. However, it is optional as well, and can be turned off. When a user executes the login procedure, NetWare checks for the existence of any of the first three login scripts. If it finds any of them, they run before or in place of the default script. Each login script serves a particular purpose. By using a combination of these scripts, you can tailor your users' environments automatically, thus reducing network maintenance.

If they exist, login scripts always execute in the same order. That order is as follows:

1. Container login script (of the object's parent container—if one exists).

2. Profile login script (if one is designated).

3. User login script (if one is specified).

4. Default login script (runs only if a User login script is not present, or if the NO_DEFAULT command is not present in the Container or Profile script).

Container Login Scripts

The *Container login script* is the first login script that can execute. Although there are other types of container objects, the Container login script is found only in the Organization or Organizational Unit container objects.

Figure 11-1

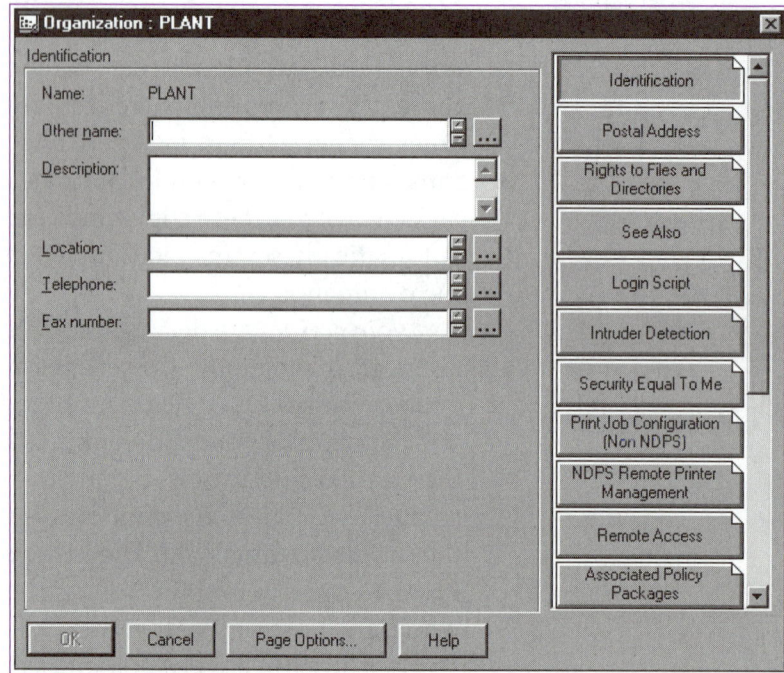

In the **TPUP PLANT** container object shown in Figure 11-1, you will notice the **Login Script** button on the right side. This is where you go to activate this property.

Figure 11-2

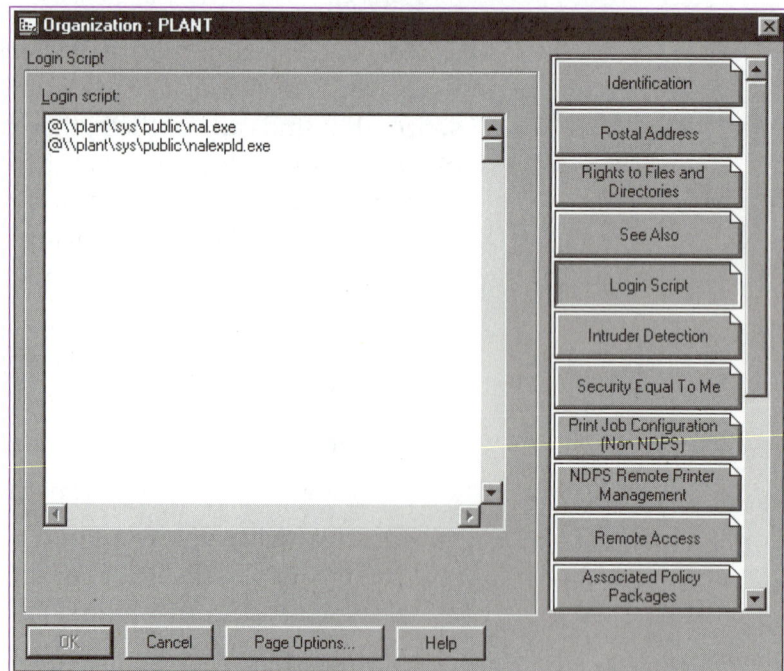

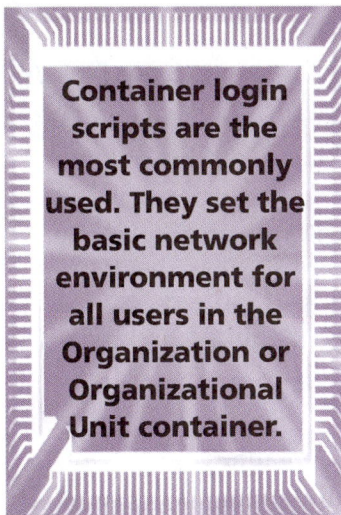

Container login scripts are the most commonly used. They set the basic network environment for all users in the Organization or Organizational Unit container.

Clicking on this button, as shown in Figure 11-2, lists the login script entries that you created when working on Network Application Launcher items.

Container login scripts are the most commonly used. They set the basic network environment for all users in the Organization or Organizational Unit container. All of the drive mappings, settings, and options are then set for every user in the container upon login. However, only the user's immediate parent Container login script is executable. If a user's container does not have a login script defined for it, the scripts for the containers above the parent are not used. NetWare will not search beyond the user's parent container for an executable login script.

As shown in the PLANT example above, you edit the Container login script using **NWAdmin** by activating the **Login Script** button to access the Login Script property.

Figure 11-3

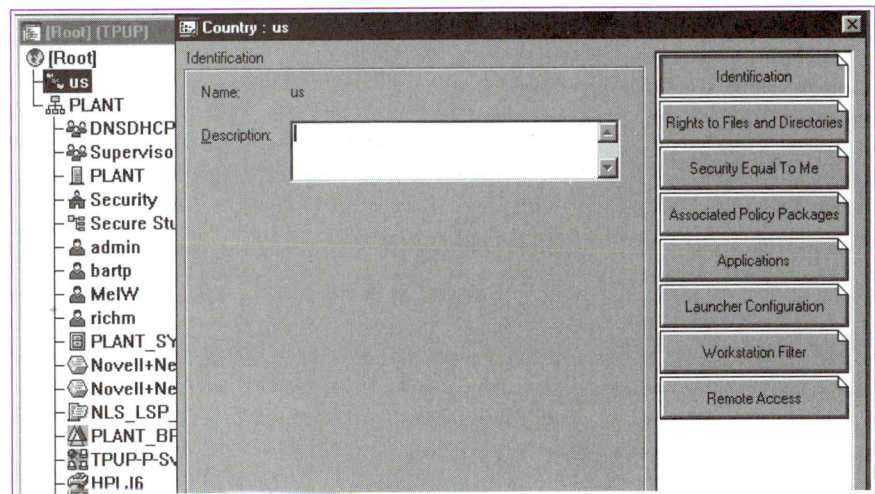

Note in Figure 11-3 above, however, that although **Country Container** is a container, there is no Login Script button when it is created in the TPUP organization.

Usually only the Admin user object is able to access and change these scripts, but any user with the proper rights can do so as well. These rights should not be distributed freely. Tampering with login scripts by unauthorized users will increase maintenance headaches.

A well-designed system of login scripts will usually have the following items in the Container login script:

- A search drive mapped to *SYS:PUBLIC*

- Search drives mapped to software applications

- Drive letters mapped for user's home directory

- Drive letters mapped for required data directories

- Messages for display to users

- User programs to execute

REMEMBER

Only O and OU containers can have Container login scripts.

REMEMBER

**CHAPTER 11
Login Scripts**

Profile Login Scripts

Profile objects are special objects that you can use to specify common environment components for multiple users.

Profile objects are special objects that you can use to specify common environment components for multiple users. One of the properties of the Profile object is the login script. Like the Container login script, the *Profile login script* can set *mappings*, *messages*, and other commands for those users associated with the profile. Unlike the Container login script, however, those users affected by a Profile login script are not required to be in the same container. The Profile login script allows you to create a login script for either a subset of users from the same container, or for a group of users that exist in two or more containers.

The Profile login script executes after the Container login script, and before the User or Default login scripts (if they exist). A Profile object should usually be created in the container where most of the affected users are located, but it can be located anywhere within the Directory. The administrator should verify that the items in the Profile login script do not conflict with those in any other login scripts.

In order to execute a Profile login script, a Profile object must be created, the user must be added as a trustee to the object, and the user must be granted the Browse Object right and the Read Property right to the object's Login Script property. The Browse Object right is granted by default, but the Read Property right must be assigned manually. If the number of users needing the Profile login script is large, you may do this using a Group object.

The following items may be in the Profile login script:

- Search drives mapped to software applications
- Drive letters mapped for required data directories
- Messages for display to users
- Commands necessary to execute user programs

In Figure 11-4, a Profile Object **Machinists** is shown with its **Login Script** property button activated. In this example, there is not yet a Profile login script.

Figure 11-4

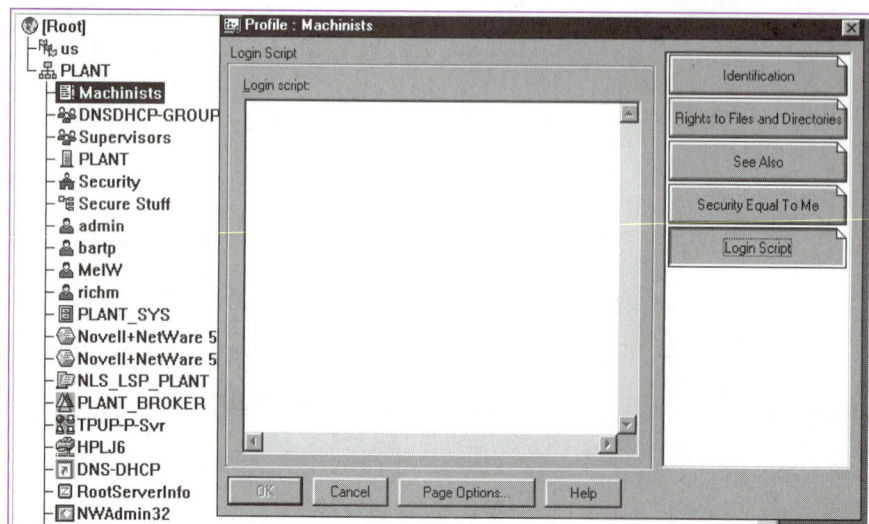

Add the following commands to the login script, as indicated in Figure 11-5. Click the **OK** button when finished.

```
WRITE "Good %GREETING_TIME, %LOGIN_NAME."
PAUSE
```

Figure 11-5

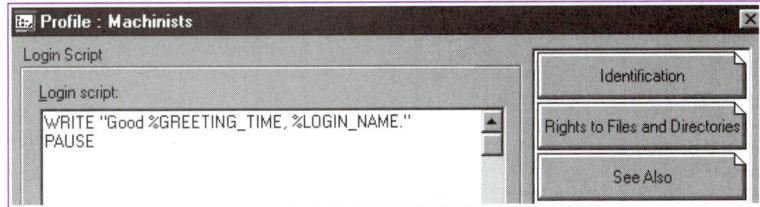

Because Bart, as a machinist, needs the items in the Machinists Profile login script, add **BartP** to the list of Trustees for the Profile Object by right clicking on the **Profile Object**. Then click on **Trustees of this Object**, click the **Add Trustee** button, and double click on **BartP**. Note that the **Browse Object** right is already granted. If you click on the **Selected Properties** radio button, however, and scroll down to the **Login Script** property, you will see that you must set this right manually. Set it by clicking on the **Profile** property, then add the **Read** right as indicated in Figure 11-6. Click **OK** to assign the rights as indicated.

Figure 11-6

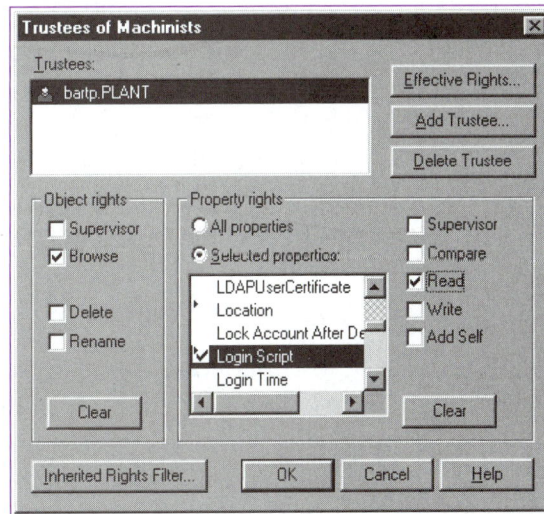

**CHAPTER 11
Login Scripts**

You must also go to the **BartP** user object and add the Profile **Machinists** to the **Login Script** properties page, as shown in Figure 11-7.

Figure 11-7

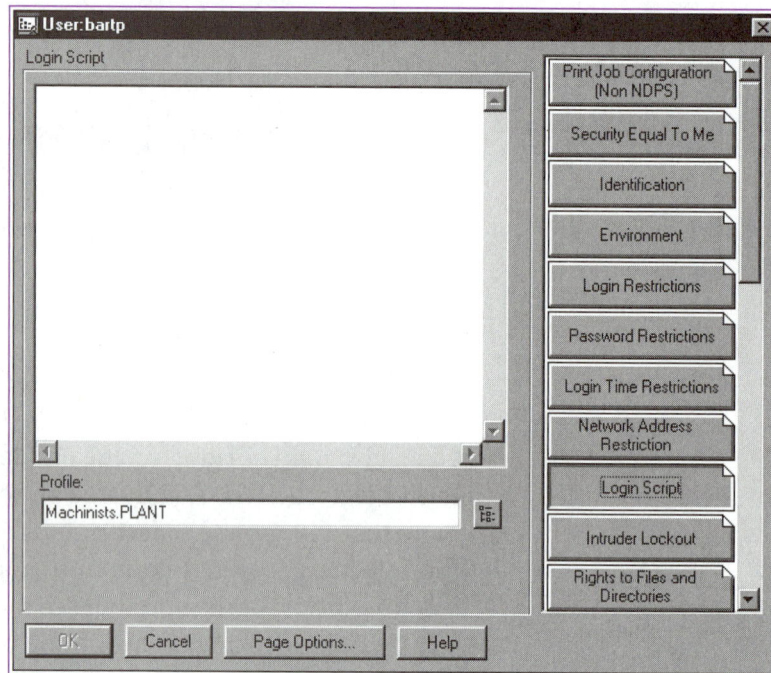

Log out, and then log back in as BartP to verify whether the Profile login script that you created works. You should see the results shown in Figure 11-8 when logging in as BartP.

The last two lines shown in the graphic are the result of the two commands that you added to the Profile login script. When you see lines similar to these on your screen, you have successfully created and verified a Profile login script. Strike any key to proceed.

Figure 11-8

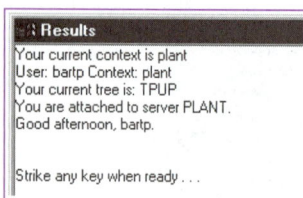

User Login Scripts

Now that you have seen and used Container and Profile login scripts to help manage groups of users, you should understand why the use of *User login scripts* is sometimes discouraged. Because login scripts are time-consuming to maintain, setting one up for each user would increase your network maintenance load significantly.

When they are used, however, User login scripts can add additional drive mappings that a user needs or display user specific messages. They create network environments for an individual user, and contain commands that pertain only to that user. If User login scripts are used, it is the network administrator's responsibility to ensure that the User login scripts do not conflict with either the Container login script or the Profile login script, if either or both will be executed. Use User login scripts only for items that you cannot include in either a Container login script or a Profile login script.

User login scripts are added to the Login Script property of the User object. They execute after both the Container login script and the Profile login script, if either, or both, exist. User login scripts

> **Use User login scripts only for items that you cannot include in either a Container login script or a Profile login script.**

execute instead of the Default login script. The Default login script will execute only if there is no User login script for a particular user. Therefore, the User login script is the last login script to execute. This is important, because if there is a conflict, the items in the last login script override any previous conflicting settings.

If you do not want the Default login script to execute, you must add the "NO_DEFAULT" entry to either the user's Container login script or the Profile login script. A User script is the only other way to disable the Default script.

Default Login Script

The *Default login script* is the only login script that the administrator cannot edit. It is part of the program *LOGIN.EXE* file in the *SYS:LOGIN* and *SYS:PUBLIC* files. The Default login script is executed when a user does not have a User login script, and when neither the Container login script nor the Profile login script have the **NO_DEFAULT** *option* added.

The Default login script's main purpose is to provide basic settings for search and drive mappings in the event that a user has no User login script. It allows new users to log into a system without creating a login script first.

The Default login script executes such commands as the following:

```
MAP DISPLAY ON
MAP ERRORS OFF
MAP *1:=SYS:
MAP *1:=SYS:%LOGIN_NAME
IF "%1"="ADMIN" THEN MAP *1:=SYS:SYSTEM
MAP INS S1:=SYS:PUBLIC
MAP INS S2:=SYS:PUBLIC\%MACHINE\%OS\%OS_VERSION
```

> The Default login script's main purpose is to provide basic settings for search and drive mappings in the event that a user has no User login script.

General Planning for Login Scripts

Remember that, as the network administrator, it is your responsibility to maintain every login script that you create. Therefore, you should use discretion when creating them, and plan ways to include large numbers of users with Container login scripts or Profile login scripts.

While it is true that the needs of the user should come first, reducing your workload allows you to spend more time taking care of your users. In other words, ease of administration will likely be your main concern when creating login scripts, especially in larger networks. It is best to create login scripts that are easy to maintain and meet your user's needs.

You will also have to take into account the types and numbers of containers, the access needs of your users, and the different groups of users who will be accessing your network. Do not make your login scripts unnecessarily long, or difficult to troubleshoot. Whenever there is a problem, you will regret any unneeded complexity.

> **Keep your format uniform. It makes it easier to avoid problems or to find them when they do occur.**

Mappings usually come first in login scripts. Keep your format uniform. It makes it easier to avoid problems or to find them when they do occur. Plan searches so that the needs of the greatest number of users are met in the higher level searches first. Make sure that you do not skip search drive mappings, because the results will be unpredictable.

Spaces and comment lines make the login scripts more readable as well as easier to troubleshoot when problems occur. Like DOS, the login script comment lines, or **REMARKS**, are designated by either **REMARK**, **REM**, *****, or **;**. Use Remarks freely when creating login scripts; you may not remember your train of thought later, when there is a problem.

Remember that none of the login scripts you create will be updated when variables used within them are changed. You will have to update them manually.

Login Script Commands

Each login script is comprised of command lines or statements. The sequence of those lines affects the outcome of the login script. Each line is a statement that performs a task. Some of those tasks are specific to login scripts, and others are available elsewhere in the NetWare operating system. For example, although many of the following **MAP** commands have been setup in the login scripts, we will be checking and verifying proper operation by testing the syntax at a command line interface.

One of the most important and most common login script commands is the **MAP** command. It provides a drive letter name to a directory location on your server. Any **MAP** command entered in the login scripts is restored each time you log in. If used in a command line entry at the workstation during normal operation, however, MAPPED drives become temporary additions, and are not restored when you log out and then log back in.

> **Any MAP command entered in the login scripts is restored each time you log in.**

Map Command

> **Directory Map Objects are NDS objects that point to an NFS directory or volume.**

You use **MAP** to associate a DOS recognizable drive letter to a NetWare Operating System item such as a volume, directory, search drive, or directory map object. Directory Map Objects are NDS objects that point to an NFS directory or volume.

Mapping a drive is a way to tell your operating system where to look for information. You may remember that we usually have at least two DOS drives (*A:* and *C:*). There really is not an *A:* drive. It is simply a descriptor that DOS recognizes, and which tells DOS where to look for whatever we are seeking at the time. If we want to tell DOS to look on a floppy disk for a file named *PAYROLL*, we would simply type *A:\PAYROLL*. DOS would understand and find the file. That command is a path to a file that DOS understands, regardless of the drive from which we were making the request. In other words, if we were running an application from the *C:* drive, but needed the *PAYROLL* file from the *A:* drive, our description above would work, and DOS could find the file. In this case, we would need the *A:* in our request, otherwise DOS would not be able to find the *PAYROLL* file—at least not the one we were seeking.

The reason for this last caveat is that there may be a file called *PAYROLL* on the *D:* drive, where we initiated our request. Because the file we want is the one on the *A:* drive, we would need to tell DOS where to search. We would have to draw DOS a MAP. We do this by typing *A:\PAYROLL*.

You learned that the normal drive map in DOS includes: a 3.5-inch floppy in the *A:* drive; sometimes a second floppy disk in the *B:* drive (this used to be used for a 5.25-inch floppy drive or a second 3.5-inch floppy drive); the first hard disk in the *C:* drive, and the CD-ROM in the *D:* drive. This can also be seen in Figure 11-9. When we start adding additional hard disks or CD-ROM players, ZIP drive units or other mass storage units, and possibly a file server, we are increasing the number of possible MAP locations that we must build for DOS. You saw that we can even use the **FDISK** command to subdivide a hard disk drive into multiple DOS drive partitions.

Figure 11-9

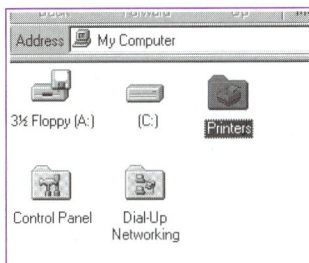

In the graphic of the DOS prompt shown in Figure 11-10, note that the drive letters *A:, B:, C:, D:,* and *E:* are all mapped to local disks. Because there are only 26 letters available, DOS recognizable drives are assigned letters first, then any remaining drive letters are made available to NetWare.

Figure 11-10

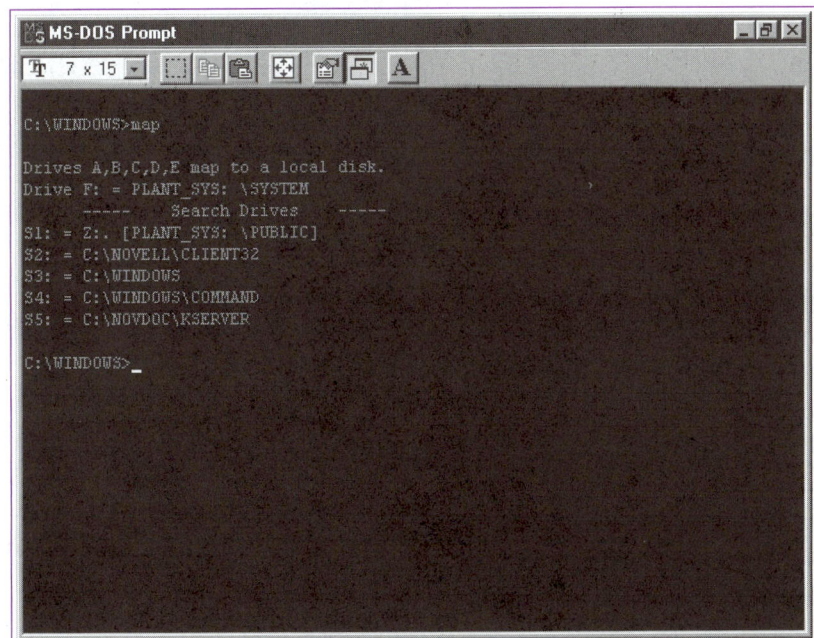

Novell NetWare's position location method is somewhat different. NetWare understands the DOS designation, but DOS does not reciprocate. For example, the designator *SYS:PUBLIC* means nothing to DOS.

> **The DOS drives and the NetWare MAP commands combine to make 26 total drive designations available.**

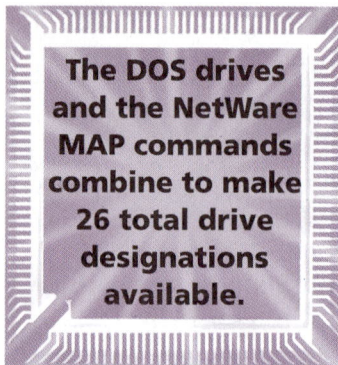

If we tell DOS to look there, the operating system will not understand. If we can associate a previously unused DOS drive letter designator to our *SYS:PUBLIC* location, however, DOS will understand. Those associations are made through **MAP** commands, and they are usually made in the login scripts. The DOS drives and the NetWare **MAP** commands combine to make 26 total drive designations available.

These drive letters can be assigned to local drives, such as hard disk drives and floppy drives, or to network drives, such as volumes and directories on the network. In addition, each user can map his own drive letters to different directories himself, or the network administrator can map them.

By going to the command prompt and typing **map?** as shown in Figure 11-11, you can see a **MAP** command *HELP* screen.

Figure 11-11

```
MS-DOS Prompt                                                    _ 回 X
Tr  7 x 15 ▼   []  [][]  [][]  []  []  A

MAP                              General Help              4.13 (970813) PTF

Purpose: To assign a drive to a directory path.
Syntax:  MAP [option | /VER] [search:=[drive:=]] | [drive:=] [path] [/W]

To:                                                        Use:
   Insert a search drive.                                    INS
   Delete a drive mapping.                                   DEL
   Map the next available drive.                             N
   Make the drive a root directory.                          R
   Map a drive to a physical volume on a server.             P
   Change a regular drive to a search drive                  C
   or a search drive to a regular drive.
   Display version information                               /VER
   Do not change master environment.                        /W

For example, to:                                           Type:
   Map the next available drive                             MAP N FS1/SYS:LOGIN
   to the login directory on server FS1
   Map drive W: as a search drive                           MAP S16:=W:=APPS:WP
   to the WP directory

C:\WINDOWS>
```

SEARCH DRIVES

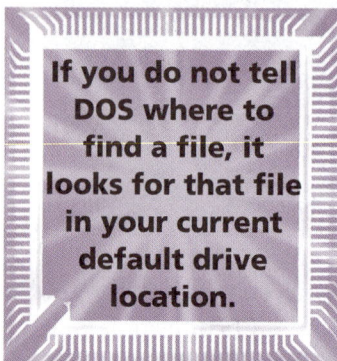

> **If you do not tell DOS where to find a file, it looks for that file in your current default drive location.**

Knowing how DOS searches for a requested file enables you to take advantage of a shortcut when designating files. If you do not tell DOS where to find a file, it looks for that file in your current default drive location. That is why you would have found the wrong *PAYROLL* file when there was a *PAYROLL* file located in the same place that we were located on the *D:* drive. When we asked for *PAYROLL*, DOS would look for our location and pick up the payroll file in that same location, even though the file we want is on the *A:* drive. If the file on the *D:* drive were the one we wanted, then we could have found a shortcut. We could use the full *D:\PAYROLL* to find our file, or the shorter *PAYROLL* designation.

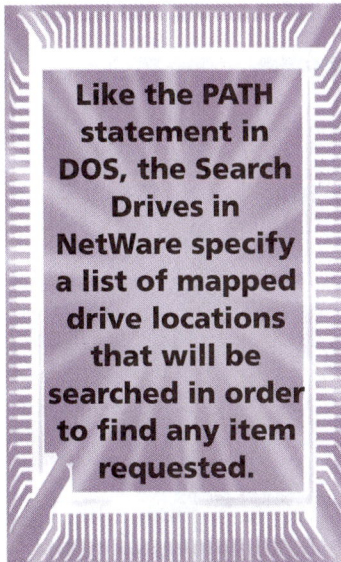

On the other hand, if you knew that there is no file named *PAYROLL* on the *D:* drive, and that DOS would immediately search the *A:* drive for the file, you could still use the shortcut designation *PAYROLL* to find the right file. DOS uses a path through whatever locations we tell it to search. We tell DOS those locations through the **PATH** statement in DOS. It goes directly to the location if it is specified completely. If you do not give complete specifications, however, DOS first looks in the current drive location, and then follows the listing of directory locations in its **PATH** statement. In either case, knowing the method DOS will use to look for your file helps to ensure that they are found.

NetWare uses **SEARCH DRIVES** that resemble the DOS **PATH** statement. Like the **PATH** statement in DOS, the **SEARCH DRIVES** in NetWare specify a list of mapped drive locations that will be searched in order to find any item requested. To search for the *PAYROLL* file we worked with earlier, the operating system starts looking for it in your present position, then in the location in the uppermost search drive listing that you have made. If it does not find it there, it continues on to the next search drive until it has searched them all.

Starting at drive letter *Z:* and working in reverse alphabetical order, you can map search drives up to the *K:* drive. This gives you a maximum of 16 search drives. In Figure 11-12, you can see that five search drives have been mapped.

> **Like the PATH statement in DOS, the Search Drives in NetWare specify a list of mapped drive locations that will be searched in order to find any item requested.**

Figure 11-12

```
C:\WINDOWS>map

Drives A,B,C,D,E map to a local disk.
Drive F: - PLANT_SYS: \SYSTEM
-----          Search Drives     -----
S1: = Z:. [PLANT_SYS: \PUBLIC]
S2: = C:\NOVELL\CLIENT32
S3: = C:\WINDOWS
S4: = C:\WINDOWS\COMMAND
S5: = C:\NOVDOC\KSERVER

C:\WINDOWS>_
```

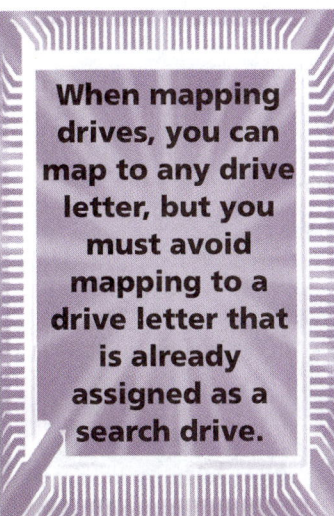

> **When mapping drives, you can map to any drive letter, but you must avoid mapping to a drive letter that is already assigned as a search drive.**

When mapping drives, you can map to any drive letter, but you must avoid mapping to a drive letter that is already assigned as a search drive. A search drive and a regular network drive cannot be mapped to the same letter. In Figure 11-12, because the drive letter *Z:* is already mapped to search drive *S1*, you would not be able to map any other drive to the drive letter *Z:* without replacing the current *Z:* drive mapping.

MAP ROOT Command

Unlike the drive letter ***F:*** in Figure 11-12, note that the drive letter *F:* in Figure 11-13 has an additional backslash after its designator.

Figure 11-13

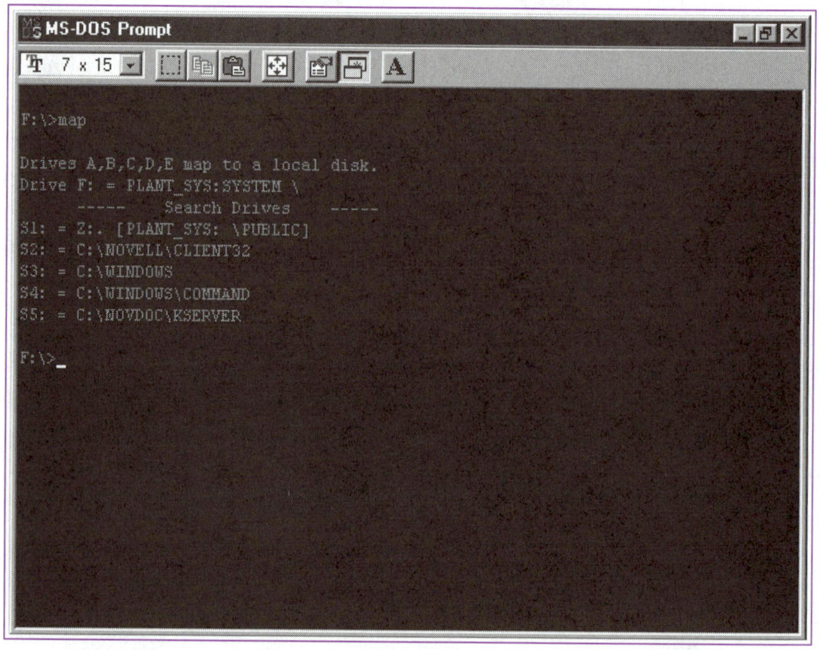

Mapping a drive as a root prevents users from exploring the directories between the "pseudo-root" and the actual root directory level.

That additional backslash specifies that drive *F:* should be considered a root directory. It is the result of the **MAP ROOT** command. This type of mapping allows you to have a letter mapped to any directory, and the drive letter will appear as if it were a root directory. Mapping a drive as a root prevents users from exploring the directories between the "pseudo-root" and the actual root directory level. Figure 11-14 illustrates an attempt to advance one level in the directory using the **CD** .. command. The result returned "Invalid Directory," even though there are higher items in the directory's *PLANT_SYS:SYSTEM* chain. Because the user cannot go further, it appears to him that he is at the top of the directory.

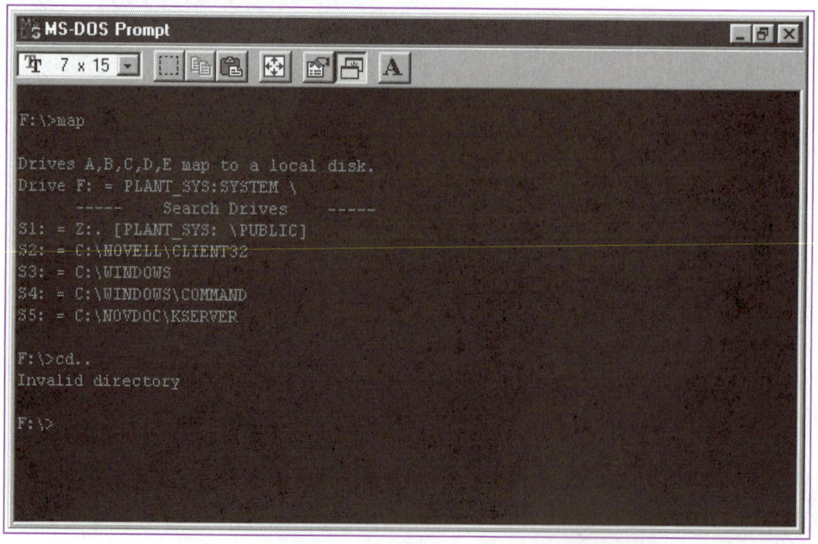

> The MAP ROOT command is another security measure that prevents the user from wandering around in places where he is not supposed to have access.

The **MAP ROOT** command is another security measure that prevents the user from wandering around in places where he is not supposed to have access. Sometimes this feature is not just a security feature.

It is also needed when applications require access to the root of their directory in order to run properly. This tricks the application into detecting that it is at the root directory of a drive, and it will run even though it is not at the real root.

Map Next

Although you can continue to add drives to the letters that you specify in the **MAP** command, those letters are not necessary. You can use the MAP NEXT shortcut feature and the drive is assigned the next available drive letter by the operating system itself.

This feature may not be available in login scripts with earlier versions of NetWare. It assumes that the assigned drive letter is not as important as making the drive available for the user object. Because this is not always the case, some administrators do not use the **MAP NEXT** command in their login scripts.

Figure 11-15 illustrates the effects of using the map next feature. The **MAP** command displayed the drive assignments before adding the *G:* drive.

Figure 11-15

The assignment `map next z:` then returned the line "`Drive G: = PLANT_SYS: \PUBLIC`." When the **MAP** command displays the drive assignments again, the *G:* drive lists the above drive mapping. This drive assignment also shows that the same directory location may be used in different drive mappings. This may be necessary when some individuals have access to one drive but not others, or when applications need particular drive letters and would return errors otherwise.

MAPPING in Windows

The above mapping actions can also be executed in Windows (95, 98, or NT). Use the **Map Drive** button (if selected in *Windows Options*) as shown in Figure 11-16 to assign your own mapping.

Figure 11-16

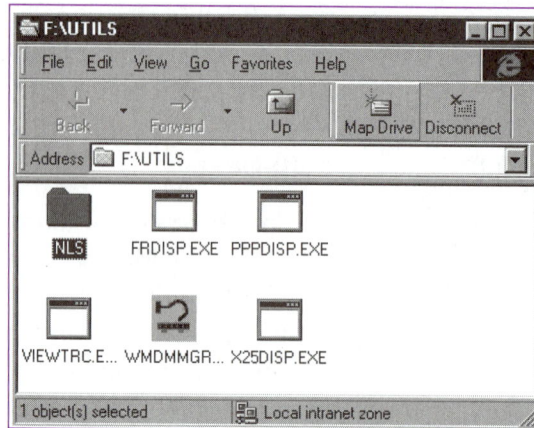

As shown in Figure 11-17, this does not assign a drive letter to the NLS folder on the *F:* drive as you would think it would. It requires you to designate the path for the new drive letter specification yourself. You must enter your own Path before it makes the drive assignment.

Figure 11-17

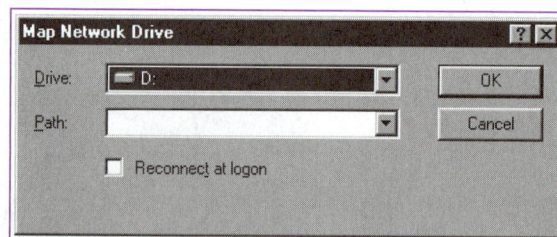

However, if you choose the folder you want assigned to the drive assignment you desire, you can simply right click on that folder and click on **Novell Map Network Drive** (as shown in Figure 11-18) to make the assignment automatically.

Figure 11-18

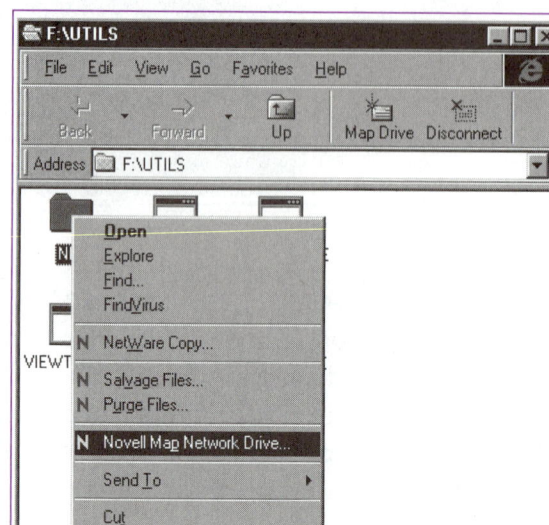

This returns the window shown in Figure 11-19.

Figure 11-19

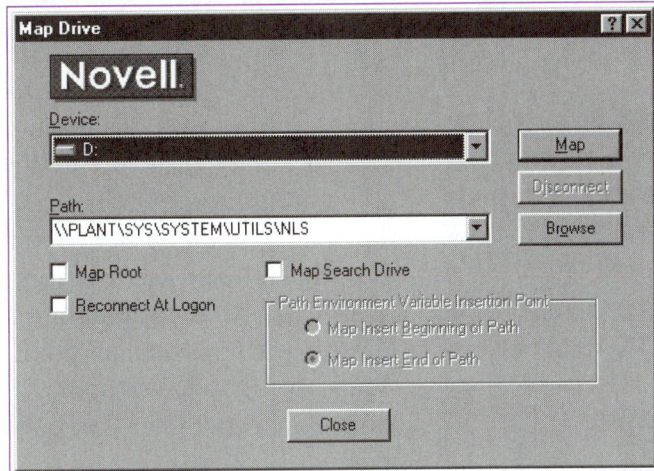

If you compare it to the earlier window, you will notice that the path is already inserted for you, and that several different mapping commands are available to you. If you want the assignment to reoccur each time your user logs in, you can even activate the "Reconnect at Logon" option.

Figure 11-20

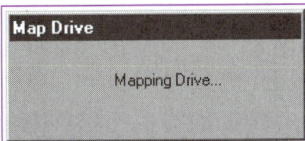

Figure 11-20 displays what occurs when the **Map** button is pressed and shows that the actions are being taken properly.

Verify that the assignment occurred by activating the MS-DOS prompt. Type the command **map** and look at the current mappings.

MAP Command Listing	
Map drive to Volume object	`map d:=plant_sys`
Map drive to Physical volume	`map d:=plant\sys:`
Map drive to existing drive	`map d:=z:`
Un-Map a drive	`map del g:`
Map drive to Root	`map root g:=plant_sys:system`
Map to the Next available drive	`map next plant_sys:system`

Search Drive Command Listing	
Create search drive and insert to 1st position	`map ins s1:= plant_sys:system`
Create search drive and replace old S2	`map s2:= plant_sys:system`
Create search drive and search it last	`map s16:= plant_sys:system`
Change network drive to a search drive	`map c: k:`
Create search drive as a root map	`map root s3:= plant_sys:system`

MAPPING to Directory Map Object

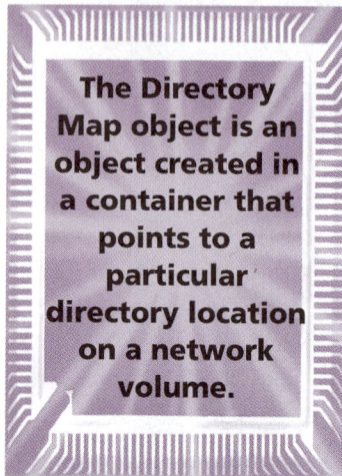

> **The Directory Map object is an object created in a container that points to a particular directory location on a network volume.**

There is another NetWare feature available for mapping a drive to a location where applications that may often change reside. Because some applications have frequent updates, it may be better to create an object in the directory and have the application pointed to by that object. In this way, when changes do occur, you need only change the pointer so that it points to the new item, either in a new location or in the updated old location. You do not have to go to each user's login scripts and change their mappings. They still map to the Directory Map object, and that object still directs them to the application at which you aim them. The Directory Map object is an object created in a container that points to a particular directory location on a network volume.

Apart from the final colon (:), Directory Map object assignments resemble the normal search mappings. When mapping a drive to the directory map object, the administrator ensures that the object points to the proper location in the object's property listings. He then uses the following format to assign the mapping for the Mail folder that he wants his user objects to use:

```
map ins s16:=mail
```

Additional Login Script Commands (There are many more!)

IF, THEN, and ELSE	conditionally execute a command or set of commands.
REMARK (also REM, ;, or *)	are used when adding descriptive remarks for clarification.
INCLUDE	allows including another login script within current script.
BREAK	is either ON to allow users to stop login script, or OFF to not allow it.
WRITE	writes a file to the user's screen.
DISPLAY	displays a message to a user.
CLS	clears screens and removes existing text.
PAUSE	halts the login script processing and waits for user input.
FIRE_PHASERS_n	makes the "Phaser" sound "n" times.
#	This symbol is placed in front of programs or batch files that are external to the login script and should be executed elsewhere.
@	This symbol is the same as above, except the login script continues as file is loaded.

Editing Scripts During Login

NetWare login allows login script editing. If the administrator allows access, the user can edit scripts in two separate locations: the script page or the variables window.

In Figure 11-21, the *script page* is activated and shows that both the **Login Script** and the **Profile Script** have pull-down windows. The **Default** selection shown can be scrolled to another location (if one exists). It also shows that the user can elect not to run the scripts or view the results window. He also can stop the results window from automatically closing as it does by default.

Figure 11-21

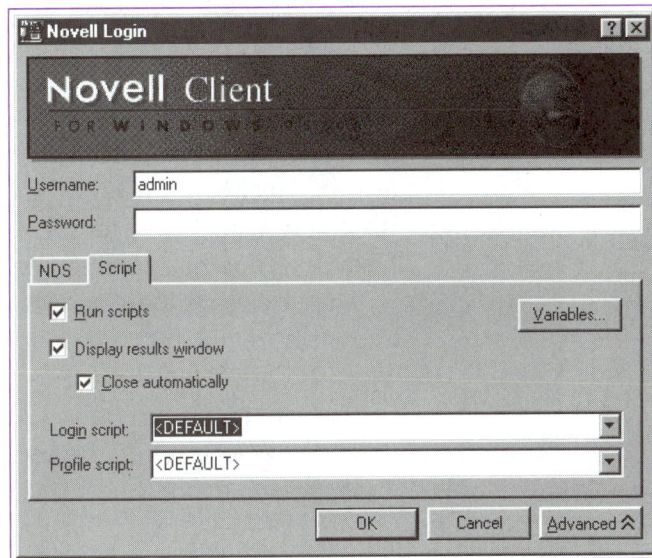

By clicking on the **Variables** button , the *variables window* shown in Figure 11-22 appears that allows the user to enter variables which can be used in scripts where the variable identifiers are called out.

Figure 11-22

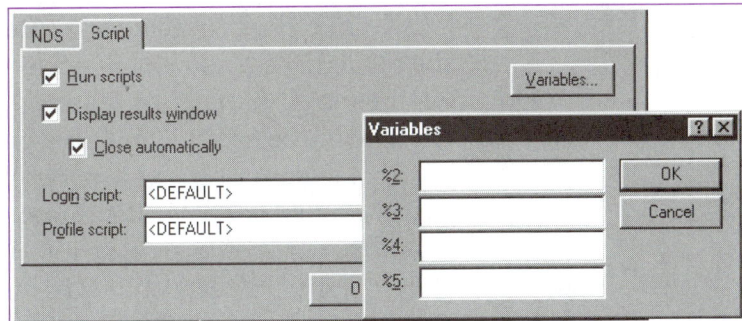

Chapter Summary

When you log into a network, you usually see a white screen with some commands flashing by on your monitor. Those commands are part of your login script. They are the instructions that executed immediately when you logged in. Login scripts are designed to help the user. He does not have to remember all of the settings and long commands needed to access his computer or the network. They are simply done for him. The administrator edits login scripts using **NWAdmin**. Because login scripts are difficult to maintain, the fewer used, the better.

There are three types of login scripts created by the administrator: Container, Profile, and User login scripts. There is also a Default login script. All four of these are optional. Using these login scripts, an administrator tailors users' environments automatically, reducing network maintenance in the process. If they exist, these login scripts always execute in the order listed above. The Default login script is used only when the User login script is not used, and only if the No-Default option has not been invoked.

The Container login scripts can be found only in Organization or Organizational Unit container objects. They are the first login scripts executed, and are the most commonly used login scripts. They set the basic network environment for all users in their respective container objects. Only the user's immediate Parent Container login script is executable.

The Profile login scripts are special objects used to specify common components for multiple users, through login scripts. The users are not necessarily in the same container. The Profile login script executes after the Container login script, if one exists. The Profile login script can be located anywhere in the Directory, but it is usually located in the container object where most of the affected users reside. In order to execute a Profile login script, a Profile object must be created, the user must be added as a trustee to the object, and the user must be granted the **Browse** object right and the **Read** property right to the object's Login Script property.

User login scripts create network environments for an individual user. Use them only for items that you cannot include in either a Container or Profile login script. User login scripts are added to the Login Script property of the User object, and they execute after the Container and Profile login scripts execute if either, or both, exist.

The only login script that the administrator cannot edit is the Default login script. It is built into the *LOGIN.EXE* file in the *SYS:LOGIN* and *SYS:PUBLIC* directories, and executes only when the user does not have a User login script, and when neither the Container login script nor the Profile login script have the **NO_DEFAULT** option activated. The Default login script's main purpose is to provide basic settings for search and drive mappings in the event that a user has no User login script. It allows new users to log into a system without creating a login script first.

Login scripts are made up of command lines, or statements, whose sequence affects the outcome of the script itself. Each line is a statement that performs a task in either the login script itself, or somewhere else in the NetWare Operating System. The **MAP** command is one of the most important, and the most common, login scripts. **MAP** commands in the login scripts are executed every time you log in, but they are only temporary when used as command line entries from the workstation.

MAP associates a DOS recognizable drive letter to a NetWare Operating System item such as a volume, directory, search drive, or directory map object. Mapping a drive is a way of telling the operating system where the drive is—like drawing a map. You can map a drive for each letter. Because there are only 26 letters, there can be only 26 mappings, minus the ones already assigned by your operating system for local disk drives. NetWare understands the DOS letter designation, but DOS does not understand NetWare volume and directory designations.

When we designate a file to look for, our operating system uses a particular search pattern to find it. DOS uses the **PATH** statement, while NetWare uses **Search Drives**, which are similar. Our operating system looks for the file first at our current location, then it goes to the next designated location. If there are no further designations, an error message is returned, and the file is not found. Assigned Search drives start at the *Z:* drive and work backward through the alphabet, providing a total of 16 possible drives.

MAP ROOT is used to make the mapping behave as if it were at the root of the directory. This can be done for security reasons, or to make applications think they have access to the root. An additional backslash is added after the mapping description when it is shown in a listing. With **MAP NEXT**, the operating system itself gives the next available drive letter to the file.

Mapping can also be accomplished in Windows using the **Map Drive** button in the normal operating window. This feature is selected in the *Windows Options*.

Another feature available in NetWare, Directory Map Object, maps a drive to a location where items that often change, like applications, are stored. When changes occur, you need only redirect the pointer to the new item.

NetWare login allows users to edit login scripts through the script page or the variables window, and allows the user to decide whether to run the scripts, view the results window, or stop the results window from closing automatically.

Networking Terms Used in Chapter 11

DOS batch files	Default login script	**BREAK**
greeting message	*LOGIN.EXE*	**WRITE**
login scripts	*SYS:LOGIN*	**DISPLAY**
Login Script property	*SYS:PUBLIC*	**CLS**
Container login script	NO_DEFAULT option	**PAUSE**
Profile object	**REMARK**, **REM**, **;**, or *	**FIRE_PHASERS_*n***
Profile login script	**MAP**	**#**
mappings	**SEARCH DRIVES**	**@**
messages	**MAP ROOT**	script page
%GREETING_TIME	**MAP NEXT**	variables window
%LOGIN_NAME	**IF**, **THEN**, and **ELSE**	
User login script	**INCLUDE**	

■ Chapter Review Questions

1. What do login scripts do when they are executed immediately each time you log in?

2. What are login scripts designed to do?

3. How many different types of login scripts are there?

4. How many login scripts can be edited by the administrator?

5. What do login scripts do for the administrator?

6. How is the Default login script prevented from running?

7. Which is the first Login script that can execute?

8. What Login script can be found in O and OU's?

9. What are the most commonly used login scripts?

10. Which login scripts will execute if the first parent container with a login script is his parent's parent container, there is no profile script, and there is no user script?

11. Which container object is missing the login script button?

12. Who is able to access and change login scripts?

13. What makes the Profile login script different from the Container login script?

14. What must happen in order for a Profile login script to be executed?

15. What happens when you use **%GREETING_TIME** in a login script?

16. Where are User login scripts added to the user object?

17. When there is a conflict between the Container login script and the User login script, which will take precedence?

18. Which is the only login script that cannot be edited?

19. What login script allows new users to log into a system without first creating a login script?

20. What is the main thing to remember, as network administrator, regarding login scripts?

21. What considerations do you have to take into account when planning for login scripts?

22. What usually comes first in login scripts?

23. How are remarks designated in login scripts?

24. How many login scripts are updated when variables used within them are changed?

25. What types of commands will you find in a login script?

26. What is one of the most important and the most common login scripts commands?

27. What is restored each time you log back into the network?

28. What do you use **MAP** commands for?

29. How do you tell your operating system where a file is?

30. How can there be a file in the directory with the same common name as another object?

31. How many drives can be mapped in NetWare?

32. What types of drives can be assigned drive letters in NetWare?

33. What do we use to tell NetWare where to look for items we request?

34. What type of drives are similar to the DOS **PATH** statement?

35. What is the first search drive letter?

36. What is the maximum number of search drives possible?

37. What is the significance of mapping to the root?

38. What happens when the **Map Next** command is used?

39. Which button in Windows is used to assign mapping?

40. Is the drive path always supplied by the operating system when assigning mapping when using the Windows methods?

41. What is the command syntax to remove a mapped drive?

42. What is the command syntax to change a network drive to a search drive?

43. What is a directory map object?

44. How many ways can a user alter scripts during login?

■ Associated Chapter Problems

1. Explain the need for login scripts.

2. Draw a chart showing the different login script options and whether or not they will be used in a login procedure.

3. Explain when the different login scripts should be used.

4. Compare the Profile login script to the Container login script.

5. Explain the process of establishing a Profile login script when one has not previously been used.

6. Why does Novell recommend not using the User login script?

7. Explain the process of deciding whether or not the Default login script is executed.

8. What are some of the general planning requirements regarding login scripts?

9. Explain the reason for using the **MAP** command.

10. Explain **Search Drives** and their use.

11. Give two examples in which the **MAP ROOT** command would be used.

12. What is the difference between using the **MAP NEXT** command and specifying that your next needed drive should be placed in the last drive position? Give an example.

13. Describe the two options for designating mapping with Windows.

14. Explain the use of Directory Map objects.

15. Explain how scripts can be edited by users during login.

CHAPTER
12
Z.E.N.
WORKS
and
WORKSTATION
MANAGEMENT

OBJECTIVES

Networks are difficult to administer. If you are running Novell's new NetWare 5, a new component for network management—Z.E.N.works—makes it easier to administer your network. Upon completion of this chapter, you will be able to:

- explain what Z.E.N.works is.

- install Z.E.N.works on the server.

- describe the benefits of Z.E.N.works.

- explain the Z.E.N.works maintenance schedule.

- explain the Z.E.N.works policies.

- explain how Z.E.N.works affects network design.

- import NDS workstations into your NDS tree.

- configure the workstation desktop.

- explain how Z.E.N.works eases remote control access for management.

Z.E.N.works

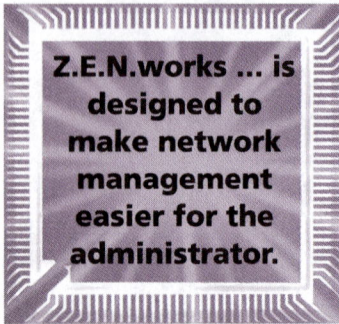

Z.E.N.works … is designed to make network management easier for the administrator.

You have already learned that it takes quite a bit of work to manage even the relatively small network that you have built. Now, imagine a network you can manage with little or no effort! That is the idea that Novell wants to convey with the newest addition to its NetWare 5 Operating system—Z.E.N.works. *Z.E.N.works (Zero Effort Networks)* is designed to make network management easier for the administrator.

Once installed, Z.E.N.works allows you to support Microsoft Windows workstations by using your NDS tree and the NDS operations that you have learned thus far. You have already found that network management, even in your classroom situation, is extremely time-consuming. The administrator is often required to go from machine to machine, making changes and fixing problems. Z.E.N.works does not remove the necessity to make changes, but it does allow the administrator to make many of the changes from a single location—presumably his office. Because less effort is required, the name Zero Effort Networks seems appropriate.

Activity 12-1   Installing Z.E.N.works

You install the Z.E.N.works *Starter Pack* to the server through a workstation when you install the new Novell Client. Notice in Figure 12-1 that the full Z.E.N.works package includes additional *Remote Control* features, a *Help Requestor*, and facilities for assistance with *Hardware Inventory*.

1. Close all open windows and insert the **Novell NetWare 5 Operating System CD**. The CD should self-start, and the Autorun feature of Z.E.N.works should start. Click on **English**.

Figure 12-1

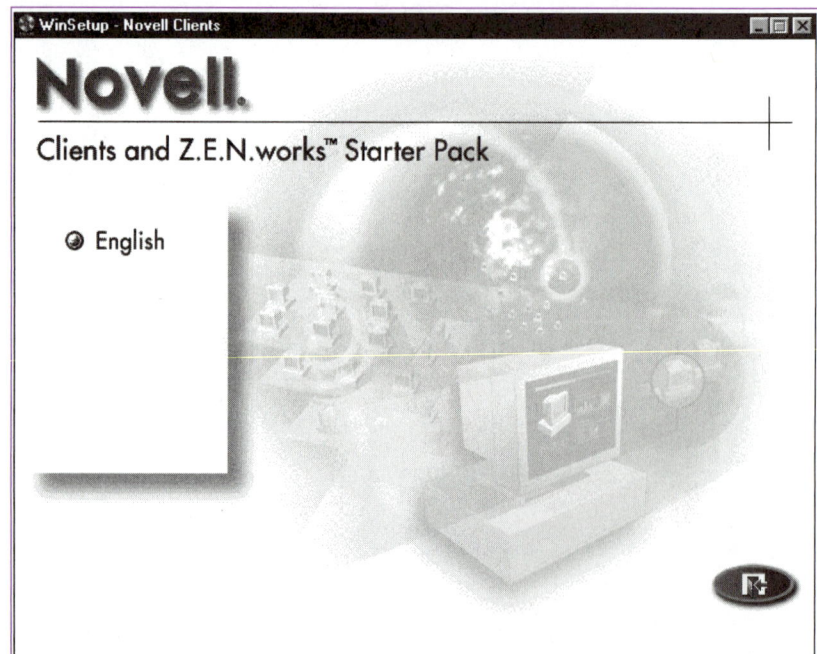

2. The window shown in Figure 12-2 should appear.

Figure 12-2

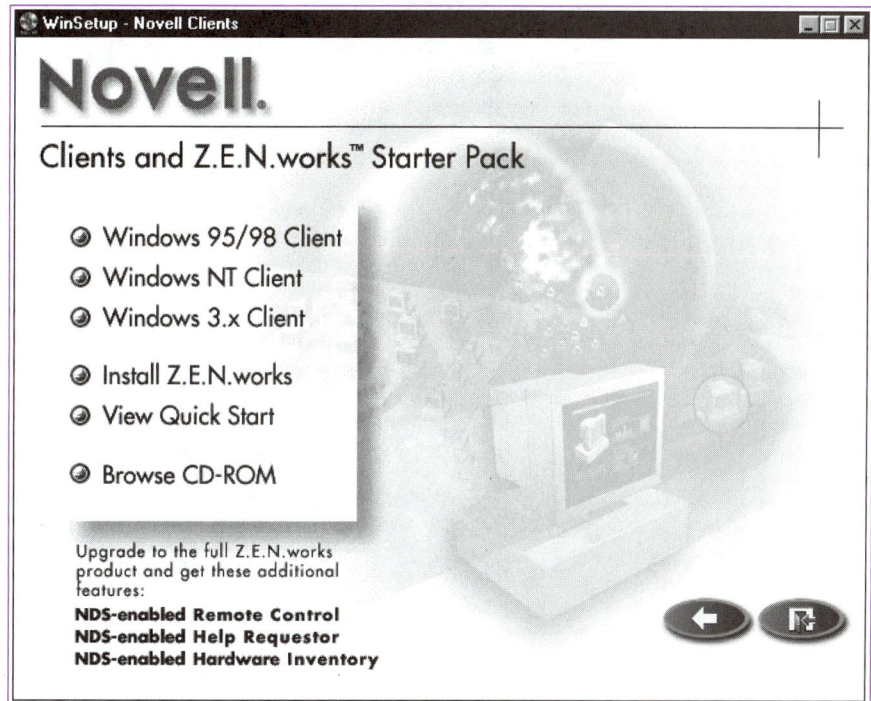

3. To install Z.E.N.works, place your cursor over the **Install Z.E.N.works** selection. The window shown in Figure 12-3 should appear. Click once when ready to proceed with the installation.

Figure 12-3

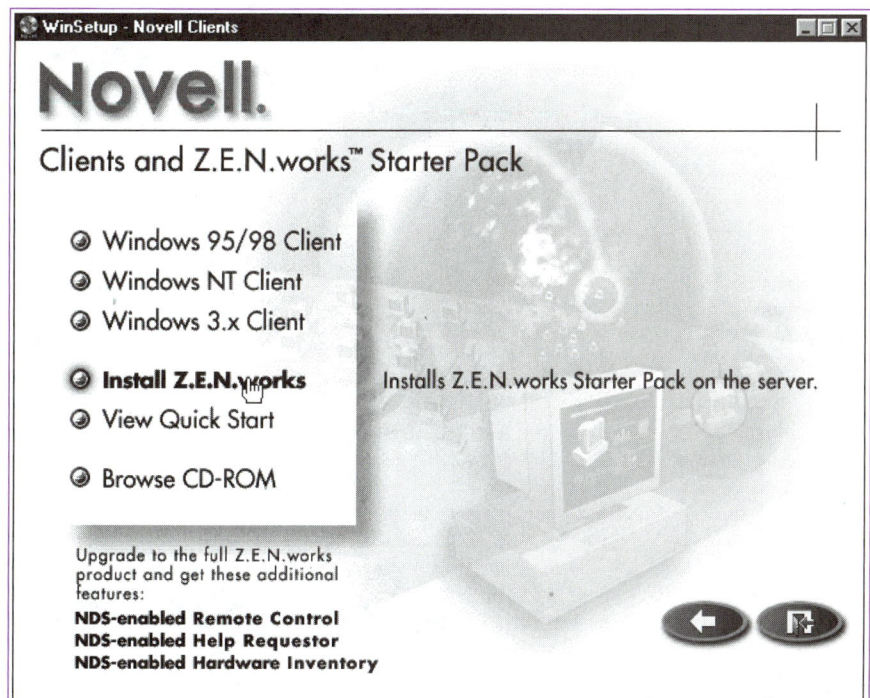

**CHAPTER 12
Z.E.N.works**

4. The *Setup* window in Figure 12-4 appears, showing the progress of the *Starter Pack Wizard installation* on the server.

Figure 12-4

5. The *Welcome to Z.E.N.works* window shown in Figure 12-5 appears, requesting that you close all programs using files in *Sys:\Public* (on the server). Press the **Next >** button when ready to proceed.

Figure 12-5

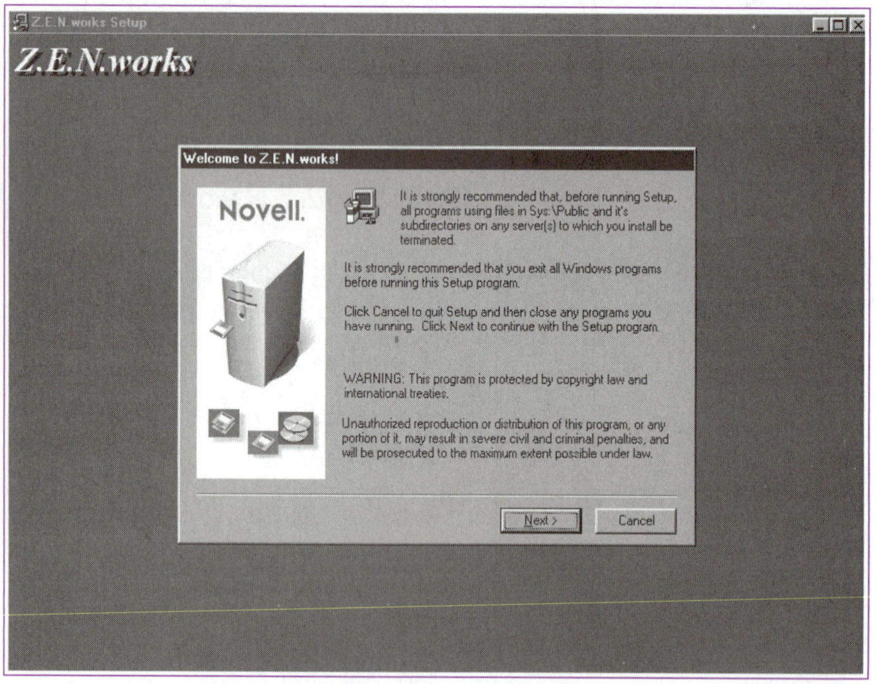

6. The ***Software License Agreement*** window shown in Figure 12-6 appears. After reading the agreement, click the **Yes** button to continue.

Figure 12-6

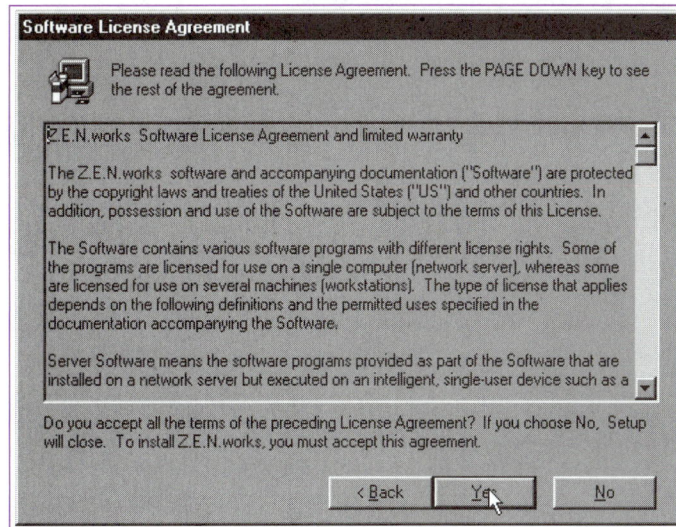

7. The ***Z.E.N.works Setup Type*** window shown in Figure 12-7 appears. Leave the radio button clicked on **Typical**, and press the **Next >** button when ready to proceed.

Figure 12-7

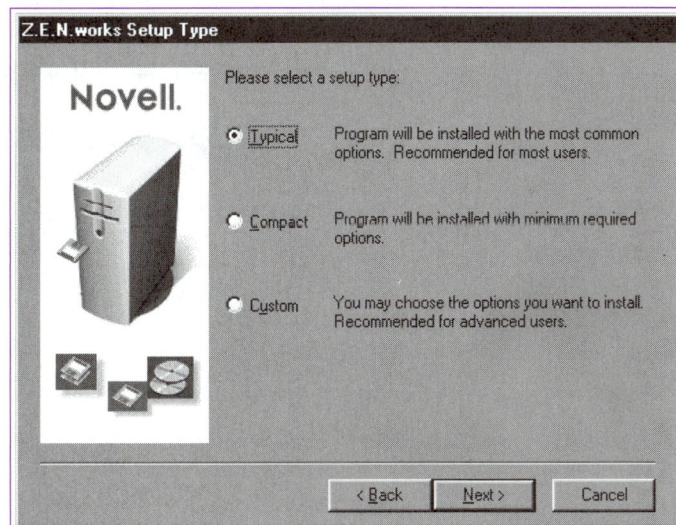

---

8. The ***Z.E.N.works List of Tree/Servers*** window shown in Figure 12-8 appears. Note that this window would include any additional networks that are able to receive Z.E.N.works. Make sure that the check mark remains in the box for the server on which you want to install Z.E.N.works, and press the **Next >** button when ready to proceed.

Figure 12-8

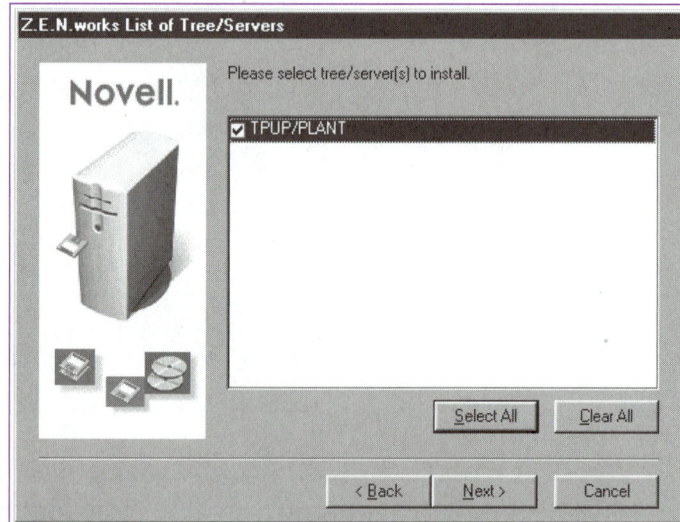

9. The ***Z.E.N.works Language Selection*** window shown in Figure 12-9 appears. Make sure that **English** is checked, and press the **Next >** button when ready to proceed.

Figure 12-9

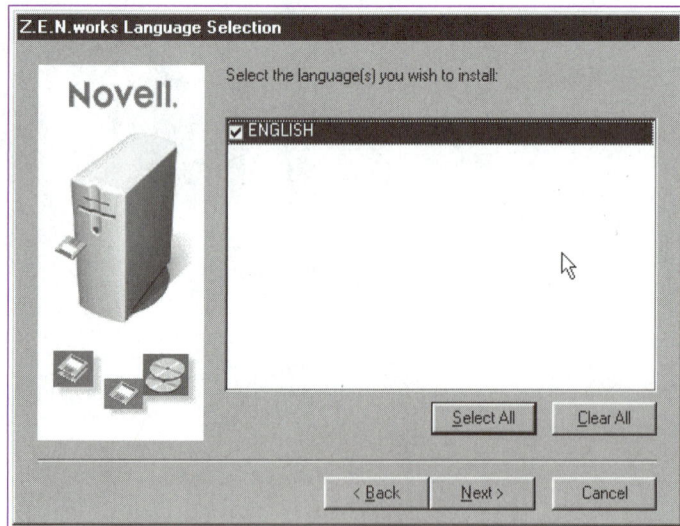

10. The *Start Copying Files* window shown in Figure 12-10 appears. Press the **Next >** button when ready to proceed.

Figure 12-10

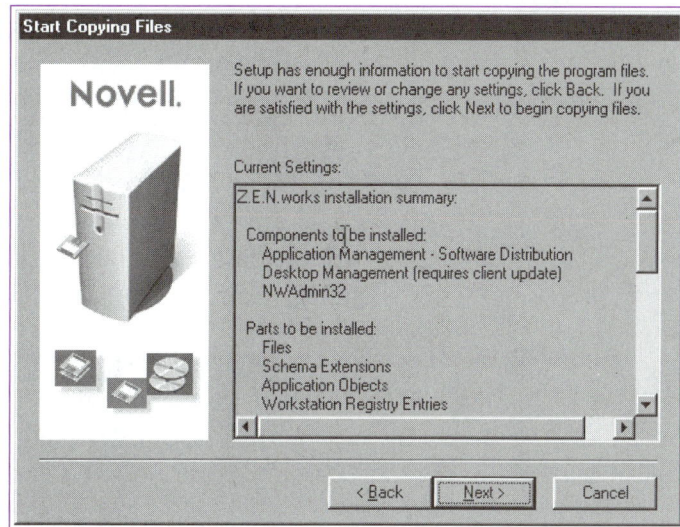

11. The *Z.E.N.works Setup* window shown in Figure 12-11 appears, showing the installation's progress.

Figure 12-11

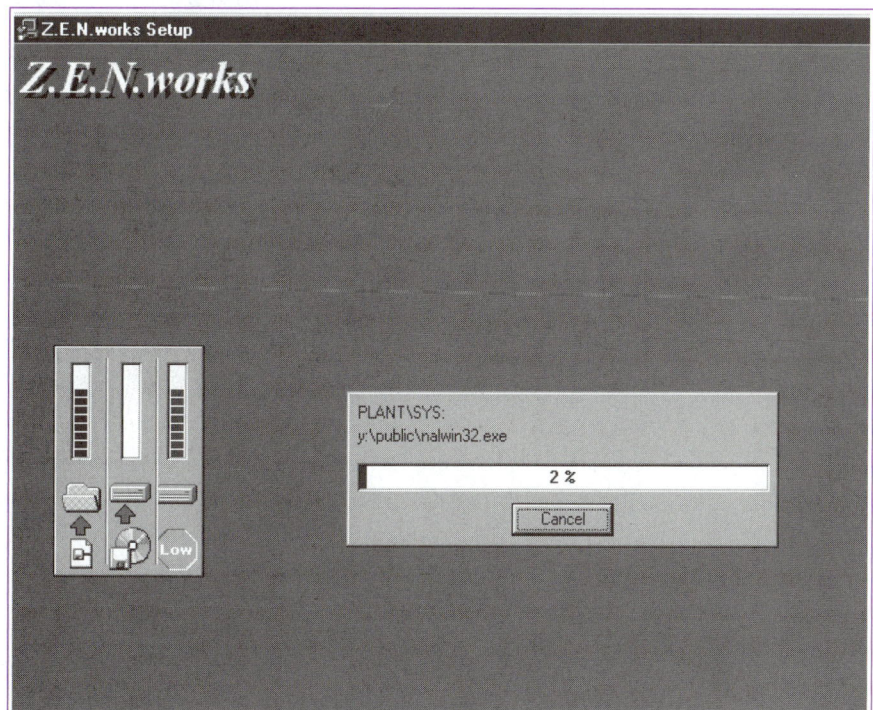

12. The ***For Server PLANT, installing: schema extension, new NDS objects*** window shown in Figure 12-12 appears.

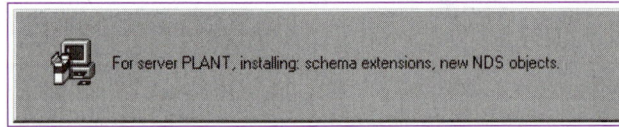

13. The ***Novell Z.E.N.works*** rights granting window shown in Figure 12-13 appears, informing you that workstations must be granted appropriate rights, and requesting a context to grant the rights to the users.

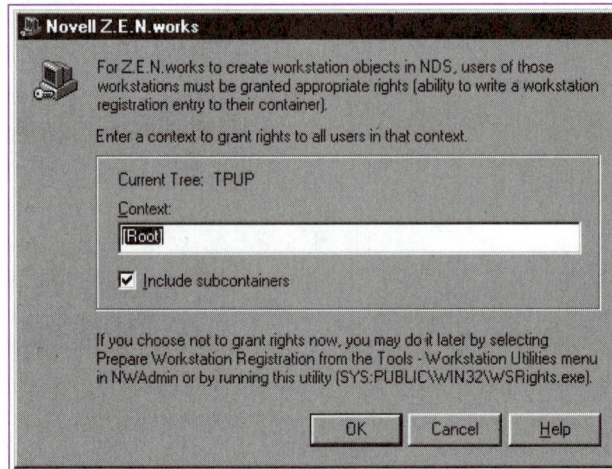

14. The ***Z.E.N.works Workstation Auto-Registration rights were successfully set up*** window shown in Figure 12-14 appears.

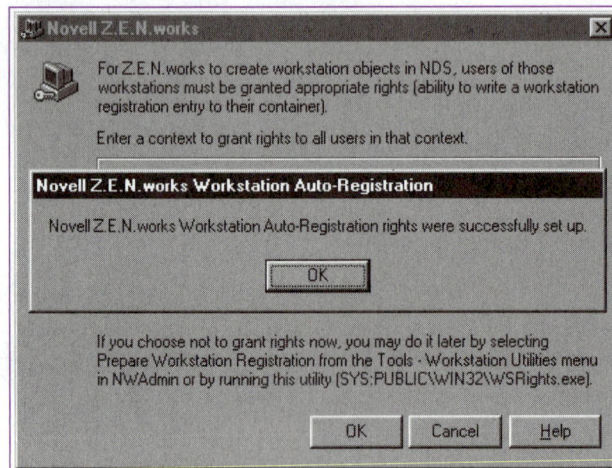

15. The *Z.E.N.works Setup* window shown in Figure 12-15 appears, informing you that Setup has finished installing Z.E.N.works on the server, and giving you the option of launching the *Read Me* file or the *Launch Setup Log* file. Press the **Finish** button when ready to proceed.

Figure 12-15

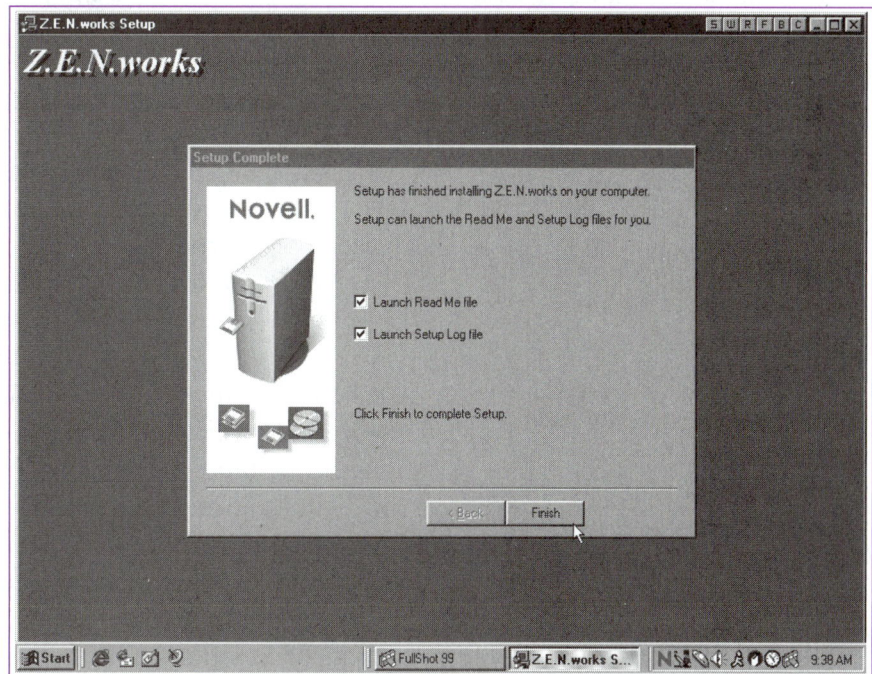

Working With Z.E.N.works

> If you do not first complete a policy for the handling of the workstations, an error will occur, and the workstations will not be imported.

During step 12 of the installation, you were informed that your schema was being extended, and that additional NDS objects were being installed into your tree. Z.E.N.works allows the addition of *Workstation objects* to your NDS tree. These new objects represent Microsoft Windows workstations on your network.

When you manage these new workstation objects, you must use particular rules. These rules are called *Policies* (similar to the policies available with Windows NT and Windows 95 or 98). They must be set before *importing* workstation objects from your network. If you do not first complete a policy for the handling of the workstations, an error will occur, and the workstations will not be imported. This is illustrated in Figures 12-16 and 12-17. Although the Import process recognized a workstation on the network, it did not import it, because a *policy package* had not yet been *associated* with the workstation.

Figure 12-16

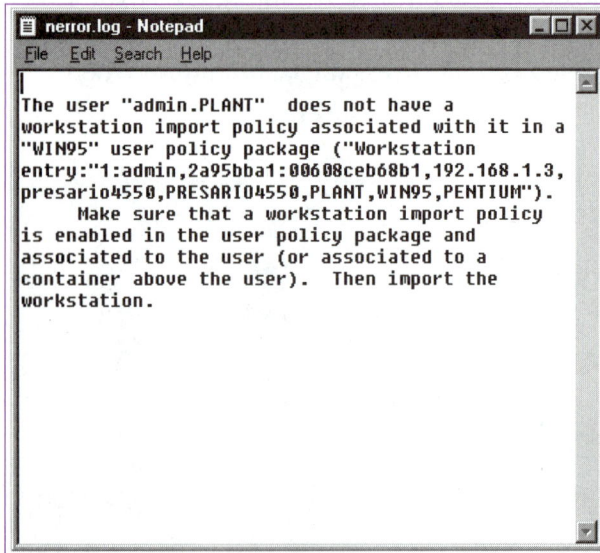

Figure 12-17

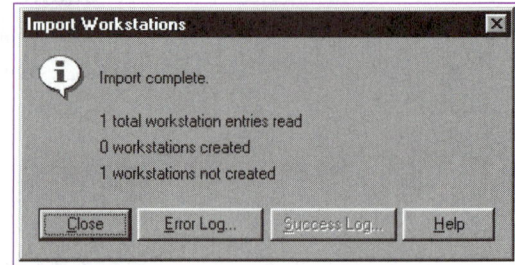

Once you have imported your workstations, you can group them into another NDS object type, *Workstation groups*, which is similar to User groups in NDS. Using these Workstation groups when creating policy packages minimizes your administration duties by reducing the number of entries you make. The group represents multiple workstations that you wish to treat in the same way. When a workstation configuration change must occur, the change process becomes easier, because although you alter only one object, all of the workstations affected by the grouping are also changed as a result of the group assignment.

For this policy packaging process to work properly, you must verify that the information being tracked by the operating system is correct. You do this by maintaining a schedule for updating the NDS workstation information. You follow a *maintenance schedule* to ensure that the data shown in NWAdmin is accurate and shows the proper network workstation configuration. When changes are made, you must make sure that they are reflected in the policy package information shown.

Some of the most important changes that must be updated include the changing out of a Network Interface Card (NIC), adding or removing a workstation, or moving a workstation from one location to another. This configuration is important, because NDS tracks the workstations through their *Media Access Control (MAC) address*. The MAC address is a unique identifier that shows the hardware address for each node (or computer workstation in this case) on the network. The workstation *naming convention* defaults to the computer name and to its MAC address, resulting in unusual workstation names like the one in step 17 of Activity 12-2.

> **Some of the most important changes that must be updated include the changing out of a Network Interface Card (NIC), adding or removing a workstation, or moving a workstation from one location to another.**

Z.E.N.works Policy Packages

There are three main types of Policy Packages that you will use when working with Z.E.N.works. They are *Container Policy Packages*, *Workstation Policy Packages*, and *User Policy Packages*. With the exception of the Container Policy Packages, each of the Windows Operating System Platforms (i.e. Win31, Win95, and Win NT) has a

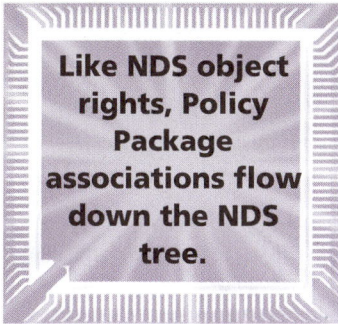

Like NDS object rights, Policy Package associations flow down the NDS tree.

Figure 12-18

different package configuration operation. This can be seen in Figure 12-18. You can access this screen by highlighting the **PLANT** container object and using the **Object** pulldown menu to **Create a Policy Package**. Use the **Select Policy Package Type**, pull down the menu to make your selection from the items below, and then name your new object. When you create your policy package, there are pages of object properties available to change the object's settings or overall configuration. Like NDS object rights, Policy Package associations flow down the NDS tree.

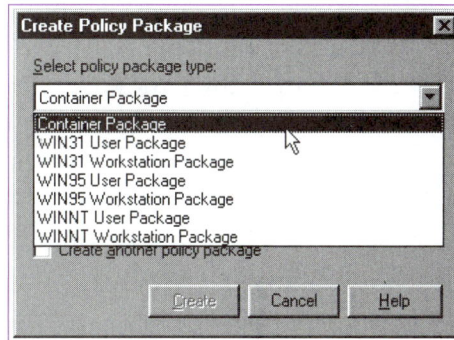

Container Policy Packages

Container Policy Packages are unique because they do not have different configurations for the three Windows operating systems. The Container Packages that you create apply to the containers in which you create them. They essentially tell the NetWare operating system which of the other Policy Packages available apply to NDS objects inside the applicable Container object. Create container policy packages at the highest level possible in the applicable network.

Create container policy packages at the highest level possible in the applicable network.

Figure 12-19

When creating a Container Package, you give the object a name, as shown in Figure 12-19. You are then given the option of conducting a search and designating which objects the search finds. This process is also shown in steps 3 and 4 of Activity 12-2. The default search order is Object, Group, and then Container up through the [Root].

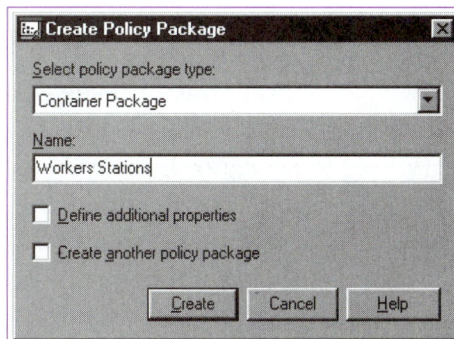

**CHAPTER 12
Z.E.N.works**

Workstation Policy Packages

Workstation Policy Packages are used to specify files you want downloaded or controls you want set for one or more workstation objects. When used, workstation policy packages apply to anyone logging in through that workstation. They apply to the specific settings of that workstation, and are not affected by the user who is logging in. Because they are workstation dependent, the controls you set are also operating system specific. The system settings that you can control for the various Windows operating systems are different for each, resulting in the need for different NetWare handling of each system. This is shown by the selection listings for the different operating systems in Figure 12-19.

You must create Workstation Policy Packages in the same container in which the workstations that will be associated with the package are located. A Win95 Policy Package creation window appears, as shown in Figure 12-20, listing the various policy configurations available.

Figure 12-20

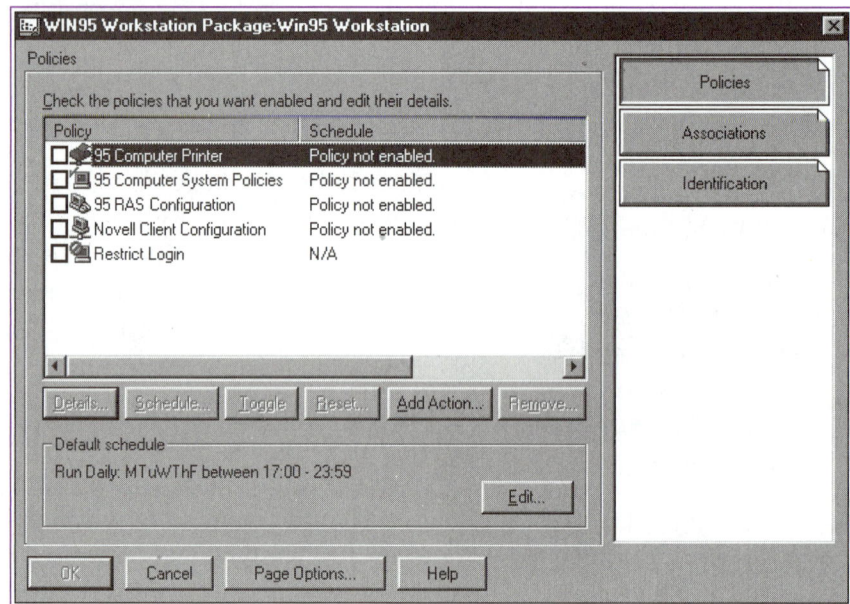

User Policy Packages

User Policy Packages are also operating system dependent, and must be configured separately for each operating system. They are used to set controls for users on whatever computer workstations they use to log into the network. However, those workstations must match the operating system platforms used in the creation process. In other words, a user policy package created for a Win31 user could not be used by that user to log in through a Win95 workstation. In addition, only one user policy package can be applicable to any user at a given time. Create user package objects in the same container in which the users who will be associated with the packages are located.

Figure 12-21 shows the various policy options available when creating a User Policy Package.

Figure 12-21

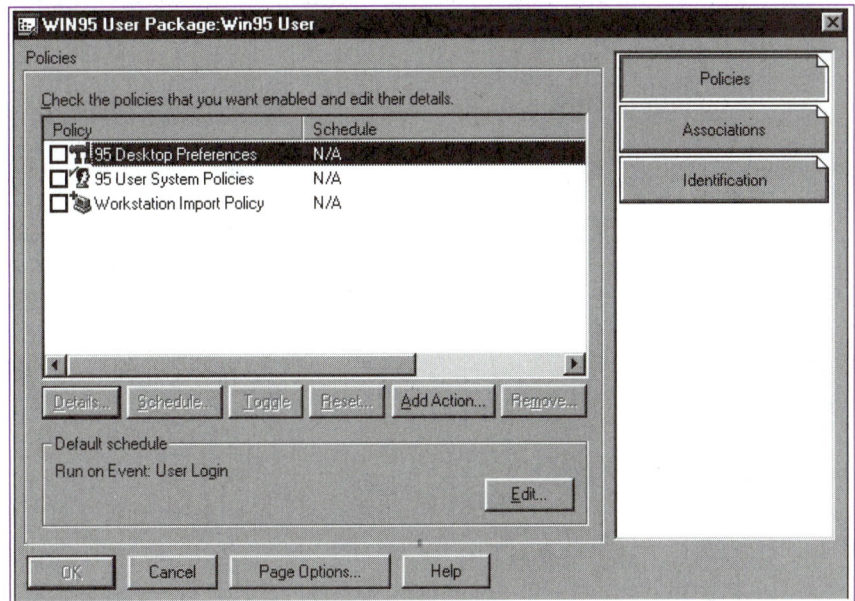

You can create multiple user policy packages in a single container object, but only one can apply to a given user at any given time.

> You can create multiple user policy packages in a single container object, but only one can apply to a given user at any given time.

Applying Policy Packages

As mentioned earlier, policy package assignments, like rights in the NDS tree, flow down through the objects. Therefore, you must use the same NDS rights assignment procedures when assigning policy packages. Avoid creating multiple user policy packages when a group assignment will work just as well. Also, try to use workstation groupings when they will reduce the number of workstation policy packages you must create. Use the Container Policy Package assignment as a security measure, and to ensure that unnecessary searches are avoided. When the container package allows only workstation policies, no user packages will be sought, and the resulting process will be expedited considerably.

Activity 12-2   Adding Workstations

1. Start in NWAdmin by creating a new object **Policy Package**, as shown in Figure 12-22.

Figure 12-22

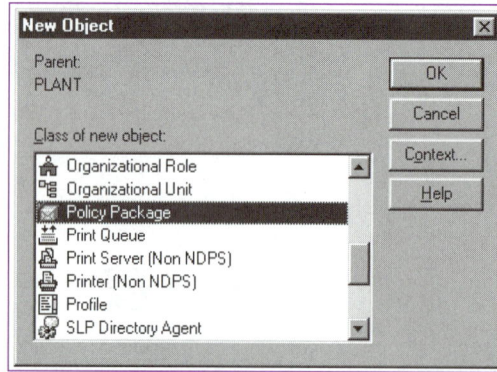

2. The *Create Policy Package* window shown in Figure 12-23 appears. Enter the name of the policy (`Workers Stations` in the figure), and click on the **Create** button to create a container policy package. The container policy package controls which policies are in effect for the objects in the container. They apply only to containers.

Figure 12-23

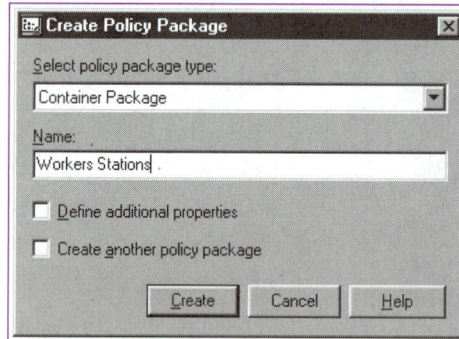

3. Double click on the new **Workers Stations** object to view the object's properties pages, as indicated in Figure 12-24. The **Search Policy** option is shown unchecked. Check this option to make the policy determine which policies are in effect in other policy packages within the container.

Figure 12-24

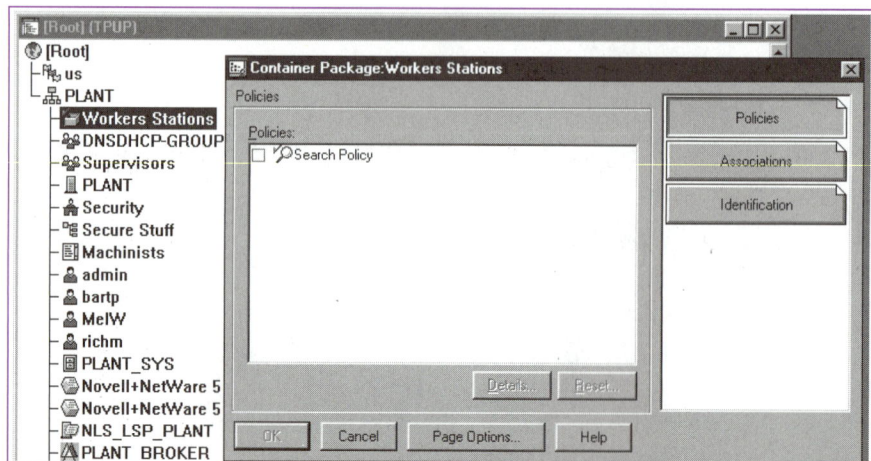

4. Clicking on **Search Policy** and selecting the **Details** button provides access to the *Search Order* allocation window, as shown in Figure 12-25. Change the order, or click on **Cancel**.

Figure 12-25

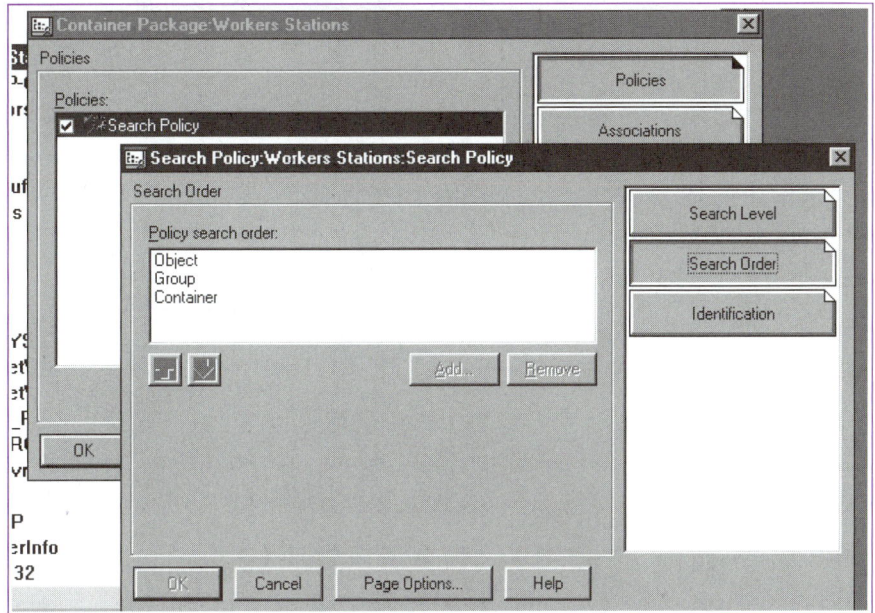

5. To create a workstation policy package, select the **Win95 Workstation Package** (or whatever user operating system type is used in your classroom), and click **Create**.

Figure 12-26

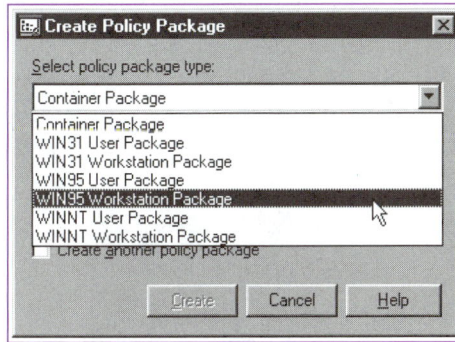

6. Choose the name for your station, as indicated in Figure 12-27, and click the **Create** button.

Figure 12-27

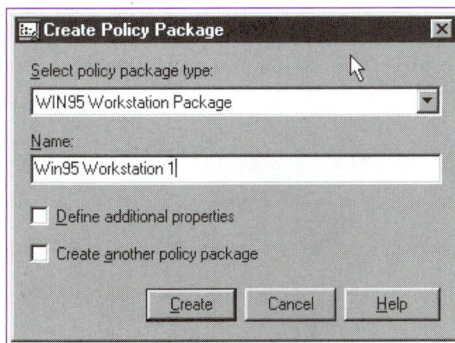

7. Double click on the object you just created to view the policies available to the workstation package you are adding.

Figure 12-28

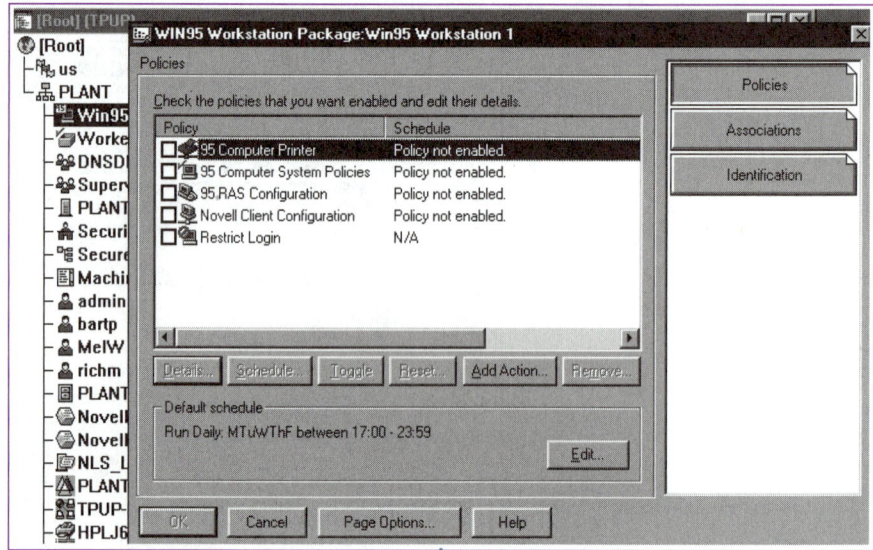

8. Select the **Win 95 Computer System Policies**, then click on the **Details** button to reveal the additional settings for the network and system, as shown in Figure 12-29.

Figure 12-29

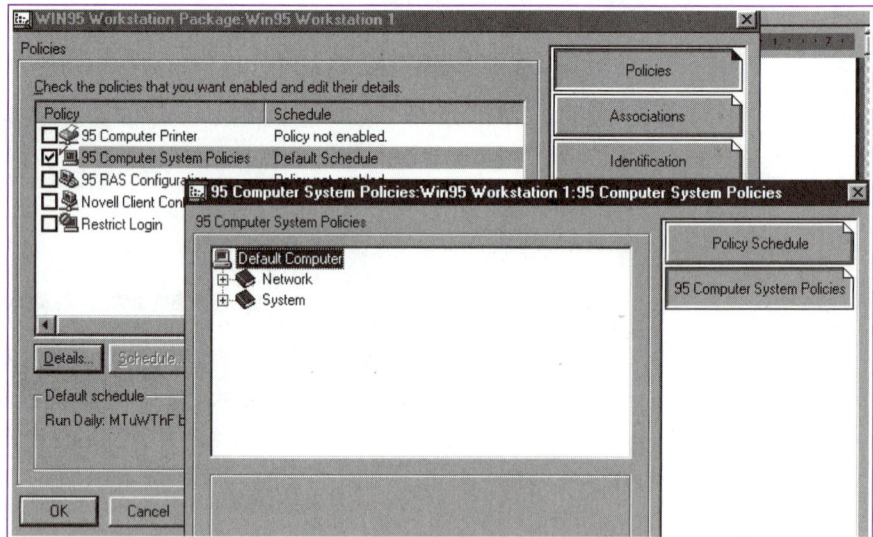

9. There is a selection of additional settings within the **Network** item, as shown in Figure 12-30.

Figure 12-30

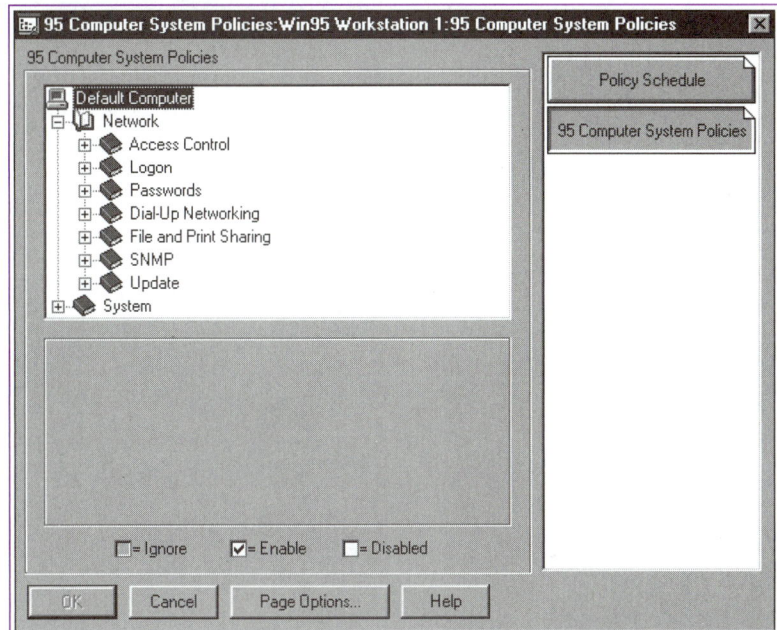

10. Clicking on a particular item in the **Network** section reveals the end items that can be changed, as well as any additional variables that can be altered (such as the length), as shown in Figure 12-31.

Figure 12-31

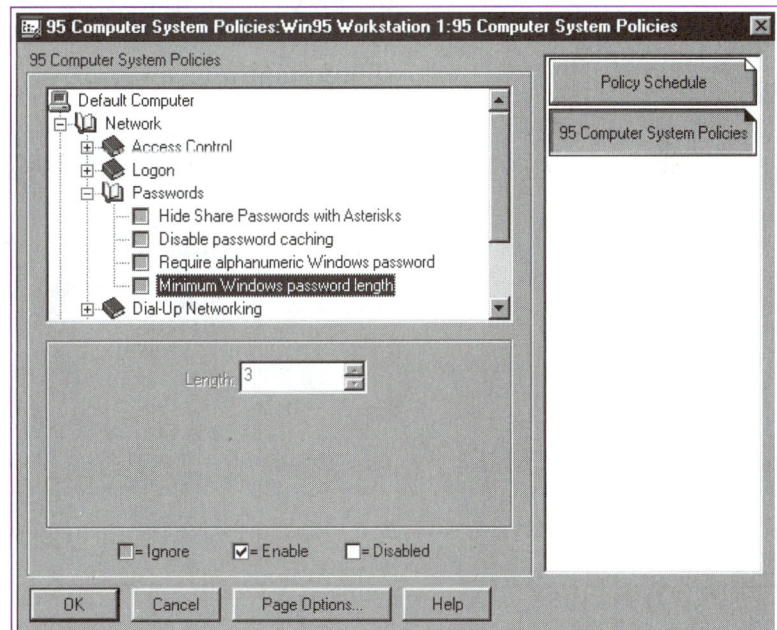

11. Similar items are available in the **System** section.

Figure 12-32

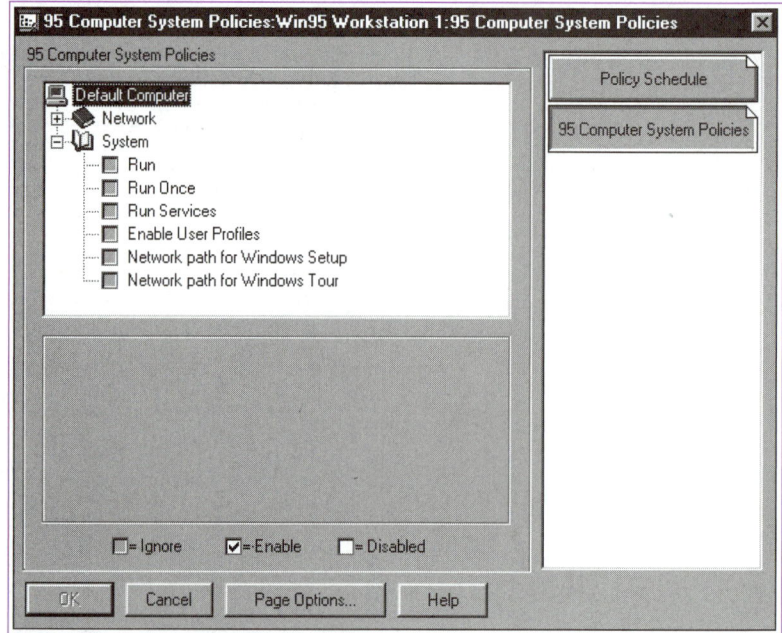

12. Through the judicious use of the available selections in the different policy packages, the administrator has a wide variety of workstation controls at his disposal.

13. Once the policy package selections have been made, the workstations can be imported. Because there are now policy package NDS objects in our Directory, the process will work properly, without returning an error.

Figure 12-33

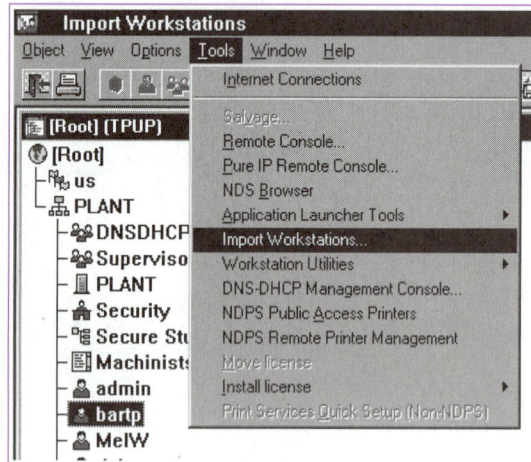

14. In **NWAdmin**, select the **Plant** container, and use the **Tools** pulldown menu as shown in Figure 12-33 to select **Import Workstations**. The window shown in Figure 12-34 appears. Click **OK**, and the import process will begin.

Figure 12-34

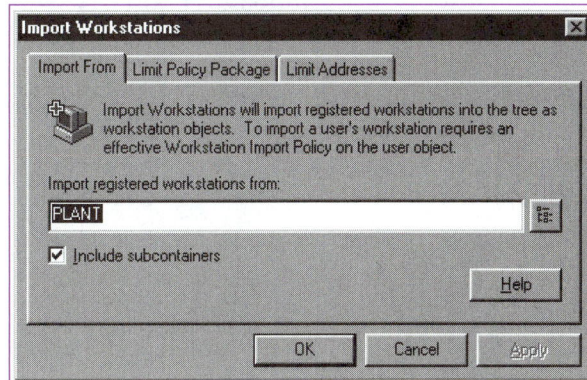

15. If your setup is correct, the window shown in Figure 12-35 should appear.

Figure 12-35

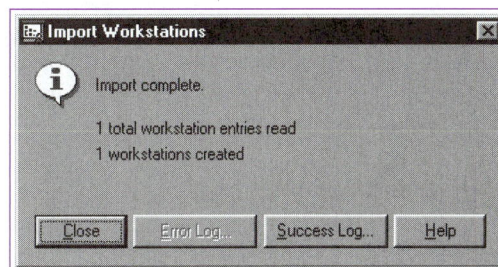

16. Once the import is complete, and no errors have occurred, you can either check the **Success Log** or go directly into the Directory to verify that your workstations do appear.

17. Go back to **NWAdmin**, double click on your **Plant** container object to close it, then double click on it again to reopen it. This refreshes the object, and adds any objects that you created in the last operation. Because it alphabetizes everything in the listing according to type, you may have to scroll through the container to find your additions. The above activity should have added the objects shown in Figure 12-36 to your list of NDS objects.

Figure 12-36

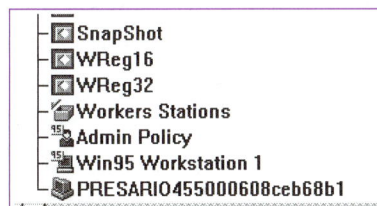

CHAPTER 12
Z.E.N.works

18. The new workstation object is easily identified by its icon; in this case, the **PRESARIO455000608ceb68b1**. Check its properties by double clicking on the object and viewing its **Details** pages. The *Effective Policies* page in particular should list the information shown in Figure 12-37. Note that the page lists a Workstation policy found for the newly-listed item.

Figure 12-37

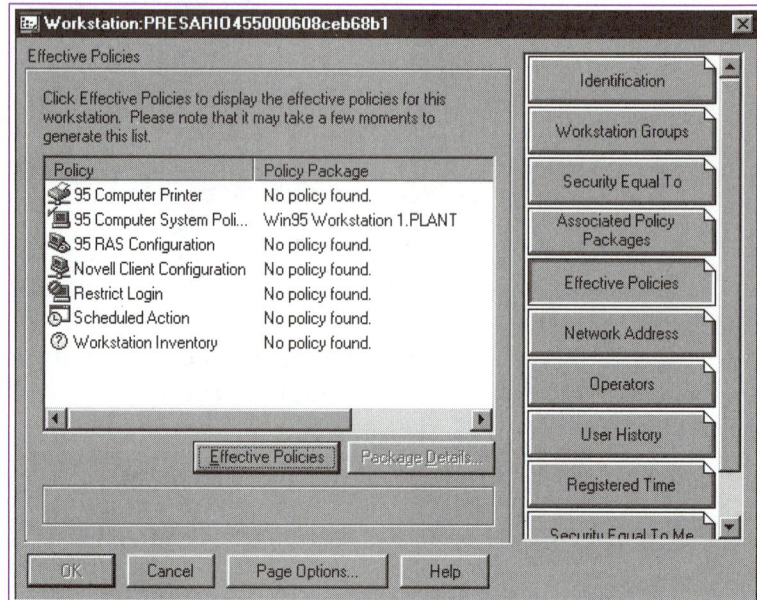

Chapter Summary

Networks are often difficult to maintain. The Novell NetWare 5 operating system's Zero Effort Networks, or Z.E.N.works, is designed to make network management easier for the administrator and reduce network maintenance.

Z.E.N.works allows you to support Microsoft Windows workstations using your NDS tree and the NDS operations that you learned during your CNA preparation. Z.E.N.works does not remove the need for network maintenance, but it does make it easier. Instead of posting changes from multiple workstations throughout your network, you are able to post them from a single location—preferably your own workstation—with little or no effort. Hence, the name "Zero Effort Networks."

Z.E.N.works is installed as part of your Novell Client installation when you install the Z.E.N.works starter pack. Additional pieces of Z.E.N.works are available that provide extra remote control features, a help requestor, and facilities for assistance with hardware inventory.

Z.E.N.works extends your schema and adds additional NDS workstation objects. These new objects represent Microsoft Windows workstations on your network. Managing these new objects is accomplished using particular sets of rules. These rules are called Policies, and are similar to the Policies found in Windows NT or Windows 95 or 98.

These rules must be set before importing workstation objects from your network.

Like user groups in NDS, imported workstations can be grouped together. Grouping and applying rules to groups of objects makes network administration easier. The groups represent multiple workstations that can be treated in the same way. When changes occur, you can post them to multiple locations through an update to a single object.

This process is effective only when the objects being tracked represent the proper locations of the workstations in the network. Whenever changes occur in the network, they must be posted to the rules configurations. This is accomplished through a maintenance schedule to ensure the accuracy of the information tracked.

Some of the most important information that must be tracked includes the changing of a network interface card, the addition or removal of a workstation, or the moving of a workstation to another location. NDS tracks workstations through their Media Access Control (MAC) address, coupled with their computer workstation's name.

There are three main types of Policy Packages: Container Policy Packages, Workstation Policy Packages, and User Policy Packages. With the exception of the Container Policy Packages, each of the Windows Operating Systems Platforms has a different package configuration operation. When you create policy packages, there are pages of object properties for changing the object's configuration. Policy package associations flow down the NDS tree.

Container Policy Packages do not have different configurations for the different Windows operating systems. They tell NetWare which of the policy packages apply to the NDS objects within the container. They should be created in the highest network level possible.

Workstation Policy Packages are used to specify the files or controls that you want set for one or more workstation objects. They apply to anyone logging in through the workstation, and are not affected by which user object is logging in. They are workstation dependent and operating system specific. You must create Workstation Policy Packages in the same container in which the workstations that will be associated with the package are located.

User Policy Packages are also operating system dependent, and must be configured separately. They are used to set controls for users on whatever computer from which they log into the network. However, the workstations they use to login must match the operating system platforms that they are authorized to use. In addition, only one User Policy Package can be applicable to any user at any given time. User package objects should be created in the same container in which the users who will be associated with the packages are located.

When assigning policy packages, use the same NDS rights assignment procedures. Avoid creating multiple user policy packages when a group assignment will work just as well. Try to use workstation groupings when they will reduce the number of Workstation Policy Packages that you have to create. Use the Container Policy Package as a security measure, and to avoid unnecessary searches.

Networking Terms Used in Chapter 12

Zero Effort Networks
   (Z.E.N.works)
Starter Pack
Remote Control
Help Requestor
Hardware Inventory

Workstation objects
Policies
importing
policy package
associated
Workstation group
   maintenance schedule

Media Access Control (MAC)
   address
naming convention
Container Policy Packages
Workstation Policy Packages
User Policy Packages

■ Chapter Review Questions

1. What does Z.E.N.works stand for?

2. When does Z.E.N.works start operating?

3. What type of workstations does Z.E.N.works allow you to support?

4. With respect to changes to workstations, what does Z.E.N.works offer to administrators?

5. How do you install Z.E.N.works?

6. What happens to the NDS schema after installing Z.E.N.works?

7. What additional NDS objects can be added to your tree through Z.E.N.works?

8. What are the rules that help you manage your new NDS objects?

CHAPTER 12
Z.E.N.works

9. Define *importing*.

10. What is a policy package?

11. Describe workstation groups.

12. What is a MAC address?

13. What are the three main types of policy packages used with Z.E.N.works?

14. Which policy package is independent of the operating systems used on the network?

15. How do policy package associations flow?

16. How many User Policy Packages can be current in a container?

17. How many User Policy Packages can be currently assigned to a user object?

18. Where should you create the different policy packages?

19. How should policy packages be applied?

20. What is one reason to use Container Policy Packages?

■ **Associated Chapter Problems**

1. Why was Z.E.N.works created?

2. How is Z.E.N.works installed?

3. Why is it important to install the Workstation and User Policy Packages according to the platforms on which they will be used?

4. Explain why a maintenance schedule should be established.

5. Describe the different policy packages available.

6. Explain what a MAC address is used for.

7. Explain the naming convention used when importing workstations.

8. Name and define each of the three policy packages used in Z.E.N.works.

9. Describe how the policy packages are further refined using the pages of properties that are available with each kind.

10. Explain how container policy packages provide additional security protection for administrators.

UNIT 4

Network Careers

CHAPTER

13

MULTICONTEXT NETWORKS

Some networks contain multiple containers that allow network users to choose the services they want to use. By the end of this chapter, you will be able to:

- describe the effects of multiple NDS tree structures.

- explain guidelines used when planning network access.

- explain the process of gaining access to network resources.

- explain how resources are offered to users in a multicontext network.

- give users adequate rights to networked resources.

- describe the entries necessary for login scripts to operate properly in a multicontext environment.

The Multicontext Environment

Although you may not be aware of it, you have worked with a *multicontext* environment throughout this text. Discussing NetWare from both the NetWare 4.11 and NetWare 5 operating system standpoints created the impression that operations were occurring concurrently in both of these systems. You saw NDS trees that illustrated more than one of these operating systems at the same time. TPUP represented the NetWare 5 section of the tree, while TPUP-HQS represented the IntranetWare 4.11 section. You can see how this impression was conveyed in Figures 13-1, 13-2, 13-3, and 13-4 from Chapter 5.

Figure 13-1

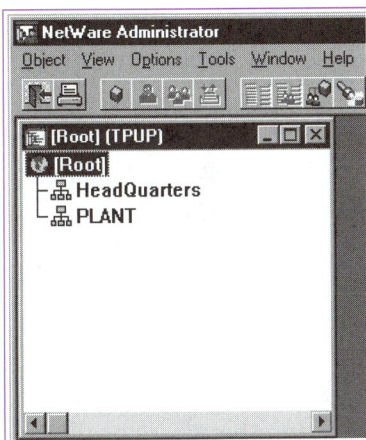

Figure 13-2

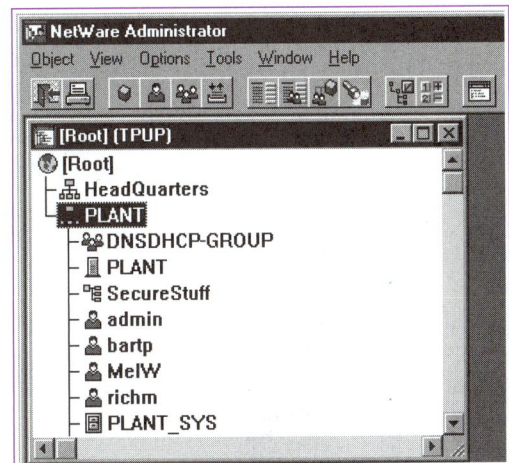

Figure 13-3

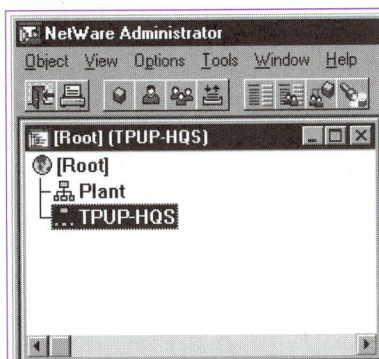

Figure 13-4

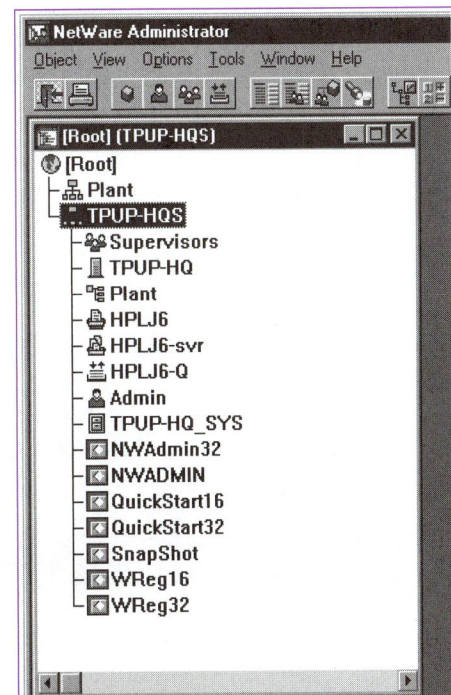

CHAPTER 13
Multicontext

Note that in the PLANT container, the server's name is *PLANT*, while in the TPUP-HQS container its name is *TPUP-HQ*. Note also that the *SYS:* volume names are *PLANT_SYS:* and *TPUP-HQ_SYS:*, respectively. This creates the impression that more than one NetWare server was running on the same network at the same time, and that either can be accessed easily from either graphic.

In reality, although the two servers were running on the same network at the same time, they could not be viewed that way on either. Although the graphics made it appear that both servers were running at the same time, each pair of graphics was actually its own multicontext network environment. Subtle differences between these two make it impossible for them to be the "same" networks. For example, the NetWare 5 container in Figure 13-1 was entitled *Headquarters*, while the same container in the IntranetWare 4.11 container in Figure 13-3 was entitled *TPUP-HQS*. In addition, the *PLANT* container used all caps in one set of graphics, but did not use them in the second set.

Both are important NDS naming rules differences, although you probably did not notice either during our NDS discussion in Chapter 5. Actually, although the two separate servers ran together on the same network tree, neither could "see" the other. Each tree had two containers, but neither had filled in both sub-containers with the necessary items, although the graphics made it appear that they did.

If either tree had filled in the two containers with the items from both sets combined, that tree would have presented a true multicontext network environment. If you remember that your *context* determines in large part your location in the tree, as well as that of the resources you wish to access, you will understand that in a multicontext environment a user can be in one container while using resources from any other.

> ... a user can be in one container while using resources from any other.

Figure 13-5

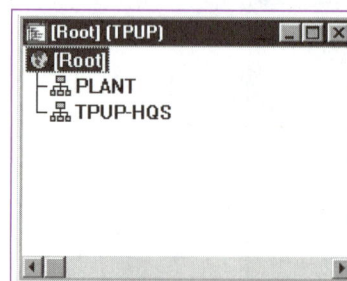

Figure 13-5 shows the multicontext environment that you will use for the remainder of this chapter. *PLANT* is a NetWare 5 server, while *TPUP-HQS* is an IntranetWare 4.11 server. You need access to both.

Network Access Planning

If you keep your users in mind when planning how to give access to your network, you will probably devise a simple login system. If you can accomplish this, and at the same time make your administrator

A simple login
system will
usually produce
an efficient
network by
minimizing the
traffic caused by
users searching
for resources.

tasks easier, then you have created an effectively planned network arrangement. A simple login system will usually produce an efficient network by minimizing the traffic caused by users searching for resources. It will also be easier to troubleshoot the network, and the network will be structured in such a way that backups are logical and easy to perform.

User access should take into account the company's general organizational information flow. For example, if the company is regionally organized around geographically separated business units (*regional organization*), you should plan the network accordingly. On the other hand, if the business is organized around departmental functions (*functional organization*), you should plan the network with those functional divisions in mind. Your company could also use a combination of both, in a hybrid organization structure.

TPUP's organizational structure, for example, combines the geographically separated business entities (Woodlands vs. Willis), and the functionally divided major units (*PLANT* vs. *HEADQUARTERS*). The server at The Woodlands is separated from the server in Willis, but they need information from each other to communicate through a connection over a Wide Area Network (WAN). It is operationally important that the two servers run different NetWare operating systems, but this will be disregarded in this planning discussion.

The company is divided geographically, as shown in Figure 13-6.

Figure 13-6

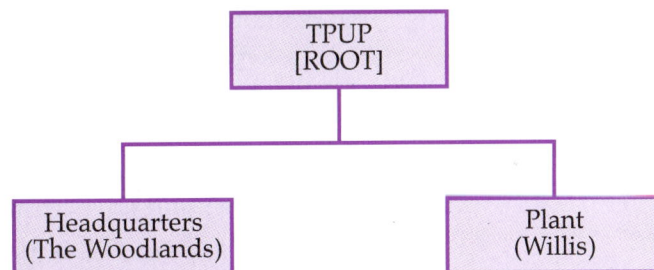

Within the Headquarters at The Woodlands, the information hierarchy is as shown in Figure 13-7.

Figure 13-7

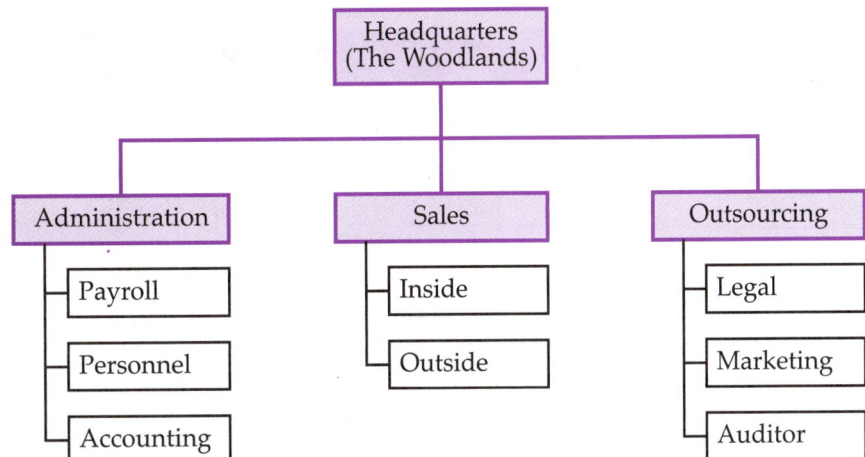

CHAPTER 13
Multicontext

Within the Plant at Willis, the information hierarchy is as shown in Figure 13-8.

Figure 13-8

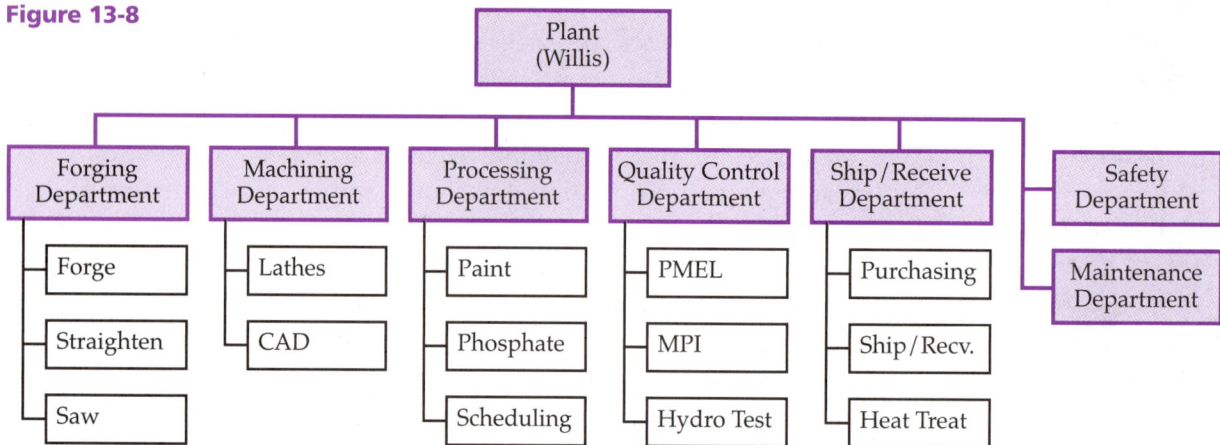

The *primary server* is located at the company's plant location, and a *backup server* is located at the headquarters building. RichM, the Plant Manager, is the network administrator at the plant's administration building. This building also houses the server and all means of network connectivity. The owners, PatH and ColleenH, located at the headquarters building, need access to the entire network. Besides the owners, BeaM is the only other person who should have open access to the personnel records, the accounting files, and the payroll.

More knowledge about the logical flow of data and individuals' data access requirements is not needed to understand the importance of effective planning in this multicontext environment. Although yours is an extremely small network, you can quickly grasp the importance of becoming involved in the early phases of network creation. You should have learned, however, that there is no "right" or "wrong" way to organize your network. However, increased efficiency can be accomplished through proper *group placement* or *group membership*, as well as through selective use of contexts during the login process.

Resource Access

As the administrator of your small classroom network, you usually controlled users' access to resources by designating their operating location in your network tree. Because of the simple nature of your network, this type of control is easy and instinctive. Regardless of the complexity or size of your network, however, you can implement the same *location-oriented controls* and simplify a great portion of your resource access decisions.

For example, if you place a user who will be using network resources in the same container where those resources are located, you have already begun to control that user's access, and have granted her access to the resources she needs.

Directing the client software on the user's workstation to set her context automatically during the login process is the easiest way to accomplish this. Check the context setting in Windows 95, as shown in Figure 13-9. To get there, right click on **Network Neighborhood**, then click on **Properties**. Once the window is opened, highlight **Novell NetWare Client** as shown, and click the **Properties** button.

Figure 13-9

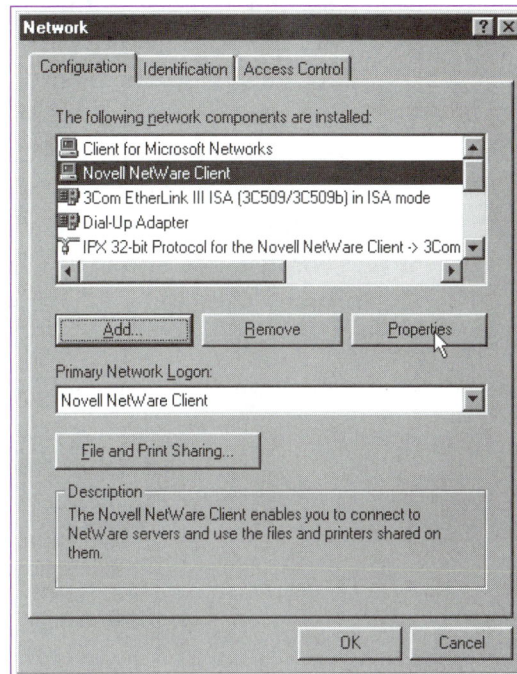

This will open the window shown in Figure 13-10, where you can alter any of the tabbed items as shown.

Figure 13-10

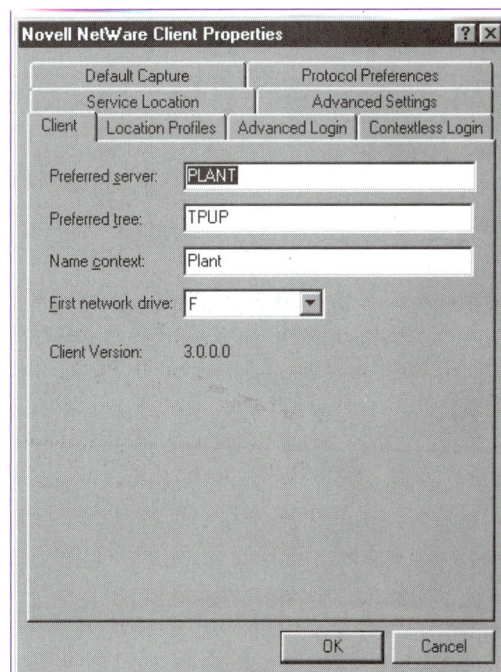

The window in Figure 13-10 shows that the *default context* is the *Plant* container, as originally desired. Your user simply logs in and specifies the resource she wants within *PLANT*. She is not required to use a long, spelled-out naming technique to gain access to her resources, unless she wants resources located outside of the *PLANT* container. If that is the case, she must enter a longer name, giving the specific location of the resource she desires. She then provides the complete name of the resource, so that the operating system can locate it. Because the user and the resource are no longer in the same container, she needs to provide more details in the name before the system can find her resource.

Another way to set this during the login process is to place the desired context in a login script activated by the user during login. For instance, enter the information shown in Figure 13-11 into the user's Container, Profile, or User login script when granting MelW access to the *SecureStuff* container shown.

Figure 13-11

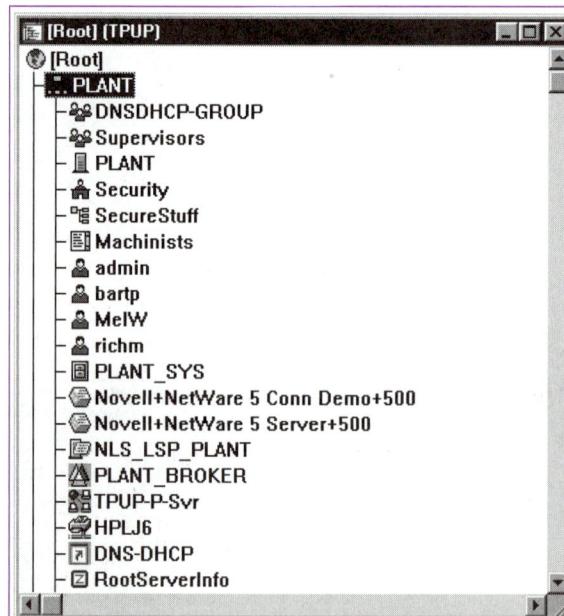

It is advantageous to set the user's context (MelW in this case) with a distinguished name in a login script (as indicated in Figure 13-11), because it does not require that the context be set correctly on the workstation from which MelW is logging into the network.

Figure 13-12

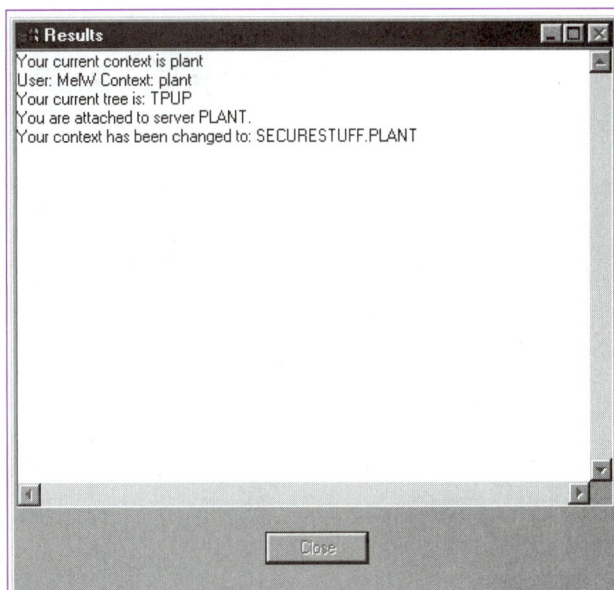

The window in Figure 13-12 shows that the login script entry does work. Using the script, MelW's context became *SECURESTUFF.Plant*, even though his user object is still in the **PLANT** container.

Note that only the User login script activated, and that it did not contain mappings. Without those mappings (found in his normal login script's actions), MelW is unable to access the *SYS:* volume. Because it is the *SYS:* volume that allows networking applications, MelW has lost his navigation capability. When MelW uses MS-DOS prompt to verify his position in the tree with CX *command*, for example, he simply receives an error message, as shown in Figure 13-13.

Figure 13-13

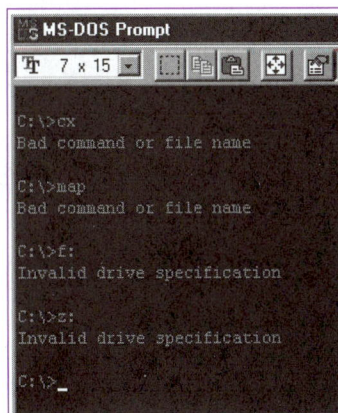

You can also see that MelW does not have an *F:* drive or a *Z:* drive mapped, so he does not have access to any networked drives, and is unable to navigate anywhere on the network. That is the power of that one context command.

Depending on the capabilities of your network users, there is yet another context selection method directly available to them when logging into the network. The administrator must have already set the **Advanced Button** feature on the Advanced Login *tab* of the ***Novell Network* Properties** button, as shown in the Figure 13-14.

Figure 13-14

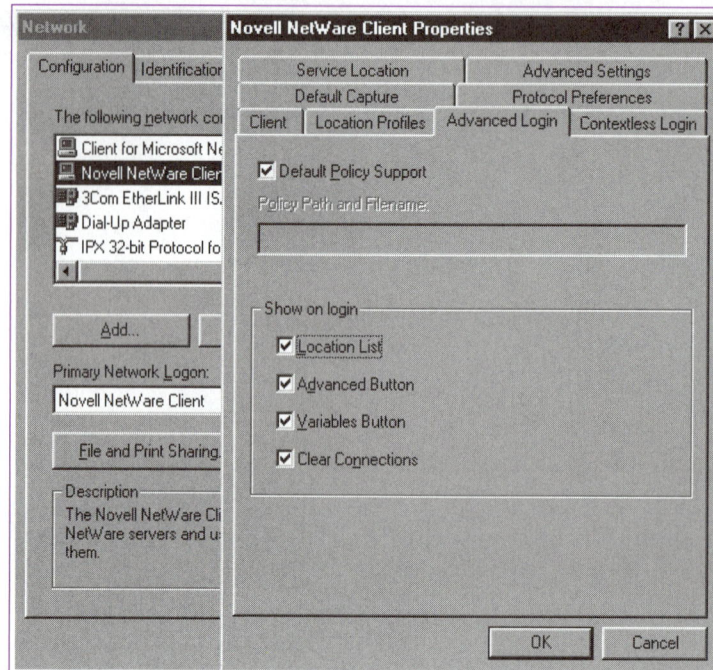

... **users are allowed to select the** Advanced **button to alter their login context.**

Figure 13-15

Once this selection is made, and the networking environment is updated by restarting the workstation, users are allowed to select the **Advanced** button to alter their login context. This is shown by the position of the selection arrow in Figure 13-15.

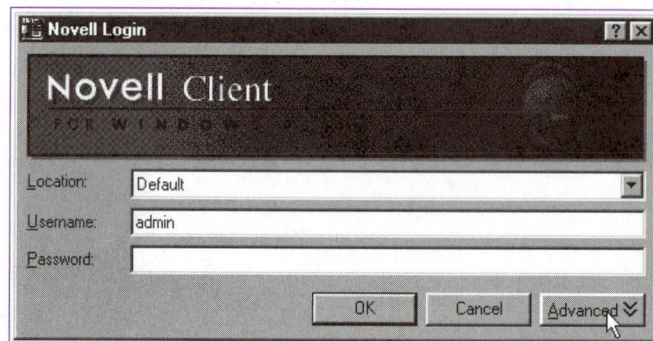

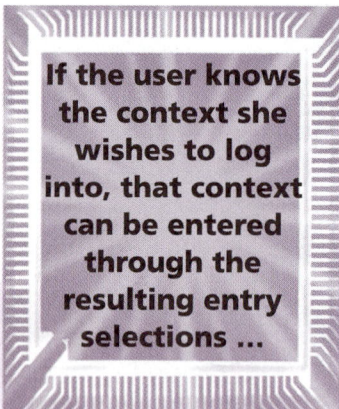

If the user knows the context she wishes to log into, that context can be entered through the resulting entry selections ...

If the user knows the context she wishes to log into, that context can be entered through the resulting entry selections, as indicated in Figure 13-16. Any of the pull down windows—**Tree**, **Context**, or **Server**—give you the choices of any contexts previously used at the workstation. In addition, the **Browse** button next to each of the selections allows the user to seek out any available selection.

Figure 13-16

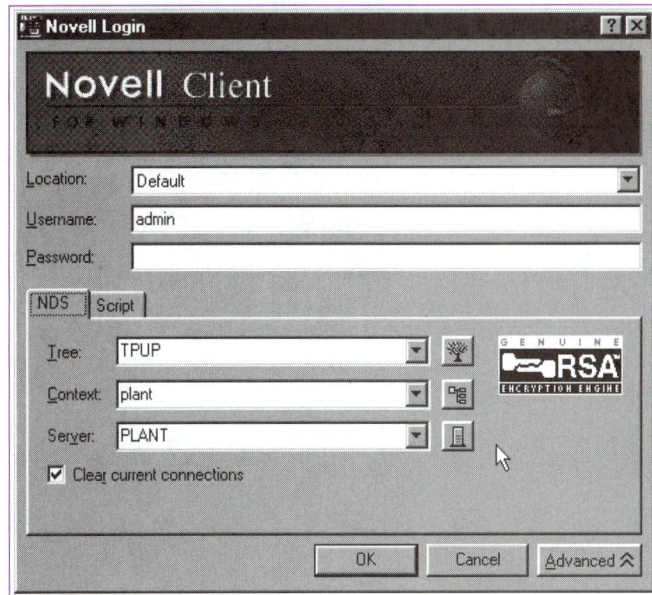

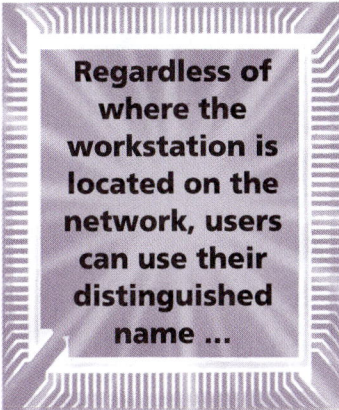

Regardless of where the workstation is located on the network, users can use their distinguished name ...

Figure 13-17

Again, depending on your users' knowledge of login procedures, there is another method to set user context when logging into your network. Regardless of where the workstation is located on the network, users can use their distinguished name, as shown in Figure 13-17, using MelW's new context developed earlier in this chapter.

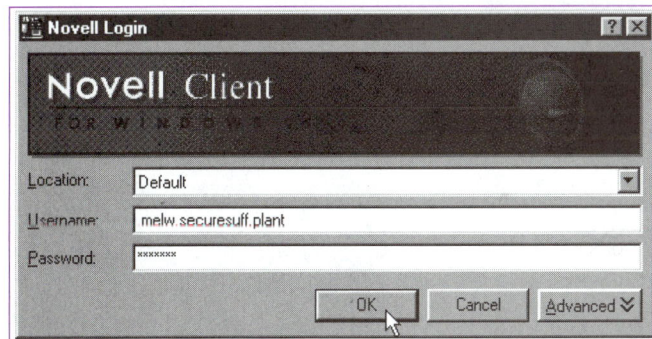

The login window shown in Figure 13-17 caused MelW to log into the location shown earlier in this discussion, even though the advanced buttons were "preset" to another location and his login script no longer forced him to go to *securestuff*. He could choose his own context as he was logging into the network.

Context Navigation

If users want to change their context, they can open a DOS prompt and navigate to where they want their context set. An example of *context navigation* is shown in Figure 13-18. To access the MS-DOS prompt, click on the **Start** button, scroll up to **Programs**, then scroll over to **MS-DOS Prompt**. Once in DOS, your prompt should show you in the *C:* drive, in *Windows*. Change drives by typing **f:** and press **<ENTER>**. The first part of the window in Figure 13-18 should appear. Change your context by typing **CX .securestuff.plant** and pressing **<ENTER>**. Your new context should be typed back to you, as indicated in Figure 13-18.

Figure 13-18

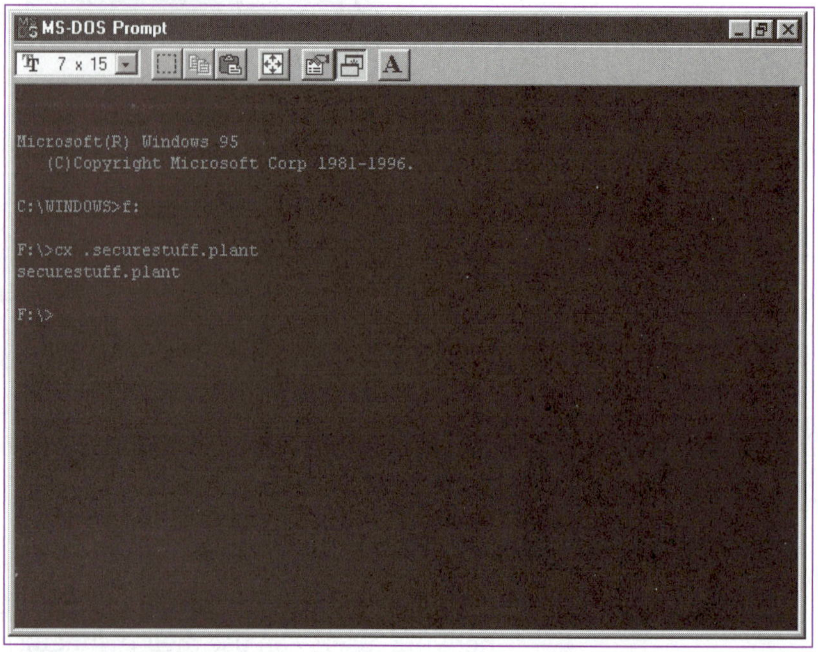

```
MS-DOS Prompt

Tr  7 x 15

Microsoft(R) Windows 95
   (C)Copyright Microsoft Corp 1981-1996.

C:\WINDOWS>f:

F:\>cx .securestuff.plant
securestuff.plant

F:\>
```

> **Once at the DOS prompt, with your context set, where you go depends on the rights you have for the location in which you find yourself.**

Once at the DOS prompt, with your context set, where you go depends on the rights you have for the location in which you find yourself. For example, if you are in the **.securestuff** container and try to login as admin from that location, you will receive the message shown in Figure 13-19.

Figure 13-19

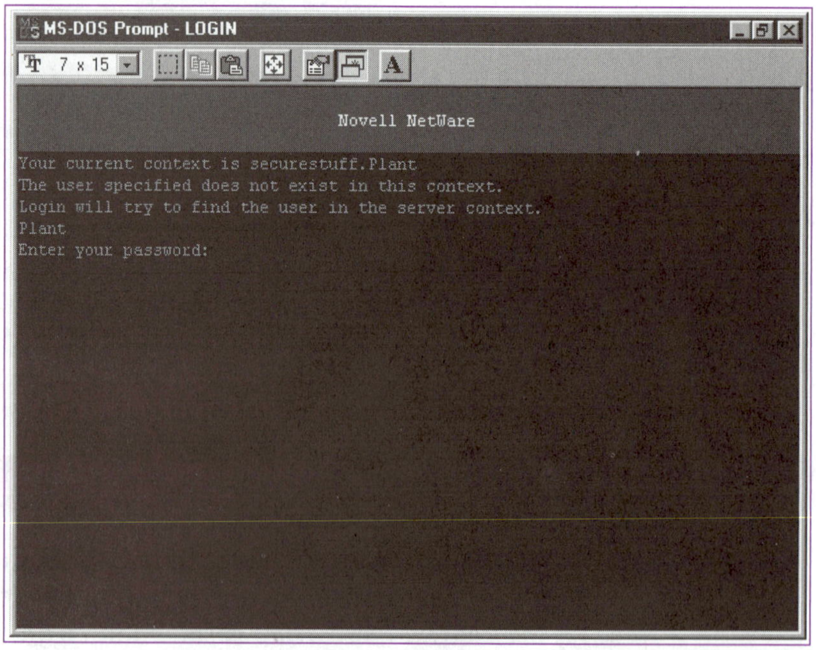

```
MS-DOS Prompt - LOGIN

Tr  7 x 15

                        Novell NetWare

Your current context is securestuff.Plant
The user specified does not exist in this context.
Login will try to find the user in the server context.
Plant
Enter your password:
```

> **... the operating system first looks for you in your current context, then it tries to find you in the server context ...**

As you can see, the operating system first looks for you in your current context, then it tries to find you in the server context *.Plant*. It does find you there, and asks you for your password in order to continue with the login procedure. If you had already been in the

.Plant context, you would have received the window shown in Figure 13-20. From there, you could have logged into the network rather than requiring the system to find the appropriate context for you.

Figure 13-20

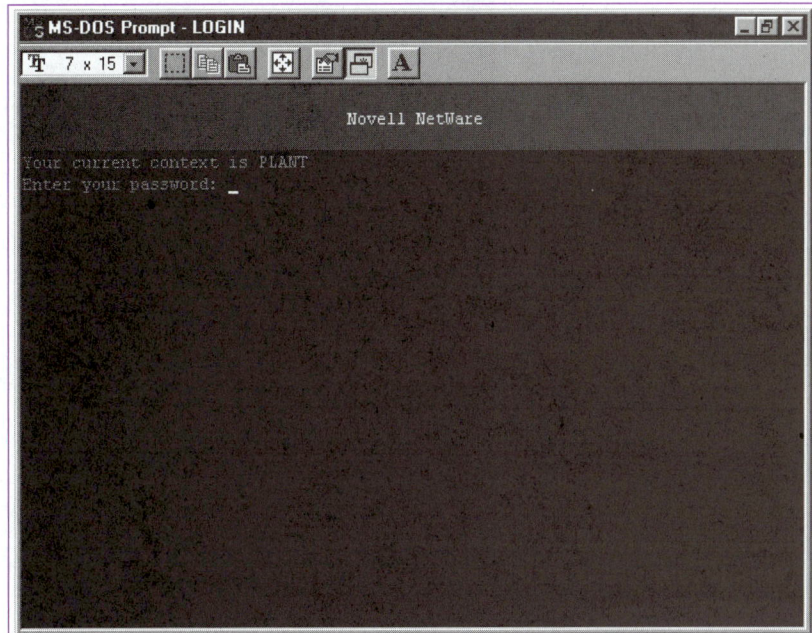

When navigating with the **CX** command, HELP is available, as shown in Figure 13-21, by entering `CX /help` and pressing **<ENTER>**.

Figure 13-21

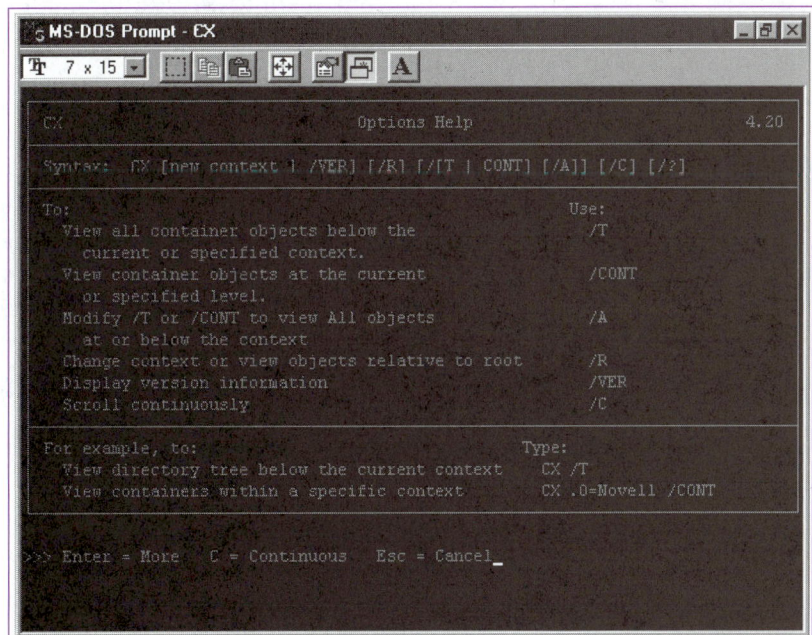

The second page shown in Figure 13-22 is available after pressing <ENTER> again.

Figure 13-22

```
MS-DOS Prompt                                              _ 8 X
Tr  7 x 15  ▼   [ ] 📋 📋 ⊠ 📁📁 A

 CX                       General Usage Help                    4.20

 Purpose: View and set current context.
 Syntax:  CX [new context | /VER] [/R] [/[T | CONT] [/A]] [/C] [/?]

 New context:
     A context can be entered either relative to your current context or
     as a distinguished name relative to the directory root.
     Use trailing periods (.) to change to a context relative to a higher
     level of your current context.
     To change to a context relative to the root of the directory put a period
     at the beginning of the new context or use the /Root flag.

 To view your current context type CX
 Current context is OU=Engineering.O=Novell

 For example, to change context:                         Type:
     O=Novell                                            CX .
     OU=Testing.OU=Engineering.O=Novell                  CX OU=Testing
     OU=Marketing.O=Novell                               CX OU=Marketing.


 F:\>
```

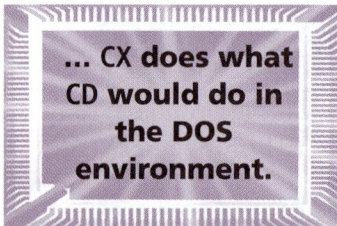

... **CX does what CD would do in the DOS environment.**

Remember that using the **CX** command is similar to using the **CD** command in DOS; **CX** does what **CD** would do in the DOS environment. This is shown in Figure 13-23. The context in the graphic was changed from *.plant* to *.securestuff.plant* using the **CX** command. The **CX** command then immediately brought the context back to *.Plant*.

Figure 13-23

```
F:\>cx .plant
plant

F:\>cx .securestuff.plant
securestuff.plant

F:\>cx
securestuff.plant
F:\>cx .
plant

F:\>cx
plant
F:\>_
```

While you are in the MS-DOS Prompt mode, you can also **MAP** drives that you wish to use. Using the **HELP** option, type `MAP /help` and press <ENTER> to view the screen in Figure 13-24, which lists the syntax and uses for the **MAP** command.

Figure 13-24

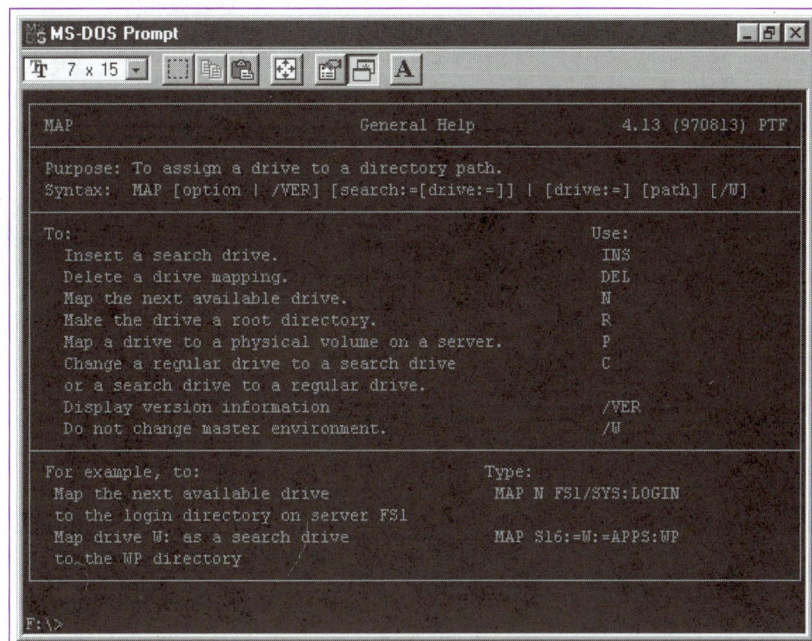

Multicontext Shortcuts

There are three shortcut methods available to make resource access easier for users and less difficult for the administrator. The three shortcuts are Aliases, Application or Directory Map Objects, and Group Objects.

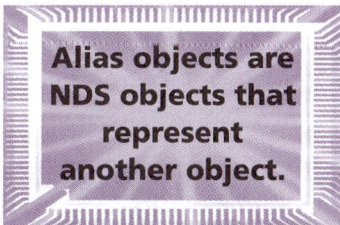

Alias Objects

> **Alias objects are NDS objects that represent another object.**

Alias objects are NDS objects that represent another object. They point to the other object and behave as if the original were actually there in the alias's place. To create an Alias object, select the **Plant** object in **NWAdmin** and use the pull down **Object** menu to **Create**. The window shown in Figure 13-25 will appear.

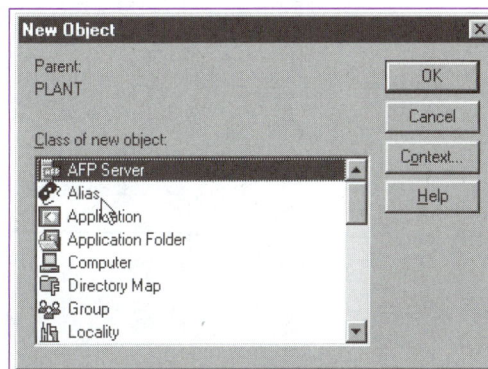

Figure 13-25

Select **Alias** and click **OK**. The window shown in Figure 13-26 appears, allowing you to specify the Alias name and the object to which it will point after it has been created. As an example, the information is completed to designate an alias which points to the File Server *PLANT_SYS.PLANT*.

Figure 13-26

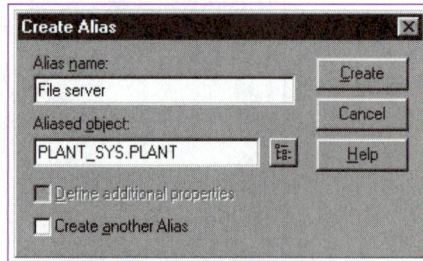

Click on **Create** to create and name the new object **File server**, as shown in Figure 13-27. The new object points to the **PLANT_SYS** object.

Figure 13-27

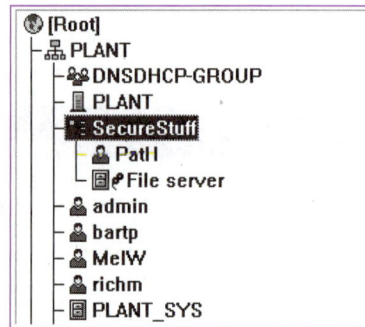

This can be demonstrated easily by right clicking on the new alias object and checking its details. They will list the details of the object to which the alias is pointing. This can be seen in Figure 13-28. Here, the alias was checked, but the main object's details appeared.

Figure 13-28

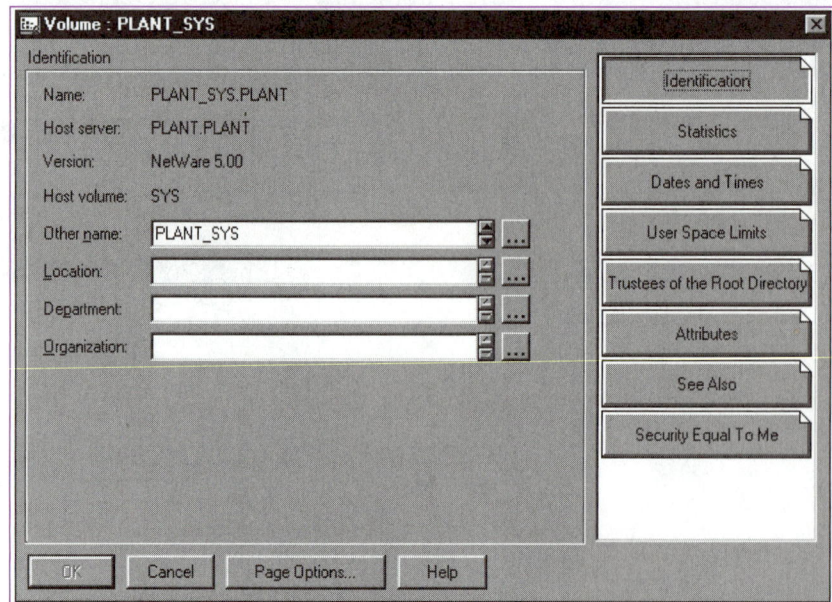

Application or Directory Map Objects

Two other NDS objects can point to other NDS objects outside of the container in which they reside. *Application objects* point to an application on another volume when the original application cannot be installed in more than one location, but must be run from another location. *Directory Map objects* point to a directory on a volume in another container when the contents of the original directory are needed elsewhere but cannot be copied. Using these two objects is similar to using aliases, with the difference that the objects can point application files and directory locations on volumes, while aliases can point only to NDS objects.

Begin to create an Application object, as shown in Figure 13-29.

Figure 13-29

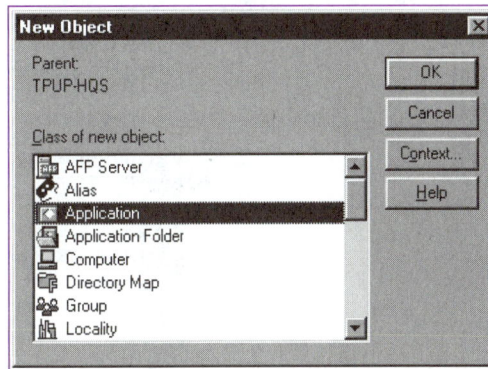

The window shown in Figure 13-30 appears. Leave the top item selected, unless you are creating a template for Application objects or duplicating an already existing Application object.

Figure 13-30

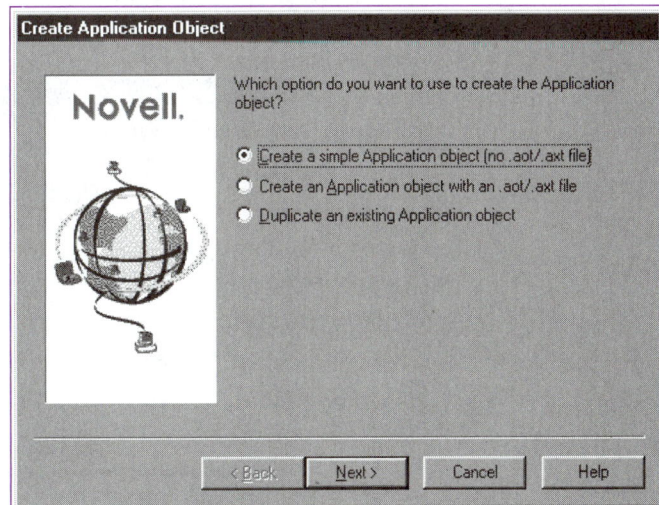

Select the application executable to which you want the new
object to point. This is indicated in the graphic sequence shown in
Figure 13-31.

Figure 13-31

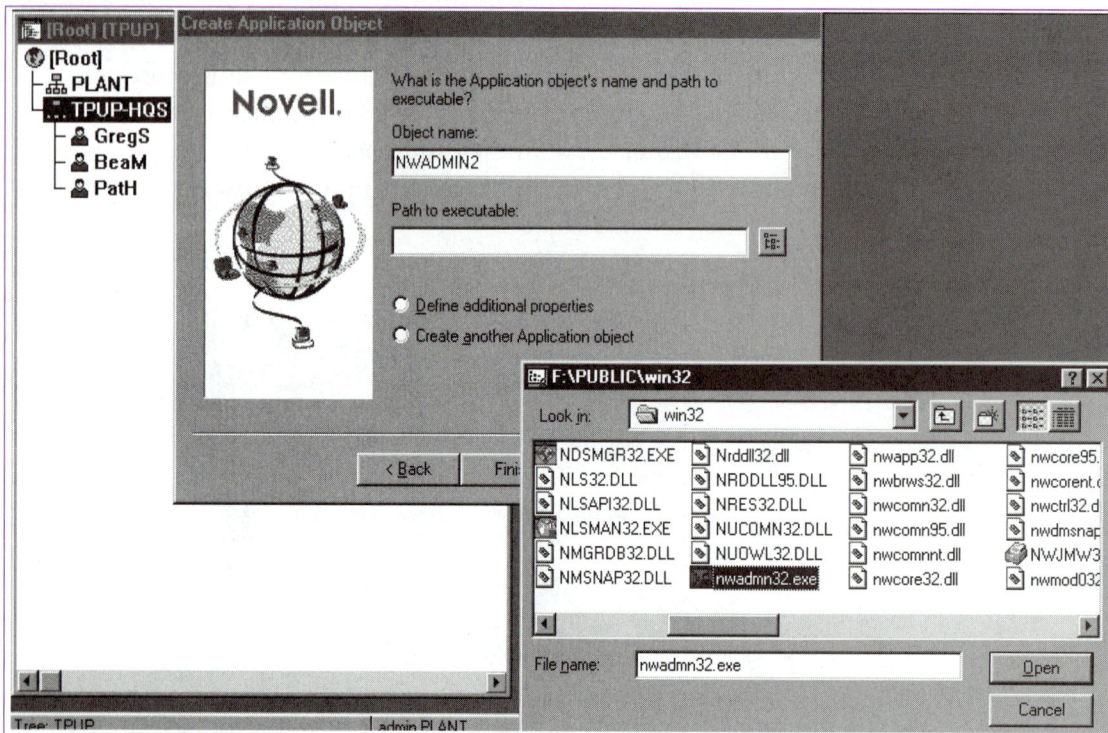

Select the executable you wish to use, and click **Open**. This adds
the path to the executable into the appropriate window, as shown in
Figure 13-32.

Figure 13-32

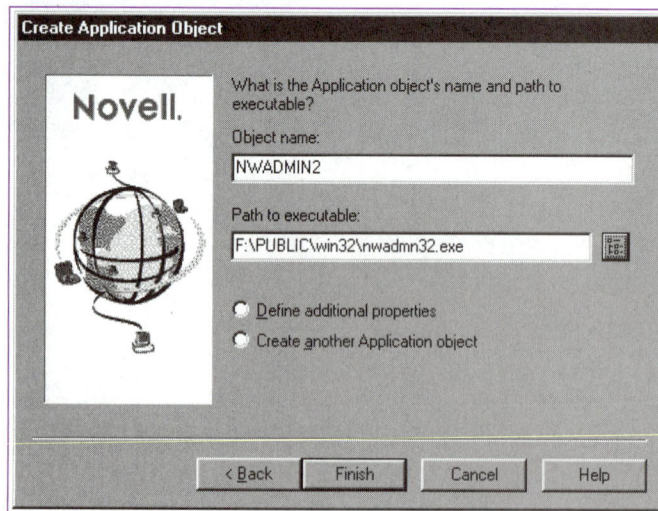

Click **Finish** in the above window to add the Application object to
the location you specified. This is shown in Figure 13-33.

Figure 13-33

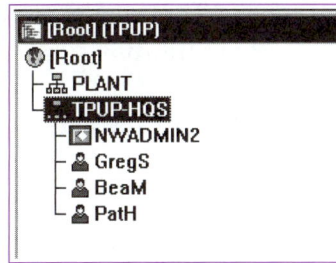

Begin to create Directory Map objects, as shown in Figure 13-34.

Figure 13-34

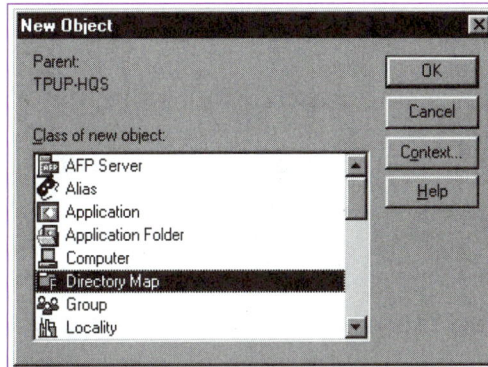

The window shown in Figure 13-35 will appear, giving you the option to specify a Directory Map object name and point to the volume and path of the original object.

Figure 13-35

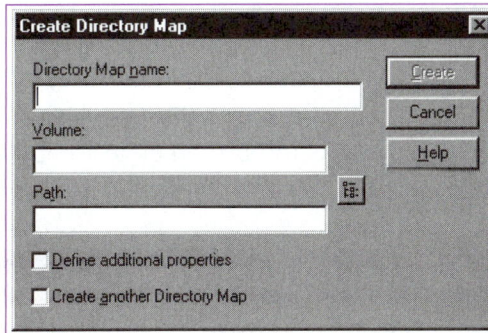

Specifying a name and choosing the path to the *Mail* directory in the *Plant* container, as indicated in Figure 13-36, allows the users in the *TPUP-HQS* container to use the original directory as if it were their own.

Figure 13-36

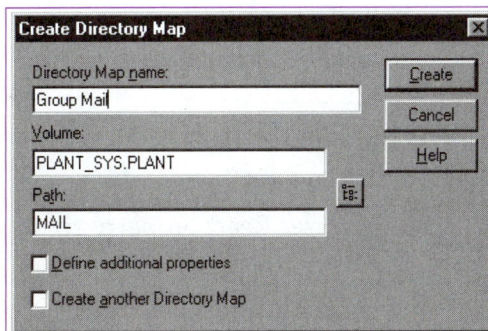

Figure 13-37

This newly created **Group Mail** Directory Map object can be seen in Figure 13-37.

Group Objects

We have already learned how to create groups within NDS. Now, we would like one object to be able to point at another in different location. *Group objects*, when used in a multicontext manner, allow the formation of a universal group comprised of users from anywhere in the network who need to be granted similar rights. Regardless of where an administrator forms such a group, adding new members to it allows them to assume the rights assignments of the group, regardless of where they are. It creates a single point where users from numerous locations can have all of their properties altered at the same time. This makes the administration of those users easier for the network administrator.

Create a Universal Group assignment as you have in previous chapters. Start with the window shown in Figure 13-38.

Figure 13-38

Figure 13-39

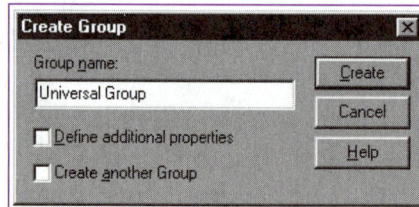

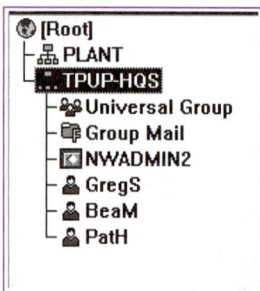

Type in the Group Name (**Universal Group** used in the example), and click **Create**. This creates the Group object shown in Figure 13-39. The desired rights assignments for the group members should then be granted to the Group object, and the individual user objects should be assigned as members of the group.

Required Access Rights for Multicontext Short Cuts

To Use Item	Do This Action	You Must Have This
Alias	Grant user rights to aliased object	Authority to grant in other container
Application	Grant application system rights to user	Supervisory right or access control
	Associate user with application object	Write property right to object and user ACLs
Directory Map	Grant directory map file system rights to user	Directory Supervisor or Access control rights
	Grant user Read property right to Map Path	Write property right to map ACL
Group	Add user to group member list of group	Write property right to member + object ACL

Chapter Summary

It is difficult to explain how two Novell networks can run on the same cabling system at the same time. Giving any user the ability to log into either of those networks and use any objects whenever he likes is a lofty goal. Multicontext networks provide means to that goal.

If you plan network access with your users in mind and manage to make your administration duties easy at the same time, you have planned an effective network environment. The login system will be efficient, and will minimize user traffic. Troubleshooting will be easier, and structured to make backups logical and easy to perform. User access should follow the company's overall organizational information flow, possibly with a regional or functional orientation. More complex companies may have a hybrid combination of the two.

In small, simple networks, it is usually easy to keep your users in the same containers where the resources that they need for their work are located. However, as companies increase in size and complexity, this becomes more difficult. Administrators should strive to use the same location-oriented controls, as they attempt to simplify their resource-access decisions. Setting the context at the user's workstation is one means of accomplishing this task. This method is set in the Client properties setup section. Administrators could also accomplish this by placing the desired context in a login script activated for the user during login. Another way to accomplish this is to give users access to the "advanced" option of the login properties windows when logging in. Finally, the user could type in his fully distinguished name for the context that he desires.

Users with access to the network and the MS-DOS prompt window can navigate through the context of their choice. The **CX** command provides navigation capability similar to that found in the DOS **CD** command. Although not generally used for network navigation since the arrival of Windows, the MS-DOS use of the **CX** command allows quick and effective login, searching, mapping, and overall network navigation capabilities. Typing **CX /help** provides you with a listing of commands and their syntax. In addition, typing **MAP /help** provides you with a listing of commands relative to the **MAP** command.

There are numerous shortcuts available when operating in the multicontext environment. Three of these shortcuts are Alias objects, Application or Directory Map objects, and Group objects. Alias objects are NDS objects that represent another NDS object's location, and point from the alias object to the original object's location. Application objects point to an application on another volume when the original application cannot be installed in more than one location, but must be run from another location. Directory Map objects point to a directory on a volume in another container when the contents of the original directory are needed elsewhere, but cannot be copied. The map objects are similar to the alias objects, although they can point to Application or Directory objects, while aliases can point only to NDS objects. Group objects allow the formation of universal groups, composed of users from anywhere in the network who can be granted similar rights. Regardless of where administrators form groups, new members added to the groups take on the rights assignments granted to the group. It creates a single point where users from numerous locations can have all of their properties altered at the same time. These objects help ease the burden of network administrators.

Networking Terms Used in Chapter 13

multicontext	group membership	`CX /help`
context	location-orientated controls	`MAP /help`
regional organization	default context	Alias objects
functional organization	**CX** command	Application objects
primary server	Advanced Login tab	Directory Map objects
backup server	context navigation	Group objects
group placement		

■ Chapter Review Questions

1. What are the benefits of multicontext networks?

2. What were the network naming conventions violated in the early discussions of this text relative to multicontext network use?

3. What are the benefits of planning for efficient network access?

4. What type of informational organization is used in the TPUP structure?

5. Where are the primary server and backup servers located in TPUP?

6. What are the benefits of a small network relative to resource access?

7. What are the different methods for user context selection during login?

8. What is the method of setting a user's context that does not rely on setting the context correctly at the workstation?

9. What command is available for users to navigate multicontext networks without using the client login windows?

10. If you try to log into the network in the wrong context, what does the operating system try to do for you?

11. What is the full **CX** command for viewing container objects at the current or specified level?

12. Write the correct **MAP** command to delete the current first search drive.

13. List the steps for creating Alias objects.

14. List the steps for creating Directory Map objects.

15. Whose properties are listed when viewing an Alias object's details?

16. How are the Alias objects differentiated from the original objects in **NWAdmin**?

17. What is the limitation on where users can come from when being added to universal groups?

18. Can aliases be used to represent NFS directories?

19. What rights must you have to allow a user access to a Directory Map object?

20. Who usually creates the Shortcut objects in a multicontext environment?

■ Associated Chapter Problems

1. Why was it important in earlier chapters to give the impression that the NetWare 4.11 and NetWare 5 networks were operating on the same network?

2. Describe how users gain access to all resources regardless of where they are on the network to which they are connected.

3. Why is it important for users to be able to operate in a multicontext environment?

4. Explain how network access planning should be performed.

5. Describe the informational constraints found in the TPUP diagrams supplied in this chapter.

6. When is the best time for resource access plans to be made? Explain.

7. Explain each of the different methods for users to alter their context during login.

8. Describe five uses of the **CX** command in multicontext network navigation.

9. Explain the difference between Alias objects and Application or Directory Map objects.

10. How can Group objects provide universal access for users and reduced workload for administrators?

CHAPTER 14
MANAGING YOUR NETWORK

OBJECTIVES

A network administrator performs numerous functions in the day-to-day routine of network environment management. By the end of this chapter, you will be able to:

- describe the network administrator's management areas.

- understand the components that make up the typical server.

- use the Server Console to monitor network operation.

- understand **VREPAIR** for Volume repairs.

- understand **DSREPAIR** for NDS repairs.

- describe how to connect to the server console using remote console methods.

- list and explain some of the more frequently used server console commands.

- list and explain some of the more frequently used NetWare Loadable Modules.

Managing the Network

Building your network and understanding the benefits of having a network are important facets of this course. How you manage the network entrusted to you, however, determines your overall success as a Novell-trained network administrator. Studying the network environment and preparing for certification through Novell's many education programs helps ensure that success. This course will try to help you become a better administrator by preparing you to become a Certified Novell Administrator (CNA). Even if you do not become certified, however, your network administrator responsibilities will involve networking functions similar to those of a CNA, regardless of the size of the network you administer. As the network administrator, you will constantly try to become better acquainted with those networking skills that help you manage your network, and your network will tend to grow rapidly.

You have already learned that there are many complicated pieces associated with networked computers. When any of the pieces break down or stop communicating with each other, the network administrator is the one who usually fixes the problem. Therefore, once your network is installed and operational, your job is to keep it up and running.

Usually the user workstation is the piece that breaks down or needs some sort of intervention. Although you may not be required to perform the repairs on the workstations if they break down, the users usually will not know what the problem is and will blame your network. Knowing how to troubleshoot and where problems originate will help you perform your primary task of administering networked resources.

Sometimes you must access the file server itself through the server console, as you did when you installed the operating system itself. You ran *commands* and loaded *NetWare Loadable Modules (NLMs)* as the system became increasingly operationally sound. Although not normally part of a new network administrator's duties, operating the server console and knowing how some of the major commands affect your network will make you a better manager of your own network and more likely to accept future managerial responsibility.

The most common administrator tasks involve working with Novell Directory Services (NDS) objects. They make up your network. Your users log into the network in order to communicate with them. The design of the network and your familiarity with NDS procedures determine how well you will be able to manage your network.

Another common administrator task involves creating and maintaining the Network File System (NFS). This is probably the most important administrator duty. Again, how you design file structures and how familiar you are with file creation and storage needs determines how successfully you will be able to manage your network.

> Knowing how to troubleshoot and where problems originate will help you perform your primary task of administering networked resources.

> Another common administrator task involves creating and maintaining the Network File System (NFS). This is probably the most important administrator duty.

Securing the two main network components above (NDS and NFS) by creating users, granting users access to networked resources, and giving users the rights necessary to work with those resources is another important network management task. Your success as an administrator, as well as your organization's livelihood, may depend on whether or not you provide a secure network. In such a network, authorized users easily gain access, and unauthorized users are kept out.

Knowledge about your environment is the strongest tool you can carry with you when you administer a network. The following will help build the base upon which your network administrator success will depend.

> Your success as an administrator, as well as your organization's livelihood, may depend on whether or not you provide a secure network.

Server Components

In Chapter 2, we learned that a server is a computer that offers its services and resources to clients and workstations over a network. In the beginning of Chapter 3, we also learned the physical requirements for servers—both Novell's 4.11 and 5 operating systems. The server is "just another computer," similar to a workstation. It does have a processor in its main structural component—the Central Processing Unit (CPU). The more powerful this processor is, the faster and stronger the server is. Like a workstation, the server also has Random Access Memory (RAM), although the server's minimum RAM requirements are much higher. Put simply, the more RAM, the better the server. The server also has disk storage associated with it, and the more it has, the better the server. In addition, like the workstations it serves, a server is connected to the network through a network interface card (NIC), network card address, and associated cabling. These components allow the server to communicate with other network members. The server also consists of additional subcomponents, however, which together facilitate network operation.

> The more powerful this processor is, the faster and stronger the server is.

The server determines the *network address* used by all the devices on the network. You install the address when you install your server software. A unique *internal network number*, created during the installation, differentiates your server from all other servers (if there are any) on the network. When multiple servers are present on the same network segment, another piece—an *external network number*—is added to the server identifier. All servers on that particular network segment use the same external network number. In addition, every segment must have its own unique external network number.

Server Console

Server management involves communication between the administrator and the server itself. This communication takes place primarily in the form of console commands and NetWare Loadable Modules (NLMs), with the majority occurring at the server console.

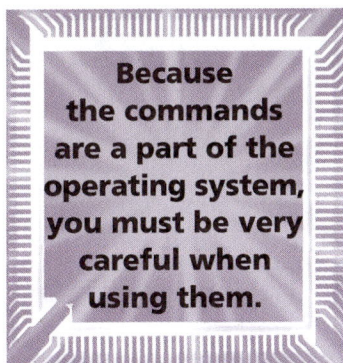

Console Commands

The NetWare Operating system includes a large number of commands through which operators interface with the file server's hardware and its loaded software. The commands are part of the operating system, just as DOS commands are part of the Disk Operating System (DOS).

Because the commands are a part of the operating system, you must be very careful when using them. They will act immediately upon whatever part of the server to which you send them, and they will do whatever you asked them to do. If your syntax (the format you use in the command) is incorrect, the command will not be understood by the software, and it will return an error. On the other hand, if your syntax is correct, but your command is for a function you do not want, it could affect your server's health. In other words, be careful what you ask for; you may just get it!

At the console prompt, type `add name space long to sys` as an example of a NetWare Command. This command is necessary to render the server capable of storing long file names in the WIN95 format instead of its customary DOS 8.3 format. This command needs to run only one time on the server for the name space capability to remain with the server. However, the appropriate NLM (*LONG.NAM*) must be loaded before it will run.

> Because the commands are a part of the operating system, you must be very careful when using them.

Common Commands	
EXIT	Command to return to DOS.
LOAD	Reads an NLM into the server's RAM.
UNLOAD	Removes an NLM from the server's RAM.
DOWN	Closes all open files and volumes and removes the server from the network.
SECURE CONSOLE	Removes DOS from the server and prevents loading NLMs from anywhere but *SYS:SYSTEM*.
MODULES	Displays all NLMs currently loaded.
CONFIG	Displays information on each connected network interface card.
NAME	Displays the name of the server.
SEND	Allows operator to send a message to all users currently logged on.
DISPLAY NETWORKS	Displays all networks to which the server has access.
DISPLAY SERVERS	Displays all servers on which the server has information.
MEMORY	Displays the total memory available to the file server.
SET TIME	Used when changing current system date and time.

NetWare Loadable Modules

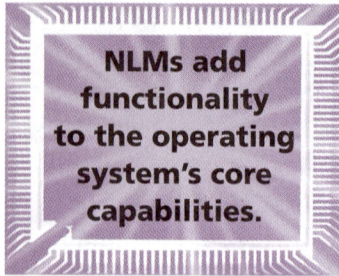

NLMs add functionality to the operating system's core capabilities.

Unlike console commands, NetWare Loadable Modules (NLMs) are external to the operating system, and must be loaded into the server's memory before they can be used. NLMs add functionality to the operating system's core capabilities. An operator must **LOAD** NLMs into the server. This action tells the server to read the module into server memory from the default *SYS:SYSTEM* location (unless another path is specified), and to execute it. The added functionality then remains in the server provided the server continues to run, or until the operator **UNLOAD**s the NLM.

At the console prompt, type `load long.nam` to initiate the addition of the long name space discussed in the previous section on commands. The NLM must be loaded before running the **Add Name Space** command. The command is run only one time at each volume where the additional space is needed. Once it has run initially and the space has been added, the NLM autoloads whenever the server restarts, and that volume is remounted.

NLM Types	
.DSK	Provides direct control of server disk drives. Located in the DOS partition.
.LAN	Controls drivers for network interface cards.
.NAM	Adds capability for server to recognize additional naming conventions.
.NLM	Adds general purpose capabilities to the server.

Common NLMs	
MONITOR.NLM	Location for general performance information on the server.
INSTALL.NLM	Allows manipulation of NetWare components. Not available in NetWare 5.
NWCONFIG.NLM	NetWare 5's replacement for INSTALL.NLM.
CDROM.NLM	Adds CDROM support to server.
DSREPAIR.NLM	Allows repairs to NDS.
VREPAIR.NLM	Allows repairs to specified Volumes.
REMOTE.NLM	Allows server console operation from workstation. Must create remote password before use.
LONG.NAM	Naming convention for Windows format.
MAC.NAM	Naming convention for Macintosh format.
3C509.LAN	Controls drivers for commonly used 3Com Network Interface Card.

Monitor

If you are responsible for the overall health of your network, you will probably spend a great deal of your time using the **MONITOR**. The server's performance and operating statistics, as well as information about the connection made to the server, are all available in Monitor.

Typing `load monitor` at the console prompt and pressing the enter key will give you a screen containing information shown in Figure 14-1.

Figure 14-1

```
NetWare 5 Console Monitor  5.19                NetWare Loadable Module
Server name: 'PLANT' in Directory tree 'TPUP'
Server version: NetWare 5.00 - August 27, 1998

                        General Information
          Utilization:                              1%  ▲
          Server up time:                  3:02:46:33  █
          Online processors:                        1  █
          Original cache buffers:              11,104  █
          Total cache buffers:                  4,951
          Dirty cache buffers:                      0  ▼

                        Available Options
          ▲ Connections
          █ Storage devices
          █ Volumes
            LAN/WAN drivers
            Loaded modules
            File open/lock activity
          ▼ Disk cache utilization

Tab=Next window     Alt+F10=Exit                         F1=Help
```

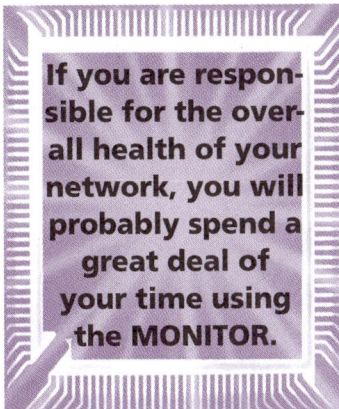

> If you are responsible for the overall health of your network, you will probably spend a great deal of your time using the MONITOR.

If nothing else is entered through the console for approximately ten seconds after loading the *monitor.nlm*, the above window opens further, and additional information becomes available when the top *Information* portion of the screen expands over the bottom *Options*. This additional information is also available through pressing the `<TAB>` key. The `<TAB>` key also toggles you back and forth between the expanded window information and the reduced screen provided initially. After ten seconds of inactivity, however, the screen expands, covering the options window, as shown in Figure 14-2.

Figure 14-2

```
NetWare 5 Console Monitor  5.19                NetWare Loadable Module
Server name: 'PLANT' in Directory tree 'TPUP'
Server version: NetWare 5.00 - August 27, 1998

                        General Information
          Utilization:                              2%
          Server up time:                  3:02:46:33
          Online processors:                        1
          Original cache buffers:              11,104
          Total cache buffers:                  4,951
          Dirty cache buffers:                      0
          Long term cache hits:                  100%
          Current disk requests:                    0
          Packet receive buffers:                 120
          Directory cache buffers:                151
          Maximum service processes:              500
          Current service processes:               19
          Current connections:                      1
          Open files:                               0

          █ File open/lock activity
          ▼ Disk cache utilization

Tab=Next window     Alt+F10=Exit                         F1=Help
```

Figure 14-3

```
   Available Options
┌─────────────────────────┐
│Connections              │
│Storage devices          │
│Volumes                  │
│LAN/WAN drivers          │
│Loaded modules           │
│File open/lock activity  │
│Disk cache utilization   │
│System resources         │
│Virtual memory           │
│Kernel                   │
│Server parameters        │
└─────────────────────────┘
```

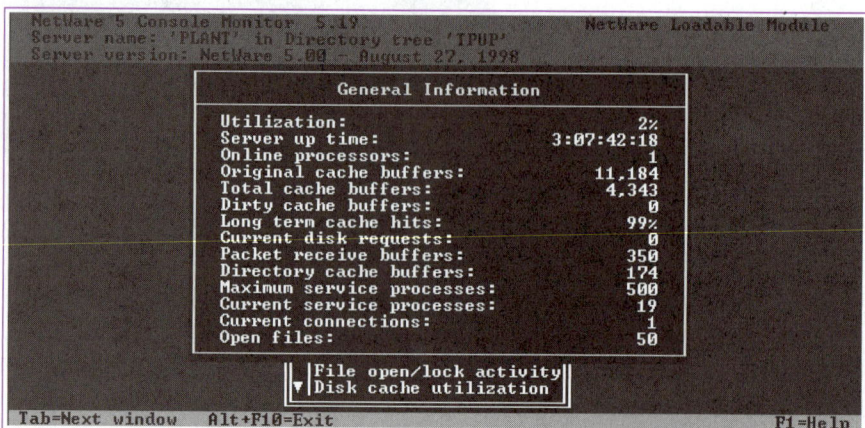

Sometimes a quick snapshot will also tell you if a problem is evident.

A large number of dirty cache buffers may indicate that your network is degrading and that you may need to install additional servers or controller cards.

The scroll bar along the right side of the **Options** window, if expanded, would reveal the additional information, as indicated in Figure 14-3.

For each available option in the graphic, there exists an information window that appears when the option is selected. Through these options, a significant amount of information about the server's operation can be accumulated. Tracking pertinent pieces of this data can alert you to a potential problem.

Sometimes a quick snapshot will also tell you if a problem is evident. For example, if the number of *total cache buffers* in the general information window falls below one half of the original cache buffers, this would indicate that the server is running low on memory, and that you should either increase memory or decrease the demands placed upon the amount you have. Either add RAM or unload NLMs.

This course is not intended to give you a complete understanding of each of the above items. However, knowing where you go to locate such information is important in times of crisis. Keeping track of trends will also help avoid potential problems.

There are also some general indicators that you can monitor. Used as "Rules of Thumb," they may help you discover where problems are developing if your network begins to act differently. The *Utilization* field tells you how much of your processor's capability is being used.

If your processor meets the demands of your network, this figure should not exceed 70%, unless there is a problem. A large number of *dirty cache buffers* may indicate that your network is *degrading* and that you may need to install additional servers or controller cards. The total dirty cache buffers should amount to less than a third of the total cache buffers, and the total cache buffers should amount to at least half of the original cache buffers.

The graphics of the server windows discussed in this section are shown in Figures 14-4 through 14-15, as captured over the remote console operation discussed later in this chapter.

Figure 14-4

```
NetWare 5 Console Monitor 5.19               NetWare Loadable Module
  Server name: 'PLANT' in Directory tree 'IPUP'
  Server version: NetWare 5.00 - August 27, 1998

┌──────────────── General Information ────────────────┐
│  Utilization:                              2%        │
│  Server up time:                  3:07:42:18         │
│  Online processors:                        1         │
│  Original cache buffers:              11,184         │
│  Total cache buffers:                  4,343         │
│  Dirty cache buffers:                      0         │
│  Long term cache hits:                   99%         │
│  Current disk requests:                    0         │
│  Packet receive buffers:                 350         │
│  Directory cache buffers:                174         │
│  Maximum service processes:              500         │
│  Current service processes:               19         │
│  Current connections:                      1         │
│  Open files:                              50         │
└─────────────────────────────────────────────────────┘
        ┌─────────────────────────────┐
        │ File open/lock activity      │
      ▼ │ Disk cache utilization       │
        └─────────────────────────────┘
 Tab=Next window    Alt+F10=Exit                      F1=Help
```

Figure 14-5

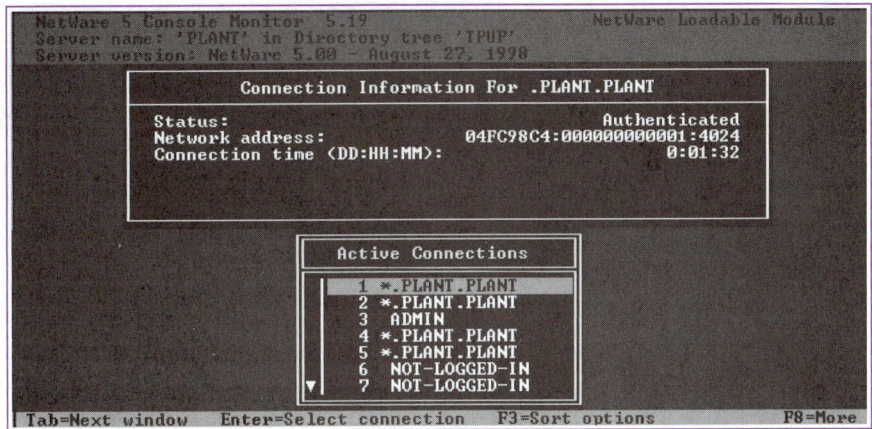

Figure 14-6

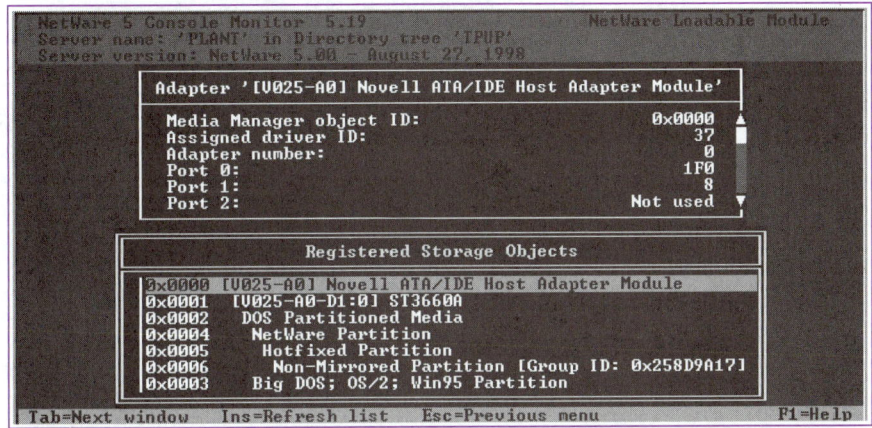

Figure 14-7

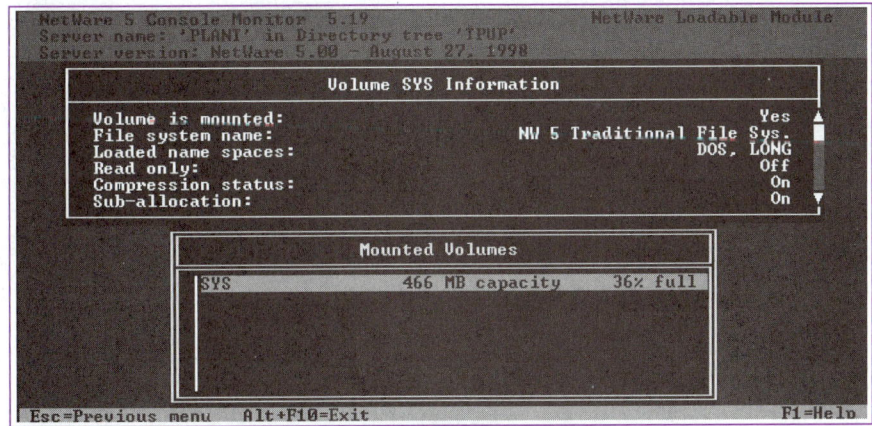

Figure 14-8

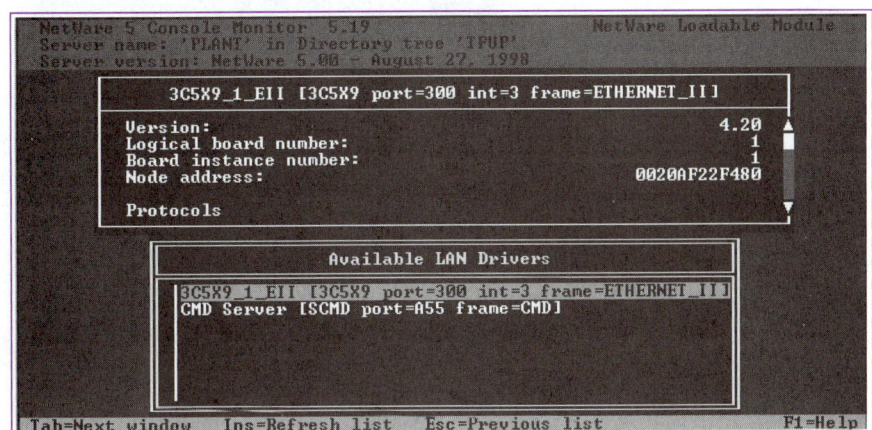

Figure 14-9

```
NetWare 5 Console Monitor  5.19              NetWare Loadable Module
Server name: 'PLANT' in Directory tree 'TPUP'
Server version: NetWare 5.00 - August 27, 1998

            Module 'SERVER.NLM' Information
  Version:                                              5.00     ▲
  Creation date:                                     8-27-1998   █
  Address space:                                           OS    █
  Bytes of memory required to load:                   1,536,000

  Allocated memory:                        3,264,512      100%   ▼

                      Loaded NLMs
  SERVER.NLM  :  NetWare Server Operating System
  XFVGA16.NLM :  XFree86 - X11R6 Server
  FILESYS.NLM :  NetWare File System NLM
  DS.NLM      :  NetWare 5.00 Directory Services
  TCPIP.NLM   :  Novell TCP/IP Module MOAB_B48_813
  MM.NLM      :  NetWare Media Manager
▼ NLSLSP.NLM  :  NLS License Service Provider

 F3=Sort options   F4=Free module memory   Enter=List resources   F8=More
```

Figure 14-10

```
NetWare 5 Console Monitor  5.19              NetWare Loadable Module
Server name: 'PLANT' in Directory tree 'TPUP'
Server version: NetWare 5.00 - August 27, 1998

               General Information
  Utilization:                              3%       ▲
  Server up time:                      3:07:54:27    █
  Online processors:                         1       █
  Original cache buffers:               11,184
  Total cache buffers:                   4,323
  Dirty cache buffers:                       0       ▼

                Select An Entry
  SYS                          <Vol>

 Tab=Next window   Enter=Select option   Alt+F10=Exit          F1=Help
```

Figure 14-11

```
              Cache Utilization Statistics
  Short term cache hits:                   100%
  Short term cache dirty hits:             100%
  Long term cache hits:                     99%
  Long term cache dirty hits:               99%
  LRU sitting time:                    1:41:13.9
  Allocate block count:                   30,788
  Allocated from AVAIL:                   25,235
  Allocated from LRU:                      5,553
  Allocate wait:                               0
  Allocate still waiting:                      0
  Too many dirty blocks:                       0
  Cache ReCheckBlock count:                    0

     | LAN/WAN drivers
     | Loaded modules
     | File open/lock activity
   ▼ | Disk cache utilization
```

Figure 14-12

```
NetWare 5 Console Monitor  5.19              NetWare Loadable Module
Server name: 'PLANT' in Directory tree 'TPUP'
Server version: NetWare 5.00 - August 27, 1998

               Server Memory Statistics
  Allocated memory pool, in bytes:      11,968,512    26%
  Cache buffer memory, in bytes:        17,686,528    39%
  Cache movable memory, in bytes:                0     0%
  Cache non-movable memory, in bytes:       20,480     0%
  Code and data memory, in bytes:       16,150,528    35%
  Total server work memory, in bytes:   45,826,048   100%

               Tracked Resource Types
  AES Process Call-Backs
  AIO Named Port Resource
  Alloc Memory (Bytes)
  Alternate Debugger Handlers
  Alternate Key Handler
  Asynchronous I/O service
▼ Audit Services

 Tab=Next window   Ins=Refresh list   Esc=Previous list        F1=Help
```

Figure 14-13

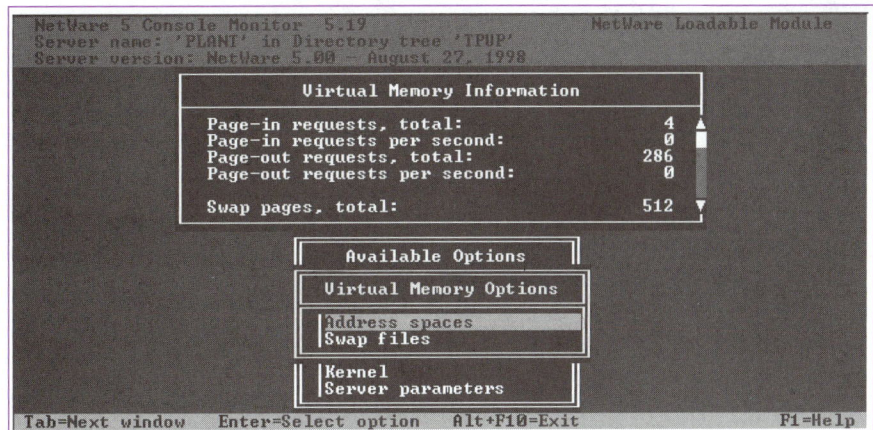

Figure 14-14

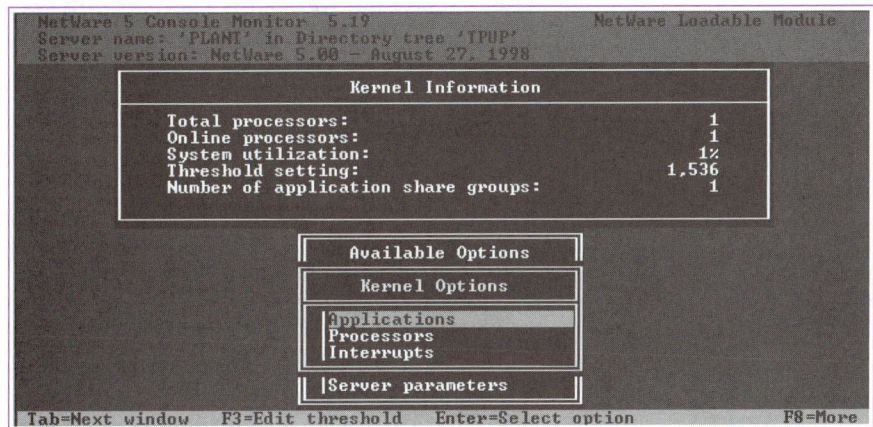

Figure 14-15

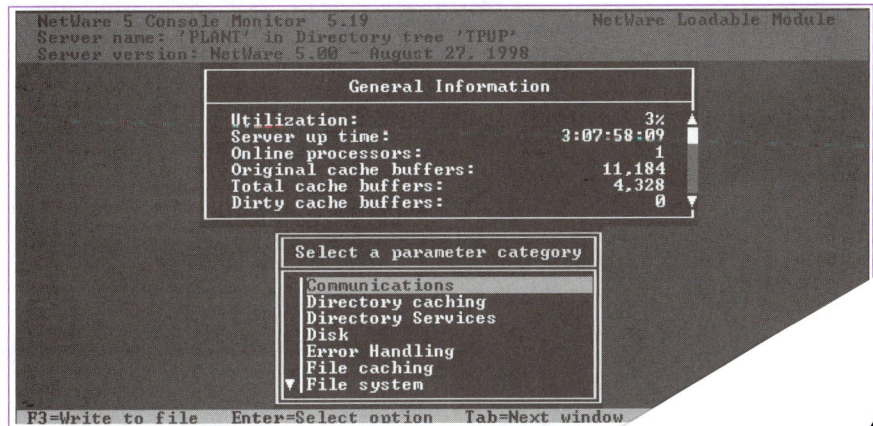

DSREPAIR

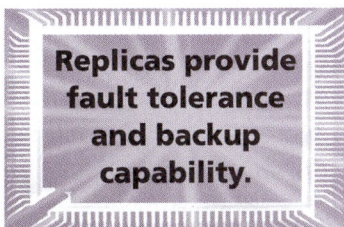

Replicas provide fault tolerance and backup capability.

Hopefully, you will not need to r...
repair it, however, you should hav...
go to initiate the repairs. Runnir...
Also, running this NLM occasi...
work problems.

In larger networks with multip...
the Directory, called "replicas," on...
around the network. Replicas provia...

> ... NDS can be-
> come disjointed
> at times.
>
> That is when
> DSREPAIR comes
> in handy.

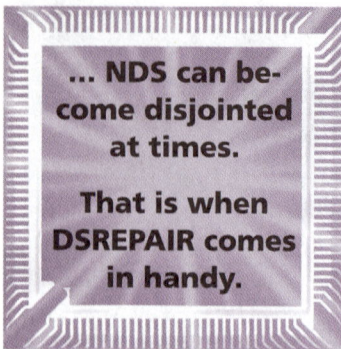

capability. The servers communicate with each other, sharing up-dates to the Directory as needed. Whether they are passed on to the next recipient is determined by the time stamp place on the update. If the recipient has data with a newer time stamp, the update is unnecessary and therefore ignored. The time stamp system depends entirely on all servers knowing what time it is. This is accomplished through a centralized time allocation system, with one main server responsible for providing accurate time.

The fact that NDS is located in several locations and that the timing of updates is critical would lead you to wonder whether NDS can be-come disjointed at times. It does. That is when **DSREPAIR** comes in handy.

DSREPAIR.NLM runs on the main server console, and brings the network back into order. From your console you can fix many of your most serious NDS problems. Typing `load dsrepair` at the console prompt and pressing `<ENTER>` will bring open a window containing information similar to that found in Figure 14-16.

Figure 14-16

```
┌─────────────────────────────────┐
│       Available Options          │
├─────────────────────────────────┤
│ Unattended full repair           │
│ Time synchronization             │
│ Report synchronization status    │
│ View repair log file             │
│ Advanced options menu            │
│ Exit                             │
└─────────────────────────────────┘
```

Highlighting each of the above options provides the following information at the bottom of the screen.

Unattended Full Repair—Automated repair that performs all possible repair operations that do not require operator assistance. Records all actions in the log file.

Time Synchronization—Collects *time synchronization* information and server status from all servers known to the local database.

Report Synchronization Status—Retrieves synchronization status of all partitions from every server that contains a replica of the partition.

View Repair Log File—Views and edits the log file that is optionally created when repair operations are performed.

Advanced Options Menu—Allows manual control of all repair operations as well as diagnostic information and global repair functions.

Highlighting and pressing **Unattended Full Repair** immediately initiates the requested repair action. Depending on the size of your network, this could take some time to complete. The Directory is locked during the repair procedure. On a small network, the process should take only a few seconds to complete. Most likely, any repairs will involve incorrect time stamps. This process should be activated during the networks' idle times so that users are not disrupted.

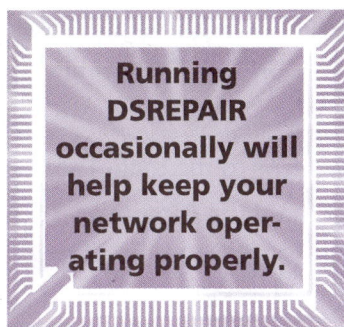

When the repair action is completed, a window appears informing you that *All automatic repair operations have been completed.* It also tells you the number of errors and the total amount of repair time that the operation required. It is not uncommon for this action to uncover numerous insignificant errors. Running **DSREPAIR** occasionally will help keep your network operating properly. You may need to run it several times when removing errors. Rerun the process until zero errors are found by **DSREPAIR**.

Highlighting the **Advanced Options Menu** and pressing **<ENTER>** provides the additional **DSREPAIR** options shown in Figure 14-17.

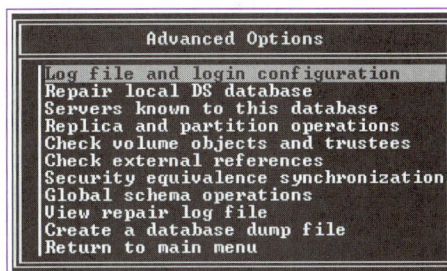

Running DSREPAIR occasionally will help keep your network operating properly.

Figure 14-17

```
                 Advanced Options
  Log file and login configuration
  Repair local DS database
  Servers known to this database
  Replica and partition operations
  Check volume objects and trustees
  Check external references
  Security equivalence synchronization
  Global schema operations
  View repair log file
  Create a database dump file
  Return to main menu
```

Highlighting each of the above options provides the following information at the bottom of the screen.

Log File And Login Configuration—Configures options for the DS repair log file. Also Login to the directory services tree which is required by some operations.

Repair Local DS Database—Repairs the Directory Services database files stored on this server.

Servers Known To This Database—Operations performed on servers that are known to this database: time synchronization, network addresses, server information.

Replica And Partition Operations—Provides functions to repair replicas, replica rings, and server objects. Also dynamically displays each server's last synchronization time.

Check Volume Objects And Trustees—Check all mounted volumes for valid volume objects and valid trustees on the volumes.

Check External References—Check for illegal external references.

Security Equivalence Synchronization—Allows user to synchronize security equivalence attributes throughout the global tree.

Global Schema Operations—Provides functions to update the schema in the tree.

View Repair Log File—Edit the log file which is optionally created when repair operations are performed.

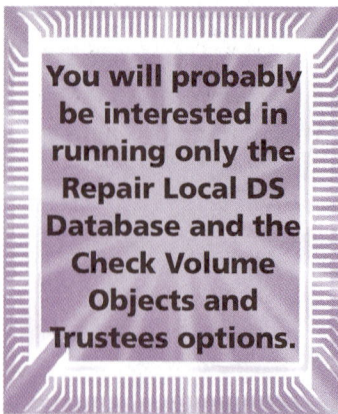

Create A Database Dump File—Copies the Directory Services database files to disk in compressed format to be used for off-line repairs and diagnostics. Not to be used as a backup method.

Return To Main Menu—Exits this menu and returns to the main list.

You will probably be interested in running only the **Repair Local DS Database** and the **Check Volume Objects and Trustees** options. The first will behave in the same way as the unattended option that you ran earlier, and the second will require that your fully distinguished administrator user name and password be used for authorization. It is useful to run both now and then, and they should not return significant errors unless there is a significant problem.

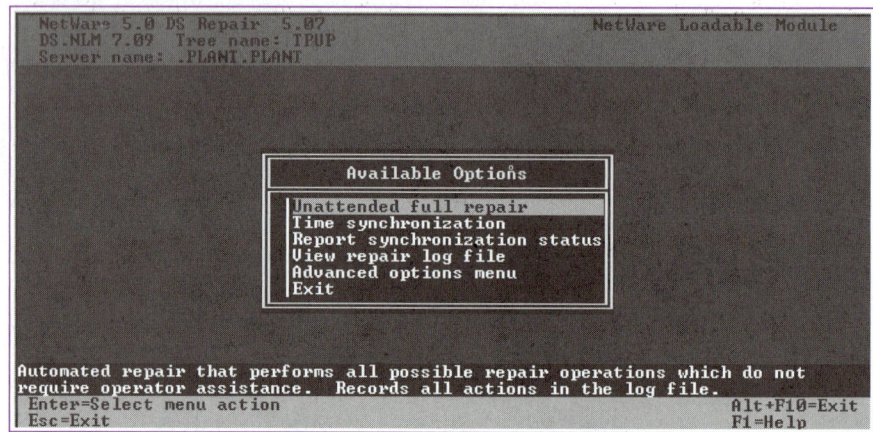

> You will probably be interested in running only the **Repair Local DS Database** and the **Check Volume Objects and Trustees options.**

Figure 14-18

VREPAIR

> If your school is located in an area that experiences power interruptions, and you do not have a UPS for each server and workstation, you should become familiar with *VREPAIR.NLM.*

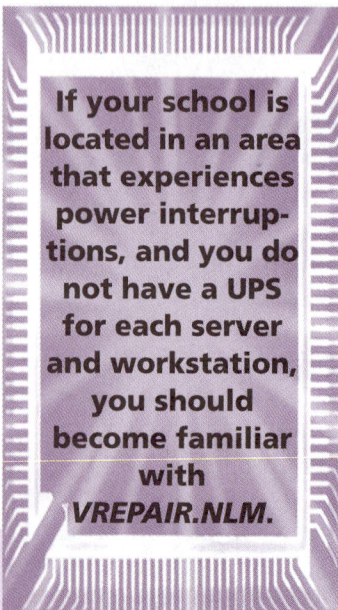

Another NLM repair option (one that you hopefully will not need) is *VREPAIR.NLM.* You will probably become acquainted with it if your server shuts down unexpectedly and will not restart. This frequently happens in school environments, because schools do not have sufficient budgets to provide an *Uninterruptible Power Supply (UPS)* for each server and workstation to prevent them from shutting down when there is an interruption in the regular power supply. If your school is located in an area that experiences power interruptions, and you do not have a UPS for each server and workstation, you should become familiar with *VREPAIR.NLM.*

VREPAIR is usually used when your system crashes. The crash may be caused by the power problem alluded to above, but may also be caused by hardware problems, software inconsistencies, or a corrupted File Allocation Table on your *SYS:VOLUME.* **VREPAIR** can be used only on volumes that are not currently mounted on the server.

Figure 14-19

```
NetWare 5.0 DS Repair 5.07                    NetWare Loadable Module
DS.NLM 7.02  Tree name: TPUP
Server name: .PLANT.PLANT

                    ┌──────────────────────────────────────┐
                    │           Advanced Options             │
                    │ Log file and login configuration       │
                    │ Repair local DS database               │
                    │ Servers known to this database         │
                    │ Replica and partition operations       │
                    │ Check volume objects and trustees      │
                    │ Check external references              │
                    │ Security equivalence synchronization   │
                    │ Global schema operations               │
                    │ View repair log file                   │
                    │ Create a database dump file            │
                    │ Return to main menu                    │
                    └──────────────────────────────────────┘

Configure options for the DS Repair log file.  Also login to the directory
services tree which is required by some operations.
Enter=Select menu action                              Alt+F10=Exit
Esc=Return to main menu                                F1=Help
```

> **If the volume on which you want to run VREPAIR is currently mounted, you must DISMOUNT it, then run the NLM.**

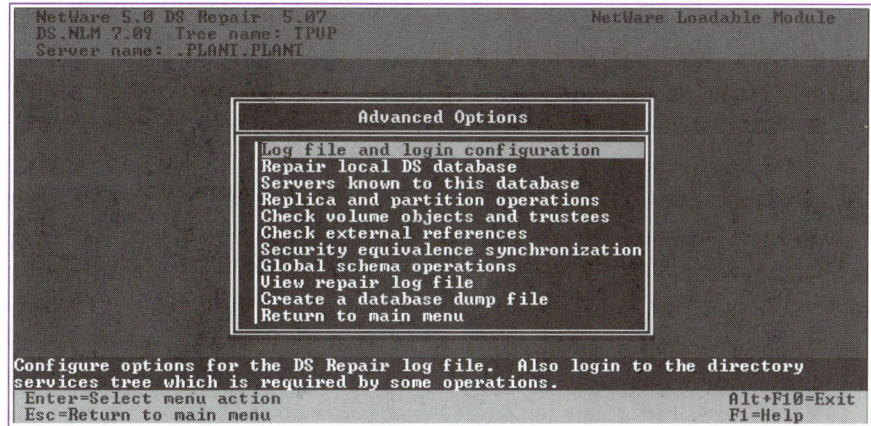

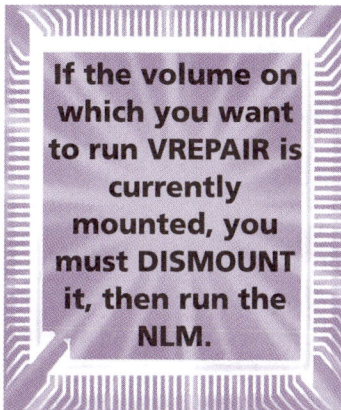

Because the *VREPAIR.NLM* is located in the *SYS:SYSTEM* directory, and this directory is located on the directory that most frequently experiences problems, you should keep a spare copy of *VREPAIR.NLM* on both a floppy disk and on the DOS partition of your server. When you are unable to mount your *SYS:*VOLUME which contains the *SYS:SYSTEM* directory, you will still be able to correct the problem by running your backup copy of *VREPAIR.NLM* from either location.

If the volume on which you want to run **VREPAIR** is currently mounted, you must **DISMOUNT** it, then run the NLM. If the volume cannot be mounted, **VREPAIR** is loaded automatically. Use dismount all 15 to dismount all volumes attached to the server. Running **VREPAIR** at the server console will then give you the options shown in Figure 14-20.

Figure 14-20

```
 NetWare Volume Repair Utility  4.32           NetWare Loadable Module

Options:

        1. Repair a volume
        2. Set VRepair options
        3. Exit

        Enter your choice: _
```

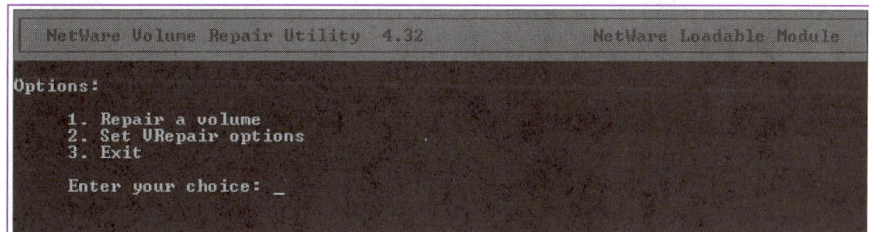

Selecting #1 from this main **VREPAIR Options** menu, when only one volume is dismounted, will automatically run the NLM. However, if you have not dismounted any volumes, and none of the volumes are failing to mount due to problems, you will receive the notice shown in Figure 14-21.

Figure 14-21

```
There are no unmounted volumes.

You need to dismount the volume you want to repair before it can be repaired.
<Press any key to continue>_
```

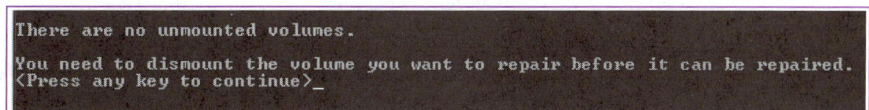

Once your volume is dismounted, the **VREPAIR** NLM is initiated, and item #1 is selected, you will again be given the option of checking your options.

This time you verify your error settings using the information shown in Figure 14-22:

Figure 14-22

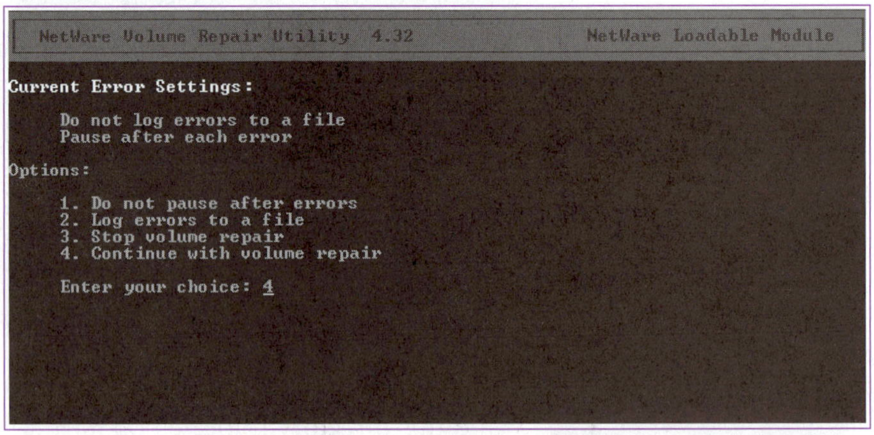

```
NetWare Volume Repair Utility  4.32          NetWare Loadable Module

Current Error Settings:

    Do not log errors to a file
    Pause after each error

Options:

    1. Do not pause after errors
    2. Log errors to a file
    3. Stop volume repair
    4. Continue with volume repair

    Enter your choice: 4
```

Item #4 is the default. When selected, it initiates your **VREPAIR** action using the selected error settings that you just verified above. It will halt whenever it encounters an error. If you want the NLM to continue the repair action without pausing, you must select #1 above, and then select #4. You should continue running **VREPAIR** until you do not encounter any errors. At the end of the repair cycle, you will receive the console prompt, where you will need to MOUNT the volume in order to verify the success of the repair action.

Selecting #2 from the main **VREPAIR Options** menu lists the **VREPAIR** setup options shown in Figure 14-23.

Figure 14-23

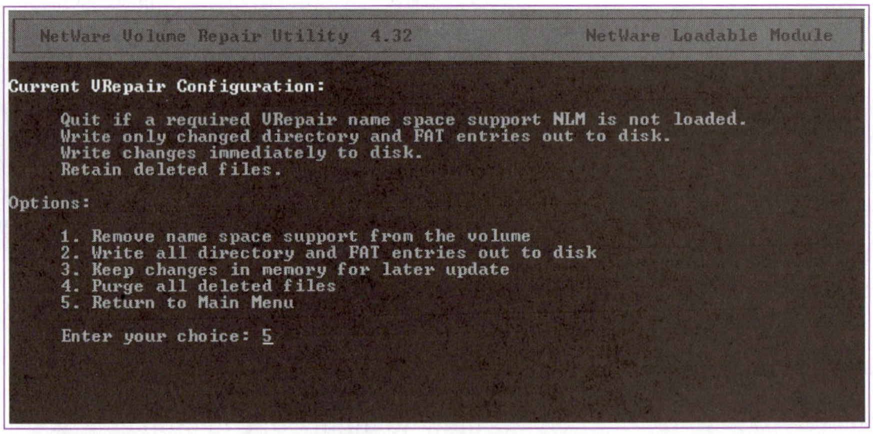

```
NetWare Volume Repair Utility  4.32          NetWare Loadable Module

Current VRepair Configuration:

    Quit if a required VRepair name space support NLM is not loaded.
    Write only changed directory and FAT entries out to disk.
    Write changes immediately to disk.
    Retain deleted files.

Options:

    1. Remove name space support from the volume
    2. Write all directory and FAT entries out to disk
    3. Keep changes in memory for later update
    4. Purge all deleted files
    5. Return to Main Menu

    Enter your choice: 5
```

NWCONFIG

If you maintain a healthy network and do not need to use **DSREPAIR** or **VREPAIR** very often, you should become familiar with another frequently used NLM—the **NWCONFIG** (*INSTALL.NLM* for NetWare 4.11 users). This is the NLM that you will use to accomplish the configuration options listed in Figure 14-24.

Figure 14-24

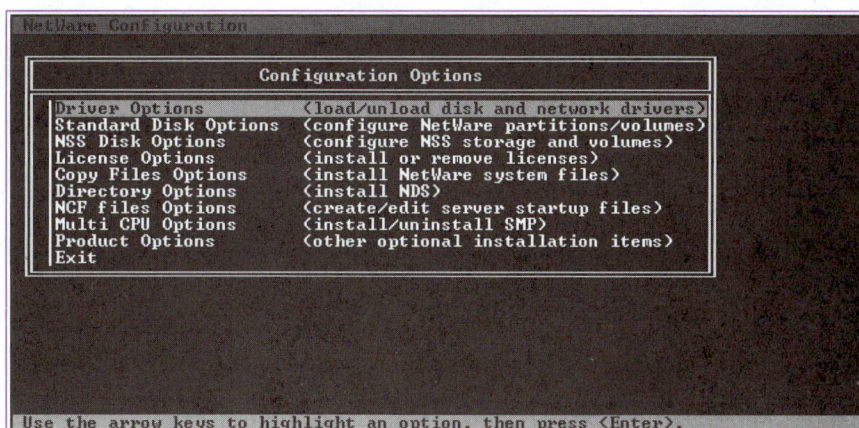

```
NetWare Configuration
        Configuration Options
 Driver Options         (load/unload disk and network drivers)
 Standard Disk Options  (configure NetWare partitions/volumes)
 NSS Disk Options       (configure NSS storage and volumes)
 License Options        (install or remove licenses)
 Copy Files Options     (install NetWare system files)
 Directory Options      (install NDS)
 NCF files Options      (create/edit server startup files)
 Multi CPU Options      (install/uninstall SMP)
 Product Options        (other optional installation items)
 Exit

 Use the arrow keys to highlight an option, then press <Enter>.
```

Most of the options are self-explanatory, although several display additional features within the selection criteria when you enter that configuration option. Licensing, for instance, not only allows you to install or remove licenses, but it also allows you to set up the licensing service new to NetWare 5.

Figure 14-25 shows what are considered Standard Disk Options.

Figure 14-25

```
        Available Disk Options
 Modify disk partitions and Hot Fix
 Mirror/Unmirror disk partitions
 Scan for additional devices (optional)
 Initialize hard disk
 NetWare Volume Options
 Return to the previous menu
```

Figure 14-26 shows some of the Directory Options available.

Figure 14-26

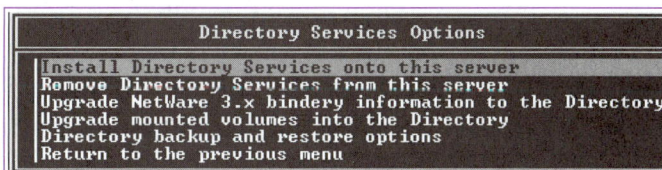

```
        Directory Services Options
 Install Directory Services onto this server
 Remove Directory Services from this server
 Upgrade NetWare 3.x bindery information to the Directory
 Upgrade mounted volumes into the Directory
 Directory backup and restore options
 Return to the previous menu
```

Embedded in each of these Configuration Options are several options that you may need from time to time. Use Figures 14-27 to 14-33 to remember where each option is located.

Figure 14-27

```
        Driver Options
 Configure disk and storage device drivers
 Configure network drivers
 Return to previous menu
```

Figure 14-28

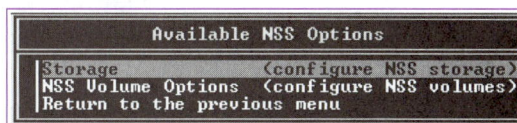

```
        Available NSS Options
 Storage              (configure NSS storage)
 NSS Volume Options   (configure NSS volumes)
 Return to the previous menu
```

Figure 14-29

```
        SMP Installation Options
 Select a Platform Support Module
 Return to previous menu
```

Figure 14-30

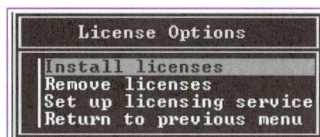

```
        License Options
 Install licenses
 Remove licenses
 Set up licensing service
 Return to previous menu
```

Figure 14-31

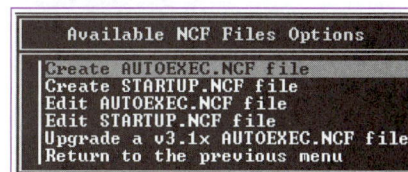

```
        Available NCF Files Options
 Create AUTOEXEC.NCF file
 Create STARTUP.NCF file
 Edit AUTOEXEC.NCF file
 Edit STARTUP.NCF file
 Upgrade a v3.1x AUTOEXEC.NCF file
 Return to the previous menu
```

Figure 14-32

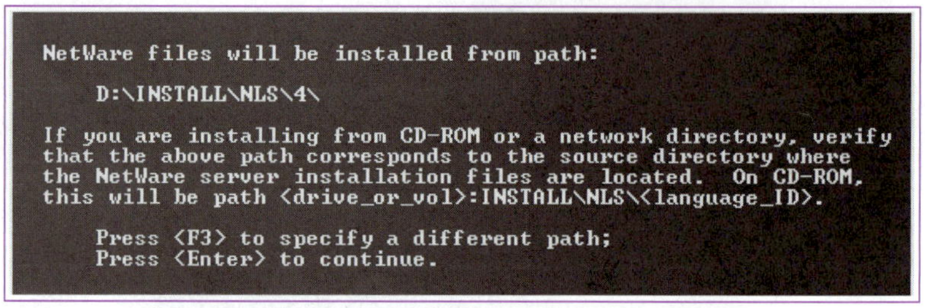

```
NetWare files will be installed from path:

     D:\INSTALL\NLS\4\

If you are installing from CD-ROM or a network directory, verify
that the above path corresponds to the source directory where
the NetWare server installation files are located.  On CD-ROM,
this will be path <drive_or_vol>:INSTALL\NLS\<language_ID>.

     Press <F3> to specify a different path;
     Press <Enter> to continue.
```

Figure 14-33

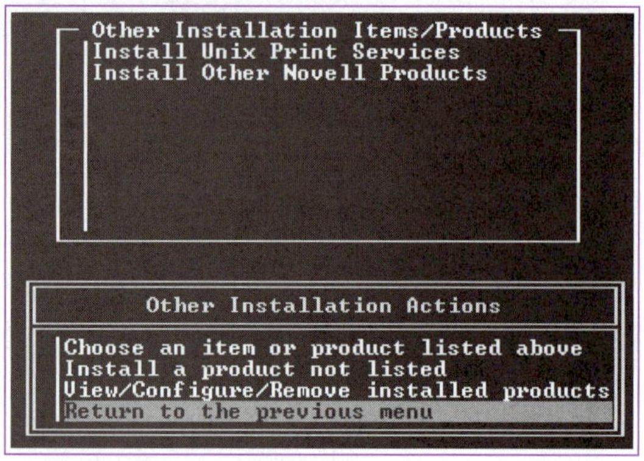

```
┌─ Other Installation Items/Products ─┐
│ Install Unix Print Services         │
│ Install Other Novell Products       │
│                                     │
│                                     │
│                                     │
│                                     │
│                                     │
└─────────────────────────────────────┘

┌─────── Other Installation Actions ───────┐
│ Choose an item or product listed above   │
│ Install a product not listed             │
│ View/Configure/Remove installed products │
│ Return to the previous menu              │
└───────────────────────────────────────────┘
```

REMOTE CONSOLE

Sometimes you simply cannot find the time to travel to the location where your server resides. In the typical classroom environment where you are probably taking this class, you are unlikely to encounter this problem, but in a business setting you could. In your class, you will go through the process of logging in from a remote console only to practice doing it, but in many businesses a remote console is a very useful option.

Novell set out to develop a Remote Console login so that administrators would not have to travel extensive distances to get to the server when only minor actions might be necessary. What they actually developed was a remote console utility that allows management of the network from a remote console. It actually rivals being at the server console itself.

Before using the Remote Console at a workstation somewhere on the network, the administrator must load *REMOTE.NLM* at the server console. Type **load remote** at the console. The server then prompts for a password. This password will then be used by anyone accessing the server from workstations. Then type **load rspx**, and press **<ENTER>**. Remote Console is ready for use.

Launch **Remote Console** through the **Tools** pulldown menu in **NWAdmin** , as shown in Figure 14-34.

Figure 14-34

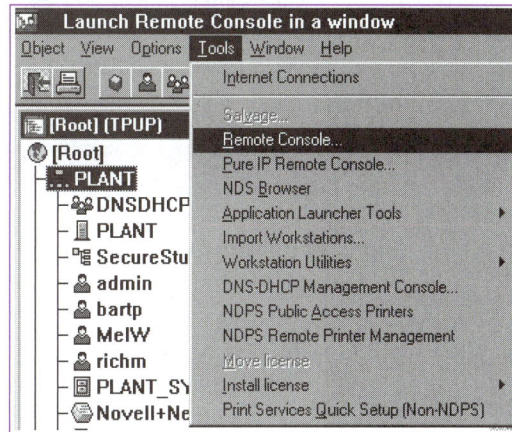

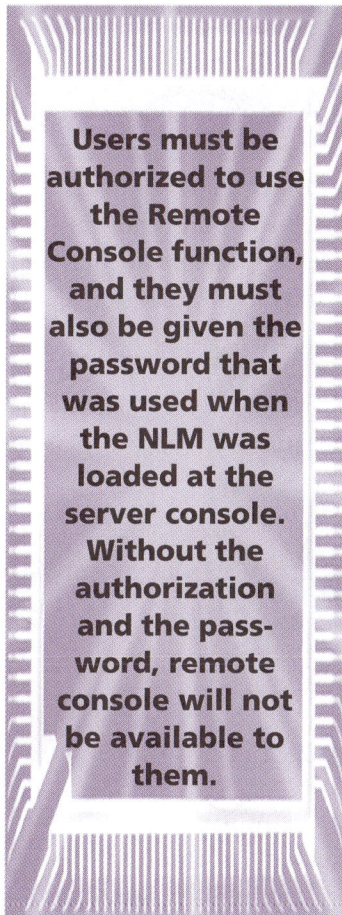

Users must be authorized to use the Remote Console function, and they must also be given the password that was used when the NLM was loaded at the server console. Without the authorization and the password, remote console will not be available to them.

Users must be authorized to use the **Remote Console** function, and they must also be given the password that was used when the NLM was loaded at the server console. Without the authorization and the password, remote console will not be available to them. There is another way to access the remote console, but this should be available only to the administrator. Remote access to the server console was created in order to make network management easier for the administrator. If the administrator wants access to the remote console function, and the *REMOTE.NLM* has been loaded, the administrator password will grant him access even if he does not know the actual **REMOTE** password.

Note in Figure 14-35 that Remote Console runs in the DOS mode. Press <ENTER> to continue. The choice shown in Figure 14-36 appears.

Figure 14-35

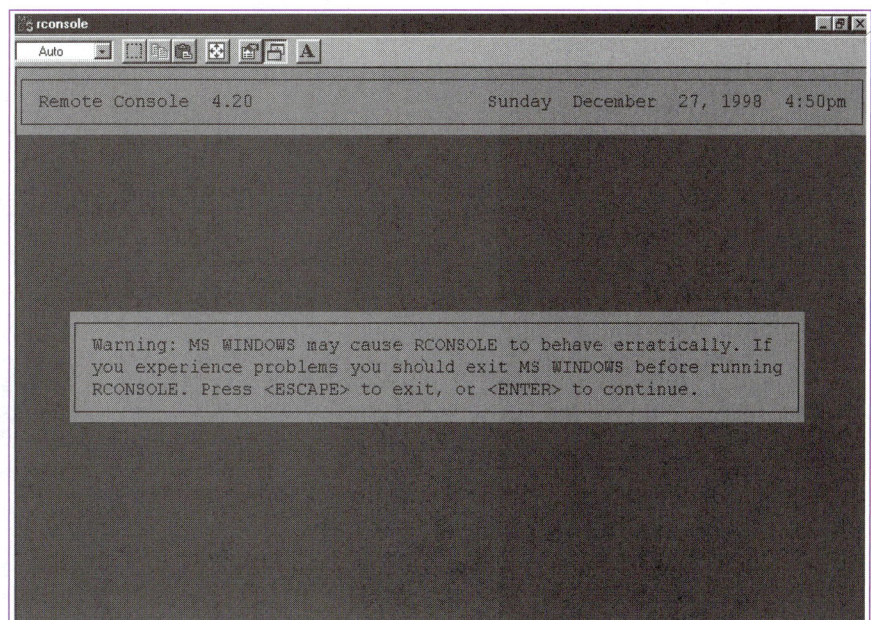

Figure 14-36

Unless you are connecting to your server through a modem connection (*asynchronous*), leave the selection on the default **LAN**, which is highlighted. You should use **LAN** when you are connected directly to the network over which you will be communicating with your server. Press **<ENTER>** to select **LAN**, and initiate remote transmission.

Pure IP Remote Console

There is another way to initiate remote operations on Novell 5 networks. Pure IP Remote Console operations are initiated in the same way as the other Remote Console method. Use the **Tools** pulldown menu and select **Pure IP Remote Console**, as shown in Figure 14-37.

Figure 14-37

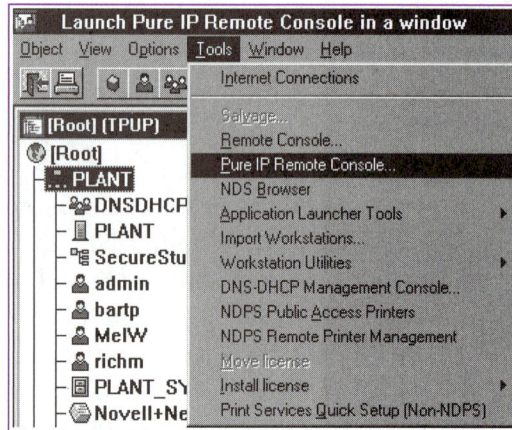

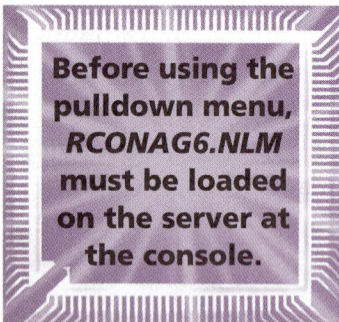

Before using the pulldown menu, *RCONAG6.NLM* must be loaded on the server at the console.

Before using the pulldown menu, *RCONAG6.NLM* must be loaded on the server at the console. In addition to the password required by the other remote method, the administrator must furnish the server's address and the remote server port number. Once the NLM is loaded and the pulldown menu is activated, you will be presented with the window shown in Figure 14-38.

Figure 14-38

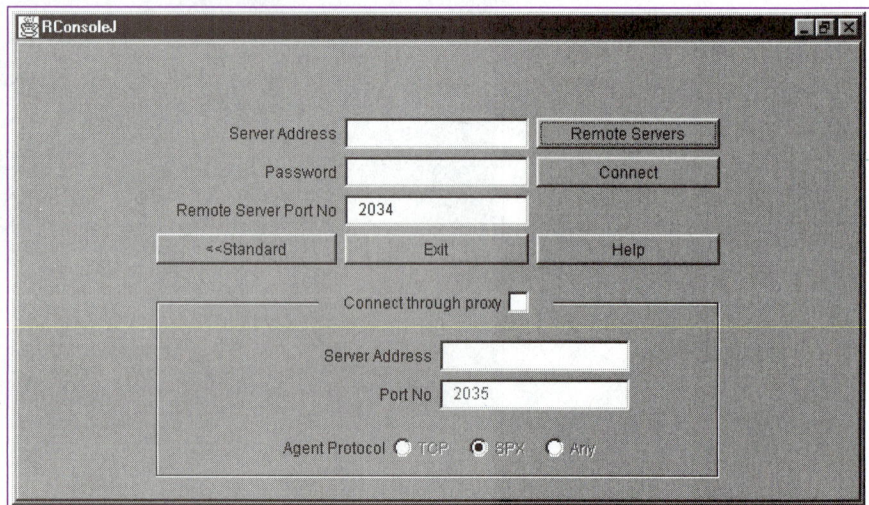

Figure 14-39

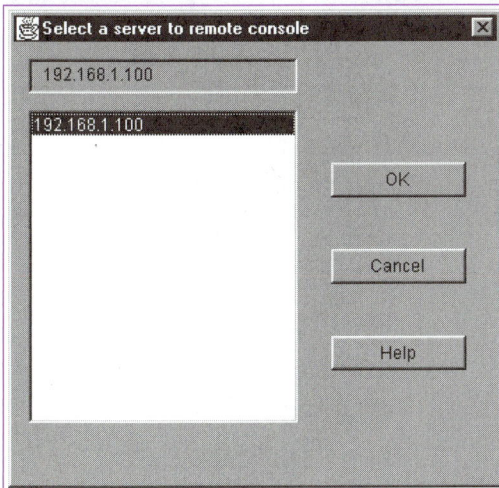

When you click on the **Remote Servers** button, the window shown in Figure 14-39 appears, listing the IP addresses of the remote servers available. Highlight the one with which you wish to establish remote operations, and the address will appear in the window at the top. Click **OK**.

The IP address that you selected appears in the window in Figure 14-40 as the "Server Address." Enter either the password entered when the NLM was loaded or your administrator password, then click on **Connect** to establish your remote session.

Figure 14-40

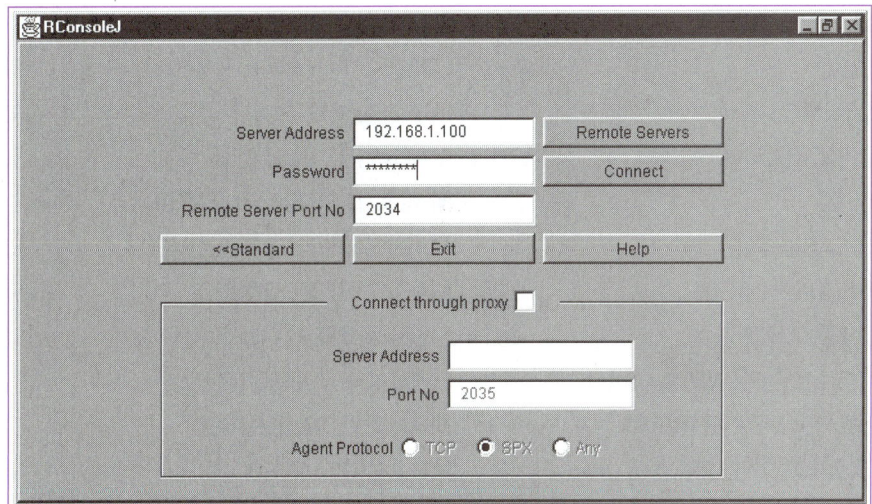

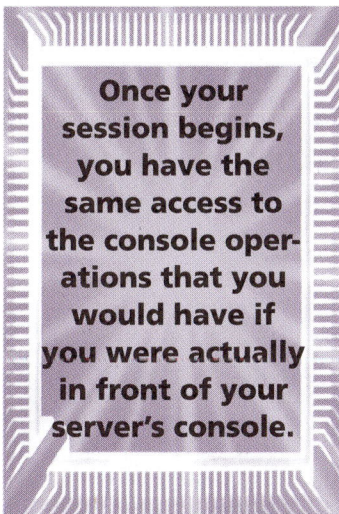

Once your session begins, you have the same access to the console operations that you would have if you were actually in front of your server's console.

Once your session begins, you have the same access to the console operations that you would have if you were actually in front of your server's console.

Figure 14-41

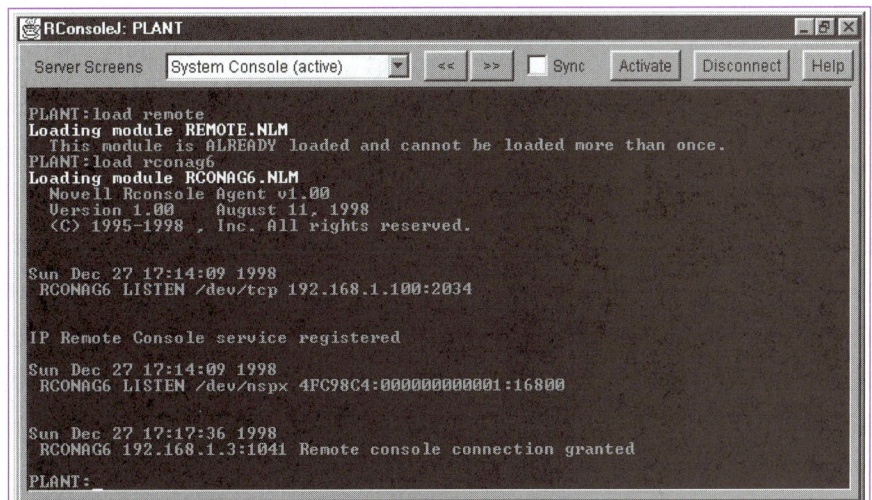

Console Command List for NetWare 5

#	JAVA-RMI.CGI	PROTOCOL REGISTER
;	JAVAC	PSM
ABORT REMIRROR	JAVADOC	PING
ADD NAME SPACE	JAVAH	REGISTER MEMORY
ALERT	JAVAKEY	REM
ALIAS	JAVAP	REMIRROR PARTITION
APPLET	JRE	REMOTE
APPLETVIEWER	LANGUAGE	REMOVE STORAGE ADAPTER
BIND	LIST STORAGE ADAPTERS	RESET ROUTER
BINDERY	LIST STORAGE DEVICE	RESET ENVIRONMENT
BROADCAST	BINDINGS	RESET SERVER
CLEAR STATION	LIST DEVICES	RESTART SERVER
CLS	LOAD	RMIC
CONFIG	LOADSTAGE	RMI REGISTRY
CPUCHECK	MAGAZINE INSERTED	SCAN ALL
CSET	MAGAZINE NOT INSERTED	SCAN FOR NEW DEVICES
DISABLE TTS	MAGAZINE NOT REMOVED	SEARCH
DISABLE LOGIN	MAGAZINE REMOVED	SECURE CONSOLE
DISMOUNT	MEDIA INSERTED	SEND
DISPLAY IPX NETWORKS	MEDIA NOT INSERTED	SERIALVER
DISPLAY IPX SERVERS	MEDIA NOT REMOVED	SET
DISPLAY INTERRUPTS	MEDIA REMOVED	SET TIME
DISPLAY PROCESSORS	MEMORY	SET TIME ZONE
DISPLAY ENVIRONMENT	MEMORY MAP	SPEED
DISPLAY MODIFIED	MIRROR STATUS	SPOOL
ENVIRONMENT	MODULES	START PROCESSORS
DOWN	MONITOR	STOP PROCESSORS
DSMERGE	MOUNT	SWAP
DSREPAIR	NAME	TIME
ECHO OFF	NATIVE2ASCII	TRACK OFF
ECHO ON	NCP ADDRESSES	TRACK ON
ENABLE LOGIN	NCP TRACE	TTS
ENABLE TTS	NCP DUMP	UNBIND
ENUSET	NCP STATS	UNLOAD
FILE SERVER NAME	OFF	VERSION
HELP	PAUSE	VMDISMOUNT
IPX INTERNAL NET	PROTECT	VMMOUNT
JAR	PROTECTION	VMVOLUMES
JAVA	PROTOCOL	VOLUME

Console Command List for NetWare 4.11

ABORT REMIRROR	ENABLE TTS	NAME
ACTIVATE SERVER	EXIT	NCOPY
ADD NAME SPACE	FILER	NCUPDATE
ADDICON	FILTCFG	NDIR
AFP	FLAG	NDS Manager
AFPCON	FPSM	NETADMIN
ALIAS	HALT	NETSYNC3
ATCON	HCSS	NETSYNC4
ATCONFIG	HELP	NETUSER
ATOTAL	HFSCD	NetWare Administrator
ATPS	HFSCDCON	NetWare Application Launcher
ATPSCON	INETCFG	NetWare Application Manager
ATXRP	INITIALIZE SYSTEM	NetWare Directory Browser
AUDITCON	INSTALL	NetWare File Migration
BIND	IPXCON	NetWare Login
BRGCON	IPXPING	NetWare Print Chooser
BROADCAST	IPXS	NetWare Tools (OS/2)
CAPTURE	KEYB	NetWare TSA (OS/2)
CD	LANGUAGE	NetWare User Tools
CDROM	LIST DEVICES	NetWare Volume Mounter
CLEAR STATION	LOAD	NIT
CLIB	LOGIN	NLIST
CLS	LOGOUT	NLMLIB
COLORPAL	MACFILE	NLS Manager
CONFIG	MAGAZINE	NMENU
CONLOG	MAP	NPAMS
CX	MATHLIB	NPATH
DHCPCFG	MATHLIBC	NPRINT
DISABLE LOGIN	MEDIA	NPRINTER.EXE
DISMOUNT	MEMORY	NPRINTER.NLM
DISPLAY NETWORKS	MEMORY MAP	NPRINTER (OS/2)
DISPLAY SERVERS	MIGPRINT	NPRINTER (Windows 95)
DOSGEN	MIGRATE	NVER
DOWN	MIRROR STATUS	NWIPCFG
DSMERGE	MODULES	NWSTART
DS Migrate	MONITOR	NWSTOP
DSREPAIR	MOUNT	NWXTRACT
EDIT	MPDRIVER	OFF
ENABLE LOGIN	MSERVER	PARTMGR

Console Command List for NetWare 4.11 *(continued)*

PCONSOLE	RIGHTS	TCPCON
PING	ROUTE	TECHWALK
PMMON	RPL	THREADS
PRINTCON	RS232	TIME
PRINTDEF	RSPX	TIMESYNC
PROTOCOL	SBACKUP	TLI
PSC	SCAN FOR NEW DEVICES	TPING
PSERVER	SCHDELAY	TRACK OFF
PUPGRADE	SEARCH	TRACK ON
PURGE	SECURE CONSOLE	UIMPORT
RCONSOLE	SEND	UNBIND
REGISTER MEMORY	SERVER	UNICON
REINITIALIZE SYSTEM	SERVMAN	UNLOAD
REMAPID	SET	UPS
REMIRROR PARTITION	SET TIME	UPS_AIO
REMOTE	SET TIME ZONE	UPS STATUS
Remote Console (Mac OS-Based Workstations)	SETPASS	UPS TIME
	SETTTS	VERSION
REMOVE DOS	SETUPDOC	VIEW
RENDIR	SPEED	VOLUME
REQUESTR	SPXCONFG	VREPAIR
RESET ROUTER	SPXS	WHOAMI
RESTART	STREAMS	WSUPDATE
RESTART SERVER	SYSTIME	WSUPGRD

Chapter Summary

Building and understanding your network are important, but managing your network will be your principal job. Preparation for Novell certifications, such as the CNA certification preparation, is the aim of this text. It will help educate you and ensure your success as a network administrator. Your studies in this course will help you regardless of the size of your network, should you decide to work in this field. The more you are required to manage a network, the more you will want to become acquainted with networking skills, because they make your job easier.

CHAPTER 14
Managing

The most frequently repaired components of your network will probably be the workstations. You may not have to repair them, but your network will be blamed for their inability to function unless you can troubleshoot the problem and get the right person to correct the problem quickly. Then you can return to your primary task of administering the networked parts.

As a beginning network administrator, you may not be responsible for console operations, or for overall management of the entire network. Knowing the basics of network administration, however, will make your job easier and more enjoyable. Your duties as an administrator will probably require you to work mostly with NDS, but from the user's point of view, your most important function is that of maintaining the file structures of the NFS. You will also secure the network by creating users, granting access to resources, and assigning rights so that users can work with the networked resources. Your organization's livelihood may even depend on how well you perform your job and succeed in preventing unauthorized users from accessing the network.

A server is simply a computer offering its services and resources to clients and workstations over a network, but it is a computer with more power and more capabilities. It usually has a faster processor and much more RAM than the other computers on the network. The server usually has much more storage space as well, and must be connected to the network through a network interface card and associated cabling. The server also creates the network addresses for the other computers on the network during installation. A unique internal network number identifies your server, and an external network number differentiates it from other servers on the same network.

Server management involves communicating between the administrator and the server. It usually occurs at the server console, and involves use of Commands and NetWare Loadable Modules. Commands are part of the operating system, and are loaded with the software. NLMs, on the other hand, are external to the operating system, and must be loaded into the server's memory by an operator before they can be used. NLMs add functionality to the operating system's core capabilities, and are executed when they are loaded.

Most of your work with NLMs will involve working with *MONITOR.NLM* and *NWCONFIG.NLM* at the server's console. Much can be learned about the network's health by using these two NLMs. Should your network experience problems, two other NLMs will probably be used. *DSREPAIR.NLM* is used to repair NDS problems, and *VREPAIR.NLM* is used for NFS repairs. In addition, depending on the physical distance your network covers, you may use *REMOTE.NLM* or *RCONAG6.NLM* in order to manage your network from a remote workstation as if you were actually at the server console.

Networking Terms Used in Chapter 14

commands	SEND	LONG.NAM
NetWare Loadable	DISPLAY NETWORKS	MAC.NAM
Modules (NLMs)	DISPLAY SERVERS	3C509.LAN
network address	MEMORY	total cache buffers
internal network number	SET TIME	utilization
external network number	.DSK	dirty cache buffers
add name space long to sys	.LAN	degrading
LONG.NAM	.NAM	time synchronization
EXIT	.NLM	Uninterruptible Power Supply
LOAD	MONITOR.NLM	(UPS)
UNLOAD	INSTALL.NLM	DISMOUNT
DOWN	NWCONFIG.NLM	MOUNT
SECURE CONSOLE	CDROM.NLM	Remote Console
MODULES	DSREPAIR.NLM	asynchronous
CONFIG	VREPAIR.NLM	Pure IP Remote Console
NAME	REMOTE.NLM	RCONAG6.NLM

■ Chapter Review Questions

1. How can this course help prepare you to become a better network administrator?

2. How will increasing your network knowledge make your job easier?

3. Why are network administrators blamed when network workstations malfunction?

4. What will help you to stay focused on your primary task of administering networked resources?

5. Where do you access the server?

6. What do the most frequently performed administrator tasks involve?

7. What is probably the most important administrator duty?

8. Define *internal network number*.

9. Define *external network number*.

10. What must every segment of a network have?

11. What are NetWare console commands used for?

12. What are NLMs?

13. What is the main difference between console commands and NLMs?

14. What is the purpose of adding name space to the server?

15. What is the NLM type *.DSK* used for?

16. What are the three most common NLMs?

17. Which NLM will you probably use most often?

18. How should total cache buffers relate to the original cache buffers?

19. What does the existence of a large number of dirty cache buffers indicate?

20. What NLM is used to repair NDS?

21. What NLM is used to repair volumes?

22. What do you have to do before repairing volumes?

23. What NLM would you use to check your licensing?

24. Which NLM operates its executable in a DOS mode on the workstation?

25. Which NLM must be loaded for a Pure IP Remote Console operation?

■ Associated Chapter Problems

1. Describe the benefits of preparing for Novell certifications.

2. Why are administrators held accountable for all activities on the networked computers, even though they may not be responsible?

3. Why are workstation troubleshooting skills important for a network administrator?

4. What are the server components, and how do they relate to those of a workstation?

5. Explain the uses for five of the most frequently used commands.

6. Explain the difference between commands and NLMs.

7. Explain the uses for *MONITOR.NLM*.

8. Why might you use **DSREPAIR** before you have experienced any problems with your network.

9. Explain **VREPAIR**.

10. Describe the processes available for Remote Console Operations.

OBJECTIVES

Networking has become almost a necessity for businesses, and the demand for networking skills is growing at a phenomenal pace worldwide. Therefore, becoming a certified networking specialist can yield significant benefits and career opportunities. It requires a substantial investment of time, money, and effort, but it is well worth it. By the end of this chapter, you will be able to:

- discuss the need for certification tracks.

- explain the origins of the Certified Novell Administrator (CNA) program.

- list the duties and benefits of a CNA.

- explain the benefits of becoming a CNA.

- describe the process of becoming a CNA.

- know the alternative sources for Novell certification courses.

- list the alternative certification tracks available.

- describe Novell's certification levels.

- describe the certification testing process.

- understand the certification objectives tested by Novell.

Certification Origins

The benefits of networks make them almost mandatory for the typical business.

By completing this course, you have started on the road to official recognition as a *qualified* network administrator. The benefits of networks make them almost mandatory for the typical business. Therefore, the demand for networking skills is high, and is continuing to grow at a phenomenal pace worldwide. Employers need trained network administrators capable of maintaining their networks.

Because it is important to standardize what "qualified" means, the major network software providers have developed *certification* programs. Graduates of these programs (certificate holders) can be expected to be highly qualified and capable of performing the duties commensurate with their level of certification. Certification is the employer's assurance that they are hiring a trained professional to whom they can entrust their network.

Novell's certification program provides a means for aspiring network professionals to demonstrate a high level of proficiency with network administration even before being hired. Novell determined that there was a need for certification standardization, and developed its own industry-standard product training and certification. In 1986, Novell began the first professional Information Services/Information Technology (IS/IT) training program in the world. Novell has issued more than 200,000 certifications. The program includes over 1,500 training and testing locations, online training, and numerous computer-based and video-oriented training products. In addition, Novell has developed its own line of "How To" textbooks.

The Certified Novell Administrator (CNA) program was begun in 1992.

Novell began the program to establish performance standards for network administrators.

Companies are increasingly using a combination of operating systems to operate their networks. Novell has responded to this global trend by adding material to its certification program to ensure that its graduates have multi-vendor capability.

The *Certified Novell Administrator (CNA)* program was begun in 1992. The CNA designation originally stood for "Certified NetWare Administrator." Novell began the program to establish performance standards for network administrators. The CNA program has helped standardize industry expectations regarding the capabilities and duties of a network administrator. The rigors of CNA training and of its certification exam assure employers that certificate holders are capable of creating and administrating an efficient and secure network.

Just What is a CNA?

Certified Novell Administrators (CNAs) provide companies direct Network Administrator support for networked users, usually at the company's location. CNAs find themselves operating in a variety of professional work environments, ranging from large office buildings to small businesses, and from single departments to entire corporate

Businesses of all sizes hire CNAs for their on-site administrative support, and they expect them to furnish a level of support that meets or exceeds the industry standards developed by Novell.

Information Services (IS) or Information Technology (IT) divisions. CNAs are expected to handle the day-to-day administration of any installed Novell networking product for which they are certified. CNA certification is expected of anyone wishing to administer Novell products. CNA certification is recognized worldwide.

As a CNA you could find yourself

- setting up workstations, servers, and printers.

- managing parts of or the entire network environment.

- installing applications and sharing them as networked resources.

- customizing and automating login capability to the network.

- determining desktop configurations for all users.

- monitoring network performance.

Businesses of all sizes hire CNAs for their on-site administrative support, and they expect them to furnish a level of support that meets or exceeds the industry standards developed by Novell.

Why Should You Certify?

The training that you receive in preparation for your CNA rating helps you develop skills that naturally lead to superior on-the-job capabilities.

When a networking giant like Novell certifies that you have passed its rigorous exam, you are recognized worldwide as highly capable of supporting Novell Netware. Furthermore, your expertise with networks in general is also recognized by employers. Therefore, Novell certification can be of value to you when you are applying for administration positions on non-Novell networks as well.

The training that you receive in preparation for your CNA rating helps you develop skills that naturally lead to superior on-the-job capabilities. As a Certified Novell Administrator, you are simply more capable of administering Novell's network environments. Companies realize that the set of skills you bring with you as a result of your CNA certification will provide them with superior overall support. In addition, companies know that because of your network-wide influence, users will be more productive.

CNA certification can also help you decide early in your career planning whether or not to choose networking as a *career path*. This path is difficult, requiring significant investments of money and time to do it properly. Training to become a CNA and completing the required certification test can help you decide whether the career is right for you. If this is not the case, you will quickly find that out. If you are ready to meet the CNA challenge, however, Novell can provide the educational foundation for this career path.

The CNA certification is only the first recognized step along that career path. You can continue to amass knowledge and skills to help you prepare for advanced Novell Certifications. Along this career path, you can train to become a *Certified Novell Engineer (CNE)*,

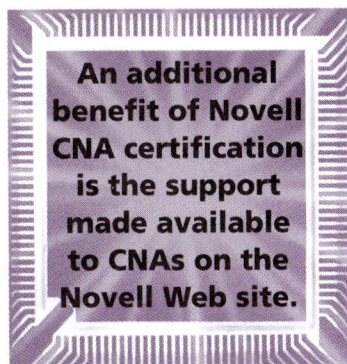

and continue on to become a *Master CNE (MCNE)*. You could also elect to become a *Certified Novell Instructor (CNI)* in order to train other aspiring network administrators. In addition, Novell has added such certifications as the *Certified Internet Professional (CIP)*, certification for World Wide Web support, and the *Certified Novell Salesperson (CNS)* certification to sell the extensive Novell product line. Once you pass your CNA exam, you have already passed one of the exams required to accede to any of Novell's CIP, CNE, Master CNE, or CNI certifications.

An additional benefit of Novell CNA certification is the support made available to CNAs on the Novell Web site. Novell has dedicated a section of their page to support CNAs. The CNE Net Web site, located at ***http://cnenet.novell.com***, includes a special section for CNAs that provides them access to Novell's latest product information. Once on the CNA section of the site, you can also check information such as your Personal certification information, as shown in Figure 15-1.

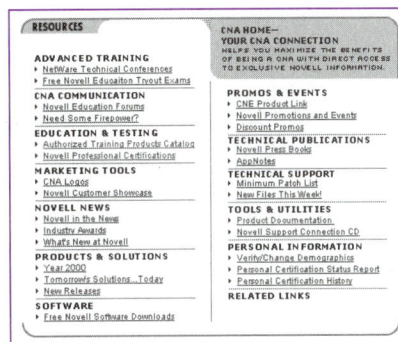

> An additional benefit of Novell CNA certification is the support made available to CNAs on the Novell Web site.

Figure 15-1

How Do I Become a Certified Novell Administrator?

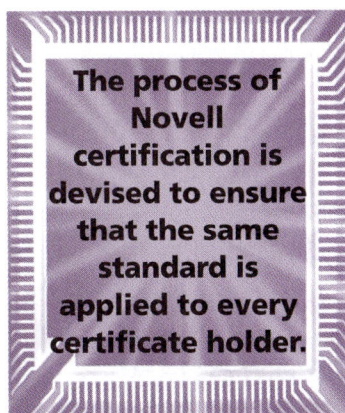

> The process of Novell certification is devised to ensure that the same standard is applied to every certificate holder.

You have already taken an important first step toward becoming certified under Novell's certification program. The fact that you have selected this course and have made it this far into the textbook demonstrates a large measure of determination on your part. Your networking potential will be determined by the extent to which you have applied yourself so far, coupled with how much you apply yourself in the future. The process of Novell certification is devised to ensure that the same standard is applied to every certificate holder.

Once you make the commitment to work diligently toward obtaining Novell's CNA certification, the process is relatively simple.

1. Complete adequate course preparation using whatever means you choose. There are several methods available for you to accomplish this step. They include:

   - Attending an independent, non-approved course that includes Novell network training (this course is a good example if it is being taught at a school that is not affiliated with Novell).

- Attending a training program at an educational facility affiliated with Novell Education. Usually the facility becomes a *Novell Education Academic Partner (NEAP)*. Secondary and post-secondary schools are eligible for this partnership agreement.

- Working with a *Novell Authorized Education Center (NAEC)* to plan your career path if you are affiliated with an employer. NAECs can help you plan your curriculum, choose a *track* that meets your career goals, and prepare you for the CNA certification test. For the nearest authorized center, visit the Authorized Training Locator at *http://education.novell.com*.

- Going to a bookstore, purchasing CNA preparation guides, studying the material, taking whatever practice tests you can find, and preparing yourself at your own pace.

- Getting a job working with Novell products and acquiring over a several year period the technical experience necessary to pass the certification exam.

2. Choose the Novell certification track for which you wish to become certified. These tracks include the following:

   - NetWare 5 CNA
   - IntraNetWare 4.11 CNA
   - NetWare 3 CNA (an earlier version of NetWare)
   - *GroupWise* 5.x CNA
   - GroupWise 4.x CNA

3. Sign and submit the agreement form.

   - Before you take your first test, read a copy of the *Certification Agreement* located on Novell's Web site at:

     http://education.novell.com

   - Text from the introductory notice on the latest version of the agreement at the time of this writing (version 1.3) follows.

Notice!

Before Novell will grant certification under any Novell certification program, you must agree and must show that you agree—to the terms and conditions of the following Novell Education Certification Agreement ("Certification Agreement"). You may show your agreement either electronically (in the manner described below) or by mailing to Novell a signed, printed copy of the Certification Agreement's Signature Form, which is available at your local Novell Authorized Education Center. In either case, PLEASE READ THE AGREEMENT CAREFULLY AFTER TAKING YOUR FIRST TEST.

ELECTRONIC AGREEMENT. You may agree to the Certification Agreement electronically at your testing center upon completion of your first test. After your first test is completed, a screen will appear asking you if you have read and agree to the terms and conditions of the Certification Agreement. Answering affirmatively to the questions on the screen will confirm your assent.

SIGNATURE FORM. Alternatively, if you sign the printed Signature Form to show your assent to the Certification Agreement, return it to the applicable Novell Education address listed on the form. We cannot accept faxed copies of the signed form.

Please note: If you are a minor under the laws of the state or country in which you reside, you must sign the Signature Form instead of agreeing electronically. The Signature Form needs to be countersigned by your parent, court-appointed curator, or legal guardian. The Certification Agreement will automatically terminate when you reach the age of majority unless you affirm the Certification Agreement by completing and signing the Novell Education Certification Agreement being used generally by Novell at that time and returning it to Novell. If you allow the Certification Agreement to lapse, your certification will be suspended and all related rights (including the right to use Novell trademarks) will terminate.

Copies of the Certification Agreement are available from your testing center and are available for downloading in each Novell certification program area on the World Wide Web. The Novell certification program areas can be accessed from the Novell Education Home Page at *http://education.novell.com*.

NOTE

Minors must sign and submit a hard copy of the Certification Agreement to Novell Education. The form must also be countersigned by a legal authority.

NOTE

Preparation through Instructor-led courses is the preferred method to prepare for any of Novell's certification exams.

- Print out, sign, and mail the Certification Agreement found on their web page at:

   http://education.novell.com/certinfo/certagrm.htm

- Commit to the agreement electronically at the end of your first certification test.

4. Register to take your exam at an approved testing facility, take the exam, and achieve a passing grade for the certification test of your chosen track.

Preparation through Instructor-led courses is the preferred method to prepare for any of Novell's certification exams. Intensive courses of a relatively short duration are available through Novell Academic Education Centers worldwide. Your local NAEC can help your company design a curriculum that meets its needs. Schools and universities that are Novell Education Academic Partners also offer Novell authorized training.

Class attendance at a Novell authorized training program is not required for CNA certification. The alternatives listed above (including your present school program and approved Novell Education courses) are provided to help you decide which method will better prepare you for your certification exam. The choice is whether you wish to study on your own or with an instructor. If you elect the instructor route, you can select the Novell-sanctioned NEAP or NAEC methods, or independent training programs such as the one your school is providing now. If you elect self-preparation, you can choose to use self-study workbooks, video programs, or one of the many computer-based training (CBT) options available.

Most self-study products are available through participating NEAPs, NAECs, and authorized Novell resellers. For more information on such courseware, contact::

CBT Systems at 1-800-929-9050 or 1-415-614-5900.

Gartner Group Learning Corporation at 1-800-532-7672 or 1-612-930-0330.

NETG at 1-800-265-1900 or 1-630-369-3000.

Which track should I choose?

There are now five CNA program tracks from which you can choose. You can specialize in one or more of the following five tracks.

1. NetWare 5   4. GroupWise 5
2. IntranetWare 4.11   5. GroupWise 4
3. NetWare 3

This text has assumed that you wish to certify in either NetWare 5 (primarily) or IntranetWare 4.11. However, if you would like to investigate other alternatives, you should go to Novell's web site for the latest information concerning the above five tracks. If possible, you should discuss your personal career goals with a networking professional at an approved Novell facility. If you are not currently working in the networking field, you should also take into account the needs of your company or of your potential employer.

What Are The Benefits Of Certification?

As An Individual

Applying for a position in a firm as a CNA distinguishes you from non-certified individuals.

Novell developed their certification program to demonstrate network administrator qualifications to potential employers. The benefits of hiring Novell's certified networking specialists are now universally recognized. Applying for a position in a firm as a CNA distinguishes you from non-certified individuals.

Once you are certified, Novell grants you access to the CNA portion of its CNENet Web site. Through this portion of the site, CNAs obtain up-to-date information that helps them keep abreast of the rapidly occurring changes in Novell's operating software. They can also keep track of their personal certification information, and update it as necessary. They can also track their progress toward advanced certifications. CNAs are authorized to use the Novell logo. (They can access electronic versions of the CNA logo on the Web site.) CNAs can also access up-to-date Novell product and technical information on Novell patches, fixes, and press releases, along with support publication updates.

The CNA program starts you on the path toward advanced certifications. Each Novell class and the exam leading toward that advanced certification builds upon what you have learned in the other Novell classes you have taken. Combined, they help prepare you for future career progress in the networking community.

From The Company's Perspective

Most companies are aware that employees with Novell certifications have studied and passed certification exams and have proven knowledge. They seek out Novell certified individuals because they expect they will deliver better job performance.

Companies also know that the increased productivity provided by employees with Novell certifications translates into financial benefits. Certified employees save the company money because they accomplish more work in less time, and perform their tasks well the first time they do them. Initial and follow-on training needs are low. System downtime is reduced, and overall support quality is enhanced. Customer support is improved because of better employee morale.

When companies decide to offer additional Novell training to their employees, they know that the benefits of the training will be worth the investment. Employees perform well at the training sessions because they are aware of the personal benefits that the certification will provide.

Novell's Basic Certification Lineup

In Novell's certifications lineup, each certification builds upon the one preceding it. For example, the knowledge that you acquired in pursuit of you CNA certification can be used in preparation for the next level of certification—the Certifed Novell Engineer (CNE). Similarly, the training involved in becoming a CNE is necessary for achieving your Master Certified Novell Engineer (MCNE). Alternatively, you could decide that you wish to become a Certified Novell Instructor (CNI).

Certified Novell Administrator (CNA)

CNAs provide a strong first line of defense against improperly operating networks. They handle the day-to-day administration tasks after the network has been designed and set up. Because of their high level of training, they usually increase system uptime and system productivity, as well as user satisfaction and user productivity.

Effective use of multiple CNAs on larger networks prevents network problems from becoming major system disasters. They also channel the usual difficulties encountered by typical users away from the upper level IT management decision makers. When problems are handled at lower levels in the organization by certified individuals, IT management is freer to deal with more important

> **The CNA program starts you on the path toward advanced certifications.**

> **Companies also know that the increased productivity provided by employees with Novell certifications translates into financial benefits.**

> **CNAs provide a strong first line of defense against improperly operating networks.**

matters. Routine tasks, such as adding users to the network, require a high degree of training, but they do not require training beyond the CNA level.

Certified Novell Engineer (CNE)

> **The Certified Novell Engineer (CNE) provides the next line of defense against improperly operating networks.**

The Certified Novell Engineer (CNE) provides the next line of defense against improperly operating networks. Obtaining your CNA certification is only the first step in the multi-step training process that leads to CNE certification. While CNAs handle the day-to-day operations of the network, CNEs concern themselves with the higher level problems that affect widespread support or require more technical training. CNEs select an area in which to specialize and concentrate their efforts on their areas of expertise. They also keep abreast of technology changes through Novell's requisite training updates.

Master Certified Novell Engineer (Master CNE)

> **The highest level of certification is Novell's Master CNE.**

The highest level of certification is Novell's Master CNE. The in-depth knowledge that the Master CNE brings to a company allows him to concentrate on highly complex, advanced network management issues. The ability to address interconnectivity issues of various networking platforms, numerous client difficulties, and internetwork connectivity issues are but a few of the capabilities expected from Master CNEs. Integrating CNAs, CNEs, and Master CNEs within a large network environment provides flexible management of networked resources.

Additional Novell Certification Offerings

Certified Novell Instructor (CNI)

> **Some individuals decide that in addition to working with Novell networks, they would enjoy teaching network installation, configuration, and overall use as well.**

Some individuals decide that in addition to working with Novell networks, they would enjoy teaching network installation, configuration, and overall use as well. These individuals can decide to become Certified Novell Instructors. Novell has recently made CNE certification a prerequisite to instructor certification. This is shown in Figure 15-3. Also shown is the dual path available for demonstrating basic teaching proficiency. Potential instructors can choose to complete the Instructor Performance Evaluation (IPE) at Novell's own training facilities, or submit proof of completion of the equally challenging Chauncy Group's Certified Technical Trainer (CTT) program. Either path ensures that only the most highly-qualified individuals become Certified Novell Instructors.

Figure 15-3

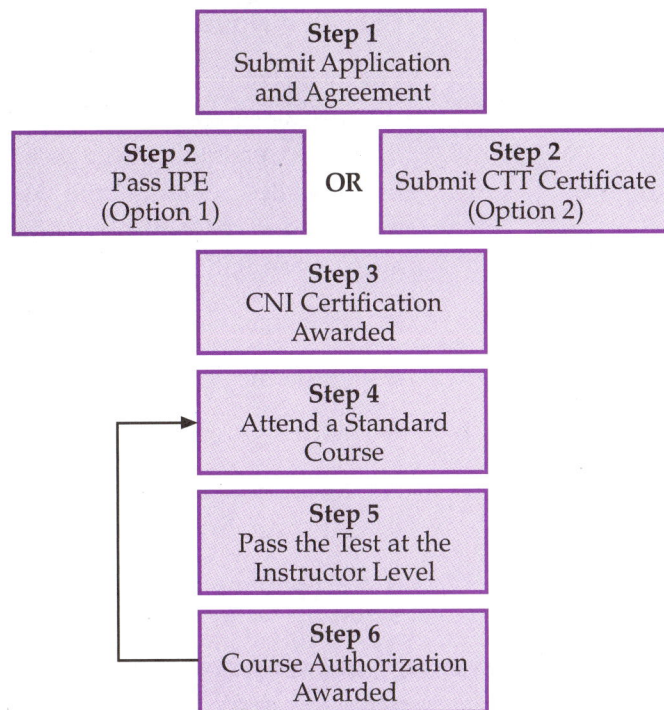

Step 1
Submit Application
and Agreement

Step 2
Pass IPE
(Option 1)

OR

Step 2
Submit CTT Certificate
(Option 2)

Step 3
CNI Certification
Awarded

Step 4
Attend a Standard
Course

Step 5
Pass the Test at the
Instructor Level

Step 6
Course Authorization
Awarded

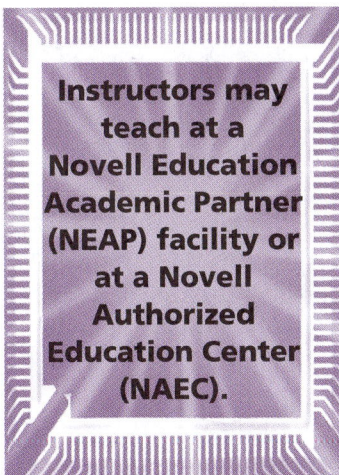

Instructors may teach at a Novell Education Academic Partner (NEAP) facility or at a Novell Authorized Education Center (NAEC).

Instructors may teach at a Novell Education Academic Partner (NEAP) facility or at a Novell Authorized Education Center (NAEC). Instructors can also elect to teach as independent contractors, provided that the courses they teach meet Novell standards. Independent contractor instructors may also offer classes at either NEAPs or NAECs.

Novell also requires CNIs to continue their certification efforts and complete additional training and testing as Novell updates its courses and releases new networking products. This assures that CNI training remains up-to-date and that CNIs are familiar with the latest Novell software.

Certified Internet Professional (CIP)

Novell has recently added a new Certified Internet Professional (CIP) program for those working with company Web sites.

Novell has recently added a new Certified Internet Professional (CIP) program for those working with company Web sites. Individuals interested in implementing, managing, and/or maintaining Internet sites or company intranets may certify as a Novell CIP. Individuals who perform Internet manager tasks will be able to:

■ create basic HTML documents for companies.

■ define page content and ensure consistency.

■ decide the design criteria used throughout the Web page.

■ develop company, department, or individual homepages.

■ manage the Web server.

Certified Novell Salesperson (CNS)

For those companies that sell Novell products and want to ensure that its sales personnel are completely qualified, Novell has developed the Certified Novell Salesperson (CNS) program. This program teaches sales personnel the skills necessary to meet customer needs and address customer concerns when choosing Novell products. As a CNS, you will acquire the sales skills necessary to:

- develop sales opportunities by asking appropriate questions.

- show the benefits of solving business networking problems.

- address customer objections.

- know how to demonstrate the benefits of the entire Novell software line.

- explain the technical capabilities of Novell products.

OK, So I Want to Become a CNA. Now What?

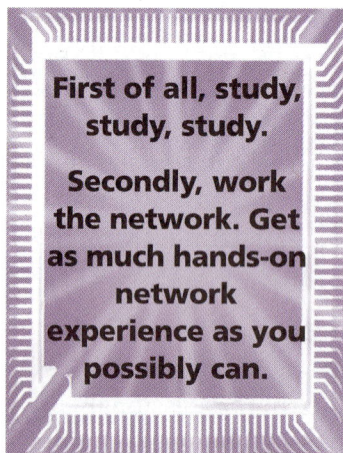

The Two Basics

> First of all, study, study, study.
>
> Secondly, work the network. Get as much hands-on network experience as you possibly can.

First of all, study, study, study. Acquire whatever learning materials you can regarding Novell Networks in order to accumulate as much networking knowledge as you can. Novell has designed its test database to simulate on-the-job experience as much as possible. Its course materials focus on the experiences of real administrators as well.

Secondly, work the network. Get as much hands-on network experience as you possibly can. Very little of the certification exam deals with the server console, so you do not need to spend a lot of time there.

NWAdmin, however, is very important, and you should spend as much time there as possible. Add users, then change everything there is about them. Understand everything you do, and know what effect your actions have on users.

Know What Will Be Required Of You

Novell ensures that you know what will be required of you before you take the test. In its own courseware, Novell clearly lists the objectives it will cover in the proficiency exam. If your method of study does not list these Novell objectives you can call Novell Education's Fax Response service at 1-800-233-3382, option 3, or 1-801-861-5363 to request a list of the objectives for your specific exam. You should obtain this information for whatever test you are preparing for. If you are planning to take the Novell NetWare 4.11 CNA exam, you should ask for information on test 50-613, which covers Course 520, IntranetWare 4.11 Administration. If you are planning to take the Novell NetWare 5 CNA exam, you should ask for test 50-639, which covers Course 560, NetWare 5 Administration. These objectives are also available on Novell's web page at *http://education.novell.com/testinfo/objectives/crsindex.htm*.

The objective listings for test 50-639 (NetWare 5 CNAs) and test 50-613 (intraNetWare 4.11 CNAs) are found at the end of this section.

Test Taking

> Successful completion of the practice exams does not guarantee that you will pass the actual proficiency test, but they are a valuable test-preparation aid.

Practice Tests

Although not a substitute for proper studying, taking practice tests on a frequent basis will help you prepare for the actual exam. Your study guide includes some written practice exams. Take them often! They should be completed right before you take the actual proficiency test. Used correctly, the practice tests can indicate whether or not you are well enough prepared to attempt the test. Successful completion of the practice exams does not guarantee that you will pass the actual proficiency test, but they are a valuable test-preparation aid.

Register For the Test

When you think you are ready to take the proficiency test, call the Novell testing facility to select a location and date. Sylvan Prometric and Virtual University Enterprises (VUE) are the companies Novell uses to conduct certification testing. You may also decide to test at one of the many NAECs that have a testing facility at their training location. Before choosing a test date, you must call a testing provider to verify site availability. Do not call to register until you are ready to take the exam. Also, do not skimp on studying or try to cram your studies into the night before the test.

The telephone number for Sylvan Prometric is 1-800-RED-EXAM (1-800-733-3926). You must tell them that you wish to check the locations available to take a Novell Proficiency Exam. They will ask you which test you plan to take, your present location's zip code, and possibly your telephone number, in order to find the testing facilities nearest you. Remember that if you are planning to take the Novell NetWare 4.11 CNA exam, you will ask for information on test 50-613, which covers Course 520, IntranetWare 4.11 Administration. If you are planning to take the Novell NetWare 5 CNA exam, you will ask for test 50-639, which covers Course 560, NetWare 5 Administration. Make sure to make record of the letter identifiers that they give you, as well as the address and telephone number of the testing facility. Request what hours and days that they offer testing. Also ask for information regarding the type of test you will be taking, the duration of the test, and whether or not you will be allowed to review and change your answers. Some of this information is available on Novell's web site at *http://education.novell.com/testinfo/testdata.htm*.

Look for a testing location where you will be comfortable while taking the test.

You may even decide to call at an early phase in your test preparation period to request a list of alternative testing sites in your area. There may be several, so make a list and scout them out. Look for a testing location where you will be comfortable while taking the test. If you have a choice of locations, choose one that is quiet. Go there before your test date to make sure that it pleases you. The day of the test is not the time to be wondering what the facility is like. Take care of as many small details as you can before testing day so that you will be able to concentrate on taking the test.

After you have chosen where you will take the test, get back to test preparation. You will have eliminated one of the major test-taking nuisances, but the test is still your primary concern. Do not let up on your studying. Keep taking the practice tests, reading any textbooks you have, and studying the on-line documentation that came with your operating software.

When you are ready to register for the exam, you must call the test provider again to tell them where you wish to take your exam. They will ask which test you plan to take, the testing facility you have chosen, and the day and time you would like them to reserve for you.

Once you have given them this information, you will need to tell them how you will pay for the test. If you have discount coupons, you should inform them that you will be using a coupon and tell them its registration number. If you intend to register by telephone, any remaining balance must be paid by credit card. Before you hang up, have them read back the information about the test for which you just registered. Confirm that the test number, the date, the time, and the test center are what you requested. Ask them to confirm the type of test, the number of questions, and ask if there are any special requirements.

Confirm that the test number, the date, the time, and the test center are what you requested. Ask them to confirm the type of test, the number of questions, and ask if there are any special requirements.

The Day Of The Test

You should sleep at least eight hours the night before the test. Eat a good breakfast, and try to test early enough in the day so that you are still wide awake and alert. If you are not a "morning person," target noon as your testing period and prepare yourself in the same way as the morning person above.

The testing center requires that you be present fifteen minutes before the exam begins. Twenty minutes early is typical, but arriving even a half-hour before the exam is not too early. The testing facility personnel use this time to check you in for the test. They must verify your identification before allowing you to take your test. You must present an official current photo ID, such as your driver's license or passport. School photos are not accepted. You will also have to show one other piece of identification, such as a credit card, with both your name and signature on it. These identification requirements are used to verify that you are the person who is registered to take the test.

If the two signatures on the two pieces of identification do not match, or if they do not match the way you sign the sign-in sheet at the test center, you will not be allowed to test. Furthermore, if the test center does not allow you to test because you could not verify your identification, they will not reimburse the testing fees. It is your job to provide that proof. If you are not sure whether your identification items are sufficient, it may be worth your while to have them verified ahead of time at the testing facility.

> **If you are not sure whether your identification items are sufficient, it may be worth your while to have them verified ahead of time at the testing facility.**

Once your identification is verified, you will sign for your test, and the test center personnel will load it up at the test booth where you will be working. Do not allow the test center personnel to rush you into the booth. Complete the check-in process, but then sit back down and refocus on your studies. Find a place where you can go over those last items that you want to be fresh in your memory when you start the exam. If you invented "memory joggers" to help you remember such things as rights assignments or any other such things, take time to review them. Commit them to short term memory.

Test centers electronically download the next day's tests on the night before your appointment. Your test is brought up on the monitor at your booth, and you will be asked to verify your identification again from the log in screen. This time, you confirm to the computer scoring system that you are the person scheduled to take this exam, and that the exam is the one for which you registered. After you log in, the computer will offer you a sample test to practice on before your test starts. You can go through it if you wish to verify that the computer works properly. You will then be asked if you are ready to begin. If anything is wrong at this point, get it corrected. It is very difficult to have any problems corrected after you have started the test.

When you go into your booth, you will have only a pencil and the paper that the center provides. Some centers will furnish dry erase markers and plastic coated work sheets. These materials are only for your scratch work. Nothing written on them will be calculated into your test score—only the answers you enter into the computer will count. You will turn in all the materials used in the booth at the end of the test, and the test center personnel will erase or destroy them.

> **Remember that your test does not start until after you sign in and either go through the practice test or decline it. Entering the booth does not automatically start the exam. Use this to your advantage.**

Remember that your test does not start until after you sign in and either go through the practice test or decline it. Entering the booth does not automatically start the exam. Use this to your advantage. As soon as you sit in your booth, write down everything you have in your short-term memory. Write out as much information as you think you will need later. Provided you write it down after you enter the booth, you can use the information during the test. In this way, you will not have to rely entirely on your memory during the test. Spread out the sheets for easy retrieval when a question requires that material. Start your test only when you are completely ready to begin. Relax. Take a deep breath. Then start your test.

> **You must finish the test before time runs out.**

You must finish the test before time runs out. If you do not, you automatically fail regardless of your score up to that point. You are required to finish. Be careful—the questions remaining could be easy multiple choice questions, but they could also be multi-step situational performance questions. Remember that if your test is adaptive, both types of questions will be asked until you pass or fail. This means that you could receive as few as fifteen and as many as twenty-five questions in the same amount of time. Plan accordingly.

Figure 15-4

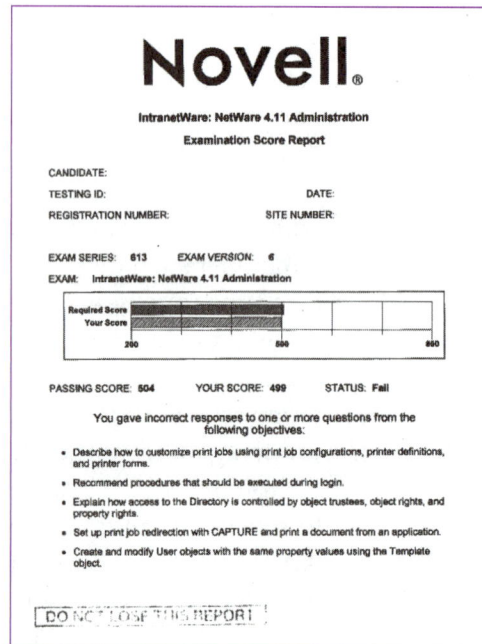

> **The report gives you your score, the score necessary to pass (the cutoff score), the pass/fail decision, and a list of objectives for further review. This is an important document—keep it.**

At the end of your test, it will be scored immediately, and any review items will appear on the screen at your booth. You will know immediately whether or not you passed. Your score report will appear on your monitor, and you will also receive a printed copy of the score report. The printed copy will be waiting for you outside your booth. The report gives you your score, the score necessary to pass (the cutoff score), the pass/fail decision, and a list of objectives for further review. This is an important document—keep it. If you did not pass, as shown in the score report in Figure 15-4, review the list of objectives on your report before retaking the test. If you passed, celebrate, because you achieved something that you can be proud of.

The Tests Themselves

Multiple-Choice All Novell Education tests begin as multiple-choice objective tests. Unlike most multiple-choice questions, more than one answer may be correct. A question may state "Choose the four steps in…", and you must know all four answers to answer correctly. When using this method, Novell incorporates the Microsoft Windows convention that changes the selection radio buttons to squares to provide a visual cue that more information is needed.

Novell also uses questions that have more than one correct answer, but you get credit for selecting any subset of the correct answers. For example, there may be a list of ten items in which five of them are correct responses. You could then be asked to choose three of the ten items. Any three of the five correct responses would be acceptable, and you cannot select more than three. Novell avoids ambiguous questions that require you to select "all that apply" without telling you how many do. Recently, Novell has also moved away from multiple graphic use in test questions because of the difficulty displaying the screens together. Older tests may still contain some multiple graphics, but newly-created tests will not.

Adaptive Novell has developed what it calls an "Adaptive" testing model. Novell has found that traditional paper-and-pencil and computerized tests that ask the same set of questions of everyone, regardless of their level of knowledge and proficiency, are not the most accurate way to measure knowledge and skills. An *adaptive test* is designed to function like an oral test.

> **An adaptive test is designed to function like an oral test.**

Novell's adaptive tests begin with a moderately difficult question. Your response is scored and your probable ability level is calculated based on the information tracked about that particular question. It then uses that probable ability level to select the next question. The test then calculates a new probable ability level based on your answer to that question and again uses it to select another question. The testing software continues this loop, revising your probable ability level as you answer the questions it selects for you. With the statistics from each answer you give, the accuracy of the probable ability level increases. After the minimum (and before the maximum) number of questions have been asked, and when the software has determined that your skill level is greater or less than the minimum level needed to pass the exam, your test ends, and you pass or fail based on that probable ability level.

> **Adaptive tests tailor the questions to your ability level.**

Adaptive tests tailor the questions to your ability level. Your score is based on the level of difficulty of the questions you answer correctly. Novell's scale has a minimum value of 200, and a maximum value of 800. Each test has its own passing (cutoff) score that lies somewhere between these two values. If your score falls at or above the cutoff score, you pass the test.

Novell Certification Test Objectives

> **NOTE**
> Test objectives are subject to change without notice.
> **NOTE**

Studying test objectives can help you prepare for certification tests. Novell-authorized student kits contain the material from which test objectives and test questions are taken. They are the best resources for test preparation. To register for a Novell test, contact your nearest test registration center. You can also call:

- Sylvan at 1-800-RED-EXAM, 1-800-RED-TEST, or 1-410-880-8700

- VUE at 1-800-511-8123, 1-888-834-8378, or 1-612-897-7370

NetWare 5 Administration Practice Test Questions

Test 050-639: CNA or CNE.

Obj. No.	Stated Objective

1. Describe what a network is and list its components.
2. Describe what NetWare is.
3. List the responsibilities of a network administrator.
4. List the resources and services you administer in NetWare 5.
5. Describe Novell Directory Services (NDS), including the NDS Directory and NDS objects.
6. Use NetWare Administrator to browse the NDS tree.
7. Explain how the NDS tree affects resource access.
8. Describe how a workstation communicates with the network.
9. Describe the function of the workstation's hardware.
10. Describe the function of the workstation's software.
11. Diagram a workstation dataflow model.
12. List the configuration options for Novell Client and Windows.
13. Install the Novell Client software.
14. Explain and perform the login procedure.
15. Browse network resources.
16. Install and configure a browser.
17. Describe the function of the user object.
18. Create and modify a user account using NetWare Administrator.
19. Create a user object using **ConsoleOne**.
20. Create a user object using **UIMPORT**.
21. Manage NetWare user licenses.
22. Identify the types of network security provided by NetWare.
23. Describe and establish login security, including login restrictions for users.
24. Describe network printing using NDPS.
25. Explain the four NDPS components and their functions.
26. List the NDPS printer types and explain the difference between public access printers and controlled access printers.
27. Configure the network for NDPS.
28. Configure a workstation to print to NDPS printers.
29. Manage printer access and print jobs.
30. Identify the basic components of the network file system.
31. Identify the basic skills involved in managing the network file system.

32. Use utilities to perform file system management tasks.

33. View file system information using Netware Administrator and Windows.

34. Access the file system by configuring drive mappings.

35. Select the correct utilities for managing the directory structure.

36. Select the correct utilities for managing files.

37. Manage volume space.

38. Explain how file system security works.

39. Plan file system rights for your organization.

40. Plan and implement file and directory attribute security.

41. Create and implement file system security.

42. Describe the types of login scripts and explain how they coordinate at login.

43. Design login scripts for containers, user groups, and users.

44. Use the **MAP** command in login scripts.

45. Create, execute, and debug login scripts.

46. Use the Login utility to edit login scripts.

47. Define NDS security and how it differs from file system security.

48. Control access to NDS objects.

49. Determine rights granted to NDS objects.

50. Block inherited rights.

51. Determine effective rights.

52. Explain guidelines for implementing NDS security.

53. Troubleshoot NDS security problems using NetWare Administrator.

54. Explain the benefits of using **Application Launcher**.

55. Explain the components of **Application Launcher**.

56. Distribute applications using **Application Launcher** and **snAppShot™**.

57. Manage applications with **Application Launcher**.

58. Identify the benefits of using **Z.E.N.works** to manage workstations.

59. Describe the **Z.E.N.works** maintenance schedule.

60. Describe **Z.E.N.works** policy packages and policies.

61. Identify NDS design considerations for **Z.E.N.works**.

62. Register workstations in NDS and import them into the NDS tree.

63. Use policies to configure the desktop environment.

64. Establish and use remote control access to manage workstations.

65. Set up and use the **Help Requester** application.

66. How does the NDS tree structure affects network administration?

67. Identify NDS planning guidelines.

68. Provide users with access to resources.

69. Create shortcuts to access and manage resources.

70. Identify guidelines for setting up resources in a multi-context environment.

71. Identify the actions to take and the rights needed to grant a user access to NDS resources.

72. Create login scripts that identify resources in other contexts.

73. Describe the function of a NetWare server and its interface, and identify the server components.

74. Perform a basic NetWare 5 server installation.

intraNetWare 4.11 Administration Practice Test Questions

Test 050-613: CNA or CNE.   Test 050-813: CNI.

Obj. No. | **Stated Objective**

1. Describe a network, including its basic function and physical components.

2. List the NetWare 4 network services individuals will learn to administer in this course.

3. Describe Novell Directory Services (NDS) and explain its role on the network.

4. Describe the Directory, including its function and basic components.

5. Describe the Directory tree, including leaf and container objects.

6. Browse the Directory tree.

7. Demonstrate correct object-naming techniques.

8. Describe how a workstation communicates with the network, and list the files required to connect a workstation to the network.

9. Describe the function of the software and hardware, including local operating systems, **Client 32**, communications protocols, and network boards necessary to connect a workstation to the network.

10. Connect a workstation to the network by executing the appropriate workstation files.

11. Explain and perform the login procedure.

12. Explain the basic concepts of network file storage, including volumes, directory structures, network drives, and search drives.

13. Display volume, directory, and file information.

14. Define NetWare command line utilities, describe how they are used, and activate Help information for them.

15. Using a Volume object and a Directory Map object, map a network drive to a volume and navigate between the volumes.

16. Using a Volume object and a Directory Map object, map a network drive to a directory and navigate the directories of a volume.

17. Using a Volume object and a Directory Map object, map a search drive to a directory containing an application.

18. Describe the basic components of network printing and how they interrelate in processing a print job.

19. Set up print job redirection and print from Windows 95 and Windows 3.1.

20. Set up print job redirection with **CAPTURE** and print a document from an application.

21. Describe the function of a User object and its property values.

22. Create a User object and enter user identification property values.

23. Create and modify User objects with the same property values using the Template object.

24. Create a user home directory automatically while creating a User object; create user home directories.

25. Modify parameters for multiple users.

26. Manage NDS objects by creating, deleting, and renaming objects, and by entering and modifying property values.

27. Create users with **UIMPORT**.

28. Identify the levels and functions of network security.

29. Describe and establish login security, including user account restrictions, time restrictions, station restrictions, and intruder detection.

30. Explain guidelines for planning and creating custom volumes and directories in the network file system.

31. List the system-created volumes and directories; describe their contents and function.

32. List suggested directories for organizing the file system.

33. Identify the strengths and weaknesses of sample directory structures.

34. Design and create a directory structure based on a given scenario.

35. Manage the file system directory structure by creating, deleting, renaming, and moving directories.

36. Manage files in the file system by copying, moving, deleting, salvaging, and purging files.

37. Manage the use of volume space by viewing volume usage statistics; restricting space usage by user and directory; changing file ownership; locating files based on usage, owner, and size; setting compression attributes; and setting data migration attributes.

38. Describe NetWare 4 file system security, including the concepts of directory and file rights, trustee assignments, inheritance, rights reassignment, Inherited Rights Filters (IRFs), security equivalence, and effective rights.

39. Determine a user's effective rights.

40. Perform basic security implementation tasks, such as assigning a trustee and granting rights, setting a directory IRF, creating a Group object and assigning members, and making a user security equivalent to another user.

41. Describe guidelines for planning a directory structure based on security considerations.

42. Given a directory structure and the function of its directories, recommend the rights that should be granted and the trustee object that will make security implementation and management easiest.

43. Describe and set the directory and file attributes that can be used to regulate access to files.

44. Based on a scenario, create and implement a file system security plan that appropriately grants directory and file rights to Container, Group, and User objects, and sets directory IRFs.

45. Describe the function of a NetWare 4 server and its interface.

46. Define console command and NetWare Loadable Module (NLM).

47. Describe the function of the **LOAD** command.

48. Describe remote console management; list the steps necessary to set up a server for both SPX and asynchronous remote connections.

49. Use **RCONSOLE** to remotely access the server console, switch between console screens, and activate the **RCONSOLE Available Options** menu.

50. Describe security strategies for a NetWare 4 server, such as setting a password on the monitor, setting a password for Remote Console, and placing the server in a secure location.

51. Set up a network printing environment by creating and configuring related Print Queue, Printer, and Print objects.

52. Set up network printing hardware by bringing up a print server on a NetWare 4 server and connecting a printer to the network through a NetWare server or DOS workstation.

53. Regulate who can do any of the following: print to a print queue, manage print jobs in the print queue, be notified by a printer when a problem occurs, view the status of the print server, or manage the print server.

54. Manage the flow of print jobs into and out of a print queue by managing the status of the print queue.

55. Manage print jobs in a print queue by pausing, rushing, delaying, and deleting print jobs in the print queue.

56. Describe how to customize print jobs using print job configurations, printer definitions, and printer forms.

57. Describe the types of login scripts and explain how they coordinate at login.

58. Recommend procedures that should be executed during login.

59. Plan login scripts with correct login script command syntax.

60. Create, execute, and debug a login script.

61. Describe how to manage and launch network applications using Application objects and the NetWare Application Launcher (NAL).

62. Configure NDS and the file system to access network applications with NAL.

63. Use NAL to launch a network application from Windows.

64. Explain how access to the Directory is controlled by object trustees, object rights, and property rights.

65. Given a Directory tree, determine effective rights for objects and properties and troubleshoot an NDS security scenario.

66. Explain guidelines and considerations for managing NDS security.

67. Implement NDS security by making trustee assignments; modifying Object, All Property, and Selected Property rights; and setting Inherited Rights Filters (IRFs).

68. Describe how the Directory tree structure affects network use and management skills.

69. Describe sample Directory structures and discuss basic guidelines for organizing resources.

70. Change the current context and access resources in the Directory tree.

71. Log in, map network drives, and redirect print jobs to resources in other contexts.

72. Grant rights to file system and network printing resources in other contexts.

73. Create shortcuts to objects in other contexts using Directory Map and Alias objects.

74. Establish an initial context at login for a DOS workstation.

75. Edit login scripts to access resources in other containers.

76. Compare and contrast back-up strategies.

77. Describe the process of backing up a NetWare server's file system with **SBACKUP**.

78. Describe the process of restoring file system information with **SBACKUP**.

Chapter Summary

Networking has become almost a necessity for most businesses, and the demand for networking skills is growing at a phenomenal pace worldwide. The number of networks is increasing, and they all require qualified administrators.

Employers who contemplate hiring these trained networking professionals need a way to determine the proficiency level at which any given candidate is operating. In short, employers need a certification program, one that will quickly answer that question for them.

In order to standardize the definition of "qualified," Novell and other major operating system companies developed certification programs. Their graduates are expected to be highly-qualified and capable of performing the duties expected of their certification level. Certification is the employer's assurance that they are hiring a trained professional to whom they can entrust their network.

Novell developed its own industry-standard product training and certification program. In 1986, Novell began the first professional IS/IT training program in the world, and has issued more than 200,000 certifications. There are now over 1,500 training and testing locations. Because companies are increasingly opting to operate their networks using a mix of numerous operating systems, Novell has added material to its certification program that ensures that its graduates have multi-vendor capability.

The CNA program was implemented in 1992 to standardize the performance capabilities of its network administrator graduates so that employers hiring a CNA could be confident that their new employee would be qualified to administer a Novell network. The program has helped standardize industry expectations regarding the duties of a network administrator.

CNAs provide companies direct Network Administrator support, and are expected to handle the day-to-day administration of any Novell networking product in which they are certified. CNA duties include setting up workstations, servers, and printers; managing parts of or entire network environments; installing applications and sharing them as network resources; customizing and automating login; determining desktop configurations; and monitoring network performance.

CNA certification is generally recognized as proof that you are capable of supporting Novell products. Potential employers usually recognize it as such without question. As a result of your CNA training, your on-the-job capabilities are superior, and often lead to increased training and responsibilities. The CNA certification process can indicate whether you should start on the advanced certification path. It is the first step in the CNE, MCNE, or CNI certification sequence. Novell also provides numerous support mechanisms to certified networking specialists.

The CNA certification process is relatively simple. You must complete adequate course preparation, choose the track in which to test, sign and submit an agreement form, register for the exam of your choice, then take and pass the exam. You can prepare through NEAPs, NAECs, independent training facilities, self-study books, or work experience. There are five CNA tracks now available— NetWare 5, IntranetWare 4.11, NetWare 3, GroupWise 5, or GroupWise 4.

Networking Terms Used in Chapter 15

qualified
certification
Certified NetWare Administrator (CNA)
career path
Certified Novell Engineer
   (CNE)

Master CNE (MCNE)
Certified Novell Instructor
   (CNI)
Certified Internet Professional
   (CIP)
Certified Novell Salesperson
   (CNS)

Novell Education Academic
   Partner (NEAP)
Novell Authorized Education
   Center (NAEC)
track
GroupWise
certification agreement
adaptive test

■ Chapter Review Questions

1. Explain why there is an increased need for certified networking specialists.

2. What does *qualified* mean?

3. What does Novell's certification program offer to individuals?

4. Who developed the first industry-standard product training and certification program?

5. How many certifications have been earned through Novell?

6. What did employers hiring CNAs expect?

7. What do CNAs do?

8. What size of business usually employs CNAs?

9. Why should an individual seek Novell certification?

10. How does CNA preparation help you on the job?

11. How does CNA testing help you on the certification path?

12. What are additional benefits made available to CNAs?

13. What are the major steps required to become a CNA?

14. What are the CNA tracks available?

15. What must you do if you are a minor seeking certification?

16. What is the preferred method to prepare for any Novell certification?

17. How many official Novell classes must you attend before obtaining certification?

18. How do you as an individual benefit by becoming a CNA?

19. How do companies benefit from hiring CNAs?

20. What certifications are in Novell's basic certification lineup?

21. What are the three additional certifications available through Novell?

22. What are the two basics of preparation for certification?

23. What are the steps to certification testing?

24. How do Novell's multiple-choice test questions differ from typical multiple-choice questions?

25. What are adaptive tests?

■ Associated Chapter Problems

1. Describe the evolution of Novell's certification process.

2. Explain the benefits of becoming a CNA from the perspective of the individual and the company.

3. Describe four typical functions you may find yourself performing if hired as a CNA.

4. Discuss how attempting to become a CNA can help you decide whether or not you want to select networking as your career.

5. Explain the difference between a NEAP and NAEC.

6. Describe how you progress through Novell's certification levels.

7. Explain how to become a CNA as if you were trying to convince someone to obtain certification.

8. Describe in detail how to prepare for a certification test.

9. What information should you know about the test before arriving at a test center?

10. Describe Novell's tests and testing process.

CHAPTER 16
CAREERS IN NETWORKING

Once you choose networking as a career, you should know where you can locate resources that can help you with your employment search. By the end of this chapter, you will be able to:

- understand what the market trends are for network specialists.

- explain the networking positions available to a beginning specialist.

- describe how to locate information about the computer industry.

- use the information available to create and post your own resume on the Internets job market.

- describe the career search resources available to you when job hunting.

Computer Related Careers

So you want to become a Certified Novell Administrator. Now what? You have already taken a giant first step in that direction by arriving at this point in the text. If you have understood even half of what has been presented, you have a good chance of achieving career success in the networking field.

If you do choose to work in the networking field, you are in for a pleasant surprise. For the past several years, networking specialists have been the most sought after professionals in the job market—worldwide! In the case of advanced networking specialists, once a company hires one, they do not let him go. Pay and benefits increases usually keep these individuals with a specific company for as long as they want to stay. Should they desire to change companies, on the other hand, they are usually snapped up quickly, and advance in the field as fast as their capabilities will allow.

Is this a rosy picture? Of course it is. If you are interested in a *networking career* and are reasonably capable, you are almost guaranteed a well-paying position. There are many career choices available to you once you decide to work with computers.

> For the past several years, networking specialists have been the most sought after professionals in the job market—worldwide!

Network Administrator

Obviously, this course points you in the direction of becoming a network administrator. If you liked working with Novell NetWare 5 or IntranetWare 4.11, and gained enough knowledge about them, obtaining Novell certification will be a relatively easy task. You could be well on your way toward entering network administration as a profession.

Network administrators work with company decision-makers to help design their network. An administrator will often do this on his or her own, but usually this task involves working with users and managers. Factors that determine network design include the number and type of computers that the company will be using, the connections needed to alternate locations, the physical layout of the networked offices, the volume of information the network will carry, the number of workers that need access, the company's data security needs, the additional components on the network, and the skill set of the users. Clearly, the administrator must be knowledgeable about the software on the network as well as the operating system itself.

Network administrators are sometimes asked to fix problems only remotely associated with their networks. Usually network administrators are highly respected, and are commonly considered capable of fixing anything associated with computers. Because of this, they are called whenever a user experiences problems, whether they concern the network or his home PC. You must enjoy troubleshooting problems, and you need to like working with people. How well you do your job depends in large part on how well you work with others.

> Network administrators are sometimes asked to fix problems only remotely associated with their networks.

Should you elect to work with the other major operating system in the networking field, Windows NT 4.0 (or Windows 2000), the transition will not be very difficult. You already know the basics of Windows, and will not find it hard to understand the networking differences that exist between the two operating system environments. Like every Novell network, every NT network has a network administrator. Many of the functions you learned for Novell apply to NT networks. The concepts are the same, even if the actions undertaken by the administrator and the capabilities of the users are different.

Help Desk Technician

If you like what you have done in this class, but do not feel quite ready to administer your own network, you could apply your skills by working as a *help desk technician*. The troubleshooting skills you acquired during these studies will help immeasurably in this type of position. As a help desk technician, you would usually answer service calls placed by PC users around a company's network. You could be the person who simply answers the phone and takes the initial trouble report directly from the user, or you could be the person to visit the user and fix the problem. Your troubleshooting and people skills have to be very good for success in this job. Usually, you must visit people who are not in the best of spirits because their computers are not working, and they cannot do their jobs without them.

> As a help desk technician, you would usually answer service calls placed by PC users around a company's network.

Applications Specialist

The *applications specialist* installs new software and adds upgrades to existing installations. When a user is hired by a company, his computer will usually be built for him with the specific software needed for the functions expected of the position. If the person is replacing a former employee, the software is usually replaced anyway in order to ensure that the software is up-to-date.

New software is being created at a rapid pace. When a large company deploys the latest version of an application, it takes time to install it, and there are usually associated problems that must be solved over time. About the time when all of the problems have been resolved and all of the users are comfortable with the software, an updated version is released, and the process starts all over again.

The applications specialist visits each location to install the software for the users. The knowledge he gains through performing the installations enables him to complete the remaining installations more efficiently. In addition, the installation process is standardized by having the same person perform all of the installations.

Usually, the applications specialist is the first one to give instructions to users regarding a particular software application. Although these introductions may often be cursory, they are important because they determine how the user initially feels about the new software.

> The applications specialist visits each location to install the software for the users.

The Computer Manager (formerly Systems Analyst)

In the US Department of Labor's Bureau of Labor Statistics article *New Occupations Emerging Across Industry Lines* (*http://stats.bls.gov/ opub/ils/pdf/opbils25.pdf*) we read:

> "Technological change continues to create emerging opportunities in computer-related occupations. *Computer managers* are responsible for an organization's computer network. They are increasingly responsible for overseeing the installation, configuration, and maintenance of both software and hardware in a local area network (LAN), wide area network (WAN), or Internet/ Intranet system. Computer managers monitor network usage to ensure that adequate computer service is available to all users. Their duties may also include keeping the computer network secure."

Computer managers monitor network usage to ensure that adequate computer service is available to all users.

In addition, the Bureau of Labor Statistics' *Occupational Outlook Handbook* (*http://stats.bls.gov/oco/ocos042.htm*) supplies the following information about the changing duties of systems analysts:

> "One obstacle associated with expanding computer use is the inability of different computer systems to communicate with each other. Because maintaining up-to-date information—accounting records, sales figures, or budget projections, for example—is important in modern organizations, systems analysts may be instructed to make the computer systems in each department compatible so that information can be shared. Many systems analysts are involved with 'networking' or connecting all the computers in an individual office, department, or establishment. A primary goal of networking is to allow users to retrieve data from a mainframe computer or a server and use it on their machine. This connection also allows data to be entered into the mainframe from a personal computer. Analysts must design the hardware and software to allow free exchange of data, custom applications, and the computer power to process it all. They study the seemingly incompatible pieces and create ways to link them so users can access information from any part of the system. Networks come in many variations and network systems and data communications analysts design, test, and evaluate systems such as Local Area Networks (LAN), Wide Area Networks (WAN), Internet, and Intranet and other data communications systems. These analysts perform network modeling, analysis and planning, and even research and recommend necessary hardware and software."

A primary goal of networking is to allow users to retrieve data from a mainframe computer or a server and use it on their machine.

Market Trends

In the past several years there has been an increasing need for people who can work in the Information Technology (IT) field. This is due in large part to increased spending in the field of networking. In the early 1990s, only about $400 million was spent for network support each year, while in 1998 alone that spending is estimated at above

> Another recent networking trend involves a shift away from working for large corporations, with multiple Management Information Systems (MIS) layers, to working for an outside agency as a temporary contracted employee.

> There is also a recent trend toward hiring younger workers in the IT field.

$2 billion. Novell currently has over 100,000 Certified Novell Engineers (CNEs). According to the Network Professionals Association (NPA) (*http://www.npa.org/*), there are 200,000 Certified Network Administrators and over 4,000 network professionals worldwide who design, integrate, manage, and maintain networked computing environments. The association also states that the world already needs at least 50,000 more individuals simply to fill currently vacant positions.

According to *Computer Reseller News*, (*http://www.crn.com*), only about a third of the personal computers in use in 1989 were connected to local area networks (LANs). In 1997, on the other hand, the vast majority of PCs were connected to LANs. What this has led to is an increasing need for networking specialists in the computer industry. This is an ideal situation if you are trying to become a networking specialist. It is much better to start a career that is in high demand, and that offers high starting salaries because there are not enough people available with the necessary skills. Once you have those skills, you become a sought after commodity.

Another recent networking trend involves a shift away from working for large corporations, with multiple *Management Information Systems (MIS)* layers, to working for an outside agency as a temporary contracted employee. Outsourcing work has become popular, so you could find yourself applying for a "temp to perm" position. In these cases, you are hired by one firm to work at another, probably larger, company for a specific period of time. If that second company is pleased with your job performance, you may be offered a permanent position. At that point, the second company acquires you from the first company by paying them a "finder's fee."

There is also a recent trend toward hiring younger workers in the IT field. You can find some of the more recent articles on this subject at the following locations on the Internet.

- The latest information on high school outlooks:
  Labor crunch an ongoing problem for IT, December 21, 1998
  http://www.zdnet.com/pcweek/stories/news/0,4153,379493,00.html

- The need for working with educational institutions:
  Making the Grade, PC Week, September 7, 1998
  http://www.zdnet.com/pcweek/news/0907/07intro.html

- Working with industry leaders:
  High-School Heroes, PC Week, April 13, 1998
  http://www.zdnet.com/pcweek/news/0413/13kids.html

- Programs already in operation:
  Going back to school, PC Week, April 13, 1998
  http://www.zdnet.com/pcweek/news/0413/13programs.html

- Student needs:
  Dealing with students, PC Week, April 13, 1998
  http://www.zdnet.com/pcweek/news/0413/13guidelines.html

■ In addition, this author's own Caney Creek High School course offering in Conroe, Texas: *It's a win-win situation with teen-age IT interns*, PC Week, February 23, 1998
http://www.zdnet.com/pcweek/news/0223/23jobsb2.html

Figure 16-1

PCWEEK
ONLINE
ZDNet's IT Resource

News
Labs
Radio
Special Reports
Spencer F. Katt
Columnists
Downloads

Click here! ▼
Click here to
sign up
now!

available
only online!
Advertisement

Search
FAQs
Subscribe
PCW Marketing

CLICK HERE!

It's a win-win situation with teen-age IT interns

By Erin Callaway, PC Week Online
02.23.98

✉ **E-mail this story**

🖨 **Easy print**

Related Stories

IT openings: All may apply

IT career change can work, but not overnight

Randy Doleman is bound for IT stardom. He's bright, technology-savvy, business-minded--and 16 years old.

High school students such as Doleman, a junior at Caney Creek High School, in Conroe, Texas, are hot prospects for corporate IT internships. And not just because companies have a benevolent impulse to mentor young hopefuls. They want to groom the students for full-time jobs. It's a long shot. But increasingly, companies are willing to take that chance.

"Realistically, it's not a big commitment. It's not like [spending] $25,000 on a finder's fee [for someone who leaves] six months later. You're paying summer employment wages," said E.P. Rogers, vice president and CIO at Mutual of New York.

Today, more companies are looking to intern students before they graduate. The caveat: Most American high schools don't have an IT curriculum. But that's changing fast. The state of Kentucky, for example, will pump $600 million into wiring its schools and developing IT courses by the year 2000. Charles Ross, a 19-year-old high school senior, is one of 16 technology assistants who operate a system for the Jessamine County, Ky., public schools.

And Caney Creek opened last August, complete with a $500,000 Windows NT lab. Meanwhile, Microsoft Corp. announced last October its plans to train high school and higher-ed instructors on Windows NT for just $150 through its Skills 2000 Educator Training Initiative. Rich McMahon, Caney Creek's IT teacher, jumped at Microsoft's training offer.

Last semester the students learned how to install PC CPU cards in Macintosh computers, load the Macs with DOS and Windows 95, and connect them to a Novell network.

Information Sources

Your own school

If your school district is like most in the country, it can provide excellent resources concerning jobs and the job-search process. The majority of districts now provide a *Career Specialist* to their enrollees. Sometimes these specialists are shared among many campuses within a district, but they provide exceptional resource support.

One resource they usually provide is The Bridges Initiative's Career Explorer (*http://www.bridges.com/*). This is an excellent source of information for individuals seeking employment.

The amount of information available concerning job searches is staggering. Discussing job possibilities with someone who is knowledgeable about job-hunting skills can be extremely valuable. Many individuals do not know what to look for or where to go for basic information. A career specialist can indicate what resources among the multiple resources available may be useful for your career search. If your district has such a program, you should take advantage of it. It will make you a more informed job applicant, and thus help you land a better position.

Government Sources

> There are numerous government resources available to the astute employment seeker.

There are numerous government resources available to the astute employment seeker. Local libraries often contain many government documents that can assist you in your search. Librarians can assist you in locating and using these documents. You can also access many of the same documents directly on the Internet. One of these resources is the US Department of Labor Bureau of Labor Statistics' *Occupational Outlook Handbook (OOH)*. You can find it at the following Internet location: *http://stats.bls.gov/oco/ocos042.htm*.

According to the OOH, computer scientists, computer engineers, and systems analysts are "expected to be the top three fastest growing occupations and among the top 20 in the number of new jobs as computer applications continue to expand throughout the economy."

You can find additional information by starting at the Bureau of Labor Statistics' web page and searching for relevant documents. For example, its *Issues* pamphlet highlights particularly interesting articles such as the *New Occupations Emerging Across Industry Lines* (*http://stats.bls.gov/opub/ils/pdf/opbils25.pdf*) from the previous section.

Another source of government information for job seekers can be found at *http://stats.bls.gov/k12/html/edu_over.htm*.

Novell Education

> Remember to use the Novell education site: *http://education.novell.com/*

Remember to use the *Novell education* site: *http://education.novell.com/*. In addition to posting updated fixes to its site, Novell also provides information about its training programs to prospective networking candidates. Newcomers to the networking field can feel comfortable starting at the location shown in Figure 16-2. They should click on training options.

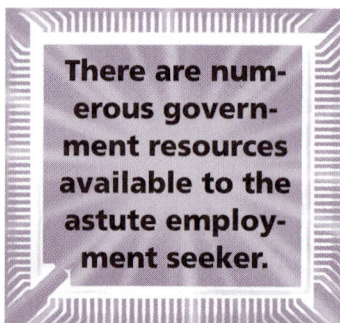

Figure 16-2

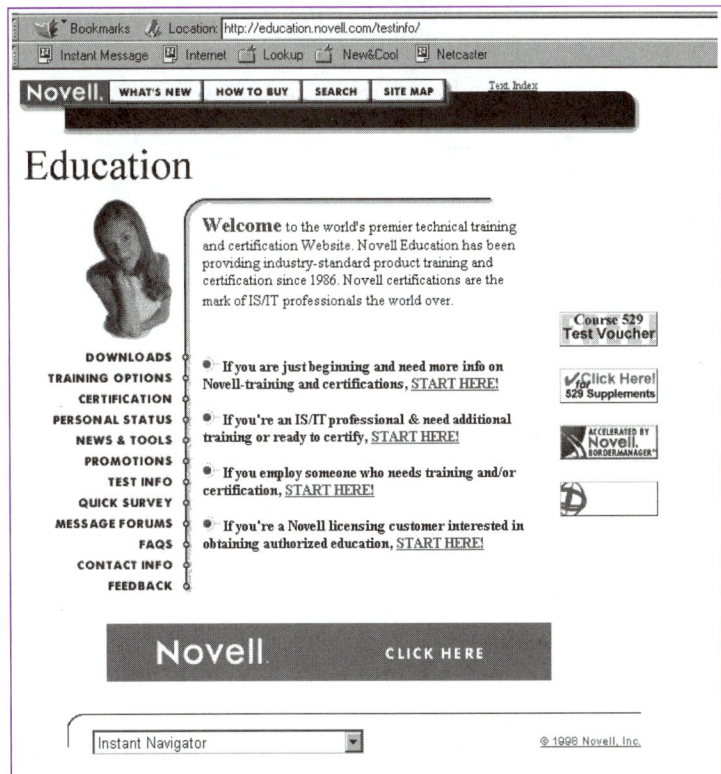

You, on the other hand, would probably find information that is more useful to you on the page shown in Figure 16-3. Click on the certification item.

Figure 16-3

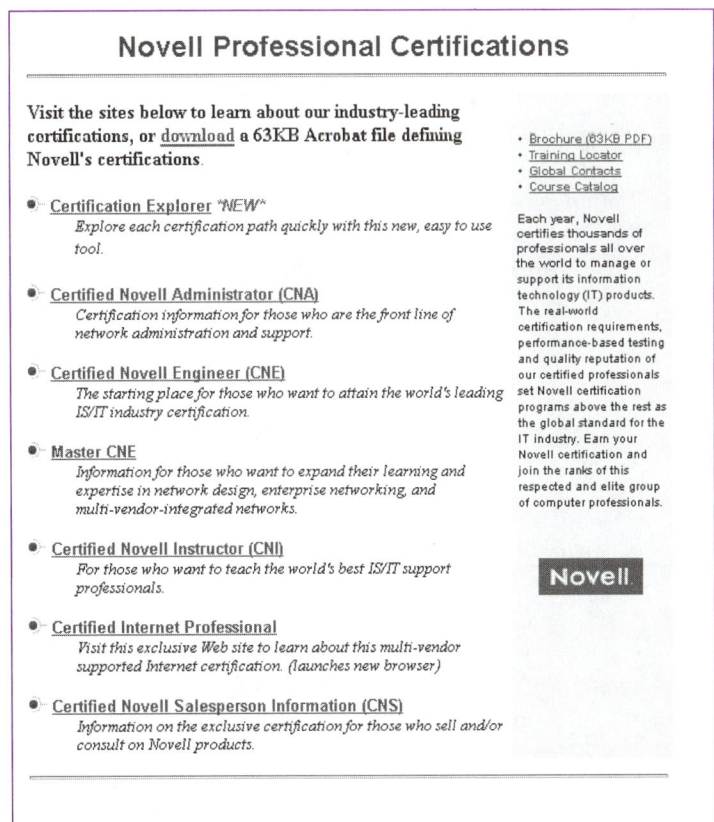

Clicking on the Certification Explorer listing in Figure 16-3 will bring you to the window shown in Figure 16-4. Here you can read more about each of Novell's certification offerings.

Figure 16-4

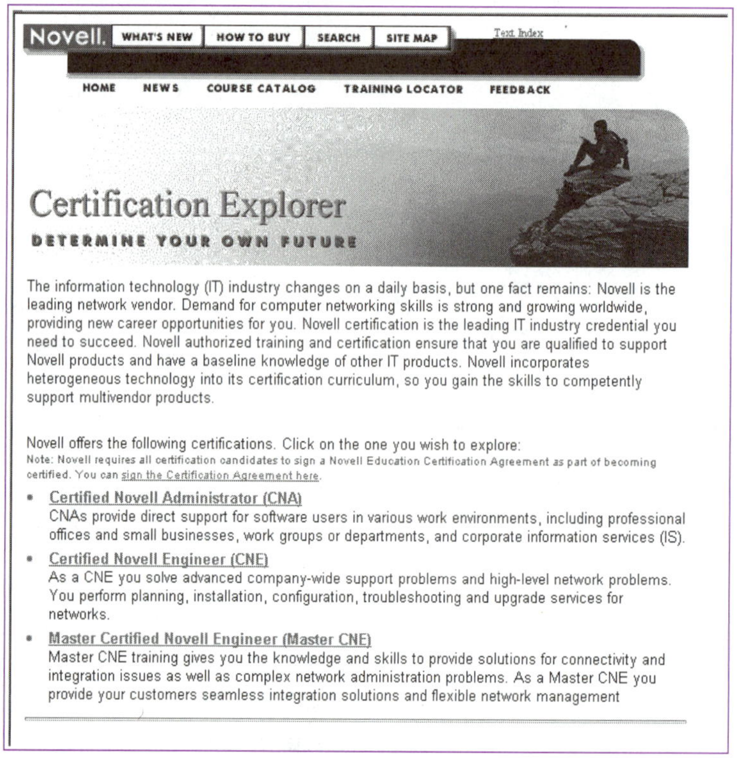

You should also visit your nearest Novell Authorized Education Center and request a copy of Novell's *The Guide CD*. It contains a very useful list of your training options, and helps map out certification paths. It also contains the best testing simulator available on the market. Random test questions are provided for any chapter or section that you should choose, and the software simulator acts exactly like the actual test session.

Figure 16-5

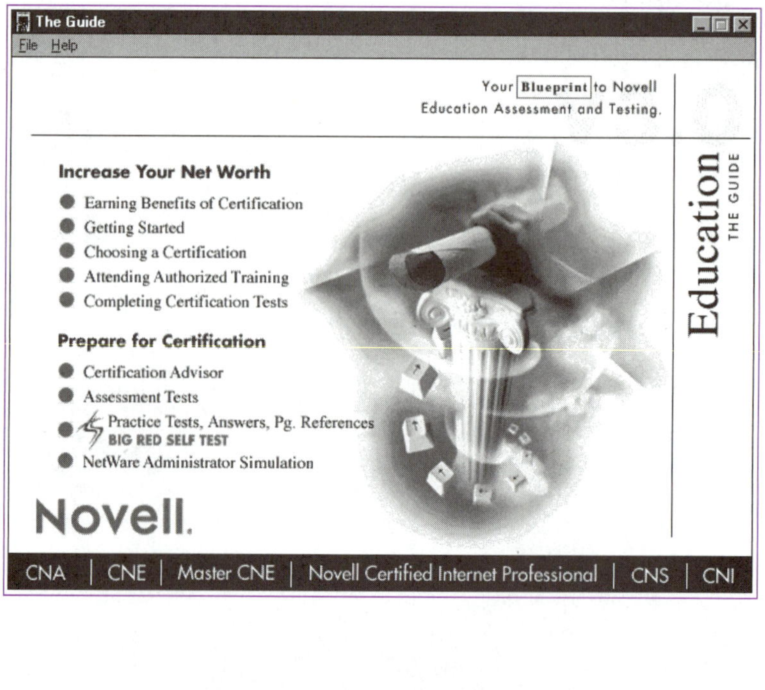

Internet Handbooks

The University of Illinois provides a *Network Administrator's Survival Handbook* (*http://www-commeng.cso.uiuc.edu/nas/nash/*) that also contains links to useful information.

Figure 16-6

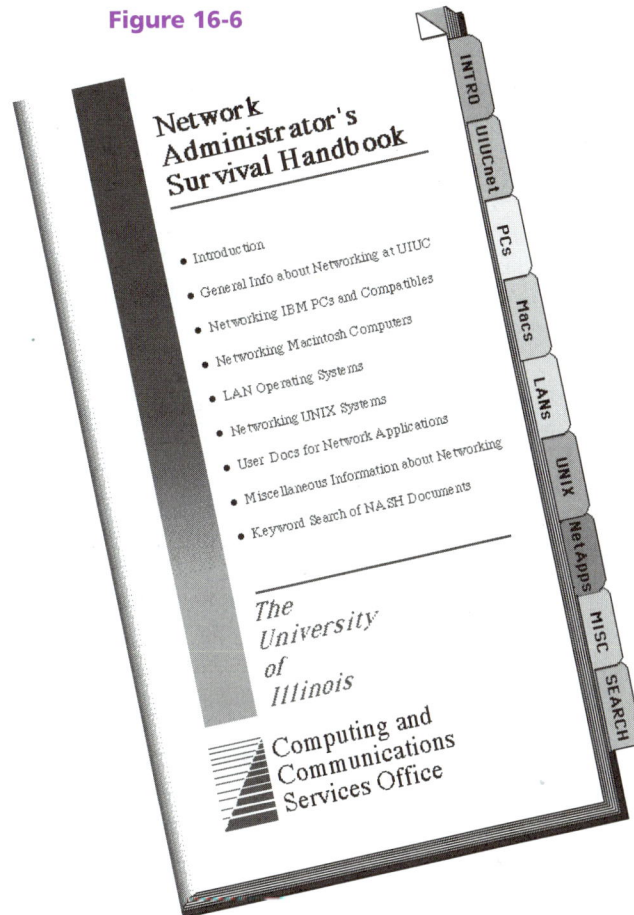

Other Internet Resources

There are numerous additional sources of information regarding IT careers. One of the most helpful is found on the Internet at *http://www.nbew.com/weddle/index.htm*.

Figure 16-7a

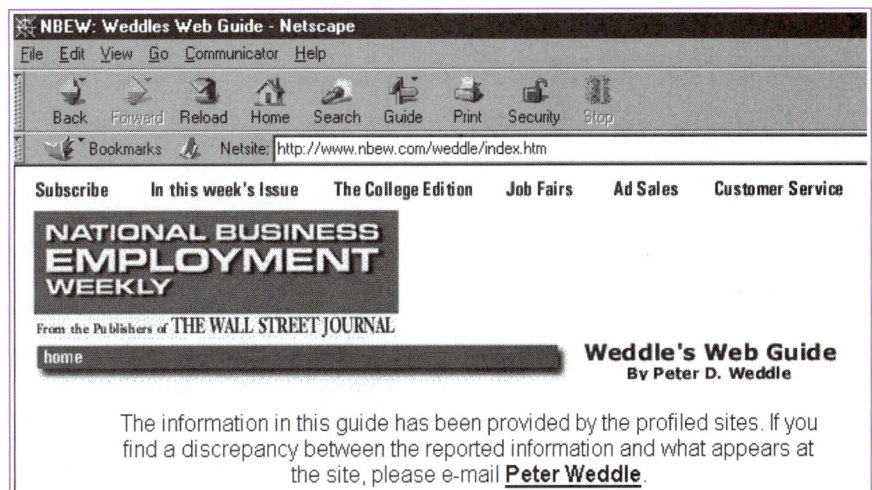

CHAPTER 16
Careers

Figure 16-7b

> **Click on a web site to read detailed information.**
>
> | | |
> |---|---|
> | ⌙ CareerWeb | ⌙ CareerExchange |
> | ⌙ CareerMosaic | ⌙ Academic Position Network |
> | ⌙ Online Career Center | ⌙ The JobMarket |
> | ⌙ Career Shop | ⌙ CareerPath.com |
> | ⌙ JOBTRAK | ⌙ Internet Career Connection |
> | ⌙ CareerMagazine | ⌙ America's Employers |
> | ⌙ Westech Virtual Job Fair | ⌙ Engineering Jobs |
> | ⌙ CareerCity | ⌙ Medhunters |
> | ⌙ E.span | ⌙ Science Online |
> | ⌙ CAREER.COM | ⌙ careers.wsj.com |
> | ⌙ NationJob Network | ⌙ NETSHARE Online |
> | ⌙ The Monster Board | ⌙ GUARANTEED |
> | ⌙ Net-Temps | Job Search Success |
> | ⌙ US RESUME | ⌙ Employnet |
> | ⌙ Best Jobs U.S.A. | ⌙ Aviation Employee |
> | ⌙ Contract Employment | Placement Service |
> | Connection at NTES | ⌙ CareerLink USA |
> | ⌙ America's Job Bank | ⌙ Accounting & Finance Jobs |
> | ⌙ America's Talent Bank | ⌙ Classifieds2000-Employment |
> | ⌙ Telecommuting Jobs | ⌙ HeadHunter.NET |
> | ⌙ Hot Jobs | ⌙ Jobnet.com |
> | ⌙ Jobs in Government | ⌙ Career Avenue |
> | ⌙ JobCenter Employment | ⌙ ITTA Connection |
> | Services | ⌙ Computerwork.com |
> | ⌙ CareerBuilder.com | ⌙ CareerCast |
> | ⌙ Town Online Working | ⌙ Federal Jobs Central |
> | ⌙ CareerSite.com | ⌙ 4work.com |
> | ⌙ PassportAccess | ⌙ Contract Employment Weekly |
> | ⌙ Data Processing | ⌙ American Banker CareerZone |
> | Independent | ⌙ Classifieds/Jobs at Infospace Inc. |
> | Consultant's Exchange | ⌙ Recruiters Online Network |
> | (DICE) | ⌙ Blackworld Career Center |
> | ⌙ World.hire ONLINE | ⌙ MarketingJobs.com |
> | ⌙ TAPS.COM | ⌙ SelectJOBS |

> **... you must be careful to not violate any school policies in an effort to speed this employment process along.**

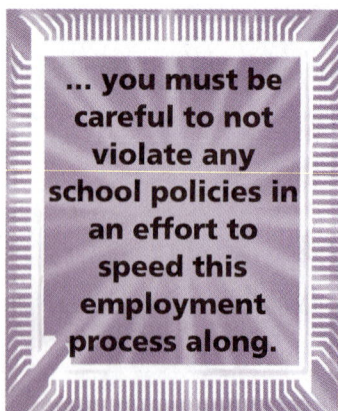

Each of the sites in the list shown in Figure 16-7b furnish information important for your employment search. Many of the sites provide online resume posting, while others provide links to other sources of information.

Most of the locations shown in Figures 16-7a and 16-7b require that you join their *online service* before allowing you to access their site. Before joining these services, or posting your resume or any other personal information from a classroom computer, you should inform your instructor of your intentions, and request authorization. You should also inform your parents or legal guardians if you are under the age of 18. Many school districts have a policy that forbids providing personal information over the Internet. Although the intent of this course is to furnish you with marketable skills that will help you obtain employment, you must be careful to not violate any school policies in an effort to speed this employment process along.

Your Net Worth

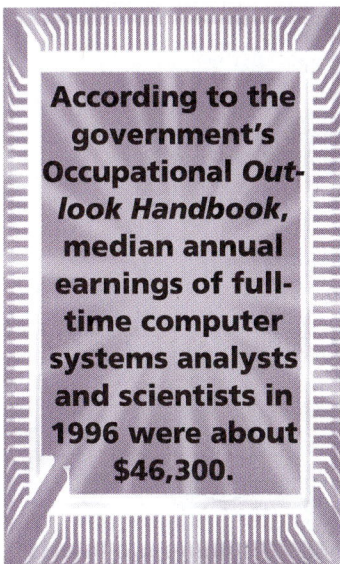

> According to the government's *Occupational Outlook Handbook*, median annual earnings of full-time computer systems analysts and scientists in 1996 were about $46,300.

According to the government's *Occupational Outlook Handbook*, median annual earnings of full-time computer systems analysts and scientists in 1996 were about $46,300. The middle 50 percent earned between $34,000 and $59,900. The lowest 10 percent earned less than $24,800, while the highest tenth earned more than $76,200.

Computer scientists with advanced degrees generally earn more than systems analysts. The starting salaries of computer scientists and computer engineers with bachelor's degrees can be significantly higher than the starting salaries of bachelor's degree holders in many other fields.

According to the National Association of Colleges and Employers, starting salary offers in 1997 for graduates with a bachelor's degree in computer engineering averaged about $39,722 a year; for those with a master's degree, $44,734 a year; and for those with a Ph.D., $63,367. Starting offers in 1997 for graduates with a bachelor's degree in computer science averaged about $36,597 a year; in information sciences, about $35,407 a year; and in systems analysis, about $43,800 a year.

Salary offers for those with the bachelor's degree in computer engineering vary according to job functions, as shown in the following table:

Computer programming	$35,167
Information systems	$34,689
Systems analysis and design	$36,261
Software design and development	$39,190
Hardware design and development	$41,237

Salary offers in 1997 for individuals with a master's degree in computer science averaged $45,853 a year, while those with a Ph.D. in computer and information sciences averaged $61,306 a year.

When you visit the "ITTA Connection" (*www.it-ta.com/*) from the previous section, you will be asked to join their listing. Should you decide to become a member (currently membership is free), you can access the salary survey listing location shown in Figure 16-8.

From there, you can locate information about the career fields for which you wish salary listings. The highlighted items indicate the salary listings investigated by this author when gathering information for this chapter.

Figure 16-8

The listings shown in Figure 16-9 came from the ITTA site, and provide information about salaries that was current at the time of the searches.

Figure 16-9

National Average Salaries for Support Professions			National Average Salaries for Communications		
Job Title	Starting Salary	Base Salary	Job Title	Starting Salary	Base Salary
Computer Hardware Engineer	$31,734	$40,091	LAN Manager	$42,864	$51,118
Help Desk Manager	$36,133	$42,969	Network Engineer	$39,170	$49,035
Other End-User Support	$27,851	$35,150	Network Manager (LAN/WAN)	$43,074	$52,990
PC Technician	$26,274	$32,574	Other Communications	$28,480	$39,385
Technical Support Analyst	$31,112	$38,936			

The site shown in Figure 16-10 also lists a free 1998 salary survey:
http://www.experienceondemand.com/features/edpstats1998.html

Figure 16-10

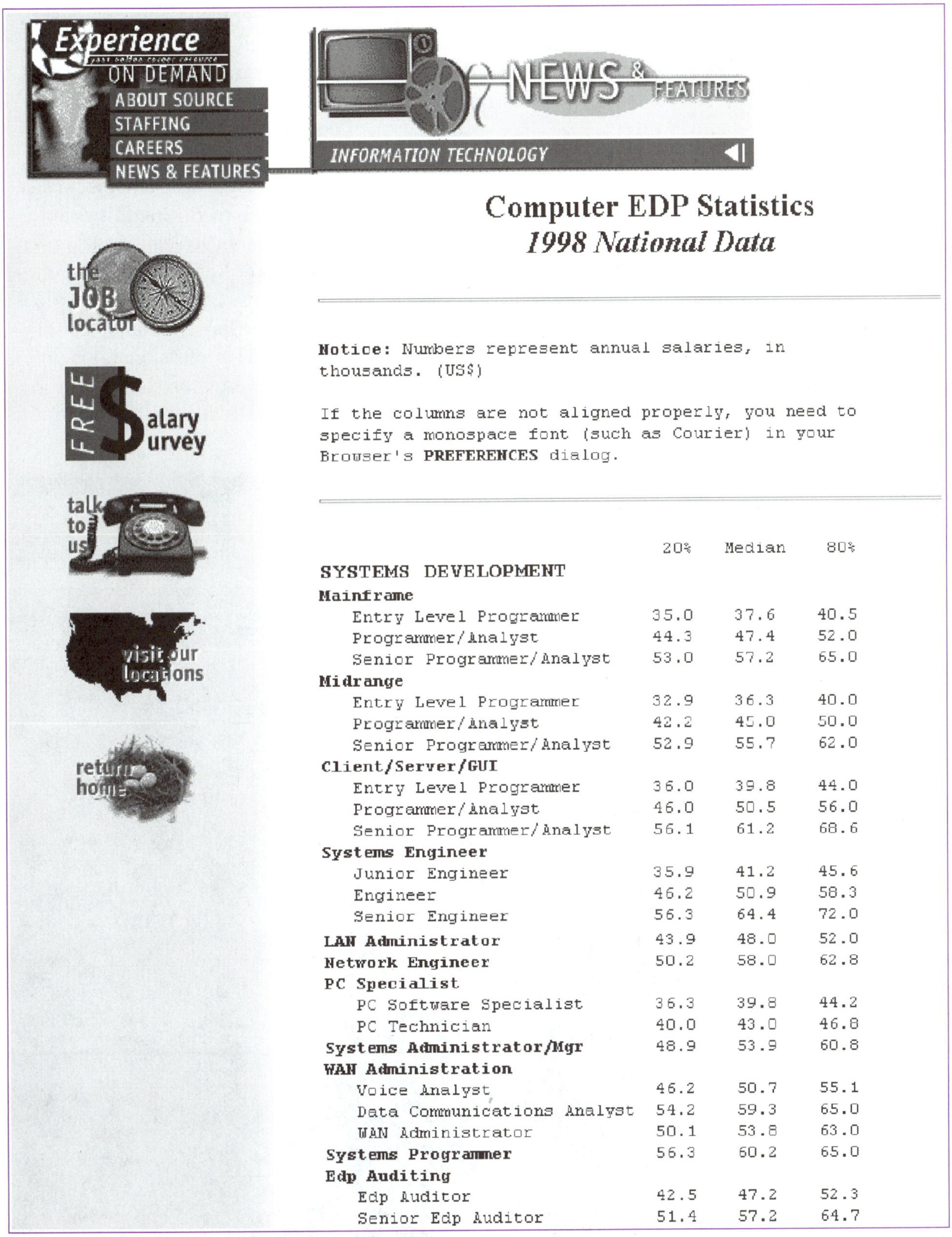

Computer EDP Statistics
1998 National Data

Notice: Numbers represent annual salaries, in thousands. (US$)

If the columns are not aligned properly, you need to specify a monospace font (such as Courier) in your Browser's **PREFERENCES** dialog.

	20%	Median	80%
SYSTEMS DEVELOPMENT			
Mainframe			
Entry Level Programmer	35.0	37.6	40.5
Programmer/Analyst	44.3	47.4	52.0
Senior Programmer/Analyst	53.0	57.2	65.0
Midrange			
Entry Level Programmer	32.9	36.3	40.0
Programmer/Analyst	42.2	45.0	50.0
Senior Programmer/Analyst	52.9	55.7	62.0
Client/Server/GUI			
Entry Level Programmer	36.0	39.8	44.0
Programmer/Analyst	46.0	50.5	56.0
Senior Programmer/Analyst	56.1	61.2	68.6
Systems Engineer			
Junior Engineer	35.9	41.2	45.6
Engineer	46.2	50.9	58.3
Senior Engineer	56.3	64.4	72.0
LAN Administrator	43.9	48.0	52.0
Network Engineer	50.2	58.0	62.8
PC Specialist			
PC Software Specialist	36.3	39.8	44.2
PC Technician	40.0	43.0	46.8
Systems Administrator/Mgr	48.9	53.9	60.8
WAN Administration			
Voice Analyst	46.2	50.7	55.1
Data Communications Analyst	54.2	59.3	65.0
WAN Administrator	50.1	53.8	63.0
Systems Programmer	56.3	60.2	65.0
Edp Auditing			
Edp Auditor	42.5	47.2	52.3
Senior Edp Auditor	51.4	57.2	64.7

Post Your Resume

If you desire a position in networking, you should compose a good resume, and then access one of the sites referenced above to post it on the Internet. Provided you can write well, and can present your skills in a way that communicates your desirability as an employee to a prospective employer in an unknown location, you should receive job offers within hours of posting your resume. That is how fast this market is operating.

According to Aileen Crowley in her *PC Week* article (October 12, 1998) about Internet-based job markets, Web recruiting fills dried up candidate pools. (Got to: *http://www.zdnet.com/pcweek/stories,news/0,4153,357991,00.html*.) Referencing Forrester Research Inc. in Cambridge, Massachusetts, she reported that only 25 percent of employers were online 1998, but 100 percent will be looking for job candidates on the Web by the year 2001. For the IT professional, the online recruiting phenomenon is a way to be constantly on the prowl for that next step in the career path without really having to take time away from a current position.

Figure 16-11

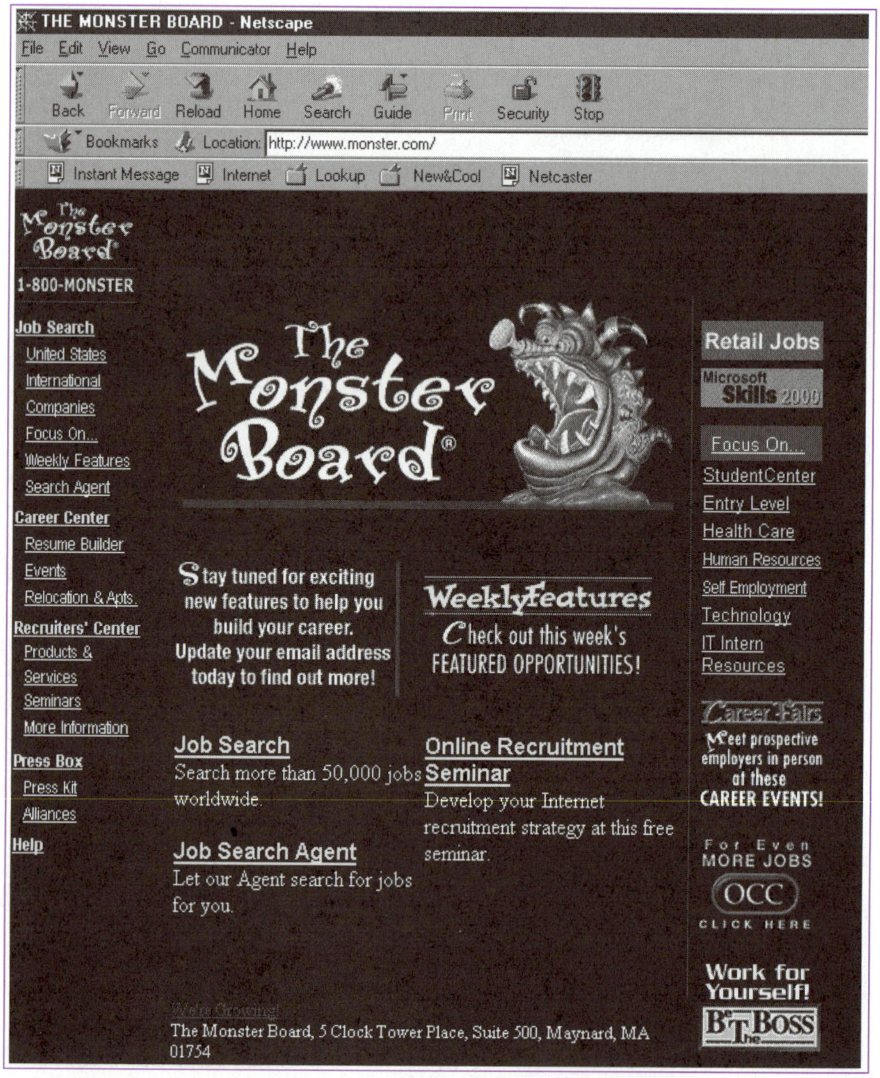

The Web provides almost real-time access to human resources departments at thousands of employer sites around the nation (or even the world, if that interests you). More and more employers are turning to the Internet as their preferred applicant source, so you would do well to begin your search with several of the online services. Along with the resume posting service that almost all of the online services provide, most offer additional services to help guide you in your job search. Some even furnish lists of questions frequently used during job interviews.

Another site for posting resumes, Online Career Center (*http://www.occ.com/*) is shown in Figure 16-12:

Figure 16-12

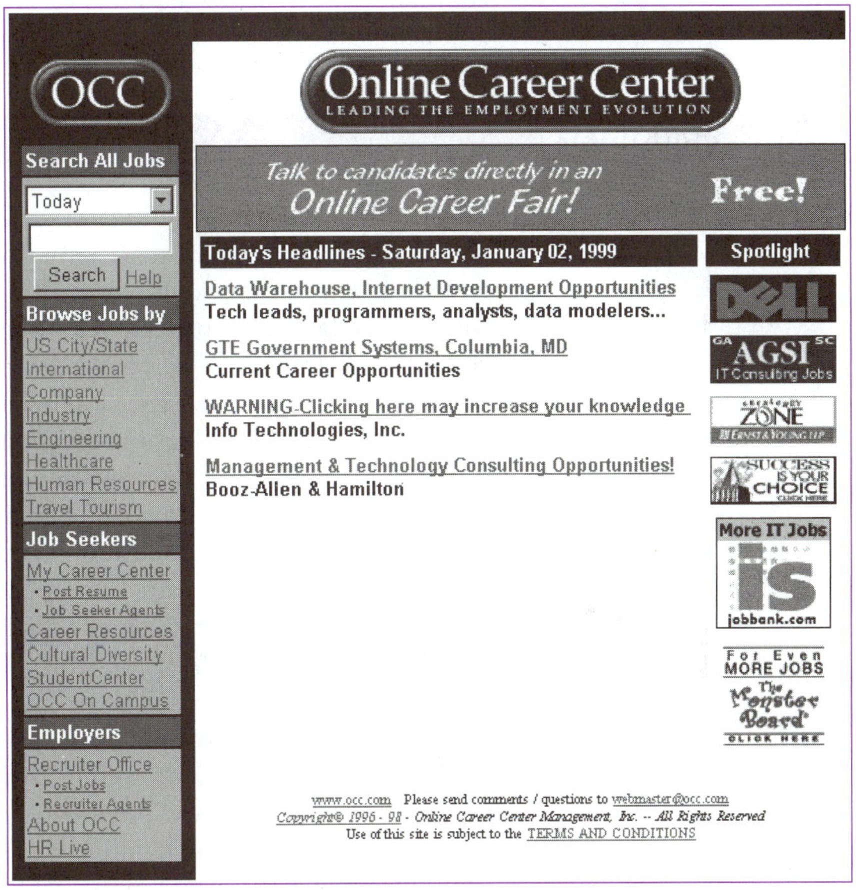

Articles like the following demonstrate how using the Web to sell yourself to potential employers is becoming more and more common.

Online Job Services Market Heats Up, Inter@ctive Week, May 29, 1998
http://www.zdnet.com/zdnn/content/inwk/0520/319802.html

Taking The Job Search To The Internet, Computer Reseller News, December 21, 1998
http://www.crn.com/sections/news/764/764pg423a.asp

Some companies are even using the Internet as the primary source of potential job candidates. Montgomery College in Conroe, Texas switched entirely to that method when it opened its new campus in 1995. All applicants were required to submit their applications through the Internet. Initially thought of as simply an interesting possibility, the process yielded thousands of highly-qualified applicants. It was so successful that all positions at the college continue to be advertised and applied for over the Internet.

Most individuals in the computer field today are insulted if a letter is sent in response to their online request for information. The environment has become so fast paced and high-tech that e-mail submissions naturally beget e-mail responses. All facets of the job search are done by computer with the exception of the interview and final hiring process. This high-tech application process is becoming common in other fields as well. For example, accounting and finance applicants have begun to use this method.

Chapter Summary

This last chapter should guide you to the resources that will help you in your employment search. By finishing this text, you have already taken an enormous step in that direction. Using the resources available to prospective employees, you have an excellent chance of finding work in the networking field.

For the past several years, networking specialists have been the most sought after new-hires in the job market worldwide. Once you find employment, you can probably remain in that position for a long period of time. If you wish to find new employment, you should be able to do so easily. It is also a field that offers excellent pay.

This text has been training you to become a Network Administrator. You have learned the Novell NetWare 5 or 4.11 networking skills that will help you obtain certification. What you have learned about networking in general will also help you work with other operating systems, such as Windows NT.

Help Desk Technicians also must know much of what you studied in this course, so the knowledge you have gained would prove useful if that is your desired area of employment. The troubleshooting skills you have learned in this text will help you answer service calls, work with users at their locations, and correct problems.

An applications specialist accomplishes many of the same tasks and works with the same people as the help desk technician. The skills you learned in this course involving software installation and computer configurations will help you obtain such a position. You would be responsible for selecting and installing the users' software and for installing all updates, usually at the user's location. The applications specialist usually introduces the user to the new software, so the position involves training users as well.

Labor statistics regarding the above career choices are typically grouped under the heading of Computer Managers. The latest information available from the US Department of Labor's Bureau of Labor Statistics demonstrates that technological change continues to create opportunities in computer-related occupations. Computer managers are responsible for an organization's computer network, and are increasingly expected to oversee the installation, configuration, and maintenance of both software and hardware in a local area network (LAN).

The market trend over the past several years has shown an increasing need for people who can work in the Information Technology (IT) field. The increased spending in this field projected annual expenditures of $400 million, while actual spending was over $2 billion. Another trend has involved a hiring shift from permanent positions to contracted personnel on temporary assignment. In "Temp-to-Perm" positions, applicants can "try out" a position before being hired permanently. Some of this trend is a result of employer's wanting to be less involved in the search process, but it is also a result of the employee's desire for more flexibility when choosing positions. A third trend is a general industry shift toward hiring younger workers in the IT field.

There are numerous sources available to prospective employees in the networking field. You should start with the resources available to you through your school guidance facilities. Usually this will involve a Career Specialist who is familiar with many of the resources commonly used by job hunters. The government also has several documents to assist people investigating a new career. Novell education does an excellent job of furnishing prospective networking specialists with information about their products and the certification programs available to them. In addition, the Internet provides handbooks and similar general purpose listings of links to helpful information.

The Internet also links you to several locations that allow you to check your current net worth through survey statistics. Based upon your training level and your experiences, you can obtain an estimate of what you should be paid for a given position. Some of the listings are regional, informing you what those in your area are being paid. All of these surveys demonstrate that over the past several years wages have risen for people who are starting careers in networking.

Once you decide that you want a position in networking, you should begin by writing a good resume and posting it on the Internet. There are several sites where this can be done easily. Some of the sites are easier to load your resume onto than others, but all provide access to employers that you would not have been able to access otherwise.

Networking Terms Used in Chapter 16

networking career
help desk technician
applications specialist
computer manager

Management Information
  Systems (MIS)
Career Specialist
Novell education

Occupational Outlook Handbook
  (OOH)
The Guide CD
online services

■ **Chapter Review Questions**

1. Name and describe three careers for which this course has helped you prepare.

2. Describe the typical duties that a network administrator can expect to perform within a typical company.

3. Why are network administrators often turned to when a user experiences problems even when they are not associated with the company's network?

4. What alternative network administrator path can you use if you do not choose to work with Novell products?

5. What are the duties of an applications specialist?

6. What does the Bureau of Labor Statistics say about the trend toward networking?

7. What are three trends in the computer industry relative to networking?

8. Describe three sources of information about networking employment possibilities.

9. Why should you attempt to obtain a copy of The Guide from Novell?

10. Where can you find information about your net worth should you decide to make networking a career?

11. According to the EDP statistics 1998 data, what should a LAN administrator expect as a minimum starting wage?

12. What resources do The Monster Board and OCC provide prospective networking professionals?

13. What should you do before posting your resume on the Internet relative to school policies?

14. Why has e-mail correspondence come to be accepted as the norm when applying for a job over the Internet?

15. What is the trend relative to applications on the Internet?

■ **Associated Chapter Problems**

1. Describe the reasons for the increasing need for qualified network administrators.

2. With the information you gained in this course, what alternative careers do you feel qualified for?

3. Discuss the increased need for "People Skills" in the computer industry.

4. Describe in detail the three national trends regarding the networking field.

5. Describe all of the job hunting information sources you can find in your community.

6. Compute your own net worth, and describe the job you intend to apply for during summer vacation.

7. Describe the process of posting your resume on the Internet.

8. Discuss the shift toward Internet-based employment offerings.

APPENDICES

Applying for a Job at TPUP

After choosing the position you would most like to fill, use the following job information, designing your own format, to complete your TPUP application. Create the form yourself to look similar to the form shown in Figure A-1 on page 428. Copies will not be allowed and an application with any mistakes will have to be entirely re-done. Fill in your information on your newly created form with a number two lead pencil only.

- Name (Last, First, Middle Initial)
  Street Address
  City, State, ZIP Code
  Telephone Number

- **Education**–List in reverse chronological order all classes taken in the past four years, giving instructors' names, grade for the class, and the school and room number the class was taught in. State the most important concept you learned in each class.

- **References**–List at least five references (excluding anyone related to you or under twenty-five years of age). Give full names, addresses, places of employment, and phone numbers for each. State the number of years they have known you.

- State whether or not you are physically capable of performing the work required to fill the position you have chosen.

You should plan on being present when your application is reviewed by the hiring official and prepare yourself by answering the following questions about the position you have chosen. (You should role play enough so that you are confident and polished, showing that you do indeed qualify for your chosen position.)

1. Why are you applying for this position?
2. What makes you qualified to fill the position you have chosen?
3. How can hiring you benefit TPUP?
4. What is the minimum salary you will accept?
5. What is the one character trait that you possess which makes you the best applicant?
6. What is the worst thing anyone you know can say about you relative to your work?
7. If given a position of responsibility, how would you get others to work efficiently?
8. When given a job to perform, how do you ensure that you complete it?
9. Where do you see yourself within TPUP in ten years?
10. What is your plan for personal growth?

Figure A-1

Job Application

GENERAL INFORMATION

Name	Date	Work Desired
Street Address	Phone Number	Full-time _____ Part-time _____
City State ZIP	Social Security Number	Seasonal _____ Temporary _____

RECORD OF EDUCATION

High School	_____ _____ _____	College Prep ☐ Business ☐ Other Voc. ☐	9 10 11 12	Yes ☐* No ☐ *Year _____	
Business College	_____ _____ _____		1 2 3 4	Yes ☐* No ☐ *Year _____	
College	_____ _____ _____		1 2 3 4	Yes ☐* No ☐ *Year _____	Major Area:

WORK EXPERIENCE

List all present and past employment, including part-time or seasonal, beginning with the most recent.

Company	Employment Dates and Salary	Describe the work you did in detail	Reason for leaving
Name: _____ Address: _____ Phone: ___ Supervisor ___	From: _____ To: _____ Salary: _____		
Name: _____ Address: _____ Phone: ___ Supervisor ___	From: _____ To: _____ Salary: _____		
Name: _____ Address: _____ Phone: ___ Supervisor ___	From: _____ To: _____ Salary: _____		

UNITED STATES MILITARY SERVICE

Veteran YES _____ NO _____ Service Branch _____
Service Dates: FROM: _____ TO: _____

REFERENCES

Please provide the name and contact information for three references who are not relatives.

Name	Address	Phone

OTHER

Please indicate other abilities, experiences, personal interests, or other special knowledge and skills which you particularly feel would qualify you for the type of work for which you are now applying, such as experience in the Armed Forces, volunteer work, etc.

_____

_____

   I authorize investigation of all statements in this application, and I understand that any false statements or deliberate omissions on this application will be cause for my discharge.

_____
Signature of Applicant

TPUP's Resume Format

Your TPUP resume is a one-page, hand-written "word snapshot" of yourself that you share with potential employers when trying to convince them to invite you in for an interview. It should be neat, clear, and concise and accurately portray all your qualifications for the position you are seeking. You should use action words as much as possible in your resume to show what you did and the results of your actions.

TPUP's format requires that you state clearly what your objective is concerning the job you would like to obtain. Include all educational institutions you have attended along with any diplomas, certificates, or awards you have received. Along with your objective and education history, you should include the following major categories in your resume: employment history, special qualifications for the position, computer qualifications, hobbies, and personal items. The page must have a one-inch margin formed by a hand-drawn, black-inked box.

Attached is a copy of a sample resume showing one layout possibility. Use your own discretion. Stay aware of the current "resume" philosophy regarding length and data you want to share. Remember, though, that your resume is a snapshot of you and everything you will bring with you to the company. Occasionally, you run into an the interviewer who is intimidated by what you have on the table—be aware of that.

1. There is no universal resume format. There are only guidelines to help you.

2. Present your job objective so that it relates to both the company and the job description.

3. Final hiring decisions are rarely based upon resume alone; however, the resume should be a concise, factual, and positive listing of your education, employment, skills, and accomplishments.

4. Test your resume for relevancy. The information included in your resume should either support your career objective directly or support your character in general. If you have no definite purpose for including something, leave it out.

5. Be conscious of the continuity of your history. The reader will be looking for reasons to eliminate as many resumes as possible. Resumes with time gaps often get eliminated.

6. Weigh your choice of words. Select strong action verbs, concrete nouns, and positive modifiers for emphasis. Use concise phrases and clauses rather than complete sentences.

7. Try your resume out on someone who knows you and who will be objective in their opinion.

8. Keep a separate list of references and make them available if requested by the employer.

9. Send a cover letter with specific reference to the company's need and your qualifications for that job. A personal letter is always best, so get the name of the individual making the hiring decision.

10. Remember your resume is only a door opener. You want a personal interview.

Answering the following four questions in a fully persuasive way will greatly increase your odds of developing a winning resume. Answering them will not only give you the material you need for building a strong resume, but will also prepare you for networking and interviewing.

1. **What do you want?** That is your Objective. Do not struggle over this. Prospective employers want a simple, specific answer. Managers and human resources people need to know how to route your resume. If your objective is too vague, they will just discard it. Change your objective for different markets.

2. **Why are you qualified to do it?** Answer succinctly why you are qualified to accomplish your objective. Ask yourself: "Why should they hire me?" (You will need this for the interview anyway!) Summarize the answer in easy-to-read bullet points. This section should satisfy your reader that the rest of your resume is worth viewing.

3. **Where have you done it?** The reader needs to relate to your experiences. Identify the company. If it is not a recognizable company, write a line about its high points. Build it up. On the resume, the reader will often equate your value with that of your employer. Describe only the parts of your job that help sell you and highlight your value.

4. **How well have you done it?** This is where you should put in your most thought and effort. Think about what you did for each employer to make that company better. It could be a big thing or something small. However, it should be enough to show value. Did you have an idea that was implemented and has saved the company money? Were you promoted due to your contributions? Were you given positive reviews, and why? Were you selected for a key program or training? Bullet these points separately from, and after, your job description. These points show your worth.

Action Verbs

accelerated	demonstrated	initiated	performed	scheduled
accomplished	designed	instructed	planned	simplified
achieved	directed	interpreted	pinpointed	set up
adapted	effected	improved	programmed	solved
administered	eliminated	launched	proposed	structured
analyzed	established	led	proved	streamlined
approved	evaluated	lectured	provided	supervised
coordinated	expanded	maintained	proficient in	supported
conceived	expedited	managed	recommended	taught
conducted	facilitated	mastered	reduced	trained
completed	found	motivated	reinforced	translated
controlled	generated	operated	reorganized	utilized
created	increased	originated	revamped	won
delegated	influenced	organized	revised	
developed	implemented	participated	reviewed	

Concrete Nouns and Positive Modifiers

ability	competent	effectiveness	qualified	technical
actively	competence	pertinent	resourceful	versatile
capacity	consistent	proficient	substantially	vigorous

My Resume Name (email@your.net)

My Address • City, State • ZIP Code
(000) 000-0000

Information Technology

CAREER HISTORY
Networking and hardware/software specialist. Experience controlling multi-million dollar software intensive projects. Documented success in supervisory-level positions. Hands-on experience defining, acquiring, installing, trouble-shooting, administering and instructing networked computer resources.

NETWORK ADMINISTRATOR
Network administrator for half-million dollar Windows NT 4.0 and Novell NetWare 4.11 lab. Certified Novell Administrator (CNA). Certified Novell Instructor (CNI). Teaching MS Office courses. Experience as network administrator Novell NetWare 3.12, 4.1, and 4.11 networks. Currently in Microsoft's "Train-the-Trainer" AATP Mentor Program. Working on MS Certified Systems Engineer (MCSE) certification. Authoring Novell NetWare 5 Textbook for an educational publisher. Beta Testing Windows 2000.

COMPUTER SKILLS
Certified in Novell 4.11. Working systems knowledge of Windows 3.1, 95, NT 3.1, NT 3.51, and NT 4.0. Installed, operated, and maintained complete Novell, Macintosh, and Windows networks. Familiar with Eudora e-mail program, Internet Explorer, and Netscape browsers. Trained in TCP/IP, IPX, and NetBEUI protocols, COBOL, FORTRAN, Linear programming, Computer Aided Systems Evaluation (CASE), ACCELERATOR, file structures, data management, and systems integration/design.

SOFTWARE MANAGEMENT
Software Division Chief for the development of over 600,000 lines of revised code. Authored developmental test-plans and procedures used for in-plant and on-site testing. In-plant and on-site test director. Sites became only Major Systems Acquisitions of Computer Resources to be turned over to the government fully operational, documented, and tested ahead of schedule and under budget. Trained and certified as U.S. Air Force software systems acquisition manager.

PROJECT MANAGEMENT
PM on $6 million four-site security sensor system, $4.6 million four-site satellite communications system, $1.4 million dual-transmission microwave network. Authored RFPs, chaired evaluations, and conducted final contract negotiations. On-site manager for construction, testing, training, and system turnover. Developed and implemented all system test and training plans, procedures, and materials. Evaluated all O&M manuals. Completed ahead of schedule and under budget. Certified as US Army contract officer's representative (COR). Plant manager in $4 million drill pipe manufacturing firm.

EDUCATION
MBA (Systems Analysis, Marketing), Hardin-Simmons University, GPA 4.0.
MS (Operations Management), University of Arkansas, GPA 3.91.
BS (Management Information Systems, Operations Management), University of Arizona, GPA 3.61.
Certified Novell Instructor (CNI), Certified Novell Administrator (CNA) Novell IntranetWare 4.11.
Certified Technical Trainer (CTT).
Microsoft Approved Academic Training Partner (AATP) Mentor.
Completed Courses in Windows NT Server and Windows NT Workstation.
Completed Course in Windows Small Business Server.
Teacher Certification (Business Administration, Industrial Technology), McMurry University, GPA 4.0.

PERSONAL
Completed military service in the U.S. Air Force with the rank of Major.
Top Secret, SCI/EBI clearance. Married. Two children. Private pilot.

The 50 Toughest Interview Questions

1. Tell me about yourself.
2. What do you know about our company?
3. Why do you want to work for us?
4. What would you do for us?
5. What do you find most attractive about the position?
6. What do you look for in a job?
7. How long would you stay with us?
8. Do you feel you're over-qualified? Why not?
9. What is your philosophy of management?
10. What is your management style?
11. Are you a good manager? Give examples.
12. What do you look for when you hire people?
13. How do you motivate subordinates?
14. What is the most difficult task in being a manager?
15. Why are you leaving (or did leave) your present job?
16. How would you evaluate your present (most recent) employer?
17. Have you helped increase sales? How?
18. Have you helped reduce costs? How?
19. Do you prefer working with people, figures, or words?
20. What do your subordinates think of you?
21. In your current or last position, what did you like most? Least?
22. What are your five most significant accomplishments?
23. What do you think of your boss?
24. What would your boss say about you?
25. What problems did you resolve in your most recent position?
26. If you had your choice of jobs and companies, where would you go?
27. Why aren't you earning more?
28. What do you feel this position should pay?
29. What kind of salary are you worth?
30. Are you creative? Give examples.
31. How would you describe your personality?
32. Are you a leader? Give examples.
33. What are your strengths?
34. What are your weaknesses?
35. Would you object to working overtime and weekends?
36. What position do you expect to have in five years?
37. What are your career and lifestyle objectives?
38. What have you done to reach those objectives?
39. If you could start again, what would you do differently?
40. What can you do for us that someone else can't?
41. How do you handle conflict with a colleague? A subordinate? Your boss?
42. What do you consider the most important aspect of your job? Least important?
43. What do you think of this job opportunity?
44. How do you go about solving problems? Making decisions?
45. How do you rectify job-related errors?
46. Are you an independent worker or a team player?
47. What do you consider ideal working conditions?
48. What are your hobbies/outside interests?
49. Why should we hire you?
50. Do you have any questions?

Introduction to Computers

Your computer is made up of four basic components. They are:

- The Monitor
- The Keyboard
- The Mouse
- The Central Processing Unit (CPU)

The monitor is just a small video display. It connects to your computer and displays the actions you are performing on your computer. It provides the computer a means of communicating with the user in the form of output. In Windows operating systems, the monitor has become an integral part of your system and has come to display more choices and available actions for the user. In some cases, such as on a bank's teller machines, a computer's monitor can also be used by the user to input data into a computer.

The keyboard is another means of communicating with the computer. Pressing the keys issues commands to the computer. Normally, the keyboard is used just like a typewriter, but in some cases special characters replace the normal letters shown on each key.

The mouse is a convenient method of communicating with the computer. It is usually tethered to the computer on a relatively small cable. It is simply a means of pointing to something on screen and communicating with the computer so that it acts upon the object to which you are pointing. The mouse is nothing more than a mechanical device used to convert up-and-down and left-and-right motions to smooth resultant vectors on the computer's screen. The mouse usually controls movement of an arrow (or another graphic depiction) shown on screen. This arrow or other moving graphic is called a cursor.

The fourth component is really the heart of the computer. The Central Processing Unit is usually the box at the center of the computer where all the essential computing components are located. The electrical components such as the processor, Random Access Memory (RAM), Read Only Memory (ROM), and Basic Input Output System (BIOS) are located in the CPU. Additionally, all the add-in components such as video cards, Compact Disc (CD) players, Floppy Disk drives, Hard Disk drives, and sound or graphics-producing devices are also located in the CPU.

What is RAM?

Random Access Memory (RAM) is made up of a series of memory chips linked together inside the computer's CPU. When the computer has electricity applied to it, RAM is activated and acts like a "thinking location" for the computer's "thought" processes. The more RAM your computer has, the more concurrent processing it can accomplish at the same time. Additionally, RAM comes in different speeds and the faster the RAM, the faster the processing accomplished by your computer.

The effect of using RAM is similar to what you are thinking when you are awake. An example is easy to demonstrate. Ask someone next to you to close their eyes and clear their thoughts. Then ask them to think of "Orange." Do not tell them any more than the one word. Their thoughts will immediately change to what you suggested. You have brought something from their memory "storage" up to a memory "using" area similar to the mechanics of a computer's RAM.

What the person brings up with your suggestion depends on the area of their storage that they bring forward. If you ask them to describe what they thought when you mention the word and they start describing an orange, tell them that you meant the color. They will then go back to storage and change their thoughts to the color. When they describe what they are thinking, their whole thought pattern will have changed. That is as close to RAM as people's minds can come.

One of the most important things to remember about RAM is that it starts fresh (empty!) whenever power is reapplied. It is a very fast scratch pad where you can do your work and keep the work you are currently doing in memory but it goes away when power is lost. That is why you lose your work in a power failure if you have not saved it to a more permanent storage medium such as your hard drive or a floppy disk.

What is ROM?

Very different from RAM, Read Only Memory (ROM) is memory built into the computer which comes on when the processor has power applied to it and stays there when power is removed. Additionally, like its name states, you can only read ROM's information. You cannot write to or save anything in ROM. Whatever you need from ROM must already be there. Keeping with our comparing memory types with our own brain functions, ROM would be the reason we wake up and already speak whatever language we have learned. Most of you reading this text learned English as your primary language and wake up speaking English. Nobody teaches it to you every time you wake up. You already know how to speak it. Again, this is a very loose similarity and is the closest we can come within our own brain. With our brains, however, we can actually save additional material there each day, whereas with ROM you cannot.

An Introduction to DOS

In order to communicate with computer storage devices, normally made up of circular media called "disks," a Disk Operating System (DOS) had to be developed. DOS is a text-based system of commands that communicates disk and file storage, management and retrieval commands to a computer.

When you want the computer to perform a task, you must communicate with it. DOS provides you with one means of communication. DOS commands allow you to direct the computer's actions. The language of DOS is the structure of those commands. Each command has its own specific format which must be used before the command will function properly.

Most of the command names are easy to understand. Some of the more familiar ones are:

Move	**Copy**	**Read**
Print	**Date**	**Time**
Open	**Save**	**Format**

However, behind the simplicity of the easily recognized intent of the command lies the cumbersome, unforgiving command format. The computer will only do what DOS tells it to, and DOS will tell it to do *exactly* what you tell it you want done. If you try to tell it to do something that it does not completely understand, it returns an error and expects you to fix it. Most of the time, it will not tell you why it is an error.

DOS operates on a computer disk much like the logic behind a multiple-drawer filing cabinet. The whole filing cabinet (lets use a three-drawer cabinet) represents your computer.

- The filing cabinet is made up of multiple drawers. Your computer is made up of multiple disks.

- Within the filing cabinet's drawers are folders. Within your computer's disks are Directories.

- Inside the filing cabinet's folders are additional folders or the filed documents themselves. Inside your computer's Directories are additional sub-directories or the filed documents themselves.

Part of being able to work successfully with DOS commands is understanding where you are located in the disk structure at the time you issue the command. Depending on whether or not you set certain DOS command switches, you could be faced with a plain DOS Command Line Prompt such as: `C:\`

The line above tells you that you are in the *C:* drive but that is about it. That is all you get. Nothing tells you what to do next. There are no indicators of where to go for help. There are no alternative entry points. You have to know where you are and what it is you want to do. You also have to know what DOS commands to use.

Setting one switch which shows you where you are all the time results in an actual DOS command line prompt like shown in Figure D-1.

Figure D-1

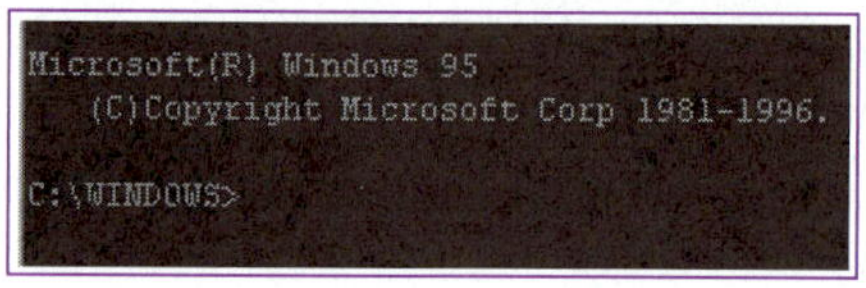

You still do not have a lot of information given to you at this point. In fact, you never get a lot of information when you use DOS. This only tells you that you are on the C drive and are currently in the Windows Directory.

If you want to see what else is in the Windows Directory you would type the DOS command **DIR** (for Directory) and hit **<ENTER>**. This would list everything in that directory. Unfortunately, it would list it all at once—without stopping. You would have to be a speed-reader to read the screens.

Should you know, however, that **DIR/P** gives you the same Directory Listing one page at a time, you would be much better off. However, the structure of DOS is such that you cannot start on the list and back up if you missed something. You would have to run the command again. If the listing is very long, you could end up doing that command numerous times before getting all your information. There are additional command switches that alphabetize the listing, list only certain files, or several other desirable actions; however, they cannot be accomplished without knowing the original command format, the switch you need, and the format and sequencing with other switches necessary for you to get what you want done. One way to learn those switches is to type the name of the command followed by a forward slash and a question mark, for example, **DIR/?**. Adding a slash and a question mark to the end of almost every DOS command provides additional information on the commands options and syntax.

Let us talk now about the file types. DOS files can only be named within the DOS 8.3 naming convention. That means that the root name of the file can only have eight characters. Those characters can then be followed by a "." and three additional characters forming an extension. Some extensions have special meaning within the DOS operating system such as *.BAT* for Batch, *.SYS* for system, *.DOC* for Document, and *.TXT* for Text. Other than the ones recognized by DOS, a user can use any other three-character extension. Many files are created and given the user's three letter initials as an extension so that his own files are easily recognized.

There are also limitations on the eight characters used in the DOS name. There are several special characters such as quotation marks, mathematical symbols, and spaces that cannot be used. Additionally, no DOS command can be used.

APPENDIX D
DOS

DOS Setup Procedures

You should have already performed the **FDISK** procedures discussed in Chapter 1 of the text before performing the following DOS installation.

1. Insert the DOS diskette number 1 into the 3-1/2 floppy disk drive and restart the computer by turning it off and then back to on. (This ensures that the computer goes through a "cold start" and all settings are re-initialized.)

2. The computer will start up on the floppy disk and gives you the information shown in Figure D-2 about MS-DOS

Figure D-2

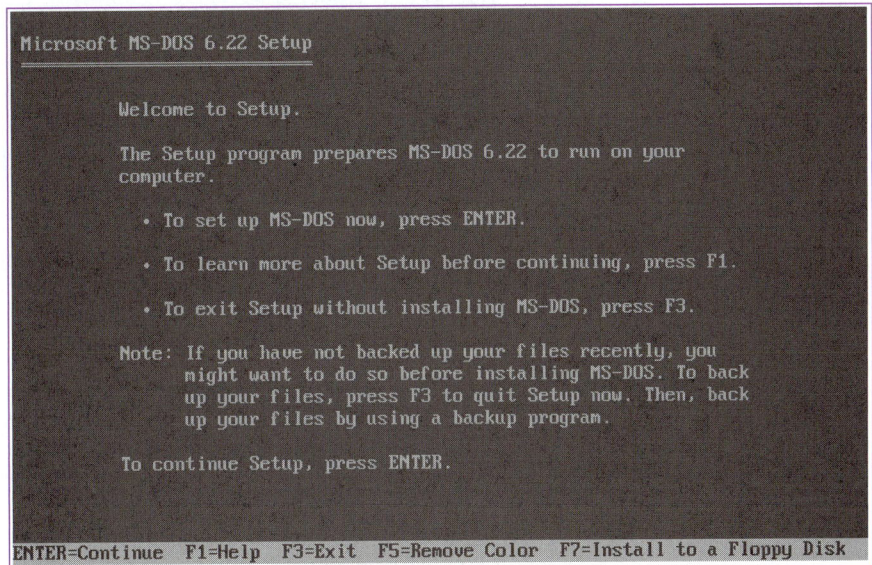

```
Microsoft MS-DOS 6.22 Setup

    Welcome to Setup.

    The Setup program prepares MS-DOS 6.22 to run on your
    computer.

        • To set up MS-DOS now, press ENTER.

        • To learn more about Setup before continuing, press F1.

        • To exit Setup without installing MS-DOS, press F3.

    Note: If you have not backed up your files recently, you
          might want to do so before installing MS-DOS. To back
          up your files, press F3 to quit Setup now. Then, back
          up your files by using a backup program.

    To continue Setup, press ENTER.

ENTER=Continue  F1=Help  F3=Exit  F5=Remove Color  F7=Install to a Floppy Disk
```

3. If you want to read about Setup, continue by pressing **F1**; otherwise, press **<ENTER>**. Since you have not yet formatted your drive after performing the **FDISK** function, DOS gives you the information choices shown in Figure D-3. Select **Format this drive** and press **<ENTER>** to continue.

Figure D-3

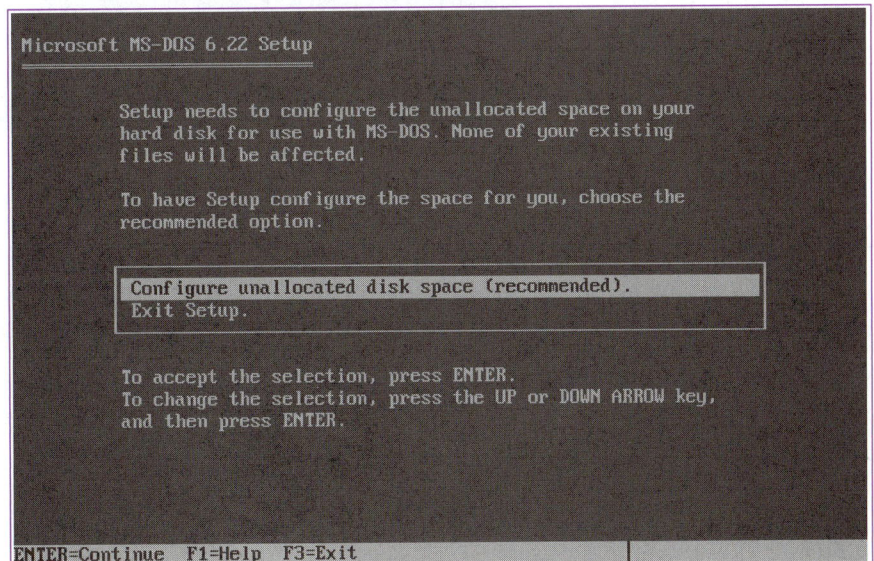

```
Microsoft MS-DOS 6.22 Setup

    Setup needs to configure the unallocated space on your
    hard disk for use with MS-DOS. None of your existing
    files will be affected.

    To have Setup configure the space for you, choose the
    recommended option.

    ┌────────────────────────────────────────────────────┐
    │ Configure unallocated disk space (recommended).     │
    │ Exit Setup.                                          │
    └────────────────────────────────────────────────────┘

    To accept the selection, press ENTER.
    To change the selection, press the UP or DOWN ARROW key,
    and then press ENTER.

ENTER=Continue  F1=Help  F3=Exit
```

4. The ***Formatting Drive C*** window will appear as shown in
Figure D-4.

Figure D-4

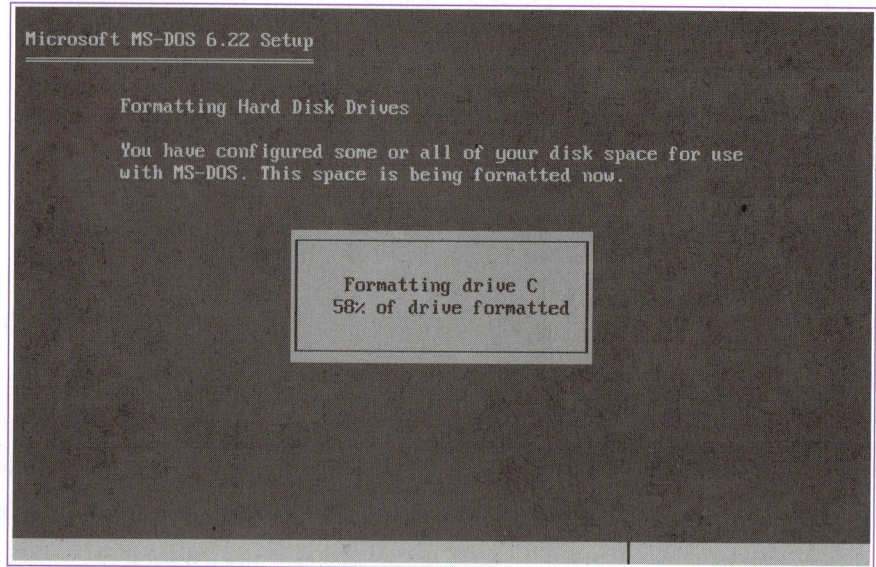

5. After the formatting is complete, the ***Setup Information Confirma-tion*** window appears. (See Figure D-5.) Press **<ENTER>** if the information is correct.

Figure D-5

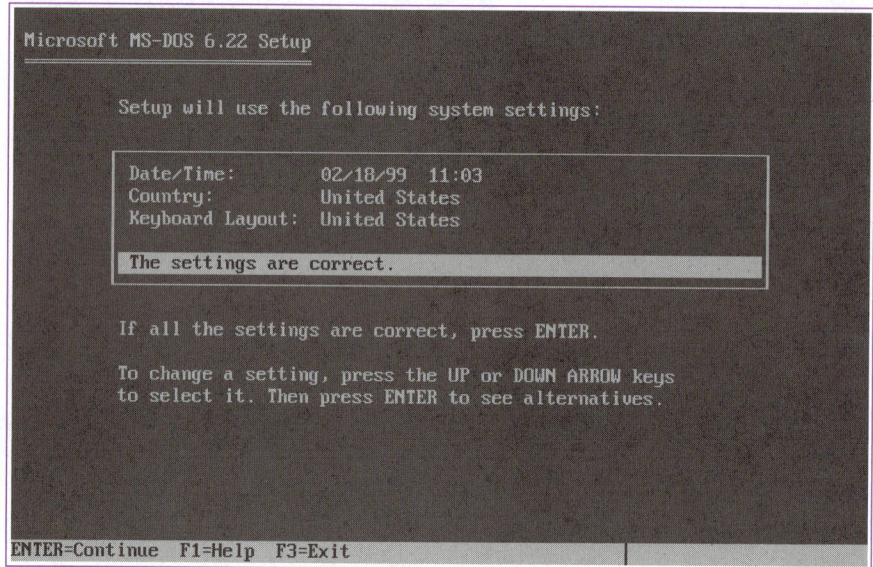

6. The window shown in Figure D-6 confirms the directory where the installation procedure will install your DOS files. Normally, this is the default directory shown in the screen below (C:\DOS) but it can be changed and any directory you want may be used. Press <ENTER> when complete.

Figure D-6

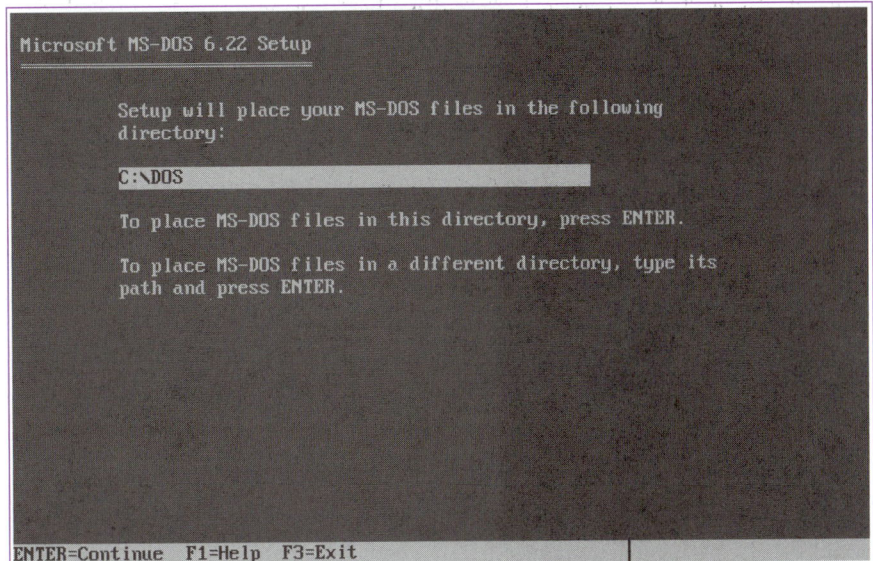

7. When the installation is complete, the window shown in Figure D-7 appears and informs you that your computer must be restarted. Press <ENTER> to restart.

Figure D-7

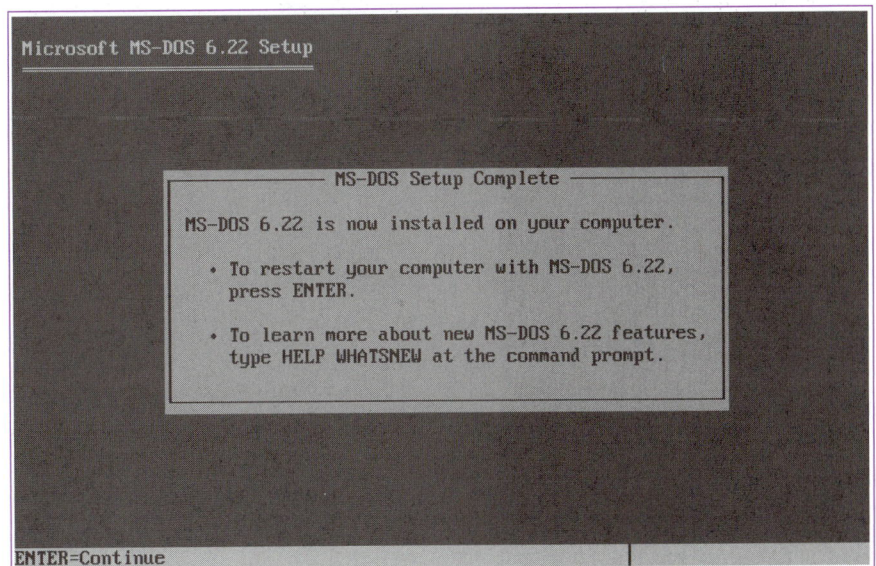

APPENDIX D
DOS

An Introduction to WIN95

Windows 95 is an operating system that lets you interact with your computer so that it responds to your commands and instructions. It replaced Windows 3.x and did away with the need for a Disk Operating System (DOS). Until recently, Windows 95 (or Win95) was the latest version of Microsoft's Windows Operating Systems. It was upgraded several times and in 1998 was replaced with a newer version called Windows 98.

Another related Windows operating system is Microsoft's Windows NT. Windows NT 3.5 was the workhorse operating system in the industry. It was upgraded to Windows NT 4.0. which is also being revised. Its replacement, originally called Windows NT 5.0, is being renamed Windows 2000.

To know Windows 95 is to know its user interface. A user interface is whatever it takes that results in you being able to have the computer do what you want when you want it. It involves both hardware and software. With Personal Computers (PCs) before Win95, the user interface was text based. You simply typed in a command string of DOS commands and the computer responded to the text-based instructions.

Windows 95, however, expanded on the interface that Microsoft apparently borrowed from Macintosh's line of computers. The Graphical User Interface (GUI) used in the early versions of Windows looked similar to the GUI that the Macintosh made popular. Windows 95 made that similarity even striking and Windows 98 goes even further. The Win95 GUI let the user work with graphics to have the computer do his bidding. It was much easier than the cumbersome, text-based DOS user interface.

When you start up your computer, the Windows Logo in Figure E-1 appears with the words Microsoft Windows 95 across the bottom and the word Microsoft across the top. The combination of items viewable on the computer's screen at one time is called a "Window." If you change views, you are supposedly looking into your computer through another "Window." Hence, the name *Windows*.

Figure E-1

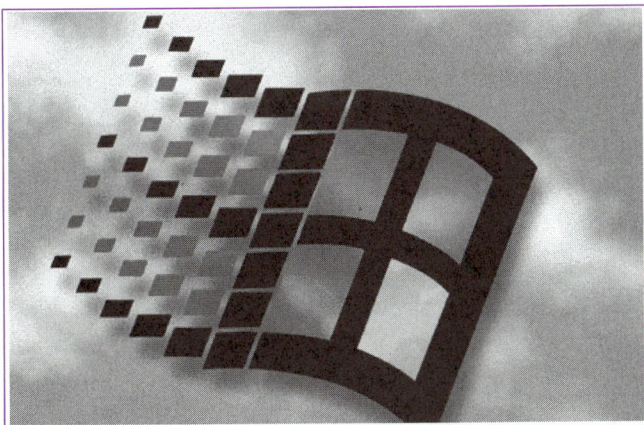

The Desktop

After startup, the computer will display a background and one or more icons on what is called the "desktop."

In the graphic shown in Figure E-2, you see a Windows 95 desktop. The background default color is green but you can change this so yours may be somewhat different. Along the left side are icons, or small pictures of items supposedly "sitting" on your desk. If you click any of them you will "open" them. Nothing actually opens up but rather you activate the software represented by the graphic icon on which you just clicked.

Figure E-2

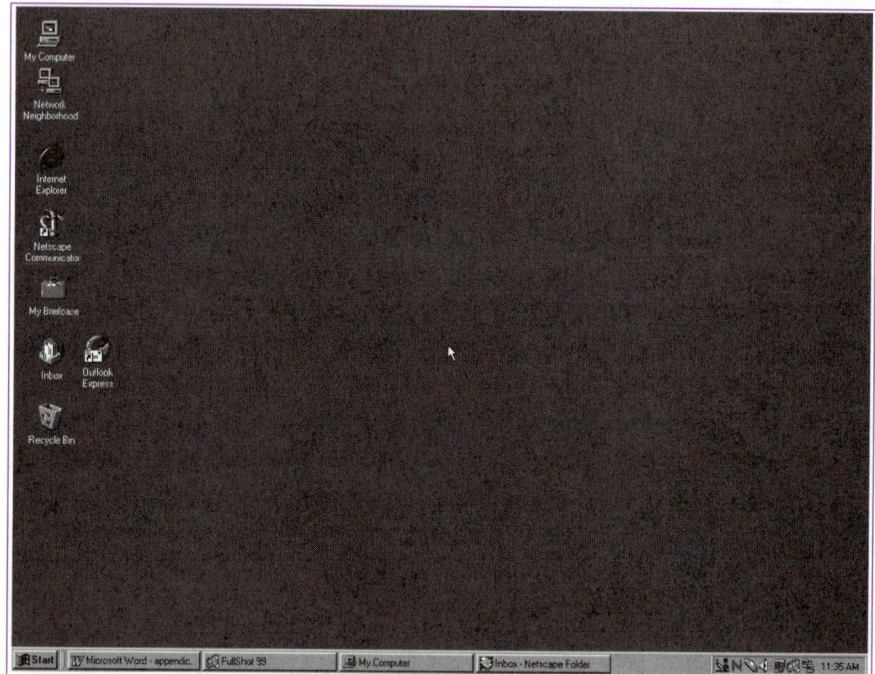

The idea of a desktop is that you have lots of workspace to accomplish tasks and store things as you work on them. Numerous components make up your desktop. They are physically located in different locations on your screen and are supposed to give you the impression that they are separate but integral parts of your own workspace.

The Start Button

In the lower left corner is the Start button. It really isn't a button at all but rather just a graphic displayed on the screen. The button is shown in Figure E-3.

Figures E-3

Figure E-4

When you activate this symbol, or any other button in Windows, it gives the appearance of being pressed in as though it is a real button. This is shown in Figure E-4. If your computer is equipped with sound, some buttons even make a sound just as if you pressed a real button.

The button graphics, the sounds, and even the desktop appearance is supposed to keep you from thinking about the mechanics of how the computer operates. They are designed to make it easy for you, the user, to operate your computer. Depending on how much you get into that mindset, you can almost start believing the buttons work and the windows let you "inside." When everything works as it should, the system makes things easy.

There are several types of pointing devices used as a mouse on computers. Some have one, two, or three buttons. Some are infrared-activated and not connected directly to your computer. Others are pad-like with no moving parts. They all operate on the same principle, however, and allow you to point and click on a displayed object. When you point and click on it, you have "selected" it and have told the computer that the next thing you do will likely be done on the item you have selected. This concept of selecting and acting upon that selection will be a consistent thought process throughout your computer use.

Clicking

Just what is "clicking?" Toward the center of the window E-4 is a graphic of an arrow. An expanded view of this arrow is shown in Figure E-5.

This is your pointer or "cursor." When you move your mouse, you move that pointer. As the arrow is expanded, you can see that it is actually composed of small dots or pixels. At the very tip of the arrow is one small dot that actually controls where the arrow is pointing. When you move your cursor so that one dot is on the icon you want to "open," you are considered "pointing" at that object and can then click your mouse to activate the computer program or software associated with that icon. For instance, left clicking your mouse pointer on the My Computer icon "opens" the window which graphically shows you the options shown as available in your computer. (See Figure E-6.)

Figure E-5

Figure E-6

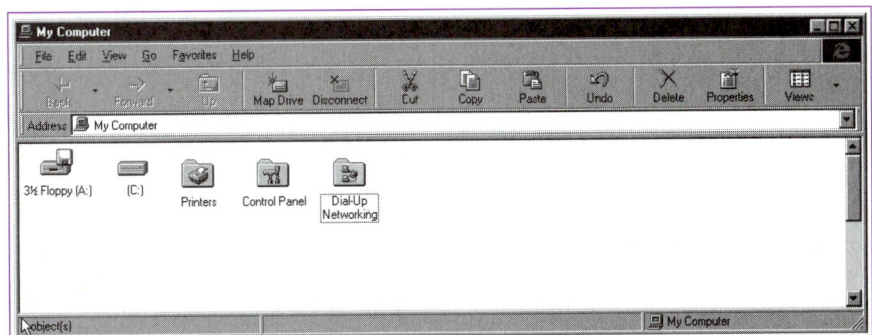

Available Clicks

Using the typical two-button Microsoft mouse, lets talk about the different clicks available. You have already learned that pointing means placing the cursor over a part of the object and clicking on it. Merely aiming the arrow at the object does not constitute "pointing" at it. You must physically have your cursor over the object.

There are still many different types of clicks. If you place your cursor over an object and click once—that is, push down on the button and release it—you have performed a single click. You do this to select an object. If you push down on the button and hold it in while over an object, you can perform a click-and-drag function and can drag that object from its present location and drop it off at a new location.

There are also double, triple, and quadruple clicks, depending on the software application that you are using at the time. Single and double clicking are the two most common button actions. Double clicks are performed by pressing and releasing the mouse button and quickly pressing and releasing it again while pointing at the same spot.

The speed of a multiple click is also adjustable. Strange as it sounds, this is necessary when you get proficient at using your computer and you start speeding around your desktop quickly. You adjust the speed through your computer's Control Panel. In the control panel, the graphic shown in Figure E-7 shows the mouse object selected.

Figure E-7

Double clicking on it opens the mouse adjustment window shown in Figure E-8.

Figure E-8

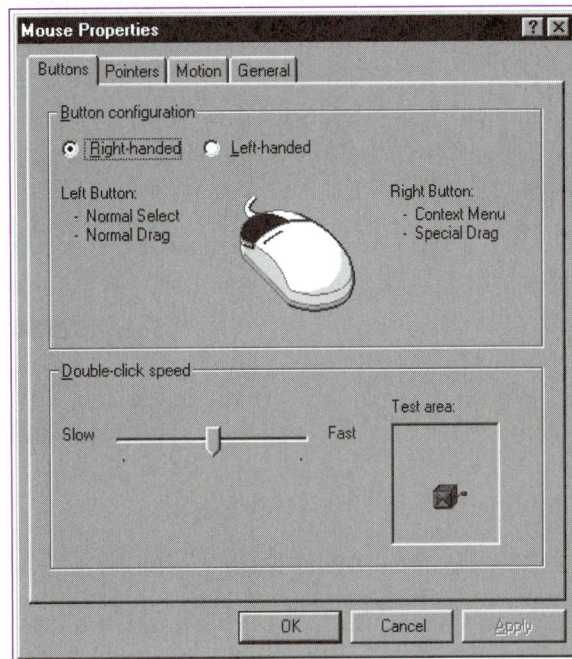

You can see that through this window you can adjust not only the speed but also whether it is a left-handed or right-handed mouse.

Clicking on the Pointers tab at the top of the window shows the choices available for graphics used to represent your cursor. (See Figure E-9.)

Figure E-9

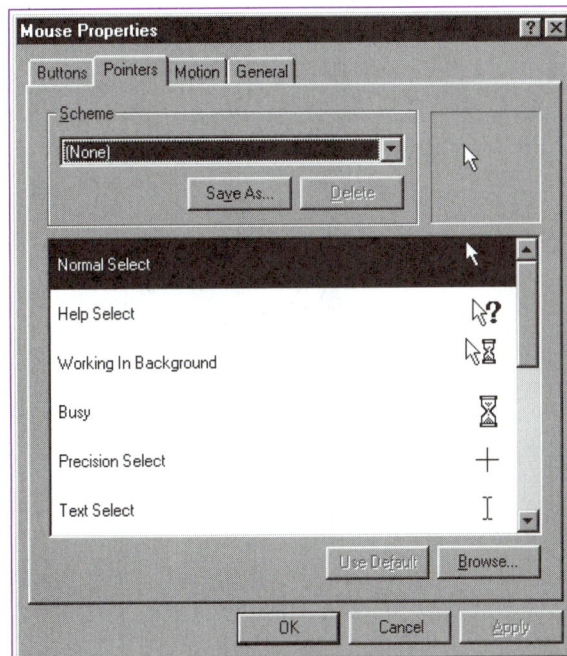

Sometimes, as shown in Figure E-9, there are additional choices available to you that cannot be shown in the space available. Next to the cursor choices there is a black "up arrow," a slider, and a black "down arrow." You use the slider by click-and-holding on it to scroll up or down through the other cursor choices. You could also click on either the up arrow or the down arrow to perform the scroll feature. The little black down arrow in the scheme section provides you with a pull-down window where you are a list of items to choose from. That pull-down feature is shown in Figure E-10. You activate the pull-down window, slide down to highlight the option you wish to choose, and click on it to make your choice.

Figure E-10

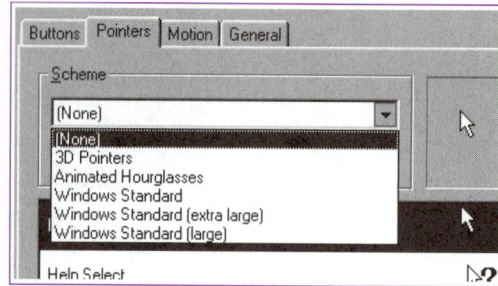

Start Menu

Figure E-11

Let us get back to the Start Menu. Using the mouse to position your pointer over this button and left clicking on it displays a pop-up menu similar to the author's shown in Figure E-12.

Once you have pressed the Start button and activated the pop-up window, you slide up to the object you want and click on it or slide to the next layer by sliding your pointer over one of those black arrows to the right of your choice.

Figure E-12

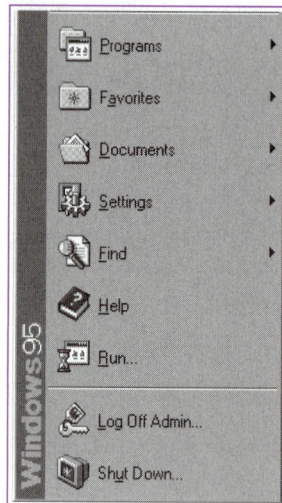

Figure E-13

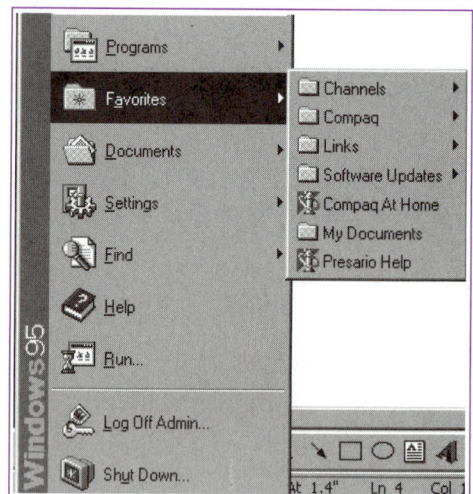

This will present you with another pop-up window similar to the one shown in Figure E-13.

As you can see in Figure E-13, you can continue in this sliding and pop-up routine until you locate the item you desire. When you find it, you simply click and activate it. In the graphic shown in Figure E-14, the Best of the Web site would be activated if it had been clicked on. If you do not wish to make any choices that are available to you after sliding through this process, just drop your slide off somewhere on your desktop (but not in any pop-up menu of the choices available). This cancels the choice process.

Figure E-14

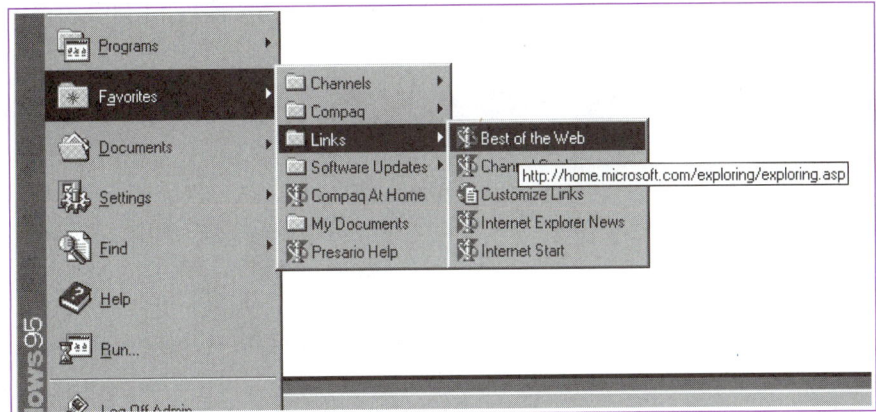

Desktop Choices

Your workspace, or desktop, is variable according to what you want it to look like and to what you have loaded and available. The same desktop in the previously shown desktop graphic is demonstrated in Figure E-15 with the Quick Launch Toolbar activated next to the start button. That feature is available if you have Internet Explorer 4.0 installed. Your desktop, therefore, can be an individual experience and can represent your personality or your mood.

Figure E-15

Figure E-16

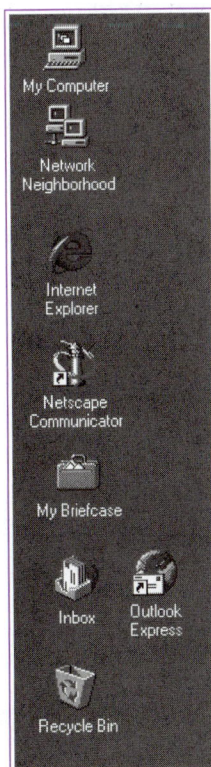

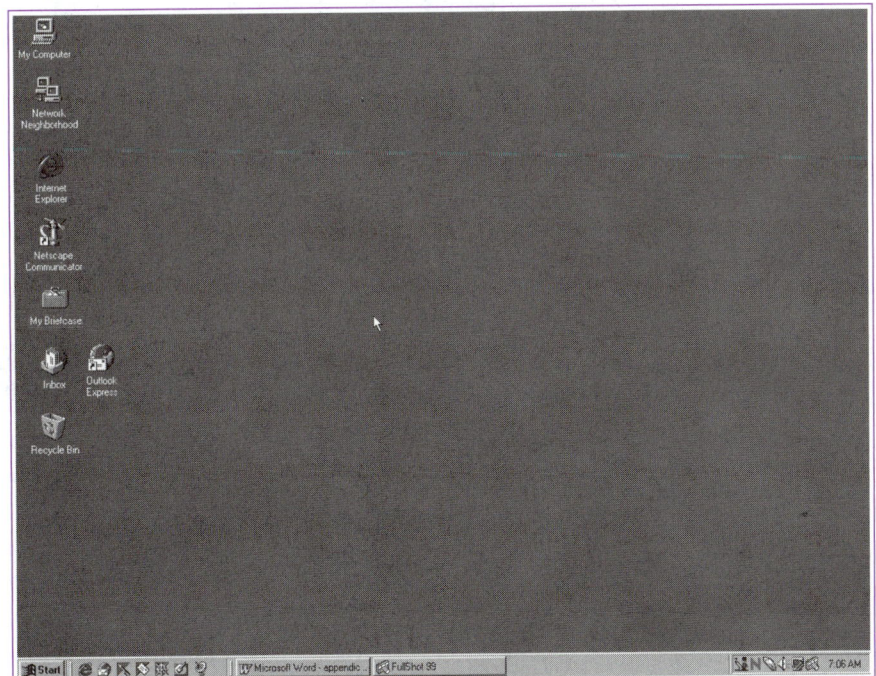

Those small graphic figures shown in Figure E-15 and shown separately in Figure E-16 are called Icons. Clicking on the My Computer icon, therefore, activates the associated software which lists the layers of your computer. If you get into the Windows mindset, you will think of this action as "opening" your computer and looking inside.

Similarly, clicking on the Network Neighborhood lets you search your network for other objects, opening your My Briefcase lets you "see" what you have in there, and dragging-and-dropping an item to your Recycle Bin gets rid of that object.

Using Windows

Double clicking on My Computer and then double clicking on your *C:* drive will provide you with a window similar to the one shown in Figure E-17. Depending on the choices you made during or after setup, the version of your operating system, and the selection of software you have installed on your computer, your desktop may appear similar to that shown in Figure E-17, but not exactly the same.

Figure E-17

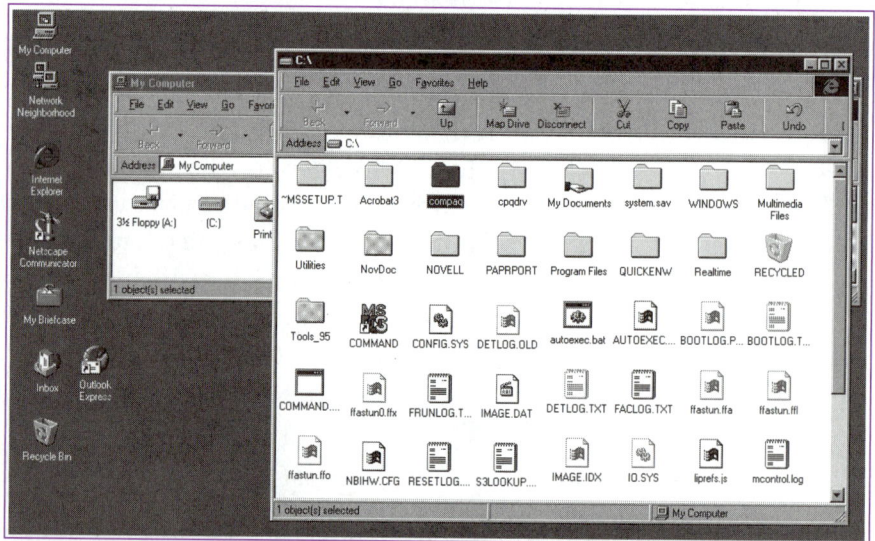

For instance, the same window shown in Figure E-17 is depicted Figure E-18 without some of the newer features available in the latest software revisions. The Standard Buttons and address line are omitted.

Figure E-18

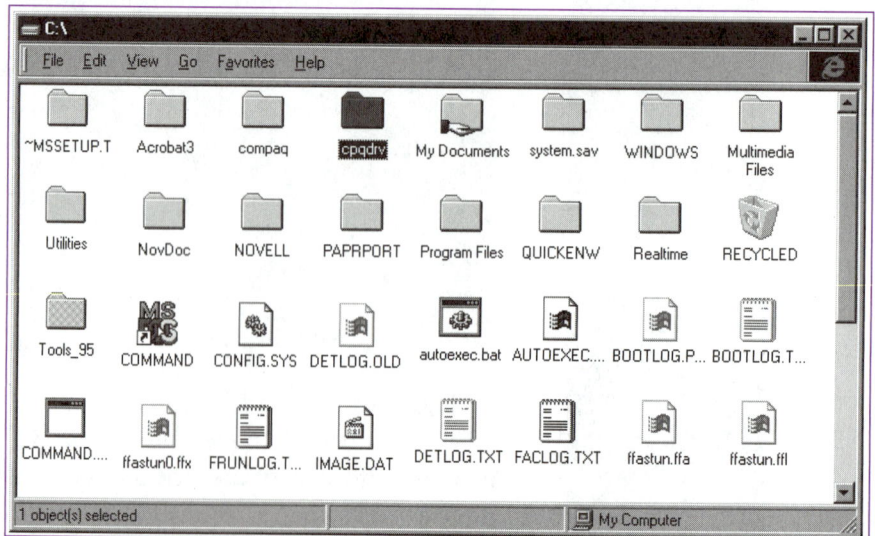

The window shown in Figure E-18 has numerous navigation features built into it that you should be aware of in order to become more proficient at using windows.

For instance, across the top of the window is a blue border. This is the Title Bar shown in Figure E-19.

Figure E-19

The mere fact that it is blue tells you that it is the currently selected window. If it is gray, as shown in Figure E-20, then another window has been selected.

Figure E-20

When this bar is blue (the window is selected), you can drag the window and drop it elsewhere by pointing your mouse in the blue area and clicking-and-dragging it to another location.

The nomenclature **C:** shown in Figure E-20 is the *Window Title* and will change according to whatever window you have open.

There are three boxes on the right side of the Title Bar. Double clicking on the icon at the far left side closes the window.

There are three sizing boxes on the right of the Title Bar. They are

Figure E-21

shown in Figure E-21. The box on the far right (✕) also closes the window. The box on the left (_) minimizes the window, or places it down in the task bar at the bottom of the desktop as shown in Figure E-22.

Figure E-22

The task bar can be moved to any of the four sides of the desktop by clicking any blank spot in the task bar and dragging it to the desired side.

The box in the middle is either the maximize button (with a large single window) as shown in Figure E-21 or the restore button (with smaller multiple windows) as shown in Figure E-23.

Figure E-21

Activating the maximize button makes the selected window fill the entire desktop space while the restore button merely returns the selected window to its size prior to being maximized.